Essentials of the D-KEFS and D-KEFS Advanced Assessment

Essentials of Psychological Assessment Series
Series Editors: Alan S. Kaufman and Nadeen L. Kaufman

Essentials of CAS2 Assessment
by Jack A. Naglieri and Tulio M. Otero

Essentials of Child and Adolescent Psychopathology, Second Edition
by Linda Wilmshurst

Essentials of Cognitive Assessment with KAIT and Other Kaufman Measures
by Elizabeth O. Lichtenberger, Debra Y. Broadbooks, and Alan S. Kaufman

Essentials of Conners Behavior Assessments™
by Elizabeth P. Sparrow

Essentials of Creativity Assessment
by James C. Kaufman, Jonathan A. Plucker, and John Baer

Essentials of Cross-Battery Assessment, Third Edition
by Dawn P. Flanagan, Samuel O. Ortiz, and Vincent C. Alfonso

Essentials of DAS-II® Assessment
by Ron Dumont, John O. Willis, and Colin D. Elliott

Essentials of Dyslexia Assessment and Intervention, Second Edition
by Nancy Mather and Barbara J. Wendling

Essentials of Evidence-Based Academic Interventions
by Barbara J. Wendling and Nancy Mather

Essentials of Executive Functions Assessment
by George McCloskey and Lisa A. Perkins

Essentials of Forensic Psychological Assessment, Second Edition
by Marc J. Ackerman

Essentials of Gifted Assessment
by Steven I. Pfeiffer

Essentials of IDEA for Assessment Professionals
by Guy McBride, Ron Dumont, and John O. Willis

Essentials of Individual Achievement Assessment
by Douglas K. Smith

Essentials of Intellectual Disability Assessment and Identification
by Alan W. Brue and Linda Wilmshurst

Essentials of KABC-II Assessment
by Alan S. Kaufman, Elizabeth O. Lichtenberger, Elaine Fletcher-Janzen, and Nadeen L. Kaufman

Essentials of KTEA™-3 and WIAT®-III Assessment
by Kristina C. Breaux and Elizabeth O. Lichtenberger

Essentials of MCMI®-IV Assessment
by Seth D. Grossman and Blaise Amendolace

Essentials of Millon™ Inventories Assessment, Third Edition
by Stephen Strack

Essentials of MMPI-A™ Assessment
by Robert P. Archer and Radhika Krishnamurthy

Essentials of MMPI-2® Assessment, Second Edition
by David S. Nichols

Essentials of Myers-Briggs Type Indicator® Assessment, Second Edition
by Naomi L. Quenk

Essentials of NEPSY®-II Assessment
by Sally L. Kemp and Marit Korkman

Essentials of Neuropsychological Assessment, Second Edition
by Nancy Hebben and William Milberg

Essentials of Nonverbal Assessment
by Steve McCallum, Bruce Bracken, and John Wasserman

Essentials of PAI® Assessment
by Leslie C. Morey

Essentials of Planning, Selecting, and Tailoring Interventions for Unique Learners
by Jennifer T. Mascolo, Vincent C. Alfonso, and Dawn P. Flanagan

Essentials of Processing Assessment, Second Edition
by Milton J. Dehn

Essentials of Psychological Assessment Supervision
by A. Jordan Wright

Essentials of Psychological Testing, Second Edition
by Susana Urbina

Essentials of Response to Intervention
by Amanda M. VanDerHeyden and Matthew K. Burns

Essentials of Rorschach® Assessment
by Tara Rose, Michael P. Maloney, and Nancy Kaser-Boyd

Essentials of Rorschach Assessment: Comprehensive System and R-PAS
by Jessica R. Gurley

Essentials of School Neuropsychological Assessment, Third Edition
by Daniel C. Miller and Denise E. Maricle

Essentials of Specific Learning Disability Identification, Second Edition
by Vincent C. Alfonso and Dawn P. Flanagan

Essentials of Stanford-Binet Intelligence Scales (SB5) Assessment
by Gale H. Roid and R. Andrew Barram

Essentials of TAT and Other Storytelling Assessments, Second Edition
by Hedwig Teglasi

Essentials of Temperament Assessment
by Diana Joyce

Essentials of Trauma-Informed Assessment and Interventions in School and Community Settings
by Kirby L. Wycoff and Bettina Franzese

Essentials of Treatment Planning, Second Edition
by Mark E. Maruish

Essentials of WAIS®-IV Assessment, Second Edition
by Elizabeth O. Lichtenberger and Alan S. Kaufman

Essentials of WISC®-IV Assessment, Second Edition
by Dawn P. Flanagan and Alan S. Kaufman

Essentials of WISC-V® Assessment
by Dawn P. Flanagan and Vincent C. Alfonso

Essentials of WISC-V Integrated Assessment
by Susan Engi Raiford

Essentials of WJ IV® Cognitive Abilities Assessment
by Fredrick A. Schrank, Scott L. Decker, and John M. Garruto

Essentials of the Tests of Dyslexia™
by Nancy Mather, R. Steve McCallum, Barbara J. Wendling and Sherry M. Bell

Essentials of WJ IV® Tests of Achievement
by Nancy Mather and Barbara J. Wendling

Essentials of WMS®-IV Assessment
by Lisa Whipple Drozdick, James A. Holdnack, and Robin C. Hilsabeck

Essentials of WNV™ Assessment
by Kimberly A. Brunnert, Jack A. Naglieri, and Steven T. Hardy-Braz

Essentials of Working Memory Assessment and Intervention
by Milton J. Dehn

Essentials of WPPSI™-IV Assessment
by Susan Engi Raiford and Diane L. Coalson

Essentials of WRAML2 and TOMAL-2 Assessment
by Wayne Adams and Cecil R. Reynolds

Essentials of WRAML3 and EMS Assessment
by Wayne V. Adams, David V. Sheslow, and Trevor A. Hall

Essentials of Evaluating Bias in Intelligence Testing
by Craig L. Frisby

Essentials of WJ V™ Assessment
by Erica M. Laforte, Nancy Mather, and W. Joel Schneider

Essentials of Cross-Battery Assessment and X-BASS, Fourth Edition
by Dawn P. Flanagan, Samuel O. Ortiz and Vincent C. Alfonso

Essentials of NIH Toolbox® Version 3 Cognition Tests
by Julie N. Hook, Amy Kovacs Giella and Erica M. LaForte

Essentials of the D-KEFS and D-KEFS Advanced Assessment
by Christopher L. Bedford, Julie A. Gettman, and Robb N. Matthews

Essentials

of the D-KEFS and D-KEFS Advanced Assessment

Christopher L. Bedford

Julie A. Gettman

Robb N. Matthews

WILEY

Published by John Wiley & Sons, Inc., Hoboken, New Jersey.

Library of Congress Cataloging-in-Publication Data applied for:

Print ISBN: 9781394316298
ePDF ISBN: 9781394316311
ePUB ISBN: 9781394316304

Cover Design: Wiley
Cover Image: Robert/stock.adobe.com

Set in 10/12pt Adobe Garamond Pro by Straive, Pondicherry, India

SKY10166710_082626

CONTENTS

FOREWORD

In 2007, our research team published a study in the *Journal of Psychoeducational Assessment* titled "Creativity Lost: The Importance of Testing Higher-Level Executive Functions in School-Age Children and Adolescents." In that article, we noted that school-based psychoeducational assessments focused primarily on evaluating overlearned verbal abilities—such as IQ and academic achievement skills—while often neglecting to include performance-based measures of higher-level executive functions. We presented empirical data showing that IQ and achievement measures demonstrate weak-to-poor correlations with performance-based measures of executive functioning. In addition, we found that one subgroup of typically functioning children and adolescents exhibited strong IQ and achievement skills but significantly weaker executive functions, while another subgroup showed the opposite profile. These findings highlighted a critical gap: standard psychoeducational assessments were often missing significant executive function deficits in children with average to above-average verbal abilities. They were also failing to identify children whose strengths lay not in their verbal skills, but in their higher-level executive abilities such as multitasking, creative thinking, and problem-solving.

Since then, I have been thrilled to see assessments broadened to incorporate evaluations of executive functions. However, I have also noticed another troubling trend in certain settings: an overreliance on behavioral rating scales to assess all aspects of executive functioning. Executive function difficulties can manifest as behavioral and emotional dysregulation (often called "hot" executive functions) or as higher-level cognitive deficits ("cold" executive functions). Research has found that behavioral rating scales are exactly that—they are valid measures of behavior, but not of cognition. Numerous studies have found that behavioral rating scales of executive functioning show weak-to-poor correlations with performance-based measures of cold executive functions, such as working memory, cognitive flexibility, verbal and nonverbal fluency, cognitive inhibition, abstract reasoning, and problem-solving.

Behavioral rating scales are essential to the assessment process, as a significant number of children and adults exhibit behavioral and emotional dysregulation. However, several commonly used rating scales also claim to assess the cognitive components of executive functioning—a practice that research simply does not support. We would never use a subjective rating scale to assess a child's IQ; the same rigor must apply to the assessment of the cognitive aspects of executive functioning.

This brings me to this superb book by Christopher Bedford, Julie Gettman, and Robb Matthews. The authors have taken the original D-KEFS and the D-KEFS Advanced and created what is, in my opinion, one of the clearest and most concise frameworks available for learning how to administer and interpret these tests across the lifespan but particularly in educational settings. By design, these tests assess complex cognitive skills. Consequently, performance on these tasks depends on a variety of fundamental cognitive abilities that support higher-level thinking. It is impossible to evaluate executive functions in isolation; results must always be interpreted in the context of a child's more basic cognitive abilities. While this principle is discussed extensively in the test manuals, Bedford, Gettman, and Matthews have transformed it into a practical, comprehensive, and highly accessible interpretive framework for use in all assessment settings involving children and adults.

For each D-KEFS test covered in this book, the authors begin with a case vignette that illustrates how the test works in practice. They then apply what they call a "hierarchical tier analysis" to interpret the results, doing so in a manner that is both sophisticated and easy to understand. They impressively illustrate how to interpret not only the core performance scores but also the numerous process measures provided by each test.

For example, a new set of process scores featured in three of the D-KEFS Advanced tests provides an assessment of speed–accuracy tradeoffs. In solving complex tasks that require rapid responding, a natural tradeoff occurs: responding too fast and impulsively often leads to errors, while responding too slowly may improve accuracy but at the cost of efficiency. Children and adults with problems in rapid multitasking often display one of three speed–accuracy profiles:

- They are too fast, impulsive, and error-prone.
- They make few errors but are atypically slow and inefficient.
- They are both atypically slow and display elevated error rates.

While the overall core performance scores on multitasking tests are essential for assessing if an individual is struggling in this area, they often fail to explain why. However, the new speed–accuracy process scores provided by the D-KEFS Advanced can illuminate the mechanism underlying a child or adult's multitasking deficit. Bedford, Gettman, and Matthews provide clear explanations of how to interpret these new speed–accuracy process scores, which are vital for developing meaningful recommendations. For example, understanding a child's speed–accuracy profile may help educators determine whether an impulsive student would benefit from strategies that encourage slower, more deliberate work with greater self-monitoring—or whether a child who is accurate but atypically slow would benefit from interventions where rapid responding is rewarded and mistakes are not penalized.

The D-KEFS Advanced was developed not to replace the original D-KEFS, but to complement it, and both versions will remain available for use by psychologists. For tests found in both versions (e.g., Trail Making Test; Color-Word Interference Test), the authors provide practical guidance regarding which version to use in different child and adult assessment situations. They also offer invaluable recommendations for other tests to use along with the D-KEFS or D-KEFS Advanced. Further, they offer excellent recommendations on when to use behavioral rating scales versus cognitive performance tests to assess hot and cold executive functions across varied clinical contexts.

Bedford, Gettman, and Matthews have provided us with an invaluable resource that will benefit school psychologists, pediatric neuropsychologists, adult neuropsychologists, and other professionals who seek a deeper understanding of executive function assessment and interpretation. I know this book will become an essential part of the resources I use in my clinical practice.

Dean C. Delis, Ph.D., ABPP/CN
Professor Emeritus of Psychiatry
University of California, San Diego, School of Medicine

SERIES PREFACE

In the *Essentials of Psychological Assessment Series*, we have provided the reader with books that deliver key *practical* information in the most efficient and accessible manner. Typically, books fall into one of two categories. The first category features specific topics in a variety of domains, such as specific learning disabilities, social-emotional learning, neuropsychological assessment, cross-battery assessment, and adaptive behavior assessment. These books are intended for professionals in psychology and education—and for graduate students in these or related disciplines—who are committed to providing assessment and intervention services.

A second category of books in this series, such as *Essentials of D-KEFS and D-KEFS Advanced Assessment*, is devoted to a single test. These books offer a concise yet thorough review of an instrument, with special attention to the details of administration, scoring, interpretation, application, and tips for best-practice use of the test. Students can rely on series books in both categories for a clear and concise overview of the important assessment tools and key topics informing skillful practice delivered efficiently and ethically in their chosen fields. Experienced clinicians will feel equally at home with this series in their efforts to remain on the cutting edge of new research and new instruments, as well as new editions of assessments in an array of diverse fields.

Wherever feasible, visual cues highlighting key points are used alongside systematic, step-by-step guidelines. Chapters are focused and succinct. Topics are organized for an easy understanding of the essential material related to a particular test or topic. Theory and research are continually woven into the fabric of each book, always to enhance the practical application of the material. With this series, we aim to challenge and assist readers interested in psychological and educational assessment to aspire to the highest level of competency by arming them with the resources they need for knowledgeable, informed practice. We have long been advocates of "intelligent" testing—the notion that numbers are meaningless unless they are brought to life by the clinical acumen and expertise of examiners. Assessment must be used to make a difference in the child's or the adult's life, or why bother testing? All books in the series—whether devoted to specific tests or general topics—are consistent with this credo. We want this series to help our readers, novice and veteran alike, benefit from the intelligent assessment approaches of the authors of each book.

In *Essentials of D-KEFS and D-KEFS Advanced Assessment*, Bedford, Gettman, and Matthews provide comprehensive guidance for administering, scoring, and interpreting both the original D-KEFS and the newer D-KEFS Advanced. Drawing on insights from test creator Dean Delis, the authors demonstrate how the hierarchical tier framework—spanning from foundational processes through complex executive integration—enables clinicians to differentiate true executive dysfunction from underlying deficits in processing speed, attention, or other component abilities. This book is designed for neuropsychologists, school psychologists, and clinical practitioners who evaluate executive functioning across the lifespan and seek systematic approaches to differential diagnosis. Chapters address the developmental trajectory of executive functions; detailed, subtest-by-subtest guidance for administration and interpretation; integration with other assessment instruments; and illustrative case studies spanning childhood through older adulthood. The extensive use of process scores and contrast analyses helps practitioners move beyond global performance measures to identify specific mechanisms underlying executive function impairment. This book not only focuses on practical test interpretation but is also designed to deepen understanding of executive function constructs and their real-world implications for intervention planning.

Alan S. Kaufman, Ph.D. and Nadeen L. Kaufman, Ed.D., Series Editors
Neag School of Education, University of Connecticut

AI DISCLOSURE

ESSENTIALS OF D-KEFS AND D-KEFS ADVANCED ASSESSMENT

AI was used in limited ways during the development of this book.

The lead author used Anthropic's Claude AI through a paid subscription with data sharing disabled. No content was used for AI training, and all data were retained for only 30 days before deletion. Claude assisted with:

- Proofreading for spelling, grammar, and mechanics
- Formatting drafts of reference tables based on chapter content
- Cross-referencing and formatting APA reference lists
- Creating drafts of end-of-chapter quizzes based on chapter content
- Comparing subtest chapters (Chapters 4–14) to ensure consistent organization, formatting, and headers were used throughout

All content was developed and thoroughly reviewed by the authors.

Part I

FOUNDATIONS

One

INTRODUCTION TO THE D-KEFS AND D-KEFS ADVANCED

This book provides comprehensive guidance for using two of the most sophisticated executive function assessment instruments available: the Delis-Kaplan Executive Function System (D-KEFS; Delis et al., 2001) and the D-KEFS Advanced (Delis & Kaplan, 2025). Whether you are new to these measures or have used them extensively, this guide will deepen your understanding of what they assess, how to interpret the rich data they provide, and how to translate findings into meaningful clinical recommendations.

The D-KEFS represented a significant advancement when it was published in 2001, applying process-oriented assessment principles to executive function measurement in ways that previous instruments had not. The D-KEFS Advanced, released in 2025, extends these capabilities through digital administration, enhanced process scores, and explicit attention to both "hot" and "cold" executive functions. Together, these instruments offer clinicians powerful tools for understanding the complex cognitive processes that enable—or impair—goal-directed behavior across the lifespan.

DON'T FORGET

Rating scales for children and adults, like the Behavior Rating Inventory of Executive Function, Second Edition (BRIEF-2), Delis Rating of Executive Functions (D-REF), and Comprehensive Executive Functions Inventory (CEFI), provide valuable information about how executive functions manifest in daily life, but they cannot identify the underlying cognitive mechanisms driving those difficulties. Direct assessment reveals *why* someone struggles—whether the issue is processing speed, working memory capacity, inhibitory control, cognitive flexibility, or some combination. This mechanistic understanding is essential for targeted intervention. A student who appears inattentive on rating scales might have primary inhibition deficits, working memory limitations, or slow processing speed, each requiring different intervention approaches. Only direct assessment can make these distinctions.

THE ASSESSMENT IMPERATIVE

Executive function concerns appear across virtually every type of psychological referral—the child who cannot organize homework despite adequate intelligence, the adolescent whose decision-making deteriorates in the presence of peers, the adult professional who excels in structured meetings but flounders with independent project management, and the older adult whose family notices increasing difficulty with financial decisions. Each presentation invokes questions about executive functioning—that collection of higher-order cognitive processes enabling goal-directed behavior, adaptive problem-solving, and successful navigation of complex environments.

Yet assessing executive functions presents unique challenges. Unlike memory or language—domains with relatively clear operational definitions—executive functioning encompasses a heterogeneous collection of processes that develop along different trajectories, rely on distributed neural networks, and manifest differently across developmental periods and contexts. This complexity has significant clinical consequences. When a patient performs poorly on an executive function measure, the clinician faces a fundamental interpretive question: Does this reflect true executive dysfunction, or could foundational processes, such as basic attention, motor speed, or language comprehension, contribute to the poor performance?

This question matters enormously for intervention. Teaching metacognitive strategies to someone whose poor Tower Test performance stems from visual–spatial processing deficits wastes time and resources. Recommending executive function coaching for a patient whose Trail Making difficulties reflect motor slowing rather than cognitive inflexibility misses the actual problem. Accurate assessment requires tools that can parse the complex contributors to task performance, distinguishing true executive dysfunction from the many foundational processes that support—but are not themselves—executive functions.

The D-KEFS and its recently released companion, the D-KEFS Advanced, were designed specifically to address this challenge. This chapter introduces these instruments and the interpretive framework that guides their use throughout this book. Through an interview with Dean Delis, the tests' lead author and a pioneer in process-oriented neuropsychological assessment, we explore the clinical needs that drove the D-KEFS development, the design philosophy that distinguishes it from earlier executive function measures, and how the D-KEFS Advanced extends these capabilities for contemporary clinical practice. Delis's perspective offers readers a unique window into the intentions behind these measures—knowledge that enriches interpretation and clinical application.

THE D-KEFS: A PROCESS-ORIENTED APPROACH

Origins and Development

The D-KEFS emerged from a convergence of clinical need and scientific innovation. In the early 1990s, Dean Delis developed a sorting test incorporating Edith Kaplan's process approach—an assessment philosophy emphasizing the breakdown of complex tasks into component processes. Research with patients who had frontal lobe lesions demonstrated the clinical value of this approach, leading to a publication in *Neuropsychologia* (Delis et al., 1992) that caught the attention of test publisher Pearson.

From Our Interview with Dean Delis:
"We started talking about doing a battery using the process approach, where you include not only core achievement scores but lots of process scores, because that approach had not been incorporated in existing executive function tests. Take the original Trail Making Test—the only thing scored was completion time. It didn't score errors or other strategies. The exception was the Wisconsin Card Sorting Test, a really brilliant test with incredible process scores. But most other executive function tests weren't rich in process data. And yet the process scores are so important, because these tests are so complex. It's really the process scores that allow you to get down to the mechanism of impairment on a task."

The intellectual foundation for this work traced back to Delis's training with Edith Kaplan and Harold Goodglass at the Boston VA. Delis describes a formative experience that shaped his entire approach to assessment:

From Our Interview with Dean Delis:
"I was in graduate school taking my first course on IQ testing while simultaneously taking an elective in cognitive science. In the cognitive science course, they were doing incredible process analysis of cognition—looking at memory in terms of strategies, processes, errors. But when I gave the original Wechsler Memory Scale, it yielded one score for the whole battery. I had a career crisis. This seemed so simplistic compared to what cognitive science was doing.

Then I happened to pull a book off the library shelf: The Assessment of Aphasia and Related Disorders by Goodglass and Kaplan [1972]. It used psycholinguistic principles to assess language disorder. It totally blew my mind. From that moment, I knew I needed to be a neuropsychologist, and I needed to work with Goodglass and Kaplan.

I wrote a letter to Harold Goodglass asking to come out for a summer externship. When I didn't hear back, I set my alarm for 5 a.m.—I was in Wyoming—so I could call the Boston VA. Goodglass picked up the phone, told me they had my letter, and said he'd bring it up at their staff meeting in ten minutes. I later heard they were shocked that anyone from Wyoming would be interested in neuropsychology. They said, 'This guy is really desperate—he had to get up at 5 a.m. Let's invite him out.'

When I got there, I clicked with everybody. It turned out my master's thesis was remarkably similar to a study Edith had done as a graduate student. It was like fate. We developed the California Verbal Learning Test together, taking principles from cognitive science and incorporating them into assessment. That's the foundation of everything."

Design Philosophy

The D-KEFS applies this process-oriented philosophy to executive function assessment through several key design features. First, each subtest includes baseline conditions that assess the foundational abilities required for higher-level task performance. On the original D-KEFS's Trail Making, for example, examinees complete visual scanning, number sequencing, and letter sequencing conditions before attempting the number-letter switching condition that assesses cognitive flexibility. This structure allows clinicians to determine whether poor switching performance reflects true executive dysfunction or limitations in prerequisite skills.

From Our Interview with Dean Delis:
"You look at the traditional Trail Making Test, and there are obviously some key component processes. There's a motor speed component. There's the number sequencing component. There's also a letter sequencing component. And when you get to the switching part of the task, all of those basic components have to be intact in order to get a more pure assessment of cognitive switching. If any of those component processes are impaired, that will compromise performance on the higher-level task, but it won't be an executive function deficit necessarily."

Second, the D-KEFS provides rich process scores and error analyses that reveal *how* examinees approach tasks, not just whether they succeed. Error patterns often prove more diagnostically informative than achievement scores, particularly for higher-functioning individuals whose global scores fall within normal limits.

From Our Interview with Dean Delis:
"Edith always said errors are the best window into brain function, and it's really true. There are a lot of tests where you look at number correct and normal performance, but there's an elevated error rate. That elevated error rate is so clinically essential to factor in. One thing we've always tried in all our process approach tests was to quantify the qualitative—that was a phrase Edith used to use."

Third, the battery includes multiple measures of similar constructs using different modalities and task demands. For example, Verbal Fluency and Design Fluency both assess generativity and cognitive flexibility, but through verbal and visual-motor channels, respectively. This design helps clinicians distinguish domain-general executive deficits from modality-specific limitations.

The Nine Original Subtests

The D-KEFS comprises nine subtests assessing different aspects of executive functioning, listed here in alphabetical order:

Color-Word Interference Test is the D-KEFS version of the Stroop paradigm, measuring inhibition and cognitive flexibility through color naming, word reading, inhibition, and inhibition/switching conditions.

Design Fluency Test assesses nonverbal fluency and cognitive flexibility through novel design generation under varying rule constraints.

Proverb Test assesses verbal abstract thinking through interpretation of common and uncommon proverbs.

Sorting Test evaluates concept formation, problem-solving, and verbal explanation abilities through free sorting and sort recognition conditions.

Tower Test evaluates spatial planning, rule learning, and problem-solving through a task requiring examinees to move disks across pegs to build target configurations in the minimum number of moves.

Trail Making Test assesses visual scanning, number sequencing, letter sequencing, number-letter switching, and motor speed through five conditions that systematically isolate component processes.

Twenty Questions Test assesses abstract thinking, hypothesis testing, and question formulation through a categorical guessing paradigm.

Verbal Fluency Test measures letter fluency, category fluency, and category switching, providing insight into generativity, lexical access, and cognitive flexibility in the verbal domain.

Word Context Test measures deductive reasoning and verbal comprehension by requiring examinees to discover word meanings through contextual clues.

Each subtest chapter in this book (Chapters 4–14) provides detailed guidance on administration, scoring, and interpretation for both original and Advanced versions where applicable, applying the hierarchical framework introduced in Chapter 3.

Rapid Reference 1.1

D-KEFS Subtests Overview

Subtest	Primary Constructs	Key Conditions/Features
Color-Word Interference	Inhibition, cognitive flexibility	Color naming, word reading, inhibition, inhibition/switching
Design Fluency	Nonverbal generativity, cognitive flexibility	Novel design generation under varying rules
Proverb	Verbal abstract thinking	Common and uncommon proverb interpretation
Sorting	Concept formation, problem-solving	Free sorting and sort recognition
Tower	Spatial planning, rule learning	Building target configurations in minimum moves
Trail Making	Visual scanning, sequencing, cognitive flexibility	Five conditions isolating component processes
Twenty Questions	Abstract thinking, hypothesis testing	Categorical guessing paradigm
Verbal Fluency	Generativity, lexical access, cognitive flexibility	Letter, category, and category switching
Word Context	Deductive reasoning, verbal comprehension	Word meaning discovery through context

THE D-KEFS ADVANCED: EXTENDING THE FRAMEWORK

Motivation for Development

The original D-KEFS established itself as a valuable clinical tool, but limitations emerged over years of use. Several subtests showed ceiling effects that reduced sensitivity to mild impairment in higher-functioning populations. The paper-and-pencil format constrained the complexity of administered tasks and the precision with which responses could be measured. And administering certain subtests—particularly the Tower Test—placed substantial demands on examiners that could compromise standardization.

From Our Interview with Dean Delis:
"Several of the original D-KEFS tests, although very helpful from a process approach, unfortunately have ceiling effects. They're not as sensitive as I would have wanted. Some worked out beautifully—Color-Word is a very sensitive test, and the switching conditions we added were very sensitive. But the Tower Test has a ceiling effect. Twenty Questions has a ceiling effect. Our Sorting Test has a ceiling effect. It's really great for moderate to severely impaired children and adults because you can do great process analysis, but it's not sensitive to subtle to mild impairment."

Around 2009, discussions began about developing an advanced version. The emergence of tablet-based assessment opened possibilities that paper-and-pencil administration could never achieve.

From Our Interview with Dean Delis:
"From the get-go, Pearson staff and I were exactly on the same page. Let's do something radically different. Let's forget print. The iPad had just come out, and we thought, let's try to do this all digital. We were immediately brainstorming all the advantages and exciting things you could do. There was no hesitation that we wanted to do more complex tests and do all digital.

One of the reasons we were excited about going all digital is that we could make cognitively demanding tasks that wouldn't be possible with just paper. We started this project in 2009 and never wavered from it."

The Six D-KEFS Advanced Subtests

The D-KEFS Advanced is made up of six subtests—four enhanced versions of original D-KEFS measures and two entirely new tests:

Color-Word Interference Test uses a matching rather than naming format for baseline conditions, while the inhibition condition creates a stronger stimulus-bound pull through response options that magnify the prepotent response.

Risk–Reward Decision Test is a new measure assessing "hot" executive functions—decision-making under conditions of motivational salience—with explicit risk–reward contingencies that minimize the learning demands of similar tests.

Social Sorting Test is a new measure of concept formation using ecologically valid social stimuli rather than abstract geometric shapes, with more challenging concept identification demands than traditional card sorting tasks.

Tower Test captures previously unscoreable process data, including zero-back, one-back, and two-back responses that reveal trial-and-error problem-solving approaches, while increasing task complexity through the introduction of striped discs and their accompanying rules alongside the standard solid discs.

Trail Making Test omits the original's visual scanning and motor speed conditions for efficiency while adding three switching conditions that isolate shifting, inhibition, and working memory contributions to multitasking performance. Clinicians can still administer the baseline conditions from the original D-KEFS if needed.

Verbal Fluency Test replaces the original's category-to-category switching with more demanding category-to-phonemic switching, increasing sensitivity to frontal involvement.

Advances in the Digital Format

The all-digital format of the D-KEFS Advanced enables several significant improvements. Response timing achieves millisecond precision, allowing for fine-grained analysis of processing speed and response patterns. The system captures process data that would be impossible to score reliably by hand, such as the "zero-back," "one-back," and "two-back" responses on the Tower Test that reveal trial-and-error problem-solving approaches.

From Our Interview with Dean Delis:
"The Tower Test is notoriously difficult to administer. The working memory demands on the examiner are enormous—you're counting moves, looking for rule violation errors, having to stop impulsive examinees, remembering what prompt to give. It's probably more difficult than manual administration of the Wisconsin Card Sorting Test.

When I would give the Tower Test, I could see incredible process data being lost. A kid or adult would pick up a chip, put it on another peg, pick it up, put it back—that's trial and error responding. Some people lift it up and put it right back on the same peg. Some put it on one peg, then another, then bring it back to the original. These are really neat qualitative features, but you're so busy trying to track everything that it's impossible to capture them reliably.

The all-digital approach allowed us to keep all the process scores we had before and add even more. It was process score heaven. Plus, it completely eliminates almost everything the examiner has to do other than read instructions. As far as observing behavior, it's incredible now. You can really focus on watching the examinee. When you need to give a prompt, it shows up on the practitioner device exactly when you're supposed to give it and exactly what to say. It freezes the client iPad so impulsive people can't keep going."

The digital format also enables more sophisticated scoring approaches, including speed-accuracy trade-off analysis—a clinically important variable seldomly formally incorporated in neuropsychological measures.

From Our Interview with Dean Delis:
"I read about speed-accuracy trade-off analysis, something rarely included in neuropsych tests. Patients with prefrontal involvement or a subgroup of ADHD are so impulsive they sacrifice accuracy for speed. It's such a critical variable, and hardly any tests incorporate it. That's something I really wanted in the D-KEFS Advanced, and we were able to include it on three of the tests with contrast scores based on regression models that tell you with clinical significance whether there's a meaningful difference."

New and Enhanced Subtests

The D-KEFS Advanced includes enhanced versions of Color-Word Interference, Tower, Trail Making, and Verbal Fluency, along with two new subtests: the Risk–Reward Decision Test and the Social Sorting Test.

The enhanced Trail Making now includes three switching conditions designed to isolate different executive components of multitasking performance:

From Our Interview with Dean Delis:
"Reading the literature and testing patients clinically, you could see that patients fail the Trail Making Test for different higher-level reasons. You can fail it for different types of executive function problems. So we wanted to build in more sophisticated assessment to parse out not only baseline abilities but different higher-level abilities.

To do the switching task—1, A, 2, B, 3, C—you need cognitive flexibility to switch between number sequencing and letter sequencing. But there's also an inhibition component. When you're at 3 and need to go to C, the semantic network activates the next automatized unit—4—and that has to be inhibited. Patients with frontal lobe lesions get pulled to that 4; they're stimulus-bound. And there's a working memory component, especially later in the sequence when you have to remember where you are.

So we developed three switching conditions to help isolate the mechanism of impairment. I tested a TBI patient with significant left temporal involvement and severe verbal memory impairment. He did well on the standard switching condition, did well on switching with distraction, but bombed the switching with working memory condition. So you could say this person has good shifting, good inhibition, but is impaired in multitasking when the demands are on working memory."

The Risk–Reward Decision Test represents an effort to assess "hot" executive functions—executive processes operating in emotionally or motivationally salient contexts—more comprehensively. Chapter 2 discusses the hot–cold distinction in detail; here we note that Delis and colleagues specifically designed this subtest to address a gap in traditional neuropsychological assessment.

From Our Interview with Dean Delis:
"Research on hot versus cold executive function has really grown in the last 20–25 years, and we wanted to include something on that. A problem I've seen with existing tests like the Iowa Gambling Task is that patients have to learn the contingencies. Patients with memory or learning impairment might struggle on that test because of the learning component, not the risk-reward decision-making itself.

So we designed our test to be very explicit on the risk-reward contingencies. If you pick the top horse to win, it's high risk because it starts furthest from the finish line, but you'll win more money. If you pick the bottom horse to win, it starts closer to the finish line but pays less. We had the contingencies right there.

It was probably the most difficult test to develop. We ran numerous pilot studies changing the risk-reward contingencies. People were all over the place; it was really hard to get consistent findings. The kid version just didn't work—results made no sense whatsoever—so painfully we had to drop it. But the adult version has clear clinical utility for TBI and other groups. It's helpful for adults who have problems with impulsivity and tolerating boredom, because you have to tolerate picking the boring, conservative option across 60 races."

The Social Sorting Test provides an ecologically valid measure of concept formation using real-world social stimuli (people, facial expressions, and hats) rather than the abstract geometric shapes of the Wisconsin Card Sorting Test.

From Our Interview with Dean Delis:

"The Wisconsin Card Sorting Test is an extraordinarily sensitive, elegant test—one of the greatest tests ever developed. We wanted to create something that could serve as an alternate form but be more ecologically valid in terms of stimuli and more challenging in concept identification. On the Wisconsin, the concepts are super high frequency—color, shape, number. Being able to do concept identification and flexibility with real-world stimuli, we felt, would be a helpful measure to have in your arsenal."

Rapid Reference 1.2

D-KEFS Advanced Subtests Overview

Subtest	Primary Constructs	Key Conditions/Features
Color-Word Interference	Inhibition, cognitive flexibility	Matching format with enhanced inhibition demands; speed-accuracy trade-off analysis
Risk–Reward Decision	Hot executive function, decision-making under motivational salience	Explicit risk–reward contingencies across 60 trials; assesses impulsivity and boredom tolerance
Social Sorting	Concept formation, cognitive flexibility, social reasoning	Ecologically valid social stimuli; derailment score and global performance measure
Tower	Spatial planning, rule learning, problem-solving efficiency	Automated administration capturing zero-back, one-back, and two-back responses; varying disc types and rules
Trail Making	Sequencing, cognitive flexibility, working memory	Number and letter sequencing plus three switching conditions isolating shifting, inhibition, and working memory
Verbal Fluency	Generativity, lexical access, cognitive flexibility	Letter, category, and category-to-phonemic switching

The Tier Framework

The D-KEFS Advanced manual introduced an explicit tiered framework for understanding the processes involved in each subtest. This framework recognizes that cognitive processes exist on a continuum from basic, nonexecutive abilities to complex executive control. Tier 1 encompasses foundational processes—sensory, motor, and basic cognitive abilities that are prerequisites for higher-level functioning but are not themselves executive functions. Tier 2 includes bridging processes that integrate foundational abilities with emerging executive control. Tiers 3 and 4 represent core and higher-order executive functions, respectively.

This book applies the tier framework systematically to both the original D-KEFS and D-KEFS Advanced subtests. Chapter 3 provides the full operational framework, explaining how to use hierarchical analysis for differential diagnosis. Each subsequent subtest chapter (Chapters 4–14) applies this framework to that specific measure.

The Interpretive Challenge

The process-oriented design of the D-KEFS helps clinicians navigate what researchers call the "impurity problem" in executive function assessment: the reality that any task designed to measure executive functions inevitably requires multiple cognitive processes. Poor performance could reflect deficits in any of these contributing processes rather than specifically indicating executive dysfunction.

From Our Interview with Dean Delis:
"In the original D-KEFS manual, we stated [the impurity problem] in an early chapter, but it didn't sink in. When I read others' reports, there's such a high frequency of psychologists interpreting even baseline scores as executive function and not interpreting the higher-level, more difficult tasks relative to all the test scores in the whole battery. That's when I thought, I have to put some flowcharts in here and drive this point—even include those flowcharts in the score reports so practitioners have it right in front of them."

The interpretive challenge extends beyond distinguishing foundational from executive processes. Clinicians must also consider ecological validity—the relationship between test performance under optimal conditions and real-world functioning.

From Our Interview with Dean Delis:
"One of the big criticisms of neuropsych testing is that it's conducted in a quiet, controlled, one-on-one structured setting. But in the real world, that's not the case. We wanted to try to add features that would systematically assess that variable.

The switching with distraction condition [on the Advanced version of Trail Making] was the single hardest test for us to develop. Our original approach used real-world stimuli—phones ringing, people talking, doors shutting. We did pilot study after pilot study with kids and older adults, trying to get as many ADHD kids as we could. And every pilot study showed no effect of the distraction. Zero.

We made it more distracting—different voices saying random numbers and letters. No effect. Our programmers had fireworks and things flying across the screen. Zero.

I woke up in the middle of the night thinking, 'Stroop effect—that's what we need.' I came up with the idea that when you hit the 4, a voice says '5' and a 5 appears on screen—instantly triggered to magnify the prepotent response. We finally got a significant effect. We had to incorporate principles of brain-behavior relationships to make the distraction clinically effective."

DON'T FORGET

The D-KEFS measures processes across a hierarchy—not all are executive functions. Poor performance on any subtest might reflect Tier 1 foundational deficits (e.g., motor speed, visual scanning, language comprehension), Tier 2 bridging process limitations (e.g., basic working memory, basic inhibition), or true Tier 3–4 executive dysfunction (e.g., cognitive flexibility, complex planning, emotional regulation under cognitive load). Chapter 3 provides the systematic framework for making these distinctions.

Rapid Reference 1.3

Key Advances in D-KEFS Advanced

Feature	Advantage
Digital administration	Millisecond timing precision; standardized prompts; reduced examiner burden
Enhanced process scores	Captures qualitative features impossible to score manually (e.g., trial-and-error patterns on Tower)
Explicit tier framework	Systematic distinction between foundational processes and executive functions
Multiple switching conditions (Trails)	Isolates shifting, inhibition, and working memory contributions to multitasking
Risk–Reward Decision Test	Assesses hot executive function—decision-making under motivational salience
Social Sorting Test	Ecologically valid concept formation with real-world social stimuli
Speed-accuracy trade-off analysis	Quantifies impulsive responding with regression-based contrast scores

Guidance from the Source

Beyond the structure and scores, effective D-KEFS interpretation requires attention to process—how examinees approach tasks, not just whether they succeed. Delis emphasizes that process scores and qualitative observations often yield the most clinically meaningful information, particularly for higher-functioning individuals.

From Our Interview with Dean Delis:
"Global scores are very helpful, but if there's a good global score with an elevated process score or qualitative feature, that can be among the most important findings, especially in high-functioning kids and adults. We tend to focus on global performance, yet some of the most meaningful clinical data are the process data.

Take someone with a slow completion time. You look at why, and it's because they were making errors and self-correcting, and the self-corrections take extra time. That's a different interpretation than someone who takes longer and doesn't make errors or takes longer and makes errors but doesn't recognize them. You get at least three different categories of people with a slow score but really different performance.

If someone's making an error and catching it, that catching is a cognitive strength—they're monitoring their performance. It explains the extended completion time; it's not just slow processing. The mechanism of that profile is probably impulsivity: they make errors but have the ability to catch them, yet they keep making them because they're not modulating their speed-accuracy trade-off."

The D-KEFS Advanced validation studies revealed some surprising clinical patterns that inform interpretation. Each chapter covering an Advanced subtest includes a detailed discussion of these validation findings, but several highlights deserve mention here:

From Our Interview with Dean Delis:
"The Color-Word Interference Test—the baseline conditions are actually easier in the Advanced version because you're simply matching from three options rather than naming. But condition three is actually harder because when you see the word 'red' in green ink and are asked to touch the ink color instead of the word, you also see the word 'red' in black ink as a response option. It creates a stronger stimulus-bound pull. You're magnifying the prepotent response that has to be inhibited.

When we got the ADHD data back, that test was extraordinarily sensitive, even on the baseline conditions. The effect sizes were especially high for condition three, inhibit—you just don't see those effect sizes in that population on cognitive tests. I kept thinking during development that the baseline conditions are like a mini continuous performance test—simple and boring but you have to sustain attention. Combined with inhibition, that's where ADHD breaks down.

Another surprise: kids with math learning disability bombed the Tower Test while ADHD kids did pretty well. The effect sizes for math LD were really large. When you think about it, a key aspect of math disability for a significant subgroup involves nonverbal skills and spatial analysis. The Tower Test is spatial planning—so that makes sense, but it was surprising."

Cultural and linguistic diversity affects performance on any measure, and the D-KEFS is no exception. Clinicians should consider these factors when interpreting results:

From Our Interview with Dean Delis:
"Some tests like Tower and Social Sorting are very nonverbal, so they're obviously useful with linguistically diverse groups. Other tests like Verbal Fluency have a significant verbal IQ component, so linguistic and cultural factors can play a really significant role, like with any verbal test.

I was on the advisory committee for the WISC-V and WAIS-5, and what we found was that even independent of language, cultural diversity and different ethnic groups still played a significant role on scores. For some of the D-KEFS Advanced tasks like Social Sorting and Tower, there's still a little bit of cultural or ethnic group difference, but it's pretty minimal and significantly less than on IQ measures. We haven't published that data yet, but it would be good to get it out there."

HOW THIS BOOK IS ORGANIZED

This book provides comprehensive guidance for using the D-KEFS and D-KEFS Advanced in clinical practice. The chapters are organized to build understanding systematically.

Part I: Foundations

Chapter 1 (this chapter) introduces the D-KEFS and D-KEFS Advanced, their development, design philosophy, and the interpretive challenges they address.

Chapter 2 examines executive functioning across the lifespan, providing the developmental and neurobiological context essential for interpreting performance at different ages. This includes the distinction between "hot" executive functions (operating in emotionally or motivationally salient contexts) and "cold" executive functions (operating in emotionally neutral conditions)—a distinction with significant implications for understanding the gap between test performance and real-world functioning.

Chapter 3 presents the hierarchical tier framework in full operational detail. This chapter is the methodological heart of the book, providing step-by-step guidance for using tier-based analysis to distinguish foundational deficits from true executive dysfunction.

Part II: Subtest Chapters

Chapters 4–14 cover individual subtests, with some chapters addressing both original D-KEFS and D-KEFS Advanced versions of the same measure. Each chapter follows a consistent structure: clinical vignette, test description, tier-by-tier analysis of processes involved, administration guidance, behavioral observations, scoring, common administration errors, interpretation using the hierarchical framework, strengths and weaknesses, alternative measures, and summary.

Part III: Integration

Chapter 15 addresses cross-subtest integration and synthesis—how to build coherent executive function profiles when multiple D-KEFS measures yield convergent or divergent patterns, and how to use the tier framework diagnostically across the battery.

Chapter 16 moves from assessment to action, providing guidance on translating tier-based profiles into functional understanding and recommendations. This includes explaining the tier framework to non-clinicians, clients, parents, educators, and treatment providers, and linking tier identification to appropriate intervention approaches.

Chapter 17 extends the tier framework beyond D-KEFS assessment, illustrating how this way of thinking about the impurity problem applies to assessment more broadly. The chapter closes with reflections from Dean Delis on the clinical philosophy underlying these instruments.

Throughout the book, you will encounter formatting conventions from the Essentials series:

Rapid Reference tables summarize key information in table format for quick access.
Caution boxes highlight critical confounds or common misinterpretations to avoid.
Don't Forget boxes emphasize essential clinical points that could easily be overlooked.

SUMMARY

The D-KEFS and D-KEFS Advanced provide clinicians with sophisticated tools for parsing the complex processes underlying executive function task performance. Their process-oriented design—baseline conditions isolating foundational abilities, rich error analyses, and multiple measures of similar constructs—addresses the impurity problem that has long plagued executive function assessment. The D-KEFS Advanced extends these capabilities through digital administration, enabling greater measurement precision, more complex task demands, enhanced process scores, and explicit attention to hot executive functions through the Risk–Reward Decision Test.

Yet tools are only as valuable as the interpretive framework guiding their use. This book provides that framework through hierarchical tier analysis that systematically distinguishes foundational processes from true executive functions, combined with attention to developmental context (Chapter 2) and the hot–cold distinction that explains why test performance may diverge from real-world functioning.

As Delis reflected on the D-KEFS Advanced development:

From Our Interview with Dean Delis:
"This approach allows us to capture and score such a rich variety of process and qualitative data that would be impossible to do otherwise. It reduces measurement error, increases reliability, and lets you address really complex cognitive questions: What is the mechanism of your multitasking deficit? Is it inhibition? Is it shifting? Is it working memory? That combination is what we're most excited about."

The chapters that follow translate this potential into practical clinical guidance, equipping you to use these instruments with the sophistication their design deserves. Chapter 2 provides the developmental and neurobiological foundation essential for interpreting executive function performance across the lifespan—from the rapid changes of childhood through the gradual declines of older adulthood. Chapter 3 then operationalizes the hierarchical tier framework into a systematic clinical method, showing how to distinguish foundational deficits from true executive dysfunction. Together, these three chapters establish the conceptual architecture for the subtest-specific guidance that follows.

TEST YOURSELF

1. The original D-KEFS was published in which year?

(a) 1995
(b) 2001
(c) 2016
(d) 2025

2. According to Dean Delis, which assessment philosophy was central to the D-KEFS development?

(a) Behavioral observation approach
(b) Process approach
(c) Ecological validity approach
(d) Functional assessment approach

3. The "impurity problem" in executive function assessment refers to:

(a) Contamination of test materials affecting standardization.
(b) Examiner bias influencing scoring decisions.
(c) Any executive function task inevitably requiring multiple cognitive processes.
(d) Cultural factors invalidating normative comparisons.

4. How many subtests comprise the original D-KEFS?

(a) Six
(b) Seven
(c) Eight
(d) Nine

5. **Which D-KEFS Advanced subtest was specifically designed to assess "hot" executive functions with explicit risk–reward contingencies?**
   (a) Social Sorting Test
   (b) Tower Test
   (c) Risk–Reward Decision Test
   (d) Color-Word Interference Test
6. **Dean Delis trained with Edith Kaplan and Harold Goodglass at which institution?**
   (a) UCLA Medical Center
   (b) Boston VA
   (c) Mayo Clinic
   (d) National Institutes of Health
7. **Which process data do the D-KEFS Advanced Tower Test capture that were impossible to score reliably with manual administration?**
   (a) Verbal mediation strategies
   (b) Eye movement patterns
   (c) Zero-back, one-back, and two-back responses
   (d) Hemispheric lateralization indices
8. **The D-KEFS Advanced Color-Word Interference Test differs from the original version primarily by:**
   (a) Eliminating the switching condition.
   (b) Using a matching format for baseline conditions.
   (c) Reducing the number of items per condition.
   (d) Removing time limits.
9. **According to the hierarchical tier framework introduced in Chapter 1, poor performance on a D-KEFS subtest might reflect all of the following EXCEPT:**
   (a) Tier 1 foundational deficits.
   (b) Tier 2 bridging process limitations.
   (c) Tier 3–4 executive dysfunction.
   (d) Tier 5 metacognitive integration failure.
10. **What key advantage does the D-KEFS Advanced's digital format provide for measuring impulsive responding?**
   (a) Automatic discontinue rules
   (b) Reduced examiner training requirements
   (c) Speed-accuracy trade-off analysis with regression-based contrast scores
   (d) Real-time normative comparisons

Answer Key: 1-b, 2-b, 3-c, 4-d, 5-c, 6-b, 7-c, 8-b, 9-d, 10-c

REFERENCES

Delis, D. C., & Kaplan, E. (2025). *Delis-Kaplan Executive Function System Advanced.* NCS Pearson.

Delis, D. C., Kaplan, E., & Kramer, J. H. (2001). *Delis-Kaplan Executive Function System*. The Psychological Corporation.

Delis, D. C., Squire, L. R., Bihrle, A., & Massman, P. (1992). Componential analysis of problem-solving ability: Performance of patients with frontal lobe damage and amnesic patients on a new sorting test. *Neuropsychologia, 30*, 683–697.

Goodglass, H., & Kaplan, E. (1972). *The Assessment of Aphasia and Related Disorders*. Philadelphia: Lea & Febiger.

Two

EXECUTIVE FUNCTIONING ACROSS THE LIFESPAN

INTRODUCTION: THE ASSESSMENT IMPERATIVE

The hierarchical framework and assessment approach introduced in Chapter 1 provides structure for interpreting executive function (EF) performance, but applying that framework effectively requires understanding how executive functions develop, mature, and change across the lifespan. The seven-year-old who cannot get ready for school, the fifteen-year-old whose academic performance has plummeted, the forty-five-year-old executive struggling after mild traumatic brain injury, and the seventy-two-year-old having difficulty with financial decisions—each presents with concerns about executive functioning, yet each must be understood within distinctly different developmental contexts. Age and premorbid abilities shape not only what we expect but how we interpret deviations from those expectations.

This chapter provides the developmental and neurobiological foundation necessary for applying the tier-based interpretive framework to individuals across the age span. We begin with a brief historical context before examining current conceptualizations of executive functioning as an integrated system of neural networks rather than isolated abilities. The developmental trajectory of executive functions from early childhood through older adulthood receives particular attention, as understanding typical development proves essential for recognizing and interpreting atypical presentations. We explore how executive functions emerge from increasingly specialized neural networks, how they change across the lifespan, and what happens when these systems are disrupted by developmental differences, injury, or disease.

The background presented here serves as the conceptual scaffolding for the practical assessment approaches detailed in subsequent chapters. While the complexity of executive functioning may seem daunting, this complexity also explains why executive dysfunction manifests so variably across individuals and why careful, systematic assessment proves so valuable for intervention planning. By grounding our assessment practices in current understanding of how executive functions develop and operate, we position ourselves to make meaningful contributions to the lives of those we assess.

BRAIN FUNCTIONS AND NEURAL DEVELOPMENT

The human brain follows a remarkably predictable developmental trajectory that provides the foundation for understanding executive functioning across the lifespan. During the first year of life, sensory pathways for hearing and vision mature rapidly, followed closely by language development and the emergence of purposeful thoughts and actions. This early neural development manifests behaviorally through developmental milestones such as object permanence, walking, and talking—each representing the underlying maturation of specific neural circuits (Anderson & Reidy, 2012; Barkat et al., 2011; Nelson, 2000; Segundo-Marcos et al., 2022).

The brain's developmental process involves two complementary mechanisms: neurogenesis, which creates new neurons, and synaptogenesis, which forms new synapses between neurons; followed by synaptic pruning, which eliminates unnecessary connections to improve neural efficiency. These processes transform the distributed networks of early life into the specialized interconnected systems of adulthood. This transition from broad, short-range regional connections focused on managing basic central nervous system functions to the long-range neural tracts that enable sophisticated environmental interaction represents a fundamental shift in neural organization (Barabási et al., 2024; Grammer et al., 2018; Koziol & Lutz, 2013; Nelson et al., 2019).

Executive function demands persist and evolve throughout adulthood. Consider the middle-aged professional who must inhibit the urge to check email during meetings (response inhibition), mentally juggle multiple project deadlines while prioritizing tasks (working memory and cognitive flexibility), or the older adult learning to navigate new banking technology while suppressing habitual responses to familiar methods (set-shifting and inhibition). These everyday challenges illustrate how executive functions remain crucial for adaptive functioning across the lifespan, though the specific contexts and demands shift with age and life stage.

Environmental experiences play a crucial role during sensitive and critical periods of brain development, with effects extending well into adolescence through ongoing cortical plasticity. While the importance of environmental input during development is well-established, ongoing research continues to examine the relative contributions of experience-dependent versus experience-expectant processes, with some evidence suggesting that certain aspects of executive function development follow more canalized, maturation-driven trajectories that are less dependent on specific environmental input than others (Best & Miller, 2010). This debate underscores the complexity of disentangling genetic, maturational, and environmental factors in executive function development. The quality and timing of these experiences can significantly influence neural structure, as demonstrated by research showing that childhood adversity affects both brain development and later executive functioning. Children who experience severe neglect, for example, often show lower global executive functioning and higher rates of psychopathology in adolescence, illustrating how environmental factors become embedded in neural architecture (Barkat et al., 2011; Fox et al., 2010; Knudsen, 2004; Nelson et al., 2019; Oberman & Pascual-Leone, 2013; Sydnor et al., 2025; Wade et al., 2020).

Individual variations in neural development reflect the complex interplay of genetic and epigenetic factors, hormonal influences, disease processes, critical illnesses, and environmental stimulation. Rather than representing discrete categories of typical versus atypical development, these variations exist along a continuum. Because the brain functions as an interconnected system of nerve cells, changes in one area rarely affect only a single functional unit but ripple throughout related networks (Barabási et al., 2024; Fox et al., 2010; Hopkins & Brett, 2005; Matthews, 2022; Nelson et al., 2019; Richter et al., 2024; Wilson, 2016). This hierarchical neural organization from primary sensory and motor cortices through association areas to prefrontal networks provides the neuroanatomical basis for the tier framework detailed in Chapter 3, where foundational processes must be intact before higher-level executive functions can be accurately assessed.

Cultural context and socioeconomic factors profoundly influence executive function development through multiple pathways. Children from lower socioeconomic backgrounds often experience chronic stress that affects prefrontal cortex development and stress-response systems, potentially compromising executive functions (Blair & Raver, 2016; Noble et al., 2015). However, these same environments may foster certain adaptive executive skills, such as enhanced cognitive flexibility in unpredictable situations (Mittal et al., 2015). Cultural values regarding emotional expression shape hot executive function development—children from cultures that value emotional restraint may demonstrate stronger delay of gratification and emotional regulation in testing situations, while those from cultures encouraging emotional expressiveness might appear more impulsive despite having age-appropriate executive control (Moriguchi, 2014). Bilingual and multilingual children often demonstrate enhanced executive control, particularly in cognitive flexibility and inhibition, suggesting that linguistic diversity serves as a form of executive function training (Bialystok, 2017; Carlson & Meltzoff, 2008). These considerations underscore that executive function assessment must account not only for neurobiological development but also for the cultural and socioeconomic contexts that shape both the development and expression of executive skills.

DEFINING EXECUTIVE FUNCTIONS

Despite dramatic advances in understanding brain development and functioning, professional consensus on the definition and measurement of executive functions remains elusive. Executive functions encompass a broad array of higher-order cognitive processes, including attentional control, working memory, inhibition, behavioral regulation, planning, problem solving, set shifting, hypothesis generation, and initiation. Early attempts at defining executive functions often cast too wide a net, attempting to include numerous potential contributors without sufficient precision. Contemporary efforts to resolve definitional disparities have focused on several contributing factors: the stepwise nature of executive development, the diverse theoretical backgrounds of researchers offering definitions, and the specific task demands used in different investigations (Doebel, 2020; Koziol & Lutz, 2013; McCloskey et al., 2009).

Some researchers have attempted to sidestep definitional challenges by focusing on observable behaviors and developing rating scales, but this approach risks conflating executive processes with their behavioral manifestations while overlooking the underlying neurocognitive mechanisms that drive executive functioning (Dias et al., 2024).

The limitation of purely behavioral approaches becomes evident when considering developmental factors that affect self-awareness and metacognition. Children consistently overestimate their abilities, with monitoring accuracy improving gradually through elementary school years (Desoete & Roeyers, 2006; Horton & Reynolds, 2021). This developmental pattern suggests that effective executive function assessment requires functional neurological measures that can be directly linked to specific abilities, such as those found in comprehensive assessment batteries like the Delis-Kaplan Executive Function System (D-KEFS; Delis et al., 2001) and its Advanced version (D-KEFS Advanced; Delis & Kaplan, 2025).

As neuroscience has evolved toward understanding the brain as an integrated, complex system, executive function conceptualizations have followed suit. This shift toward more elegant, brain-based definitions has enhanced clinical flexibility in applying executive function concepts to individual circumstances while generating interest across multiple professional domains, including academic performance, mental health, psychosocial functioning, and sports performance (Dias et al., 2024; Gioia et al., 2015; Koziol & Lutz, 2013; Matthews, 2023).

The hierarchical nature of executive abilities adds further complexity to developing unified models of executive functioning. More complex executive functions emerge from combinations of simpler component processes, making it difficult to study higher-order abilities in isolation. Planning, for example, requires successful coordination of working memory, inhibition, cognitive flexibility, and attentional control—illustrating how executive functions build upon and integrate multiple foundational components (Ferguson et al., 2021; Karr et al., 2022; Miyake et al., 2000). This hierarchical organization means that apparent deficits in complex executive tasks may actually reflect weaknesses in underlying component processes rather than impairment in the higher-order function itself. Biological findings reveal additional individual variability that complicates modeling efforts: the lateral prefrontal cortex shows individual differences in sulcal morphology that predict reasoning ability, while neuroimaging sometimes reveals paradoxical relationships such as inverse correlations between right frontal pole activation and creative performance, possibly reflecting the suppression of inhibitory processes during creative thinking (Kutsche et al., 2025; Voorhies et al., 2021). These findings underscore why consensus on executive function definitions remains elusive. The construct encompasses not only multiple interrelated processes but also substantial individual variation in both neural architecture and functional expression.

NEURAL NETWORKS SUPPORTING EXECUTIVE FUNCTIONS

Executive functions emerge from the coordinated activity of multiple brain regions and networks that change systematically across development. Research has identified several key brain regions that consistently activate across diverse executive tasks. The mid-dorsolateral prefrontal cortex (DLPFC), mid-ventromedial prefrontal cortex (VMPFC), and dorsal anterior cingulate cortex (ACC) form the core of what researchers term the "multi-demand cortex." This network coordinates multiple brain functions and serves as a foundation for intellectual thought and action. This finding established the crucial principle that executive functions emerge from network activity rather than isolated brain regions, fundamentally changing how we understand executive control (Duncan, 2010; Duncan & Owen, 2000).

The thalamus contributes to executive functioning through hierarchically organized influences on cortical development, following a timeline that mirrors the maturation of other executive function brain structures. This region also mediates the impact of environmental experiences on neural development, serving as a bridge between external influences and internal neural organization. The cerebellum enhances executive functioning by improving the automaticity of information processing—anticipating cognitive needs, adjusting responses in real-time, and increasing the precision of executive control (Koziol & Lutz, 2013; Sydnor et al., 2025).

A particularly important network for executive functioning is the default mode network (DMN), which includes distributed and interconnected regions across the frontal, temporal, and parietal lobes. This network activates during internally directed thought and action, supporting complex behaviors such as mental arithmetic, visual scanning, reasoning, judgment, memory encoding, and autobiographical recall. The DMN's function varies based on specific task demands, highlighting the flexible, context-dependent nature of executive control (Bartoli et al., 2024; Beaty & Kenett, 2023; Kutsche et al., 2025; Paquola et al., 2025).

Within the DMN, specialized subnetworks support creative thinking and innovation—the integration of disparate information toward novel outcomes. These microarchitectural networks respond primarily to sensory input and appear relatively resistant to environmental influences, suggesting a fundamental biological basis for certain aspects of executive creativity. Both semantic and episodic memory can trigger DMN activation, creating pathways for executive functions to access and manipulate stored knowledge (Bartoli et al., 2024; Beaty & Kenett, 2023; Paquola et al., 2025).

The ACC deserves special attention for its role in integrating cognitive and emotional processes within executive functioning. This region supports empathy and prosocial behaviors, modulating responses based on social cues and contextual interpretations. Research demonstrates that the ACC contributes to the effort required for prosocial actions and links to both empathy and helping behaviors. Even sleep quality affects prosocial behavior through ACC-mediated mechanisms, illustrating how executive functions extend far beyond purely cognitive domains to encompass social and emotional regulation (Ben Simon et al., 2022; Keum & Shin, 2019; Lockwood et al., 2022; Segundo-Marcos et al., 2022).

THE CHALLENGE OF EXECUTIVE FUNCTION MEASUREMENT

Chapter 1 introduced the "impurity problem"—the reality that any executive function task inevitably requires multiple cognitive processes. The neurobiological foundations reviewed in this chapter reveal why this problem is unavoidable: the brain's interconnected network architecture means that changes in one region ripple throughout related systems. A task intended to assess inhibition, for example, also draws upon working memory, attention, processing speed, and often language comprehension. This overlap means that poor performance could reflect deficits in any of these contributing processes rather than specifically indicating executive dysfunction (Anderson & Reidy, 2012; Miyake et al., 2000; Tervo-Clemmens et al., 2023).

Multitasking research illustrates this complexity particularly well. Effective multitasking requires the integration of general cognitive abilities such as response speed, cognitive efficiency, and inhibition, combined with demand-specific resources like working memory capacity. The ability to efficiently reorganize information emerges as a necessary component that changes with increasing task complexity. Since many executive function tasks depend on recognizing and correcting errors, and since the contributing processes may not be immediately apparent, disentangling specific aspects of executive functioning from supporting cognitive processes remains challenging (Lui et al., 2025).

The predominance of emotionally neutral, decontextualized measures in standardized assessment batteries further complicates the impurity problem. Traditional neuropsychological instruments such as the Tower Test, Trail Making Test, and Stroop Color-Word Test present stimuli under controlled conditions that minimize emotional salience, reward processing, and motivational factors. This methodological constraint means that even when we successfully parse the cognitive components contributing to task performance, we may still miss clinically significant executive dysfunction that emerges only in emotionally charged or motivationally complex situations. The impurity problem thus operates on two levels: the challenge of isolating specific cognitive processes within tasks, and the limitation of assessing executive functions primarily through emotionally neutral paradigms when emotional and motivational factors may drive the functional impairments that prompt referral. As we will see in the following section, this challenge becomes particularly salient when we consider the distinction between executive processes that operate in emotionally neutral versus emotionally salient contexts.

The interconnected nature of brain networks compounds this measurement challenge. Changes in one neurological network inevitably affect functioning in associated networks, with alterations in regions that coordinate large volumes of information producing particularly broad functional changes. Brain diseases such as epilepsy and serious mental illnesses like bipolar disorder and schizophrenia continue to impact cortical functions and network connectivity even during periods of apparent clinical stability, demonstrating the pervasive influence of executive function networks throughout the brain (Grammer et al., 2018; Matthews, 2022; Nissen et al., 2017; Royer et al., 2022; Wilson, 2016).

HOT AND COLD EXECUTIVE FUNCTIONS: AFFECTIVE AND COGNITIVE CONTROL SYSTEMS

CAUTION

Given the impurity problem, poor performance on any executive function task could reflect deficits in contributing processes (e.g., working memory, attention, processing speed, language comprehension) rather than true executive dysfunction. Always consider whether foundational processing weaknesses may account for observed difficulties before attributing them to executive impairment.

The heterogeneity of executive functions extends beyond distinctions between working memory, inhibition, and cognitive flexibility to encompass a fundamental division between executive processes that operate in emotionally neutral versus emotionally salient contexts. This distinction between "cold" and "hot" executive functions has emerged as an essential framework for understanding both the neurobiological architecture of executive control and the frequent discrepancies between performance in structured assessment settings and real-world functioning (Welsh & Peterson, 2014; Zelazo & Carlson, 2012).

Cold executive functions encompass the cognitive control processes typically assessed in traditional neuropsychological evaluation: abstract reasoning, working memory manipulation, set-shifting, and response inhibition deployed in affectively neutral, decontextualized conditions. These processes operate when solving arithmetic problems, organizing geometric designs, generating words from phonemic cues, or alternating between cognitive sets—tasks that require cognitive control but lack emotional significance or motivational salience. The standardized testing environment, with its quiet room, clear instructions, and emotionally neutral stimuli, creates ideal conditions for assessing cold executive functions while simultaneously limiting opportunities to observe hot executive processes (Zelazo, 2020).

Hot executive functions engage when cognitive control must be maintained in the presence of emotional arousal, motivational conflict, or reward contingencies. These processes encompass delay of gratification, affective decision-making, emotion regulation in service of goals, and the inhibition of prepotent (overlearned) responses when rewards or punishments are salient. The child who must share toys despite wanting them all, the adolescent navigating peer pressure while maintaining long-term academic goals, and the adult managing workplace frustration while preserving professional relationships all require hot executive functions. These situations demand not only cognitive control but the integration of that control with emotional processing and motivational systems (Happaney et al., 2004; Poon, 2018).

Neurobiological Distinctions

The hot–cold distinction maps onto partially dissociable neural circuits, though considerable overlap exists given the integrated nature of executive control networks. Cold executive functions primarily recruit dorsolateral prefrontal cortex and associated frontoparietal networks. These circuits support abstract manipulation of information independent of affective significance. Neuroimaging studies consistently demonstrate activation of these regions during traditional executive tasks such as n-back working memory paradigms, Stroop interference, and task-switching protocols conducted with emotionally neutral stimuli (Miller & Cohen, 2001; Niendam et al., 2012).

Hot executive functions preferentially engage ventromedial and orbitofrontal prefrontal regions that maintain dense reciprocal connections with limbic and paralimbic structures, including the amygdala, ventral striatum, and hypothalamus. These circuits evolved to support decision-making in contexts where choices have emotional or motivational consequences. The orbitofrontal cortex particularly contributes to the representation of reward values and the flexible updating of these values based on changing contingencies. The ventromedial prefrontal cortex integrates emotional signals from limbic regions with cognitive representations from dorsolateral regions, enabling decisions that balance immediate emotional impulses with longer-term goals (Kringelbach & Rolls, 2004; Zelazo & Carlson, 2012).

The ACC, particularly its dorsal and rostral subdivisions, serves as a critical interface between hot and cold executive systems. This region supports both cognitive control and emotional processing, with dorsal regions more associated with cold executive functions and rostral/ventral regions more linked to hot executive processes. This anatomical arrangement facilitates the flexible recruitment of appropriate executive

Rapid Reference 2.1

Brain Regions and Networks Involved in EF

Brain Region/Network	Functions and Contributions to EF	Key References
Prefrontal cortex (mid-dorsolateral, mid-ventromedial, dorsal ACC)	Activated across diverse EF tasks; basis for the *multi-demand (MD) cortex* concept (intellectual thought, action, coordination of functions)	Duncan and Owen (2000) and Duncan (2010)
Developmental brain connectivity	*Early life*: Short-range regional connections (CNS management); *Adulthood*: Long-range tracts (environmental action, integration)	Koziol and Lutz (2013) and Paquola et al. (2025)
Thalamus	Hierarchical contributions to cortical development; reflects both biological growth and environmental influence	Sydnor et al. (2025)
Cerebellum	Enhances automaticity, anticipates needs, adjusts responses, improves precision	Koziol and Lutz (2013)
Default mode network (DMN)	Interwoven frontal, temporal, parietal cortices; task-variable; supports reasoning, memory, mental arithmetic, scanning, judgment	Paquola et al. (2025), Bartoli et al. (2024), and Beaty and Kenett (2023)
DMN subnetworks	Support creative thinking and innovation; linked to sensory-driven activity, relatively environment-independent. Stimulated by semantic/episodic memory	Beaty and Kenett (2023) and Bartoli et al. (2024)
Anterior cingulate cortex (ACC)	Empathy and prosocial behaviors; integrates cognitive-emotional processes, modulated by social cues and sleep quality	Keum and Shin (2019), Lockwood et al. (2022), and Ben Simon et al. (2022)
Task-based EF measurement	Tasks often measure overlapping processes (e.g., inhibition + working memory); multitasking requires both general abilities and demand-specific resources; highlights "impurity problem"	Miyake et al. (2000), Anderson and Reidy (2012), Lui et al. (2025), and Tervo-Clemmens et al. (2023)
Cross-network effects	Changes in one network ripple to others; brain diseases and psychiatric disorders disrupt connectivity even during remission	Grammer et al. (2018), Matthews (2022), Wilson (2016), Royer et al. (2022), and Nissen et al., 2017
Cold EF circuits (DLPFC, frontoparietal)	Abstract reasoning, working memory, set-shifting in emotionally neutral contexts; consistent with multi-demand cortex functions	Miller and Cohen (2001) and Niendam et al. (2012)
Hot EF circuits (VMPFC, OFC, limbic connections)	Decision-making with emotional/motivational salience; reward processing, delay of gratification; integration of emotion with cognitive control	Zelazo and Carlson (2012) and Happaney et al. (2004)

resources based on task demands, though it also creates vulnerability when coordination between systems fails (Bush et al., 2000; Stevens et al., 2011).

Developmental Considerations

Hot and cold executive functions follow distinct developmental trajectories that have important implications for understanding behavior across childhood and adolescence. Cold executive functions show relatively rapid development during the preschool and early elementary years, with many components reaching near-adult levels by early adolescence. The developmental progression of working memory, inhibition, and cognitive flexibility between ages 5 and 11 primarily reflects cold executive function maturation (Best & Miller, 2010).

Hot executive functions demonstrate more protracted development, with some components not reaching maturity until the mid-twenties. This extended developmental timeline particularly characterizes decision-making under emotional arousal and the ability to resist immediately rewarding choices in favor of long-term goals. The Iowa Gambling Task (IGT; Bechara, 2007), which requires participants to learn to avoid immediately rewarding but ultimately disadvantageous choices, reveals continued improvements through late adolescence. Similarly, delay of gratification tasks show ongoing development well into the second decade of life, with individual differences in childhood performance predicting academic achievement, social competence, and psychological adjustment decades later (Mischel et al., 1989).

This developmental asymmetry—whereby cold executive functions mature earlier than hot executive functions—creates a period during adolescence characterized by strong abstract reasoning capabilities coexisting with immature emotional decision-making. The adolescent brain possesses the cognitive capacity to understand long-term consequences and generate sophisticated problem-solving strategies, yet when emotional arousal increases or peers are present, hot executive functions may fail to regulate behavior effectively. This maturational gap partially explains heightened risk-taking, emotional volatility, and susceptibility to peer influence that characterize adolescence (Casey et al., 2011; Somerville et al., 2010). For clinicians applying the tier framework, this asymmetry means that an adolescent may demonstrate intact Tier 3 cold executive functions on standardized testing while showing significant hot executive deficits that emerge only in emotionally salient contexts. This underscores the importance of integrating behavioral observations, rating scales, and functional history with test performance.

> **DON'T FORGET**
>
> Hot and cold EF follow different developmental trajectories. Cold executive functions reach near-adult levels by early adolescence, while hot executive functions continue developing into the mid-twenties. Age-appropriate performance on traditional (cold) measures cannot rule out significant hot executive deficits that manifest primarily in emotionally charged contexts.

Clinical Populations and Diagnostic Patterns

Different clinical populations show characteristic patterns of hot and cold executive functioning that inform both assessment and intervention approaches. Children with attention-deficit/hyperactivity disorder (ADHD) typically demonstrate impairments in both domains, though hot executive deficits often prove most impairing for daily functioning. Difficulties with delay of gratification, emotion regulation, and reward processing frequently drive the behavioral problems that prompt referral, even when cold executive deficits also contribute to academic struggles (Castellanos et al., 2006; Sonuga-Barke, 2003).

Autism spectrum disorder often presents with a different profile: relatively preserved or even superior cold executive functions alongside significant hot executive challenges, particularly in social–emotional contexts. These individuals may excel at abstract reasoning tasks and demonstrate strong working memory for nonsocial information yet struggle profoundly when executive control must integrate emotional understanding or navigate social reward contingencies. This dissociation helps explain why some individuals with autism perform well on performance-based executive function measures despite experiencing significant real-world executive challenges (Kouklari et al., 2018; Zimmerman et al., 2017).

Bipolar disorder and severe emotional dysregulation disorders frequently involve primary disruption of hot executive functions, with cold executive impairments emerging secondarily when emotional dysregulation interferes with cognitive performance. During euthymic periods, cold executive functions may normalize while hot executive deficits persist, suggesting fundamental differences in the stability and treatment responsiveness of these systems (Wegbreit et al., 2016).

Assessment Implications of the Hot–Cold Distinction

The hot–cold framework reveals a critical blind spot in traditional neuropsychological assessment: our standardized instruments systematically exclude emotional and motivational contexts that often drive the very behaviors prompting referral. This exclusion is not accidental but methodological—standardized administration requires controlling for emotional variables to ensure reliable measurement. Yet this necessary standardization means we primarily capture cold executive capacity while potentially missing hot executive impairments entirely (Welsh & Peterson, 2014; Zelazo & Carlson, 2012).

Consider how different measures align with hot versus cold systems. The Wisconsin Card Sorting Test, Trail Making Test, and Digit Span assess cold executive functions—abstract set-shifting, sequencing, and working memory in emotionally neutral contexts. Even when these tasks become frustrating, they lack intrinsic emotional significance or meaningful reward contingencies. In contrast, delay of gratification tasks, gambling paradigms, and go/no-go tasks with reward/punishment feedback tap hot executive functions by incorporating motivational conflict and emotional salience (Mischel et al., 1989). The child who sorts cards perfectly but cannot resist grabbing a peer's toy demonstrates intact cold but impaired hot executive functioning, a distinction our standard batteries may miss entirely (Toplak et al., 2013).

The developmental asynchrony between these systems creates particular assessment challenges. During adolescence, near-adult cold executive abilities coexist with still-developing hot executive functions. An adolescent may demonstrate sophisticated abstract reasoning on the WISC-V Matrix Reasoning subtest yet show profound impairment when reward contingencies and loss potential are introduced. This developmental gap means that age-appropriate performance on traditional measures cannot rule out significant hot executive deficits that manifest primarily in emotionally charged contexts (Casey et al., 2011; Somerville et al., 2010).

Clinical populations show characteristic hot–cold dissociations that inform differential diagnosis. The child with ADHD who completes the Tower Test successfully in a quiet testing room but cannot organize homework when siblings are playing nearby shows context-dependent executive failure—performance degrades specifically when hot executive functions must regulate behavior despite emotional distractors (Castellanos et al., 2006; Sonuga-Barke, 2003). Conversely, the anxious adult whose worry interferes with cold executive tasks during testing may demonstrate adequate hot executive functions in familiar emotional contexts. Recognizing these patterns requires deliberate assessment of both systems rather than inferring global executive functioning from cold executive measures alone (Zelazo, 2020).

Intervention Considerations Based on Hot–Cold Profiles

The hot–cold distinction directly informs intervention selection, as strategies effective for cold executive deficits may fail when hot executive functions are primarily impaired. Cold executive interventions, such as working memory training, cognitive rehabilitation exercises, and strategy instruction for planning and organization, assume the individual can deploy these skills when emotionally aroused. This assumption breaks down when hot executive deficits prevent strategy implementation despite adequate cold executive capacity (Diamond & Ling, 2016).

For hot executive deficits, interventions must explicitly address the integration of cognitive control with emotional processing. Dialectical behavior therapy's distress tolerance modules, for example, specifically target maintaining executive control during emotional dysregulation. The Zones of Regulation curriculum teaches children to recognize their emotional state and select appropriate regulatory strategies—bridging awareness of hot states with cold executive planning. These approaches differ fundamentally from cognitive training by acknowledging that executive control must function within emotional contexts rather than despite them (Zelazo & Carlson, 2012).

The interaction between hot and cold systems suggests value in integrated interventions. The Promoting Alternative Thinking Strategies (PATHS) curriculum exemplifies this integration, teaching emotional understanding alongside problem-solving skills (Riggs et al., 2006). Children learn to recognize emotional triggers (hot), generate alternative solutions (cold), evaluate consequences considering feelings (hot–cold integration), and implement chosen strategies despite emotional arousal (hot). This scaffolded approach builds both systems while strengthening their coordination.

Treatment planning should consider whether deficits are primary or secondary. Hot executive deficits that secondarily impair cold performance (anxiety disrupting working memory) require a different intervention than primary cold deficits with intact hot functions. Similarly, cold executive deficits may prevent effective emotion regulation strategy use, suggesting the need to build foundational cognitive skills before attempting complex emotional regulation training. The hierarchical framework introduced in Chapter 3 provides a systematic approach for determining where in this integrated system intervention should begin.

EXECUTIVE FUNCTIONS ACROSS THE LIFESPAN

Large-scale research examining individuals from ages 3 to 85 reveals a characteristic pattern of executive function change across the lifespan. Performance improves rapidly during childhood and adolescence, remains relatively stable throughout much of adulthood, and shows an accelerating decline in older age. This pattern reflects the underlying maturation and eventual aging of the neural networks that support executive control (Karr et al., 2022). Critically, these changes do not occur uniformly across the hierarchy of processes introduced in Chapter 1. Tier 1 foundational processes, such as processing speed, show the earliest maturation and the most consistent age-related decline, while Tier 3–4 executive functions follow more protracted developmental trajectories and may be relatively preserved in early aging even as foundational processes slow.

Having established the distinction between hot and cold executive functions and their different neural substrates, we can now examine how these systems develop across the lifespan. Executive function development begins in infancy and follows a predictable but variable course that extends into early adulthood, with some aspects continuing to mature throughout the lifespan. Early developmental markers such as visual attention patterns and recognition abilities predict later executive functioning, suggesting that the foundations for executive control emerge much earlier than traditionally recognized. Research has identified associations between infant gaze duration and later executive efficiency, with "short-lookers" who process information quickly showing stronger executive functioning throughout early childhood (Anderson & Reidy, 2012; Cuevas & Bell, 2014; Ferguson et al., 2021; Hendry et al., 2016; Horton & Reynolds, 2021; Roebers, 2017; Segundo-Marcos et al., 2022).

These early executive capacities link directly to the maturation of frontal lobe regions and the development of connectivity within broader neurological networks, including the cerebellum and parietal lobes. As these neural connections strengthen, children demonstrate increasing executive control and application. The progression from basic attention regulation to sophisticated planning and problem-solving reflects this underlying neural maturation and explains why early executive function differences may signal future difficulties or emerging developmental conditions (Hendry et al., 2016; Koziol & Lutz, 2013; Segundo-Marcos et al., 2022).

Preschool and Early Elementary Development

Executive functions undergo rapid development during the preschool years, with dramatic improvements in planning, organization, and decision-making. Cognitive flexibility emerges between ages 3 and 4, increases in complexity between ages 7 and 9, and traditionally reaches maturity around age 12, though some research suggests continued development into the early 20s. This developmental progression coincides with the cognitive demands of academic performance, emotional management, and social functioning, highlighting the practical importance of executive maturation (Ferguson et al., 2021; Segundo-Marcos et al., 2022).

Meta-analytic research spanning nearly two decades reveals consistent age-related improvements in executive functioning from ages 5 to 22. Planning abilities show the most prominent growth between ages 5 and 8 and after age 17, with steady improvements during intervening years. Verbal fluency demonstrates significant growth between ages 5–8, 8–11, and after 17, while design fluency shows the most dramatic improvement between ages 5–8 and 8–11.

Inhibitory control exhibits large gains between ages 5–8 and 8–11, with smaller improvements continuing through age 14. Working memory follows a similar pattern, with substantial growth in the ability to maintain and manipulate information through task completion occurring primarily between ages 5 and 11 (Romine & Reynolds, 2005).

The relationship between executive function development and academic achievement becomes particularly evident during elementary school years. Stronger executive functioning predicts school readiness and mathematical ability, with effects extending beyond simple behavioral regulation to encompass information processing efficiency. Metacognitive abilities—the capacity to think about thinking—account for substantial variance in mathematical problem-solving, though children's self-assessments of their abilities remain notably inaccurate until later elementary years (Desoete & Roeyers, 2006; Roebers, 2017; Vitiello & Greenfield, 2017).

Late elementary and early middle school represent particularly important periods for executive development. Longitudinal research reveals coordinated maturation in working memory, cognitive flexibility, inhibition, planning, and emotional reasoning. These improvements support alternating attention and successful adaptation to new situations while facilitating essential elements of written and spoken language and mathematical reasoning. Interestingly, collaborative learning approaches appear more effective than individualistic methods for promoting working memory and self-regulation, suggesting that environmental factors can optimize executive development (Grammer et al., 2018; Karr et al., 2022; Segundo-Marcos et al., 2022).

Adolescent Development

Executive function development accelerates during adolescence, with particularly rapid changes in efficiency and accuracy occurring between ages 10 and 15. Performance generally stabilizes between ages 18 and 20, earlier than many previous models suggested. Rather than reflecting the emergence of entirely new capacities, adolescent executive development appears to involve refinements in the accuracy and efficiency of existing abilities (Tervo-Clemmens et al., 2023).

Adult Development

Executive function development does not cease in early adulthood. Adult executive functioning typically peaks during young adulthood, when the cognitive demands of higher education, career development, and independent living require sophisticated executive control. Throughout middle and older adulthood, executive functions show both stability and change, with some abilities (such as accumulated knowledge-based problem-solving) continuing to improve while others (particularly processing speed-dependent executive tasks) may show age-related decline. Some aspects of executive functioning begin declining earlier than previously recognized, with working memory changes detectable in the 30s and inhibitory control decreasing in older age. These changes reflect the ongoing maturation and eventual aging of frontal brain regions that support executive control, occurring within a context of vast individual differences shaped by factors including cognitive reserve, physical health, social engagement, and continued learning opportunities (Ferguson et al., 2021; Tervo-Clemmens et al., 2023). Understanding this continued developmental trajectory helps clinicians distinguish between typical age-related changes and pathological decline requiring intervention.

Rapid Reference 2.2

Developmental Trajectory of EF

Age Range	Key EF Developments	Research Highlights
Infancy (0–2 yrs)	• *Early markers*: Visual attention, recognition, gaze duration • "Short-lookers" have more efficient processing and stronger later EF	Cuevas and Bell (2014) and Hendry et al. (2016)

Age Range	Key EF Developments	Research Highlights
Preschool (3–5 yrs)	• Rapid growth in planning, organization, decision-making • Cognitive flexibility begins (3–4 yrs) • Inhibition and working memory deficits linked to dysregulation	Diamond and Doar (1989), Anderson and Reidy (2012), Schoemaker et al. (2012), and Ferguson et al. (2021)
Early elementary (5–8 yrs)	• Significant growth in planning, verbal fluency, design fluency, inhibition, working memory • EF linked to school readiness, early math, metacognition	Romine and Reynolds (2005), Vitiello and Greenfield (2017), and Desoete and Roeyers (2006)
Later childhood (8–11 yrs)	• Continued growth in fluency, inhibition, WM • Error monitoring matures; need for external input decreases	Romine and Reynolds (2005) and Grammer et al. (2018)
Early adolescence (11–14 yrs)	• Gains in WM, fluency, inhibition, planning • EF supports adaptation, alternating attention, emotional reasoning	Segundo-Marcos et al. (2022) and Romine and Reynolds (2005)
Late adolescence (15–20 yrs)	• Rapid changes in EF efficiency and accuracy • Stabilization by ~18–20 yrs (earlier than some models)	Tervo-Clemmens et al. (2023)
Young adulthood (20s–30s)	• Peak cognitive performance • EF supports independence, abstract reasoning, higher education/work demands • Some WM decline is detectable in 30s	Ferguson et al. (2021) and Voorhies et al. (2021)
Middle adulthood (40s–60s)	• Generally stable EF performance • Adaptive networks (ACC and LPFC) support task/environmental demands • Creativity linked to paradoxical right frontal pole activity	Grammer et al. (2018) and Kutsche et al. (2025)
Older adulthood (60s–85+ yrs)	• Declines in inhibitory control, WM, processing speed • Downward slope in EF performance accelerates with age	Karr et al. (2022) and Ferguson et al. (2021)

The stability of adult executive functioning can be disrupted by various factors including disease processes, genetic influences, health status, and physical well-being. Reduced health behaviors such as poor dietary choices, inadequate self-regulation of eating, and difficulties adapting behaviors related to health often reflect executive dysfunction. Given the prevalence of metabolic syndrome and related conditions in middle adulthood, examining executive function interventions for health promotion represents an important clinical application (Dohle et al., 2018).

Barring mitigating factors such as central nervous system diseases, brain injuries, severe mental illnesses, substance abuse, or certain medical treatments, executive functions begin declining as frontal brain regions undergo age-related changes during early to middle adulthood. The DMN faces particularly prominent changes in older adulthood, including decreases in both functionality and efficiency. Semantic fluency typically declines after age 70, with phonemic fluency (word generation by specific letters) showing reductions by age 80. Decreases in working memory, inhibitory control, planning, and cognitive flexibility characterize older age, though research reveals inconsistent patterns regarding the specific trajectories of these changes (Ferguson et al., 2021; Horton & Reynolds, 2021; Kutsche et al., 2025; Oberman & Pascual-Leone, 2013).

EXECUTIVE FUNCTIONS IN CONTEXT: BRIDGING THE ASSESSMENT–REALITY GAP

The discrepancy between test performance and daily functioning represents one of the most persistent challenges in executive function assessment, extending beyond the hot–cold distinction to encompass fundamental questions about ecological validity. Teachers describe students who "fall apart" with multistep assignments despite strong test scores. Parents report children who navigate complex video games yet cannot organize their backpacks. Employers note workers who excel in structured meetings but fail at independent project management. These observations highlight a critical gap: standardized assessment captures executive capacity under optimal conditions, but life rarely provides such conditions.

The ecological validity research reveals modest but meaningful relationships between formal assessment and functional outcomes. Meta-analyses consistently find correlations in the 0.30 to 0.50 range between office-based executive measures and real-world functioning (Burgess et al., 1998; Chaytor & Schmitter-Edgecombe, 2003; Finnanger et al., 2022). These moderate correlations suggest our measures capture real variance in executive functioning while simultaneously confirming that substantial aspects of daily executive performance remain unmeasured. This limitation reflects not test inadequacy but the fundamental complexity of translating laboratory-based measurement to naturalistic contexts where multiple factors—social dynamics, competing priorities, fluctuating motivation, cumulative fatigue, and environmental supports—continuously modulate executive demands (Suchy, 2009; Suchy et al., 2024).

This reality necessitates a multi-method, multi-informant approach to executive function assessment. Rating scales completed by informants who observe the individual across settings and time—parents and teachers for children, spouses or partners, adult children, coworkers, or supervisors for adults—provide insights into EF expression that may not emerge during brief testing sessions. Self-report measures offer additional perspectives for adolescents and adults, though insight into one's own executive difficulties may itself be compromised by the very deficits being assessed. These instruments assess the consistency and pervasiveness of executive difficulties, though they bring their own limitations, including rater bias, variable interpretation of items, and the conflation of EF deficits with other behavioral or emotional concerns. Observational data, including structured observations in classroom or workplace settings and careful behavioral observations during testing offer additional perspectives on how individuals recruit and sustain executive control under varying demands. The qualitative aspects noted during D-KEFS administration (e.g., strategy use, self-correction, response to feedback, frustration tolerance) often prove as informative as scaled scores in understanding an individual's executive profile.

The integration of these multiple data sources—formal testing, rating scales, observations, developmental history, and functional reports—allows clinicians to triangulate toward a more complete understanding of executive functioning. Convergent evidence across methods strengthens diagnostic confidence, while discrepancies between data sources often prove diagnostically informative. The child who performs well on structured EF tasks but receives poor ratings on behavioral measures may have adequate executive skills but lack the self-awareness or motivation to deploy them independently. Alternatively, they may rely heavily on external structure and struggle when such scaffolding is absent. Adolescents with strong behavioral ratings but poor test performance might have developed effective compensatory strategies for familiar situations but lack the flexible problem-solving required for novel tasks. Similarly, the adult who demonstrates intact performance on assessment measures yet receives concerning reports from family members about financial decisions, medication management, or workplace performance may be drawing on cognitive reserves to meet circumscribed task demands while failing to deploy executive skills consistently in complex, real-world contexts. The older adult whose informant ratings suggest significant decline but who performs adequately on standardized measures may benefit from environmental supports that preserve functioning, whereas discrepant findings in the opposite direction—poor test performance despite reassuring informant reports—may suggest emerging deficits not yet apparent in well-practiced daily routines. Chapter 3 provides further guidance on integrating these multiple data sources within the tier framework.

Understanding these patterns has direct implications for intervention planning. A student whose executive deficits emerge primarily in unstructured settings may benefit more from environmental modifications and strategy instruction than from cognitive rehabilitation targeting component executive skills. An adult returning to work after traumatic brain injury whose testing reveals intact executive capacity but whose supervisor reports difficulty with independent project management may need workplace accommodations and compensatory strategy training rather than cognitive remediation. Conversely, foundational executive deficits identified through formal assessment may require direct intervention before environmental accommodations can be effective for the elementary student learning organizational systems or the older adult implementing memory strategies to support medication adherence. The ecological validity challenge thus becomes not merely a limitation to acknowledge but a clinical data point that informs our understanding of how executive functions manifest across the complexity of human experience.

DON'T FORGET

Discrepancies are data. When formal testing, rating scales, and functional reports yield conflicting pictures, the discrepancy itself is diagnostically informative. These patterns reveal whether deficits are context-dependent, whether compensatory strategies mask underlying weaknesses, or whether environmental structure is supporting—or will need to support—daily functioning.

The assessments detailed in the following chapters attempt to bridge this ecological gap through varied task demands, multiple response modalities, and process-oriented scoring that captures not just achievement but approach. However, no single assessment tool can fully capture the dynamic, context-dependent nature of executive functioning. The clinical skill lies in integrating multiple sources of information, understanding the factors that influence EF expression, and translating assessment findings into interventions that address both the underlying executive capacities and the real-world contexts in which they must be deployed.

Rapid Reference 2.3

Clinical Pearls for EF Assessment

Assessment Challenge	**Clinical Implication**	**Best Practice**
Impurity problem	Poor performance may reflect non-EF deficits (e.g., language, motor, visual–spatial)	Use a hierarchical interpretation framework; assess foundational skills first
Hot vs. cold EF gap	Standard measures miss emotional/motivational EF deficits	Integrate rating scales, observations, and clinical history with test scores
Performance vs. competence	Structured testing may mask real-world EF problems	Triangulate data from multiple sources and settings
Developmental variability	EF components mature at different rates	Interpret profiles considering age-expected developmental patterns
Ecological validity limits	Correlations between tests and function are modest (0.30–0.50)	View assessment data as hypothesis-generating, not definitive

THE ASSESSMENT CHALLENGE REVISITED

The theoretical and neurobiological foundations presented in this chapter add developmental complexity to the assessment challenges introduced in Chapter 1. Not only must clinicians determine whether poor performance reflects true executive dysfunction versus foundational processing deficits, but they must also consider where an individual falls along the developmental trajectory and whether observed performance aligns with age-expected patterns.

A child who cannot complete the Tower Test successfully might have executive dysfunction, or might have visual–spatial processing difficulties, motor planning problems, comprehension issues, or developmental immaturity in prefrontal systems that will resolve with time. This interpretive complexity extends across the lifespan. An older adult who struggles with medication management might exhibit executive dysfunction, or might have visual processing difficulties reading labels, memory problems recalling instructions, motor coordination issues opening pill bottles, or age-related slowing that affects timed performance without reflecting true executive impairment. Similarly, a working adult who misses deadlines consistently might have deficits in planning and organization (executive functions), or might have unaddressed anxiety that disrupts concentration, sleep deprivation that impairs cognitive efficiency, or simply an unrealistic workload that would overwhelm anyone's executive capacities. The developmental context shapes not only what we expect but how we interpret deviations from those expectations.

The hierarchical framework introduced in Chapter 1—distinguishing between Tier 1 foundational processes, Tier 2 bridging processes, Tier 3 core executive functions, and Tier 4 higher-order integration—provides the structure for navigating these interpretive challenges. The developmental perspective offered in this chapter adds the essential temporal dimension: understanding not only *what* is being assessed but *when* in the developmental trajectory we are assessing it. Together, these perspectives enable clinicians to distinguish between developmental delay and disorder, between age-appropriate limitation and pathological decline, and between performance that reflects current capacity and performance that predicts future trajectory. This approach honors the neurobiological complexity discussed throughout this chapter while providing the practical structure necessary for clinical decision-making.

SUMMATION OF THE EF RESEARCH

Executive functions remain a theoretical construct without widely accepted definitions at the time of this writing. However, major advances in conceptualizing executive functioning as a complex, integrated system that varies with time, experience, and genetic factors bring us closer to definitional consensus. Literature reviews, meta-analyses, enhanced computerized measurement strategies, and functional magnetic resonance imaging studies continue to refine our understanding of these crucial cognitive processes.

The authors hope this review of executive function history, biological and social contributors to development, and impact on daily life enhances professional understanding and improves the health and well-being of those we serve. Executive functions clearly represent higher-level cognitive processes that contribute to multiple aspects of daily functioning throughout the lifespan, emerging from sophisticated neural networks that develop predictably but with significant individual variation.

LOOKING FORWARD: FROM THEORY TO PRACTICE

The neurobiological and developmental foundations explored in this chapter provide the essential context for understanding executive functioning across the lifespan. As the research reviewed here demonstrates, executive functions are neither unitary nor static; they emerge from complex neural networks, develop along predictable but variable trajectories, and manifest differently across developmental periods and clinical populations. This complexity explains why executive dysfunction manifests so variably and why the tier framework introduced in Chapter 1 proves so essential for accurate interpretation.

Chapter 3 operationalizes the tier framework into a systematic clinical method. Where this chapter explained *why* foundational processes, bridging abilities, and true executive functions follow different developmental trajectories, Chapter 3 shows *how* to determine which level is compromised in a given individual. The hierarchical approach provides the structure for distinguishing Tier 1 foundational deficits from Tier 3–4 executive dysfunction—a distinction with direct implications for intervention. Together, these three foundational chapters equip clinicians to approach the subtest-specific guidance that follows with both the conceptual understanding and practical framework necessary for sophisticated interpretation.

TEST YOURSELF

1. The "impurity problem" in executive function assessment refers to:

(a) The tendency for test materials to become contaminated over repeated use.

(b) The reality that any single task designed to measure one executive function inevitably requires multiple cognitive processes.

(c) The difficulty in obtaining unbiased ratings from parents and teachers.

(d) The challenge of maintaining standardized testing conditions across different settings.

2. Which brain network activates during internally directed thought and supports complex behaviors such as reasoning, judgment, and autobiographical recall?

(a) The frontoparietal attention network

(b) The salience network

(c) The default mode network (DMN)

(d) The sensorimotor network

3. Hot executive functions are BEST characterized as:

(a) Executive processes that operate under time pressure.

(b) Executive processes that engage when cognitive control must be maintained in the presence of emotional arousal or motivational conflict.

(c) Executive processes that are measured by generative tasks.

(d) Executive processes that activate during physical exertion.

4. According to the chapter, which brain regions form the core of the "multi-demand cortex"?

(a) Hippocampus, amygdala, and hypothalamus

(b) Mid-dorsolateral prefrontal cortex, mid-ventromedial prefrontal cortex, and dorsal anterior cingulate cortex

(c) Primary motor cortex, primary sensory cortex, and occipital lobe

(d) Cerebellum, brainstem, and thalamus

5. The developmental asymmetry between hot and cold executive functions during adolescence is characterized by:

(a) Hot executive functions maturing before cold executive functions.

(b) Both systems maturing at the same rate.

(c) Cold executive functions reaching near-adult levels while hot executive functions continue developing into the mid-twenties.

(d) Neither system showing significant development during adolescence.

6. Meta-analyses examining the relationship between office-based executive measures and real-world functioning consistently find correlations in which range?

(a) 0.80 to 0.95

(b) 0.60 to 0.75

(c) 0.30 to 0.50

(d) 0.05 to 0.15

7. Which clinical population typically presents with relatively preserved or superior cold executive functions alongside significant hot executive challenges, particularly in social-emotional contexts?

(a) Attention-deficit/hyperactivity disorder

(b) Autism spectrum disorder

(c) Bipolar disorder

(d) Major depressive disorder

8. **According to meta-analytic research, which executive function shows the most prominent growth between ages 5 and 8 and after age 17?**
   (a) Inhibitory control
   (b) Working memory
   (c) Planning
   (d) Shifting
9. **The process by which the brain eliminates unnecessary neural connections to improve efficiency is called:**
   (a) Neurogenesis.
   (b) Synaptogenesis.
   (c) Synaptic pruning.
   (d) Myelination.
10. **Cold executive functions primarily recruit which brain region?**
    (a) Orbitofrontal cortex
    (b) Ventromedial prefrontal cortex
    (c) Dorsolateral prefrontal cortex
    (d) Amygdala

Answer Key: 1-b, 2-c, 3-b, 4-b, 5-c, 6-c, 7-b, 8-c, 9-c, 10-c

REFERENCES

Anderson, P. J., & Reidy, N. (2012). Assessing executive function in preschoolers. *Neuropsychology Review, 22*(4), 345–360. https://doi.org/10.1007/s11065-012-9220-3.

Barabási, D. L., Schuhknecht, G. F. P., & Engert, F. (2024). Functional neuronal circuits emerge in the absence of developmental activity. *Nature Communications*, 15, 364. https://doi.org/10.1038/s41467-023-44681-2.

Bartoli, E., Devara, E., Dang, H. Q., Rabinovich, R., Mathura, R. K., Anand, A., Pascuzzi, B. R., Adkinson, J., Kenett, Y. N., Bijanki, K. R., Sheth, S. A., & Shofty, B. (2024). Default mode network electrophysiological dynamics and causal role in creative thinking. Brain, 147(10), 3409–3425. https://doi.org/10.1093/brain/awae199.

Barkat, T. R., Polley, D. B., & Hensch, T. K. (2011). A critical period for auditory thalamocortical connectivity. Nature Neuroscience, 14(9), 1189–1194. https://doi.org/10.1038/nn.2882.

Beaty, R. E., & Kenett, Y. N. (2023). Associative thinking at the core of creativity. *Trends in Cognitive Sciences*, 27(7), 671–683. https://doi.org/10.1016/j.tics.2023.04.004.

Bechara, A. (2007). *Iowa Gambling Task Professional Manual.* Psychological Assessment Resources, Inc.

Ben Simon, E., Vallat, R., Rossi, A., & Walker, M. P. (2022). Sleep loss leads to the withdrawal of human helping across individuals, groups, and large-scale societies. *PLOS Biology, 20*(8), e3001733. https://doi.org/10.1371/journal.pbio.3001733.

Best, J. R., & Miller, P. H. (2010). A developmental perspective on executive function. *Child Development, 81*(6), 1641–1660.

Bialystok, E. (2017). The bilingual adaptation: How minds accommodate experience. *Psychological Bulletin, 143*(3), 233.

Blair, C., & Raver, C. C. (2016). Poverty, stress, and brain development: New directions for prevention and intervention. *Academic Pediatrics, 16*(3), S30–S36.

Burgess, P. W., Alderman, N., Evans, J., Emslie, H., & Wilson, B. A. (1998). The ecological validity of tests of executive function. *Journal of the International Neuropsychological Society*, *4*(6), 547–558. https://doi.org/10.1017/S1355617798466037.

Bush, G., Luu, P., & Posner, M. I. (2000). Cognitive and emotional influences in anterior cingulate cortex. *Trends in Cognitive Sciences, 4*(6), 215–222.

Carlson, S. M., & Meltzoff, A. N. (2008). Bilingual experience and executive functioning in young children. *Developmental Science, 11*(2), 282–298.

Casey, B. J., Somerville, L. H., Gotlib, I. H., Ayduk, O., Franklin, N. T., Askren, M. K., et al. (2011). Behavioral and neural correlates of delay of gratification 40 years later. *Proceedings of the National Academy of Sciences, 108*(36), 14998–15003.

Castellanos, F. X., Sonuga-Barke, E. J., Milham, M. P., & Tannock, R. (2006). Characterizing cognition in ADHD: Beyond executive dysfunction. *Trends in Cognitive Sciences, 10*(3), 117–123.

Chaytor, N., & Schmitter-Edgecombe, M. (2003). The ecological validity of neuropsychological tests: A review of the literature on everyday cognitive skills. *Neuropsychology Review, 13*(4), 181–197. https://doi.org/10.1023/B:NERV.0000009483.91468.fb.

Cuevas, K., & Bell, M. A. (2014). Infant attention and early childhood executive function. *Child Development*, 85(2), 397–404. https://doi.org/10.1111/cdev.12126.

Delis, D. C., & Kaplan, E. (2025). *Delis-Kaplan Executive Function System Advanced: Manual.* NCS Pearson.

Delis, D. C., Kaplan, E., & Kramer, J. H. (2001). *The Delis-Kaplan Executive Function System: Examiner's Manual.* The Psychological Corporation.

Desoete, A., & Roeyers, H. (2006). Metacognitive macroevaluations in mathematical problem solving. Learning and Instruction, 16(1), 12–25. https://doi.org/10.1016/j.learninstruc.2005.12.003.

Diamond, A., & Doar, B. (1989). The performance of human infants on a measure of frontal cortex function, the delayed response task. Developmental Psychobiology, 22(3), 271–294. https://doi.org/10.1002/dev.420220307.

Diamond, A., & Ling, D. S. (2016). Conclusions about interventions, programs, and approaches for improving executive functions that appear justified and those that, despite much hype, do not. *Developmental Cognitive Neuroscience, 18*, 34–48.

Dias, N. M., Helsdingen, I. E., Lins, E. K. R. M. d., Etcheverria, C. E., A., D.,. V. d., Steffen, L., O., C.,. C. d., & Lopes, F. M. (2024). Executive functions beyond the "Holy Trinity": A scoping review. Neuropsychology, 38(2), 107–125. https://doi.org/10.1037/neu0000922.

Doebel, S. (2020). Rethinking executive function and its development. Perspectives on Psychological Science, 15(4), 942–956. https://doi.org/10.1177/1745691620904771.

Dohle, S., Diel, K., & Hofmann, W. (2018). Executive functions and the self-regulation of eating behavior: A review. *Appetite, 124*, 4–9.

Duncan, J. (2010). The multiple-demand (MD) system of the primate brain: Mental programs for intelligent behaviour. *Trends in Cognitive Sciences, 14*(4), 172–179.

Duncan, J., & Owen, A. M. (2000). Dissociative methods in the study of frontal lobe function. *Attention and Performance, 18*, 566–576.

Ferguson, H. J., Brunsdon, V. E. A., & Bradford, E. E. F. (2021). The developmental trajectories of executive function from adolescence to old age. *Scientific Reports, 11*, 1382. https://doi.org/10.1038/s41598-020-80866-1.

Finnanger, T. G., Andersson, S., Chevignard, M. P., Johansen, G. O., Brandt, A. E., Hypher, R. E., Risnes, K., Rø, T. B., & Stubberud, J. (2022). Assessment of executive function in everyday life—Psychometric properties of the Norwegian adaptation of the Children's Cooking Task. *Frontiers in Human Neuroscience, 15*, 761755. https://doi.org/10.3389/fnhum.2021.761755.

Fox, S. E., Levitt, P., & Nelson, C. A. I. I. I. (2010). How the timing and quality of early experiences influence the development of brain architecture. Child Development, 81(1), 28–40. https://doi.org/10.1111/j.1467-8624.2009.01380.x.

Gioia, G. A., Isquth, P. K., Guy, S. C., & Kenworthy, L. (2015). *Behavior Rating Inventory of. Executive Function* (2nd ed.). Lutz, FL: PAR Inc.

Grammer, J. K., Gehring, W. J., & Morrison, F. J. (2018). Associations between developmental changes in error-related brain activity and executive functions in early childhood. *Psychophysiology, 55*(3), e13040. https://doi.org/10.1111/psyp.13040.

Happaney, K., Zelazo, P. D., & Stuss, D. T. (2004). Development of orbitofrontal function: Current themes and future directions. *Brain and Cognition, 55*(1), 1–10.

Hendry, A., Jones, E. J. H., & Charman, T. (2016). Executive function in the first three years of life: Precursors, predictors and patterns. Developmental Review, 42, 1–33. https://doi.org/10.1016/j.dr.2016.06.005.

Horton, A. M., Jr., & Reynolds, C. R. (2021). Trajectory of the development of executive functioning: Implications for death as a penalty as applied to the late adolescent class. Journal of Pediatric Neuropsychology, 7(1–2), 66–73. https://doi.org/10.1007/s40817-021-00103-z.

Hopkins, R. O., & Brett, S. (2005). Chronic neurocognitive effects of critical illness. Current Opinion in Critical Care, 11(4), 369–375. https://doi.org/10.1097/01.ccx.0000166399.88635.a5.

Karr, J. E., Rodriguez, J. E., Goh, P. K., Martel, M. M., & Rast, P. (2022). The unity and diversity of executive functions: A network approach to life span development. Developmental Psychology, 58(4), 751–767. https://doi.org/10.1037/dev0001313.

Keum, S., & Shin, H. S. (2019). Neural basis of observational fear learning: A potential model of affective empathy. *Neuron, 104*(1), 78–86. https://doi.org/10.1016/j.neuron.2019.09.013.

Knudsen, E. I. (2004). Sensitive periods in the development of the brain and behavior. Journal of Cognitive Neuroscience, 16(8), 1412–1425. https://doi.org/10.1162/0898929042304796.

Kouklari, E. C., Tsermentseli, S., & Monks, C. P. (2018). Hot and cool executive function in children and adolescents with autism spectrum disorder: Cross-sectional developmental trajectories. *Child Neuropsychology, 24*(8), 1088–1114.

Koziol, L. F., & Lutz, J. T. (2013). From movement to thought: The development of executive function. Applied Neuropsychology: Child, 2(2), 104–115. https://doi.org/10.1080/21622965.2013.748386.

Kringelbach, M. L., & Rolls, E. T. (2004). The functional neuroanatomy of the human orbitofrontal cortex: Evidence from neuroimaging and neuropsychology. *Progress in Neurobiology, 72*(5), 341–372.

Kutsche, J., Taylor, J. J., Erkkinen, M. G., et al. (2025). Mapping neuroimaging findings of creativity and brain disease onto a common brain circuit. JAMA Network Open, 8(2), e2459297. https://doi.org/10.1001/jamanetworkopen.2024.59297.

Lockwood, P. L., Wittmann, M. K., Nili, H., Matsumoto-Ryan, M., Abdurahman, A., Cutler, J., Husain, M., & Apps, M. A. J. (2022). Distinct neural representations for prosocial and self-benefiting effort. Current Biology, 32(20), 4172–4185. https://doi.org/10.1016/j.cub.2022.08.010.

Lui, K. F. H., Ng, H. T. Y., Fan, P., Wong, Y. K., & Wong, A. C.-N. (2025). Bridging concurrent multitasking, task switching, and complex multitasking: The general and specific skills involved. Journal of Experimental Psychology: Human Perception and Performance, 51(7), 875–894. https://doi.org/10.1037/xhp0001332.

Matthews, R. N. (2022). Assessing and intervening with children with seizure disorders. In D. C. Miller, D. E. Maricle, C. L. Bedford, & J. A. Gettman (Eds.), Best Practices in School Neuropsychology: Guidelines for Effective Practice, Assessment, and Evidence-Based Intervention (2nd ed., pp. 359–371). Wiley.

Matthews, R. N. (2023, October 7). Executive functions: From development to intervention School Neuropsychology Institute training program. Online presentation.

McCloskey, G., Perkins, L. A., & Van Divner, B. (2009). Assessment and Intervention for Executive Function Difficulties. School-Based Practice in Action Series. New York, NY, US: Routledge/Taylor & Francis Group.

Miller, E. K., & Cohen, J. D. (2001). An integrative theory of prefrontal cortex function. *Annual Review of Neuroscience, 24*(1), 167–202.

Mischel, W., Shoda, Y., & Rodriguez, M. L. (1989). Delay of gratification in children. *Science, 244*(4907), 933–938.

Mittal, C., Griskevicius, V., Simpson, J. A., Sung, S., & Young, E. S. (2015). Cognitive adaptations to stressful environments: When childhood adversity enhances adult executive function. *Journal of Personality and Social Psychology, 109*(4), 604.

Miyake, A., Friedman, N. P., Emerson, M. J., Witzki, A. H., Howerter, A., & Wager, T. D. (2000). The unity and diversity of executive functions and their contributions to complex "frontal lobe" tasks: A latent variable analysis. Cognitive Psychology, 41(1), 49–100. https://doi.org/10.1006/cogp.1999.0734.

Moriguchi, Y. (2014). The early development of executive function and its relation to social interaction: A brief review. *Frontiers in Psychology, 5*, 388.

Nelson, C. A. (2000). The neurobiological bases of early intervention. In J. P. Shonkoff & S. J. Meisels (Eds.), Handbook of Early Childhood Intervention (pp. 204–228). Cambridge: Cambridge University Press.

Nelson, C. A., III, Zeanah, C. H., & Fox, N. A. (2019, 2019). How early experience shapes human development: The case of psychosocial deprivation. Behavioural Neurology, 1676285. https://doi.org/10.1155/2019/1676285.

Niendam, T. A., Laird, A. R., Ray, K. L., Dean, Y. M., Glahn, D. C., & Carter, C. S. (2012). Meta-analytic evidence for a superordinate cognitive control network subserving diverse executive functions. Cognitive, Affective, & Behavioral Neuroscience, *12*(2), 241–268.

Nissen, I. A., Stam, C. J., Reijneveld, J. C., van Straaten, I. E. C. W., Hendriks, E. J., Baayen, J. C., De Witt Hamer, P. C., Idema, S., & Hillebrand, A. (2017). Identifying the epileptogenic zone in interictal resting-state MEG source-space networks. Epilepsia, 58(1), 137–148. https://doi.org/10.1111/epi.13622.

Noble, K. G., Houston, S. M., Brito, N. H., Bartsch, H., Kan, E., Kuperman, J. M., et al. (2015). Family income, parental education and brain structure in children and adolescents. Nature Neuroscience, *18*(5), 773–778.

Oberman, L., & Pascual-Leone, A. (2013). Changes in plasticity across the lifespan: Cause of disease and target for intervention. Progress in Brain Research, 207, 91–120. https://doi.org/10.1016/B978-0-444-63327-9.00016-3.

Paquola, C., Garber, M., Frässle, S., Jessica Royer, Yigu Zhou, Shahin Tavakol, …, Boris C. Bernhardt (2025). The architecture of the human default mode network explored through cytoarchitecture, wiring, and signal flow. Nature Neuroscience, 28, 654–664. https://doi.org/10.1038/s41593-024-01868-0.

Poon, K. (2018). Hot and cool executive functions in adolescence: Development and contributions to important developmental outcomes. Frontiers in Psychology, *8*, 2311.

Richter, S., Winzeck, S., Correia, M. M., Czeiter, E., Whitehouse, D., Yeo, B. T. T., Menon, D. K., & Cole, J. H. (2024). Predicting recovery in patients with mild traumatic brain injury and a normal CT using serum biomarkers and diffusion tensor imaging (CENTER-TBI): An observational cohort study. EClinicalMedicine. https://doi.org/10.17863/CAM.110.18.

Riggs, N. R., Greenberg, M. T., Kusché, C. A., & Pentz, M. A. (2006). The mediational role of neurocognition in the behavioral outcomes of a social-emotional prevention program in elementary school students: Effects of the PATHS curriculum. *Prevention Science, 7*(1), 91–102.

Roebers, C. M. (2017). Executive function and metacognition: Towards a unifying framework of cognitive self-regulation. Developmental Review, 45, 31–51. https://doi.org/10.1016/j.dr.2017.04.001.

Romine, C. B., & Reynolds, C. R. (2005). A model of the development of frontal lobe functioning: Findings from a meta-analysis. Applied Neuropsychology, 12(4), 190–201. https://doi.org/10.1207/s15324826an1204_2.

Royer, J., Bernhardt, B. C., Larivière, S., Gleichgerrcht, E., Vorderwülbecke, B. J., Vulliémoz, S., & Bonilha, L. (2022). Epilepsy and brain network hubs. Epilepsia, 63(3), 537–550. https://doi.org/10.1111/epi.17171.

Schoemaker, K., Bunte, T., Wiebe, S. A., Espy, K. A., Deković, M., & Matthys, W. (2012). Executive function deficits in preschool children with ADHD and DBD. Journal of Child Psychology and Psychiatry, 53(2), 111 120. https://doi.org/10.1111/j.1469-7610.2011.02468.x.

Segundo-Marcos, R., Carrillo, A. M., Fernández, V. L., & González, M. T. D. (2022). Development of executive functions in late childhood and the mediating role of cooperative learning: A longitudinal study. Cognitive Development, 63, 101219. https://doi.org/10.1016/j.cogdev.2022.101219.

Somerville, L. H., Jones, R. M., & Casey, B. J. (2010). A time of change: Behavioral and neural correlates of adolescent sensitivity to appetitive and aversive environmental cues. *Brain and Cognition*, *72*(1), 124–133.

Sonuga-Barke, E. J. (2003). The dual pathway model of AD/HD: An elaboration of neuro-developmental characteristics. *Neuroscience & Biobehavioral Reviews*, *27*(7), 593–604.

Stevens, F. L., Hurley, R. A., & Taber, K. H. (2011). Anterior cingulate cortex: unique role in cognition and emotion. *The Journal of Neuropsychiatry and Clinical Neurosciences*, *23*(2), 121–125.

Suchy, Y. (2009). Executive functioning: Overview, assessment, and research issues for non-neuropsychologists. *Annals of Behavioral Medicine*, *37*(2), 106–116. https://doi.org/10.1007/s12160-009-9097-4.

Suchy, Y., DesRuisseaux, L. A., Gereau Mora, M., Brothers, S. L., & Niermeyer, M. A. (2024). Conceptualization of the term "ecological validity" in neuropsychological research on executive function assessment: A systematic review and call to action. *Journal of the International Neuropsychological Society*, *30*(3), 247–263. https://doi.org/10.1017/S1355617723000735.

Sydnor, V. J., Bagautdinova, J., Larsen, B., et al. (2025). Human thalamocortical structural connectivity develops in line with a hierarchical axis of cortical plasticity. Nature Neuroscience, 28, 1772–1786. https://doi.org/10.1038/s41593-025-01991-6.

Tervo-Clemmens, B., Calabro, F. J., Parr, A. C., Fedor, J., Foran, W., & Luna, B. (2023). A canonical trajectory of executive function maturation from adolescence to adulthood. Nature Communications, 14, 6922. https://doi.org/10.1038/s41467-023-42540-8.

Toplak, M. E., West, R. F., & Stanovich, K. E. (2013). Practitioner review: Do performance-based measures and ratings of executive function assess the same construct? *Journal of Child Psychology and Psychiatry*, *54*(2), 131–143.

Vitiello, V. E., & Greenfield, D. B. (2017). Executive functions and approaches to learning in predicting school readiness. Journal of Applied Developmental Psychology, 53, 1–9. https://doi.org/10.1016/j.appdev.2017.08.004.

Voorhies, W. I., Miller, J. A., Yao, J. K., Bunge, S. A., & Weiner, K. S. (2021). Cognitive insights from tertiary sulci in prefrontal cortex. Nature Communications, 12, 5122. https://doi.org/10.1038/s41467-021-25162-w.

Wade, M., Zeanah, C. H., Fox, N. A., & Nelson, C. A. (2020). Global deficits in executive functioning are transdiagnostic mediators between severe childhood neglect and psychopathology in adolescence. Psychological Medicine, 50(10), 1687–1694. https://doi.org/10.1017/S0033291719001764.

Wegbreit, E., Cushman, G. K., Weissman, A. B., Bojanek, E., Kim, K. L., Leibenluft, E., & Dickstein, D. P. (2016). Reversal-learning deficits in childhood-onset bipolar disorder across the transition from childhood to young adulthood. *Journal of Affective Disorders*, *203*, 46–54.

Welsh, M., & Peterson, E. (2014). Issues in the conceptualization and assessment of hot executive functions in childhood. *Journal of the International Neuropsychological Society*, *20*(2), 152–156.

Wilson, S. M. (2016). Lesion-symptom mapping in the study of spoken language understanding. Language, Cognition and Neuroscience, 32(7), 891–899. https://doi.org/10.1080/23273798.2016.1248984.

Zelazo, P. D. (2020). Executive function and psychopathology: A neurodevelopmental perspective. *Annual Review of Clinical Psychology*, *16*(1), 431–454.

Zelazo, P. D., & Carlson, S. M. (2012). Hot and cool executive function in childhood and adolescence: Development and plasticity. *Child Development Perspectives*, *6*(4), 354–360.

Zimmerman, D., Ownsworth, T., O'Donovan, A., Roberts, J., & Gullo, M. J. (2017). Associations between executive functions and mental health outcomes for adults with autism spectrum disorder. *Psychiatry Research*, *253*, 360–363.

Three

HOW TO USE THIS BOOK

This chapter introduces the hierarchical tier framework that organizes all subsequent subtest chapters. We recommend reading this chapter completely before proceeding to individual subtests, as understanding the tier system fundamentally changes how you interpret test performance. Each subtest chapter will reference this framework, applying it to that specific measure's unique demands. The Rapid Reference boxes can serve as quick reminders when you're deep into individual subtest chapters and need to recall tier distinctions or differential diagnosis steps.

FROM THEORY TO PRACTICE

Chapter 1 introduced the Delis-Kaplan Executive Function System (D-KEFS; Delis et al., 2001) instruments and the process-oriented philosophy underlying their design. Chapter 2 provided the developmental and neurobiological foundation for understanding how executive functions emerge, mature, and change across the lifespan. This chapter brings those elements together into a systematic clinical method—the hierarchical tier framework that will guide interpretation throughout the remainder of this book.

The practical challenge is clear: How do we accurately assess executive functions when any test performance involves multiple cognitive processes, when emotional factors profoundly influence cognitive control, and when structured testing may miss the very deficits that manifest most problematically in daily life? The tier framework provides the answer. By distinguishing foundational processes (Tier 1) from bridging abilities (Tier 2) and true executive functions (Tiers 3–4), and by attending to both hot and cold executive demands, clinicians can parse the complex contributors to test performance and identify precisely where intervention should target.

Central to effective use of the D-KEFS and D-KEFS Advanced is understanding that not all processes measured by these tests are executive functions. Performance on any D-KEFS subtest depends on a foundation of basic cognitive processes, bridging abilities, and true executive functions. This distinction is crucial: poor performance might reflect deficits at any level of this hierarchy, and accurate identification of the affected level is essential for appropriate intervention.

Each subtest chapter follows a consistent format to facilitate comparison and application. Whether you're new to these instruments or an experienced user seeking to deepen your understanding, this section will enhance your ability to interpret and apply the rich information the D-KEFS and D-KEFS Advanced can provide. The framework presented here directly addresses the "impurity problem" discussed in earlier chapters—the reality that no executive function task measures a single cognitive process in isolation. By systematically parsing performance across hierarchical tiers and considering both hot and cold executive demands, clinicians can identify which level and type of processing is compromised.

EXECUTIVE FUNCTION DOMAINS FRAMEWORK: A HIERARCHICAL APPROACH

The D-KEFS Advanced manual introduced a tiered system of processes involved in each of the subtests (Delis & Kaplan, 2025). Throughout this book, we take two approaches with this framework. First, we apply the tiered analysis retrospectively to the original D-KEFS subtests, which predate this organizational system. Second, for the D-KEFS Advanced subtests, we occasionally build upon Pearson's tier designations to reflect insights from our clinical practice. Readers will find our tier frameworks similar to those in the official manual, but sometimes expanded based on what we have observed in applied assessment contexts.

This hierarchical organization corresponds with neuroanatomical functioning from primary sensory and motor cortices through association areas to the prefrontal networks that support executive control (Luria, 1980; Mesulam, 1998). Specifically, lower-tier processes map onto posterior brain regions and primary cortices, while higher-tier executive functions increasingly engage prefrontal and frontoparietal networks (Badre & D'Esposito, 2009; Stuss & Alexander, 2000).

THE HIERARCHICAL MODEL: DISTINGUISHING EXECUTIVE FROM NONEXECUTIVE PROCESSES

The tiered framework shows that cognitive processes exist on a continuum from basic, nonexecutive abilities to complex executive control. Understanding this continuum fundamentally changes how we interpret performance and select interventions. Working memory, for example, may function as a Tier 2, 3, or 4 process depending on task complexity. Basic memory maintenance represents lower-tier processing, while complex manipulation and integration represent higher-tier executive control. For each subtest, different abilities fall within each tier. Here, we describe each tier and present an overarching method for understanding, assessing, and interpreting executive functions.

This hierarchical approach provides a systematic solution to the impurity problem by helping clinicians identify which specific processes—executive or otherwise—explain test performance. When a client performs poorly on Trail Making, is it because they cannot visually scan efficiently (Tier 1), cannot hold a straightforward sequence in immediate memory span (Tier 2), cannot flexibly shift between number and letter sequences (Tier 3), or cannot manage the complex attentional demands while inhibiting overlearned responses (Tier 4)? The answer changes our understanding of the deficit and our approach to intervention.

Tier 1: Foundational Processes (Nonexecutive)

At the base of the hierarchy lie the foundational cognitive processes that must be intact for any higher-level processing to occur. These are not executive functions but rather the cognitive infrastructure upon which executive functions depend. When evaluating an individual's performance on the D-KEFS, clinicians must first ensure these basic abilities are intact before attributing poor performance to executive dysfunction. The impurity problem often manifests most problematically at this level, where foundational deficits masquerade as executive dysfunction, leading to misdiagnosis and ineffective interventions.

Perceptual-Motor Foundations

The perceptual-motor foundations include motor speed and motor control—the physical execution of movement with minimal cognitive involvement. Motor speed can be evaluated through tools like the Purdue Pegboard Test (Tiffin & Asher, 1948) for fine motor control, the original D-KEFS Trail Making Motor Speed condition, or the Oral Agility subtest from the Boston Diagnostic Aphasia Examination (BDAE-3; Goodglass et al., 2001) for oral-motor speed. Motor speed should be distinguished from processing speed, a Tier 2 bridging process that involves cognitive mediation beyond simple motor execution. A client with essential tremor or bradykinesia from Parkinson's disease might fail timed D-KEFS tasks not because of executive dysfunction but because of Tier 1 motor limitations.

Visual scanning and tracking abilities form another crucial foundation, as deficits here can look like executive problems on tasks like Trail Making or Design Fluency. The Developmental Eye Movement Test (Richman, 2009) or simple letter cancellation tasks can help identify whether poor visual tracking, rather than executive dysfunction, explains performance deficits. Color perception, often taken for granted, becomes critical for tests like the Color-Word Interference Test, where inability to distinguish colors would invalidate any conclusions about inhibitory control. Color vision can be evaluated with tools like the Ishihara test plates (Ishihara, 1917) or the Farnsworth-Dichotomous Test for color blindness (Farnsworth, 1947). Basic graphomotor control, assessed through measures like the Beery VMI (Beery & Beery, 2010) or the graphomotor index from the Feifer Assessment of Writing (FAW; Feifer, 2020), underlies performance on any test requiring written or drawn responses.

Language Foundations

Language foundations represent another critical tier of nonexecutive processes that significantly impact D-KEFS performance. Language comprehension, both receptive and expressive, affects test performance across nearly all D-KEFS subtests. The Clinical Evaluation of Language Fundamentals (CELF-5; Wiig et al., 2013) or the Test of Language Development (TOLD; Newcomer and Hammill, 2008) can evaluate whether language limitations rather than executive deficits explain poor performance. Letter and number knowledge (orthographic knowledge) must be automatic for tests involving alphanumeric sequencing. A recent immigrant who learned numbers in Mandarin script might fail Trail Making not because of sequencing problems but because of unfamiliar orthographic symbols.

Basic reading skills and word recognition speed directly impact performance on the original Color-Word Interference Test's baseline conditions. The Test of Word Reading Efficiency (TOWRE-2; Torgesen et al., 2012) or the Gray Oral Reading Tests (GORT-5; Wiederholt & Bryant, 2012) can assess whether reading fluency issues, rather than inhibitory deficits, explain poor performance. Verbal retrieval and articulation abilities affect all verbal fluency measures, and deficits here could be mistaken for executive dysfunction if not properly evaluated through measures like the Boston Naming Test-2 (Kaplan et al., 2001) or NEPSY-II Speeded Naming tasks (Korkman et al., 2007). Phonological processing, assessed via the Comprehensive Test of Phonological Processing (CTOPP-2; Wagner et al., 2013), underlies the ability to manipulate speech sounds as required in phonemic fluency tasks.

Basic Cognitive Foundations

The cognitive foundations include basic attention and vigilance, measurable through continuous performance tests like the Conners Continuous Performance Test (Conners CPT-3; Conners, 2014) or the Integrated Visual and Auditory Continuous Performance Test (IVA-2; Sandford & Turner, 2000). These provide the platform for more complex attentional control but are not themselves executive functions. The distinction is crucial: basic attention to a simple task (Tier 1) differs fundamentally from strategically allocating or sustaining attention across multiple competing demands (Tier 4).

Immediate memory span without manipulation represents pure storage capacity rather than the working memory manipulation that characterizes executive function. Digit Span Forward (e.g., Wechsler, 2014) or Corsi Blocks Forward (e.g., Wechsler & Kaplan, 2015) assess this basic capacity. Visual–spatial perception underlies performance on tests like the Tower Test, where poor spatial processing could be mistaken for planning deficits. The Rey Complex Figure Test's (Meyers & Meyers, 1995) initial Copy condition (without memory demands) or Judgment of Line Orientation (Benton et al., 1978) can help determine whether spatial perception rather than executive dysfunction explains poor performance.

Task Engagement

Finally, a willingness to engage in the task, while not strictly cognitive, significantly impacts test performance, particularly on challenging tasks. This bridges into hot executive function territory but at a basic level represents the ability to remain engaged with tasks—a prerequisite for any cognitive assessment.

Tier 2: Bridging Processes

The second tier contains processes that bridge between basic cognition and true executive control. This level presents particular diagnostic challenges because it contains both emerging executive components and complex nonexecutive processes. The key distinction lies in whether the process involves control, regulation, or coordination of other cognitive resources. This is where the hot–cold distinction begins to emerge more clearly, as emotional factors can significantly impact these bridging processes.

Processing Speed

Processing speed reflects the efficiency with which an individual can perceive information, make basic decisions, and execute responses. Unlike Tier 1 motor speed, processing speed engages cognitive resources—it is slowed by factors affecting mental efficiency, not just physical execution. The Wechsler Intelligence Scale for Children (WISC-V) or Wechsler Adult Intelligence Scale (WAIS-5) Processing Speed Index (Wechsler, 2014, 2024) provides a useful comparison point when interpreting D-KEFS performance on speeded subtests. Reduced processing speed is common in normal aging, traumatic brain injury, and various neurological and psychiatric conditions. Critically, slowed processing speed is not an executive function deficit; it represents foundational efficiency that constrains higher-level performance. An examinee with globally slow processing who performs proportionally across D-KEFS conditions demonstrates intact executive functions operating within reduced processing capacity.

Emerging Executive Control

Emerging executive control at this level includes basic working memory tasks that require holding information in mind while using it, such as those measured by Digit Span Backward (e.g., Wechsler, 2014) or basic mental arithmetic. This represents a step beyond simple storage (Tier 1) but doesn't yet reach the complex manipulation required at higher tiers. Basic inhibition emerges when individuals must follow a single rule to stop automatic responses, as in simple Go/No-Go tasks or the baseline conditions of the Color-Word Interference Test. The individual can stop when told "don't read the words," but this single-rule inhibition differs from the flexible, context-dependent inhibition required at Tier 3.

Elementary cognitive shifting involves switching between two clear tasks or rules, a simpler form of the complex flexibility required in higher-tier executive functions. The original D-KEFS Trail Making Conditions 2 and 3 (numbers only, letters only) assess this basic sequencing ability. Basic sequencing and planning begin to emerge here, as seen in the early items of the Tower Test or straightforward picture arrangement tasks. The individual can plan 2–3 moves ahead but may struggle with the complex, hierarchical planning required for difficult items.

Even at this bridging level, the hot–cold distinction matters. In our clinical experience, a child might demonstrate basic inhibition in emotionally neutral contexts (stopping when told "red light" in a calm game) but fail when emotionally invested (unable to wait their turn for a preferred toy). These differences reflect the emerging separation between cold and hot executive systems discussed previously, where emotional salience fundamentally changes task demands (Zelazo & Carlson, 2012).

Complex Nonexecutive Processes

Complex nonexecutive processes at this tier include pattern recognition abilities assessed through Matrix Reasoning (Wechsler, 2014) or Ravens Progressive Matrices (Raven et al., 2018). These tasks require complex processing but don't necessarily involve executive control—they can be solved through perceptual analysis without planning or flexibility. The distinction is important: failing a pattern recognition task doesn't indicate executive dysfunction unless the failure stems from inflexibility or poor strategy use rather than pattern perception itself.

Affect and facial recognition, measured through tools like the NEPSY-II Affect Recognition subtest (Korkman et al., 2007), represent sophisticated perceptual processing that supports but doesn't constitute executive function. These abilities become crucial for the Social Sorting Test on the D-KEFS Advanced, where affect recognition provides the perceptual foundation for higher-tier social-executive reasoning.

Learning through repetition (procedural learning) can be observed across repeated trials of any task and represents a form of implicit learning distinct from executive control. When a client improves across Tower Test items of similar difficulty, this might reflect procedural learning rather than executive planning. Sustained attention with basic interference resistance begins to bridge toward executive attention but remains primarily a capacity rather than a control function. The ability to maintain focus despite mild distractions differs from the strategic attentional allocation that characterizes Tier 4 executive attention.

Tier 3: Core Executive Functions

The upper tiers of the hierarchy represent genuine executive control processes that orchestrate, regulate, and direct lower-level cognitive resources. These are the actual executive functions that the D-KEFS aims to measure, though their accurate assessment depends on intact lower-tier processes. Here, the hot–cold distinction becomes particularly important for understanding performance variability and real-world applications.

Cold Executive Functions

Inhibitory control at this level involves suppressing automatic or strongly ingrained responses when they're not appropriate for the current context (Miller & Cohen, 2001). This goes beyond basic rule following to include managing multiple rules simultaneously, resisting interference from distracting information, and stopping oneself from saying or doing the first thing that comes to mind. The original D-KEFS' Color-Word Interference Test Conditions 3 and 4 exemplify this level of inhibitory control, requiring not just suppression of the reading response but flexible application of inhibition based on changing task demands. The cognitive load is substantial; the individual must maintain the task goal, monitor their responses, suppress the automatic reading response, and produce the correct color name, all within time constraints.

Cognitive flexibility and switching represent the ability to shift mental sets in response to changing demands or priorities (Miyake et al., 2000). This involves mental set shifting between different concepts or perspectives, spontaneous flexibility in generating alternative approaches, and the capacity to adapt when task demands change unexpectedly. The ability to maintain and coordinate multiple mental sets simultaneously distinguishes this from simpler forms of shifting seen in Tier 2. Trail Making Condition 4 and Verbal Fluency Condition 3 assess this complex flexibility by requiring rapid shifts between conceptual categories while maintaining overall task goals. The individual must not only switch but must track what category they're in, remember what they've already said, and generate novel responses within each category. The D-KEFS Advanced subtests have increased the complexity of these demands.

The executive component of working memory involves managing multiple pieces of information simultaneously while actively updating and integrating information streams. This includes dual-task coordination and mental workspace management—keeping multiple pieces of information active and accessible while performing cognitive operations on them. The D-KEFS Advanced's Trail Making with Working Memory condition specifically targets this level of working memory function, distinguishing it from basic storage capacity. The individual must maintain number-letter sequences while tracking their position, updating after each response, and inhibiting previously used items.

Planning and organization at the executive level involve goal formulation and prioritization, strategic sequencing of steps toward objectives, efficient resource allocation, and the crucial ability to anticipate outcomes and potential obstacles. The Tower Test, particularly in its advanced form with more complex rules and constraints, requires all these components as examinees must mentally simulate moves, evaluate alternative strategies, and execute complex multistep plans while adhering to task rules and learning from feedback.

Abstract reasoning and concept formation represent the ability to move beyond concrete, surface-level features to identify underlying principles or patterns. This includes hypothesis generation and testing, finding commonalities across seemingly disparate items, and maintaining conceptual flexibility when initial hypotheses prove incorrect. The Sorting Test, Twenty Questions, and Word Context all exemplify these abilities by requiring examinees to identify abstract categorization principles and systematically test hypotheses to arrive at solutions.

Hot Executive Functions

At Tier 3, hot executive demands begin to significantly affect performance even on ostensibly "cold" tasks (Zelazo & Carlson, 2020). Based on clinical observation, frustration during difficult Tower Test items can derail planning abilities. Anxiety about timed performance on Trail Making can interfere with cognitive flexibility. Emotional reactions to errors on the Color-Word Interference Test can cascade into subsequent mistakes. The interaction between hot and cold systems becomes clinically relevant—intact cold executive functions can be compromised by poor hot executive regulation.

This is where we see the clearest manifestation of the performance-competence distinction discussed in Chapter 2. An individual might possess the cold executive capacity to inhibit responses or shift sets, but emotional arousal in real-world settings overwhelms these abilities (Welsh & Peterson, 2014). A child with attention deficit hyperactivity disorder (ADHD) might successfully complete the Color-Word Interference Test in the structured testing environment but be unable to inhibit verbal outbursts when excited or frustrated in the classroom.

Tier 4: Higher-Order Integration and Metacognition

Tier 4 encompasses the highest level of executive control—the capacity to coordinate multiple executive processes, monitor one's own cognition, and adapt strategically based on self-evaluation. These abilities are difficult to assess through single scores but reveal themselves through qualitative observation and patterns across tasks.

Problem-solving integration represents one of the most complex executive functions, requiring the coordination of multiple executive processes toward novel solutions. This involves using feedback to adjust strategies dynamically, generating creative solutions to unfamiliar problems, and systematically evaluating alternatives before committing to a course of action. Complex Tower Test items and the D-KEFS Advanced's more challenging conditions require this level of integrated problem-solving, as they present novel challenges that cannot be solved through routine application of learned strategies. The individual must simultaneously plan, inhibit impulsive moves, maintain multiple rules in working memory, and flexibly adjust their approach based on feedback.

Self-monitoring and metacognition involve the ability to observe and evaluate one's own cognitive processes. This includes error detection and correction, performance tracking across time, strategy evaluation and adjustment, and self-awareness of cognitive processes. While not assessed by a single D-KEFS subtest, these abilities can be evaluated through error analysis across multiple tests, observing whether examinees recognize and attempt to correct mistakes, and how they adjust their approach based on performance feedback. The clinician should note whether the individual spontaneously comments on their performance, attempts to self-correct, or shows awareness of when they're struggling.

Complex attentional control at Tier 4 involves strategic allocation of attention resources based on task priorities and changing demands. This includes managing divided attention across multiple domains simultaneously, maintaining selective and sustained attention under high interference conditions, and demonstrating attentional flexibility by shifting focus based on changing task relevance. The D-KEFS Advanced subtests with distraction conditions specifically target this level of attentional control, distinguishing it from basic attention. The individual must not only maintain attention but strategically deploy it, ignoring salient distractors while attending to less obvious but task-relevant information.

Strategic adaptation—recognizing when an approach is not working and adjusting accordingly—distinguishes Tier 4 from lower-tier executive functions. An examinee who persists with an ineffective strategy despite clear feedback demonstrates Tier 4 weakness even if component Tier 3 abilities are intact. Conversely, an examinee who begins haphazardly but develops a systematic approach as the task progresses demonstrates intact metacognitive learning. This capacity for self-directed adjustment is central to real-world executive functioning, where external feedback is inconsistent and structure is often absent.

Emotional and motivational regulation at Tier 4 involves maintaining cognitive control under affective challenge. This domain includes delayed gratification (Mischel et al., 1989)—the ability to forgo immediate rewards for larger future benefits. Managing frustration during complex tasks, persisting despite repeated failure, and maintaining a strategic approach rather than devolving into impulsive responding all reflect mature Tier 4 functioning (Casey et al., 2011). The individual who can work through difficult Tower Test items despite multiple failed attempts, maintaining planful behavior rather than random moves, demonstrates this capacity. The D-KEFS Advanced Risk–Reward Decision Test explicitly assesses this integration. Success requires not just understanding probabilities but managing the emotional pull of potential rewards and the frustration of losses.

> **CAUTION**
>
> The Risk–Reward Decision Test deserves special attention as it explicitly measures the integration of cognitive and emotional executive functions. Success requires calculating probabilities and tracking outcomes while managing the emotional impact of gains and losses. Individuals with intact cognitive executive functions but impaired emotional regulation might understand the probabilities but be unable to resist the emotional pull of high-risk, high-reward options.

Social judgment and perspective-taking, assessed through the D-KEFS Advanced Social Sorting Test, represent perhaps the most complex form of Tier 4 functioning. The task requires coordinating cognitive processes (categorization, flexibility) with social–emotional understanding (recognizing emotions, understanding social categories) while managing one's own responses to the social stimuli.

Rapid Reference 3.1

The Hierarchical Tier Framework

Tier	Label	Description	Examples of Processes	D-KEFS Relevance
Tier 1	Foundational processes (nonexecutive)	Basic cognitive infrastructure that must be intact for higher-level processing; NOT executive functions	Motor speed/control, visual scanning/tracking, color perception, graphomotor control, language comprehension, orthographic knowledge, basic reading, verbal retrieval, sustained attention, immediate memory span, visual–spatial perception, task engagement	Deficits here masquerade as executive dysfunction; rule out first using baseline conditions (e.g., Motor Speed, Visual Scanning, Color Naming, Word Reading)
Tier 2	Bridging processes	Processes that bridge basic cognition and true executive control; includes emerging executive components and complex nonexecutive processes	Processing speed, simple working memory (maintenance), basic inhibition (single-rule), elementary cognitive shifting, simple sequencing, pattern recognition, affect recognition, procedural learning, sustained attention with basic interference resistance	Deficits produce proportional slowing/difficulty across conditions; contrast scores remain normal despite weak absolute scores
Tier 3	Core executive functions	Genuine executive control processes that orchestrate, regulate, and direct lower-level resources; includes both cold and hot EF	**Cold:** Inhibitory control, cognitive flexibility/switching, executive working memory (manipulation), planning/organization, abstract reasoning, concept formation. **Hot:** Frustration tolerance, anxiety management, emotional interference with cognition	Primary target of D-KEFS assessment; accurate measurement depends on intact Tiers 1–2; switching conditions, inhibition conditions, and complex planning items
Tier 4	Higher-order integration and metacognition	Capacity to coordinate multiple executive processes, monitor one's own cognition, and adapt strategically	Problem-solving integration, self-monitoring, error detection/correction, complex attentional control, strategic adaptation, delayed gratification, social judgment/perspective-taking	Often observed qualitatively rather than through single scores; look for spontaneous strategy adaptation, self-correction, metacognitive insight

Key Principle: Poor D-KEFS performance might reflect deficits at ANY tier. Always identify the lowest tier at which consistent weakness appears. Deficits at lower tiers contaminate performance at higher tiers.

UNDERSTANDING TRAIL MAKING THROUGH THE HIERARCHICAL LENS: AN EXAMPLE

To illustrate how the tier framework applies to a specific D-KEFS subtest, consider the Trail Making Test from the original D-KEFS, a visual-motor sequencing task that assesses multiple levels of processing from basic to complex. Each subsequent subtest chapter will provide a similar tier-by-tier analysis specific to that measure.

Tier 1 Requirements

The test requires visual scanning efficiency to locate numbers and letters across the page, number and letter recognition, motor speed and control to connect stimuli with pencil lines, and basic processing speed to complete tasks within time limits. An examinee with visual scanning deficits, unfamiliarity with Arabic numerals, motor tremor, or generalized slowing might perform poorly due to Tier 1 limitations rather than executive dysfunction.

Tier 2 Processes

Straightforward sequencing ability is needed to follow numerical or alphabetical order, basic attention maintains focus on task-relevant stimuli while filtering distractors, and procedural learning occurs as the examinee becomes familiar with task demands across conditions. These bridging processes support but don't constitute executive function.

Tier 3 Functions

Cognitive flexibility becomes critical in Condition 4, where examinees must alternate between numbers and letters. Working memory maintains the sequencing rules (1-A-2-B-3-C...) while tracking position. Inhibition of automatic/overlearned responses prevents continuing with numbers when a letter is required, or vice versa. These represent true executive functions at the core level.

Tier 4 Demands (Advanced Version)

Trail Making's scored measures do not formally assess Tier 4 processes—the test provides explicit rules and clear feedback, eliminating the need for self-directed strategy generation or metacognitive problem-solving. The D-KEFS Advanced's additional switching conditions (Switching-Working Memory and Switching-Distraction) remain Tier 3 measures, assessing working memory integration and inhibition under interference, respectively. However, Tier 4 functioning can be qualitatively observed during administration through spontaneous strategy adaptation, error monitoring and self-correction, and metacognitive insight about task demands. These observations provide clinically valuable information even though the test's scored indices capture only Tiers 1–3.

Hot EF Factors

Even this ostensibly "cold" task engages hot executive functions. Based on our clinical observations, frustration with errors can lead to poor performance on subsequent items. Anxiety about timed performance may increase errors and slow completion. Emotional response to perceived failure on a straightforward task can derail remaining test performance. The adolescent who becomes frustrated after making an error and then rushes through remaining items, making more errors, demonstrates how hot EF factors compromise cold EF performance.

This example illustrates how a single subtest engages all four tiers and both hot and cold executive systems. When an individual performs poorly, the tier framework guides differential diagnosis: Is this a Tier 1 visual scanning problem? A Tier 2 sequencing deficit? A Tier 3 flexibility impairment? Or a Tier 4 integration failure? Is hot EF (frustration, anxiety) compromising otherwise intact cold EF abilities? Each possibility has different implications for diagnosis and intervention.

Rapid Reference 3.2

Hot Versus Cold Executive Functions in D-KEFS Interpretation

Dimension	Cold Executive Functions	Hot Executive Functions
Definition	Cognitive processes operating in emotionally neutral, abstract contexts	Regulatory processes engaged when emotion, motivation, or reward are involved
Core processes	Inhibitory control, cognitive flexibility, working memory, planning, abstract reasoning	Frustration tolerance, delay of gratification, risk assessment, emotional inhibition under load, effort regulation
Deficits appear as	Poor strategy generation, inflexible thinking, cannot shift between rules, working memory failures, systematic planning errors, perseverative responses	Giving up when frustrated, impulsive responding for rewards, emotional interference with performance, test-reality performance gaps, inconsistent performance across sessions, deteriorating performance after errors
Primary D-KEFS measures	Color-Word Interference (Conditions 3–4), Trail Making (Number-Letter Switching), Verbal Fluency (Switching), Tower, Sorting, Twenty Questions	Risk–Reward Decision Test (explicit), Social Sorting Test (social–emotional integration), behavioral observations across all subtests
Assessment approach	Standardized scores, contrast scores, error analysis	Behavioral observation, rating scales (BRIEF-2, CEFI), functional history, test–retest variability
Real-world manifestation	Difficulty with novel problems, poor organization, rigid approaches	Poor decisions despite knowing better, inconsistent performance based on emotional state, difficulty in high-stakes situations

Clinical Note: Hot and cold systems interact—intact cold EF can be compromised by poor hot EF regulation. An anxious examinee who slows dramatically on Trail Making may appear cognitively inflexible when the primary problem is anxiety management. Always consider both systems when interpreting performance.

CULTURAL AND LINGUISTIC CONSIDERATIONS IN TIER-BASED ASSESSMENT

The tier framework requires careful application with culturally and linguistically diverse individuals (Ardila, 2005; Manly, 2008). At foundational levels, orthographic differences (Arabic, Hindi, or Chinese number systems), directional scanning patterns in right-to-left reading cultures, and language proficiency can all affect performance without indicating cognitive impairment (Chua et al., 2005). Educational background shapes familiarity with the flexible problem-solving and novel strategy generation that many D-KEFS tasks reward (Nisbett & Miyamoto, 2005). Hot executive function expression also varies by cultural norms—emotional restraint valued in some cultures may appear as superior regulation, while expressive norms elsewhere might be misread as impulsivity (Markus & Kitayama, 1991). Risk tolerance and delayed gratification carry cultural meaning that should not be confused with executive dysfunction (Weber & Hsee, 2000). True executive deficits should manifest across culturally neutral tasks, while cultural factors typically affect specific modalities or content areas.

Assessment adaptations should account for these factors systematically. When possible, supplement the D-KEFS battery with nonverbal measures or tests in the individual's primary language when evaluating suspected

Tier 1 deficits. Consider whether the individual has had adequate exposure to the types of tasks and materials used in testing. Someone who grew up without access to board games or puzzles may perform poorly on the Tower Test, not because of planning deficits but because of task unfamiliarity. Most importantly, avoid pathologizing cultural or linguistic differences as cognitive deficits. A comprehensive evaluation includes careful consideration of the individual's cultural background, language history, and educational experiences in interpreting test performance (Nell, 2000).

DEVELOPMENTAL CONSIDERATIONS

The developmental trajectories detailed in Chapter 2 align predictably with the tier framework. Tier 1 foundational processes mature earliest, with processing speed continuing to improve through adolescence. Tier 2–3 cold executive functions show rapid development during preschool and elementary years, reaching near-adult levels by mid-adolescence. Tier 4 integration and hot executive functions follow more protracted trajectories, not fully maturing until the mid-twenties. In older adults, Tier 1 processing speed shows the most consistent decline, while Tier 3 core functions may remain relatively preserved. Clinicians should reference Chapter 2 for detailed developmental expectations at each age.

IDENTIFYING AND LEVERAGING COGNITIVE STRENGTHS ACROSS TIERS

The hierarchical framework serves not only to identify deficits but also to recognize cognitive strengths that can support compensation and intervention. Understanding an individual's pattern of strengths across tiers, and distinguishing between superficial performance and underlying competence, is crucial for effective intervention planning. Too often, assessment focuses solely on what's impaired, missing the cognitive resources that could support recovery and adaptation.

The Strength-Masking Problem

Consider a common scenario that illustrates this critical interpretive challenge: An individual completes the original D-KEFS' Trail Making Condition 4 in average time, suggesting intact performance. However, careful observation reveals they achieved this through rapid visual-motor processing (Tier 1 strength) that compensated for chaotic visual scanning and lack of systematic strategy (Tier 3 deficit). They darted across the page, made multiple self-corrections, and showed no evidence of a planned approach, yet they finished within normal limits due to sheer processing speed.

This pattern has fundamentally different implications than slow but methodical completion. In our clinical experience, the fast-but-chaotic performer has Tier 1 resources available for compensation but lacks an executive strategy. Intervention should focus on strategy instruction, as processing resources are abundant. The individual might benefit from "slow down to speed up" approaches, deliberately reducing Tier 1 speed to allow Tier 3 planning to engage. Their strength could become a liability if it prevents them from recognizing their strategy deficit.

Conversely, someone with slow processing speed (Tier 1 weakness) but excellent strategy (Tier 3 strength) shows methodical, organized scanning patterns but takes longer to complete tasks. This person needs time accommodations, while their strategic abilities could be leveraged in untimed contexts. Their careful approach might make them excellent at tasks requiring accuracy over speed.

Strength Patterns and Compensation Strategies

Different tier strength patterns suggest different compensation approaches and intervention strategies. The following patterns emerge from our clinical observations and case experience:

Tier 1 Strengths with Higher-Tier Deficits

Individuals with strong foundational abilities but executive weaknesses often initially compensate well, which can delay identification of executive dysfunction. Their rapid processing, strong language skills, or excellent visual perception might mask executive deficits until task complexity overwhelms their compensation capacity. Rapid processing can compensate for poor planning in straightforward tasks, but fails with complexity. Strong language abilities can support verbal mediation strategies for visual–spatial executive tasks. Intact visual processing can support visual organizers and graphic strategies for executive deficits. Superior motor speed might hide poor planning on construction tasks. *Intervention approach*: Leverage processing strengths while building executive strategies; teach the individual to deliberately slow down to engage in planning; use their strengths as a bridge to developing weaker executive skills.

Tier 2 Strengths with Tier 3–4 Deficit

When bridging processes are intact but higher-level executive functions are impaired, individuals can often function well with appropriate environmental structuring. Good basic working memory can support external organizational systems. Strong pattern recognition can compensate through environmental structuring and routine. Intact procedural learning allows habit formation to reduce executive demands. Basic inhibition abilities can work with clear, consistent rules. *Intervention approach*: Create structured routines that utilize bridging strengths; use consistent patterns and rules; build habits that reduce executive demands.

Tier 3 Strengths with Variable Lower Tiers

Some individuals show the paradoxical pattern of strong executive abilities despite foundational weaknesses. These individuals often develop sophisticated compensatory strategies spontaneously. Strong cold EF can compensate for mild Tier 1–2 weaknesses through strategic approaches. Good cognitive flexibility helps develop workarounds for specific deficits. Intact planning can organize environments to minimize lower-tier demands. Strategic thinking can identify and utilize assistive technology effectively. *Intervention approach*: Teach metacognitive strategies that leverage executive strengths; help them systematize their spontaneous compensations; provide tools that bypass lower-tier weaknesses.

Hot EF Strengths with Cold EF Deficits

The individual with strong emotional regulation despite cognitive executive deficits represents an important pattern often overlooked. Strong emotional regulation maintains performance despite cognitive challenges. Good frustration tolerance allows persistence through inefficient strategies. Social motivation drives compensation efforts. Emotional insight supports self-advocacy. *Intervention approach:* Use emotional strengths to support cognitive intervention engagement; leverage motivation and persistence; build on social awareness for strategy development.

Clinical Assessment of Strengths

When conducting D-KEFS assessment, systematically document strengths alongside deficits. Quantitatively, scaled scores ≥12 indicate relative strengths, while contrast scores may reveal superior performance in specific conditions. Faster completion times with maintained accuracy, low error rates despite complex demands, and consistent performance across trials all suggest good strategy and cognitive resources.

Qualitatively, observe a systematic approach, self-correction showing good monitoring, verbal mediation or self-talk during tasks, creative problem-solving approaches, persistence despite difficulty, emotional regulation under stress, and effective use of feedback. Document not just whether tasks are completed successfully, but how. Does speed compensate for strategy? Does verbal mediation support visual–spatial tasks? Does emotional regulation maintain performance despite frustration? Do environmental cues trigger effective performance? Does the individual spontaneously develop compensatory strategies?

CAUTION

Fast task completion may mask poor executive strategy. Always observe HOW tasks are completed, not just WHETHER they're completed successfully. Process observations and error analysis reveal whether success comes from executive competence or lower-tier compensation.

FROM TEST PERFORMANCE TO DAILY FUNCTION: INTEGRATING ASSESSMENT METHODS

Comprehensive executive function assessment requires both standardized testing and ecological methods—each provides information that the other cannot capture (Suchy, 2009). There has been a concerning trend toward evaluating executive functions primarily through rating scales without direct, performance-based testing. No competent evaluator would assess intellectual functioning or academic achievement solely through ratings, yet many practitioners apply this less rigorous standard to executive function assessment.

Standardized testing uniquely provides normative comparisons against age-matched peers, controlled conditions that isolate cognitive processes and reveal maximum capability, objective measurement that supports tracking change over time, sensitivity to subtle deficits that may not yet manifest behaviorally, and the systematic variation of task demands that supports differential diagnosis. The D-KEFS measures what an individual *can* do under optimal conditions—one-on-one attention, minimal distractions, clear instructions, and immediate feedback.

As discussed in Chapter 2, the assessment-reality gap reflects both methodological constraints and the hot–cold distinction. Ecological methods, including rating scales such as the Behavior Rating Inventory of Executive Function (BRIEF-2; Gioia et al., 2015) and Behavior Rating Inventory of Executive Function-Adult version (BRIEF-A; Roth et al., 2005), Comprehensive Executive Function Inventory (CEFI; Naglieri & Goldstein, 2013) and Comprehensive Executive Function Inventory Adult (CEFI Adult; Naglieri & Goldstein, 2017), and Delis-Rating of Executive Functions (D-REF; Delis, 2012) and Delis-Rating of Executive Functions, Adult (D-REF Adult; Delis, 2021), along with behavioral observations and functional history, reveal what individuals actually do when managing multiple demands, navigating social contexts, experiencing emotional stress, and operating without external structure. Rating scales are particularly valuable for assessing hot executive functions, which standardized testing rarely captures directly.

When rating scales indicate significant impairment despite normal test performance, this discrepancy itself is diagnostically meaningful, suggesting that environmental demands, emotional factors, or lack of external structure may be driving functional difficulties. Conversely, an individual who performs poorly on structured tests but functions adequately in daily life may have developed effective compensatory strategies. Neither data source alone tells the complete story; together they provide the comprehensive picture necessary for accurate diagnosis and intervention planning.

Rapid Reference 3.3

Seven Critical Interpretation Errors to Avoid

Error	Description	How to Avoid
1. Attributing Tier 1 deficits to executive dysfunction	Interpreting slow motor speed, poor visual scanning, or language limitations as executive impairment	Always evaluate baseline conditions first; compare performance across conditions with different foundational demands
2. Ignoring processing speed as an alternative explanation	Concluding executive dysfunction when global slowing explains the pattern	Check whether contrast scores are normal despite slow absolute times; if proportional slowing across all conditions, suspect Tier 2 processing speed rather than Tier 3 EF deficit
3. Confusing hot EF problems with cold EF deficits	Interpreting anxiety-driven slowing as cognitive inflexibility, or frustration-driven errors as inhibitory control deficits	Observe behavioral signs of emotional interference; note whether errors cluster after difficult items; compare structured testing to real-world function

Error	Description	How to Avoid
4. Relying on a single subtest for diagnostic conclusions	Drawing conclusions about executive dysfunction from one measure	Require converging evidence across multiple subtests tapping similar processes through different modalities
5. Interpreting successful completion as intact executive function	Assuming average scores indicate no executive deficits	Observe HOW tasks are completed; fast-but-chaotic performance may reflect Tier 1 compensation masking Tier 3 deficits
6. Pathologizing cultural or linguistic differences	Attributing poor performance to cognitive deficits when cultural factors explain the pattern	Consider orthographic familiarity, educational background, and cultural norms for emotional expression; true deficits manifest across culturally neutral tasks
7. Dismissing test-reality discrepancies	Ignoring when rating scales indicate impairment but test scores are normal (or vice versa)	Recognize that structured testing measures maximum capability under optimal conditions; real-world function involves hot EF, competing demands, and absent external structure

Remember: The tier framework exists to prevent misattribution of deficits. When in doubt, rule out lower tiers before concluding higher-tier dysfunction, and always consider whether hot EF factors are compromising cold EF performance.

UNDERSTANDING SUBTEST CHAPTER STRUCTURE

The next 11 chapters focus on a specific D-KEFS or D-KEFS Advanced subtest and follow a consistent structure designed to support hierarchical analysis of performance. Familiarizing yourself with this structure will help you efficiently navigate these chapters and apply the tier framework to clinical interpretation.

The subtest chapters vary in their coverage depending on the test's history. Some chapters address subtests that appear only in the original D-KEFS (e.g., Twenty Questions, Word Context), while others cover subtests introduced exclusively in the D-KEFS Advanced (i.e., Risk–Reward Decision Test, Social Sorting Test). Several chapters address subtests that appear in both batteries (e.g., Trail Making, Color-Word Interference, Verbal Fluency), and these chapters integrate discussion of both versions, highlighting how the Advanced conditions extend assessment into higher tiers. Regardless of coverage scope, all chapters apply the same hierarchical tier framework and hot–cold analysis to guide interpretation.

Clinical Vignette

Each chapter begins with a case example demonstrating the subtest in use, illustrating how hierarchical analysis reveals the true nature of performance deficits.

Test Description

This overview explains what the test measures and how it's designed, helping clinicians understand the full range of cognitive processes engaged.

Hierarchical Tier Analysis

This section maps the subtest onto the executive function domains, distinguishing between Tier 1–2 requirements and Tier 3–4 executive functions actually being assessed. This includes a discussion of the input, processing, and output demands of the test.

Administration

The administration section includes details about the materials needed to conduct the subtest and the standard instructions for administration. It serves as a complement rather than a replacement for the test manual.

Behavioral Observations

This practical section describes behaviors indicating which tier might be affected and whether hot or cold EF problems are primary, providing crucial qualitative information beyond standardized scores.

Scoring

Information about primary and supplementary measures, with guidance on how different scores may reflect deficits at different tiers or in hot versus cold systems.

Common Administration Errors

Highlights pitfalls that could invalidate assessment of specific tiers or lead to misattribution of deficits.

Interpretation

This section explains how to use the hierarchical framework and hot–cold distinction to identify specific causes of poor performance, with implications for real-world functioning.

Strengths and Weaknesses

Assessment of what each subtest measures well at each tier, and where caution in interpretation is warranted.

Alternative Measures

Discussion of other tools for assessing specific tiers when D-KEFS results are inconclusive or when foundational abilities need separate evaluation. This includes other subtests within the D-KEFS family as well as measures beyond the D-KEFS.

SUMMARY

This chapter has provided an integrated framework combining the hierarchical tier system with the hot–cold executive function distinction from Chapter 2. This dual-lens approach directly addresses the impurity problem, explains performance variability, and guides differential diagnosis. By recognizing that D-KEFS subtests measure a spectrum of processes from foundational through executive, and that executive functions themselves divide into hot and cold domains, clinicians can parse the complex contributors to test performance and provide precisely targeted interventions.

The hierarchical framework fundamentally changes how we conceptualize executive function assessment. Rather than viewing the D-KEFS as a collection of executive function tests, we understand it as a sophisticated tool for parsing the hierarchy of cognitive processes from foundational through executive levels. Combined with the hot–cold distinction, this framework ensures accurate diagnosis and effective intervention planning. No single subtest should serve as the sole basis for diagnostic conclusions; accurate interpretation requires converging evidence across measures that tap similar processes through different modalities or task demands. The subsequent chapters will demonstrate how to apply this framework to each specific D-KEFS and D-KEFS Advanced subtest, providing the practical guidance necessary for skilled clinical practice.

TEST YOURSELF

1. An individual performs poorly on Color-Word Interference but performs well on Verbal Fluency. What should you assess first?

(a) Executive flexibility
(b) Color perception and reading fluency
(c) Working memory capacity
(d) Attention span

2. Which statement best describes the relationship between D-KEFS performance and executive functions?

(a) All processes measured by the D-KEFS are executive functions
(b) Only Tier 3 and Tier 4 processes are measured by the D-KEFS
(c) D-KEFS subtests measure foundational, bridging, and executive processes
(d) Executive functions cannot be measured by standardized tests

3. Which of the following is a Tier 1 (foundational) process rather than an executive function?

(a) Cognitive flexibility
(b) Strategic planning
(c) Visual scanning
(d) Inhibitory control

4. A child performs well on the Tower Test during structured testing but demonstrates poor planning and impulsive decision-making at home and school. This discrepancy most likely suggests:

(a) Invalid testing.
(b) Tier 1 foundational deficits.
(c) Hot EF deficits that emerge outside structured testing conditions.
(d) The child is malingering at home.

5. The Risk–Reward Decision Test primarily assesses:

(a) Cold executive function.
(b) Tier 1 processing.
(c) Integration of hot and cold EF.
(d) Visual-spatial planning.

6. An examinee shows weakness on Visual Scanning and Motor Speed conditions with proportionally impaired Number-Letter Switching, but contrast scores are in the average range. The appropriate interpretation is:

(a) Tier 3 cognitive flexibility deficit requiring executive function intervention.
(b) Tier 1 foundational deficits affecting all conditions, with intact executive functions.
(c) Hot EF anxiety interfering with performance.
(d) Poor effort invalidating the results.

7. An examinee shows globally slow performance across all D-KEFS conditions but normal contrast scores. This pattern most likely indicates:

(a) Tier 3 executive dysfunction.
(b) Tier 2 processing speed weakness with intact executive functions.
(c) Poor effort or motivation.
(d) Hot EF deficits.

8. What distinguishes Tier 2 from Tier 3 working memory?

(a) The amount of information stored.

(b) Basic maintenance versus complex manipulation.

(c) Verbal versus visual-spatial content.

(d) Speed of processing.

9. An adolescent with ADHD performs well on structured D-KEFS tasks but poorly in school. This pattern most likely suggests:

(a) Invalid testing.

(b) Learning disability.

(c) Hot EF deficits affecting real-world performance.

(d) Tier 1 problems.

10. The hierarchical tier framework directly addresses which problem discussed in Chapter 1?

(a) Developmental trajectories.

(b) The impurity problem.

(c) Neural network organization.

(d) Cultural factors.

Answer Key: 1-b, 2-c, 3-c, 4-c, 5-c, 6-b, 7-b, 8-b, 9-c, 10-b

REFERENCES

Ardila, A. (2005). Cultural values underlying psychometric cognitive testing. *Neuropsychology Review, 15*(4), 185–195.

Badre, D., & D'Esposito, M. (2009). Is the rostro-caudal axis of the frontal lobe hierarchical? *Nature Reviews Neuroscience, 10*(9), 659–669.

Beery, K. E., & Beery, N. A. (2010). *The Beery-Buktenica Developmental Test of Visual-Motor Integration* (6th ed.). Pearson.

Benton, A. L., Varney, N. R., Hamsher, K., & d. S. (1978). Visuospatial judgment: A clinical test. *Archives of Neurology, 35*(6), 364–367.

Casey, B. J., Somerville, L. H., Gotlib, I. H., Ayduk, O., Franklin, N. T., Askren, M. K., et al. (2011). Behavioral and neural correlates of delay of gratification 40 years later. *Proceedings of the National Academy of Sciences, 108*(36), 14998–15003.

Chua, H. F., Boland, J. E., & Nisbett, R. E. (2005). Cultural variation in eye movements during scene perception. *Proceedings of the National Academy of Sciences, 102*(35), 12629–12633.

Conners, C. K. (2014). *Conners Continuous Performance Test* (3rd ed.). Multi-Health Systems.

Delis, D. C. (2012). *Delis Rating of Executive Functions.* Pearson.

Delis, D. C. (2021). *Delis Rating of Executive Functions–Adult.* Pearson.

Delis, D. C., & Kaplan, E. (2025). *Delis-Kaplan Executive Function System Advanced.* Pearson.

Delis, D. C., Kaplan, E., & Kramer, J. H. (2001). *Delis-Kaplan Executive Function System.* Pearson.

Farnsworth, D. (1947). *Farnsworth Dichotomous Test for Color Blindness: Panel D-15.* Psychological Corporation.

Feifer, S. G. (2020). *Feifer Assessment of Writing.* PAR.

Gioia, G. A., Isquith, P. K., Guy, S. C., & Kenworthy, L. (2015). *Behavior Rating Inventory of Executive Function* (2nd ed.). PAR.

Goodglass, H., Kaplan, E., & Barresi, B. (2001). *Boston Diagnostic Aphasia Examination* (3rd ed.). Pro-Ed.

Ishihara, S. (1917). *Tests for Colour-Blindness.* Handaya.

Kaplan, E., Goodglass, H., & Weintraub, S. (2001). *Boston Naming Test* (2nd ed.). Pro-Ed.

Korkman, M., Kirk, U., & Kemp, S. (2007). *NEPSY-II.* Pearson.

Luria, A. R. (1980). *Higher Cortical Functions in Man* (2nd ed.). Basic Books.

Manly, J. J. (2008). Critical issues in cultural neuropsychology: Profit from diversity. *Neuropsychology, 22*(3), 329–333.

Markus, H. R., & Kitayama, S. (1991). Culture and the self: Implications for cognition, emotion, and motivation. *Psychological Review, 98*(2), 224–253.

Mesulam, M. M. (1998). From sensation to cognition. *Brain, 121*(6), 1013–1052.

Meyers, J., & Meyers, K. R. (1995). *Rey Complex Figure Test and Recognition Trial.* Psychological Assessment Resources, Incorporated.

Miller, E. K., & Cohen, J. D. (2001). An integrative theory of prefrontal cortex function. *Annual Review of Neuroscience, 24*(1), 167–202.

Mischel, W., Shoda, Y., & Rodriguez, M. L. (1989). Delay of gratification in children. *Science, 244*(4907), 933–938.

Miyake, A., Friedman, N. P., Emerson, M. J., Witzki, A. H., Howerter, A., & Wager, T. D. (2000). The unity and diversity of executive functions and their contributions to complex "frontal lobe" tasks: A latent variable analysis. *Cognitive Psychology, 41*(1), 49–100.

Naglieri, J. A., & Goldstein, S. (2013). *Comprehensive Executive Function Inventory.* Multi-Health Systems.

Naglieri, J. A., & Goldstein, S. (2017). *Comprehensive Executive Function Inventory–Adult.* Multi-Health Systems.

Nell, V. (2000). *Cross-Cultural Neuropsychological Assessment: Theory and Practice.* Psychology Press.

Newcomer, P. L., & Hammill, D. D. (2008). *Test of Language Development* (4th ed.). Pro-Ed.

Nisbett, R. E., & Miyamoto, Y. (2005). The influence of culture: Holistic versus analytic perception. *Trends in Cognitive Sciences, 9*(10), 467–473.

Raven, J., Rust, J., Chan, F., & Zhou, X. (2018). Raven's 2 Progressive Matrices, Clinical Edition (Raven's 2). Pearson: Nonverbal IQ test.

Richman, J. E. (2009). Developmental Eye Movement Test, Examiner's Manual, Version 2.0. South Bend, IN: Bernell Corporation.

Roth, R. M., Isquith, P. K., & Gioia, G. A. (2005). *Behavior Rating Inventory of Executive Function–Adult Version.* PAR.

Sandford, J. A., & Turner, A. (2000). *Integrated Visual and Auditory Continuous Performance Test.* BrainTrain.

Stuss, D. T., & Alexander, M. P. (2000). Executive functions and the frontal lobes: A conceptual view. *Psychological Research, 63*(3–4), 289–298.

Suchy, Y. (2009). Executive functioning: Overview, assessment, and research issues for non-neuropsychologists. *Annals of Behavioral Medicine, 37*(2), 106–116.

Tiffin, J., & Asher, E. J. (1948). The Purdue Pegboard: Norms and studies of reliability and validity. *Journal of Applied Psychology, 32*(3), 234–247.

Torgesen, J. K., Wagner, R. K., & Rashotte, C. A. (2012). *Test of Word Reading Efficiency* (2nd ed.). Pro-Ed.

Wagner, R. K., Torgesen, J. K., Rashotte, C. A., & Pearson, N. A. (2013). *Comprehensive Test of Phonological Processing* (2nd ed.). Pro-Ed.

Weber, E. U., & Hsee, C. (2000). Cross-cultural differences in risk perception, but cross-cultural similarities in attitudes towards perceived risk. *Management Science, 46*(9), 1205–1217.

Wechsler, D. (2014). *Wechsler Intelligence Scale for Children* (5th ed.). Pearson.

Wechsler, D. (2024). *Wechsler Adult Intelligence Scale* (5th ed.). Pearson.

Wechsler, D., & Kaplan, E. (2015). *Wechsler Intelligence Scale for Children Integrated* (5th ed.). Pearson.

Welsh, M., & Peterson, E. (2014). Issues in the conceptualization and assessment of hot executive functions in childhood. *Journal of the International Neuropsychological Society, 20*(2), 152–156.

Wiederholt, J. L., & Bryant, B. R. (2012). *Gray Oral Reading Tests* (5th ed.). Pro-Ed.

Wiig, E. H., Semel, E., & Secord, W. A. (2013). *Clinical Evaluation of Language Fundamentals* (5th ed.). Pearson.

Zelazo, P. D., & Carlson, S. M. (2012). Hot and cool executive function in childhood and adolescence: Development and plasticity. *Child Development Perspectives, 6*(4), 354–360.

Zelazo, P. D., & Carlson, S. M. (2020). The neurodevelopment of executive function skills: Implications for academic achievement gaps. *Psychology & Neuroscience, 13*(3), 273–298.

Part II

SUBTEST CHAPTERS

Four

COLOR-WORD INTERFERENCE TEST

CLINICAL VIGNETTE

Fifteen-year-old Tyler Jackson was referred following an attention deficit hyperactivity disorder (ADHD) diagnosis and concerns about academic underachievement despite high IQ. Teachers reported Tyler understood material quickly but made "careless errors" on tests, particularly on multistep problems requiring him to ignore irrelevant information. For example, he struggled with math word problems where he often incorporated numeric information from the word problem that was not needed to solve the problem.

On the Color-Word Interference Test (CWIT), Tyler demonstrated strong Tier 1 processing on Condition 1 (Color Naming scaled score = 12) and Condition 2 (Word Reading scaled score = 13). However, Condition 3 (Inhibition) revealed significant Tier 2 difficulty (scaled score = 6); he made three uncorrected errors, saying the word rather than the ink color, with errors clustering together. The contrast score comparing Inhibition to baseline was significantly impaired (scaled score = 5). Condition 4 (Inhibition/Switching) amplified these difficulties (scaled score = 4), with six errors, most occurring on switch trials rather than pure inhibition trials.

Throughout testing, Tyler showed intact metacognitive awareness, frequently commenting on his errors and attempting to slow down. However, emotional factors contributed; as errors accumulated, frustration increased, and he began rushing, creating a negative feedback loop. When prompted to take breaks, performance temporarily improved.

The hierarchical analysis indicated Tier 2 inhibitory control deficits that worsened under Tier 3 dual-task demands, with hot executive factors (frustration, impulsivity) exacerbating cold executive weaknesses. Recommendations included teaching explicit inhibition strategies, breaking multistep problems into phases, and emotion regulation training. Six months later, teachers reported improved test performance when using these strategies.

TEST DESCRIPTION

The CWIT is based on the classic Stroop (1935) paradigm and represents one of the most widely used measures of inhibitory control in neuropsychology. Both the original (Delis et al., 2001) and Advanced (Delis & Kaplan, 2025) versions assess the capacity to suppress automatic reading responses while identifying conflicting ink colors—a central executive function essential for adaptive behavior when automatic reactions must be overridden.

Original D-KEFS Color-Word Interference Test (CWIT)

The original version (ages 8–89) consists of four conditions administered in paper-and-pencil format, a digital replication version via Q-global, or a tablet version via Q-interactive. Examinees verbally respond to stimuli presented on a paper or digital Stimulus Booklet while the examiner times performance and records errors either on a paper Record Form or on the examiner's tablet if using Q-interactive. Condition 1

(Color Naming) and Condition 2 (Word Reading) establish baseline processing speed for fundamental skills. Condition 3 (Inhibition) presents the classic Stroop interference task—color words printed in dissonant ink colors where examinees must name the ink color while suppressing the reading response. Condition 4 (Inhibition/Switching) adds cognitive flexibility demands by requiring examinees to switch between naming ink colors and reading words based on whether the word appears inside a box. Administration typically requires 5–10 minutes.

D-KEFS Advanced Color-Word Interference Test (CWIT)

The Advanced version (ages 8–90) provides an alternative digital presentation on a tablet. Rather than verbalizing responses, examinees use a stylus to touch one of three response choices displayed at the bottom of the screen. This response format fundamentally alters task demands: it eliminates motor speech and word-finding confounds and lowers the floor for individuals with language production difficulties. The four conditions parallel the original version—Color Identification, Word Identification, Inhibition, and Inhibition/Switching—but the digital format enables more precise error tracking and timing while adding contemporary norms collected in the 2020s. Visual distractions are increased for Condition 4 with the addition of a dissonant color box behind the word-reading items. For example, when required to read the word GREEN, not only is the word printed in RED or BLUE, but the box behind it may also be RED or BLUE. Visual tracking requirements are decreased as the Advanced version shows one item at a time versus requiring scanning and tracking of an entire page of all items for each condition. Administration typically requires 10–15 minutes.

Both versions provide rich normative data, contrast scores that quantify executive dysfunction relative to baseline abilities, and detailed error analysis. The tests' ecological validity stems from their direct relevance to real-world situations requiring inhibitory control and cognitive flexibility—from classroom behavior (raising a hand rather than blurting out answers) to driving (inhibiting a braking response when acceleration would prevent a skid) to social interactions (suppressing an inappropriate comment) to workplace demands (abandoning a planned approach when circumstances suddenly change).

DON'T FORGET

The Color-Word Interference Test measures response inhibition in structured cognitive tasks, not general impulse control in emotionally charged situations. Performance reflects cognitive capacity to suppress automatic verbal responses under controlled conditions. Deficits on this test do not necessarily predict behavioral disinhibition when hot executive functions dominate, where emotional regulation plays a larger role than cold cognitive control.

Rapid Reference 4.1

Color-Word Interference Test Overview

Element	Original D-KEFS	D-KEFS Advanced
Age range	8–89 years	8–90 years
Conditions	Condition 1: Color naming	Condition 1: Color identification
	Condition 2: Word reading	Condition 2: Word identification
	Condition 3: Inhibition	Condition 3: Inhibition
	Condition 4: Inhibition/switching	Condition 4: Inhibition/switching
Time limits	Conditions 1–2: 90 seconds	Conditions 1–2: 60 seconds
	Conditions 3–4: 180 seconds	Condition 3: 120 seconds
		Condition 4: 180 seconds

Element	Original D-KEFS	D-KEFS Advanced
Response format	Verbal (examinee speaks responses aloud)	Touch screen (examinee touches response word with stylus)
Materials	Examiner's manual, stimulus booklet, record form, timer	Examiner's manual, client device, practitioner device, stylus
Primary score metric	Completion time in seconds	Net correct responses within time limit
Discontinuation	Marked difficulty or four uncorrected errors on practice items	Software auto-discontinues at time limit
Primary constructs	Inhibitory control, cognitive flexibility, processing speed	Inhibitory control, cognitive flexibility, processing speed

CHOOSING BETWEEN ORIGINAL AND ADVANCED VERSIONS

The decision between versions depends on examinee characteristics, referral questions, examiner preferences, and clinical context. Each version offers distinct advantages for specific assessment scenarios.

When the Original Version Is Preferred

Motor Speech and Word-Finding Concerns are Minimal
If the examinee has intact verbal output, the original version provides a valid assessment for most school-age children and adults without neurological conditions affecting speech production because the verbal response format poses no significant barrier.

Fine and Gross Motor Deficits Exist
Only verbal responses are required on the original version, which reduces confounds of motor impairment.

More In-Depth Error Analysis Is Needed
The original version allows examiners to track corrected and uncorrected errors, which isn't possible in the Advanced version. Analysis of errors that were caught and corrected versus errors that were made without recognition of the error can be helpful in some clinical contexts, such as gauging the ability to self-monitor, even if unable to effectively inhibit responses.

Traditional Administration Is Required
Some assessment contexts (e.g., forensic evaluations, disability determinations, research protocols) may require paper-and-pencil administration with established procedures. The original version's longer history also provides extensive research validation across diverse clinical populations.

Cost and Equipment Constraints Exist
The original paper-and-pencil version requires only a Stimulus Booklet, Record Form, and timer—no digital equipment. For practices with limited access to digital resources, this may be an important consideration.

When the Advanced Version Is Preferred

Speech or Language Production Difficulties Are Present or Suspected
Individuals with dysarthria, aphasia, apraxia of speech, word-finding deficits, or language-based learning disabilities may perform poorly on the original version due to output demands rather than true inhibitory control deficits. The Advanced version's touch screen response format bypasses these confounds, providing more direct assessment of executive functions. This may be particularly valuable for adults with stroke, TBI, or neurodegenerative conditions.

Higher Cognitive Ceiling Is Needed

The Advanced version deliberately increases task difficulty through its response format. In the Inhibition condition, the to-be-inhibited word appears visually among the response choices, magnifying its prepotency and making it harder to suppress. Furthermore, visual distractions are increased for Condition 4 with the addition of a dissonant color box surrounding the word-reading items. This enhanced sensitivity helps detect subtle executive deficits in high-functioning individuals who might score in the average range on the original version.

Precise Error Tracking Is Important

The digital interface automatically captures all errors with exact timestamps, eliminating the examiner's burden of simultaneously timing, cueing, and recording errors. This reduces measurement error and allows examiners to focus on behavioral observation rather than clerical recording.

Contemporary Normative Comparison Is Desired

The Advanced version's norms were collected in the 2020s, providing a comparison to current populations. While Pearson maintains that the original version's 2001 norms remain appropriate for most clinical purposes, some clinicians prefer the most recent normative data, particularly when assessing younger examinees whose development has occurred in substantially different educational and technological contexts than the early 2000s cohort.

When Either Version Works Equally Well

For adolescents and adults with average cognitive abilities, intact verbal output, and no specific motor or language concerns, either version provides a valid inhibitory control assessment. The choice may depend on which other D-KEFS subtests are being administered (maintaining consistent original versus Advanced format has advantages), examiner familiarity, or equipment availability.

Returning to Tyler

The Advanced version would not necessarily have helped Tyler. His ADHD-related inhibitory control deficits manifested clearly on the original version, with normal baseline speed but marked inhibition difficulty. The original version's verbal response format posed no barrier for this adolescent with intact language skills. However, the Advanced version's increased prepotency of the to-be-inhibited response (visually displayed among choices) might have further challenged his inhibitory control, potentially making his deficits even more apparent. The key

Rapid Reference 4.2

Choosing Between Original and Advanced Versions

Consider Original When	Consider Advanced When
Motor speech and word-finding concerns are minimal	Speech or language production difficulties are present or suspected
Fine or gross motor deficits exist (only verbal responses required)	Higher cognitive ceiling is needed for high-functioning individuals
More in-depth error analysis is needed (corrected vs. uncorrected errors)	Precise error tracking with automated timing is important
Traditional paper-and-pencil administration is required (forensic, research)	Contemporary normative comparison from 2020s is desired
Cost and equipment constraints exist	Examiner burden reduction through automated administration is valued
	Magnified interference demands are clinically useful

clinical question—"Can Tyler inhibit automatic responses effectively?"—received a clear answer from the original version, though the Advanced version's enhanced difficulty could have provided additional sensitivity had Tyler's deficits been more subtle.

HIERARCHICAL TIER ANALYSIS

The CWIT maps onto a three-tier hierarchical framework, distinguishing foundational verbal processing speed from response inhibition and cognitive flexibility. The D-KEFS Advanced explicitly incorporates this tiered structure into its design, while the same framework emerges through clinical analysis of the original version. Both versions assess through Tier 3 but lack substantial Tier 4 metacognitive demands present in subtests like Tower or Sorting.

Tier 1: Foundational Processes (Nonexecutive)

Color-Word performance depends critically on rapid verbal processing—the speed at which examinees access and produce responses to visual stimuli. Conditions 1 and 2 quantify these foundational abilities that undergird all subsequent executive demands, though the response modality differs between versions.

Color Naming and Identification Speed

The original version's Condition 1 requires rapidly naming colored patches (red, green, blue) presented in rows. This seemingly easy task engages multiple cognitive processes: visual perception and discrimination of colors, semantic access to color labels, phonological retrieval of color words, and motor speech production. Examinees must maintain focus across 50 items while working quickly under time pressure. The Advanced version's Color Identification condition simplifies this demand through visual-verbal matching. Examinees see a colored box and touch the corresponding word among three choices, eliminating word-retrieval and articulation demands while maintaining speed requirements. This modification makes the task accessible for individuals with speech or language production difficulties. Performance establishes baseline color processing efficiency, essential for interpreting Condition 3. An examinee who names or identifies colors slowly due to word-finding difficulties, reduced processing speed, or motor speech problems will naturally perform slowly on the Inhibition condition. Without the Condition 1 baseline, clinicians might misattribute this slowing to poor inhibitory control rather than foundational processing limitations.

Word Reading and Identification Speed

Condition 2 requires rapidly reading or matching color words. For most literate individuals, reading is highly automatic and faster than Color Naming. This automaticity creates the interference effect in Condition 3—the faster, more automatic reading response must be inhibited to produce the slower, more effortful naming response. On the original version, examinees read color words printed in black ink aloud. The Advanced version requires touching the word that matches a printed word at the top of the screen—again eliminating oral production demands. Reading speed varies substantially based on reading skill development. Individuals with dyslexia or other reading difficulties may read slowly, creating an unusual pattern where Color Naming/Color Identification (Condition 1) speed matches or exceeds Word Reading/Word Identification (Condition 2) speed. This reversal has important implications for interpreting Condition 3: when reading is not automatic, interference effects diminish because the reading response lacks automaticity.

Processing Speed as a Foundational Variable

Beyond specific color naming and word reading skills, general processing speed affects all Color-Word conditions. Notably, Color-Word processing speed relies on verbal output (original version) or simple touch responses (Advanced version) rather than the graphomotor demands of measures like Trail Making Test A or Coding, which is an important distinction when fine motor impairment may confound other processing speed tasks. Processing speed reflects the efficiency of cognitive operations—how quickly an examinee can perceive stimuli, access semantic information, select responses, and execute motor actions. Reduced processing speed can result from numerous factors: neurological conditions (TBI, stroke, dementia; Su et al., 2014), psychiatric conditions such as depression (Nuño et al., 2021) and anxiety (Mishra et al., 2023), medications (sedatives, anticonvulsants, antipsychotics; Sherman et al., 2022), or normal aging (Gonzales et al., 2022). While common age-related processing speed weaknesses are controlled for by the D-KEFS's age-based norms, the other concerns may result in reduced normed performance. Critically, slowed processing speed is not an executive function deficit. It represents Tier 1 foundational efficiency that constrains higher-level performance. An examinee with globally slow processing who performs proportionally across all four conditions demonstrates intact executive functions operating within reduced foundational capacity. In contrast, an examinee with age-appropriate processing speed who struggles specifically on Conditions 3–4 demonstrates true executive dysfunction.

Sustained Attention During Repetitive Processing

Both baseline conditions require maintaining consistent focus across 50 items (original version) or 60 seconds of continuous responding (Advanced version). The repetitive nature of these tasks requires sustained attention—the ability to maintain performance consistency without attention lapses across the full trial array. Examinees must resist mind-wandering, maintain processing speed throughout rather than slowing as the condition progresses, and avoid skipping items or losing their place. Attention lapses on baseline conditions manifest as inconsistent response timing, sporadic errors on easy tasks, or line-skipping that requires examiner redirection. Examinees with ADHD, fatigue, or reduced arousal may show attention difficulties even on these baseline conditions, reflected in slowing across the trial array, variable response pacing, or errors despite adequate color perception and reading ability. Importantly, baseline attention difficulties predict proportional difficulties across all subsequent conditions and should not be misattributed to executive dysfunction.

CAUTION

Color perception deficits can masquerade as processing speed or executive deficits. Color blindness affects approximately 8% of males and 0.5% of females (Almustanyir, 2025). The Color-Word test uses red, green, and blue stimuli—the colors most affected by common color vision deficiencies. Individuals with red-green color blindness may perform poorly on all conditions, particularly Color Naming/Identification. Always screen for color vision problems before administering this test. Examinees who cannot reliably discriminate between the red, green, and blue stimuli during practice items should not continue with standard administration. Individuals with mild color vision deficiency who demonstrate consistent, accurate discrimination across practice items may proceed, as the critical task demand—suppressing an automatic reading response—remains valid when color identification is functionally intact.

Tier 1 Impairment Pattern

Tier 1 impairment manifests as slow performance across all four conditions with proportional contrast scores. The examinee struggles with Color Naming/Identification and Word Reading/Identification, and this foundational slowness carries through to Inhibition and Inhibition/Switching conditions, but contrast scores remain in the expected range because higher-level performance is proportional to baseline limitations. Key indicators include globally slow completion times or low net correct scores, few errors relative to speed (accuracy preserved despite slowness), and no disproportionate difficulty when inhibition or switching demands are added. This pattern suggests processing speed limitations, word-finding difficulties, motor speech problems (original version), or fine motor slowness (Advanced version) rather than executive dysfunction. Corroborating evidence includes slow performance on other processing speed measures and intact performance on untimed executive tasks.

Tier 2: Bridging Processes

Tier 2 contains processes that bridge between foundational verbal abilities and true executive control. On the CWIT, Condition 3 (Inhibition) represents the primary Tier 2 measure, requiring examinees to inhibit the prepotent reading response to name dissonant ink colors. This introduces the hallmark Stroop interference task that has defined inhibitory control assessment for nearly a century.

Prepotent Response Suppression

Reading is automatic for literate individuals—seeing a word activates its pronunciation automatically and rapidly. When the word "blue" appears in red ink, two competing responses activate: the automatic reading response ("blue") and the task-appropriate naming response ("red"). Successfully naming the ink color requires actively suppressing the stronger automatic response while executing the weaker controlled response. This inhibitory demand is substantial. Examinees must inhibit the reading response on every single item across the full array. The inhibitory demand does not habituate. Even experienced psychologists taking the test for the twentieth time still feel the pull of the reading response and must actively suppress it. Practice effects can temporarily reduce the interference effect but do not fully eliminate it (Davidson et al., 2003; MacLeod, 1992). The Advanced version magnifies this inhibitory demand through its response format. The to-be-inhibited word appears twice: once as the target stimulus (e.g., "blue" printed in red letters) and again as one of the three response options at the bottom of the screen. This visual presentation of the interfering response increases its prepotency beyond traditional Stroop tasks, raising the ceiling for detecting subtle executive deficits in high-functioning individuals. The cognitive cost of this inhibition manifests as slowing (Scarpina & Tagini, 2017). Examinees who complete Condition 1 in 25 seconds and Condition 2 in 20 seconds might require 60–70 seconds for Condition 3 on the original version. This slowing is normal and expected—it quantifies the interference effect. The critical question is whether the slowing is proportionate to baseline abilities or disproportionate, suggesting true inhibitory control deficits.

Working Memory for Task Rules
Successful Condition 3 performance requires maintaining the task rule in working memory while executing repeated trials (Kane & Engle, 2003). This represents simple, single-rule working memory—not the complex multi-rule demands of Tier 3 tasks, but nonetheless requiring active maintenance of task instructions. Examinees who lose track of the rule mid-task make characteristic errors, suddenly reading words instead of naming colors. These "set-loss" errors indicate failure to maintain the task set, distinct from errors where examinees attempt to name colors but produce incorrect responses due to difficulty inhibiting the reading response.

Sustained Attention During Interference
Condition 3 requires sustained focus across all trials while managing continuous interference. This sustained attention under cognitive load goes beyond the basic attention demands of Conditions 1–2. Attention lapses manifest as error clusters. Examinees perform well for several items, then make multiple consecutive errors as attention wavers. This pattern differs from consistent difficulty inhibiting throughout the condition, suggesting attention dysregulation rather than pure inhibitory control deficit.

Tier 2 Deficit Pattern
Tier 2 deficits produce a characteristic dissociation: adequate baseline performance with disproportionate difficulty on the Inhibition condition. The examinee completes Color Naming/Identification and Word Reading/Identification at expected speed but slows dramatically or makes excessive errors when required to suppress the prepotent reading response. Contrast scores comparing Inhibition to baseline fall below expected range (7 or lower), confirming the inhibition difficulty exceeds what foundational abilities would predict. Error analysis typically reveals classic Stroop errors—saying the printed word instead of naming the ink color—indicating failed suppression of the automatic reading response. Behavioral observations may show visible conflict when processing incongruent stimuli, self-corrections indicating the examinee recognizes errors after making them, or impulsive responding where words are produced before adequate processing occurs. This pattern commonly appears in ADHD, frontal lobe dysfunction affecting inferior frontal regions, and impulse control disorders.

Tier 3: Core Executive Functions

Tier 3 represents the core executive functions that Condition 4 (Inhibition/Switching) is designed to assess. This condition elevates task demands by requiring cognitive flexibility in addition to inhibitory control. Examinees must switch between naming ink colors and reading words based on visual cues, integrating inhibition, working memory, and set-shifting. These processes can be divided into cold executive functions involving the cognitive mechanisms of flexible responding and hot executive functions involving frustration tolerance, anxiety management, and emotional regulation under demanding conditions.

Cold Executive Functions

Cold executive functions on the CWIT involve the cognitive machinery of flexible inhibition and set-shifting, operating in relatively affect-neutral contexts where logical analysis drives performance.

Mental Set-Shifting

Examinees must flexibly shift between two different response rules based on a visual cue. On the original version, they name ink colors when words are not in boxes and read words when words are inside boxes. On the Advanced version, they touch the word matching the letter color when the box background is white and touch the word matching the printed word when the box background is colored. The box that surrounds the printed word is a dissonant color in addition to the ink color, adding complexity. After processing items with one rule, examinees must recognize the cue change, switch mental sets, and apply the alternate rule—then switch back when the cue changes again. This alternating requirement creates switching costs: slowing and errors at transition points when examinees must disengage from one response mode and engage another. Set-shifting difficulty manifests in two ways: transition-point slowing (examinees slow down specifically when switching between rules) and perseverative errors (examinees continue applying the previous rule despite the cue to switch). Both patterns indicate cognitive flexibility deficits distinct from the basic inhibition problems measured in Condition 3.

Dual-Rule Working Memory

Unlike Condition 3's single-rule maintenance, Condition 4 requires maintaining two rules simultaneously while tracking which rule applies to each item. This dual-rule working memory represents greater executive demand than single-rule maintenance. Working memory limitations create characteristic errors where examinees lose track of which rule to apply, essentially "guessing" rather than using the visual cue systematically. These errors differ from set-loss errors (forgetting the task entirely) or perseverative errors (difficulty switching)—they reflect working memory overload from tracking multiple rules.

Inhibitory Control Under Alternating Demands

Condition 4 does not eliminate the inhibition demands of Condition 3. Examinees still must inhibit the reading response when naming colors. However, the alternation requirement adds variability: on half the trials, reading is correct (words in boxes on original; colored box backgrounds on Advanced); on the other half, reading must be inhibited (words without boxes on original; white box backgrounds on Advanced). This inconsistency increases inhibitory demands because the response that must be inhibited on one trial becomes correct on the next. The Advanced version's colored box backgrounds create additional interference. When the target is the word "red," the ink color may be green or blue, and the box in the background may also be green or blue. This magnified visual-verbal prepotency makes the incorrect response of ink or box color extremely salient, requiring strong inhibitory control to select "red" correctly. The interplay between inhibition and switching creates the condition's cognitive complexity. Examinees must inhibit flexibly—sometimes suppressing reading, sometimes executing it—based on rapidly updating task demands.

Tier 3 Cold EF Impairment Pattern

Tier 3 Cold EF deficits manifest as specific difficulty on Inhibition/Switching beyond what Inhibition performance would predict. The examinee may perform adequately on baseline conditions and show only modest difficulty on Inhibition, but struggle markedly when required to flexibly alternate between naming ink colors and reading words. The Inhibition/Switching versus Inhibition contrast score falls below the expected range, isolating the switching component as the primary deficit. Error analysis reveals perseverative errors at transition points—continuing to apply the previous rule despite visual cues signaling a switch—and slowing concentrated at rule changes rather than distributed across all trials. Behavioral observations may show confusion about which rule applies, verbalization of rules as a compensatory strategy, or visible frustration, specifically when switching demands increase. This pattern indicates cognitive flexibility deficits distinct from basic inhibition problems and commonly appears in frontal lobe dysfunction affecting dorsolateral prefrontal regions, autism spectrum disorders with cognitive rigidity, and conditions producing perseverative tendencies.

Hot Executive Functions

Hot executive functions involve the motivational and emotional aspects of executive control that influence how effectively cold executive processes are deployed. On the CWIT, hot EF factors become increasingly prominent as task demands escalate across conditions.

Frustration Tolerance and Error Recovery

Condition 4 places maximum demands on cognitive resources, and errors are common even among neurotypical examinees. How individuals respond to these errors reveals hot executive functioning. Examinees with strong frustration tolerance acknowledge errors without emotional disruption and continue working methodically. Those with poor frustration tolerance show deteriorating performance after errors. The frustration itself disrupts inhibitory control, creating a negative cascade where emotional dysregulation compounds cognitive difficulty. This pattern is particularly common in examinees with ADHD, anxiety disorders, or frontal lobe dysfunction.

Anxiety Management and Performance Pressure

The timed nature of Color-Word conditions creates performance pressure that anxious examinees may struggle to manage. Some respond by slowing dramatically, essentially "overthinking" each response to avoid errors—transforming an inhibitory control task into an anxiety management challenge. Others rush impulsively, sacrificing accuracy for speed in an attempt to escape the uncomfortable experience. Neither pattern reflects true cold executive capacity; both reflect hot EF factors overwhelming cognitive control.

Persistence Under Cognitive Load

Condition 4 requires sustained effort across an extended, demanding task. Examinees must persist despite accumulating fatigue, errors, and frustration. Those who give up, request breaks, or show marked deterioration toward the end of the condition demonstrate hot EF limitations in persistence and sustained motivation. Behavioral observations of emotional state, self-talk, and effort maintenance help distinguish cold EF deficits (consistent difficulty throughout) from hot EF deficits (deterioration linked to emotional or motivational factors).

Tier 3 Hot EF Pattern

Hot EF difficulties produce a distinctive pattern where performance deteriorates in connection with emotional state rather than remaining consistently impaired throughout. The examinee may begin Inhibition or Inhibition/Switching conditions adequately but show progressive deterioration as errors accumulate and frustration mounts. Behavioral observations are essential for identifying this pattern: visible agitation after errors, negative self-talk, rushing that sacrifices accuracy, or requests to stop. Error clustering provides diagnostic information: errors distributed randomly suggest attention fluctuations, but errors that increase specifically after initial mistakes suggest frustration disrupting cognitive control. The Advanced version's First-Half versus Second-Half contrast score can quantify this deterioration pattern. The key diagnostic indicator is that cognitive capacity exists—evidenced by periods of adequate performance—but emotional dysregulation prevents sustained deployment. This pattern commonly appears in examinees with ADHD, anxiety disorders, low frustration tolerance, or frontal lobe dysfunction affecting ventromedial regions, and indicates that intervention should prioritize emotional regulation before cognitive strategy training.

Bottom-Up Tier Effects

The explicit tier framework emphasizes the bottom-up nature of tier effects: impairments at lower tiers typically affect all higher-tier performance, while impairments at higher tiers often leave lower-tier performance intact. An examinee with Tier 1 processing speed deficits will struggle across all conditions. An examinee with Tier 2 inhibition deficits will typically perform adequately on Tier 1 baselines but struggle on both Inhibition and Inhibition/Switching. An examinee with specific Tier 3 cold executive deficits may perform adequately on baselines and basic inhibition while faltering only on the switching condition. Hot EF deficits create a different pattern—performance that varies with emotional state, deteriorates after errors, or improves with encouragement and breaks.

Rapid Reference 4.3

Tier Structure at a Glance

Tier	Processes
Tier 1: Foundational processes (nonexecutive)	Color naming and identification speed
	Word reading and identification speed
	General processing speed
	Sustained attention during repetitive processing
	Color perception and discrimination
Tier 2: Bridging processes	Prepotent response suppression (inhibiting automatic reading response)
	Working memory for a single task rule
	Sustained attention during interference
Tier 3: Cold executive functions	Mental set-shifting (switching between response rules)
	Dual-rule working memory
	Inhibitory control under alternating demands
Tier 3: Hot executive functions	Frustration tolerance and error recovery
	Anxiety management under performance pressure
	Persistence under cognitive load

ADMINISTRATION

NOTE: Refer to the Examiner's Manual for complete and detailed administration instructions. The Examiner's Manual provides verbatim instructions, and clinicians should follow these precisely to ensure standardized administration.

Administration procedures differ between versions primarily in response format and error recording but share common principles: ensure comprehension through practice items, maintain standardized timing and prompting, and observe response patterns and emotional reactions throughout.

Original D-KEFS Color-Word Interference Test, Paper and Pencil or Q-Global Digital Assets

Materials

For paper-and-pencil administration, the Color-Word Interference Test requires the Examiner's Manual, Record Form, Stimulus Booklet (flat position, landscape orientation), and timer. Pearson also offers digital options: Q-global digital assets provide an Examiner's Manual, Stimulus Book, and Stimulus Book Administration Directions. Q-interactive provides tablet-based administration on the Practitioner Device with error recording and automatic timing.

General Procedures

Position the Stimulus Booklet flat on the table directly in front of the examinee. The examiner sits across from or beside the examinee to observe the booklet while timing and recording responses. All four conditions are administered in fixed order: Color Naming, Word Reading, Inhibition, and Inhibition/Switching. Do not alter this sequence, as each condition builds on skills practiced in previous conditions.

For each condition, the examinee is provided an opportunity to practice on two lines of five items each. If the examinee has marked difficulty or makes four uncorrected errors on the two practice lines, discontinue the condition and proceed to the next condition. The exception is that if they do not meet the practice requirement on Condition 3, do not administer Condition 4.

For each condition, allow the examinee to use a finger to maintain their place on the stimulus page. If the examinee skips a line accidentally, redirect immediately while keeping the timer running. Record the time needed to arrive at the last item on the page or say "Stop" at the time limit if the examinee does not complete the task. Indicate on the Record Form the last item attempted at the time limit.

Condition 1: Color Naming
The examinee names the color of 50 colored patches (red, green, blue) arranged in rows as quickly as possible. Start timing when the examinee says the first color; stop when the final response completes. Record errors by writing the first letter of the incorrect color name beneath the correct response and write any nonsense words verbatim. Indicate self-corrections by drawing a slash through the word. *Time limit:* 90 seconds.

Condition 2: Word Reading
The examinee reads 50 color words (red, green, blue) printed in black ink as quickly as possible. Follow Color Naming timing and error recording procedures. Most examinees complete this condition faster than Color Naming because reading is more automatic. *Time limit*: 90 seconds.

Condition 3: Inhibition
The examinee names the ink color of 50 color words printed in dissonant ink colors (e.g., the word red printed in blue ink), suppressing the automatic reading response. This condition is substantially more difficult, and most examinees slow considerably. Encourage effort using neutral statements without providing accuracy feedback during scored trials. On the Record Form, correct answers are noted with a single letter in parentheses that indicates the first letter of the word that is stated if an error is made. For example, if the word is "blue" printed in red ink, the protocol is marked red(b). If the examinee makes an error and says "blue," circle the letter in parentheses. Indicate self-corrections by drawing a slash through the letter or word. Write any nonsense words verbatim. If the examinee makes three consecutive errors, provide one prompt to name the ink color while continuing timing. *Time limit:* 180 seconds.

Condition 4: Inhibition/Switching
The examinee switches between naming ink colors (words not in boxes) and reading words (words in boxes) for 50 items. A visual key is provided to help remember the rules. This condition combines inhibition difficulty with cognitive flexibility demands. Follow the same error recording and three-consecutive-error prompting procedures as Condition 3. *Time limit*: 180 seconds.

Examiner Demands
Simultaneous timing, error recording, and line-skip monitoring create a substantial examiner burden, particularly during the faster-paced Conditions 1–2 and with impulsive examinees who respond rapidly.

Original D-KEFS Color-Word Interference Test, Q-Interactive

Administration and scoring rules for the Q-interactive version of the original D-KEFS are the same as the paper-and-pencil version, but administration via the Practitioner Device reduces examiner demands through instructions for each condition, streamlined error recording (single-click for errors, double-click for self-corrections), and automatic scoring. Additionally, Q-interactive allows audio recording of examinee responses, which can be replayed after administration to verify error recording accuracy during rapid response sequences. The examiner must turn the timer on and off, indicate the last item attempted by touching the hand icon corresponding to that item, and remember to provide the three-consecutive-error prompt manually, if needed, as no automatic notification appears.

D-KEFS Advanced Color-Word Interference Test

Materials and Setup
The Advanced version (ages 8–90) requires the Examiner's Manual, Client Device, Practitioner Device, and stylus. Before beginning, ensure both devices are charged, connected, and the stylus is functional. Position the Client Device flat in landscape orientation directly in front of the examinee. Verify a comfortable stylus grip and ensure no screen glare.

Response Format
Unlike the original version's oral responses, examinees touch one of three response words (red, green, or blue printed in black) displayed at the bottom of the client device screen. This touch-response format eliminates motor speech confounds and enables millisecond-precision response time capture for each item.

Condition Structure
The four conditions parallel the original version: Color Identification (60 seconds), Word Identification (60 seconds), Inhibition (120 seconds), and Inhibition/Switching (180 seconds). Each condition begins with at least one demonstration and sample item. Demonstration items can be repeated as needed and corrective feedback notifications appear for incorrect responses and pauses longer than 10 seconds between responses. Test items are initiated when the examiner starts the timer. The software automatically advances items, records errors, and discontinues when time limits expire. No verbal feedback is provided if errors are made on test items, but general encouragement is allowed (e.g., "That's OK, just keep going").

It is recommended to administer all four conditions, but if marked difficulties are indicated on earlier conditions, the test may be manually discontinued after any condition. Once the discontinuation decision is made, later conditions should not be administered.

Magnified Interference
The Advanced version creates stronger interference than the original. On Inhibition and Inhibition/Switching conditions, the to-be-inhibited response appears among the three response options—examinees must select the correct word while the incorrect option is visually present. On Inhibition/Switching, dissonant colored box backgrounds add additional visual-verbal interference beyond the original version's simple box presence/absence cue.

Behavioral Observation Opportunities
The automated administration frees the examiner to observe behavioral nuances: response hesitations suggesting planning versus rapid responding suggesting impulsivity; frustration escalation across conditions; self-talk or strategy verbalization; emotional reactions to errors. These qualitative observations provide critical information about hot executive function influences that quantitative scores alone cannot capture.

Administration Considerations Common to Both Versions

Color Vision Screening
Before beginning, verify adequate color perception during practice items. Examinees who cannot reliably distinguish red, green, and blue should not proceed with testing, as poor performance would reflect sensory limitations rather than executive dysfunction.

Timing Precision
Start timing when the first response begins (original version) or when timed trials activate (Advanced version). Maintain consistent timing throughout—variations affect completion time and net correct scores.

Neutral Encouragement
Provide neutral encouragement without accuracy feedback during scored trials. Statements like "Keep going" or "Do your best" are appropriate; comments indicating correctness compromise standardization.

Finger Tracking
Some examinees use a finger to track position on the stimulus page (original version), indicating awareness of spatial organization challenges or adaptive strategy use. This is permitted and may be clinically informative.

BEHAVIORAL OBSERVATIONS

Color-Word testing provides rich behavioral information beyond timed scores. Systematic observation of examinees' approaches, error patterns, emotional responses, and strategic adjustments reveals which cognitive and emotional systems are functioning well versus poorly. These observations help localize deficits to specific tiers and determine whether cold or hot executive factors predominate.

Response Patterns and Pacing

Observe how examinees approach the tasks. Some maintain steady pacing across all items, suggesting efficient processing with adequate cognitive control. Others show variable pacing—slowing at certain points, speeding at others—indicating fluctuating effort, attention, or strategy use.

In baseline conditions, extremely fast responding with errors suggests impulsivity overwhelming accuracy goals; extremely slow responding without errors suggests excessive caution or anxiety. On interference conditions, examinees typically slow substantially. This is normal and expected. However, those who alternate between very fast and very slow responses may be inconsistently applying inhibitory control.

Distinguishing impulsivity from rapid processing is crucial. Fast responders with high accuracy demonstrate efficient processing; fast responders with high error rates demonstrate impulsivity. On the original version, examinees who begin speaking before fully processing the stimulus—starting one color, stopping mid-word, and self-correcting—show poor response control. The Advanced version's touch screen format reveals similar patterns through immediate touching without adequate processing or rapid multiple touches, indicating a trial-and-error approach.

Error Patterns and Self-Monitoring

Error analysis reveals specific deficit localization. In the Inhibition condition, the most common error is producing the printed word instead of naming the ink color—the classic Stroop error demonstrating failed inhibition. High rates of these errors localize to Tier 2 inhibitory control deficits. Other error types (producing an entirely wrong color, perseverating on the previous response) suggest different mechanisms.

On Inhibition/Switching, perseverative errors are particularly diagnostic. Examinees who continue naming colors when they should read words (or vice versa) despite clear cues demonstrate cognitive inflexibility. These errors occur most commonly at transition points and reveal the switching cost.

Error clustering provides critical information: errors distributed randomly suggest attention fluctuations; errors clustering at task beginning suggest inadequate rule learning; errors clustering after frustration emerges suggest hot EF factors disrupting performance; errors at transitions indicate specific set-shifting difficulty.

Self-correction indicates intact error monitoring. Examinees detect mistakes and attempt repair, suggesting preserved metacognitive awareness despite errors occurring. Consistent errors without self-correction may indicate poor self-monitoring or such severe cognitive load that examinees cannot track accuracy while executing responses.

Strategy Use and Adaptation

Note whether examinees develop strategies to manage task demands. Some verbalize the rule to themselves ("color of ink, not the word"), using self-directed speech to maintain task set. Others visibly slow down after making errors, suggesting metacognitive awareness and strategic adjustment. Some spontaneously use a finger to track position on the original version's booklet, indicating awareness of spatial organization challenges and adaptive strategy deployment.

The presence of strategy adaptation indicates preserved metacognitive abilities—examinees monitor their performance, recognize difficulties, and attempt strategic solutions. Absence of strategy adaptation despite poor performance suggests either a lack of metacognitive awareness or such severe cognitive overload that no resources remain for strategic thinking.

Emotional Regulation and Sustained Effort

Color-Word testing often triggers frustration, particularly in interference conditions. The task is designed to be difficult—errors are common even in neurotypical samples. How examinees handle this difficulty reveals hot executive functioning.

Some examinees maintain composure despite errors, continuing effort without visible frustration. Others show progressive agitation, such as sighing, negative self-talk, physical tension, rushing, or requesting to stop.

This deteriorating emotional regulation often cascades into worsening performance as frustration disrupts cognitive control. The relationship between emotional state and performance clarifies whether poor performance reflects cold EF deficits (struggles from the start with neutral affect), hot EF deficits (begins adequately but deteriorates as frustration mounts), or both.

Observe whether performance deteriorates across conditions. Examinees who start strong but fade demonstrate fatigue or waning motivation. Those who maintain consistent effort show better sustained attention and persistence. Young examinees, individuals with ADHD, and those with frontal lobe dysfunction often show pronounced hot EF influences and may need frequent encouragement or breaks—the amount of support required reflects real-world demands.

SCORING

Both versions provide multiple score types that enable clinicians to isolate specific executive components from foundational processing speed. The original version uses completion times with subtraction-based contrast scores; the Advanced version uses net correct responses with regression-based contrast scores.

Original D-KEFS Color-Word Interference Test

Primary Scores

Raw scores for each condition are completion times in seconds, with lower times reflecting better performance. Raw times convert to scaled scores (M = 10, SD = 3) based on age-corrected norms spanning 16 age groups from 8 to 89 years. Condition 1 (Color Naming), Condition 2 (Word Reading), Condition 3 (Inhibition), and Condition 4 (Inhibition/Switching) each yield separate completion time scaled scores. A Combined Naming + Reading time completion score is also provided to gauge time required for the two baseline conditions. Scaled scores of 8–12 represent the average range, scores of 13+ indicate above-average performance, and scores of 7 or below indicate below-average performance.

Contrast Scores

Simple scaled score comparisons are misleading because examinees with slow baseline processing naturally perform slowly on interference conditions. Contrast scores address this by empirically determining whether interference performance is worse than expected given baseline abilities. Three primary contrast scores and two additional contrast scores are provided (M = 10, SD = 3). Contrast scores of 8–12 indicate performance within expected range; scores of 7 or lower indicate disproportionately impaired inhibition; scores of 13+ indicate unexpectedly strong inhibition.

The Inhibition versus Color Naming Contrast compares Condition 3 to Condition 1 performance, calculated as Condition 3 scaled score minus Condition 1 scaled score, then converted to a contrast scaled score. The Inhibition/Switching versus Combined Naming + Reading Contrast compares Condition 4 to the combined score of Conditions 1 and 2, asking whether switching performance is proportional to combined baseline abilities. The Inhibition/Switching versus Inhibition Contrast isolates the switching component by comparing Condition 4 to Condition 3, determining whether switching adds disproportionate difficulty beyond inhibition alone.

The two additional contrast scores individually isolate performance on either the color naming (Inhibition/Switching versus Color Naming) or word reading (Inhibition/Switching versus Word Reading) component from performance on the Inhibition/Switching condition.

Error Scores

The test distinguishes self-corrected errors (examinee spontaneously corrects) from uncorrected errors (error stands). Condition 1 and 2 errors (Total Color Naming Errors and Total Word Reading Errors) are uncommon among adolescents and adults, so the error score reflects the sum of corrected and uncorrected errors. High error rates suggest word-finding deficits, reading problems, perseveration, or inattention. Condition 3 and 4 errors are more common, and the test provides separate corrected, uncorrected, and total scores for each (Corrected Inhibition Errors, Uncorrected Inhibition Errors, Total Inhibition Errors, Corrected Inhibition/Switching Errors, Uncorrected Inhibition/Switching Errors, Total Inhibition/Switching Errors). High uncorrected errors suggest poor self-monitoring; high self-corrected errors with lower uncorrected errors indicate intact error monitoring despite difficulty. Cumulative percentile ranks are provided for all error scores except the Total Inhibition and Inhibition/Switching Errors scores, which produce scaled scores.

D-KEFS Advanced Color-Word Interference Test

Core Scaled Scores

Rather than measuring time to completion, the Advanced version measures net correct responses—correct responses minus errors within fixed time limits. The Net Correct Responses are provided for each condition: Color Identification, Word Identification, Inhibition, and Inhibition/Switching. Core scores are provided as scaled scores (M = 10, SD = 3) by age group.

Combined Scores

Three index scores are derived from meaningful combinations of scaled scores. Color Identification and Word Identification Net Correct Responses Index is derived from the two scaled scores provided by the baseline conditions. This composite provides a single foundational score for contrast score calculations. CWIT Multitasking Index is derived from the two scaled scores provided by the advanced conditions—Inhibition and Inhibition/Switching—providing an overall executive function composite. Combined Inhibition and Inhibition/Switching Mean Pure Response Time (Correct and Incorrect) Index is computed from the mean time to make any response on these two conditions and serves as a measure of latency for responding. The final combined score provides an overall error score for conditions 3 and 4 (Combined Inhibition and Inhibition/Switching Total Errors).

Two combined scores are used to compute a Speed-Accuracy Tradeoff Graph. The graph interprets the relationship between an examinee's pure speed across the two higher level conditions (Combined Inhibition and Inhibition/Switching Mean Pure Response Time [Correct and Incorrect] Index) relative to their accuracy across the two conditions (Combined Inhibition and Inhibition/Switching Total Errors). The position of the two scores plotted on a graph provides information about whether accuracy was sacrificed for speed, speed was sacrificed for accuracy, if both were balanced weaknesses, or if both were balanced strengths.

Contrast Scores

The Advanced version's contrast scores answer the question of whether performance on the more complex condition is above, at, or below the predicted level given the examinee's performance on the less complex condition. The measures employ regression-based contrast scores rather than simple subtraction, which corrects for the statistical problem that scaled score discrepancies are more common when someone has especially strong or weak performance on one condition. The regression-based contrast scores in the D-KEFS Advanced help correct this problem by determining whether performance on more complex conditions (e.g., Inhibition or Inhibition/Switching) is better than, on par with, or worse than expected given performance on less complex conditions (e.g., Color Identification or Word Identification). Contrast scores between 8 and 12 indicate that performance on the more complicated task is within the range predicted by the performance on baseline/less complex task. Scores of 7 or lower indicated that performance on the complex task was worse than expected given baseline abilities (likely a sign of higher-tier deficits), and scores of 13 or higher suggest that better performance on the complex task than baseline abilities would have predicted.

Regression-based contrast scaled scores are provided across different pairs of conditions: Combined Identification versus Inhibition Net Correct Responses, Combined Identification versus Inhibition/Switching Net Correct Responses, and Inhibition versus Inhibition/Switching Net Correct Responses. An additional contrast score compares performance on the first half of a condition with the second half of the same condition (Combined Identification First-Half versus Second-Half Net Correct Responses) and provides information about consistency in responding across a condition. A final contrast score is a regression-based version of the Speed-Accuracy Tradeoff combined score described earlier. This score provides information regarding whether the examinee exhibits an expected level of errors given their speed of responding.

> **DON'T FORGET**
>
> Contrast scores answer whether performance is disproportionately impaired, not whether performance is absolutely impaired. An examinee might have below-average Inhibition (scaled score 6) but obtain an expected-range contrast score (10) if their baselines are also below-average (Combined Index 80). This indicates the inhibition problem reflects underlying processing speed limitations, not additional executive dysfunction. Conversely, an examinee with average Inhibition (scaled score 9) might obtain an impaired contrast score (6) if their baselines are superior (Combined Index 120), indicating underperformance relative to cognitive potential.

Process Scores

Additional insights into the reasons why an examinee may be having difficulties when completing tasks are provided by several process scores. Some scores compare performance on the first half to the second half of each condition to flag difficulties with initiation, attention, or fatigue. Other process scores compare differences in response time when producing correct versus incorrect responses. A complete list of process scores is listed in Table 6.3 of the Examiner's Manual.

Additional Raw Scores

Additional raw scores provide insight into the types of responses made by the examinee, such as pure response time for correct and incorrect responses, total number and type of responses (overall, correct, errors) for conditions, and percent of responses made for the left, middle, and right response boxes. Table 6.4 in the Examiner's Manual provides a complete listing of the types of scores provided (standard, scales, or base rate).

Behavioral Observations

Several base rate scores are provided for a select number of behaviors that examinees may exhibit during assessment. These quantitative scores complement behavioral observations and provide context for interpreting how behaviors or emotional reactions may have affected an examinee's performance. See Table 6.5 in the Examiner's Manual for a listing.

Rapid Reference 4.4

Scoring Summary

Score Type	Original D-KEFS	D-KEFS Advanced
Primary scores	Completion time (seconds) for each condition; converts to scaled scores (M = 10, SD = 3)	Net correct (correct minus errors) within fixed time limits; converts to scaled scores (M = 10, SD = 3)
Baseline measures	Condition 1 (Color Naming) and Condition 2 (Word Reading) scaled scores	Color Identification and Word Identification Net Correct Responses Index (M = 100, SD = 15)
Inhibition vs. baseline contrast	Condition 3 minus Condition 1; subtraction-based	Combined Identification vs. Inhibition Net Correct Responses; regression-based
Switching vs. baseline contrast	Condition 4 minus Combined Conditions 1 + 2; subtraction-based	Combined Identification vs. Inhibition/Switching Net Correct Responses; regression-based
Switching vs. inhibition contrast	Condition 4 minus Condition 3; isolates switching component	Inhibition vs. Inhibition/Switching Net Correct Responses; isolates switching component
Error scores	Self-corrected and uncorrected errors; separate percentile rankings	Incorporated into net correct; Combined Inhibition and Inhibition/Switching Total Errors also provided separately
Speed-accuracy tradeoff	Not provided	Graph plotting speed against errors; regression-based contrast score quantifies whether error rate is expected given response speed
First-half vs. second-half	Not provided	Contrast score comparing performance consistency within conditions; flags initiation difficulties, attention decline, or fatigue
Interpretation	Contrast ≤7 = disproportionate impairment; 8–12 = expected range; ≥13 = relative strength	Same interpretation; regression-based method more accurate at performance extremes

COMMON ADMINISTRATION ERRORS

Color-Word administration presents different challenges depending on the version, though certain errors compromise validity across both formats.

Failing to Screen for Color Vision Deficits

Always verify color perception during practice items before proceeding with scored trials. Examinees who cannot reliably distinguish red, green, and blue should not continue testing, as poor performance would reflect sensory limitations rather than executive dysfunction. This applies equally to both original and Advanced versions.

Stopping the Timer During Corrections

On the original version, when examinees skip lines, examiners must immediately redirect to the correct line while keeping the timer running. Stopping timing during corrections invalidates the completion time score. The Advanced version eliminates this concern through presenting only one item at a time and automated timing.

Providing Feedback on Accuracy During Scored Trials

After practice items conclude, examiners should offer only neutral encouragement ("Keep going," "Do your best") without indicating whether specific responses are correct or incorrect. Accuracy feedback during scored trials compromises standardization by providing external monitoring that the examinee should perform independently. The Q-interactive version of the original assists by providing feedback suggestions at appropriate times.

Inadequate Error Recording

On the original version's Conditions 3–4, examiners must simultaneously time, monitor for line-skipping, and record all errors with their type (corrected versus uncorrected). Missing errors or failing to distinguish correction status compromises valuable interpretive data about self-monitoring abilities. The Advanced version captures error data automatically, eliminating this concern.

Inadequate Device Positioning or Stylus Instruction

On the Advanced version, examinees unfamiliar with stylus use may struggle with the response format itself rather than the cognitive demands. Verify comfortable stylus grip, ensure the Client Device lies flat in landscape orientation with no screen glare, and confirm devices are adequately charged before beginning.

Assuming Automated Scoring Eliminates Observation Needs

On the Advanced version, while the software captures response accuracy and timing automatically, examiners must still observe behavioral responses—frustration, impulsivity, strategy use, and emotional regulation. The freed attention from manual recording should enhance, not replace, qualitative observation.

Misinterpreting Slow Baseline Performance as Executive Dysfunction

Slow completion times on Conditions 1–2 (original) or low Color Identification and Word Identification Net Correct Responses Index scores (Advanced) indicate Tier 1 processing speed limitations, not executive dysfunction. Always examine contrast scores to determine whether higher-level performance is disproportionately impaired relative to baseline abilities. This interpretive error occurs post-administration but reflects inadequate understanding of the test's design.

INTERPRETATION

CWIT interpretation requires integrating timed performance with error patterns within a systematic framework that distinguishes foundational processing speed limitations from true executive dysfunction.

Using the Hierarchical Framework for Differential Diagnosis

CWIT interpretation begins by systematically evaluating performance across tiers to identify where breakdown occurs. Always evaluate tiers hierarchically from bottom to top, ruling out lower-tier explanations before concluding higher-tier deficits exist.

Step 1: Rule Out Tier 1 Limitations

Before interpreting executive performance, confirm adequate prerequisite abilities. Color perception must be intact—individuals with color blindness may struggle depending on the extent of their difficulties with color vision. Reading ability must be adequate for age. On the original version, speech articulation and word-finding must be adequate; individuals with dysarthria, aphasia, or anomia may perform poorly due to output difficulties rather than cognitive deficits. The Advanced version's touch screen format bypasses verbal output confounds but requires fine motor control.

Next, examine baseline condition performance. On the original version, review Color Naming and Word Reading scaled scores. On the Advanced version, review the Color Identification and Word Identification Net Correct Responses Index (Combined Identification Index). Scores in the average range or above (scaled scores 8+, Index 85+) indicate adequate foundations. Below-average scores indicate Tier 1 processing speed limitations that will affect all subsequent conditions. If Tier 1 is impaired, consider general processing speed deficits, age effects, neurological conditions, medications, or psychiatric conditions. Critically, processing speed deficits are not executive dysfunction—they represent foundational efficiency limitations. Interventions should target processing speed (reducing environmental demands, allowing extra time) rather than executive strategy training.

Step 2: Evaluate Tier 2 Bridging Processes

Examine Inhibition condition performance relative to baseline using contrast scores. Disproportionate inhibition impairment (contrast scores 7 or below) localizes to Tier 2 response inhibition deficits. These examinees can process verbal information at an adequate speed but cannot effectively suppress prepotent responses when required. This pattern appears in ADHD (particularly combined and hyperactive–impulsive presentations), frontal lobe lesions (especially inferior frontal and anterior cingulate regions), early-stage dementias, and impulse control disorders (Lansbergen et al., 2007; McDonald et al., 2005).

Interventions for Tier 2 deficits focus on external inhibitory supports and strategy training: removing distractors to reduce competing response options, using self-talk to verbalize the correct response rule before acting, implementing "stop and think" strategies, and gradually increasing task difficulty as inhibitory control strengthens. Proportional inhibition performance (adequate contrast scores despite low absolute scaled scores) indicates Tier 1 processing speed limitations explain the inhibition difficulty and that no specific executive deficit exists.

Step 3: Analyze Tier 3 Cold Executive Patterns

Examine Inhibition/Switching performance relative to both baselines and Inhibition condition using multiple contrast scores. If Inhibition/Switching versus Inhibition contrast is low (7 or below), switching specifically adds difficulty beyond inhibition alone. This indicates Tier 3 cognitive flexibility deficits. Examinees can inhibit adequately when the inhibitory demand is consistent, but cannot flexibly switch between different task rules. This pattern appears in frontal lobe dysfunction (particularly dorsolateral prefrontal cortex), moderate-to-severe ADHD, cognitive rigidity in autism spectrum disorders, epilepsy (McDonald et al., 2005), and perseverative tendencies in various neurological conditions.

Interventions for Tier 3 flexibility deficits include explicit transition warnings, visual cues highlighting rule changes, practice with set-shifting tasks to build flexibility skills and reducing the number of rule changes required in complex activities.

Step 4: Evaluate Tier 3 Hot Executive Factors

Behavioral observations clarify whether cold EF capacity limitations or hot EF dysregulation primarily drive poor performance. Cold EF deficit pattern: consistent difficulty from task beginning, visible cognitive effort, neutral emotional tone, errors despite trying, and maintaining persistence. Hot EF deficit pattern: adequate performance initially that deteriorates as frustration mounts, emotional reactivity to errors, impulsive responding, giving up, and improved performance after emotional support. Combined deficits show difficulty from the start that worsens with frustration.

Hot EF factors are particularly important when error patterns suggest speed-accuracy tradeoffs. High total errors with average speed indicate examinees work quickly but sacrifice accuracy, suggesting limited response control that often reflects hot EF factors (poor impulse control, frustration intolerance) rather than pure cold EF capacity limitations. Interventions focus on slowing response speed deliberately, implementing accuracy feedback, teaching self-monitoring strategies, and addressing emotional regulation.

Note on Tier 4

Unlike D-KEFS subtests such as Tower or Twenty Questions that require coordinating multiple executive processes simultaneously, Color-Word Interference primarily assesses Tier 2 inhibition and Tier 3 cognitive flexibility in relatively discrete conditions. While examinees certainly engage metacognitive monitoring during the task (evident in self-corrections), this represents error detection rather than the strategic coordination of multiple executive systems that characterizes Tier 4 functioning. Clinicians seeking to assess higher-order integration should supplement Color-Word with measures designed for that purpose.

PERFORMANCE PATTERNS AND CLINICAL IMPLICATIONS

CWIT performance yields several recognizable patterns, each with distinct clinical implications and intervention considerations. Identifying these patterns helps clinicians move beyond global scores to understand the specific nature of an examinee's inhibitory and flexibility difficulties.

Normal Baselines with Impaired Interference

Condition 1–2 scaled scores of 8 or above with Condition 3–4 scaled scores of 7 or below, accompanied by Inhibition versus Color Naming Contrast scores of 7 or below, indicates Tier 2–3 executive dysfunction with intact Tier 1 foundations. This pattern localizes deficits to true inhibitory control and/or cognitive flexibility problems rather than foundational processing speed limitations. These examinees process verbal information adequately but cannot suppress prepotent responses or flexibly shift between task demands. This pattern commonly appears in ADHD, frontal lobe lesions, and impulse control disorders. Interventions should target executive strategy training, environmental modifications to reduce interference demands, and self-regulatory supports.

Proportionally Impaired Across All Conditions

All scaled scores of 7 or below with contrast scores of 8–12 indicate Tier 1 deficits affecting all performance proportionally. No specific executive dysfunction exists beyond baseline limitations. The examinee's inhibition and switching abilities are proportional to their foundational processing speed. This pattern appears in conditions affecting general cognitive efficiency: neurological conditions affecting processing speed, medication effects, fatigue, or age-related slowing. Interventions should target foundational processing speed rather than executive strategies—reducing time pressure, simplifying environmental demands, and allowing additional processing time.

Specific Switching Deficit

Conditions 1–3 in the adequate range with Condition 4 impaired, accompanied by Inhibition/Switching versus Inhibition contrast scores of 7 or below, indicates Tier 3 cognitive flexibility deficits with intact Tier 2 inhibition. These examinees can suppress prepotent responses when the inhibitory demand is consistent, but cannot flexibly alternate between different response rules. This dissociation between inhibition and flexibility has important clinical implications: the examinee may function adequately in contexts requiring sustained response suppression but struggle when task demands shift. This pattern appears in frontal lobe dysfunction affecting dorsolateral prefrontal regions, autism spectrum disorders with cognitive rigidity, and conditions producing perseverative tendencies. Interventions should emphasize explicit transition warnings, environmental cues signaling rule changes, and graduated practice with set-shifting demands.

Speed-Accuracy Tradeoff Pattern

Average completion times or net correct scores with elevated error rates indicates examinees who work quickly but sacrifice accuracy. This pattern suggests limited response control under interference demands—examinees can process information at adequate speed but cannot maintain precision while doing so. The speed-accuracy tradeoff often reflects hot EF factors (impulsivity, frustration intolerance, inadequate self-monitoring) rather than pure cold EF capacity limitations. Whether this pattern is maladaptive depends on real-world context; some settings reward speed over detailed accuracy. The D-KEFS Advanced provides a regression-based Speed-Accuracy Tradeoff contrast score that quantifies whether error rates are expected given response speed, enabling more precise identification of this pattern. Interventions focus on deliberately slowing response speed, implementing accuracy feedback systems, teaching self-monitoring strategies, and addressing underlying emotional regulation difficulties that may drive impulsive responding.

Intact Error Monitoring with Execution Difficulty

High self-corrected errors with low uncorrected errors indicate examinees who struggle to execute correct responses but detect and repair their mistakes. (*Note*: The original version provides separate self-corrected and uncorrected error scores that enable this analysis; the Advanced version incorporates errors into net correct calculations, though similar patterns may be observable during administration.) This pattern reveals intact metacognitive monitoring despite response inhibition difficulty—a relative strength that can be leveraged therapeutically. These examinees know when they've erred and attempt correction, suggesting the cognitive capacity for accurate responding exists but cannot be consistently deployed under interference demands. Interventions can build on this self-monitoring strength, using the examinee's error awareness as a foundation for developing more proactive response control strategies.

Poor Self-Monitoring Pattern

High uncorrected errors with low self-corrected errors indicate examinees who make mistakes without detecting them. (*Note*: This analysis requires the original version's separate error scores; behavioral observation during Advanced administration may reveal similar patterns.) This pattern suggests impaired error monitoring—either failures in metacognitive awareness or such severe cognitive load that resources for self-evaluation are unavailable. Poor self-monitoring has significant real-world implications: these individuals may not recognize when their behavior is ineffective and thus fail to self-correct in academic, vocational, or social contexts. Interventions require external accuracy feedback systems and explicit metacognitive training, as the examinee cannot rely on internal error detection to guide behavioral adjustment.

Hot EF Predominant Pattern

Adequate performance initially that deteriorates as frustration mounts, with emotional reactivity to errors, impulsive responding, or premature task abandonment, indicates hot EF dysregulation compromising initially adequate cold EF capacity. Behavioral observations are essential for identifying this pattern. The score profile alone may show only modest impairment that fails to capture the underlying mechanism. The D-KEFS Advanced provides a First-Half versus Second-Half contrast score that can quantify this deterioration pattern. These examinees possess the cognitive capacity for inhibition and flexibility, but cannot deploy these abilities when emotionally activated. Interventions should prioritize emotional regulation strategies, frustration tolerance building, and environmental supports that reduce emotional load before targeting cognitive strategy training.

Rapid Reference 4.5

Distinguishing Tier-Level Deficits

Tier Level	Indicators	Clinical Implications
Tier 1 deficit	Slow performance across all conditions proportionally; baseline scaled scores below average; contrast scores within expected range despite slow absolute performance	Processing speed or foundational verbal abilities limit performance; executive functions may be intact relative to foundational capacity; interventions target processing speed, not inhibitory control
Tier 2 deficit	Normal baselines but impaired Inhibition condition; low Inhibition vs. Color Naming Contrast score (≤7); errors predominantly on Inhibition condition; struggles extend to Inhibition/Switching	Primary inhibitory control deficit; difficulty suppressing prepotent responses; interventions target response inhibition strategies; consider ADHD, frontal dysfunction
Tier 3 cold deficit	Normal baselines and adequate Inhibition, but disproportionately impaired Inhibition/Switching; low Inhibition/Switching vs. Inhibition Contrast score (≤7); perseverative errors at transition points	Specific cognitive flexibility deficit beyond basic inhibition; difficulty shifting mental sets; interventions target flexibility training and explicit cues for rule changes
Tier 3 hot deficit	Performance deteriorates after errors or as frustration mounts; adequate initial performance with declining trajectory; visible emotional dysregulation; improvement with breaks or encouragement	Emotional regulation difficulties compromising cognitive control; hot EF factors overwhelm cold EF capacity; interventions target frustration tolerance, anxiety management, and emotional regulation
Combined cold and hot deficit	Poor performance throughout, with worsening emotional state; struggles from start with escalating frustration	Both cognitive limitations and emotional dysregulation present; comprehensive interventions needed to address both cold EF strategies and hot EF regulation

ECOLOGICAL VALIDITY AND FUNCTIONAL IMPLICATIONS

Color-Word performance relates directly to real-world situations requiring response inhibition and cognitive flexibility. Understanding these connections helps clinicians predict functional difficulties and design ecologically valid interventions.

Academic Functioning

The Color Naming condition functions as a rapid automatized naming (RAN) task, and decades of research demonstrate that naming speed predicts reading fluency development independent of phonological awareness (Wolf & Bowers, 1999; Norton & Wolf, 2012). Children with slow color naming often show corresponding difficulties with reading rate and automaticity—a connection clinicians can explore when Color Naming is disproportionately weak.

Beyond this foundational link, students constantly face situations requiring inhibition of automatic responses. Reading comprehension requires inhibiting surface-level word meanings to derive deeper inferences. Mathematics requires inhibiting memorized procedures when new problems demand different approaches. Test-taking requires inhibiting the automatic tendency to answer quickly without carefully reading questions. Students with

Color-Word inhibition deficits often struggle with these academic demands, with teachers reporting they "don't think before answering" or "make careless errors despite understanding material."

The switching condition predicts additional difficulties when academic tasks require flexible rule application—shifting between operations in math, alternating between reading and writing during note-taking, or adapting study strategies to different subject demands. Interventions include explicit rule reminders, self-talk strategies, deliberate slowing practice, and error-checking routines.

Vocational and Daily Living

Workplace demands frequently require response inhibition and cognitive flexibility. Following procedures requires inhibiting habitual shortcuts. Quality control requires inhibiting the automatic tendency to continue without checking. Customer service requires inhibiting negative emotional reactions. Multitasking requires flexibly switching between work demands. Interaction with coworkers requires monitoring and inhibiting comments that may be appropriate among friends but not in professional contexts. Adults with Color-Word deficits may receive feedback about "rushing through tasks," "not following new procedures," or "struggling to handle multiple priorities." Workplace interventions include checklist systems providing external reminders, self-pacing strategies, job restructuring to reduce multitasking demands, and explicit transition time when switching between major tasks.

Many safety-critical daily living situations also demand rapid response inhibition and cognitive flexibility. Driving requires inhibiting automatic responses in unusual traffic situations. Cooking requires inhibiting automatic timing when recipes differ from familiar routines. Medication management requires inhibiting routine schedules when doses change. Older adults with Color-Word deficits may show declining driving safety, medication errors, or household accidents from perseverating on habitual procedures when circumstances require flexibility.

Social Functioning

Social interactions demand continuous response inhibition: conversational turn-taking requires inhibiting interruption urges; disagreeing respectfully requires inhibiting harsh criticism; managing frustration requires inhibiting angry outbursts. Individuals with Color-Word deficits often show social difficulties stemming from poor response inhibition, such as blurting inappropriate comments, interrupting others, or reacting impulsively to frustration. The switching condition predicts difficulties flexibly adapting social behavior to changing contexts, like shifting communication style between professional and casual settings or adjusting behavior when social dynamics change.

However, critical limitations exist in generalizing from Color-Word to social functioning. Color-Word measures cold EF in emotionally neutral contexts, while social situations often involve emotionally charged hot EF demands. An individual may demonstrate adequate inhibition on Color-Word yet struggle with social inhibition when emotions are activated.

CAUTION

Color-Word predicts real-world inhibition and flexibility only when those real-world demands resemble test conditions: emotionally neutral, clear rules, immediate feedback on errors, structured one-on-one context. Real-world executive demands often differ dramatically: emotionally charged, ambiguous rules, delayed or absent error feedback, chaotic, unstructured contexts. Always integrate Color-Word results with rating scales, behavioral observations, and functional assessment to accurately predict real-world executive functioning.

PRELIMINARY CLINICAL VALIDATION OF THE D-KEFS ADVANCED COLOR-WORD INTERFERENCE TEST

Clinical group studies conducted during D-KEFS Advanced standardization provide initial evidence of the Advanced CWIT's sensitivity to executive dysfunction across several populations (Delis & Kaplan, 2025). These preliminary findings require replication and should not be used as sole diagnostic criteria, but they establish useful reference points for clinical interpretation.

Attention-Deficit/Hyperactivity Disorder

The ADHD sample (n = 55 children and adolescents) performed below matched controls on all four CWIT conditions. Effect sizes were notably robust for a population that historically shows inconsistent performance-based cognitive deficits. The Inhibition condition produced the strongest differentiation (d = 0.80, $p < 0.01$), while baseline conditions also separated groups meaningfully (Color Identification d = 0.58; Word Identification d = 0.73). The Multitasking Index showed similar sensitivity (d = 0.74, $p < 0.01$). Clinically, the Advanced CWIT's combination of monotonous sustained responding with inhibitory demands may tap the specific attentional vulnerabilities characteristic of ADHD, namely performance breaks down when examinees must maintain focus on repetitive stimuli while simultaneously suppressing prepotent responses.

Autism Spectrum Disorder

The ASD sample (n = 31 children and adolescents) showed pronounced difficulty on foundational conditions, with both Color Identification (d = 1.13, $p < 0.01$) and Word Identification (d = 0.93, $p < 0.01$) producing large effect sizes. The Inhibition condition similarly differentiated groups (d = 1.06, $p < 0.01$). Interestingly, the Inhibition/Switching condition did not reach significance (d = 0.47, p = 0.07), raising the possibility that cognitive flexibility difficulties in this sample were proportional to—rather than exceeding—their baseline processing limitations. This pattern underscores the clinical importance of contrast score interpretation: apparent executive deficits may actually reflect Tier 1 foundations struggling to support adequate response speed, rather than true inhibitory control problems.

Specific Learning Disorder–Mathematics

The SLD-Math sample (n = 26 children) showed a more muted pattern. The Inhibition/Switching condition approached but did not reach significance (p = 0.07), yielding a moderate effect size consistent with shared cognitive demands between mathematical reasoning and task-switching. Whether the nonsignificant findings reflect true absence of inhibitory deficits in this population or simply insufficient statistical power remains unclear. The moderate effect sizes suggest clinically meaningful differences that larger samples might confirm.

Mild Cognitive Impairment

The mild cognitive impairment (MCI) sample (n = 18 adults) presented a clinically informative dissociation: baseline Color Identification was significantly impaired with a large effect size, while higher-level Inhibition and Inhibition/Switching conditions remained intact. This pattern aligns with MCI's primary memory rather than executive presentation and demonstrates that the CWIT appropriately identifies foundational slowing without over-pathologizing executive functioning in populations whose deficits lie elsewhere. Clinicians can take some reassurance that the test does not simply label all impaired populations as "executive dysfunction"—it distinguishes where in the processing hierarchy difficulties emerge.

Clinical Implications

Across these clinical samples, the Advanced CWIT demonstrated meaningful sensitivity to processing speed and inhibitory control deficits, with the Inhibition condition appearing particularly useful for identifying ADHD-related difficulties. The varying patterns across diagnostic groups support hierarchical interpretation: baseline versus higher-level condition comparisons help localize whether foundational or executive processes drive performance problems. These group-level patterns provide useful benchmarks, though substantial individual variation within each diagnostic category means the CWIT should complement rather than replace comprehensive clinical evaluation.

STRENGTHS AND WEAKNESSES

The CWIT offers distinct advantages for assessing inhibitory control and cognitive flexibility while also presenting limitations that clinicians should consider when selecting measures and interpreting results.

Strengths

Several features make the CWIT a valuable component of a comprehensive executive function evaluation.

Extensive Research Validation

The Stroop paradigm has 90 years of research validation, with thousands of studies documenting its neural correlates, cognitive mechanisms, and clinical sensitivity across diverse populations. This robust empirical foundation provides clinicians with confidence in the construct validity of their interpretations and allows meaningful comparison to the extensive clinical and research literature.

Systematic Component Separation

Unlike omnibus executive function measures that yield global scores conflating multiple processes, Color-Word systematically separates foundational processing speed from inhibitory control from cognitive flexibility. The baseline conditions isolate Tier 1 naming and reading speed, the Inhibition condition adds Tier 2 response suppression demands, and the Inhibition/Switching condition adds Tier 3 cognitive flexibility requirements. This hierarchical structure enables precise deficit localization rather than vague conclusions about "executive dysfunction."

Contrast Score Methodology

The contrast scores quantify whether executive deficits exist beyond baseline abilities, preventing misattribution of processing speed limitations as executive dysfunction. An examinee with slow processing speed will naturally perform slowly on interference conditions; contrast scores determine whether this slowness is proportional to baseline limitations or reflects disproportionate executive difficulty. This methodology represents sophisticated psychometric thinking that many competing measures lack.

Broad Clinical Sensitivity and Efficient Administration

The test detects executive deficits across diverse clinical populations including ADHD, traumatic brain injury (Hacker et al., 2024), stroke, dementia, psychiatric conditions, and developmental disorders. Brief administration time (5–15 minutes) provides efficient assessment without a lengthy testing burden, and minimal language demands beyond basic color words make the test accessible to diverse populations. The Advanced version further reduces language demands by eliminating speech production requirements entirely.

Contemporary Normative Sample (Advanced Version)

The D-KEFS Advanced provides recently collected normative data based on contemporary populations, addressing concerns about the original version's two-decade-old norms and ensuring accurate comparison to current demographic standards.

Weaknesses and Limitations

Despite its strengths, the CWIT has several limitations that clinicians should consider when selecting measures and interpreting results.

Limited Hot EF and Tier 4 Assessment

The test measures executive functions in emotionally neutral, highly structured contexts with clear rules and immediate error feedback. Performance may not predict hot EF functioning in emotionally charged or unstructured real-world situations where rules are ambiguous and feedback is delayed. Additionally, unlike D-KEFS subtests such as Tower or Twenty Questions that require coordinating multiple executive processes simultaneously, Color-Word provides minimal assessment of higher-order metacognitive integration (Tier 4). Self-monitoring and strategy adjustment are observable but not formally measured.

Cultural, Linguistic, and Reading Limitations
Color words must be highly automatic for the interference effect to emerge (Manly, 2008; Ardila, 2005; Chua et al., 2005). English Language Learners, individuals with limited literacy, or those with reading disabilities may show reduced interference unrelated to inhibitory control capacity. The baseline reading condition helps identify this confound, but clinicians must carefully consider whether apparent inhibitory deficits actually reflect foundational reading or language limitations.

Floor and Ceiling Effects
Individuals with profound disability or advanced dementia may be unable to complete even baseline conditions, limiting utility in severe populations. Conversely, high-functioning individuals often obtain scaled scores of 12–13 on all conditions, providing limited differentiation of executive abilities in superior-range examinees. The Advanced version partially addresses ceiling effects through increased difficulty and finer-grained timing precision, but both limitations remain relevant for extreme populations.

Practice Effects and Technology Requirements
Repeated administrations show significant practice effects as examinees develop strategies for managing interference demands, limiting utility for monitoring intervention effects or tracking progressive conditions over short intervals. Additionally, the original version on Q-interactive and the Advanced version require tablet devices, proprietary software, and technical expertise—equipment failures or examiner unfamiliarity with digital platforms can disrupt standardized administration.

Dated Norms (Original Version)
The original D-KEFS normative data were collected over two decades ago. While the test's construct validity remains strong, norm accuracy for contemporary populations may be compromised, particularly given demographic and educational shifts since standardization.

ALTERNATIVE MEASURES

Color-Word should be interpreted within a comprehensive assessment, including complementary measures that assess related but distinct aspects of inhibitory control and cognitive flexibility.

Within the D-KEFS Suite

Several D-KEFS subtests provide complementary or converging evidence for inhibitory control and cognitive flexibility.

Trail Making Test
Assesses cognitive flexibility through sequential number-letter switching, providing convergent evidence for flexibility deficits when Condition 4 performance parallels Color-Word Inhibition/Switching difficulties. However, Trail Making uses predictable alternation while Color-Word uses cued switching, so discrepancies between tests may reveal important distinctions in switching mechanisms.

Sorting Test
Requires generating sorting rules and flexibly shifting between categorization approaches, assessing verbal and conceptual flexibility with minimal inhibitory demands. Useful for determining whether flexibility deficits extend beyond interference contexts to conceptual reasoning.

Verbal Fluency Test
The Category Switching condition assesses generative flexibility—producing responses while alternating between categories—complementing Color-Word's reactive flexibility assessment, where examinees respond to externally presented stimuli.

Social Sorting Test (D-KEFS Advanced)
Assesses cognitive flexibility within social-cognitive contexts, measuring whether flexibility deficits observed on Color-Word extend to social categorization and reasoning. This comparison is particularly relevant for individuals

with autism spectrum disorders or social cognitive impairments, where flexibility difficulties may be more pronounced in social versus nonsocial domains.

Beyond D-KEFS

Measures beyond the D-KEFS battery provide additional perspectives on inhibitory control and cognitive flexibility.

Other Stroop Paradigms

Alternative Stroop formats exist with varying administration procedures and normative samples. The Victoria Stroop Test (Regard, 1981) and Stroop Neuropsychological Screening Test (Trenerry et al., 1989) provide similar interference paradigms useful when specific normative populations are needed or when D-KEFS stimuli have been previously administered.

Motor Response Inhibition Measures

Go/No-Go and Stop-Signal tasks assess motor response inhibition—suppressing prepotent motor responses rather than verbal responses. Discrepancies between Color-Word and motor inhibition tasks help determine whether inhibitory deficits are modality-specific or reflect general response control difficulties.

Continuous Performance Tests

CPTs such as the Conners CPT-3 (Conners, 2014) measure sustained attention and response inhibition over extended periods, assessing whether inhibitory deficits are specific to interference tasks or reflect broader vigilance problems. CPTs also provide process scores distinguishing inattention from impulsivity, complementing Color-Word's inhibition focus.

Set-Shifting Measures

The Wisconsin Card Sorting Test (Heaton et al., 1993) requires discovering sorting rules through feedback and shifting rules when they change, assessing self-directed rule inference and feedback-based shifting that complements Color-Word's explicit rule switching.

Behavioral Rating Scales

Executive function rating scales capture real-world executive behaviors that may or may not align with performance-based measures. For children and adolescents, the Behavior Rating Inventory of Executive Function, Second Edition (BRIEF-2; Gioia et al., 2015), Comprehensive Executive Function Inventory (CEFI; Naglieri & Goldstein, 2013), and Delis Rating of Executive Functions (D-REF; Delis, 2012) provide parent and teacher perspectives on daily executive functioning. For adults, the BRIEF-A (Roth et al., 2005), CEFI Adult (Naglieri & Goldstein, 2017), and D-REF Adult (Delis, 2021) offer self-report and informant-report options. Relevant scales across these measures include Inhibit (paralleling Color-Word's response suppression demands), Shift (cognitive flexibility required for the Inhibition/Switching condition), and Emotional Control (hot EF factors that may compromise cold EF capacity during testing). Discrepancies between Color-Word performance and rating scale elevations provide diagnostic information: adequate test performance with elevated rating scales may indicate that the structured, emotionally neutral testing environment does not capture inhibitory and flexibility challenges that emerge in unstructured, emotionally charged daily situations. Conversely, poor Color-Word performance with unremarkable rating scales might suggest test-specific factors such as performance anxiety under timed conditions, unfamiliarity with testing demands, or successful real-world compensation through environmental supports rather than pervasive executive dysfunction.

SUMMARY

The CWIT, in both original and Advanced versions, provides essential assessment of response inhibition and cognitive flexibility—core executive functions with clear real-world relevance. The hierarchical tier framework guides interpretation, distinguishing foundational verbal processing speed (Tier 1) from true inhibitory control (Tier 2) and cognitive flexibility (Tier 3). This systematic approach prevents misattributing processing speed limitations as executive dysfunction and ensures interventions target the appropriate cognitive level.

The original version's verbal response format provides a valid assessment for most examinees while quantifying color naming and word reading baselines separately. The Advanced version's touch screen format eliminates speech production confounds, increases inhibitory demands through magnified response prepotency, and provides contemporary norms with precise digital timing and error tracking. Preliminary clinical validation studies demonstrate strong sensitivity across multiple populations, with particularly robust findings for ADHD and ASD. Version selection depends on examinee characteristics, referral questions, and clinical context.

Critical to skilled Color-Word interpretation is recognizing that test performance reflects cold executive functions in emotionally neutral, structured contexts. Hot executive factors—frustration tolerance, emotional regulation, impulsivity—profoundly influence performance, and real-world executive demands often involve hot EF challenges not captured by Color-Word testing. Recognizable performance patterns from proportionally impaired profiles indicating Tier 1 limitations to specific switching deficits revealing Tier 3 flexibility problems guide differential diagnosis and intervention planning. Integration with behavioral rating scales, functional assessment, and other neuropsychological measures bridges the assessment-reality gap.

Ultimately, Color-Word data become clinically meaningful when translated into functional predictions and intervention recommendations. An examinee's specific pattern of strengths and weaknesses across tiers, conditions, and error types should directly inform individualized interventions targeting the appropriate level—whether foundational processing accommodations, inhibitory control strategies, cognitive flexibility training, or emotional regulation support.

TEST YOURSELF

1. What is the primary difference in response format between the original and Advanced Color-Word Interference Tests?

(a) The original uses verbal responses; the Advanced uses touch screen responses.

(b) The original uses written responses; the Advanced uses verbal responses.

(c) Both use identical response formats but different stimuli.

(d) The original uses pointing; the Advanced uses verbal responses.

2. According to Pearson's tier framework for the Advanced CWIT, Tier 1 includes all of the following EXCEPT:

(a) Verbal processing speed

(b) Sustained attention

(c) Inhibition of prepotent responses

(d) Basic reading skills

3. A contrast score of 7 on the Inhibition versus Color Naming comparison indicates:

(a) Performance is within the expected range

(b) Disproportionately poor inhibition beyond baseline abilities

(c) Better-than-expected inhibition performance

(d) Invalid test results requiring readministration

4. Which condition of the Color-Word Interference Test specifically assesses cognitive flexibility through set-shifting?

(a) Condition 1: Color Identification

(b) Condition 2: Word Identification

(c) Condition 3: Inhibition

(d) Condition 4: Inhibition/Switching

5. **When should the Advanced Color-Word version be preferred over the original version?**
   (a) When the examinee has intact verbal output and motor speech
   (b) When traditional paper-and-pencil administration is required
   (c) When speech articulation or word-finding difficulties are present
   (d) When cost constraints limit access to digital equipment
6. **An examinee obtains scaled scores of 12 on both baseline conditions but a scaled score of 6 on Inhibition with a contrast score of 5. This pattern indicates:**
   (a) Tier 1 processing speed deficit
   (b) Tier 2 inhibitory control deficit
   (c) Tier 3 cognitive flexibility deficit
   (d) Invalid results due to poor effort
7. **High self-corrected errors with low uncorrected errors on the Inhibition condition suggest:**
   (a) Severe inhibitory control impairment
   (b) Poor self-monitoring and metacognitive awareness
   (c) Intact error monitoring despite response execution difficulty
   (d) Processing speed limitations rather than executive dysfunction
8. **The Advanced version increases inhibitory demands by:**
   (a) Using longer color words that are harder to read.
   (b) Presenting more items within the same time limit.
   (c) Displaying the to-be-inhibited word as a response choice.
   (d) Removing all baseline conditions.
9. **The most common error type on the Inhibition condition—saying the printed word instead of naming the ink color—specifically indicates:**
   (a) Tier 1 processing speed limitations
   (b) Tier 2 Failure to suppress the prepotent reading response
   (c) Tier 3 cognitive flexibility deficit
   (d) Tier 4 metacognitive monitoring failure
10. **An examinee shows adequate performance initially but deteriorates as frustration mounts, with increasing errors after mistakes. This pattern primarily reflects:**
   (a) Cold EF deficits in inhibitory capacity
   (b) Hot EF dysregulation compromising cognitive control
   (c) Tier 1 processing speed limitations
   (d) Invalid results requiring test discontinuation

Answer Key: 1-a, 2-c, 3-b, 4-d, 5-c, 6-b, 7-c, 8-c, 9-b, 10-b

REFERENCES

Almustanyir, A. (2025, August). A global perspective of color vision deficiency: Awareness, diagnosis, and lived experiences. Healthcare (Basel), 13(16), 2031. MDPI.

Ardila, A. (2005). Cultural values underlying psychometric cognitive testing. Neuropsychology Review, *15*(4), 185–195.

Chua, H. F., Boland, J. E., & Nisbett, R. E. (2005). Cultural variation in eye movements during scene perception. Proceedings of the National Academy of Sciences, *102*(35), 12629–12633.

Conners, C. K. (2014). Conners Continuous Performance Test–Third Edition (Conners CPT-3). Multi-Health Systems.

Davidson, D. J., Zacks, R. T., & Williams, C. C. (2003). Stroop interference, practice, and aging. *Aging, Neuropsychology, and Cognition*, *10*(2), 85–98.

Delis, D. C. (2012). Delis Rating of Executive Functions (D-REF). Pearson.

Delis, D. C. (2021). Delis Rating of Executive Functions–Adult Version (D-REF Adult). Pearson.

Delis, D. C., & Kaplan, E. (2025). Delis-Kaplan Executive Function System–Advanced (D-KEFS Advanced). Pearson.

Delis, D. C., Kaplan, E., & Kramer, J. H. (2001). Delis-Kaplan Executive Function System (D-KEFS). San Antonio, TX: The Psychological Corporation.

Gioia, G. A., Isquith, P. K., Guy, S. C., & Kenworthy, L. (2015). Behavior Rating Inventory of Executive Function–Second Edition (BRIEF-2). Lutz, FL: Psychological Assessment Resources.

Gonzales, M. M., Garbarino, V. R., Pollet, E., Palavicini, J. P., Kellogg, D. L., Kraig, E., & Orr, M. E. (2022). Biological aging processes underlying cognitive decline and neurodegenerative disease. The Journal of Clinical Investigation, *132*(10).

Hacker, D., Jones, C. A., Chan, Y. M., Yasin, E., Clowes, Z., Belli, A., Cooper, J., Bose, D., Hawkins, A., Davies, H., & Paton, E. (2024). Examining the validity of the Delis–Kaplan Executive Function System (DKEFS) in traumatic brain injury. *Journal of Neuropsychology*, 18(1), 81–99.

Heaton, R. K., Chelune, G. J., Talley, J. L., Kay, G. G., & Curtiss, G. (1993). *Wisconsin Card Sorting Test Manual: Revised and Expanded.* Psychological Assessment Resources.

Kane, M. J., & Engle, R. W. (2003). Working-memory capacity and the control of attention: The contributions of goal neglect, response competition, and task set to Stroop interference. *Journal of Experimental Psychology: General, 132*(1), 47.

Lansbergen, M. M., Kenemans, J. L., & van Engeland, H. (2007). Stroop interference and attention-deficit/hyperactivity disorder: A review and meta-analysis. *Neuropsychology, 21*(2), 251.

MacLeod, C. M. (1992). "The Stroop task: The gold standard" of attentional measures. *Journal of Experimental Psychology: General, 121*(1), 12.

Manly, J. J. (2008). Critical issues in cultural neuropsychology: Profit from diversity. *Neuropsychology Review, 18*(3), 179–183.

McDonald, B. C., Delis, D. C., Norman, M. A., Wetter, S. R., Tecoma, E. S., & Iragui, V. J. (2005). Response inhibition and set shifting in patients with frontal lobe epilepsy or temporal lobe epilepsy. *Epilepsy & Behavior, 7*(3), 438–446.

Mishra, A. K., Varma, A. R., & Varma, A. (2023). A comprehensive review of the generalized anxiety disorder. *Cureus, 15*(9).

Naglieri, J. A., & Goldstein, S. (2013). *Comprehensive Executive Function Inventory (CEFI).* Multi-Health Systems.

Naglieri, J. A., & Goldstein, S. (2017). *Comprehensive Executive Function Inventory–Adult (CEFI Adult).* Multi-Health Systems.

Norton, E. S., & Wolf, M. (2012). Rapid automatized naming (RAN) and reading fluency: Implications for understanding and treatment of reading disabilities. *Annual Review of Psychology, 63*, 427–452.

Nuño, L., Gómez-Benito, J., Carmona, V. R., & Pino, O. (2021). A systematic review of executive Function and information processing speed in major depression disorder. *Brain Sciences, 11*(2), 147.

Regard, M. (1981). *Cognitive rigidity and flexibility: A neuropsychological study.* [Unpublished doctoral dissertation]. University of Victoria.

Roth, R. M., Isquith, P. K., & Gioia, G. A. (2005). *Behavior Rating Inventory of Executive Function–Adult Version (BRIEF-A).* Psychological Assessment Resources.

Scarpina, F., & Tagini, S. (2017). The Stroop color and word test. *Frontiers in Psychology, 8*, 557.

Sherman, E. M. S., Brooks, B. L., Akdag, S., Connolly, M. B., & Wiebe, S. (2022). Cognitive effects of anti-seizure medications in pediatric epilepsy: A critical review of clinically relevant changes in standard scores. *Developmental Neuropsychology, 47*(5), 221–243.

Stroop, J. R. (1935). Studies of interference in serial verbal reactions. *Journal of Experimental Psychology, 18*(6), 643–662.

Su, C. Y., Wuang, Y. P., Lin, Y. H., & Su, J. H. (2014). The role of processing speed in post-stroke cognitive dysfunction. *Archives of Clinical Neuropsychology*, 30(2), 148–160.

Trenerry, M. R., Crosson, B., DeBoe, J., & Leber, W. R. (1989). *Stroop Neuropsychological Screening Test manual.* Psychological Assessment Resources.

Wolf, M., & Bowers, P. G. (1999). The double-deficit hypothesis for the developmental dyslexias. *Journal of Educational Psychology, 91*(3), 415–438.

Five

DESIGN FLUENCY TEST

CLINICAL VIGNETTE

Fourteen-year-old Elena Rodriguez was referred for neuropsychological evaluation following concerns about declining academic performance and organizational difficulties after starting high school. Her parents reported that Elena had always been bright, but teachers noted she struggled with open-ended assignments and seemed to "run out of ideas" when creativity was required.

During assessment, Elena performed well on tests of vocabulary, reading comprehension, and factual knowledge, with scores in the high average to superior range. Her attention and memory functions were intact, and she demonstrated good visual–spatial abilities. However, on the D-KEFS Design Fluency Test, a distinctive pattern emerged.

On Condition 1 (Filled Dots), Elena had no trouble with visual scanning or motor control (Tier 1 intact), and she could hold the basic rules in mind (Tier 2 intact). However, her productivity was below average with only 6 correct designs in 60 seconds (scaled score = 7). Initially, she drew two or three designs quickly using simple "chain" patterns (connecting dots sequentially), but then she paused for several seconds before each subsequent design, occasionally starting and stopping midway, saying, "I already did that one." This suggested Tier 3 difficulties with fluent generation of novel patterns and cognitive flexibility.

On Condition 2 (Empty Dots Only), her performance was similar: 8 correct designs (scaled score = 8). Notably, she made no set-loss errors, indicating adequate basic inhibition and self-monitoring capacity. The similarity between Conditions 1 and 2 suggested her fundamental issue was generating novel designs, not inhibiting responses to irrelevant stimuli.

The most striking finding emerged on Condition 3 (Switching), where performance declined dramatically to only 2 correct designs (scaled score = 4). However, both designs correctly showed alternation between filled and empty dots, indicating Elena understood and could apply the rule. The problem was productivity. She couldn't generate many designs while managing the switching demand. The contrast score (Switching versus Combined Conditions 1 + 2) was significantly low (contrast scaled score = 6), indicating a specific deficit in cognitive flexibility when generation demands were increased.

Throughout testing, Elena maintained good effort and frustration tolerance (Hot EF relatively intact) and demonstrated metacognitive awareness by recognizing when she was about to repeat a design (Tier 4 self-monitoring present). The hierarchical analysis indicated her deficit was specifically at the Tier 3 cold executive function level—difficulty with fluent generativity and cognitive flexibility under increased demands.

These findings explained Elena's real-world difficulties with open-ended assignments requiring creative idea generation. Recommendations included teaching specific strategies for brainstorming, breaking complex assignments into smaller components, and providing graphic organizers.

TEST DESCRIPTION

The D-KEFS Design Fluency Test is for individuals aged 8–89 and provides a nonverbal assessment of generative fluency and executive functioning. It is a measure of the ability to generate novel visual patterns, inhibit previously drawn responses, and engage in cognitive flexibility when task demands require switching between stimulus types (Delis et al., 2001).

The test consists of three conditions, each administered for 60 seconds. Total administration time is approximately 8–10 minutes, including instructions and practice items. The examinee is presented with a Response Booklet containing rows of boxes, and each box contains an array of dots. The task is to draw different designs in each box using four straight lines, ensuring each line touches at least one other line at a dot.

Condition 1: Filled Dots presents boxes containing only five filled (blackened) dots. The examinee connects these dots to create as many unique four-line designs as possible in 60 seconds. This condition assesses basic nonverbal generativity and fluency—the ability to produce novel visual patterns at Tier 3.
Condition 2: Empty Dots Only presents boxes containing five filled dots and five empty dots. The examinee must connect only the empty dots, inhibiting responses to the filled dots. This condition maintains the generativity demand while adding an inhibitory requirement, allowing assessment of response inhibition at Tier 2–3.
Condition 3: Switching presents boxes with both filled and empty dots. The examinee must alternate between the two types. Each line must connect an empty dot to a filled dot, then to an empty dot, then to a filled dot. This condition combines the generativity demand with cognitive flexibility, requiring continuous, rapid shifting embedded within each design. Unlike tasks requiring occasional switching between two clear conditions, Condition 3 demands set shifting with each line drawn (Delis et al., 2001).

DON'T FORGET

The three-condition structure is specifically designed to separate different executive processes. Condition 1 provides a baseline measure of nonverbal fluency. Comparing Condition 2 to Condition 1 reveals whether inhibiting competing stimuli impairs performance. Comparing Condition 3 to the combined Conditions 1 + 2 isolates cognitive flexibility demands. This structured interpretation helps differentiate whether poor performance reflects generativity deficits (low across all conditions), inhibition problems (specific decline on Condition 2), or flexibility impairment (specific decline on Condition 3).

The administration is straightforward for each condition: the examiner presents three practice boxes, provides standardized instructions emphasizing the specific rules for that condition, allows practice with corrective feedback, and then presents the test array with instructions to generate as many different designs as possible in 60 seconds. Responses are drawn directly in the Response Booklet and later scored for correctness. The examiner can choose between reading the instructions from the Stimulus Booklet or using instructions provided on a tablet through Q-interactive.

The Design Fluency Test evaluates the ability to generate novel responses in the nonverbal domain, a capacity essential for creative problem-solving, adaptive thinking, and cognitive flexibility (Jones-Gotman & Milner, 1977; Ruff et al., 1987). Performance reflects both visual–spatial constructional abilities and higher-level executive functions, including initiation, fluent production of novel patterns, simultaneous processing while monitoring rules and previous responses, and inhibition of repetitive responses.

CAUTION

Because nonverbal fluency develops throughout childhood and continues maturing into adolescence, younger children will typically produce fewer designs than adolescents and adults, even with intact executive functioning. Always interpret performance in the context of age-appropriate norms. Additionally, performance peaks in young adulthood and shows a gradual decline with normal aging, particularly on the Switching condition, which may reflect age-related changes in processing speed and executive flexibility.

HIERARCHICAL TIER ANALYSIS

The Design Fluency Test can be analyzed through the four-tier framework, with performance reflecting processes from basic visual-motor abilities to higher-order metacognitive integration.

Tier 1: Foundational Processes (Nonexecutive)

The Design Fluency Test requires intact foundational abilities before any executive processing can occur. Deficits at this level will compromise performance but do not indicate executive dysfunction.

Rapid Reference 5.1

Design Fluency Test Overview

Element	Description
Age range	8–89 years
Conditions	Condition 1: Filled Dots (baseline fluency)
	Condition 2: Empty Dots Only (fluency + inhibition)
	Condition 3: Switching (fluency + cognitive flexibility)
Time limit	60 seconds per condition
Response format	Draw four-line designs connecting dots in Response Booklet
Materials	Stimulus Booklet, Design Fluency Response Booklet, pen, timer
Discontinuation	None—administer all three conditions
Primary constructs	Nonverbal fluency, cognitive flexibility, response inhibition

Visual Processing and Perception

The test relies on adequate visual acuity to perceive the dots clearly, visual scanning efficiency to locate dots within each box, and visual–spatial perception to understand spatial relationships. Examinees must distinguish between filled and empty dots (particularly important for Conditions 2 and 3), scan the array to identify available dots, and recognize geometric patterns. Visual processing deficits, scanning inefficiencies, figure-ground discrimination problems, or visual–spatial deficits may impair performance independent of executive capacity.

Visual-Motor Coordination and Processing Speed

Drawing straight lines between dots requires adequate fine motor control, visual-motor integration and motor planning. The task demands coordinating visual perception with motor execution to connect specific dots accurately. Motor disorders (tremor, bradykinesia, ataxia), visual-motor integration deficits, or poor motor planning may result in slow, inaccurate drawing. The 60-second time limit makes processing speed a significant factor; examinees must process visual information and execute motor responses quickly enough to produce multiple designs. Generalized psychomotor slowing—whether from normal aging, medication effects, depression, or neurological conditions—will reduce productivity across all conditions regardless of executive capacity.

Task Comprehension and Attention

Examinees must understand the verbal instructions for each condition, including the concepts of "design," "four lines," "start and end," "touching," and "different." Particularly for Condition 3, understanding the alternating switching rule is essential. Language comprehension deficits, or intellectual disability, may result in poor performance due to comprehension limitations. The test also requires sustained attention for 60 seconds per condition and consistent engagement across three separate conditions. At a foundational level, examinees must tolerate the challenge sufficiently to remain attentive and engaged.

Tier 1 Impairment Pattern

Poor performance across all conditions with observable visual-motor difficulties, motor control problems, or a consistent slow work pace suggests Tier 1 limitations. These examinees work steadily but slowly throughout, without the long pauses between designs seen in Tier 3 executive deficits. Productivity may be equally low across all three conditions without a differential effect of condition demands. These examinees need foundational assessment (vision testing, motor evaluation, processing speed measures), not executive function intervention.

Tier 2: Bridging Processes

Tier 2 encompasses processes that bridge foundational visual-motor abilities and true executive control. On the Design Fluency Test, these bridging processes involve maintaining task rules in working memory, recognizing basic geometric patterns, and demonstrating elementary inhibition of rule violations. These abilities must be intact for a valid assessment of Tier 3 executive functions.

Working Memory and Rule-Following

At Tier 2, examinees must briefly hold the visual image of dots while planning which to connect, representing simple working memory without complex manipulation. The task requires understanding and consistently applying simple task rules: use four lines, each line starts and ends at a dot, make each line touch at least one other line at a dot, and create different designs. The ability to follow these straightforward rules throughout each 60-second condition represents basic procedural working memory and rule-following capacity. Within a single design, examinees must monitor whether they've used four lines that start and end at a dot, whether each line touches another, and whether lines connect the appropriate dot types.

> **DON'T FORGET**
>
> The distinction between Tier 2 rule-following and Tier 3 flexible generation is critical. An examinee who consistently applies rules (uses four lines, makes them touch) but produces very few designs has adequate Tier 2 but impaired Tier 3. An examinee who produces many attempts but frequently violates rules may have Tier 2 difficulties with basic rule-following or Tier 3 Hot EF issues (impulsivity) rather than Tier 3 cold EF generativity problems.

Pattern Recognition

Recognizing basic geometric patterns and understanding what constitutes a "design" represents Tier 2 perceptual processing. Examinees must grasp the concept that they are creating visual configurations rather than simply drawing lines, recognizing that certain arrangements of lines form coherent patterns versus random arrangements. Examinees who use common strategies like "chain" patterns (connecting dots sequentially) or "fan" patterns (all lines radiating from a central dot) demonstrate basic pattern recognition. These typical configurations emerge naturally for most examinees and represent fundamental spatial relationship understanding. Many examinees also show procedural learning across conditions, becoming more efficient at applying rules and generating designs as they gain experience with the task format, providing the foundation for later variation and elaboration at Tier 3.

Basic Inhibition

At Tier 2, examinees must demonstrate basic inhibition of rule-violating behaviors—the fundamental level of behavioral control needed to follow explicit, clearly stated rules. This differs from the more sophisticated Tier 3 inhibition required to suppress prepotent response patterns or previously successful strategies. Tier 2 basic inhibition involves inhibiting random motor responses (not drawing haphazardly or making disorganized marks outside designated boxes), inhibiting rule violations (consistently using exactly four lines, ensuring lines connect to dots at both endpoints, and making lines touch each other), and maintaining basic task structure (staying within boxes, moving systematically across rows as instructed). An examinee with Tier 2 basic inhibition deficits might understand what they're supposed to do but struggle to consistently apply these constraints. Their designs might frequently include three or five lines instead of four; lines might not connect properly at dots or they might engage in scribbling behavior. Importantly, this pattern differs from Tier 3 Hot EF impulsivity; the Tier 2 deficit reflects difficulty maintaining basic procedural rules rather than being driven by emotional dysregulation or time pressure.

Tier 2 Deficit Pattern

Examinees with Tier 2 deficits may show frequent rule violations (not using four lines, lines not touching), suggesting difficulty with basic rule-following. They might appear to understand instructions but inconsistently apply rules throughout conditions.

Tier 3: Core Executive Functions

Tier 3 represents the Design Fluency Test's primary assessment target—the executive functions that enable flexible, productive generation of novel visual patterns. These processes can be divided into cold executive functions involving the cognitive mechanisms of fluent generation, inhibition, and flexibility, and hot executive functions involving frustration tolerance and emotional regulation under timed, demanding conditions.

Cold Executive Functions

Cold executive functions on the Design Fluency Test involve the cognitive machinery of productive ideation, response inhibition, and cognitive flexibility, operating in relatively affect-neutral contexts where systematic generation drives performance.

Fluent Generation of Novel Patterns (Primary Measure)

This is the core Tier 3 cold executive function assessed by the Design Fluency Test. Examinees must spontaneously generate multiple unique visual patterns within the time limit. This requires nonverbal creativity, productive capacity, and the ability to vary one's approach systematically to produce novel designs. The fluency demand is heavily taxed across all three conditions—examinees must initiate problem-solving, maintain productivity throughout the time period, and continually generate new solutions without external prompts.

Low productivity across all three conditions suggests fundamental difficulties with nonverbal fluency at Tier 3. Better performance on Conditions 1 and 2 than Condition 3 suggests that basic generativity is adequate, but flexibility in generation under complex demands is impaired.

Strategic Approach and Inhibition

Successful performance requires developing and applying strategies for systematically varying designs. Some examinees use spatial strategies (starting from different dot positions), configurational strategies (alternating between chain and fan patterns), or directional strategies (varying the orientation of designs). Some examinees create closed-shape designs, which can be an effective strategy. However, this may lead to a self-imposed requirement to end designs on the same starting dot, which can slow performance and limit design options.

Tier 3 also requires sophisticated inhibition of previously drawn designs. Examinees must self-monitor what they have produced, suppress the impulse to repeat patterns to increase the number completed in the time limit, resist "getting stuck" or perseverating on a particular configuration, and overcome prepotent responses even when they're appealing (Jones-Gotman & Milner, 1977). This becomes increasingly difficult as more designs are drawn and working memory for previous responses becomes taxed. High rates of repeated designs suggest Tier 3 inhibitory deficits, particularly when the examinee doesn't recognize the repetitions.

Inhibition of Competing Stimuli and Cognitive Flexibility

Condition 2 specifically assesses the ability to inhibit responses to perceptually salient but irrelevant stimuli—the filled dots. This requires focused attention on task-relevant stimuli (empty dots) while actively suppressing attention to distractors. Set-loss errors (connecting filled dots) indicate Tier 2–3 inhibitory difficulties. The filled dots function as "capture stimuli" designed to pull attention away from the correct targets (Delis et al., 2001).

Cognitive flexibility is most directly assessed by Condition 3, which requires continuous set-shifting with each line drawn. The contrast score comparing Condition 3 to Combined Conditions 1 + 2 provides a direct measure of cognitive flexibility over and above basic fluency. A large discrepancy indicates specific difficulties with flexibility when generation demands remain constant.

Working Memory and Simultaneous Processing

While Tier 2 involves straightforward maintenance of visual information, Tier 3 working memory provides a performance advantage through active tracking. Previous designs remain visible in the Response Booklet, so examinees can visually scan their prior work to check for repetitions. However, those who can maintain a mental representation of recently drawn designs work more efficiently. They spend less time looking back and more time generating new patterns. Examinees with stronger working memory can quickly recognize "I already did something like that" without pausing to visually search, while those with weaker working memory must repeatedly scan the page, consuming valuable seconds. This efficiency advantage becomes more pronounced as designs accumulate and visual scanning becomes more time-consuming.

Throughout each condition, examinees must simultaneously generate ideas for new designs, monitor adherence to rules, track previous responses, and execute motor responses. The capacity to maintain productivity while monitoring quality (avoiding rule violations and repetitions) requires dividing attention between generative and supervisory processes. Examinees who produce many designs but with high error rates may struggle with simultaneous processing—they can generate OR monitor, but not both effectively.

Tier 3 Cold EF Impairment Pattern

This is the classic executive dysfunction pattern. Examinees show low productivity with adequate basic skills—they can draw lines well, understand rules, but produce few designs. Qualitatively, they may pause frequently between designs, repeat similar patterns, or become "stuck" generating variations of the same configuration. High repetition rates despite adequate effort indicate Tier 3 problems with inhibition of perseverative responses. Specific difficulty during Condition 3, with better performance on Conditions 1–2, indicates Tier 3 cognitive flexibility impairment.

Hot Executive Functions

Hot executive functions involve the motivational and emotional aspects of executive control that influence how effectively cold executive processes are deployed. On the Design Fluency Test, hot EF factors become prominent as examinees encounter creative blocks, recognize repetitions, or struggle to maintain productivity under time pressure.

Frustration Tolerance and Emotional Regulation

Beyond basic Tier 1 engagement, Tier 3 hot executive function involves managing emotional responses. When an examinee experiences "creative block," struggles to generate new ideas, or realizes they're repeating designs, they must regulate frustration and anxiety sufficiently to persist productively. The time pressure creates emotional pressure: some examinees respond with impulsivity—rushing to draw designs without checking whether they're unique or follow rules—while others become paralyzed by anxiety or perfectionism, working slowly despite adequate motor and processing speed abilities. Perfectionistic tendencies regarding line quality or the "rightness" of each design may result in low productivity that superficially resembles Tier 1 or Tier 3 cold EF deficits but actually reflects emotional interference.

Some examinees become visibly distressed when they recognize their limited output or notice repetitions, yet the ability to manage these emotional reactions while continuing to engage productively represents intact hot EF capacity. Performance may decline specifically on Conditions 2 or 3, not because of increased cognitive demands, but because the added complexity triggers anxiety or perfectionism that disrupts otherwise adequate executive abilities. The capacity to maintain productivity despite emotional reactions to task difficulty—whether by inhibiting impulsive responding under time pressure or persisting despite anxiety—represents the core hot EF demand at Tier 3.

CAUTION

Hot EF difficulties can look like cold EF deficits. An examinee with intact Tier 3 generativity who becomes anxious about performance may produce fewer designs, not because they cannot generate patterns, but because emotional dysregulation disrupts their cognitive processing. Behavioral observation during testing is essential for distinguishing these patterns, and intervention approaches differ substantially—anxiety management versus fluency training.

Motivation

Sustaining motivation across three 60-second conditions, particularly when the task is challenging, requires hot executive function. Some examinees show strong effort on Condition 1, decreased effort on Condition 2, and minimal effort on Condition 3, which may reflect declining motivation rather than declining cognitive capacity.

Tier 3 Hot EF Pattern

Examinees with hot EF difficulties show performance that varies with emotional state. They may start well but deteriorate as frustration builds or show anxiety-driven, rushed responding leading to errors. Visible frustration, pressure on the pencil, anxious comments, or emotional reactions to difficulty distinguish this from cold EF deficits.

Tier 4: Higher-Order Integration and Metacognition

Tier 4 processes involve the highest level of executive integration—monitoring one's own cognitive performance and strategically adjusting approaches based on self-evaluation. On the Design Fluency Test, Tier 4 functioning manifests as awareness of repetitive responding, spontaneous strategy shifts, and effective balancing of speed and accuracy.

Metacognitive Monitoring and Strategic Flexibility

Tier 4 metacognition involves observing and evaluating one's own pattern generation to recognize when designs are becoming repetitive. Examinees must spontaneously monitor "Am I making designs that are actually different?" and adjust their approach accordingly. Examinees who spontaneously comment, "I think I'm starting to repeat myself," or who deliberately shift strategies demonstrate this metacognitive awareness.

At Tier 4, examinees can evaluate their generative strategy and adjust based on effectiveness. After producing several designs using chain patterns and noticing they're running out of variations, some examinees will spontaneously shift to fan patterns or other approaches. This strategic adjustment represents higher-order executive integration.

Integration Across Systems

While productivity (Tier 3 generativity) and accuracy (avoiding errors and repetitions) are separable processes, Tier 4 involves integrating them. The sophisticated examinee balances speed and accuracy by working quickly enough to produce many designs while carefully enough to avoid repetitions and rule violations. Tier 4 also involves coordinating the planning of designs with motor execution smoothly—beginning to draw while still refining the plan rather than planning completely before drawing (inefficient) or drawing impulsively (leading to errors).

Perhaps most sophisticated is the integration of hot and cold executive systems at Tier 4. The examinee who begins feeling frustrated but uses metacognitive awareness to recognize "I'm getting stressed and it's making me repeat patterns—let me take a breath and try a different approach" demonstrates integration of emotional awareness (hot) with strategic cognitive adjustment (cold).

Tier 4 Integration Difficulties

Some examinees show adequate fluency but lack metacognitive awareness or strategic flexibility. They may produce many designs, but with high repetition rates because they don't monitor for uniqueness. They might persist with one strategy without recognizing it's becoming exhausted and spontaneously shifting.

ADMINISTRATION

NOTE: Refer to the Examiner's Manual for complete and detailed administration instructions. The Examiner's Manual provides verbatim instructions, and clinicians should follow these precisely to ensure standardized administration.

Rapid Reference 5.2

Tier Structure at a Glance

Tier	Processes
Tier 1: Foundational processes	Visual scanning and perception Visual-motor coordination Fine motor control and drawing speed Sustained attention Processing speed Task comprehension
Tier 2: Bridging processes	Basic rule-following (four lines, lines start and end at a dot, lines touch at dots, correct dot types) Procedural learning across conditions Basic pattern recognition
Tier 3: Cold executive functions	Generativity (fluent production of novel designs) Cognitive flexibility (switching between dot types in Condition 3) Inhibition of previously drawn responses Inhibition of competing stimuli (Condition 2) Working memory for tracking previous designs
Tier 3: Hot executive functions	Frustration tolerance under time pressure Managing impulsivity vs. perfectionism Emotional response to task difficulty
Tier 4: Higher-order integration and metacognition	Metacognitive monitoring of design uniqueness Strategic flexibility and adjustment Hot–cold EF integration Speed–accuracy integration

Materials and Setup

The paper-and-pencil version of the Design Fluency Test requires the Examiner's Manual, Record Form, Response Booklet, Stimulus Booklet, and timer. A digital version of the Examiner's Manual, Stimulus Booklet, and Stimulus Booklet Administration Directions is also available through Q-global digital assets. If administering using the tablet-based Q-interactive platform, the examiner will use the instructions provided on the Practitioner Device versus the Stimulus Booklet. The examiner should ensure a quiet testing environment and position the Response Booklet directly in front of the examinee in portrait (vertical) orientation for practice items and landscape (horizontal) orientation for test conditions.

Standard Instructions

Each condition begins with three practice items. The examiner provides standardized instructions specific to each condition, demonstrates if needed, and allows the examinee to complete practice items with corrective feedback. The instructions emphasize the specific rules for that condition—connecting filled dots (Condition 1), only empty dots (Condition 2), or alternating between filled and empty dots (Condition 3). Instructions are clear that each design is made using *only four straight lines* to connect the dots, that each line starts at a dot and ends at a dot, that each line touches at least one other line at a dot, and that each design is different. The inclusion of these rules creates restrictions on the types of designs that can be drawn and increases the difficulty level of the task. The Stimulus Booklet (paper or digital) and Client Device (Q-interactive) provide a listing of the instructions to help the client remember them.

For each condition, examiners may provide the following prompts, but each prompt may be used only once per condition:

If the examinee draws three consecutive incorrect designs, briefly explain the error. If the examinee states they have made a mistake, say, "That's OK. Try to get the next one right." If the examinee fails to respond for 15 seconds, say, "Keep going."

Condition Administration Sequence

Condition 1: Filled Dots is administered first, providing a baseline measure of nonverbal fluency without inhibitory or switching demands. Condition 2: Empty Dots Only follows, adding the inhibitory demand. Condition 3: Switching is administered last, incorporating both fluency and flexibility demands. This sequence is standardized and must be maintained, as performance on later conditions may be influenced by practice effects from earlier conditions.

Timing Considerations

Each condition is timed for exactly 60 seconds. The examiner should start timing immediately upon saying "Begin" and stop promptly at 60 seconds. If an examinee is in the process of drawing a design when time expires, they are allowed to complete that design, and it is scored as completed within the time limit.

BEHAVIORAL OBSERVATIONS

Behavioral observations during administration provide critical qualitative data that complement quantitative scores and inform tier-based interpretation.

Approach and Response Patterns

Observe whether the examinee employs systematic design strategies or generates designs haphazardly. Two common approaches are the "chain" strategy, where lines connect sequentially from one dot to the next, and the "fan" strategy, where all lines originate from the same dot, with each extending to a different dot. Note whether the examinee relies exclusively on one strategy, flexibly alternates between strategies, or generates designs without an apparent systematic approach. Rigid adherence to a single strategy may suggest cognitive inflexibility, while flexible strategy use indicates intact Tier 4 strategic adjustment. Some examinees discover that the fan strategy works efficiently on Condition 3 when the central dot is one type and extending lines reach dots of the other type, demonstrating effective problem-solving and strategic adaptation. Note whether strategies become more organized across conditions (suggesting learning) or remain disorganized throughout.

The pattern of responding also provides diagnostic information. Does the examinee work steadily throughout the 60 seconds, or show long pauses between designs? Pauses suggest difficulty with Tier 3 generation rather than Tier 1 motor speed. Do pauses become longer as the condition progresses, suggesting depletion of readily accessible patterns?

Self-Monitoring and Rule Adherence

Observe whether the examinee checks previous designs before drawing new ones (Tier 4 monitoring), makes spontaneous comments about repetition ("I think I did that one"), or shows signs of recognizing when they're "stuck." Do they correct themselves mid-design if they realize they're violating a rule? Notice whether the examinee consistently applies rules or makes errors. Do errors cluster at certain points (beginning of condition suggesting comprehension difficulties, end of condition suggesting fatigue or frustration)?

Emotional Responses

Note visible frustration, anxiety, or emotional reactions to difficulty. Does the examinee maintain composure throughout or show emotional dysregulation? Comments like "This is hard," "I can't think of any more," or "I'm bad at this" indicate hot EF factors.

SCORING

The Design Fluency Test yields scaled scores for individual conditions, composite measures, a contrast score isolating cognitive flexibility, and optional process measures for detailed analysis.

Primary Scores

Condition 1 Filled Dots Total Correct. This score reflects the number of correct designs generated within the 60-second time limit for Condition 1, where examinees connect filled dots.

Condition 2 Empty Dots Only Total Correct. This score reflects the number of correct designs generated within the 60-second time limit for Condition 2, where examinees must connect only empty dots while inhibiting responses to filled dots.

Condition 3 Switching Total Correct. This score reflects the number of correct designs generated within the 60-second time limit for Condition 3, where each line must alternate between connecting an empty dot and a filled dot.

Design Fluency Total Correct Composite. This composite scaled score reflects overall performance across all three conditions.

Combined Filled Dots + Empty Dots Only Total Correct. This composite sums performance on Conditions 1 and 2, providing a measure of design fluency without the cognitive switching demand. This serves as the comparison baseline for the Contrast Measure.

Contrast Measure

Switching Versus Combined Filled Dots + Empty Dots Only. This Contrast Score directly compares Condition 3 performance to the Combined Conditions 1 + 2 Composite, isolating the impact of cognitive flexibility demands on fluency. This Contrast Score is particularly valuable for identifying examinees whose generativity is adequate but who struggle specifically when switching requirements are added.

Optional Measures

Total Set-Loss Designs. This score sums rule violations across all three conditions, reflecting failures to maintain the cognitive set of each task.

Total Repeated Designs. This score sums exact duplicates across conditions, indicating inhibitory failures in suppressing previously drawn responses.

Total Attempted Designs. This score counts all designs drawn (correct, set-loss, and repeated), reflecting overall productivity independent of accuracy.

Percent Design Accuracy. Calculated as ([Design Fluency: Total Correct ÷ Total Attempted Designs] x 100), this score represents the percentage of correct designs relative to total attempted, revealing whether low scores reflect poor generation, poor accuracy, or both.

Scoring Criteria

Correct Designs

For a design to be counted as correct, it must be constructed with exactly four lines; each line connects two dots, one at each endpoint; each line touches at least one other line at one of its endpoints; and the design is novel for that condition. For Condition 2, all lines must also connect only empty dots. For Condition 3, each line must have an empty dot at one endpoint and a filled dot at the other endpoint. Lines may cross each other.

Set-Loss Designs

A design is counted as a set-loss if it contains more or fewer than four lines, has at least one isolated line that is not adjacent to another line, has at least one partially connected line, has at least one free-floating line with no dots at endpoints, has a line that forms a curved angle of 90° or less, or was made by simply scribbling. In addition, a design is a set-loss if any line connects one or more filled dots for Condition 2 or connects two filled dots or two empty dots for Condition 3. Each design can only be counted as one set-loss error, even if it contains two or more errors.

Repeated Designs

A design is considered a repeated design error if the same design is drawn two or more times (the first design is correct). The repeated design must be an exact duplicate—rotations and mirror images are scored as correct, not as repetitions. If a set-loss design is repeated, the repetition is scored as both a set-loss and a repeated design.

Special Considerations

Liberal scoring criteria apply when motor control issues create ambiguity. If the examinee's intent was clearly to connect specific dots and slight motor inaccuracy resulted in a line being slightly off-target (within ½ centimeter), credit may be given. The test measures fluency, not motor precision. Shaky or wavy lines are acceptable.

Rapid Reference 5.3

Scoring Summary

Criterion	All Conditions	Condition 2 Additional	Condition 3 Additional
Line count	Exactly four lines	—	—
Line endpoints	Each line connects two dots (one at each endpoint)	All lines connect only empty dots	Each line connects one empty dot to one filled dot
Line connections	Each line touches at least one other line at a dot	—	—
Novelty	Design is not an exact duplicate of a previous design in that condition	—	—
Set-loss	Violation of any criterion above; see text for complete list	Any line touching a filled dot	Any line connecting same dot types
Repetition	Exact duplicate only; rotations and mirror images are correct	—	—

COMMON ADMINISTRATION ERRORS

Several administration errors can compromise test validity. Awareness of these common pitfalls enables quality control and accurate interpretation.

Inadequate Practice and Feedback

A common error is insufficient practice before beginning timed conditions. Each condition requires three practice items with corrective feedback to ensure the examinee understands requirements. Failing to provide adequate practice, particularly for Condition 3's complex switching rule, may result in poor performance due to misunderstanding rather than executive dysfunction.

Improper Timing

Starting timing before the examinee is ready, stopping prematurely, or allowing excessive time beyond 60 seconds compromises standardization. The examinee is allowed to finish a design that was in process at 60 seconds.

Inappropriate Prompting or Assistance

Examiners sometimes provide cues or assistance during timed conditions when examinees struggle. Only use the provided prompts once for each of the Conditions 1–3. Conversely, it is important that for each Condition, the examiner explains the error the first time an examinee draws three consecutive incorrect designs. Failure to do so may result in a low score achieved differently from the standardization sample.

Scoring Errors

Common scoring errors include incorrectly scoring rotations or reflections as repetitions (they should NOT be marked as repetitions), being too lenient with set-loss errors, being too strict with line connections (not applying liberal criteria for minor motor inaccuracies), miscounting total correct designs, incorrectly computing Percent Design Accuracy, and failing to double-check for true repetitions (exact duplicates) across the entire condition.

Failure to Observe Tier-Relevant Behaviors

Examiners focused solely on timing and rule enforcement may miss critical behavioral observations that inform tier-based interpretation.

INTERPRETATION

Design Fluency interpretation requires integrating productivity scores with error patterns and qualitative observations within a systematic framework that distinguishes foundational processing limitations from true executive dysfunction.

Using the Hierarchical Framework for Differential Diagnosis

When interpreting Design Fluency performance, systematic tier-based analysis prevents the common error of attributing all deficits to executive dysfunction. Always evaluate tiers hierarchically from bottom to top.

Step 1: Rule Out Tier 1 Limitations

Before concluding executive dysfunction, ensure foundational processes are intact. Were visual scanning and perception adequate? Could the examinee distinguish filled from empty dots and locate targets efficiently? Was fine motor control sufficient for drawing straight lines between specific dots? Was processing speed adequate, or did generalized psychomotor slowing limit productivity regardless of executive capacity? Qualitative observation is critical here: steady but slow work throughout each condition suggests Tier 1 speed limitations, whereas normal drawing speed with long pauses between designs points toward Tier 3 generativity deficits. Were task instructions understood, particularly the complex switching rule for Condition 3? If Tier 1 deficits are present, supplementary assessment (processing speed measures, visual-motor evaluation) takes priority over executive function interpretation.

Step 2: Evaluate Tier 2 Bridging Processes

If Tier 1 is intact, assess bridging functions. Could the examinee consistently follow basic rules—using exactly four lines, lines starting and ending at a dot, ensuring lines touch at dots, connecting the appropriate dot types for each condition? Frequent rule violations despite apparent comprehension suggest Tier 2 difficulties with basic procedural working memory rather than Tier 3 executive deficits. Was there evidence of procedural learning across conditions—did the examinee become more efficient at applying rules after practice? Basic pattern recognition should be present, with examinees grasping that they are creating visual configurations rather than simply drawing random lines. Tier 2 deficits manifest as inconsistent rule application throughout conditions, not the strategic or generativity problems characteristic of Tier 3.

Step 3: Analyze Tier 3 Cold Executive Patterns

With Tiers 1–2 intact, evaluate cold executive function capacity. Is productivity low despite adequate foundational skills? Low output across all three conditions suggests fundamental nonverbal fluency deficits. Examine whether Condition 3 shows a specific decline relative to Conditions 1 + 2—a low contrast score indicates cognitive flexibility impairment when generation demands remain constant. High repetition rates (exact duplicates, not rotations) suggest inhibitory difficulties in suppressing previously drawn responses. Note whether the examinee uses systematic strategies or persists rigidly with one approach, indicating potential cognitive inflexibility. The pattern of errors also informs interpretation: set-loss errors on Condition 2 suggest difficulty inhibiting attention to competing stimuli, while set-loss errors on Condition 3 indicate problems implementing the switching rule.

Step 4: Evaluate Tier 3 Hot Executive Factors

Determine whether emotional regulation factors contribute to performance. Did frustration or anxiety visibly affect productivity? Some examinees respond to time pressure with impulsivity—rushing to draw designs without checking for uniqueness or rule adherence—leading to high error rates despite adequate cold EF capacity. Others become paralyzed by anxiety or perfectionism, working slowly and cautiously despite adequate motor speed. Perfectionistic tendencies regarding line quality or design "correctness" can masquerade as cold EF deficits. Note whether performance declined specifically on later conditions, not because of increased cognitive demands, but because accumulated difficulty triggered emotional interference. Behavioral observations during testing are essential for distinguishing hot EF contributions from cold EF deficits, as intervention approaches differ substantially.

Step 5: Assess Tier 4 Integration and Metacognition

For examinees with adequate Tier 3 core functions, evaluate higher-order integration: Is there metacognitive awareness of repetitive responding? Does the examinee spontaneously adjust strategies? Is there smooth integration of planning and execution? Can the examinee balance speed and accuracy effectively? Tier 4 deficits manifest as adequate basic fluency without strategic flexibility or production of many designs without monitoring for repetitions.

PERFORMANCE PATTERNS AND CLINICAL IMPLICATIONS

Several recognizable performance patterns emerge on the Design Fluency Test, each with distinct clinical implications and tier-level associations.

Low Productivity Across All Conditions

Consistently low production across all conditions with similar scaled scores suggests fundamental difficulties with nonverbal fluency at Tier 3 or may indicate any Tier 1 limitation. Qualitative observations help distinguish between these: steady, slow work suggests Tier 1 speed limitations, while long pauses between designs suggest Tier 3 generativity deficits. These individuals struggle with generating multiple solutions to open-ended problems, brainstorming, or creative production in timed situations.

Specific Decline on Condition 2

Disproportionately lower performance on Condition 2 relative to Condition 1, with many set-loss errors, suggests Tier 2–3 inhibitory difficulties. The examinee struggles to inhibit attention to competing stimuli (filled dots) while maintaining focus on targets (empty dots). These individuals may be vulnerable to distraction by irrelevant but salient stimuli or struggle in busy environments with competing inputs.

Specific Decline on Condition 3

Markedly worse performance on Condition 3 compared to Combined Conditions 1 + 2, reflected in a low contrast score, indicates specific cognitive flexibility impairment at Tier 3. The examinee can generate designs when rules are simple, but struggles with continuous micro-shifting. These individuals may function adequately in routine situations with stable demands but struggle when tasks require frequent shifting, multitasking, or adapting approaches dynamically.

High Repetition Rate Pattern

Adequate or even high total productivity, but with many repeated designs (exact duplicates, not rotations or reflections), indicates Tier 3 inhibitory or perseveration difficulties. If the examinee becomes aware of repetitions and shows frustration, this suggests Tier 4 metacognitive awareness is intact, but Tier 3 inhibitory control is impaired. If the examinee seems unaware of repetitions even when pointed out, this suggests combined Tier 3–4 problems. These individuals may show perseverative tendencies, getting "stuck" on particular approaches or solutions.

Strategy and Error Patterns

Examinees who use organized strategies typically produce more unique designs efficiently. Some persist rigidly with one strategy throughout, suggesting Tier 3 cognitive rigidity or Tier 4 lack of strategic flexibility. The optimal pattern shows initial strategy use followed by spontaneous strategy shifting, demonstrating Tier 4 metacognitive awareness. High set-loss errors, specifically on Conditions 2–3, help localize deficits. Errors early in a condition suggest comprehension difficulties (Tier 1) or working memory problems (Tier 2), while errors late suggest fatigue, frustration (Tier 3 Hot EF), or breakdown under sustained cognitive load.

Comparison Between Conditions and Measures

Condition 1 Versus Condition 2 Comparison
Most examinees show similar or slightly better performance on Condition 2 than on Condition 1, likely due to practice effects. The normative sample averaged 8.7 designs on Condition 1 and 9.3 designs on Condition 2 (Delis et al., 2001). Better Condition 2 performance reflects intact inhibition despite added demands. However, some examinees, particularly those with frontal or diffuse pathology, show disproportionate impairment on Condition 2, often related to perseverative tendencies.

Condition 3 Relative to Conditions 1 + 2
The contrast score directly compares flexibility demands. Large discrepancies warrant investigation of cognitive flexibility specifically. Is the problem productivity (fewer designs with similar error rates) or accuracy (many set-loss errors indicating switching failures)? Productivity problems suggest flexibility affects generation, while accuracy problems suggest difficulties implementing the switching rule consistently.

Productivity Versus Accuracy
Compare total attempted designs to total correct designs or calculate Percent Design Accuracy. High productivity with low accuracy suggests impulsive responding (Tier 3 Hot EF) or poor simultaneous processing (Tier 3 Cold EF—can generate OR monitor but not both). Low productivity with high accuracy suggests a cautious approach or anxiety limiting productivity. Optimal performance shows both high productivity and high accuracy, reflecting successful Tier 4 integration.

Rapid Reference 5.4

Distinguishing Tier-Level Deficits

Tier Level	Indicators	Clinical Implications
Tier 1: Deficit	Poor performance across all conditions proportionally; observable visual-motor or processing speed difficulties; steady, slow work without pauses between designs	Foundational limitations limit performance; executive functions may be intact; assess vision, motor function, processing speed rather than EF
Tier 2: Deficit	Frequent rule violations (wrong line count, lines not touching); understands instructions but inconsistently applies rules; set-loss errors across all conditions	Basic rule-following difficulties; interventions target procedural learning and rule maintenance
Tier 3: Cold deficit	Low productivity despite adequate basic skills; long pauses between designs; high repetitions; gets "stuck" on configurations; low Condition 3 contrast score	Classic executive dysfunction; generativity or flexibility impairment; interventions target fluency training and flexibility strategies
Tier 3: Hot deficit	Performance varies with emotional state; deteriorates as frustration builds; rushed responding with errors; visible frustration or anxiety	Emotional dysregulation compromising cognition; interventions target anxiety management and frustration tolerance
Tier 4: Deficit	Adequate fluency but high repetitions without awareness; persists with exhausted strategy; no spontaneous strategy shifting or self-correction	Metacognitive monitoring failure; interventions target self-monitoring and strategic flexibility training

ECOLOGICAL VALIDITY AND FUNCTIONAL IMPLICATIONS

Design Fluency performance relates to real-world demands for creative generation, flexible problem-solving, and adaptive responding across academic, vocational, and social contexts.

Academic Functioning

Nonverbal fluency capacity predicts performance in contexts requiring creative generation of solutions and productive capacity under time constraints. Students with low Design Fluency performance may struggle with open-ended projects requiring idea generation, brainstorming activities, visual–spatial creative tasks such as art or design assignments, and timed tests requiring multiple responses. Generating alternative approaches when initial solutions fail—a common academic demand—draws directly on the generativity and flexibility capacities this test measures.

Students with specific Condition 3 deficits may perform adequately on structured assignments with clear expectations but struggle when tasks require shifting between different approaches or integrating multiple strategies. Interventions might include providing frameworks for brainstorming, allowing additional time for creative production, teaching specific strategies for varying approaches, and breaking complex projects into smaller components with explicit structure.

Vocational and Daily Living

Design fluency relates to flexible problem-solving capacity in occupational and daily contexts. Individuals with flexibility deficits (poor Condition 3) may approach problems rigidly, struggle to generate alternative solutions when initial approaches fail, or perseverate with ineffective strategies. Real-world situations requiring these capacities include troubleshooting when equipment or technology malfunctions, adapting plans when circumstances change unexpectedly, and generating multiple options when faced with logistical challenges.

Occupations requiring rapid generation of novel solutions—design, engineering, emergency response, culinary arts, or any role demanding creative problem-solving under time pressure—may be challenging for individuals with nonverbal fluency deficits. Those with intact fluency but impaired flexibility may function adequately in routine work with stable demands but struggle when job requirements shift or when multitasking is required. Workplace accommodations might include additional time for problem-solving tasks, structured decision-making frameworks, and advance notice when procedures change.

Social Functioning

While Design Fluency is a nonverbal measure without direct social content, the underlying capacities have social implications. Social interactions often require rapid generation of conversational responses, flexible adaptation when social dynamics shift, and the ability to generate multiple approaches when initial social strategies are unsuccessful. Individuals with generativity deficits may appear socially "flat" or struggle to contribute ideas in group settings, while those with flexibility deficits may have difficulty adapting their social approach when context changes, such as shifting from casual to formal interaction or adjusting behavior based on social feedback.

The cognitive flexibility assessed by Condition 3 supports perspective-taking and adapting communication style to different social partners. Deficits in this area may manifest as social rigidity or difficulty navigating situations requiring rapid social adjustment. However, clinicians should interpret social implications cautiously—direct assessment of social cognition through measures like the D-KEFS Advanced Social Sorting Test (Delis & Kaplan, 2025) provides more specific information about social reasoning capacities.

> **DON'T FORGET**
>
> Design Fluency deficits don't occur in isolation. Consider performance across multiple D-KEFS measures. An individual with low Design Fluency and low Verbal Fluency likely has broad generativity deficits affecting both verbal and nonverbal domains. An individual with low Design Fluency but adequate Verbal Fluency shows domain-specific deficits. Someone with poor Design Fluency Condition 3 and poor Trail Making Condition 4 (Number-Letter Switching) shows convergent evidence for cognitive flexibility deficits across measures.

STRENGTHS AND WEAKNESSES

The Design Fluency Test offers several distinctive strengths for executive function assessment, alongside limitations that clinicians should consider when selecting measures and interpreting results.

Strengths

The Design Fluency Test offers several notable advantages for assessing nonverbal fluency and cognitive flexibility within a comprehensive executive function evaluation.

Nonverbal Assessment and Multi-Condition Design

The Design Fluency Test provides an assessment of executive functions in the nonverbal domain, complementing primarily verbal measures like Verbal Fluency and Proverbs. This is particularly valuable for individuals with language limitations, English Language Learners, or verbal learning disabilities. The three-condition structure allows separation of different executive processes—Condition 1 provides baseline fluency, Condition 2 adds inhibition, and Condition 3 adds flexibility. The systematic separation of executive components within a single test helps pinpoint the root of difficulties.

Contrast Score Utility

The contrast score comparing Condition 3 to Combined Conditions 1 + 2 provides a direct, normed measure of cognitive flexibility's impact on performance. This is particularly valuable for identifying subtle flexibility deficits that may be missed when examining individual condition scores alone.

Quantitative and Qualitative Information
Beyond quantitative scores, the test provides rich qualitative data through observation of approach, strategy use, emotional responses, and error patterns. The design production remains in the Response Booklet for later review, allowing detailed analysis.

Developmental and Age-Range Appropriateness
With norms from ages 8–89, the test covers a broad developmental span. The task is engaging for children while remaining challenging for adults, making it appropriate across the lifespan. For people who struggle to comprehend the verbal instructions, there are ample opportunities to correct errors during the sample design practice items and an additional corrective prompt during the timed items.

Weaknesses and Limitations

Despite its strengths, the Design Fluency Test has several limitations that clinicians should consider when selecting measures and interpreting results.

Processing Speed and Motor Confounds
The 60-second time limit makes processing speed and motor speed significant confounds, representing the most challenging interpretive issue for this test. Distinguishing whether low productivity reflects foundational speed limitations or executive fluency deficits requires careful qualitative observation and supplementary assessment.

Practice Effects and Limited Item Pool
Condition 2 performance typically equals or exceeds Condition 1 performance in the normative sample, likely reflecting practice effects as examinees become more efficient after the first condition. Because this pattern is built into the standardization, the norms account for expected practice gains. Clinically, this means that a decline from Condition 1 to Condition 2 is particularly noteworthy—it suggests the inhibitory demand outweighed the expected practice benefit. Repeated administration across evaluations is problematic, as examinees may remember effective strategies or specific designs. With only 60 seconds per condition and a finite number of possible four-line designs, the test provides a relatively limited sample of performance, making it more susceptible to random variation.

Limited Generalizability and Visual–Spatial Confound
While Design Fluency assesses nonverbal fluency and flexibility, the relationship between connecting dots with four-line designs and real-world creative problem-solving is not entirely clear. The highly structured format differs from open-ended creative tasks encountered in daily life. While intended as an executive function measure, the test has significant visual–spatial processing demands. Individuals with visual–spatial perception difficulties may perform poorly, not due to executive dysfunction but due to challenges with spatial planning or visual–spatial working memory.

Hot EF Not Systematically Measured
While hot EF factors can be observed qualitatively, they are not systematically quantified. Frustration tolerance, impulsivity, and anxiety affect performance but aren't captured by derived scores.

ALTERNATIVE MEASURES

Comprehensive assessment of nonverbal fluency and cognitive flexibility often benefits from complementary measures that clarify Design Fluency findings.

Within the D-KEFS Suite

Several D-KEFS subtests provide complementary or converging evidence for fluency and cognitive flexibility.

Verbal Fluency Test (Original and Advanced)
Provides assessment of fluency and flexibility in the verbal domain. Comparing Verbal Fluency to Design Fluency helps determine whether fluency deficits are broad or domain-specific. The Category Switching condition parallels

Design Fluency Condition 3 in requiring flexible switching during generative production. The Advanced version adds more demanding switching conditions that tax working memory and retrieval, helping clarify whether generativity and flexibility deficits are modality-specific or reflect broader executive control limitations under increased cognitive load.

Trail Making Test (Original and Advanced)
Condition 4 (Number-Letter Switching) assesses cognitive flexibility through alternating between numbers and letters, providing convergent evidence for flexibility deficits when combined with Design Fluency Condition 3. However, Trail Making involves sequencing familiar information rather than solution generation, helping distinguish whether flexibility deficits are specific to generative contexts. The Advanced version adds working memory and distraction conditions that further increase cognitive demands during flexible switching, helping determine whether flexibility deficits worsen under increased working memory load or competing stimuli, suggesting Tier 4 integration limitations.

Color-Word Interference Test (Original and Advanced)
Assesses inhibition in the verbal domain, with the original D-KEFS requiring a verbal response and the Advanced version using a nonverbal response. Comparing inhibition across verbal (Color-Word) and nonverbal (Design Fluency Condition 2) domains helps determine whether inhibitory deficits are broad or narrow. Set-loss errors on Design Fluency Condition 2, combined with inhibition difficulties on Color-Word suggest broad Tier 3 inhibitory control deficits.

Beyond D-KEFS

Measures outside the D-KEFS family can provide converging evidence or assess related constructs when additional information is needed.

Processing Speed Measures
Given the speed confound in Design Fluency, a supplementary processing speed assessment is essential. The WAIS-5/WISC-V Processing Speed Index (Coding, Symbol Search; Wechsler, 2024; Wechsler, 2014) and Trail Making Condition 5 (Motor Speed; Delis et al., 2001) help clarify whether speed limitations contribute to Design Fluency performance. Consistent processing speed deficits across measures suggest Tier 1 limitations; normal processing speed with low Design Fluency suggests Tier 3 executive deficits.

Visual–Spatial and Visual-Motor Measures
The Beery-Buktenica Developmental Test of Visual-Motor Integration (VMI; Beery & Beery, 2010), WAIS-5 Block Design and Visual Puzzles (Wechsler, 2024), and NEPSY-II Design Copying (Korkman et al., 2007) help assess visual–spatial and constructional abilities. The Rey Complex Figure Test (RCFT; Meyers & Meyers, 1995) copy condition provides additional visual–spatial constructional assessment. Comparing performance on these measures to Design Fluency helps distinguish visual–spatial processing deficits (Tier 1–2) from executive fluency problems (Tier 3). Good visual–spatial performance with poor Design Fluency suggests executive deficits; poor performance on both suggests visual–spatial contributions.

Motor Speed and Dexterity Measures
The Grooved Pegboard Test (Lafayette Instrument Company, 2015) provides a purer measure of fine motor speed and dexterity than Design Fluency. Finger tapping tests (Reitan & Wolfson, 1993) examine motor speed and persistence. Comparing performance on these measures to Design Fluency helps distinguish motor control limitations (Tier 1) from executive fluency problems (Tier 3).

Alternative Fluency Measures
The Ruff Figural Fluency Test (RFFT; Ruff, 1996) provides an alternative nonverbal fluency measure using a five-dot array with varying patterns and multiple-line designs. It is available for ages 16–70 and may be appropriate when avoiding practice effects or seeking convergent validity. The Controlled Oral Word Association Test (COWAT; Benton et al., 1994) assesses verbal fluency similar to D-KEFS Verbal Fluency, allowing comparison between verbal and nonverbal generativity domains.

Cognitive Flexibility Measures

The Wisconsin Card Sorting Test (WCST; Heaton et al., 1993) assesses cognitive flexibility through rule-learning and set-shifting in a conceptual categorization task. Unlike Design Fluency's continuous micro-shifting within each design, WCST requires recognizing when rules change and adapting to new sorting principles. Comparing performance helps determine whether flexibility deficits are specific to generative contexts or reflect broader set-shifting impairment.

Behavior Rating Scales

Executive function rating scales capture real-world executive behaviors that may or may not align with performance-based measures. For children and adolescents, the Behavior Rating Inventory of Executive Function, Second Edition (BRIEF-2; Gioia et al., 2015), Comprehensive Executive Function Inventory (CEFI; Naglieri & Goldstein, 2013), and Delis Rating of Executive Functions (D-REF; Delis, 2012) provide parent and teacher perspectives on daily executive functioning. For adults, the BRIEF-A (Roth et al., 2005), CEFI Adult (Naglieri & Goldstein, 2017), and D-REF Adult (Delis, 2021) offer self-report and informant-report options. Relevant scales across these measures include Initiate (paralleling fluent generation of novel designs), Shift (cognitive flexibility required for Condition 3 switching), Inhibit (suppressing repetitive responses and attending to correct stimuli), and Plan/Organize (strategic approach to design generation). Discrepancies between Design Fluency performance and rating scale elevations provide diagnostic information: adequate test performance with elevated rating scales may indicate that the structured testing environment with explicit rules does not capture flexibility and generativity challenges that emerge in ambiguous, open-ended real-world situations requiring spontaneous creative problem-solving. Conversely, poor Design Fluency performance with unremarkable rating scales might suggest test-specific factors such as visual-motor demands, performance anxiety under timed conditions, or poor metacognitive awareness of daily creative and flexibility difficulties, rather than pervasive executive dysfunction.

SUMMARY

The D-KEFS Design Fluency Test provides an assessment of nonverbal fluency and cognitive flexibility through systematic manipulation of task demands across three conditions. By evaluating free generation (Condition 1 baseline), generation with inhibition (Condition 2), and generation with cognitive flexibility (Condition 3), the test offers insights into multiple aspects of executive functioning analyzed through the hierarchical tier framework.

Optimal use requires systematic tier-based analysis, beginning with Tier 1 foundational processes (visual processing, motor control, processing speed, visual-motor integration), evaluating Tier 2 bridging functions (simple working memory, basic rule-following, procedural learning), distinguishing Tier 3 cold and hot EF (fluency, flexibility, inhibition; emotional regulation), and assessing Tier 4 integration (metacognitive monitoring, strategic flexibility, hot–cold integration).

The test's strengths include its nonverbal format, multi-condition design separating different executive processes, and rich qualitative information. The contrast score provides a valuable assessment of cognitive flexibility. Limitations include processing speed and motor confounds, practice effects, and a limited item pool.

The most significant interpretive challenge is distinguishing whether low productivity reflects Tier 1 processing speed/motor limitations or Tier 3 executive fluency deficits. This requires qualitative observations, behavioral analysis, and supplementary processing speed assessment. Similarly, distinguishing visual–spatial processing deficits from executive fluency problems requires integration with visual–spatial measures.

When appropriately administered and interpreted through the hierarchical tier framework, the Design Fluency Test contributes valuable information to comprehensive neuropsychological assessment, particularly regarding nonverbal generativity and cognitive flexibility within the broader D-KEFS framework.

TEST YOURSELF

1. What is the age range for the D-KEFS Design Fluency Test?

(a) 8–15 years
(b) 16–89 years
(c) 8–89 years
(d) 12–89 years

2. How long is each condition of the Design Fluency Test administered?

(a) 30 seconds
(b) 45 seconds
(c) 60 seconds
(d) 90 seconds

3. Which tier represents the primary executive function assessed by Design Fluency?

(a) Tier 1: Foundational processes
(b) Tier 2: Bridging processes
(c) Tier 3: Core executive functions
(d) Tier 4: Higher-order integration

4. What is the sequence of condition administration?

(a) Switching, Filled Dots, Empty Dots Only
(b) Filled Dots, Empty Dots Only, Switching
(c) Empty Dots Only, Filled Dots, Switching
(d) Can be administered in any order

5. Significantly worse performance on Condition 3 compared to Conditions 1 + 2 suggests:

(a) Visual-motor integration problems.
(b) Processing speed deficits.
(c) Cognitive flexibility impairment at Tier 3.
(d) Language comprehension difficulties.

6. Which executive function domain is considered the primary Tier 3 cold EF assessed by this test?

(a) Working Memory Manipulation
(b) Fluent Generation of Novel Patterns
(c) Processing Speed
(d) Motor Planning

7. An examinee who produces many designs but with high repetition rates and no apparent awareness of the repetitions most likely has deficits at which tier(s)?

(a) Tier 1: Visual processing
(b) Tier 2: Simple working memory
(c) Tier 3: Inhibition with possible Tier 4 monitoring deficits
(d) Tier 1: Motor control

8. Set-loss errors in Condition 2 (connecting filled dots instead of empty dots) primarily indicate:

(a) Tier 1 visual discrimination problems.
(b) Tier 2–3 inhibition of competing stimuli difficulties.
(c) Tier 4 metacognitive deficits.
(d) Language comprehension problems.

9. What is the most significant confound that makes Design Fluency interpretation challenging?
- (a) Cultural differences in creativity
- (b) Processing speed and motor speed limitations
- (c) Educational background
- (d) Language proficiency

10. Two examinees produce the same number of correct designs (8 each). Examinee A works steadily but slowly throughout each condition. Examinee B draws quickly but shows long pauses between designs. This pattern suggests:
- (a) Both have identical deficits.
- (b) Examinee A likely has Tier 1 processing speed limitations; Examinee B likely has Tier 3 generativity problems.
- (c) Both have Tier 3 executive dysfunction.
- (d) Examinee A has executive problems; Examinee B has processing speed problems.

Answer Key: 1-c, 2-c, 3-c, 4-b, 5-c, 6-b, 7-c, 8-b, 9-b, 10-b

REFERENCES

Beery, K. E., & Beery, N. A. (2010). *The Beery-Buktenica Developmental Test of Visual-Motor Integration* (6th ed.). Pearson.

Benton, A. L., Hamsher, K., & deS., & Sivan, A. B. (1994). *Multilingual Aphasia Examination* (3rd ed.). AJA Associates.

Delis, D. C. (2012). *Delis Rating of Executive Functions (D-REF)*. Pearson.

Delis, D. C. (2021). *Delis Rating of Executive Functions—Adult (D-REF Adult)*. Pearson.

Delis, D. C., & Kaplan, E. (2025). *Delis-Kaplan Executive Function System—Advanced (D-KEFS Advanced)*. Pearson.

Delis, D. C., Kaplan, E., & Kramer, J. H. (2001). *Delis-Kaplan Executive Function System (D-KEFS)*. The Psychological Corporation.

Gioia, G. A., Isquith, P. K., Guy, S. C., & Kenworthy, L. (2015). *Behavior Rating Inventory of Executive Function* (2nd ed.). PAR.

Heaton, R. K., Chelune, G. J., Talley, J. L., Kay, G. G., & Curtiss, G. (1993). *Wisconsin Card Sorting Test Manual: Revised and Expanded*. Psychological Assessment Resources.

Jones-Gotman, M., & Milner, B. (1977). Design fluency: The invention of nonsense drawings after focal cortical lesions. *Neuropsychologia, 15*(4–5), 653–674.

Korkman, M., Kirk, U., & Kemp, S. (2007). *NEPSY-II: A Developmental Neuropsychological Assessment* (2nd ed.). The Psychological Corporation.

Lafayette Instrument Company (2015). *Grooved Pegboard Test*. Lafayette Instrument.

Meyers, J. E., & Meyers, K. R. (1995). *Rey Complex Figure Test and Recognition Trial Professional Manual*. Psychological Assessment Resources.

Naglieri, J. A., & Goldstein, S. (2013). *Comprehensive Executive Function Inventory (CEFI)*. Multi-Health Systems.

Naglieri, J. A., & Goldstein, S. (2017). *Comprehensive Executive Function Inventory Adult (CEFI Adult)*. Multi-Health Systems.

Reitan, R. M., & Wolfson, D. (1993). *The Halstead-Reitan Neuropsychological Test Battery: Theory and Clinical Interpretation* (2nd ed.). Neuropsychology Press.

Roth, R. M., Isquith, P. K., & Gioia, G. A. (2005). *Behavior Rating Inventory of Executive Function—Adult Version (BRIEF-A)*. PAR.

Ruff, R. M. (1996). *Ruff Figural Fluency Test Professional Manual*. Psychological Assessment Resources.

Ruff, R. M., Light, R. H., & Evans, R. W. (1987). The Ruff Figural Fluency Test: A normative study with adults. *Developmental Neuropsychology, 3*(1), 37–51. https://doi.org/10.1080/87565648709540362.

Wechsler, D. (2014). *Wechsler Intelligence Scale for Children—Fifth Edition (WISC-V)*. Pearson.

Wechsler, D. (2024). *Wechsler Adult Intelligence Scale—Fifth Edition (WAIS-5)*. Pearson.

Six

PROVERBS TEST

CLINICAL VIGNETTE

James Kurowski is a 45-year-old high school English teacher referred for neuropsychological testing three months after a moderate traumatic brain injury from a cycling accident. While he could still teach basic grammar and literature competently, he struggled following faculty discussions, noting that colleagues "communicate in shorthand that I can't understand."

Testing revealed mild divided attention difficulties but relatively preserved memory. On the D-KEFS Proverbs Test, James had no trouble reading proverbs or articulating his thoughts (Tier 1 intact), and his verbal working memory appeared adequate (Tier 2 intact). However, on the Free Inquiry condition, he provided partially abstract interpretations. For "the early bird catches the worm," he explained, "it means you should get up early to be successful," missing the broader implication about proactivity and initiative. This suggested Tier 3 difficulty with abstract concept generation and cognitive flexibility.

His performance declined notably with uncommon proverbs, where he struggled beyond literal interpretations. However, in Multiple Choice, James performed significantly better, often selecting fully abstract interpretations even for items he had interpreted concretely in Free Inquiry. This difference pointed to a Tier 3 generation deficit rather than a Tier 4 integration problem. James could recognize abstract concepts but struggled independently generating them.

Throughout testing, James maintained good effort and appropriate frustration tolerance (Hot EF intact) and demonstrated metacognitive awareness by commenting when uncertain (Tier 4 self-monitoring present). The hierarchical analysis indicated his deficit was specifically at the Tier 3 cold executive function level—difficulty with independent abstract concept generation and cognitive flexibility.

The results explained James's workplace difficulties. He struggled independently interpreting figurative language and implied meanings in meetings, though he understood these concepts when explicitly presented. Targeted interventions included communication strategies for his team (providing more explicit context) and cognitive rehabilitation focused on independent generation of abstract interpretations, resulting in significant improvement six months later.

TEST DESCRIPTION

The Delis-Kaplan Executive Function System (D-KEFS; Delis et al., 2001) Proverbs Test is designed for individuals aged 16–89. The test is not administered to examinees aged 8–15, making it unusual among D-KEFS subtests. The Risk–Reward Decision Test on D-KEFS Advanced (Delis & Kaplan, 2025) is the only other subtest that isn't normed for younger test takers. Administration typically requires 10–15 minutes for both conditions. This higher starting age reflects the developmental requirements for abstract metaphorical reasoning and cultural knowledge necessary for proverb interpretation, which typically emerge during adolescence as the rostrolateral prefrontal cortex matures (Dumontheil, 2014). It is a measure of abstract verbal reasoning and executive functioning that assesses the ability to interpret metaphorical language and form conceptual abstractions (Delis et al., 2001).

DON'T FORGET

The two-condition structure is specifically designed to separate Tier 3 generation (Free Inquiry) from recognition (Multiple Choice) demands. This distinction is critical for differential diagnosis. Examinees who perform much better on Multiple Choice than Free Inquiry have intact Tier 3 abstract reasoning capacity but difficulty with independent generation, which has very different intervention implications than true abstract reasoning deficits.

The test consists of 8 proverbs total: 5 common proverbs frequently encountered in American culture, and 3 uncommon proverbs intended to be less familiar. The proverbs are presented in two distinct conditions: Free Inquiry and Multiple Choice. During Free Inquiry, examinees explain the meaning of proverbs in their own words, requiring them to independently generate abstract interpretations (primarily a Tier 3 cold executive function). In Multiple Choice, examinees select the best interpretation from four options, which changes the task demand from generation to recognition of abstract meanings (reducing executive demands while maintaining the Tier 3 requirement for abstract reasoning).

The administration begins with the Free Inquiry condition, where all 8 proverbs are presented. The examiner reads each proverb aloud and asks, "What does that saying mean?" Responses are recorded verbatim for later scoring. Following completion of the Free Inquiry condition, the Multiple Choice condition is administered using the same 8 proverbs. For each item, the examinee is presented with four interpretation options and asked to select the best one.

The Proverbs Test evaluates the ability to look beyond the literal meaning of language to understand underlying abstract, metaphorical, or implied meaning. The ability to engage in abstract thinking and conceptualization is essential for complex reasoning and problem-solving (Dumontheil, 2014; Ferrer et al., 2009), social functioning and pragmatic communication (Colston, 2015; Norbury, 2004), and academic performance, including reading comprehension and critical analysis (Nippold, 2016). The test provides valuable information about an individual's capacity for metaphorical thinking, which is crucial for understanding implied meanings in communication, literary interpretation, humor comprehension, and navigating social situations where indirect communication is common (Norbury, 2004). Performance reflects both the integrity of verbal executive functions and the development of cultural knowledge and abstract reasoning abilities that continue to mature through adolescence and into early adulthood (Marini & Case, 1994; Dumontheil, 2014).

CAUTION

Because abstract metaphorical reasoning develops throughout adolescence, 16-year-olds will typically perform more poorly than adults even with intact executive functioning. Always interpret adolescent performance in the context of age-appropriate norms rather than adult-level expectations.

Rapid Reference 6.1

Proverbs Test Overview

Element	Description
Age range	16–89 years
Conditions	Free inquiry (generation) followed by multiple choice (recognition)
Number of items	8 proverbs total: 5 common, 3 uncommon
Time limit	None
Response format	Verbal explanation (free inquiry); selection from four options (multiple choice)
Materials	Examiner's manual, record form, stimulus book
Discontinuation	None—administer all eight proverbs in both conditions
Primary construct	Tier 3 Cold EF: Verbal abstract reasoning and concept generation/recognition

HIERARCHICAL TIER ANALYSIS

The Proverbs Test can be analyzed through the four-tier framework, with performance reflecting processes ranging from basic perception and language to higher-order metacognitive integration.

Tier 1: Foundational Processes (Nonexecutive)

The Proverbs Test requires intact foundational abilities before any executive processing can occur. Deficits at this level will compromise performance but do not indicate executive dysfunction.

Sensory and Language Processing

The test relies on auditory processing when proverbs are presented orally and visual processing for reading in the Multiple Choice condition. Examinees must accurately perceive verbal input, comprehend literal meaning of individual words and sentence structure, and, in Multiple Choice, demonstrate adequate reading fluency. Language comprehension difficulties—whether from hearing impairment, limited English proficiency, receptive language disorders, or reading disorders—will prevent accurate interpretation regardless of executive capacity. An examinee who performs worse on Multiple Choice than Free Inquiry might have reading difficulties rather than executive problems.

Vocabulary and Lexical Access

Understanding proverbs requires adequate vocabulary to comprehend individual words. Research demonstrates that lexical knowledge is a powerful predictor of proverb interpretation—vocabulary accounts for 42.2% of variance in proverb interpretation performance (Dosi, 2019). An examinee with limited vocabulary may struggle not because of poor abstract reasoning but because they don't understand keywords.

Basic Attention and Task Engagement

The test requires sustained attention and basic task engagement. An examinee who appears distracted, repeatedly asks for repetition, or provides rushed responses without reflection may have attentional difficulties rather than executive dysfunction. Similarly, examinees must tolerate the challenge sufficiently to remain engaged and must be able to articulate verbal responses (Free Inquiry) or communicate their selections (Multiple Choice). Expressive language disorders or severe frustration preventing task participation represent Tier 1 limitations that preclude assessment of higher-level processes.

Tier 1 Impairment Pattern

Poor performance across both conditions, with observable language comprehension difficulties, reading struggles, or communication deficits, suggests Tier 1 problems. Performance may be inconsistent based on vocabulary difficulty rather than metaphorical complexity. These examinees need a foundational language assessment, not an executive function intervention.

Tier 2: Bridging Processes

Tier 2 encompasses processes that bridge foundational language abilities and true executive control. On the Proverbs Test, these bridging processes involve holding proverb content in working memory, recognizing that proverbs carry metaphorical meaning, and demonstrating basic inhibition of overly literal responses. These abilities must be intact for a valid assessment of Tier 3 abstract reasoning.

Working Memory and Semantic Processing

At Tier 2, examinees must hold the proverb content in active awareness while processing it—basic working memory without complex manipulation. They must also access semantic knowledge and make elementary associations between concepts (connecting "bird" with "early morning" or "stone" with "movement"). An examinee who frequently asks for repetition or seems to forget the proverb mid-response may have Tier 2 working memory limitations.

DON'T FORGET

Better performance on common versus uncommon proverbs suggests the examinee is relying on Tier 2 crystallized cultural knowledge rather than Tier 3 fluid abstract reasoning. This pattern has important intervention implications. The individual may function adequately in familiar cultural contexts but struggle with novel situations requiring independent abstract thinking.

Pattern Recognition and Cultural Knowledge

Recognizing that proverbs have metaphorical intent ("this saying probably means something beyond just birds and worms") represents Tier 2 pattern recognition. For common proverbs, examinees may activate preexisting cultural schemas due to familiarity from having heard the expression before. This represents Tier 2 memory retrieval of crystallized knowledge rather than Tier 3 active reasoning. An examinee might recall "I've heard people say that about being early" without being able to explain why.

Basic Inhibition

At Tier 2, examinees must inhibit the tendency to simply repeat the proverb or describe the literal scenario. The ability to recognize "this isn't asking me to explain what birds do" represents basic inhibition, distinct from the Tier 3 inhibition required to suppress concrete interpretations in favor of abstract ones.

Tier 2 Deficit Pattern

Examinees with Tier 2 deficits may show very literal or incomplete responses even on common proverbs. They recognize that proverbs are metaphorical but cannot access the semantic associations or maintain the content long enough to work with it. They might say, "I know it means something, but I can't think of what."

Tier 3: Core Executive Functions

Tier 3 represents the Proverbs Test's primary assessment target—the executive functions that enable abstract interpretation and metaphorical reasoning. These processes can be divided into cold executive functions involving the cognitive mechanisms of concept generation, verbal reasoning, and cognitive flexibility, and hot executive functions involving frustration tolerance and anxiety management when encountering challenging or unfamiliar proverbs.

Cold Executive Functions

Cold executive functions on the Proverbs Test involve the cognitive machinery of abstract reasoning, verbal analysis, and flexible thinking, operating in relatively affect-neutral contexts where logical interpretation drives performance.

Concept Generation and Abstract Reasoning (Primary Measure)

This is the core Tier 3 cold executive function assessed by the Proverbs Test. Examinees must identify the underlying principle embedded within each proverb and express it in abstract, generalizable terms. This requires moving beyond concrete interpretation to identify metaphorical relationships and recognize how specific scenarios represent broader conceptual patterns. In the Free Inquiry condition, concept generation is heavily taxed as individuals independently formulate abstract meanings. The Multiple Choice condition shifts emphasis to concept recognition. Examinees must identify the most appropriate abstract interpretation among options, which reduces executive generation demands while still requiring Tier 3 abstract reasoning capacity.

The depth of abstraction required varies across items. The distinction between common and uncommon proverbs helps differentiate crystallized cultural knowledge (Tier 2) from active abstract reasoning (Tier 3). Better performance on common proverbs may reflect cultural learning rather than executive function, while performance on uncommon proverbs provides a purer measure of Tier 3 abstract reasoning.

Verbal Reasoning and Logical Analysis

Verbal reasoning at Tier 3 requires applying logical analysis to metaphorical content and drawing appropriate inferences. This process integrates linguistic knowledge with reasoning abilities to derive meaning beyond literal interpretation. Successful performance demonstrates the ability to identify relevant verbal relationships, analyze verbal analogies, and construct logical verbal explanations. This ability to think abstractly begins to develop in childhood with meaningful advances in adolescence and continued development in early adulthood (Blakemore & Choudhury, 2006; Dumontheil, 2014).

Cognitive Flexibility and Mental Set Shifting

Cognitive flexibility is essential for shifting from literal to metaphorical interpretative frames (Kasirer & Mashal, 2014). Examinees must disengage from the concrete meaning (what the words literally say) and shift to an abstract perspective (what the saying means more broadly). This flexibility is particularly evident with uncommon proverbs, where novelty may initially trigger a concrete interpretation, but the examinee must instead switch to an abstract conceptualization.

Inhibition of Concrete Responses

While Tier 2 involves basic inhibition of immediate associations, Tier 3 requires sophisticated inhibition of concrete interpretations even when they seem compelling. Examinees must suppress the tendency to focus exclusively on literal meaning and resist associations that are concrete rather than abstract (McDonald et al., 2008). This aspect of executive control is particularly evident with less familiar proverbs. The frontal systems supporting this inhibition are vulnerable to disruption, with medial frontal lesions particularly associated with increased concrete responses (Murphy et al., 2013).

Working Memory (Complex Manipulation)

While Tier 2 involves simply holding information, Tier 3 working memory requires active manipulation (Kiang et al., 2007; Pierce et al., 2010). Examinees must maintain the proverb content while simultaneously generating potential interpretations, evaluating these possibilities, and organizing a verbal response while maintaining focus on abstract rather than literal meaning. This is particularly demanding in the Free Inquiry condition, where examinees must access relevant knowledge, generate interpretations, and organize their response without external scaffolding.

Problem-Solving and Strategic Thinking

Each proverb presents a cognitive problem requiring analysis, inference, and solution generation. Examinees must identify key elements, analyze relationships, generate potential interpretations, evaluate these possibilities, and select or articulate the most appropriate abstract meaning. This systematic approach to verbal problem-solving reflects Tier 3 executive functions related to strategic thinking and analytical reasoning.

Tier 3 Cold EF Impairment Pattern

This is the classic executive dysfunction pattern. Examinees show concrete interpretations despite intact language comprehension and working memory. For "the early bird catches the worm," they might explain "birds that wake up early get food to eat." Performance is typically worse on uncommon proverbs and may improve significantly in Multiple Choice, suggesting recognition ability exceeds generation capacity. This pattern is associated with frontal lobe dysfunction (Murphy et al., 2013).

Hot Executive Functions

Hot executive functions involve the motivational and emotional aspects of executive control that influence how effectively cold executive processes are deployed. On the Proverbs Test, hot EF factors become prominent when examinees encounter unfamiliar proverbs, struggle to generate abstract interpretations, or experience uncertainty about response adequacy.

CAUTION

Hot EF difficulties can present as cold EF deficits. An examinee with intact Tier 3 abstract reasoning who becomes anxious or frustrated may produce concrete responses not because they cannot think abstractly, but because emotional dysregulation disrupts their cognitive processing. Behavioral observation during testing is essential for distinguishing these patterns, and intervention approaches differ substantially—anxiety management versus cognitive training.

Frustration Tolerance and Anxiety Management
Beyond basic Tier 1 engagement, Tier 3 hot executive function involves managing frustration and anxiety during cognitively challenging moments. When an examinee encounters an unfamiliar proverb or realizes their interpretation may be inadequate, they must regulate emotion sufficiently to persist with the task. The ability to maintain effort despite uncertainty reflects hot executive capacity (Zelazo & Carlson, 2012). An examinee who becomes visibly frustrated and then provides quick, unconsidered responses demonstrates how hot EF difficulties can compromise cold EF performance.

Emotional Response to Ambiguity
Proverb interpretation, particularly for uncommon items, involves tolerating ambiguity (Ounis, 2021). There isn't always a single correct interpretation, and some examinees become distressed by ambiguity and retreat to concrete, "safe" responses. The ability to remain cognitively engaged with abstract reasoning despite this emotional discomfort reflects hot EF capacity.

Tier 3 Hot EF Pattern
Examinees with hot EF difficulties show performance that varies with emotional state. They may perform well on early items but deteriorate as frustration builds or show anxiety-driven concrete responses. Behavioral observations are crucial—visible frustration, anxious comments, or emotional reactions distinguish this from cold EF deficits.

Tier 4: Higher-Order Integration and Metacognition

Tier 4 processes involve the highest level of executive integration—monitoring one's own cognitive performance and strategically adjusting approaches based on self-evaluation. On the Proverbs Test, Tier 4 functioning manifests as awareness of interpretation quality, spontaneous self-correction from concrete to abstract responses, and strategic adjustment across items.

Metacognitive Monitoring and Self-Evaluation.
Tier 4 metacognition involves observing and evaluating one's own cognitive processes and interpretation quality. Examinees must recognize when their initial response is too concrete and adjust accordingly. The ability to spontaneously comment "I'm not sure if that's abstract enough" or to self-correct mid-response "Well, it's not really about birds, it's about…" demonstrates Tier 4 self-monitoring. This differs from simply generating an abstract interpretation (Tier 3) by requiring awareness of the quality of one's own cognitive processing.

Strategy Evaluation and Adjustment
At Tier 4, examinees can evaluate their interpretive strategy and adjust based on feedback. After receiving neutral prompting—tell me a little more about what you mean—on an early item, some examinees will modify their approach on subsequent items, recognizing they need to "think more broadly." This strategic adjustment represents higher-order executive integration.

Integration Across Systems
Tier 4 involves coordinating different cognitive approaches for common versus uncommon proverbs, recognizing when to rely on cultural knowledge versus novel analysis. Perhaps most sophisticated is the integration of hot and cold executive systems. The examinee who becomes frustrated during a difficult proverb but uses metacognitive awareness to recognize "I'm getting frustrated and that's making me think less clearly" demonstrates integration of emotional awareness (hot) with strategic cognitive adjustment (cold).

Tier 4 Integration Difficulties
Some examinees show adequate abstract reasoning on individual items but lack metacognitive awareness or strategic flexibility. They may provide abstract interpretations but show no awareness of whether their responses are complete or adequate. This represents difficulty with the highest level of executive integration rather than core abstract reasoning problems.

Rapid Reference 6.2

Tier Structure at a Glance

Tier	Processes
Tier 1: Foundational processes (Nonexecutive)	Language comprehension and vocabulary
	Auditory processing
	Visual processing and reading (Multiple Choice)
	Expressive language ability
	Basic sustained attention
Tier 2: Bridging processes	Simple verbal working memory
	Basic semantic processing
	Cultural knowledge and familiarity
	Elementary pattern recognition
	Basic inhibition of literal responses
Tier 3: Cold executive functions	Abstract concept generation/recognition (primary)
	Verbal reasoning and logical analysis
	Cognitive flexibility (literal to metaphorical)
	Inhibition of concrete responses
	Complex working memory manipulation
Tier 3: Hot executive functions	Frustration tolerance during challenge
	Anxiety management
	Emotional response to ambiguity
Tier 4: Higher-order integration	Metacognitive monitoring and self-evaluation
	Strategic adjustment and flexibility
	Integration of cultural knowledge with active reasoning
	Hot-cold EF integration

ADMINISTRATION

NOTE: Refer to the Examiner's Manual for complete and detailed administration instructions. The Examiner's Manual provides verbatim instructions and clinicians should follow these precisely to ensure standardized administration.

Materials and Setup

The paper-and-pencil version of the Proverbs Test requires the Examiner's Manual, Record Form, and Stimulus Book. A digital version of the Examiner's Manual, Stimulus Booklet, and Stimulus Booklet Administration

Directions is also available through Q-global digital assets. The examiner should ensure a quiet testing environment free from distractions, as the verbal nature of the task makes it particularly susceptible to auditory interference.

Condition 1: Free Inquiry

The test begins with standardized instructions for the Free Inquiry condition: "I am going to read some sayings. After each one, tell me what the saying means." The examiner reads each prompt exactly as it is printed on the Record Form. Responses should be recorded verbatim. Prompts are provided in the Examiner's Manual and include encouragement to take a guess and clarifying what is meant if a response is vague.

Condition 2: Multiple Choice

After completing all Free Inquiry items, the examiner transitions to the Multiple Choice condition. Position the stimulus booklet in the easel position so each proverb and response choice can be easily read. Provide these instructions: "Here are the same sayings. Each saying has four different possible meanings written below it. For each saying, read all four possible meanings and tell me which one you think is best. You can say the letter a, b, c, or d if you like." If an examinee seems to have trouble reading the sayings, the examiner can read the sayings and response choices aloud. Circle the letter corresponding to the examinee's response choice for each item.

Discontinuation Rules

Unlike many D-KEFS subtests, the Proverbs Test does not have specific discontinuation rules. All 8 proverbs are administered in both conditions regardless of performance level. This ensures a comprehensive assessment across both familiar and unfamiliar content.

Timing Considerations

The Proverbs Test is not timed, allowing examinees to reflect on their responses without pressure. However, examiners should note unusually long response latencies or quick, impulsive responses, as these patterns may provide qualitative information about the examinee's approach to the task and may indicate Tier 3 hot EF factors (e.g., anxiety, impulsivity) affecting performance.

BEHAVIORAL OBSERVATIONS

Behavioral observations during administration provide critical qualitative data that complement quantitative scores and inform tier-based interpretation.

Approach and Self-Monitoring

Observe how the examinee approaches the task: Do they take time to reflect before responding, or do they respond impulsively? Do examinees self-correct or refine their interpretation spontaneously? Comments like "Actually, I think it means…" or "No, that's too literal, it's really about…" demonstrate Tier 4 metacognitive awareness. Some examinees explicitly articulate their reasoning: "Well, it's not really about birds, so it must mean something about people…" This verbalized metacognition demonstrates Tier 4 awareness.

Note whether examinees explicitly recognize when they are uncertain. Comments like "I'm not sure what that means" or "I've never heard that one before" provide insight into self-awareness and might predict better performance in Multiple Choice. Examinees who confidently provide concrete interpretations without recognizing their inadequacy demonstrate Tier 4 monitoring deficits in addition to any Tier 3 reasoning problems.

Emotional Response and Effort

Note the examinee's emotional response to the task—frustration with difficult items, anxiety about performance, or engagement with the intellectual challenge. These hot EF factors at Tier 3 can significantly impact cold EF performance. Observe signs of effort and persistence with challenging items versus premature abandonment. Defensive responses such as dismissing the task as meaningless may indicate awareness of difficulty and attempts to protect self-esteem, representing Tier 3 hot EF combined with potential Tier 4 awareness that performance is inadequate.

Note any signs of fatigue as the test progresses, distinguishing between genuine cognitive fatigue (Tier 1), frustration-based disengagement (Tier 3 hot EF), and strategic effort allocation (Tier 4).

Condition-Specific Observations

In Free Inquiry, observe whether the examinee demonstrates a systematic approach (Tier 4 strategy) or responds haphazardly. Note the richness and completeness of responses—are all elements addressed? In Multiple Choice, observe whether examinees read all four options before selecting or choose impulsively. Systematic evaluation suggests Tier 4 strategic processing.

Compare the examinee's approach across conditions. An examinee who is reflective in Multiple Choice but impulsive in Free Inquiry may struggle specifically with Tier 3 generation demands. A similar approach across conditions with better recognition and generation suggests that generation demands explain performance differences rather than effort or strategy.

SCORING

Free Inquiry Condition

For each item, the degree of accuracy and the degree of abstraction are scored. Accuracy is a reflection of whether the answer could be considered a feasible abstract or concrete interpretation of the proverb. Score 2 points for Mostly Accurate (all or most of the key elements), 1 point for Partially Accurate (some of the key elements are described), and 0 points for Mostly Inaccurate (none of the key elements is described). Degree of abstraction is rated according to the level of generalization represented by the response. Mostly Accurate is a response that applies to more situations, people, or concepts than the literal descriptions and earns 2 points. Mostly Concrete refers to literal descriptions and earns 0 points. The Total Achievement Score is indicated by circling the sum of the Accuracy and Abstraction Scores. The Examiner's Manual provides comprehensive scoring instruction and examples for each item.

Pay particular attention to the level of abstraction demonstrated. Some examinees provide responses that are partially abstract but still too concrete to receive full credit. For example, interpreting "a watched pot never boils" as "if you watch something too closely, it takes longer" captures some metaphorical thinking but misses the broader principle about patience and the subjective experience of time. These partial abstractions suggest Tier 3 difficulties with achieving full conceptual generalization.

A concrete response to "the early bird catches the worm" might be "birds that wake up early get food," rather than recognizing the principle about being proactive. The pattern across items helps distinguish between Tier 1 language comprehension problems (inconsistent, related to vocabulary), Tier 2 difficulties (vague recognition without elaboration), and Tier 3 executive deficits (consistent concreteness despite apparent comprehension).

Some examinees provide responses that are too vague: "It means you should do things" or "It's about being smart." These may reflect Tier 2 working memory difficulties, Tier 3 generation deficits, or Tier 4 metacognitive limitations. Perseverative elements across different proverbs—examinees who apply the same interpretive framework to multiple proverbs—might demonstrate Tier 3 cognitive inflexibility.

The examiner should record No/Don't Know Responses (1 point each) if the examinee provided no response even after being prompted. Repeated Responses are also recorded (1 point each) if an examinee repeats an interpretation that was given for an earlier proverb.

Multiple Choice Condition

The Record Form is designed so that the choice that is circled identifies the score that the item obtains for Multiple Choice Condition. The examiner does not need to analyze the response to determine how many points it receives. After circling the response choice, circle the score that is immediately under the response choice letter. Choices that are Unrelated or Phonemically Related earn 0 points. Choices that are Concrete earn 2 points. Choices that are Abstract earn 4 points.

NORMED VARIABLES

Free Inquiry Condition

Total Achievement Score

This primary measure reflects overall performance on the free response condition, where examinees generate their own interpretations. Raw scores can range from 0 to 32 (0–4 points per item across 8 items) and convert to scaled scores (M = 10, SD = 3) corrected for age. Assuming foundational processes are intact, this score assesses Tier 3 cold executive functions including concept generation, abstract reasoning, and cognitive flexibility, with significant Tier 3 hot EF influence from frustration tolerance and anxiety management during the open-ended task demands.

Free Inquiry Optional Process and Error Measures

The subtest provides optional measures that enable more precise tier-based interpretation.

Common Proverbs Achievement Score: This measure reflects performance on the five familiar proverbs (Items 1–5) that most examinees have encountered previously. Raw scores range from 0 to 20 and convert to scaled scores corrected for age. Lower scores may reflect limited cultural exposure (Tier 1–2) rather than executive dysfunction, as familiar proverb interpretation draws heavily on crystallized knowledge.

Uncommon Proverbs Achievement Score: This measure reflects performance on the three less familiar proverbs (Items 6–8) that examinees are unlikely to have heard before. Raw scores range from 0 to 12 and convert to scaled scores corrected for age. Because examinees cannot rely on memorized interpretations, this score provides a purer measure of Tier 3 abstract reasoning capacity with reduced Tier 2 cultural knowledge contribution.

Accuracy Only Score: This measure isolates the accuracy dimension by summing only accuracy scores (0–2 points) across all eight items, with raw scores ranging from 0 to 16 and converting to scaled scores corrected for age. The normative sample mean was 10.4. This score helps distinguish comprehension of proverb meaning from ability to express understanding abstractly, clarifying whether deficits are at Tier 1–2 (understanding) or Tier 3 (abstraction).

Abstraction Only Score: This measure isolates the abstraction dimension by summing only abstraction scores (0 or 2 points) across all eight items, with raw scores ranging from 0 to 16 and converting to scaled scores corrected for age. The normative sample mean was 13.2. This score targets Tier 3 cold EF capacity for abstract conceptualization independent of comprehension accuracy.

No/Don't Know Responses: This error measure counts items where the examinee provides no response or responds "I don't know" even after prompting. Raw scores convert to cumulative percentile ranks corrected for age. High scores may indicate Tier 3 hot EF difficulties (e.g., anxiety, low frustration tolerance), Tier 4 initiation limitations, or non-neurological factors such as depression or insufficient effort.

Repeated Responses: This error measure counts items where the examinee repeats an interpretation given for an earlier proverb. Raw scores convert to cumulative percentile ranks for all age groups combined. Elevated scores suggest perseverative tendencies, indicating Tier 3 cognitive inflexibility in the verbal modality.

Multiple Choice Condition

Total Achievement Score

This primary measure reflects overall performance on the recognition condition where examinees select interpretations from four alternatives. Raw scores can range from 0 to 32 and convert to cumulative percentile ranks corrected for age. This condition reduces Tier 3 generation demands while maintaining assessment of Tier 3 abstract reasoning capacity, making it valuable for distinguishing generation deficits from recognition abilities.

Multiple Choice Optional Measures

The recognition condition provides the additional scores of Common and Uncommon Proverbs Achievement Scores (paralleling the Free Inquiry measures). In addition, the Endorsement Measures score counts how frequently the examinee selected each response type—correct abstract, correct concrete, incorrect phonemic, and incorrect unrelated—with each converting to cumulative percentile ranks corrected for age. Elevated incorrect phonemic responses suggest severe stimulus-bound tendencies characteristic of extensive frontal or diffuse pathology (Tier 1 language processing or Tier 3 executive dysfunction), while elevated unrelated responses may indicate tangential thinking, severe global cognitive deficits, or insufficient effort.

Rapid Reference 6.3

Scoring Summary

Score	Description	Tier Implications
Free inquiry total achievement	Overall performance in free response condition	Tier 3 cold EF generation
Multiple choice total achievement	Overall performance on recognition condition	Tier 3 cold EF recognition
Free inquiry: common proverbs	Performance on 5 familiar proverbs	Tier 2–3 (cultural scaffolding)
Free inquiry: uncommon proverbs	Performance on 3 less familiar proverbs	Purer Tier 3 measure
Free inquiry: accuracy only	Elements identified regardless of abstraction	Tier 1–2 comprehension
Free inquiry: abstraction only	Level of abstract conceptualization	Tier 3 cold EF isolation
No/don't know responses	Frequency of nonresponses	May indicate Tier 3 hot EF or Tier 4
Repeated responses	Perseverative response patterns	Tier 3 cognitive inflexibility
Multiple choice: endorsement measures	Types of answers chosen (abstract, concrete, phonemic, unrelated)	Error pattern analysis
Total incorrect phonemic/ unrelated	Frequency of 0-point responses	Tier 1–2 deficits

COMMON ADMINISTRATION ERRORS

Several administration errors can compromise test validity. Awareness of these common pitfalls enables quality control and accurate interpretation.

Inadequate Recording of Responses

A common error is failing to record the examinee's verbal responses verbatim in the Free Inquiry condition. Complete and accurate recording is essential for precise scoring and tier-based analysis. A partial or paraphrased recording may lose critical elements that inform whether deficits are at Tier 1 (language output), Tier 2 (incomplete semantic processing), Tier 3 (concrete reasoning), or Tier 4 (incomplete self-monitoring).

Inappropriate Prompting

Examiners sometimes provide excessive prompting when examinees struggle, such as offering hints or asking leading questions. The standardized administration permits only specific neutral prompts to encourage responding and when responses are unclear (e.g., "Tell me a little more about what you mean"). Additional prompting compromises standardization and inflates scores. Conversely, failure to use permitted prompts when responses are vague may underestimate abilities, particularly when Tier 1 expressive language limitations are present.

Inconsistent Presentation

Variations in how proverbs are presented—including vocal emphasis, pacing, or repetition—can affect comprehension and performance. Proverbs should be presented clearly, at a moderate pace, and with neutral emphasis.

Scoring Errors

Scoring the Free Inquiry condition requires clinical judgment about abstraction level, creating opportunities for systematic errors. One common mistake involves overvaluing articulate but concrete explanations, mistaking Tier 1 expressive ability for Tier 3 abstraction—an examinee who eloquently describes the literal meaning of a proverb may receive undeserved abstraction credit. The converse error involves under-scoring abstract ideas expressed with limited vocabulary, confusing Tier 1 expression limitations with Tier 3 reasoning deficits. Inconsistently applying scoring criteria across different proverbs undermines reliability, particularly when some proverbs have more obvious abstract meanings than others. Cultural differences in interpretation can inappropriately influence scoring when examiners fail to recognize that valid abstract principles may be expressed differently across cultural frameworks. Finally, failing to recognize partial abstractions that deserve credit even if incomplete penalizes examinees who demonstrate emerging abstract reasoning capacity.

Failure to Observe Tier-Relevant Behaviors

Examiners focused solely on recording verbal responses may miss critical behavioral observations that inform tier-based interpretation. Failure to note frustration (Tier 3 hot EF), struggle with reading (Tier 1), self-corrections (Tier 4), or effortful working memory processing (Tier 2) limits the interpretive value beyond quantitative scores.

INTERPRETATION

Proverbs Test interpretation requires integrating quantitative scores with qualitative observations within a systematic framework that distinguishes foundational limitations from true executive dysfunction.

Using the Hierarchical Framework for Differential Diagnosis

When interpreting Proverbs Test performance, systematic tier-based analysis prevents the common error of attributing all deficits to executive dysfunction. Always evaluate tiers hierarchically from bottom to top.

Step 1: Rule Out Tier 1 Limitations
Before concluding executive dysfunction, ensure foundational processes are intact: Were comprehension difficulties observed? Were reading difficulties evident in Multiple Choice? Were expressive language limitations apparent? Were basic attention and task engagement sufficient? If Tier 1 deficits are present, avoid over-attributing problems to executive dysfunction. Interventions should address foundational limitations first.

Step 2: Evaluate Tier 2 Bridging Processes
If Tier 1 is intact, assess bridging functions: Was working memory adequate? Could the examinee access basic semantic associations? Was there recognition that proverbs are metaphorical? Did performance suggest cultural knowledge gaps versus reasoning deficits? Tier 2 deficits manifest as incomplete or vague responses with apparent effort.

Step 3: Analyze Tier 3 Cold Executive Patterns

With Tiers 1–2 intact, evaluate cold executive function capacity for abstract reasoning. Are responses consistently concrete across both conditions despite adequate comprehension? Consistent concreteness suggests fundamental Tier 3 abstract reasoning deficits. Examine whether there is a discrepancy between common and uncommon proverbs. Significantly better performance on common proverbs suggests heavy reliance on Tier 2 crystallized cultural knowledge rather than active Tier 3 abstract reasoning. Compare Free Inquiry and Multiple Choice performance: markedly better recognition than generation indicates a specific Tier 3 generation deficit with intact abstract reasoning capacity, which has different intervention implications than global abstract reasoning impairment. Note whether responses show partial abstractions (capturing some but not all elements at an abstract level), which suggests emerging but incomplete Tier 3 capacity. Examine accuracy versus abstraction scores—better accuracy than abstraction indicates the examinee understands proverb meaning but cannot achieve full conceptual generalization. Finally, look for perseverative elements across different proverbs (applying the same interpretive framework repeatedly), which may indicate Tier 3 cognitive inflexibility.

Step 4: Evaluate Tier 3 Hot Executive Factors

Determine whether emotional regulation factors are contributing to performance. Does performance deteriorate with frustration or anxiety? Some examinees respond to difficult proverbs (particularly uncommon ones) with visible frustration and then provide quick, unconsidered concrete responses, not because they lack abstract reasoning capacity, but because emotional dysregulation disrupts cognitive processing. Others become anxious about "getting it wrong" and retreat to safe, concrete interpretations rather than risking an incorrect abstract response. Note whether the examinee shows defensive reactions—dismissing proverbs as "stupid" or "meaningless"—which may indicate awareness of difficulty and attempts to protect self-esteem. Compare performance on early versus later items: deterioration over time may reflect accumulated frustration rather than fatigue or increasing difficulty. Hot EF deficits require anxiety management and emotional regulation strategies before cognitive interventions targeting abstract reasoning will be effective.

Step 5: Assess Tier 4 Integration and Metacognition

For examinees with adequate Tier 3 core functions, evaluate higher-order integration: Is there metacognitive awareness of response quality? Does the examinee spontaneously self-correct? Is there a strategic adjustment across items? Can the examinee integrate cultural knowledge with active reasoning? Tier 4 deficits manifest as adequate basic abstract reasoning without awareness of when responses are incomplete.

PERFORMANCE PATTERNS AND CLINICAL IMPLICATIONS

Several recognizable performance patterns emerge on the Proverbs Test, each with distinct clinical implications and tier-level associations.

Concrete Thinking Pattern

Consistently literal interpretations across both common and uncommon proverbs suggest fundamental Tier 3 difficulties with abstract reasoning. This pattern is associated with conditions affecting frontal lobe functioning, including traumatic brain injury (McDonald et al., 2008), behavioral variant frontotemporal dementia (Johnen & Bertoux, 2019), and autism spectrum disorder (Green et al., 2014). These individuals may struggle across multiple contexts requiring abstract thinking. Academic performance in subjects requiring abstract reasoning will likely be impaired, and social functioning may be compromised as the individual interprets social communication literally and misses implied meanings (Norbury, 2004).

Familiarity Effect Pattern

Significantly better performance on common than uncommon proverbs suggests heavy reliance on Tier 2 cultural knowledge rather than Tier 3 active abstract reasoning. In this pattern, cultural learning masks limited abstract reasoning on the more common proverbs. Alternatively, it could reflect difficulties applying abstract reasoning skills to novel/unfamiliar content. These individuals may function adequately in familiar situations where cultural scripts are available but struggle when confronted with novel contexts requiring independent abstract reasoning.

Generation Deficit Pattern

Markedly better performance on Multiple Choice than Free Inquiry suggests stronger Tier 3 recognition than generation abilities. This dissociation may reflect executive difficulties with independent concept formation, language production deficits (Tier 1 confound), or working memory limitations (Tier 2 confound). It may be seen in expressive language disorders, frontal lobe dysfunctions affecting initiation, and conditions affecting strategic generation. These individuals may benefit from providing options or frameworks rather than requiring independent generation.

Evaluation Difficulty Pattern

Better performance on Free Inquiry than Multiple Choice suggests challenges with evaluating multiple options or difficulty inhibiting appealing but incorrect interpretations. This uncommon pattern may indicate problems with comparative judgment (Tier 4), susceptibility to distraction by plausible alternatives (Tier 3 hot EF—impulsivity), or atypical conceptual frameworks. These individuals may struggle in situations requiring evaluation of multiple alternatives.

Inconsistent Abstraction Pattern

Variability in abstraction level across items without a clear relationship to familiarity suggests inconsistent Tier 3 executive functioning or fluctuating cognitive control. This pattern is associated with conditions characterized by variable performance, attention-deficit/hyperactivity disorder (ADHD), mood disorders, and early stages of neurodegenerative conditions. These individuals may show significant day-to-day or situation-to-situation variability in abstract reasoning capacity.

COMPARISON BETWEEN CONDITIONS AND MEASURES

Free Inquiry Versus Multiple Choice

Compare performance between conditions for insights into specific cognitive strengths and challenges. Superior performance on Multiple Choice compared to Free Inquiry might indicate stronger Tier 3 recognition than generation abilities, Tier 1 expressive language limitations masking intact conceptual understanding, Tier 2 working memory limitations, or Tier 4 strategic deficits. Conversely, better performance on Free Inquiry might suggest Tier 3 hot EF difficulties (impulsivity), Tier 4 problems with evaluating multiple alternatives, or atypical but valid conceptual frameworks.

Common Versus Uncommon Proverb Performance

Compare performance between common and uncommon proverbs within each condition. Large discrepancies may indicate heavy reliance on Tier 2 cultural knowledge versus Tier 3 active abstract reasoning, adequate Tier 3 capacity when familiar contexts provide scaffolding, Tier 3 flexibility deficits, or cultural knowledge gaps. Examinees who perform significantly better on common proverbs may be drawing on memorized interpretations rather than demonstrating flexible Tier 3 abstract thinking.

Accuracy Versus Abstraction Performance

Compare accuracy and abstraction scores. Better accuracy than abstraction scores might indicate good Tier 1–2 verbal skills, difficulty achieving Tier 3 abstract conceptualization despite understanding literal meaning, or a specific Tier 3 cold EF deficit in abstraction. This pattern suggests interventions targeting abstract thinking specifically rather than broader language training.

Rapid Reference 6.4

Distinguishing Tier-Level Deficits

Tier Level	Indicators	Clinical Implications
Tier 1 deficit	Poor performance across both conditions; observable language comprehension difficulties, reading struggles, or communication deficits; inconsistent, based on vocabulary difficulty rather than metaphorical complexity	Foundational language deficits limit performance; assess language abilities rather than executive function; interventions target vocabulary and comprehension
Tier 2 deficit	Very literal or incomplete responses even on common proverbs; recognizes proverbs are metaphorical but cannot access semantic associations; may say "I know it means something, but I can't think of what"	Working memory or semantic access problems; can recognize the task demands but cannot retrieve or maintain relevant content; interventions target semantic retrieval strategies
Tier 3 cold deficit	Concrete interpretations despite intact language and working memory; worse on uncommon proverbs; significant improvement in Multiple Choice over Free Inquiry; recognition exceeds generation	Classic executive dysfunction; difficulty with abstract concept generation and cognitive flexibility; associated with frontal dysfunction; interventions target abstract reasoning training
Tier 3 hot deficit	Performance varies with emotional state; deteriorates as frustration builds; anxiety-driven, concrete responses; visible frustration or anxious comments	Emotional dysregulation compromising cognition; intact abstract reasoning disrupted by anxiety or frustration; interventions target anxiety management and frustration tolerance
Tier 4 deficit	Adequate abstract reasoning but no self-correction; poor awareness of response quality; no spontaneous strategy adjustment; unaware when responses are incomplete	Metacognitive monitoring failure; can reason abstractly but fails to evaluate own performance; interventions target self-monitoring and metacognitive awareness training

ECOLOGICAL VALIDITY AND FUNCTIONAL IMPLICATIONS

Performance on the Proverbs Test relates to real-world functioning across multiple domains. Abstract reasoning capacity—the core Tier 3 cold EF construct assessed by this test—underlies success in academic, professional, social, and adaptive contexts.

Academic Functioning

Abstract reasoning capacity predicts performance in contexts requiring conceptual thinking: comprehending complex texts, identifying themes and patterns, applying principles across contexts, and engaging in critical analysis (Nippold, 2016). Limitations may manifest as difficulty understanding implicit information in advanced texts, struggle recognizing underlying principles, problems transferring learning to new situations, or difficulty with subjects requiring abstract reasoning. Students with concrete thinking patterns may perform adequately on factual recall but struggle with literary analysis, thematic interpretation, or applying learned concepts to novel problems.

Vocational and Daily Living

Abstract reasoning facilitates effective problem-solving by supporting identification of underlying patterns, application of principles to new situations, and generation of innovative solutions (Holyoak, 2012). Concrete thinking may limit problem-solving to familiar approaches or lead to a focus on surface features rather than deeper structural elements. In James's case (clinical vignette), his Tier 3 generation deficit directly impacted his ability to follow implied meanings in professional meetings. He struggled to interpret the "shorthand" communication common in workplace discussions. In daily life, abstract reasoning supports adaptation to changing circumstances, understanding complex instructions, interpretation of safety warnings and social rules, and navigation of systems with implicit rules (Lezak et al., 2012).

> **DON'T FORGET**
>
> Problem-solving difficulties attributed to "executive dysfunction" may actually reflect Tier 3 abstract reasoning limitations specifically. An individual who can plan adequately for concrete, familiar problems but struggles with novel situations requiring abstract principles has a different intervention need than someone with broader planning deficits across all contexts.

Social Functioning

Abstract verbal reasoning supports understanding implied meanings, interpreting nonliteral communication, recognizing social principles, and adapting to social rules (Colston, 2015; Norbury, 2004). Research demonstrates that difficulties with figurative language comprehension are associated with social communication challenges and pragmatic language deficits (Paul & Norbury, 2012). Concrete thinking may contribute to social difficulties when individuals miss social nuances, interpret communication overly literally, struggle to understand unstated social expectations, or have difficulty with humor, sarcasm, and figurative language (Pexman, 2008).

> **CAUTION**
>
> Don't assume social difficulties reflect autism spectrum disorder or primary social–emotional deficits without considering whether Tier 3 abstract reasoning limitations could explain the social challenges. An individual with concrete thinking due to frontal lobe dysfunction may present with social communication difficulties that look similar to autism but have different underlying mechanisms and require different interventions.

STRENGTHS AND WEAKNESSES

The Proverbs Test offers several distinctive strengths for executive function assessment, alongside limitations that clinicians should consider when selecting measures and interpreting results.

Strengths

The Proverbs Test offers several notable advantages for assessing verbal abstract reasoning within a comprehensive executive function evaluation.

Clear Tier Structure

The Proverbs Test provides a relatively pure measure of Tier 3 verbal abstract reasoning with clear Tier 1 requirements (language comprehension/production) and minimal Tier 2 confounds. The two-condition format allows separation of Tier 3 generation from recognition demands, making it particularly useful for tier-based differential diagnosis.

Cultural Knowledge Assessment

The inclusion of both common and uncommon proverbs allows examination of both culturally acquired knowledge (Tier 2) and novel abstract reasoning (Tier 3). This design helps distinguish between rote learning of familiar metaphors and active abstract reasoning capacity, providing insight into how cultural knowledge interfaces with executive functions (Biesok et al., 2024).

Multiple Response Formats
The inclusion of both free response and multiple-choice conditions allows assessment of both generation (Tier 3 cold EF) and recognition (lower executive demand) of abstract concepts. This design accommodates individuals with Tier 1 expressive language limitations while still providing information about independent Tier 3 concept formation abilities.

Ecological Relevance
Abstract verbal reasoning is crucial for many real-world contexts, including educational settings, professional environments, social interactions, and independent daily functioning. The test assesses Tier 3 cognitive skills that directly relate to adaptive functioning across multiple domains, making findings readily translatable to functional recommendations.

Qualitative Richness
Beyond quantitative scores, responses provide rich qualitative data about thinking processes across tiers. The nature of concrete responses, specific misinterpretations, and patterns of partial abstraction offer valuable insights into which tier is compromised. Observation of self-correction reveals Tier 4 metacognition, while emotional reactions inform Tier 3 hot EF assessment.

Developmental Appropriateness
The age restriction to 16+ years reflects appropriate developmental considerations, as abstract metaphorical reasoning requires sufficient cognitive maturity and cultural exposure. This targeted age range enhances the test's validity for its intended population.

Weaknesses and Limitations

Despite its strengths, the Proverbs Test has several limitations that clinicians should consider when selecting measures and interpreting results.

Cultural and Educational Bias
Despite efforts to include both common and uncommon proverbs, performance is inevitably influenced by cultural exposure, educational background, and language proficiency. Research demonstrates that understanding proverbs involves both crystallized intelligence (cultural knowledge—Tier 2) and fluid intelligence (abstract reasoning—Tier 3), with these factors difficult to fully separate (Biesok et al., 2024). The test may underestimate Tier 3 abstract reasoning abilities in individuals with limited exposure to Western cultural frameworks, lower educational attainment, or non-Western cultural backgrounds, while potentially overestimating Tier 3 executive capacity in highly educated individuals who can rely on Tier 2 crystallized knowledge.

Intellectual Ability and Vocabulary Confound
Research suggests that performance is significantly mediated by general intellectual ability, particularly vocabulary knowledge and crystallized intelligence (Tier 1–2), rather than purely Tier 3 abstract reasoning. Dosi (2019) found that lexical knowledge was the strongest predictor of accurate proverb interpretation, accounting for 42.2% of variance, while abstract thinking variables showed no significant correlation. This indicates that Tier 1 vocabulary knowledge may be a far stronger predictor than Tier 3 executive capacity. Individuals with extensive vocabulary may perform well regardless of Tier 3 abstract reasoning capabilities (false negatives), while those with weaker lexical knowledge but intact Tier 3 executive functions may perform poorly (false positives).

Language Dependency
The heavy reliance on language comprehension (Tier 1 input) and expressive language abilities (Tier 1 output in Free Inquiry) limits utility with individuals who have language impairments, communication disorders, or limited English proficiency. Distinguishing between Tier 1 language deficits and Tier 3 abstract reasoning limitations requires careful behavioral observation and often supplementary language assessment.

Limited Domain Coverage
The test focuses specifically on verbal abstract reasoning through metaphorical interpretation (Tier 3 cold EF in the verbal domain), providing limited information about abstract reasoning in nonverbal domains, Tier 4 integration across multiple executive systems, Tier 3 hot EF (though observable, not systematically measured), or other Tier 3 cold EF domains. A comprehensive assessment requires additional measures addressing different modalities.

Sensitivity Versus Specificity Limitations
While sensitive to Tier 3 abstract reasoning deficits, the test does not specify the underlying cause or tier of impairment without careful analysis. Poor performance may reflect limitations at any tier, requiring tier-based interpretation in the context of a comprehensive assessment rather than relying on scores alone.

Practice Effects and Coaching Vulnerability
Common proverbs are susceptible to practice effects, as their interpretations can be learned through exposure or coaching. This limits utility in repeated assessment and may mask genuine Tier 3 deficits if examinees have been specifically prepared.

Limited Item Pool
With only 8 proverbs total, the test provides a relatively small sample of performance. This limited item pool may not fully capture the range of Tier 3 abstract reasoning abilities, makes the test more susceptible to random variation, and provides relatively few items at each familiarity level (5 common, 3 uncommon). This emphasizes the importance of qualitative observation and integration with other measures.

ALTERNATIVE MEASURES

When Proverbs Test results suggest abstract reasoning difficulties or when Tier 1–2 confounds limit interpretability, complementary measures can clarify the clinical picture.

Within the D-KEFS Suite

Several D-KEFS subtests provide complementary or converging evidence for abstract reasoning and related executive functions.

Word Context Test
Provides an alternative measure of Tier 3 verbal abstract reasoning through deductive thinking about word meanings. Like the Proverbs Test, it assesses the ability to derive abstract concepts from verbal information but uses a deductive rather than metaphorical paradigm. This test may be more appropriate for examinees with limited cultural exposure to Western proverbs, reducing Tier 2 cultural knowledge demands while maintaining assessment of Tier 3 verbal reasoning capacity.

Twenty Questions Test
Assesses Tier 3 abstract categorization and strategic thinking through question formulation. Though different in format, it similarly requires identification of abstract categories and conceptual relationships. This measure provides complementary information about how individuals generate and test conceptual hypotheses, with significant Tier 4 demands for strategic planning and metacognitive monitoring.

Sorting Test
Evaluates Tier 3 concept formation through card sorting, offering insights into both verbal and visual-perceptual conceptualization. While broader in scope, it similarly assesses the ability to identify abstract relationships and articulate conceptual principles. This test may be more appropriate when assessing concept formation across modalities or when Tier 1 verbal comprehension limitations might compromise Proverbs Test performance.

Social Sorting Test (D-KEFS Advanced)
Assesses Tier 3 abstract reasoning in the social–emotional domain, requiring identification and articulation of abstract social–emotional principles and sorting based on emotional expressions. Like Proverbs, it requires moving beyond concrete, surface features to identify underlying relationships, but in social rather than linguistic content. This may be particularly valuable for distinguishing whether abstract reasoning difficulties are domain-general or specific to verbal-metaphorical material.

Beyond D-KEFS

Measures outside the D-KEFS family can provide converging evidence or assess related constructs when additional information is needed.

Verbal Abstract Reasoning Measures
The Similarities subtest (WAIS-5, Wechsler, 2024; WISC-V, Wechsler, 2014) assesses Tier 3 verbal abstract reasoning through identification of conceptual relationships between word pairs. Like the Proverbs Test, it evaluates verbal concept formation and abstraction but uses direct comparison rather than metaphorical interpretation. This brief measure provides complementary information about verbal abstraction in a different paradigm with less Tier 2 cultural loading. Davies and Piovesana (2015) found the Similarities test to be a very strong measure of verbal abstract reasoning in adults. The Comprehension subtest (WAIS-5/WISC-V) evaluates social reasoning and practical judgment through questions about social rules and practical problems. While broader than abstract reasoning alone, it assesses application of verbal concepts to social and practical situations, complementing the more purely abstract focus of the Proverbs Test with more Tier 3–4 hot EF demands in social–emotional contexts.

Language and Vocabulary Assessment
Given the strong influence of vocabulary on Proverbs Test performance (Dosi, 2019), supplementary language assessment is often essential for accurate tier-based interpretation. The Peabody Picture Vocabulary Test, Fifth Edition (PPVT-5; Dunn, 2019) assesses receptive vocabulary with minimal verbal reasoning and oral expression demands, helping clarify whether poor Proverbs performance reflects Tier 1 vocabulary limitations versus Tier 3 abstract reasoning deficits. The WAIS-5/WISC-V Vocabulary subtest provides additional information about word knowledge but conflates vocabulary with verbal expression abilities. The Clinical Evaluation of Language Fundamentals, Fifth Edition (CELF-5; Wiig et al., 2013) includes pragmatic language subtests that may complement proverb interpretation findings. The Understanding Spoken Paragraphs and Semantic Relationships subtests help distinguish between Tier 1 general language comprehension difficulties and Tier 3 specific challenges with abstract verbal reasoning.

Nonverbal Abstract Reasoning
Raven's Progressive Matrices (Raven et al., 2018) provides assessment of Tier 3 abstract reasoning in the nonverbal domain. While not directly comparable to verbal metaphorical reasoning, convergent findings across verbal (Proverbs) and nonverbal (Raven's) abstract reasoning suggest domain-general Tier 3 executive capacity, while discrepancies suggest domain-specific deficits. Interestingly, Murphy et al. (2013) found no correlation between proverb interpretation and Raven's performance in frontal lesion patients, suggesting that different neural mechanisms may support verbal versus nonverbal abstract reasoning despite both being Tier 3 functions. This finding underscores the importance of assessing abstract reasoning across modalities rather than assuming performance in one domain generalizes to another.

Informal Figurative Language Assessment
Clinicians can assess metaphor, idiom, and sarcasm comprehension informally to determine whether difficulties are specific to proverbs or reflect broader Tier 3 abstract language challenges. Tasks requiring interpretation of common idioms (e.g., "raining cats and dogs," "break a leg") or recognizing sarcasm in social vignettes complement formal Proverbs Test findings and provide ecologically relevant information about figurative language comprehension in everyday contexts.

Behavior Rating Scales

Executive function rating scales capture real-world behaviors that may or may not align with performance-based measures. For children and adolescents, the Behavior Rating Inventory of Executive Function, Second Edition (BRIEF-2; Gioia et al., 2015), Comprehensive Executive Function Inventory (CEFI; Naglieri & Goldstein, 2013), and Delis Rating of Executive Functions (D-REF; Delis, 2012) provide parent and teacher perspectives on daily executive functioning. For adults, the BRIEF-A (Roth et al., 2005), CEFI Adult (Naglieri & Goldstein, 2017), and D-REF Adult (Delis, 2021) offer self-report and informant-report options. Relevant scales across these measures include Shift (cognitive flexibility required for moving from literal to abstract interpretations), Plan/Organize (strategic approach to complex verbal reasoning), and Initiate (spontaneous generation of abstract concepts). Discrepancies between Proverbs performance and rating scale elevations provide diagnostic information: adequate test performance with elevated rating scales may indicate that the one-on-one, untimed testing environment does not capture abstract reasoning challenges that emerge in fast-paced conversations, workplace meetings, or socially complex situations requiring rapid interpretation of implied meanings. Conversely, poor Proverbs performance with unremarkable rating scales might suggest test-specific factors such as vocabulary limitations, cultural unfamiliarity with Western proverbs, performance anxiety, or poor metacognitive awareness of daily figurative language difficulties rather than pervasive executive dysfunction.

SUMMARY

The D-KEFS Proverbs Test provides a sophisticated assessment of Tier 3 verbal abstract reasoning through the interpretation of metaphorical language. By evaluating both free generation (higher Tier 3 executive demand) and recognition (lower executive demand) of abstract concepts across familiar and novel content, the test offers insights into multiple aspects of conceptual thinking and executive functioning analyzed through the hierarchical tier framework.

Optimal use requires systematic tier-based analysis. Clinicians must first ensure Tier 1 foundational processes (language comprehension, vocabulary, expressive ability) are intact before attributing poor performance to executive dysfunction. Tier 2 processes (working memory, semantic access, cultural knowledge) must be evaluated to distinguish bridging function deficits from true Tier 3 executive impairment. Within Tier 3, both cold EF (abstract reasoning, cognitive flexibility, concept generation) and hot EF (frustration tolerance, anxiety management) must be considered. Finally, Tier 4 integration (metacognitive monitoring, strategic flexibility, self-correction) provides information about higher-order executive functions.

The test's strengths include its relatively pure measure of Tier 3 verbal abstract reasoning, multiple response formats accommodating different executive demands, and rich qualitative information about thinking processes across tiers. The two-condition structure allows valuable differentiation between Tier 3 generation and recognition abilities, informing intervention planning. Limitations include significant Tier 1–2 confounds (cultural knowledge, vocabulary, language proficiency), domain specificity (verbal reasoning only), and the small item pool. The research demonstrating that vocabulary accounts for more variance than abstract reasoning in proverb interpretation underscores the critical importance of tier-based differential diagnosis.

When appropriately administered and interpreted through the hierarchical tier framework, the Proverbs Test contributes valuable information to comprehensive neuropsychological assessment, particularly regarding Tier 3 higher-order thinking skills that impact academic achievement, professional functioning, social comprehension, and adaptive problem-solving. Its integration within the broader D-KEFS framework allows examination of abstract reasoning in relation to other executive functions, supporting a nuanced understanding of cognitive strengths and challenges across all tiers. However, clinicians should be aware that the test's focus on culturally bound metaphorical language creates Tier 2 confounds that may limit its utility with certain populations. Tier-based analysis combined with alternative measures ensures accurate differential diagnosis and appropriate intervention planning.

TEST YOURSELF

1. What is the age range for the D-KEFS Proverbs Test?

(a) 8–89 years

(b) 16–89 years

(c) 12–89 years

(d) 18–89 years

2. Which tier represents the primary executive function assessed by the Proverbs Test?

(a) Tier 1: Foundational processes

(b) Tier 2: Bridging processes

(c) Tier 3: Core executive functions

(d) Tier 4: Higher-order integration

3. In the Free Inquiry condition, what is the maximum combined score that can be earned for a single response?

(a) 2 points

(b) 3 points

(c) 4 points

(d) 5 points

4. Which condition is administered first?

(a) Free Inquiry

(b) Multiple Choice

(c) Either can be administered first

(d) They are administered simultaneously

5. What does significantly better performance on Multiple Choice compared to Free Inquiry suggest?

(a) Superior abstract reasoning capacity

(b) Cultural knowledge deficits

(c) Tier 3 recognition stronger than generation abilities

(d) Tier 1 attention problems

6. Which executive function domain is considered the primary Tier 3 function assessed by this test?

(a) Working Memory Manipulation

(b) Processing Speed

(c) Concept Generation/Recognition and Abstract Reasoning

(d) Motor Planning

7. An examinee who understands all words in a proverb but provides a consistently literal interpretation most likely has a deficit at which tier?

(a) Tier 1: Language comprehension

(b) Tier 2: Semantic processing

(c) Tier 3: Abstract reasoning (cold EF)

(d) Tier 4: Metacognitive monitoring

8. Significantly better performance on common versus uncommon proverbs suggests:

(a) Superior Tier 3 abstract reasoning.

(b) Reliance on Tier 2 cultural knowledge rather than Tier 3 active reasoning.

(c) Tier 1 attention deficit.

(d) Tier 4 metacognitive problems.

9. Research by Dosi (2019) found which factor as the strongest predictor of proverb interpretation?

(a) Abstract reasoning abilities (Tier 3)

(b) Executive functioning (Tier 3–4)

(c) Lexical knowledge/vocabulary (Tier 1)

(d) Working memory (Tier 2)

10. What is a major limitation of the Proverbs Test that requires tier-based analysis?

(a) It takes too long to administer.

(b) Cultural, educational, and vocabulary factors (Tier 1–2) significantly confound Tier 3 executive function measurement.

(c) It requires motor coordination.

(d) It has poor reliability.

Answer Key: 1-b, 2-c, 3-c, 4-a, 5-c, 6-c, 7-c, 8-b, 9-c, 10-b

REFERENCES

Biesok, J., Ziegler, M., Montag, C., & Nenchev, I. (2024). Proverb comprehension: Unveiling the role of crystallized and fluid intelligence. *Intelligence, 102,* 101808. https://doi.org/10.1016/j.intell.2023.101808.

Blakemore, S. J., & Choudhury, S. (2006). Development of the adolescent brain: Implications for executive function and social cognition. *Journal of Child Psychology and Psychiatry, 47*(3–4), 296–312. https://doi.org/10.1111/j.1469-7610.2006.01611.x.

Colston, H. L. (2015). *Using Figurative Language.* Cambridge University Press.

Davies, K., & Piovesana, A. (2015). The roles of executive functions in verbal abstract reasoning. *Australian Journal of Psychology, 67*(1), 49–56.

Delis, D. C. (2012). *Delis Rating of Executive Functions (D-REF).* Pearson.

Delis, D. C. (2021). *Delis Rating of Executive Functions—Adult (D-REF Adult).* Pearson.

Delis, D. C., Kaplan, E., & Kramer, J. H. (2001). *Delis-Kaplan Executive Function System (D-KEFS).* The Psychological Corporation.

Dosi, I. (2019). Do proverbs measure abstract or metaphorical thinking: Evidence from healthy Greek-speaking adults. *European Journal of Psychological Research, 6*(1), 75–83.

Dumontheil, I. (2014). Development of abstract thinking during childhood and adolescence: The role of rostrolateral prefrontal cortex. *Developmental Cognitive Neuroscience, 10,* 57–76.

Dunn, D. M. (2019). *Peabody Picture Vocabulary Test* (5th ed.). Pearson.

Ferrer, E., O'Hare, E. D., & Bunge, S. A. (2009). Fluid reasoning and the developing brain. *Frontiers in Neuroscience, 3*(1), 46–51.

Gioia, G. A., Isquith, P. K., Guy, S. C., & Kenworthy, L. (2015). *Behavior Rating Inventory of Executive Function* (2nd ed.). PAR.

Green, A. E., Kenworthy, L., Mosner, M. G., Gallagher, N. M., Fearon, E. W., Balhana, C. D., & Yerys, B. E. (2014). Abstract analogical reasoning in high-functioning children with autism spectrum disorders. *Autism Research, 7*(6), 677–686.

Holyoak, K. J. (2012). Analogy and relational reasoning. In K. J. Holyoak & R. G. Morrison (Eds.), *The Oxford Handbook of Thinking and Reasoning* (pp. 234–259). Oxford University Press.

Johnen, A., & Bertoux, M. (2019). Psychological and cognitive markers of behavioral variant frontotemporal dementia–A clinical neuropsychologist's view on diagnostic criteria and beyond. *Frontiers in Neurology, 10,* 594.

Kasirer, A., & Mashal, N. (2014). Verbal creativity in autism: Comprehension and generation of metaphoric language in high-functioning autism spectrum disorder and typical development. *Frontiers in Human Neuroscience, 8*, 615.

Kiang, M., Light, G. A., Prugh, J., Coulson, S., Braff, D. L., & Kutas, M. (2007). Cognitive, neurophysiological, and functional correlates of proverb interpretation abnormalities in schizophrenia. *Journal of the International Neuropsychological Society, 13*(4), 653–663.

Lezak, M. D., Howieson, D. B., Bigler, E. D., & Tranel, D. (2012). *Neuropsychological Assessment* (5th ed.). Oxford University Press.

Marini, Z., & Case, R. (1994). The development of abstract reasoning about the physical and social world. *Child Development, 65*(1), 147–159. https://doi.org/10.2307/1131372.

McDonald, S., Delis, D. C., Norman, M. A., Tecoma, E. S., & Iragui-Madozi, V. J. (2008). A componential analysis of proverb interpretation in patients with frontal lobe epilepsy and temporal lobe epilepsy: Relationships with disease-related factors. *The Clinical Neuropsychologist, 22*(3), 480–496. https://doi.org/10.1080/13854040701363828.

Murphy, P., Shallice, T., Robinson, G., MacPherson, S. E., Turner, M., Woollett, K., Bozzali, M., & Cipolotti, L. (2013). Impairments in proverb interpretation following focal frontal lobe lesions. *Neuropsychologia, 51*(11), 2075–2086.

Naglieri, J. A., & Goldstein, S. (2013). *Comprehensive Executive Function Inventory (CEFI)*. Multi-Health Systems.

Naglieri, J. A., & Goldstein, S. (2017). *Comprehensive Executive Function Inventory Adult. (CEFI Adult)*. Multi-Health Systems.

Nippold, M. A. (2016). *Later Language Development: School-Age Children, Adolescents, and Young Adults* (4th ed.). PRO-ED.

Norbury, C. F. (2004). Factors supporting idiom comprehension in children with communication disorders. *Journal of Speech, Language, and Hearing Research, 47*(5), 1179–1193. https://doi.org/10.1044/1092-4388(2004/087).

Ounis, M. (2021). Relationship between creativity and tolerance of ambiguity to understand metaphorical polysemy: A pilot study. In *The Sixth International Conference on Languages, Linguistics, Translation and Literature* (Vol. 2, pp. 91–103). Ahwaz, Iran.

Paul, R., & Norbury, C. F. (2012). *Language Disorders from Infancy Through Adolescence: Listening, Speaking, Reading, Writing, and Communicating* (4th ed.). Elsevier.

Pexman, P. M. (2008). It's fascinating research: The cognition of verbal irony. *Current Directions in Psychological Science, 17*(4), 286–290. https://doi.org/10.1111/j.1467-8721.2008.00591.x.

Pierce, R. S., MacLaren, R., & Chiappe, D. L. (2010). The role of working memory in the metaphor interference effect. *Psychonomic Bulletin & Review, 17*(3), 400–404.

Raven, J., Rust, J., Chan, F., & Zhou, X. (2018). *Raven's 2 Progressive Matrices, Clinical Edition*. Pearson.

Roth, R. M., Isquith, P. K., & Gioia, G. A. (2005). *Behavior Rating Inventory of Executive Function—Adult Version (BRIEF-A)*. PAR.

Wechsler, D. (2014). *Wechsler Intelligence Scale for Children* (5th ed.). Pearson.

Wechsler, D. (2024). *Wechsler Adult Intelligence Scale* (5th ed.). Pearson.

Wiig, E. H., Semel, E., & Secord, W. A. (2013). *Clinical Evaluation of Language Fundamentals* (5th ed.). Pearson.

Zelazo, P. D., & Carlson, S. M. (2012). Hot and cool executive function in childhood and adolescence: Development and plasticity. *Child Development Perspectives, 6*(4), 354–360. https://doi.org/10.1111/j.1750-8606.2012.00246.x.

Seven

RISK–REWARD DECISION TEST

CLINICAL VIGNETTE

Marcus Green is a 28-year-old referred for neuropsychological evaluation following concerns about poor financial decision-making and job instability. His partner reported that Marcus made impulsive choices undermining his long-term goals, including high-risk financial gambles and quitting jobs over minor frustrations. Marcus acknowledged understanding consequences intellectually but said he "can't resist in the moment."

During the D-KEFS Advanced Risk–Reward Decision Test, the examiner carefully observed which tier contributed to Marcus's risk-taking pattern. He had no difficulty with Tier 1 visual processing, quickly scanning options and tracking outcomes accurately. His Tier 2 basic comprehension was intact; he grasped instructions immediately and could articulate the probability structure: "So the high-risk one pays more points but doesn't hit as often—got it."

His Tier 3 cold executive functions appeared adequate. After several trials, he correctly identified that "the low-risk option is consistently better over time." Despite this understanding, Marcus's performance revealed profound Tier 3 hot executive dysfunction. He persistently selected the high-risk option, accumulating significantly less money than expected. When the examiner commented on this pattern after the test was completed, Marcus acknowledged it: "Yeah, I know the odds weren't great, but I felt like the big win was coming." Even after repeated losses, he couldn't resist the emotional pull of potential high rewards.

This dissociation—intact cold executive understanding but impaired hot executive management of emotional arousal and delayed gratification—explained why traditional cognitive interventions hadn't identified his risky or impulsive decision-making in real life. Recommendations included targeting emotional regulation and tolerance for delayed gratification, specifically in motivationally salient contexts.

TEST DESCRIPTION

The D-KEFS Advanced Risk–Reward Decision Test (RISK) represents an innovation in executive function assessment by explicitly measuring the interplay between hot and cold executive functions within a single, ecologically valid task. Designed for adults aged 19–90 years, RISK is comprised of 60 trials in a virtual horse racing game where examinees employ both cold executive functions (problem-solving, feedback utilization, abstract reasoning) and hot executive functions (emotional inhibition, risk aversion, delayed gratification) to maximize gains while minimizing losses. Most people can complete the test in 6–7 minutes.

For each race, three horses appear at varying distances from the finish line, with the bottom horse closest (highest probability of winning, $25 payout, lowest monetary loss potential), the middle horse at intermediate distance (moderate probability of winning, $50 payout, moderate monetary loss potential), and the top horse farthest away (lowest probability of winning, $100 payout, highest monetary loss potential). The examinee selects one horse per race and immediately sees the animated outcome. If their horse finishes first, they gain the corresponding amount; if third, they lose that amount; if second, their total remains unchanged. The goal is to accumulate at least $300 by the 60th race.

The test's design clarifies risk–reward contingencies upfront, both visually through horses' starting positions and verbally through explicit instructions. This reduces the trial-and-error learning component seen in similar measures like the Iowa Gambling Task (Bechara, 2016), creating a more homogeneous assessment of decision-making style. The emotional engagement fostered by animated races, galloping sounds, and visual rewards (medals, coins dropping) intentionally heightens visceral reactions, increasing hot executive function demands.

DON'T FORGET

RISK assesses the integration of hot and cold executive functions within a single measure. Success requires not just understanding probabilities (cold EF) but also managing the emotional pull of potential rewards and the frustration of losses (hot EF). This integration makes it valuable for evaluating real-world decision-making where cognitive understanding doesn't always translate to adaptive choices.

RISK provides four core scaled scores: Total Net Earnings (overall performance across all 60 trials) and three block scores reflecting performance across races 1–20, 21–40, and 41–60. Process scores include percentage of selections for each horse type, risky selections following wins, and conservative selections following losses, helping clinicians parse whether difficulties stem primarily from cold executive function deficits (poor problem-solving, inadequate feedback utilization), hot executive function problems (impulsivity, poor delayed gratification), or both.

CAUTION

RISK does not involve the examinee's actual money, limiting how personally meaningful the outcomes may be compared to real-world financial decisions. When formulating interpretations about hot executive functions based on RISK performance, always assess whether the examinee exhibits similar emotional dysregulation, impulsivity, and risky behaviors in their real-world functioning through clinical interview, collateral reports, and behavioral rating scales.

Rapid Reference 7.1

RISK Test Overview

Element	Description
Age range	19–90 years (adults only)
Format	Virtual horse racing game with 60 trials
Time limit	10 seconds per trial; approximately 6–7 minutes total
Response format	Stylus selection on Client Device
Materials	Client Device, Practitioner Device, stylus
Discontinuation	After 60 races OR 5 time-elapsed races (consecutive or nonconsecutive)
Minimum for scoring	55 races completed (including time-elapsed races)
Primary constructs	Tier 3 Cold EF (feedback utilization, trend analysis); Tier 3 Hot EF (emotional inhibition, delayed gratification, risk calibration)

HIERARCHICAL TIER ANALYSIS

RISK can be analyzed through the four-tier framework, with performance reflecting processes ranging from basic perception and language to higher-order metacognitive integration.

Tier 1: Foundational Processes (Nonexecutive)

RISK requires several foundational abilities before higher-level executive functions can be assessed.

Language Comprehension
Understanding risk–reward contingencies explained in instructions is necessary—specifically that the bottom horse is most likely to win but offers the smallest payout, while the top horse is least likely to win but offers the largest payout. While the visual display reinforces these contingencies (horses' starting positions relative to the finish line), verbal instructions provide explicit clarification. Examinees with significant language impairments or receptive aphasia may struggle with Tier 1 demands.

Visual Processing
Examinees must perceive the three horses, their relative positions, the finish line, and monetary values displayed. They must visually track the race animation and perceive outcomes (first, second, or third place ribbons). Individuals with visual field deficits, significant visual acuity problems, or visuoperceptual impairments may experience Tier 1 limitations affecting performance independent of executive function.

Basic Motor Control
Using the stylus to select a horse within the 10-second time limit requires minimal motor demands—a tap on the chosen horse—but examinees with severe tremor, paralysis, or motor planning deficits may struggle to execute responses efficiently.

Tier 1 Impairment Pattern
When an examinee performs poorly on RISK, the examiner should first rule out these Tier 1 limitations. Did the examinee understand the instructions and risk–reward structure? Could they perceive the visual display adequately? Were motor limitations evident? Tier 1 limitations manifest as fundamental difficulty understanding or executing the task, with examinees asking repeated questions about instructions, seeming confused about which horse to select, or having difficulty tracking the visual display. This pattern is relatively rare but might occur with significant language impairment, dementia, or severe cognitive limitation. Practitioners may want to consider the utility of giving RISK (or any other instrument) based on known client deficits.

Tier 2: Bridging Processes

Tier 2 bridging functions include processes more complex than basic sensory-motor abilities but not yet full-fledged executive functions.

Sustained Attention
Maintaining engagement across 60 trials is required. Unlike tests requiring sustained attention over longer durations, RISK presents discrete trials with immediate feedback, visual animation, and auditory stimulation, potentially making attention maintenance more engaging and therefore less demanding. Nevertheless, examinees must remain engaged throughout all trials. Attentional lapses might manifest as time-elapsed trials where no selection is made within the 10-second limit, or increasingly random selections suggesting disengagement.

Working Memory
Working memory demands are relatively modest compared to tests like the Tower Test. Examinees must hold in mind the general risk–reward structure (which horse represents which level of risk) and track their running total

to monitor progress toward the $300 goal. However, the visual display continuously shows the current total, reducing memory load. Examinees with significant working memory impairments might forget which horse represents which risk level, but most adults can meet these Tier 2 demands without difficulty.

Basic Procedural Learning

Examinees become familiar with the selection-race-outcome sequence as the test progresses. They learn that selecting a horse immediately triggers the race, that outcomes are displayed via ribbons and updated totals, and that the next race begins promptly. This procedural aspect is straightforward, and most examinees adapt quickly.

Tier 2 Deficit Pattern

Tier 2 difficulties are relatively uncommon on RISK given its straightforward structure and engaging format. When suspected, consider whether the examinee has more pervasive attention or working memory deficits, or if their difficulties are more likely due to decreased stamina from conditions like chronic pain, migraine headaches, or illness. Multiple time-elapsed trials suggest attentional problems, while repeatedly forgetting which horse represents which payout, despite a visual display, suggests working memory limitations.

Tier 3: Core Executive Functions

RISK's primary assessment value lies at Tier 3, where it uniquely measures both cold and hot executive functions within an integrated, emotionally engaging task. The distinction between these two domains is central to interpreting performance patterns.

Cold Executive Functions

RISK assesses multiple cold executive functions that operate in emotionally neutral, analytical contexts.

Problem-Solving Through Feedback Utilization

This is central to RISK performance. At the test's outset, examinees don't know whether the high-risk, medium-risk, or low-risk strategy will produce the best outcomes. Examinees must use win/loss feedback after each race to deduce which strategy is most effective. RISK's predetermined outcomes are calibrated such that consistently selecting the $25 horse yields the largest net gains, the $50 horse produces moderate gains, and the $100 horse results in net losses. However, this pattern emerges only across multiple trials; individual races can produce misleading feedback. Examinees with strong cold executive functions integrate feedback across trials to identify the optimal strategy despite intermittent contradictory outcomes. Deficits manifest as persistent selection of suboptimal strategies even after experiencing poor outcomes.

Abstract Reasoning (Trend Analysis)

Feedback on RISK is probabilistic rather than absolute. Unlike tasks where a specific response always yields the same outcome, any horse selection can win, lose, or place second on any given trial. To succeed, examinees must recognize that the key is identifying trends across multiple trials rather than reacting to individual outcomes. An examinee might notice that the $25 horse wins more frequently than it loses over time, even though it doesn't win every race. Recognizing this trend requires abstracting beyond single instances to identify patterns. Deficits often manifest as trial-by-trial selections, with the examinee shifting to the horse that just won, pursuing a recency-based strategy rather than recognizing broader trends.

Planning and Strategic Thinking

Effective performance involves formulating an overarching approach to the task rather than responding impulsively to immediate contingencies. An examinee with strong planning skills might explicitly articulate a strategy: "I'm going to stick mostly with the safe horse but occasionally try the medium one." Deficits manifest as reactive, moment-to-moment decision-making without a coherent strategy. When asked about their approach, they may say, "I just picked whatever felt right."

Cognitive Flexibility

This becomes relevant when examinees recognize that their initial strategy isn't working and need to shift approaches. Deficits appear as rigid adherence to an initial strategy despite poor outcomes. The examinee might repeatedly select the same horse throughout all 60 trials, never adjusting, even as their total stagnates or declines.

Tier 3 Cold EF Impairment Pattern

Cold executive deficits manifest as persistent poor performance across all blocks without improvement. The examinee shows no learning trajectory despite repeated feedback. Net Earnings remain below average on races 1–20, 21–40, and 41–60 alike. Process scores reveal scattered selections across all three horse types without clear pattern or strategy shift over time. The examinee cannot articulate why they're struggling or what strategy might work better. This pattern reflects deficits in feedback utilization, trend analysis, or strategic planning that prevent the examinee from solving the problem, even given 60 trials of explicit feedback.

Hot Executive Functions

RISK's most distinctive feature is its explicit assessment of hot executive functions—cognitive control processes operating under emotionally arousing or motivationally salient conditions (Zelazo & Carlson, 2012).

Emotional Inhibition and Delayed Gratification

These are perhaps the most critical hot executive functions assessed. To maximize long-term gains, examinees must tolerate the lack of excitement associated with consistently selecting the $25 horse. This conservative strategy requires patience—the willingness to accept small, steady gains over an extended period rather than pursuing the emotional rush of potentially large payouts. The marshmallow test research demonstrates that the ability to delay gratification in childhood predicts numerous life outcomes decades later (Casey et al., 2011; Mischel et al., 1989), and RISK provides a window into these capacities in adults.

The test's design intentionally amplifies this emotional challenge. The animated races, galloping sounds, ribbons, and coin-dropping audio for wins all heighten emotional engagement. When the $100 horse wins, the examinee experiences a strong positive emotional response. This intermittent reinforcement creates a powerful emotional pull toward risky selections despite poor long-term outcomes. Consistently choosing the $25 horse feels boring. There's less excitement, less drama, smaller victories. Tolerating this boredom requires emotional inhibition.

Deficits in delayed gratification manifest as a strong preference for the high-risk, high-reward option despite poor outcomes. The examinee understands intellectually that the risky choice isn't optimal—they may even verbalize this understanding—but they cannot resist the emotional allure of potential big wins. This dissociation between cold (knowing) and hot (doing) executive functions characterizes many real-world decision-making failures and has been documented in individuals with ventromedial prefrontal damage, who demonstrate intact problem-solving but impaired real-world decision-making (Bechara et al., 1994).

Marcus's case vignette illustrates this pattern. He correctly identified that "the low-risk option is mathematically better over time" (intact cold executive function) yet persistently selected the high-risk option, explaining "I feel like the big win is coming" (impaired hot executive function). This inability to resist immediate emotional gratification despite understanding long-term consequences parallels problems seen in individuals with Attention-Deficit/Hyperactivity Disorder (ADHD) (Castellanos et al., 2006), substance use disorders, or ventromedial prefrontal damage. This can also be seen in a variety of psychiatric conditions with frontally prominent deficits, like bipolar disorder, obsessive compulsive disorder (OCD), post-traumatic stress disorder (PTSD), eating disorders, and others.

Risk Aversion and Tolerance for Negative Outcomes

These represent complementary hot executive functions. Some examinees demonstrate heightened aversion to losses, compelling them to make increasingly conservative selections. After experiencing a loss, they may become anxious or fearful about future losses, driving them toward the safest option regardless of strategic considerations. While this emotional reaction happens to benefit performance on RISK (since the conservative strategy is optimal), excessive risk aversion can be maladaptive in real-world contexts where calculated risks are sometimes necessary.

A lack of risk aversion—diminished arousal or fear response to potential losses—can be equally problematic. Some examinees appear emotionally unaffected by losses, showing minimal distress when they lose $100. This insensitivity to loss can combine with impulsivity to produce highly risky decision-making, similar to the diminished psychophysiological arousal to losses documented in ventromedial prefrontal clients (Bechara et al., 1994).

Frustration Tolerance and Emotional Regulation
These become increasingly relevant as the test progresses, especially for examinees performing poorly. As net earnings stagnate or decline, frustration may mount. Some examinees become visibly upset, making comments like "This is ridiculous!" or "Nothing's working!" Additionally, the repetitive nature of 60 trials can itself trigger frustration independent of performance quality. Some examinees, particularly those with attention difficulties, low frustration tolerance, or reduced engagement capacity, express boredom or irritation with the task length itself: "This is taking forever," "Do I really have to do all of these?" This task-fatigue frustration differs from performance-based frustration but similarly compromises hot EF, leading to increasingly impulsive or careless selections just to "get it over with" or, in extreme cases, refusing to continue. This emotional arousal can further impair decision-making, creating a negative spiral: poor performance causes frustration, leading to impulsive decisions that result in worse performance and fuel more frustration. Examinees with strong hot executive functions maintain emotional control even when frustrated, while those with hot executive deficits may become dysregulated, abandoning any coherent approach as emotional arousal overrides cognitive control.

Response Time as a Hot EF Indicator
The 10-second response deadline reveals hot EF individual differences. Impulsive examinees with poor emotional inhibition typically respond very quickly, often tapping immediately without adequate consideration. In contrast, anxious or perfectionistic examinees may exceed the 10-second limit repeatedly, paralyzed by indecision or fear of making mistakes. These time-elapsed trials incur financial penalties (after the first one), creating a secondary source of frustration for already-anxious examinees. Multiple time-elapsed trials suggest either Tier 2 attentional lapses (neglecting to respond) or hot EF anxiety/perfectionism overwhelming decision-making capacity. Observing whether time-elapsed trials cluster early (learning the response format) versus throughout (persistent indecision) helps distinguish these mechanisms.

Tier 3 Cold EF Impairment Pattern
Hot executive deficits with intact cold functions produce a distinctive dissociation. The examinee may explicitly verbalize understanding of the optimal strategy, "I know the $25 horse is the smart choice," yet continue selecting riskier options. They might explain, "But it's so boring," "I feel like taking a chance," or "Maybe I'll hit the big one." Net Earnings remain below average across all blocks despite cognitive understanding. Process scores reveal persistently high selection of the $100 or $50 horses and elevated Risky Selection Following a Win scores. This pattern parallels Marcus's vignette and suggests primary hot executive dysfunction.

Combined Cold and Hot Executive Deficits

When both systems are impaired, performance is poor across all blocks without improvement. The examinee neither figures out the optimal strategy (cold EF deficit) nor manages emotional impulses effectively (hot EF deficit). They may make increasingly desperate or random selections as frustration mounts. Net Earnings scores fall below average across all three blocks, process scores

> **CAUTION**
>
> Hot executive function deficits on RISK can present as cold executive problems, and vice versa. An examinee with poor feedback utilization might appear impulsive, while someone with strong emotional reactions might seem to lack problem-solving skills. The key distinction lies in examining the pattern over time and comparing cold versus hot executive functions. Does the examinee understand the optimal strategy but fail to implement it (hot EF deficit), or do they genuinely not figure out which strategy is best (cold EF deficit)? Process scores and behavioral observations help make this critical distinction.

show scattered selections across all horse types without a clear pattern, and behavioral observations reveal both strategic confusion and emotional dysregulation.

Tier 4: Higher-Order Integration and Metacognition

RISK assesses executive functioning through Tier 3 but does not substantially engage Tier 4 metacognitive processes. The task structure remains constant across trials, requiring identification and implementation of an optimal strategy (Tier 3 cold and hot EF) rather than metacognitive strategy evaluation, performance monitoring, or adaptive switching based on self-assessment. Unlike tests requiring ongoing strategy evaluation and adjustment (e.g., Tower Test, Sorting Test), success on RISK depends on discovering and consistently applying an effective approach.

Some examinees spontaneously demonstrate metacognitive awareness through verbal comments—"I'm not doing well; I need to change my approach"—but this reflection is not required for successful performance and is not systematically assessed by the test. An examinee could succeed by consistently selecting the $25 horse without any metacognitive reflection about their strategy or performance. Conversely, strong metacognitive awareness doesn't guarantee success if Tier 3 hot EF deficits prevent implementation. When present, such metacognitive comments provide qualitative context for interpretation but don't represent a distinct level of assessment within RISK's structure.

Rapid Reference 7.2

Tier Structure at a Glance

Tier	Processes
Tier 1: Foundational processes (nonexecutive)	Language comprehension (understanding instructions and contingencies) Visual processing (perceiving horse positions, monetary values) Basic motor control (stylus selection within time limit)
Tier 2: Bridging processes	Sustained attention (maintaining focus across 60 trials) Working memory (tracking wins/losses and running total) Basic procedural learning (understanding task mechanics)
Tier 3: Cold executive functions	Problem-solving through feedback utilization Abstract reasoning (trend analysis across variable outcomes) Planning and strategic thinking Cognitive flexibility (adjusting strategy based on outcomes)
Tier 3: Hot executive functions	Emotional inhibition and delayed gratification Risk aversion and tolerance for negative outcomes Frustration tolerance and emotional regulation
Tier 4: Higher-order integration and metacognition	Not substantially engaged by RISK administration

ADMINISTRATION

NOTE: Refer to the Examiner's Manual for complete and detailed administration instructions. The Examiner's Manual provides verbatim instructions and clinicians should follow these precisely to ensure standardized administration.

RISK administration is largely automated through the digital platform, with the system controlling stimulus presentation, recording responses, timing, and computing scores. The examiner's primary role is to explain the task, monitor engagement, and note behavioral observations.

Materials and Setup

RISK requires the Examiner's Manual, Client Device, Practitioner Device, and Stylus. Before beginning, ensure both devices are charged, connected, and the stylus is functional. Verify a comfortable stylus grip and ensure no screen glare. The Client Device is placed flat in landscape orientation in front of the examinee, who receives a stylus for responding. The test begins with a sound check to ensure comfortable volume, as auditory feedback (galloping hooves during races, coins dropping for wins) is integral to the experience. The Practitioner Device displays all administration instructions, which should be read verbatim in a natural, conversational manner.

Standard Administration Procedure

Instructions explain that three horses will race, each starting at a different distance from the finish line. The bottom horse starts closest and is most likely to win, but pays only $25. The top horse starts farthest and is least likely to win, but pays $100. The middle horse represents intermediate risk and payout at $50. The examinee learns they have 10 seconds to select a horse for each race, and the goal is to accumulate at least $300 by race 60. If their horse finishes first, they gain the corresponding amount; if third, they lose it; if second, their total stays the same.

After reading instructions, the examiner touches the timer on the Practitioner Device to begin timing and activate the Client Device. The examinee uses the stylus to tap their chosen horse, immediately triggering the race animation. The race plays out with galloping sounds until a winner crosses the finish line. Visual and auditory feedback automatically displays the outcome (ribbons for 1st, 2nd, or 3rd place), money gained or lost, and updated total earnings.

Critical Administration Points

Never provide guidance on which horse to select or hint about strategy (e.g., "Maybe try betting less money"). If asked which strategy to use, respond: "I can't tell you; just try to end up with at least $300 by the 60th race." The Speech Bubble button on the practitioner tablet includes prompts for how to respond.

The first time the examinee doesn't respond within 5 seconds, a prompt appears on the practitioner's device. Read the prompt: "Go ahead and make your choice." The test doesn't pause for this prompt.

The first time the examinee doesn't respond within 10 seconds, a notification pauses the test. Read: "You didn't make a choice in time for this race. Your money will stay the same this time, but you'll lose money each time this happens again. Let's try another one." After reading this, press OK to continue.

After a fifth time-elapsed race (consecutive or nonconsecutive), the test discontinues. Read: "Time's up" and press Discontinue.

If the examinee completes fewer than 55 races (including time-elapsed races), the overall score cannot be derived, though raw response data for completed races will be available.

Encourage examinees to make selections for each race. Provide general encouragement as needed—"This is hard for many people," "Just do your best"—but avoid specific strategy suggestions. Although unusual, some examinees may become genuinely upset during the task. Be especially attentive to negative emotional reactions, provide support and encouragement, and document emotional responses in the Observations Checklist. If an examinee is struggling and further administration is unlikely to yield clinically useful results, the manual discontinue button may be used, though normative scores may not be calculated if fewer than 55 races are completed.

BEHAVIORAL OBSERVATIONS

Qualitative observations during RISK administration provide useful information for interpreting performance, particularly regarding hot executive functions.

Emotional Responses

RISK can elicit strong emotional reactions—this is by design. Note whether the examinee becomes visibly excited after wins, distressed after losses, or frustrated as the task progresses. Many examinees become animated during races, even rooting for their selected horse. While emotional engagement is normal, extreme or poorly regulated reactions warrant documentation—dysregulation after losses with angry comments or visible agitation, exaggerated excitement after wins, or remarkably flat affect throughout with no reaction to wins or losses (suggesting depression, apathy, or lack of investment).

Response Timing and Decision-Making Style

Observe whether the examinee responds quickly or deliberately. Some examinees tap a horse immediately, suggesting impulsive decision-making without careful consideration. Others pause, perhaps looking between horses or visibly thinking before selecting. While there's no "correct" response time, consistently impulsive responding (especially when coupled with poor outcomes) suggests hot executive dysfunction with behavioral inhibition. Note whether selections demonstrate a consistent strategy or appear random without a discernible pattern.

Verbalizations and Self-Monitoring

Many examinees verbalize thoughts during RISK. Comments like "I know I should pick the safe one, but…" reveal intact cognitive understanding undermined by emotional impulses—the hallmark of hot executive dysfunction. Some examinees demonstrate metacognitive awareness: "I need to play it safer," suggesting intact self-monitoring even if implementation is impaired. Others show limited awareness, expressing surprise at poor outcomes despite persistently selecting high-risk options. Frustration-related comments often increase as examinees fall behind their goal. Note whether these coincide with strategic changes (e.g., increasingly desperate selections) or reflect emotional dysregulation affecting decision-making.

Change Across Blocks

Observe whether approach, emotional reactions, or engagement changes across the three 20-race blocks. Some examinees start enthusiastically but become visibly frustrated or bored by the third block. Others show increasing strategic sophistication, with early random selections giving way to more consistent approaches. Deteriorating engagement and attention to task in later blocks might explain performance declines in races 41–60 despite adequate early performance.

SCORING

RISK generates all scores automatically through the digital administration system. The system records each selection, tracks outcomes, computes running totals, and calculates all core and process scores without examiner intervention. This automated scoring eliminates calculation errors and provides immediate access to comprehensive performance data.

Core Scaled Scores

RISK provides four core scaled scores (M = 10, SD = 3) reflecting net earnings across the full test and within each 20-race block.

Total Net Earnings

This score provides the best measure of global performance because it factors in gains and losses across all 60 races. The raw score represents the examinee's net earnings—total money earned minus total money lost—across the 55–60 races completed (at least 55 races must be completed for this score to be derived). Higher scaled scores reflect better performance (larger net gains), while lower scaled scores reflect smaller net gains or net losses.

Net Earnings Races 1–20

This score reflects net earnings during the first block of 20 trials, when examinees are initially learning the task contingencies. The starting amount is $0; no earnings from subsequent blocks are included. Performance during this block typically reflects early problem-solving attempts before the optimal strategy has been identified.

Net Earnings Races 21–40

This score reflects net earnings during the middle block of 20 trials. Performance often improves during this block as examinees begin recognizing that conservative selections yield better long-term outcomes. Comparing this score to Net Earnings Races 1–20 reveals a learning trajectory.

Net Earnings Races 41–60

This score reflects net earnings during the final block of 20 trials. By this point, most examinees with intact cold executive functions have identified the optimal strategy. Decline during this block, despite adequate earlier performance, may suggest hot executive dysfunction—boredom with the conservative approach leading to increased risk-taking.

Process Scores

RISK provides five process scores reported as base rates that help distinguish whether performance difficulties reflect cold executive dysfunction, hot executive dysfunction, or both. Time-elapsed races or races past the discontinue are not included in the calculation.

Percent $25 Horse Selections

This score reflects the percentage of races for which the $25 horse selection was made. Consistently choosing the $25 horse is the best long-term strategy; a higher base rate reflects better overall performance. Lower base rates indicate the examinee frequently selected riskier options, suggesting possible difficulties with delayed gratification or feedback utilization.

Percent $50 Horse Rejections

This score reflects the percentage of races for which the $50 horse was not selected. Higher base rates reflect better performance, indicating the examinee avoided this intermediate-risk option.

Percent $100 Horse Rejections

This score reflects the percentage of races for which the $100 horse was not selected. Higher base rates reflect better performance. A tendency to select the $100 horse (low base rate on rejections) indicates greater problems with the hot executive function components, including impulsivity and lack of risk aversion.

Risky Selection Following a Win

This score reflects the percentage of races following a win where the examinee selected a horse of higher value or stayed with the $50 or $100 horse. Frequent use of this strategy draws the examinee away from the safest long-term selection. A higher base rate reflects better performance (the examinee refrained from this ineffective strategy). A lower base rate suggests the examinee exhibited problems with emotional inhibition and risk aversion by seeking excitement after positive reinforcement rather than maintaining a conservative approach.

Conservative Selection Following a Loss

This score reflects the percentage of races following a loss where the examinee selected a lower value horse or stayed with the $25 horse. This conservative response to losses benefits long-term performance. A higher base rate reflects better performance. A lower base rate suggests the examinee took greater risks after losses, possibly reflecting impulsivity, lack of risk aversion, or weakness in abstract reasoning (failing to recognize that a single loss doesn't change the optimal strategy).

Additional Raw Scores

Beyond scaled scores, two raw scores provide information about test completion and engagement.

Total Races Completed

This raw score indicates the number of races completed by the examinee, excluding time-elapsed races. Most examinees complete all 60 races; however, this score provides information about how far an examinee advanced if they did not complete all races.

Total Time-Elapsed Races

This raw score indicates the number of races for which a horse selection was not made within 10 seconds. This score provides insight into whether an examinee had difficulty making decisions quickly. Elevated time-elapsed races may reflect Tier 2 attentional lapses, anxiety-driven indecision, or perfectionism overwhelming decision-making capacity.

Behavioral Observations

Several base rate scores are provided for a select number of behaviors that examinees may exhibit during assessment. These quantitative scores compliment behavioral observations and provide context for interpreting how behaviors or emotional reactions may have affected an examinee's performance. See Table 9.4 in the Examiner's Manual for a listing.

Rapid Reference 7.3

Scoring Summary

Score Type	Score Name	What It Measures
Core scaled scores ($M = 10$, $SD = 3$)	Total net earnings	Global performance across all 60 races
	Net earnings races 1–20	Early learning phase; initial problem-solving
	Net earnings races 21–40	Middle block; strategy identification phase
	Net earnings races 41–60	Final block; strategy maintenance; decline may indicate hot EF dysfunction
Process scores (base rates)	Percent $25 horse selections	Conservative strategy use; higher = better
	Percent $50 horse rejections	Avoidance of intermediate risk; higher = better
	Percent $100 horse rejections	Avoidance of high risk; lower suggests hot EF difficulties
	Risky selection following a win	Emotional inhibition after positive reinforcement; higher = better
	Conservative selection following a loss	Appropriate response to negative feedback; higher = better
Additional raw scores	Total races completed	Number of races completed (typically 60)
	Total time-elapsed races	Selections not made within 10 seconds; may indicate attention or anxiety issues

COMMON ADMINISTRATION ERRORS

Although RISK administration is largely automated, several errors can compromise the validity of results or limit the clinical utility of the data obtained.

Providing Strategic Guidance

The most critical administration error is suggesting which horse to select or hinting at a strategy. Comments like "Maybe try betting less" or "That's a risky choice" invalidate test results by providing information the examinee should derive independently through feedback utilization. If the examinee asks which strategy to use, respond only with the scripted prompt: "I can't tell you; just try to end up with at least $300 by the 60th race."

Failing to Read Prompts Verbatim

The 5-second warning, 10-second time-elapsed notification, and discontinue prompt should be read exactly as written. Paraphrasing or elaborating on these prompts introduces variability that may affect examinee responding. The prompts are specifically worded to provide standardized information without strategic guidance.

Not Monitoring Engagement

Because RISK administration is largely automated, some examiners disengage from the testing process. However, continuous observation is essential for documenting behavioral observations that inform interpretation—emotional reactions to wins and losses, response timing patterns, verbalizations about strategy, and signs of frustration or boredom. These qualitative observations are critical for distinguishing cold from hot executive dysfunction.

Interrupting During Races

Once the examinee selects a horse and the race animation begins, avoid interrupting with comments or encouragement until the race concludes and feedback is displayed. Interruptions during the race can distract the examinee from attending to the outcome, potentially affecting subsequent selections.

Inadequate Device Positioning

The Client Device must be placed flat in landscape orientation directly in front of the examinee. Improper positioning can affect response accuracy and timing, particularly for examinees with visual or motor limitations. Ensure the sound check is completed at a comfortable volume before beginning, as auditory feedback is integral to the emotional engagement the test is designed to elicit.

Discontinuing Prematurely

Some examiners may be tempted to discontinue when examinees become frustrated or perform poorly. However, completing all 60 races (or reaching the automatic discontinue after 5 time-elapsed races) provides the most clinically useful data. The pattern of performance across all three blocks—including deterioration in later blocks—yields important diagnostic information. Use the Manual Discontinue button only when further administration is truly unlikely to yield clinically useful results, recognizing that normative scores may not be reported if fewer than 55 races are completed.

INTERPRETATION

RISK provides a unique window into the interplay between cold and hot executive functions during decision-making under conditions of risk and reward. Interpretation focuses on identifying whether performance difficulties reflect cold executive dysfunction (problem-solving, feedback utilization, trend analysis), hot executive dysfunction (emotional inhibition, delayed gratification, risk aversion), or both. The hierarchical tier framework guides systematic analysis from foundational processes through higher-order executive functions.

Using the Hierarchical Framework for Differential Diagnosis

The following five-step framework ensures systematic evaluation of RISK performance, moving from foundational abilities through executive functions to identify the primary locus of dysfunction.

Step 1: Rule Out Tier 1 Limitations
Evaluate whether foundational abilities were adequate for a valid assessment. Did the examinee understand the instructions and risk–reward structure? Could they perceive the visual display adequately, including the three horses, their positions relative to the finish line, and the monetary values? Were motor limitations evident that interfered with timely stylus responses? Examinees with significant receptive language impairment may not have understood the risk–reward contingencies despite both visual and verbal explanation.

Step 2: Evaluate Tier 2 Bridging Processes
Assess whether sustained attention and working memory were adequate throughout the 60 trials. Multiple time-elapsed races may suggest attentional difficulties, particularly if they occur throughout the test rather than clustering early (learning phase) or late (fatigue/frustration). Examinees must maintain in working memory the general risk–reward structure and track their running total, though the visual display reduces memory load by continuously showing current earnings.

Step 3: Analyze Tier 3 Cold Executive Patterns
Examine whether the examinee successfully identified the optimal strategy through feedback utilization and trend analysis. The key indicators include the pattern of Net Earnings across the three blocks and the Percent $25 Horse Selections base rate. Gradually improving performance across blocks—below average in Races 1–20, improving in Races 21–40, average in Races 41–60—suggests intact but slow cold executive problem-solving. The examinee eventually figured out that conservative selections yield better outcomes. Persistently poor performance across all three blocks, with low Percent $25 Horse Selections, suggests more significant cold executive dysfunction: the examinee never identified the optimal strategy despite 60 trials of feedback. Compare behavioral observations: Did the examinee verbalize understanding of the optimal strategy? If they articulated that "the safe horse is probably best" but didn't implement this understanding, the deficit is more likely hot than cold executive dysfunction.

Step 4: Evaluate Tier 3 Hot Executive Factors
This is the critical distinction on RISK. Examine whether emotional factors compromised the implementation of an understood strategy. The hallmark of hot executive dysfunction is the dissociation between knowing and doing. The examinee verbalizes understanding that conservative selections are optimal, but cannot resist the emotional pull of riskier choices. Key indicators include low base rates on Risky Selection Following a Win (the examinee increased risk after positive reinforcement despite knowing better) and elevated $100 horse selections. Behavioral observations are essential: Did the examinee show visible excitement during races? Express boredom with conservative selections? Make comments like "I know I should pick the safe one, but..." or "Maybe I'll get lucky this time"? Late deterioration—adequate performance in Races 1–40 followed by decline in Races 41–60—often reflects hot executive dysfunction, as examinees become bored with the repetitive conservative approach and seek excitement through riskier selections.

Step 5: Assess Tier 4 Integration and Metacognition
RISK does not substantially engage Tier 4 metacognitive processes. The task structure remains constant across trials, requiring identification and implementation of an optimal strategy (Tier 3) rather than metacognitive strategy evaluation, performance monitoring, or adaptive integration across changing task demands. However, clinicians can note whether the examinee demonstrated metacognitive awareness during testing. Comments like "I'm not doing well—I need to change my approach" reflect intact metacognition even if strategy implementation was impaired. Absence of such self-monitoring despite poor performance may suggest broader metacognitive limitations worth exploring through other measures.

PERFORMANCE PATTERNS AND CLINICAL IMPLICATIONS

RISK performance yields several recognizable patterns, each with distinct clinical implications and intervention considerations. Identifying these patterns helps clinicians move beyond global performance scores to understand the specific nature of an examinee's decision-making difficulties.

Gradual Learning Pattern

Improving Net Earnings across blocks—below average in Races 1–20, borderline in Races 21–40, average in Races 41–60—suggests intact learning potential with slow cold executive functions. The examinee eventually identified the optimal strategy but required extended exposure to feedback. Real-world implications include needing more time to master new procedures, benefiting from explicit instruction rather than discovery learning, and performing better once routines are established. These individuals may struggle initially in novel situations but adapt successfully given adequate time and experience.

Cold-Hot Dissociation Pattern

Demonstrating understanding of the optimal strategy but failing to implement it represents the hallmark hot executive deficit pattern. The examinee may verbalize "I know the safe horse is better," yet persistently select riskier options, explaining "but it's so boring" or "I feel like taking a chance." Net Earnings remain below average across all blocks despite cognitive understanding. Process scores reveal persistently high Risky Selection Following a Win and low Percent $25 Horse Selections. This pattern has profound real-world implications: these individuals analyze situations rationally, but hot executive functions fail when emotional arousal increases. This dissociation appears in ADHD (impulsive presentation), substance use disorders, bipolar disorder, and ventromedial prefrontal damage. Effective interventions target emotion regulation, mindfulness, and delay of gratification exercises.

Pervasive Executive Dysfunction Pattern

Below-average performance across all three blocks without improvement suggests severe multidimensional impairment affecting both cold and hot executive systems. The examinee neither figures out the optimal strategy nor manages emotional impulses effectively. Selections appear scattered without a coherent pattern, and behavioral observations often reveal both strategic confusion and emotional dysregulation. This pattern may appear in moderate-to-severe TBI, moderate-to-advanced dementia, and severe ADHD. These individuals require comprehensive interventions with substantial environmental supports, an external structure for decision-making, and reduced autonomy in high-stakes situations until functioning improves.

Late Deterioration Pattern

Adequate performance in Races 1–40 followed by a decline in Races 41–60 suggests intact cold executive functions with hot executive vulnerability to boredom or fatigue. The examinee identified and initially implemented the optimal strategy, but couldn't sustain the emotionally unrewarding conservative approach. This pattern may reflect low frustration tolerance, sensation-seeking traits, or difficulty maintaining effortful control over extended periods. Intervention implications include structuring tasks to maintain engagement, building in breaks or variety, and developing self-monitoring strategies for recognizing when boredom threatens performance.

Risk-Seeking Pattern

Persistently elevated $100 horse selections with low Percent $100 Horse Rejections despite experiencing losses suggests diminished risk aversion or sensation-seeking that overrides feedback learning. These examinees may show minimal distress after losses and visible excitement in pursuing high-risk options. When combined with impulsivity, this pattern creates particular vulnerability to poor judgment in high-stakes situations. Real-world concerns include financial decision-making, substance use risk, and safety behaviors. The pattern has been documented in individuals with ventromedial prefrontal involvement who show diminished psychophysiological arousal to potential losses.

Excessive Risk Aversion Pattern

Extremely conservative responding with near-exclusive $25 horse selections may reflect heightened anxiety, excessive fear of negative outcomes, or rigid adherence to a "safe" approach. While this pattern produces good RISK performance, it may indicate maladaptive real-world functioning when calculated risks are appropriate or necessary. Behavioral observations of visible anxiety, relief after avoiding losses, or distress at any negative outcome support this interpretation. These individuals may benefit from graduated exposure to tolerable risk-taking and cognitive interventions addressing catastrophic thinking about negative outcomes.

Rapid Reference 7.4

Distinguishing Tier-Level Deficits

Tier Level	Indicators	Clinical Implications
Tier 1 deficit	Fundamental difficulty understanding instructions or task structure; repeated questions about rules; confusion about which horse to select; difficulty tracking visual display; motor difficulties executing selections	Foundational limitations (language, visual processing, motor); rare on RISK; consider utility of administering given known deficits; address sensory-motor issues before executive function assessment
Tier 2 deficit	Multiple time-elapsed trials suggesting attentional lapses; forgetting which horse represents which payout despite visual display; random selections suggesting disengagement	Sustained attention or working memory limitations; consider supplementary attention (CPT-3; Conners, 2014) or working memory (WAIS-5 Digit Span; Wechsler, 2024) measures; relatively uncommon given engaging task format
Tier 3 cold deficit	Persistently poor performance across all blocks; low Percent $25 Horse Selections; scattered selections suggesting trial-and-error without pattern recognition; cannot articulate optimal strategy; gradual improvement suggests slow but intact learning	Problem-solving and feedback utilization deficits; benefits from explicit instruction and extended practice; needs more time to master new procedures; performs better once routines established
Tier 3 hot deficit	Verbalizes understanding but doesn't implement ("I know I should pick $25, but..."); elevated Risky Selection Following a Win; low Percent $100 Horse Rejections; late deterioration pattern; visible excitement, boredom with conservative choices, impulsive responding	Emotional regulation overriding cognitive insight; knowing-doing dissociation; requires emotion regulation, mindfulness, delay of gratification interventions
Tier 4	Not substantially assessed by RISK	Task structure remains constant; note metacognitive comments if present ("I need to change my approach"); explore with other measures if metacognitive limitations suspected

ECOLOGICAL VALIDITY AND FUNCTIONAL IMPLICATIONS

RISK performance relates to real-world functioning across multiple domains. The core abilities assessed—feedback utilization, trend analysis, delayed gratification, and risk calibration—underlie success in contexts where individuals must make decisions under uncertainty, resist impulsive choices, and prioritize long-term outcomes over immediate rewards.

Academic Functioning

Although RISK is administered only to adults ages 19–90, academic implications remain relevant for young adults in postsecondary education and for understanding developmental history in older examinees. Academic success requires sustained effort toward long-term goals (graduation, career preparation) despite competing short-term temptations. Students with hot executive dysfunction may understand that studying yields better outcomes than socializing but struggle to implement this knowledge when faced with immediate social rewards. The cold executive components—feedback utilization and trend analysis—support academic learning from graded assignments and recognizing which study strategies yield improvement over time. Adults returning to education or professional certification programs face similar demands.

Vocational and Daily Living

Financial decision-making represents the most direct real-world parallel to RISK performance. Managing personal finances requires resisting impulsive purchases, tolerating the delayed gratification of saving, and using feedback (account balances, debt accumulation) to adjust spending patterns. Individuals with the cold-hot dissociation pattern may understand budgeting principles intellectually but fail to implement them when confronted with appealing purchases. Occupational functioning similarly requires calibrated risk-taking: knowing when to pursue safer established approaches versus when innovation justifies risk. Career advancement often depends on tolerating extended periods of unrewarded effort (the "conservative selection" approach) rather than seeking immediate but unsustainable gains. Health behaviors—medication adherence, diet, exercise, substance use—all involve choosing smaller immediate rewards (skipping medication, eating dessert, avoiding exercise, using substances) versus larger delayed benefits. The RISK paradigm directly models these decisions: immediate emotional satisfaction versus long-term cumulative outcomes.

> **DON'T FORGET**
>
> RISK's ecological validity has inherent limitations because it doesn't involve actual monetary stakes, personal consequences, or social–emotional context. Always corroborate RISK findings with clinical interview and collateral reports about real-world decision-making (Chaytor & Schmitter-Edgecombe, 2003). Some individuals perform well on RISK's emotionally neutral decision-making but show poor judgment in personally meaningful contexts, while others show RISK difficulties that don't fully generalize to real life. RISK is best viewed as one piece of evidence about executive functioning in risk–reward contexts, not a definitive predictor of all real-world decision-making.

Social Functioning

Interpersonal relationships require risk calibration and delayed gratification. Individuals must decide how much emotional vulnerability to risk in forming connections, tolerate the delayed rewards of relationship investment, and use social feedback to adjust their approach. Those with diminished risk aversion may over-disclose prematurely or make impulsive relational decisions, while those with excessive risk aversion may avoid social engagement entirely. The hot executive components assessed by RISK—emotional inhibition and frustration tolerance—directly support managing interpersonal conflict, resisting impulsive reactions during disagreements, and maintaining relationships through inevitable periods of reduced reward. Social decision-making under uncertainty (trusting others, investing in relationships with unknown outcomes) parallels the RISK structure of making choices with probabilistic rather than guaranteed outcomes.

PRELIMINARY CLINICAL VALIDATION OF THE D-KEFS ADVANCED RISK

Clinical group studies conducted during D-KEFS Advanced standardization provide initial evidence of RISK's sensitivity to executive dysfunction (Delis & Kaplan, 2025). Because RISK is administered only to adults ages 19–90, no child clinical groups (ADHD, ASD, SLD-Math) were tested. These preliminary findings require replication and should not be used as sole diagnostic criteria, but they establish useful reference points for clinical interpretation.

Traumatic Brain Injury

The adult TBI sample (n = 30; mean GCS = 8.5) demonstrated significantly lower Total Net Earnings compared to matched controls, with a moderate effect size (d = 0.56, p = 0.01). This finding is noteworthy given RISK's minimal time demands. Unlike timed measures such as the TMT and CWIT where the TBI group showed slowed processing with preserved accuracy, the RISK deficit reflects decision-making quality rather than speed. The moderate effect size, while smaller than those observed on the TMT and CWIT, carries particular clinical significance because RISK assesses a dimension of executive functioning not captured by traditional instruments. As the D-KEFS Advanced Manual notes, RISK had the lowest correlations with WAIS-5 subtests and with other D-KEFS Advanced tests, yet remained sensitive to TBI-related deficits. This pattern suggests that RISK taps hot executive functions (emotional inhibition, delayed gratification, risk calibration) that operate somewhat independently from the cold executive functions assessed by other measures.

The TBI findings invite further investigation into whether performance difficulties reflect hot executive dysfunction (impaired emotional inhibition, diminished risk aversion), cold executive dysfunction (impaired feedback utilization, weak trend analysis), or both. RISK process scores, particularly Risky Selection Following a Win and Percent $100 Horse Rejections, may help differentiate these contributions, though additional research examining subgroup patterns is needed. Given the heterogeneity of cognitive profiles in TBI depending on lesion location and severity, individual-level analysis using the process scores is essential rather than assuming uniform impairment patterns.

Other Clinical Populations

Because RISK administration is limited to adults, no data are available for child clinical groups studied with other D-KEFS Advanced tests (ADHD, ASD, SLD-Math). The MCI sample (n = 18) was too small for reliable analysis and is not reported. Future research examining RISK performance in adults with ADHD, substance use disorders, ventromedial prefrontal lesions, and bipolar disorder would be valuable, given the theoretical relevance of hot executive dysfunction in these populations.

STRENGTHS AND WEAKNESSES

RISK offers several distinctive strengths for executive function assessment, alongside limitations that clinicians should consider when selecting measures and interpreting results.

Strengths

RISK possesses notable advantages for clinical assessment of executive functions, particularly in its unique capacity to examine hot–cold integration within a single measure.

Explicit Assessment of Hot–Cold Executive Function Integration
RISK's primary strength is its explicit measurement of both hot and cold executive functions within a single task. Most executive function measures assess predominantly cold EF (e.g., WCST; Heaton et al., 1993) or primarily hot EF (behavioral rating scales), but few integrate both. RISK requires understanding probabilities and learning from feedback (cold EF) while simultaneously managing emotional arousal and resisting impulsive gratification (hot EF).

Explicit Risk–Reward Contingencies
Unlike the Iowa Gambling Task, where examinees discover risk–reward contingencies through trial-and-error (Bechara et al., 1994), RISK explicitly clarifies them upfront both visually and verbally. This design choice reduces the learning and memory component, creating a purer assessment of decision-making style. Examinees who fail RISK do so not because they didn't learn the contingencies but because they can't implement optimal strategies despite understanding them.

Strong Ecological Validity
The engaging, game-like format with animation, sound effects, and immediate feedback creates an emotionally engaging experience paralleling real-world decision-making contexts (Parsons, 2015). This may enhance generalizability to actual decision-making compared to more abstract executive function measures.

Rich Process Scores

Beyond overall performance, RISK's process scores illuminate specific aspects of decision-making: preferred risk level, learning from wins versus losses, and consistency of strategy. These scores help distinguish cold from hot executive deficits and characterize individual decision-making styles with greater specificity than global scores alone provide.

Automated Administration and Scoring

The fully digital format eliminates scoring errors and administration variability, enhancing reliability. Automated timing, response recording, and score computation reduce examiner burden while ensuring standardized administration.

Weaknesses and Limitations

Despite its strengths, RISK has several limitations that clinicians should consider when selecting measures and interpreting results.

Limited Age Range

RISK is normed only for adults ages 19–90, excluding children and adolescents. Given that hot executive functions show protracted development through adolescence (Best & Miller, 2010), a version appropriate for younger ages would be valuable. Clinicians assessing adolescents must use alternative risk–reward measures (e.g., Iowa Gambling Task) that lack RISK's specific advantages.

Play Money Reduces Personal Stakes

RISK's most significant limitation is that outcomes involve "play money" with no real consequences. This reduces personal significance compared to actual financial decisions, potentially limiting how strongly emotions are aroused and how well performance generalizes to real-world stakes. Some examinees explicitly comment that they're "just playing a game," suggesting insufficient emotional investment. Distinguishing genuine executive dysfunction from insufficient test-taking engagement or motivation can be challenging, requiring examiner judgment based on observations and broader assessment context.

Multiple Trials

Completing 60 trials, even if they are quick, may feel like a long time for a single executive function measure. Some examinees, particularly those with ADHD, dementia, or motivational problems, may experience flagging engagement in later blocks, potentially affecting performance through attentional factors rather than core executive dysfunction.

Cannot Distinguish All Hot Executive Components

While RISK broadly assesses hot executive functions, it cannot fully distinguish among its components. Is poor performance due to impaired delayed gratification, excessive reward-seeking, insufficient risk aversion, poor frustration tolerance, or some combination? Behavioral observations provide clues, but the task doesn't systematically parse these components.

ALTERNATIVE MEASURES

When RISK administration is not feasible or when converging evidence is needed, several alternative approaches can assess risk–reward decision-making and related hot executive functions.

Within the D-KEFS Suite

No other D-KEFS Advanced subtest directly assesses risk–reward decision-making or hot executive functions to the same degree as RISK. However, several measures tap related processes. The Social Sorting Test (SST) assesses feedback utilization and cognitive flexibility in a social context, sharing the cold executive demands of learning from variable feedback. The Color-Word Interference Test Inhibition condition assesses response inhibition, a cold executive function that interacts with hot executive control during decision-making. From the original D-KEFS (Delis et al., 2001), the Tower Test requires planning and impulse control. Examinees must inhibit impulsive moves in favor of planned sequences, a demand that parallels RISK's requirement to inhibit impulsive high-risk selections. None of these alternatives captures the hot–cold executive integration that makes RISK unique, but they can provide converging evidence about component processes when RISK cannot be administered.

Beyond D-KEFS

Several measures outside the D-KEFS family assess related constructs and can provide converging evidence for clinical interpretation.

Gambling and Risk–Reward Tasks

Multiple gambling paradigms assess decision-making under conditions of uncertain reward. The Iowa Gambling Task, Second Edition (IGT2; Bechara, 2016) presents examinees with four card decks yielding different risk–reward contingencies. Unlike RISK, the IGT2 does not explicitly explain the contingencies—examinees must discover through trial and error which decks are advantageous. This implicit learning demand increases the cold executive load and can make it difficult to isolate hot executive contributions. The IGT2 has extensive research support across clinical populations, particularly substance use disorders and ventromedial prefrontal lesions. The Balloon Analogue Risk Task (BART; Lejuez et al., 2002) requires examinees to inflate a virtual balloon, earning money with each pump but risking total loss if the balloon pops. This paradigm assesses tolerance for escalating risk and has been validated in substance use and impulse control research. The Columbia Card Task (CCT; Figner et al., 2009) presents a card game where examinees choose how many cards to turn over, balancing potential gains against loss probability. The CCT provides separate indices for "hot" (affective) and "cold" (deliberative) decision-making components, offering more granular differentiation than most risk–reward measures.

Delay Discounting Measures

Delay discounting tasks assess preference for smaller immediate rewards versus larger delayed rewards, directly indexing delayed gratification capacity. Various versions exist with different administration formats and normative data, including computerized and questionnaire-based approaches. Delay discounting correlates with real-world outcomes, including substance use, financial behavior, and health decisions, making these measures valuable complements to RISK when assessing hot executive functioning.

Behavioral Rating Scales

Executive function rating scales capture real-world executive behaviors that may or may not align with performance-based measures. Because RISK is administered only to adults aged 19–90, adult versions are appropriate: the Behavior Rating Inventory of Executive Function-Adult Version (BRIEF-A; Roth et al., 2005), Comprehensive Executive Function Inventory Adult (CEFI Adult; Naglieri & Goldstein, 2017), and Delis Rating of Executive Functions-Adult (D-REF Adult; Delis, 2021) offer self-report and informant-report options. Relevant scales across these measures include Inhibit (paralleling emotional inhibition demands), Emotional Control (assessing emotional regulation in daily contexts), and the D-REF Adults' specific subscales for impulsivity and risk-taking tendencies. Discrepancies between RISK performance and rating scale elevations provide diagnostic information: adequate RISK performance with elevated rating scales may indicate that the structured, emotionally neutral testing environment does not capture hot executive challenges that emerge in personally meaningful, emotionally arousing real-world situations. Conversely, poor RISK performance with unremarkable rating scales might suggest test-specific factors such as task disengagement or comprehension issues rather than pervasive hot executive dysfunction.

SUMMARY

The D-KEFS Advanced Risk–Reward Decision Test uniquely assesses the integration of hot and cold executive functions within a single, ecologically valid measure. Through 60 trials of virtual horse racing, examinees must employ cold executive functions (problem-solving, feedback utilization, and abstract reasoning) to identify optimal risk–reward strategies, while simultaneously managing hot executive functions (emotional inhibition, delayed gratification, and risk aversion) to implement those strategies despite the emotional pull of high-risk, high-reward options.

The hierarchical tier framework guides systematic interpretation. Tier 1 requires basic language comprehension, visual processing, and motor control. Tier 2 demands sustained attention and working memory to maintain engagement across trials. Tier 3 cold executive functions include problem-solving through feedback utilization, abstract reasoning to recognize trends in variable outcomes, planning to formulate coherent strategies, and cognitive flexibility to adjust approaches when initial strategies prove ineffective. Tier 3 hot executive functions encompass emotional inhibition and delayed gratification to tolerate the boredom of conservative choices, risk aversion to appropriately avoid losses, and frustration tolerance to maintain emotional control despite setbacks. RISK assesses through Tier 3 but does not engage Tier 4 metacognitive processes, as the task structure remains constant and success depends on consistent strategy implementation rather than ongoing metacognitive evaluation.

RISK's process scores—percentages of selections for each horse type, risky selections following wins, and conservative selections following losses—help clinicians distinguish cold from hot executive deficits. An examinee who verbalizes understanding of optimal strategies but fails to implement them demonstrates the classic hot executive dysfunction pattern: intact cognitive analysis undermined by emotional impulses. Conversely, gradually improving performance across blocks with increasing adoption of conservative strategies suggests slow cold executive functions—adequate learning potential with inefficient problem-solving.

Critical to clinical interpretation is recognizing that RISK involves "play money" without real consequences, potentially limiting generalization to personally meaningful real-world decisions. Always corroborate RISK findings with clinical interviews, collateral reports about real-world decision-making, and behavioral rating scales. Some individuals show RISK difficulties that don't fully generalize to daily functioning, while others perform well on RISK's relatively neutral context but struggle when actual personal stakes heighten emotional arousal.

Within comprehensive executive function assessment, RISK proves particularly valuable for evaluating individuals with suspected hot executive dysfunction affecting real-world judgment: impulsive financial decisions, substance use, ADHD with prominent impulsivity, personality disorders involving poor impulse control, ventromedial prefrontal damage, and any presentation where "they know better but don't do better." The test explicitly measures whether cognitive understanding translates to adaptive behavior under emotionally engaging conditions—a critical question for predicting real-world functioning and targeting interventions appropriately.

TEST YOURSELF

1. A 32-year-old examinee verbalizes understanding that "the $25 horse wins most often and is the smart choice," but consistently selects the $100 horse throughout the test, explaining, "I just feel like the big payout is coming." This pattern most directly reflects:

(a) Tier 1 language comprehension deficit.

(b) Tier 3 cold executive function deficit in abstract reasoning.

(c) Tier 3 hot executive function deficit in emotional inhibition and delayed gratification.

(d) Tier 2 working memory deficit.

2. An examinee's Net Earnings scores are 6 (Races 1–20), 8 (Races 21–40), and 10 (Races 41–60). Process scores show gradually increasing Percent $25 Horse Selections from 30% to 70% across blocks. This pattern suggests:

(a) Primary hot executive dysfunction.

(b) Pervasive combined cold and hot executive deficits.

(c) Slow cold executive functions with intact learning potential.

(d) Tier 1 limitations affecting consistent performance.

3. During RISK administration, an examinee asks, "Which horse should I pick to win?" The examiner's most appropriate response is:

(a) "Try the bottom horse—it wins most often."

(b) "I can't tell you; just try to end up with at least $300 by the 60th race."

(c) "Pick whichever one you think is best."

(d) "The goal is to make the most money, so think about which strategy will work."

4. The primary advantage of RISK's explicit risk-reward contingencies (compared to the Iowa Gambling Task's trial-and-error discovery) is:

(a) Faster administration time.

(b) Better normative data available.

(c) Creates a purer assessment of decision-making style rather than learning ability.

(d) Eliminates the need for working memory.

5. An examinee completes only 48 races before the test discontinues after five time-elapsed trials. Which of the following is true?

(a) Total Net Earnings scaled score can still be derived

(b) No scaled scores can be derived; only raw data is available

(c) Scores are valid but should be interpreted with caution

(d) The test should be readministered after a break

6. High Percent $25 Horse Selections, high Conservative Selection Following a Loss scores, and behavioral observations of visible anxiety after any loss most likely indicate:

(a) Optimal RISK strategy implementation.

(b) Excessive risk aversion potentially reflecting generalized anxiety.

(c) Intact hot executive functions.

(d) Cold executive function deficit.

7. RISK assesses functioning through which tier level(s)?

(a) Tier 3 only (cold and hot EF)

(b) Tiers 1–3 (but not Tier 4)

(c) Tiers 1–4 (all levels)

(d) Tier 3 and Tier 4 only

8. The most critical limitation of RISK for predicting real-world decision-making is:

(a) Limited age range (ages 19–90 only).

(b) Long administration time (10–15 minutes).

(c) Play money outcomes lack personal consequences and real stakes.

(d) Automated administration prevents examiner flexibility.

9. A 45-year-old with documented ventromedial prefrontal damage performs poorly on RISK with high $100 horse selections despite verbalizing understanding of optimal strategy. This pattern is most consistent with research showing ventromedial PFC clients demonstrate:

(a) Impaired abstract reasoning and problem-solving.

(b) Intact cognitive understanding but impaired emotional regulation in decision-making.

(c) Primary language comprehension deficits.

(d) Slowed processing speed affecting reaction time.

10. An examinee performs well on Races 1–40 (Net Earnings scores of 11 and 10) but declines significantly in Races 41–60 (Net Earnings score of 7), accompanied by comments like "This is taking forever" and increasingly impulsive selections. This pattern most likely reflects:

(a) Progressive cold executive function declining during the task.

(b) Emerging hot executive dysfunction under cognitive load.

(c) Flagging motivation and engagement rather than core executive deficits.

(d) Tier 1 visual processing fatigue.

Answer Key: 1-c, 2-c, 3-b, 4-c, 5-b, 6-b, 7-b, 8-c, 9-b, 10-c

REFERENCES

Bechara, A. (2016). *Iowa Gambling Task Professional Manual.* Psychological Assessment Resources.

Bechara, A., Damasio, A. R., Damasio, H., & Anderson, S. W. (1994). Insensitivity to future consequences following damage to human prefrontal cortex. Cognition, 50(1–3), 7–15.

Best, J. R., & Miller, P. H. (2010). A developmental perspective on executive function. Child Development, 81(6), 1641–1660.

Casey, B. J., Somerville, L. H., Gotlib, I. H., Ayduk, O., Franklin, N. T., Askren, M. K., et al. (2011). Behavioral and neural correlates of delay of gratification 40 years later. Proceedings of the National Academy of Sciences, 108(36), 14998–15003.

Castellanos, F. X., Sonuga-Barke, E. J., Milham, M. P., & Tannock, R. (2006). Characterizing cognition in ADHD: Beyond executive dysfunction. Trends in Cognitive Sciences, 10(3), 117–123.

Chaytor, N., & Schmitter-Edgecombe, M. (2003). The ecological validity of neuropsychological tests: A review of the literature on everyday cognitive skills. Neuropsychology Review, 13(4), 181–197.

Conners, C. K. (2014). *Conners Continuous Performance Test* (3rd ed.). Multi-Health Systems.

Delis, D. C. (2021). *Delis Rating of Executive Functions-Adult (D-REF Adult).* Pearson.

Delis, D. C., & Kaplan, E. (2025). *Delis-Kaplan Executive Function System Advanced (D-KEFS Advanced).* Pearson.

Delis, D. C., Kaplan, E., & Kramer, J. H. (2001). *Delis-Kaplan Executive Function System (D-KEFS).* Pearson.

Figner, B., Mackinlay, R. J., Wilkening, F., & Weber, E. U. (2009). Affective and deliberative processes in risky choice: Age differences in risk taking in the Columbia Card Task. *Journal of Experimental Psychology: Learning, Memory, and Cognition, 35*(3), 709–730.

Heaton, R. K., Chelune, G. J., Talley, J. L., Kay, G. G., & Curtiss, G. (1993). *Wisconsin Card Sorting Test Manual: Revised and Expanded.* Psychological Assessment Resources.

Lejuez, C. W., Read, J. P., Kahler, C. W., Richards, J. B., Ramsey, S. E., Stuart, G. L., Strong, D. R., & Brown, R. A. (2002). Evaluation of a behavioral measure of risk taking: The Balloon Analogue Risk Task (BART). *Journal of Experimental Psychology: Applied, 8*(2), 75–84.

Mischel, W., Shoda, Y., & Rodriguez, M. L. (1989). Delay of gratification in children. Science, 244(4907), 933–938.

Naglieri, J. A., & Goldstein, S. (2017). *Comprehensive Executive Function Inventory Adult (CEFI Adult).* Multi-Health Systems.

Parsons, T. D. (2015). Virtual reality for enhanced ecological validity and experimental control in the clinical, affective and social neurosciences. Frontiers in Human Neuroscience, 9, 660.

Roth, R. M., Isquith, P. K., & Gioia, G. A. (2005). *Behavior Rating Inventory of Executive Function-Adult Version (BRIEF-A).* Psychological Assessment Resources.

Wechsler, D. (2024). *Wechsler Adult Intelligence Scale* (5th ed.). Pearson.

Zelazo, P. D., & Carlson, S. M. (2012). Hot and cool executive function in childhood and adolescence: Development and plasticity. Child Development Perspectives, 6(4), 354–360.

Eight

SOCIAL SORTING TEST

CLINICAL VIGNETTE

Talia Hunt is a 13-year-old with autism spectrum disorder (ASD) referred for comprehensive evaluation to inform educational planning. Her parents and teachers described her as academically capable with strong rote memory and logical reasoning, but struggling profoundly with peer relationships. They noted she seemed "blind" to social cues and often misinterpreted others' emotions, leading to conflict and isolation.

During the D-KEFS Advanced Social Sorting Test (SST), which presents cards depicting faces with various emotional expressions, a specific pattern emerged. The examiner observed Talia's performance carefully across the hierarchical framework. Her Tier 1 baseline skills were excellent. She quickly scanned the cards and had no difficulty with visual perception or attention to the task. Her Tier 2 bridging abilities remained largely intact. She held task rules in working memory without difficulty and demonstrated adequate basic executive control for categorization and cognitive flexibility when sorting by concrete features.

The breakdown emerged at Tier 3, where cold executive demands integrate with social–emotional processing. Talia was able to sort cards based on physical appearance and apparel, but when tasked to sort by emotional display, she struggled to see any pattern in right and wrong sorts. Careful observation showed that Talia eventually started consistently sorting happy faces, but she struggled to properly sort the other emotional displays.

Notably, she demonstrated no difficulty with executive flexibility demands. She could switch strategies readily when given concrete categories to use. Her limitation was in recognizing and categorizing the social–emotional content itself. This profile—intact cold executive abilities for abstract rule-following and set-shifting but impaired integration when executive control must incorporate emotional recognition—explained the discrepancy between her cognitive test scores and real-world social functioning, guiding intervention toward social–emotional learning rather than traditional executive function training.

TEST DESCRIPTION

The D-KEFS Advanced SST extends the methodology originally developed in the 1940s for the Wisconsin Card Sorting Test (WCST; Grant & Berg, 1948) into the realm of social cognition. SST assesses problem-solving that requires facial and affect recognition, concept identification, feedback utilization, cognitive switching, and inhibition of perseverative responses, all within the context of ecologically valid social stimuli (Delis & Kaplan, 2025). Designed for ages 8 through 90, the test is administered via tablet and typically requires 8–12 minutes to complete.

Following standardized D-KEFS Advanced administration protocols, SST consists of 128 virtual cards displayed on the Client Device. Each card features a photograph showing one of four individuals displaying one of four emotional expressions (happy, sad, angry, or surprised) while wearing one of four types of hats (cap, beanie, cowboy hat, or hard hat). The examinee uses a stylus to drag each card from the stack and place it below one of four key cards shown at the top of the screen, matching according to rules they must discover through trial and error. The key cards display all four individuals, each with one of the emotional expressions and one of the types of hats.

Three sorting categories exist: Person (which of four individuals), Hat (which of four hat types), and Emotion (which of four emotional expressions). After each sort, the examinee receives visual feedback—a green overlay with a checkmark for correct sorts, a red overlay with X for incorrect sorts. The rules change after the examinee completes 10 consecutive correct sorts in a category. The examinee must rely solely on the visual feedback to identify the current sorting rule, maintain that rule despite ambiguous feedback that sometimes reinforces multiple categories simultaneously, and flexibly shift to new rules when the correct category changes without warning.

The test automatically discontinues when the examinee successfully completes all six target categories (Person, Hat, Emotion, repeated twice) or after 128 cards have been sorted. An optional Affect Matching screening measure can be administered at the end to evaluate whether difficulties with the Emotion category stemmed from problems recognizing emotional expressions versus problems with the executive demands of the task.

DON'T FORGET

SST's primary value lies in its ecological validity—it assesses executive functioning using stimuli that closely resemble real-world social perception demands. This makes it sensitive to deficits in individuals who perform adequately on abstract executive function tasks but struggle when executive control must integrate with social–emotional processing. The test is especially useful for differential diagnosis in ASD, social communication disorders, and conditions affecting ventromedial prefrontal cortex function.

Rapid Reference 8.1

Social Sorting Test Overview

Feature	Description
Age range	8–90 years
Administration time	8–12 minutes
Administration format	Digital (tablet with stylus)
Stimuli	128 virtual cards showing one of four individuals displaying one of four emotional expressions (happy, sad, angry, surprised) wearing one of four hat types
Sorting categories	Person (4 individuals), Hat (4 types), Emotion (4 expressions); each category completed twice
Response format	Drag card to match one of four key cards; green checkmark (correct) or red X (incorrect) feedback after each sort
Discontinue rule	After 6 categories completed or 128 cards sorted
Primary constructs	Tier 3 Cold EF (concept identification, feedback utilization, set-shifting, inhibition); integration of executive control with social–emotional processing
Optional measure	Affect Matching (10 items; differentiates Tier 2 affect recognition from Tier 3 executive dysfunction)

HIERARCHICAL TIER ANALYSIS

The SST can be analyzed through the four-tier framework, with performance reflecting processes ranging from basic perception and language to higher-order metacognitive integration.

Tier 1: Foundational Processes (Nonexecutive)

SST requires several foundational abilities to be intact before executive functioning can be meaningfully assessed. These baseline skills represent requisite capacities rather than executive functions themselves. Note that in this book, we have expanded the hierarchical analysis beyond Pearson's model to reflect our experience using the test in clinical settings.

Visual Processing and Perception

The examinee must perceive the photographs on the screen, distinguish between the four key cards at the top and the card to be sorted, and track the visual feedback after each response. Examinees with visual field defects (such as left hemispatial neglect following right parietal damage), significantly impaired visual acuity, or severe visual perceptual deficits will struggle with the fundamental task demands before executive functions can be evaluated.

Attention and vigilance

Examinees must maintain focus across up to 128 sorting trials spanning 8–12 minutes, with each trial requiring attention to the card being sorted, the four key cards, and the visual feedback. Unlike brief executive tasks with only a few trials, SST's extended demands mean that attentional lapses can accumulate and compromise performance even when executive functions are intact. Examinees with attention-deficit/hyperactivity disorder (ADHD), traumatic brain injury affecting arousal systems, or fatigue may show deteriorating performance across the test. This can manifest as early categories completed efficiently but later categories marked by increased errors, longer response times, and reduced systematic approach. This progressive decline pattern suggests attentional fatigue rather than primary executive dysfunction.

Language Comprehension

The examiner's instructions are intentionally nonspecific. Examinees are told only to match cards but are not told how to match them or that the rules will change. This deliberate lack of explicit guidance is fundamental to the task, as examinees must use feedback to discover the sorting principles. However, examinees must understand concepts like "match," "correct," and "wrong," and the spatial terms needed to understand where to place cards. Individuals with significant receptive language impairments may struggle to understand what they are supposed to do rather than demonstrating executive dysfunction.

Motor Control

Basic fine motor control and coordination are necessary to manipulate the stylus and drag cards to the appropriate locations on the screen. The motor demands are minimal, but examinees with severe motor impairments, significant tremor, or marked bradykinesia may have difficulty with the mechanical aspects of responding.

Processing Speed

Unlike many executive function measures, SST has no strict time limits—examinees can take as long as needed to make each sort. However, significantly slowed processing can affect performance indirectly through working memory failures if too much time elapses between seeing the feedback and making the next sort.

Tier 1 Impairment Pattern

Confused or random responding from the outset, with errors lacking systematic patterns. The examinee may fail to complete even the first category and show poor understanding of what they are supposed to do, suggesting the task's fundamental requirements exceed their capabilities. This pattern might result from visual-perceptual problems or language comprehension deficits.

Tier 2: Bridging Processes

SST demands several mid-level abilities that bridge basic cognitive functions and high-level executive control. These skills operate relatively automatically in most individuals but can be selectively impaired in various clinical conditions.

Working Memory

Working memory is essential throughout the task. Examinees must maintain the general task rules while simultaneously tracking the category they have chosen to match and what they have learned from previous sorts. However, the working memory requirements are primarily for holding information in mind rather than actively manipulating it. Examinees need to remember "I'm currently sorting by hat type" but do not need to perform mental operations on that information. A specific working memory demand involves remembering to match each card to one of the four key cards displayed at the top of the screen rather than to the card just placed. Some examinees, particularly those with working memory deficits or attentional lapses, lose track of this fundamental rule and begin matching new cards to the previously sorted cards instead of to the stable key cards. This error pattern—matching to the last card placed rather than to the key cards—produces elevated Other responses and random-appearing sorts that reflect working memory failure rather than executive dysfunction. Examinees may verbalize confusion about why they're getting incorrect feedback despite appearing to match correctly, not recognizing they've shifted their matching reference point.

Facial Recognition

Recognizing that different cards show the same person requires perceptual expertise with faces (McKone et al., 2009)—the ability to identify an individual with different clothes or emotional expressions. This skill typically develops early (Slater & Quinn, 2001) and operates relatively automatically in most individuals but can be selectively impaired in prosopagnosia. The task provides a prompt after Sort 33 if the examinee has not completed the Person category, which helps identify individuals for whom facial perception may be compromising performance.

Affect Recognition

Perhaps the most critical Tier 2 skill for SST, affect recognition involves the ability to perceive and identify emotional expressions on faces. This requires specialized perceptual processing of facial features, particularly around the eyes and mouth. This skill operates largely automatically in neurotypical individuals but can be selectively impaired in several clinical conditions, including ASD, schizophrenia, and focal brain lesions affecting the amygdala or related circuitry (Suchy, 2023).

Critically, affect recognition difficulties are not executive deficits per se—they reflect problems with social perception rather than problem-solving, cognitive flexibility, or inhibition. An examinee may have intact executive abilities but fail to complete the emotion category because they cannot adequately perceive the emotional expressions, not because they cannot identify concepts, use feedback, or shift sets. The optional Affect Matching task, administered after the main test, helps disentangle these possibilities. If the examinee can successfully sort by emotion when explicitly told to do so, this suggests intact affect recognition with executive dysfunction preventing discovery of the emotion rule. Conversely, poor performance even when explicitly instructed to match emotions suggests the primary deficit lies in affect recognition itself.

Preliminary clinical validation data offer some reassurance on this point: in the D-KEFS Advanced standardization study, children with ASD were able to engage meaningfully with SST despite the well-documented affect recognition challenges in this population, and their performance pattern reflected executive dysfunction (elevated total errors) rather than selective failure on emotion-based sorting (Delis & Kaplan, 2025). However, this single study with a modest sample size (n = 31) cannot definitively resolve the

DON'T FORGET

The relationship between Tier 2 affect recognition and Tier 3 executive demands on the SST creates unique interpretive opportunities and challenges. Theoretically, an examinee with ASD might show intact Tier 1 visual perception and adequate Tier 2 facial recognition but impaired Tier 2 affect recognition, manifesting as successfully completing Person and Hat categories but failing to complete Emotion—not because of executive dysfunction but because of social perception deficits. Preliminary clinical validation data suggest this concern may be less problematic than anticipated: children with ASD in the standardization sample showed a pattern of general executive dysfunction rather than selective emotion-category failure, and they engaged meaningfully with the task despite known face processing challenges in this population. Nevertheless, clinicians should still consider whether social perception deficits might be contributing to an individual examinee's SST performance. Conversely, an examinee with frontal lobe damage might have intact Tier 2 affect recognition but fail on the SST because of Tier 3 executive deficits in set-shifting or inhibition. The SST's process scores and optional Affect Matching task help distinguish these patterns.

question, and clinicians should remain attentive to the possibility that affect recognition deficits may confound SST interpretation in individual cases—particularly given the heterogeneity of social perception abilities within the autism spectrum.

Tier 2 Impairment Patterns
These manifest differently depending on which mid-level ability is impaired. Working memory difficulties present as inconsistent performance where the examinee discovers a sorting principle but then "loses" it. Facial perception problems appear as a specific difficulty with the Person category, with the examinee verbalizing confusion about whether cards show the same person or resorting to sorting by superficial features. Affect recognition deficits manifest as a specific failure in the emotion category despite successfully completing Person and Hat.

Tier 3: Core Executive Functions

The Tier 3 demands of SST represent the core executive functions the test was designed to assess. These processes require the integration of cognitive control, problem-solving, and—uniquely for this test—social–emotional processing capabilities.

Cold Executive Functions
SST assesses multiple cold executive functions that operate in the analytical, emotionally neutral domain of sorting social stimuli by conceptual categories.

Concept Identification
This primary executive function manifests behaviorally in observable ways during testing. Examinees with strong concept identification quickly lock onto potential sorting principles, often verbalizing hypotheses ("Maybe it's the hats?") or showing systematic exploration patterns—methodically trying one potential category, then switching to test another when feedback indicates the first wasn't correct. They demonstrate what looks like purposeful hypothesis testing.

In contrast, concept identification difficulties appear as random or inconsistent responding that lacks systematic structure. The examinee may sort by superficial perceptual features not corresponding to any target category—grouping by hair length or whether mouths are open. When the Emotion category is being reinforced, an examinee with concept identification problems might sort by smile/no smile (a perceptual feature) rather than recognizing the underlying emotional states. They struggle to generate potential sorting dimensions and test them systematically, appearing confused or making statements like "I don't know what you want me to do."

Feedback Utilization (Problem-Solving)
Strong feedback utilization appears when examinees demonstrate immediate responsiveness to error feedback. After an incorrect sort, they pause visibly, sometimes looking back at previous cards, and adjust their next response. They maintain tentative hypotheses, continuing to test a category after one correct response, but not becoming rigidly committed until multiple confirmations. When ambiguous sorts occur (matching both current category and another), they recognize that correct feedback doesn't necessarily validate all matching dimensions.

Poor feedback utilization manifests as an apparent disregard for the visual feedback. The examinee receives a red X (incorrect) but continues making the same type of sort, as if the feedback provided no information. They may verbalize confusion: "I don't understand—why is that wrong?" without adjusting their approach. Some examinees show evidence of attempting to use feedback but doing so ineffectively. They recognize errors but cannot determine why the sort was incorrect or what to change, leading to haphazard modifications that don't improve performance.

Set-Shifting (Cognitive Flexibility)
Set-shifting difficulties manifest differently depending on when they occur. At category boundaries—immediately after completing 10 consecutive correct sorts when the target changes—poor set-shifting appears as perseveration. The examinee receives incorrect feedback after the 10th consecutive sort (the first sort of the new category), but

continues sorting by the just-completed category despite clear evidence that it's wrong. They may verbalize frustration ("But I was doing it right!") while persisting with the old rule for multiple trials. Some examinees show awareness ("I know this isn't working") but cannot generate or commit to an alternative strategy.

Within-category set-shifting problems appear differently. Some examinees get "stuck" on one exemplar within a category—if sorting by Person, they correctly identify that individual #1 matches with individual #1, but when individual #2 appears, they seem unable to flexibly apply the same "match the person" rule to the new exemplar. This reflects difficulty maintaining the abstract sorting principle while shifting between specific instances.

Pattern Recognition and Anticipatory Shifting

SST employs a fixed, predictable sequence—Person, Hat, Emotion, then repeating Person, Hat, Emotion for the second cycle. Savvy test-takers may explicitly or implicitly recognize this pattern during testing, which fundamentally changes the cognitive demands of set-shifting. Once an examinee completes the first cycle and begins the second Person category, they may anticipate that Hat comes next, then Emotion, reducing the executive load required for category discovery and facilitating more rapid, efficient shifting. Some test takers might even begin to recognize the pace of the shifting requirement and be prepared to switch to a new category.

This pattern recognition advantage manifests behaviorally in several ways. Some examinees verbalize their insight: "Oh, it's going to be hats again now" immediately after completing the second Person category, demonstrating explicit awareness of the sequence. Others show the advantage implicitly through markedly improved performance on categories 4–6 compared to 1–3—faster trials-to-complete, fewer errors, and more confident, decisive sorting. They may not articulate that they've detected the pattern, but their performance reveals they're no longer discovering categories through trial-and-error feedback; they're anticipating them based on sequential regularity.

This pattern learning capability can significantly mask executive dysfunction. An examinee with moderate set-shifting deficits might show many perseverative errors when transitioning from Person to Hat in the first cycle (a true cold shift requiring discovery), but few perseverative errors when transitioning from Person to Hat in the second cycle (an anticipated shift requiring less executive control). Their Tier 3 set-shifting abilities haven't improved. Rather, the predictable sequence has reduced the genuine executive demand. When interpreting performance, clinicians should examine whether improvement across cycles reflects true learning and executive adaptation or simply reflects reduced cognitive load once the pattern becomes evident.

Conversely, examinees who fail to benefit from the predictable sequence—showing similar performance patterns and error rates on both cycles—may have difficulties with either implicit pattern detection or the ability to use recognized patterns to facilitate performance. This can occur in individuals with procedural learning deficits, those with severe working memory limitations preventing them from maintaining information about the sequence across categories, or those whose executive dysfunction is so profound that even anticipated shifts remain difficult.

Derailment Inhibition

SST assesses two distinct types of inhibition that manifest in different error patterns. Derailment inhibition is required when the examinee is correctly sorting by one category but makes an ambiguous sort—a card that matches both the current correct category and one or two other categories. When this ambiguous sort receives correct feedback, the examinee must inhibit switching to the other categories that were coincidentally reinforced. Derailment errors occur when this inhibition fails—the examinee abandons the correct strategy after an ambiguous sort and begins sorting by the newly reinforced but actually incorrect category. Behaviorally, this appears as sudden strategy shifts following ambiguous sorts, often with the examinee seeming to "discover" a new pattern ("Oh! It's the hats!") when actually being pulled off-track.

Retroactive Inhibition

Retroactive inhibition is required after completing a category, when that previously correct and heavily reinforced response pattern must be suppressed. The completed category has gained substantial prepotency through 10+ consecutive reinforcements. Failures of retroactive inhibition appear as perseverative errors immediately following category completion. The examinee continues sorting by the old rule for the sorts after the switch in rules despite repeated incorrect feedback. Some examinees show graded recovery, demonstrated by strong perseveration immediately after the switch in rules that then gradually diminishes, suggesting effortful but eventually successful inhibition. Others show persistent retroactive inhibition failure, continuing to revert to the previous category throughout the remainder of testing.

Tier 3 Cold EF Impairment Pattern

These produce characteristic patterns depending on which executive process is primarily impaired. Concept identification deficits appear as prolonged random responding before discovering categories, with elevated Trials to Complete First Category but subsequent improvement. Problem-solving deficits manifest as failure to benefit from feedback—continuing the same ineffective approach despite repeated errors. Set-shifting impairments appear as an inability to abandon a previously correct category when the target changes, with perseverative errors accumulating primarily at category boundaries. Inhibition deficits produce either derailment errors (problems maintaining the current set when ambiguous feedback reinforces multiple categories) or retroactive inhibition problems (perseveration back to a previously reinforced category).

Hot Executive Functions

SST requires emotional control and frustration tolerance. The task can be highly frustrating, particularly for examinees who make numerous incorrect sorts. While the visual feedback system (red X rather than examiner saying "wrong") might reduce emotional impact compared to verbal feedback, examinees who become significantly upset during testing may experience hot executive dysfunction that interferes with their cold executive abilities.

Examinees with poor hot executive control may become increasingly frustrated as errors accumulate, leading to impulsive responding, giving up, or emotional outbursts that prevent them from effectively using their intact cognitive abilities. This is particularly relevant for individuals with mood disorders, externalizing disorders, or damage to ventromedial prefrontal regions (Anderson et al., 2006; Eslinger et al., 2004). Behavioral observations during testing help identify when emotional dysregulation is contributing to poor performance.

CAUTION

Hot executive dysfunction can look like cold executive deficits on SST. An examinee with intact cognitive flexibility, problem-solving, and inhibition who becomes frustrated by accumulating errors may show impulsive responding or giving up—patterns that superficially resemble cold EF deficits. Behavioral observations during testing help differentiate these presentations: visible frustration, emotional outbursts, or performance that deteriorates after errors suggest hot EF interference with otherwise intact cold EF capacity. Intervention approaches differ substantially—emotion regulation strategies versus cognitive training.

Tier 3 Hot EF Pattern

Examinees with Hot EF difficulties show performance compromised by emotional dysregulation rather than cognitive limitations. They may begin sorting systematically but deteriorate as frustration builds from accumulating errors, leading to impulsive responding, giving up, or emotional outbursts. The key diagnostic indicator is that executive capacity exists—evidenced by an initial systematic approach or periods of organized sorting—but emotional factors prevent sustained deployment. Behavioral observations are essential: visible frustration, performance that deteriorates specifically after errors, or emotional reactions disproportionate to task difficulty suggest hot EF interference with otherwise intact cold EF capacity.

Integration of Cold and Hot Executive Functions with Social–Emotional Processing

SST's contribution to executive functioning assessment lies in its requirement to integrate cold executive functions with social–emotional processing. When the Emotion category is being reinforced, examinees must not only demonstrate cognitive flexibility, problem-solving, and inhibition, they must do so while processing affective information. This integration reflects the operation of executive functions in real-world social contexts where abstract problem-solving must incorporate emotional and social cues.

This integration requirement makes SST sensitive to deficits in specific populations, including individuals with ASD who may show intact cold executive functioning on abstract tasks but struggle when those same executive processes must operate on social–emotional stimuli. The discrepancy between performance on abstract executive measures and SST can reveal important information about an individual's capacity for social–emotional executive integration.

CAUTION

The increased difficulty of identifying the target categories on SST, particularly the Emotion category, means that longer trials-to-complete and lower categories completed do not always indicate executive dysfunction. Many neurotypical examinees require more trials to discover the Emotion category than they needed for Person or Hat. The key differentiating features are: (1) whether the examinee eventually completes all categories, even if slowly; (2) whether errors reflect perseveration or random exploration; (3) whether the examinee demonstrates learning across the test or continues making similar errors throughout; and (4) how performance on the SST compares to performance on other executive measures.

Tier 4: Higher-Order Integration and Metacognition

Tier 4 processes involve the highest level of executive integration—monitoring one's own cognitive performance, recognizing when strategies are failing, and flexibly adjusting the approach based on self-evaluation.

Metacognitive Monitoring

Successful SST performance requires awareness of one's own understanding and confusion. Examinees with strong metacognitive abilities demonstrate this through self-correction behaviors, pausing when uncertain, and verbalizing their thinking process ("I'm not sure if this is right"). Those with metacognitive deficits may not recognize when they're confused or when their strategy isn't working, continuing ineffective approaches without the self-awareness needed to prompt strategy change.

Strategic Flexibility and Adjustment

Beyond basic set-shifting (Tier 3), strategic flexibility involves adjusting one's overall approach based on success patterns. For example, an examinee might realize after struggling with random exploration that a more systematic hypothesis-testing approach would be more effective. This meta-level strategic adjustment represents a higher-order integration than simply shifting from one category to another.

Integration of Multiple Executive Systems

SST ultimately requires coordination of concept identification, feedback utilization, set-shifting, and inhibition—all operating simultaneously. Examinees must hold their current hypothesis in mind (working memory), test it systematically (problem-solving), inhibit incorrect alternatives (inhibition), and shift when needed (cognitive flexibility), all while managing frustration (hot executive control). This multisystem integration represents Tier 4 demands that go beyond any single executive function operating in isolation.

Tier 4 Integration Deficits

These appear as difficulty coordinating multiple executive demands simultaneously. An examinee might demonstrate adequate performance on each executive component when tested in isolation, but struggle when required to integrate concept identification, feedback utilization, set-shifting, and inhibition all at once. Poor metacognitive awareness may manifest as continuing ineffective strategies without recognizing the need to change the approach.

Rapid Reference 8.2

Tier Structure at a Glance

Tier	Processes
Tier 1: Foundational processes (Nonexecutive)	Visual processing and perception
	Sustained attention and vigilance across 128 trials
	Language comprehension of instructions
	Basic motor control (stylus use)
	Processing speed (indirect effect on working memory)
Tier 2: Bridging processes	Working memory (maintaining sorting rule and tracking feedback)
	Facial recognition (identifying same person across expressions)
	Affect recognition (perceiving emotional expressions)
Tier 3: Cold executive functions	Concept identification (discovering sorting categories)
	Feedback utilization (problem-solving from visual feedback)
	Set-shifting (switching categories after rule change)
	Derailment inhibition (resisting ambiguous reinforcement)
	Retroactive inhibition (suppressing previously correct responses)
	Integration of executive control with social–emotional content
Tier 3: Hot executive functions	Frustration tolerance during repeated errors
	Emotional regulation preventing impulsive responding
	Persistence despite negative feedback
Tier 4: Higher-order integration	Metacognitive monitoring (awareness of confusion/understanding)
	Strategic flexibility (adjusting overall approach)
	Coordination of multiple executive systems simultaneously

ADMINISTRATION

NOTE: Refer to the Examiner's Manual for complete and detailed administration instructions. The Examiner's Manual provides verbatim instructions and clinicians should follow these precisely to ensure standardized administration.

Materials and Setup

SST requires the Examiner's Manual, Client Device, Practitioner Device, and Stylus. Before beginning, ensure both devices are charged and connected, and the stylus is functional. Verify a comfortable stylus grip and ensure no screen glare. The examiner places the Client Device flat in landscape orientation in front of the examinee and provides a stylus for responding.

Starting Point and Discontinuation

The examiner begins with Sort 1. There are no practice items. The task automatically discontinues either when the examinee successfully completes all six categories or after 128 sorts have been made.

Instructions and Feedback

All instructions appear on the Practitioner Device and should be read verbatim in a natural, conversational manner. The basic instructions inform the examinee to match each card from the stack to one of the four key cards displayed at the top of the screen by dragging it with the stylus. Critically, the examiner does not tell the examinee how to match the cards or which categories to use. The intentional ambiguity of the instructions is fundamental to the task—examinees must discover the sorting principles through trial and error.

After each sort, visual feedback appears automatically: a green overlay with a checkmark for correct responses, a red overlay with X for incorrect responses. The examiner provides no verbal feedback about whether responses are correct or incorrect.

Timing

Timing is tracked but not limited. The examinee can take as long as needed to make each sort.

Prompts

Several prompts appear as notifications that the Examiner reads for the following conditions.

First Other Sort

The first time an examinee places a card under a key card that does not match Person, Hat, or Emotion, a notification appears and the examiner reads, "Each card you place should match the key card above it in some way."

No Response after 20 Seconds

A 20-second timer appears on the Practitioner Device, and if the examinee does not respond within 20 seconds, a prompt notification appears that the examiner reads aloud: "Keep going."

No Correct Category Before Sort 33

If the examinee has not completed the Person category (10 consecutive correct sorts to Person) by Sort 33, the Client Device darkens and a notification appears on the Practitioner Device instructing the examiner to tell the examinee: "Try matching by the person." This prompt was added to lower the floor of the test and reduce frustration in examinees with moderate to severe executive dysfunction who might never complete even the first category without assistance. After providing this prompt, testing continues normally. The prompt is provided only once and only for the first category.

Critical Administration Rule

The examiner must never provide information about the sorting categories or switching rules, even if the examinee directly asks: "How should I sort these?" or "What do you want me to do?" The examiner should respond with the scripted prompt: "I can't tell you how to match the cards, but each time you'll see if your sort is right or wrong." Providing any hints about categories (e.g., "Look at their hats") invalidates the test results, as discovery through feedback utilization is the core executive demand being assessed. The only exception is the standardized Sort 33 prompt for the Person category if that category has not been completed.

> **DON'T FORGET**
>
> The digital administration system automatically provides correct/incorrect visual feedback to the examinee, switches the sorting rule when needed, scores all responses, and discontinues the test at the appropriate point. The examiner's role is to read prompts when they appear, provide encouragement as needed, and observe the examinee's approach and reactions.

Optional Affect Matching Task

Following completion of SST, examiners will be provided the option to also administer the Affect Matching task. The task should only be administered after completion of the standard SST and provides no normative data. The task can be useful for the examinee who performs well on the Person and Hat categories but not the Emotion category. Do not administer the Affect Matching task if the examinee had at least some correct sorts on the Emotion category, did not complete any categories successfully, or if the examinee may undergo future reevaluation and the examiner wants to reduce practice effects.

BEHAVIORAL OBSERVATIONS

Systematic observation during SST administration provides qualitative information that enhances interpretation of quantitative scores. The digital administration format allows the examiner to focus on the examinee's approach and reactions rather than managing test materials and scoring. Organize observations into three major categories: Approach and Strategy, Emotional Responses and Task Engagement, and Self-Monitoring and Error Awareness.

Approach, Strategy, and Feedback Utilization

Note how the examinee initially approaches the task. Some examinees immediately begin sorting by an obvious category (often Person or Hat), suggesting efficient concept identification. Others spend considerable time examining the key cards before making their first sort, indicating careful analysis. Still others begin sorting seemingly randomly, suggesting either a trial-and-error approach or difficulty identifying relevant categories.

Observe whether the examinee's strategy evolves as testing progresses. Effective problem-solvers adjust their approach based on feedback; if random exploration isn't working, they shift to more systematic hypothesis testing and might verbalize their thinking. Examinees with problem-solving difficulties continue using ineffective strategies even after repeated failures.

Note how quickly and effectively the examinee uses feedback. Strong executive functioning is evident when examinees make an error, pause to consider what went wrong, and adjust their next response accordingly. They systematically test hypotheses and modify them based on results. Weak feedback utilization appears when examinees seem to ignore the feedback, continuing the same approach despite repeated errors. Pay attention to reactions to ambiguous feedback—examinees with strong inhibition maintain their current strategy when a sort matches multiple categories and receives correct reinforcement, recognizing that correct feedback on an ambiguous sort doesn't necessarily mean all matching categories are correct.

Emotional Responses and Task Engagement

Observe what happens when the reinforced category changes after the examinee completes 10 consecutive correct sorts. Strong set-shifting ability is evident when examinees quickly recognize from feedback that the rule changed and efficiently identify the new category. They might verbalize surprise but rapidly adjust. Poor set-shifting manifests as perseveration—continuing to sort by the previous category despite repeated incorrect feedback. After a few completed sets, some examinees show anticipatory shifting. They complete a category and immediately try a different sorting principle even before receiving feedback that the rule changed, which can be problematic if excessive.

Document emotional responses throughout testing. SST can be frustrating, particularly for examinees who make many errors. Note signs of frustration, anxiety, sadness, or anger, and specify when these reactions occur: throughout testing, only during the Emotion category, primarily after category shifts, or increasingly as testing progresses. Distinguish between emotional reactions that briefly disrupt performance versus sustained emotional dysregulation that significantly compromises functioning.

Assess the examinee's engagement with the task. Strong engagement is evident when examinees focus on the cards, appear to be actively thinking about their responses, and persist despite difficulty. Poor engagement appears as rushed responding without apparent thought, and obviously random card placement. Note any unusual sorting behaviors, such as sorting to the response piles rather than matching to the key cards at the top.

Self-Monitoring and Error Awareness

After incorrect sorts, do examinees appear to recognize the error and verbalize a self-correction? Or do they seem surprised by negative feedback, suggesting poor error monitoring? Strong executive functioning includes metacognitive awareness, knowing when you understand versus when you're confused, recognizing errors and their patterns. Examinees with poor self-monitoring may make the same types of errors repeatedly without recognizing the pattern or adjusting their approach.

SCORING

SST generates a comprehensive set of scores automatically through the digital administration system. These scores include one core standard score reflecting global performance, ten process scaled scores describing specific aspects of sorting performance, seven base rate process scores for variables with restricted ranges, and raw scores for additional descriptive information.

Core Score

Global Performance Index

The Global Performance Index (GPI) is the primary outcome measure and represents overall performance across the entire test. This standard score ($M = 100$, SD = 15) integrates three components: number of categories completed (0–6), total number of sorts administered (60–128), and percentage of correct responses. The GPI was developed to overcome limitations of traditional WCST summary scores, which individually didn't adequately capture global performance.

Process Scaled Scores

Ten process scaled scores ($M = 10$, SD = 3) provide detailed information about specific aspects of sorting performance.

Total Number of Perseverative Responses and Percent Perseverative Responses

The total number and percentage of perseverative responses reflect sorts to the same category used previously, regardless of whether they receive correct or incorrect feedback. This measure includes both perseverative errors (incorrect perseverative sorts) and perseverative correct responses (sorts that continue using the previous category but accidentally match the new correct category on ambiguous cards). For example, if an examinee completes the Person category and the target changes to Hat, but they continue sorting by Person and place a card that happens to match both Person and Hat, this receives correct feedback but is still scored as perseverative because the examinee likely hadn't recognized the category change. Higher raw scores yield lower scaled scores, indicating more perseveration.

Total Number Perseverative Errors and Percent Perseverative Errors

These measures capture only incorrect perseverative sorts—continuing to sort by a previous category after receiving clear feedback that it's no longer correct. This is the classic WCST perseveration measure and reflects failures of cognitive flexibility and response inhibition to prepotent (recently reinforced) categories.

Total Number Nonperseverative Errors and Percent Nonperseverative Errors

These scores reflect incorrect responses that don't meet criteria for perseverative errors, including "Other" responses (sorts that match no category), sorts to incorrect categories that aren't the perseverative category, and various other error types. High nonperseverative errors typically suggest problems with concept identification, problem-solving, or random responding.

Total Number of Errors

This simple sum of all incorrect responses provides an overall measure of sorting accuracy. The specific pattern of errors provides more diagnostic information than the total alone.

Percent Correct Responses

The percentage of sorts that correctly matched the target category provides another perspective on accuracy. This measure is one of the three components used to calculate the GPI raw score.

Total Number of Conceptual Level Responses and Percent Conceptual Level Responses

These measures capture correct responses occurring within runs of three or more consecutive correct sorts. Three consecutive correct responses are unlikely to occur by chance; they indicate the examinee has identified the correct category and is sorting conceptually rather than randomly.

Base Rate Process Scores

Seven process scores with restricted raw score ranges are normed as base rates.

Number of Categories Completed

This traditional WCST measure ranges only from 0 to 6. Completing all six categories places an examinee at high base rates (common, good performance); completing 0–2 categories places them at low base rates (rare, impaired performance).

Trials to Complete First Category

This score reflects how many sorts were required before the examinee completed 10 consecutive correct responses to the Person category. Lower scores indicate efficient concept identification for the first category. However, elevated scores may reflect either difficulty with concept identification and problem-solving or problems with facial recognition that specifically compromise performance on the Person category. If an examinee requires many trials to complete the first category despite receiving the Sort 33 prompt, consider whether facial perception deficits may be contributing to their difficulty.

Failure to Maintain Set

This score counts instances when an examinee makes incorrect responses after five or more consecutive correct responses but before completing the category. These failures suggest instability of conceptual set.

Derailment Errors

This score, developed specifically for SST, counts instances when an examinee is correctly sorting by one category, receives correct feedback on an ambiguous sort (matching multiple categories), and then begins incorrectly sorting by one of the other categories that was reinforced on that ambiguous card. Derailment errors reflect problems with inhibitory control in the face of competing reinforcement.

Other Responses

These scores count as sorts that match no category on any dimension. Other responses can occur for multiple reasons: forgetting or misunderstanding instructions, working memory failure, stimulus-bound responding, very poor concept identification, or inadequate effort.

Additional Raw Scores

The score report provides several raw scores offering additional descriptive information, including Number of Sorts Administered and Number of Responses, Correct Responses, Errors, Perseverative Errors, Nonperseverative Errors, and Other Responses per Category (Person, Hat, Emotion). If the optional Affect Matching screening task was administered, a raw score for total correct responses (0–10 correct) is provided.

The category-specific scores reveal important differential patterns that enhance clinical interpretation. Disproportionate difficulty with the Emotion category is particularly clinically significant. When an examinee completes Person and Hat successfully but accumulates many errors during Emotion trials, this suggests either affect recognition deficits (Tier 2) or difficulty integrating executive control with emotional content (Tier 3). The optional Affect Matching task helps distinguish these possibilities with good performance (8–10 correct) indicating intact affect recognition, pointing toward Tier 3 integration difficulties. Poor Affect Matching (<6 correct) suggests the primary deficit lies in emotion perception itself. Specific difficulty with the Person category, particularly when Hat and Emotion are completed successfully, may indicate facial perception or facial recognition problems rather than executive dysfunction. This pattern warrants consideration of prosopagnosia or related perceptual deficits, especially if the Sort 33 prompt was needed and provided some benefit.

Behavioral Observations

Several base rate scores are provided for a select number of behaviors that examinees may exhibit during assessment. These quantitative scores complement behavioral observations and provide context for interpreting how behaviors or emotional reactions may have affected an examinee's performance. See Table 8.5 in the Examiner's Manual for a listing.

Rapid Reference 8.3

Scoring Summary

Score Type	Score Name	What It Measures
Core standard score (*M* = 100, SD = 15)	Global performance index (GPI)	Overall performance integrating categories completed, sorts administered, and percent correct
Process scaled scores (*M* = 10, SD = 3)	Perseverative responses	Total sorts to previously used category (correct or incorrect)
	Perseverative errors	Incorrect sorts continuing previous category despite error feedback
	Nonperseverative errors	Incorrect sorts not meeting perseveration criteria; suggests concept identification problems
	Total errors	Sum of all incorrect responses
	Correct responses	Percentage of sorts matching target category
	Conceptual level responses	Correct responses within runs of 3+ consecutive correct
Base rate process scores	Categories completed	Number of sorting categories completed (0–6)
	Trials to complete first category	Sorts required to complete first category; concept identification efficiency
	Failure to maintain set	Errors after 5+ correct but before category completion
	Derailment errors	Strategy switches after ambiguous reinforcement
	Other responses	Sorts matching no target category
Additional Raw Scores	Affect matching	Optional screening (0–10); good performance (8–10) with emotion failure indicates Tier 3 integration deficit

COMMON ADMINISTRATION ERRORS

Several administration errors can compromise SST validity or make interpretation difficult.

Providing Hints About Categories

Examiners sometimes provide hints about sorting categories, even inadvertently. Statements like "Try looking at the faces more carefully" or "Pay attention to what they're wearing" give information about relevant categories and invalidate the test. The examinee must discover categories through visual feedback alone. The only exception is the standardized Sort 33 prompt to "Try matching by the person" if needed.

Verbal Feedback About Correctness

Examiners occasionally provide verbal feedback about correctness in addition to the automated visual feedback. Even brief verbal confirmations alter the feedback provided and may make it more salient or emotionally charged than the standardized visual feedback. All feedback must come from the automated system—the examiner should remain neutral and not verbally indicate whether responses are correct.

Premature Discontinuation

Some examiners discontinue testing prematurely when examinees appear frustrated or seem to be struggling significantly. While examiner judgment about continuing testing is important when examinees are in significant distress, premature discontinuation limits the information obtained. Some examinees start poorly but improve as testing progresses. Discontinuing early misses this improvement and underestimates capabilities.

Inadequate Behavioral Documentation

Examiners sometimes fail to record important behavioral observations because they're focused on the digital administration system. Qualitative observations about approach, strategy, emotional reactions, and verbalization are critical for interpretation and should be documented systematically during testing.

Inappropriate Use of Affect Matching

Some examiners administer the optional Affect Matching task inappropriately. This task should be used sparingly and only for examinees who completed Person and Hat successfully but failed to complete Emotion. It should not be administered to examinees who will likely need repeat testing in the future, where practice effects would be problematic (annual school evaluations, disability or forensic exams, treatment efficacy studies).

INTERPRETATION

SST interpretation requires integrating quantitative scores with qualitative observations within a systematic framework that distinguishes foundational limitations from true executive dysfunction.

Using the Hierarchical Framework for Differential Diagnosis

Interpreting SST performance requires systematic evaluation across the four-tier framework, beginning with the foundational requirements and progressing to executive functions only after ruling out lower-level confounds. The GPI provides the initial determination of whether performance is impaired, but understanding why requires tier-based analysis.

Step 1: Rule Out Tier 1 Limitations
Begin by considering whether the examinee had adequate foundational abilities to perform the task. Review behavioral observations for evidence of visual perception difficulties, processing speed deficits, language comprehension difficulties, or motor impairments that might compromise performance independently of executive functioning.

Step 2: Evaluate Tier 2 Bridging Processes
If Tier 1 processes appear intact, evaluate mid-level abilities. Working memory can be assessed through other tests in the battery and through SST observations—did the examinee forget the general task rules or show inconsistent application of discovered strategies? Face perception should be considered if the examinee struggled specifically with the Person category. Affect recognition is the most critical Tier 2 consideration for SST. If the examinee completed Person and Hat successfully but never completed Emotion, the optional Affect Matching task becomes informative. Good Affect Matching performance (8–10 correct) suggests affect recognition is intact, and the Emotion category difficulty stemmed from Tier 3 executive demands. Poor Affect Matching (<6 correct) suggests the primary deficit lies in emotion perception itself.

Step 3: Analyze Tier 3 Cold Executive Patterns
If Tier 1 and 2 abilities appear adequate, attention turns to cold executive functions. High perseverative error scores suggest problems with cognitive flexibility and response inhibition to prepotent categories. Low categories completed with relatively few perseverative errors but high nonperseverative errors, and Other responses suggest concept identification and problem-solving difficulties. High derailment errors indicate specific problems with inhibitory control in the face of ambiguous feedback. Low conceptual level responses relative to total correct responses indicate unstable hypothesis maintenance.

Step 4: Evaluate Tier 3 Hot Executive Factors
Consider how emotional and motivational factors influenced executive performance. Did frustration with repeated negative feedback lead to impulsive responding or task disengagement? Did anxiety about performance interfere with systematic hypothesis testing? SST's use of emotionally expressive faces may elicit affective responses that interact with executive control. Some examinees find the emotional content engaging and motivating, while others find it distracting or aversive. Behavioral observations regarding frustration tolerance, persistence after errors, and affective responses to the social stimuli inform this step.

Step 5: Assess Tier 4 Integration and Metacognition
The unique interpretive question for SST concerns integration of executive functions with social–emotional content. Examinees who complete Person and Hat efficiently but struggle disproportionately with Emotion (assuming intact affect recognition per Affect Matching) demonstrate difficulty integrating executive control with affective processing. Consider how SST performance compares to performance on the traditional D-KEFS Sorting Test or other abstract executive function measures—substantially better performance on abstract measures than SST suggests the social–emotional integration requirement was particularly challenging. Also consider metacognitive awareness: Did the examinee recognize when strategies were ineffective? Did they spontaneously adjust their approach, or persist rigidly despite poor outcomes?

Performance Patterns and Clinical Implications

Several recognizable performance patterns emerge on SST, each with distinct clinical implications and tier-level associations.

Pattern 1: Low Categories Completed, High Perseverative Errors
The examinee completes the first category relatively efficiently but completes few additional categories and makes many perseverative errors, particularly immediately after completing categories. This pattern indicates cognitive inflexibility and deficits in retroactive inhibition. The examinee can initially identify concepts but cannot jettison previous response patterns to shift sets. This is common in individuals with prefrontal cortex damage, particularly dorsolateral regions (Delis, 2012a; Stuss & Knight, 2013), and in conditions affecting cognitive flexibility like ASD and obsessive-compulsive disorder.

Pattern 2: Low Categories Completed, High Nonperseverative Errors, High Other Responses
The examinee completes a few categories and makes many errors that are not predominantly perseverative. They make many Other responses and seem to sort randomly. This pattern suggests problems with concept identification, problem-solving, or understanding the task demands. It may indicate Tier 1 or 2 limitations (language comprehension, visual perception, affect recognition) or Tier 3 deficits in hypothesis generation and testing. Consider administering measures to assess component abilities.

Pattern 3: Person and Hat Completed Efficiently, Emotion Not Completed
The examinee completes the first two cycles with few errors and good efficiency, but never completes the Emotion category, despite it being reinforced for many trials. If Affect Matching is administered and performance is good (8–10 correct), this pattern suggests specific difficulty integrating executive control with emotional content. This pattern is particularly associated with ASD, where individuals demonstrate intact cold executive functions on abstract tasks but struggle when executive processes must operate on social–emotional stimuli.

Pattern 4: Slow Start with Improvement
The examinee requires many trials to complete the first category with many initial errors, but subsequent categories are completed more efficiently with fewer errors. This pattern suggests initial concept identification difficulties that resolve once the examinee understands the task structure and relevant categories. This "slow starter" pattern is common in individuals with intact executive functions but poor tolerance for ambiguity or novel problem-solving situations. Once they grasp the general principles, their executive abilities are adequate.

Rapid Reference 8.4

Distinguishing Tier-Level Deficits

Tier Level	Indicators	Clinical Implications
Tier 1 deficit	Confused or random responding from outset; errors lacking systematic patterns; poor task understanding; fails to complete first category	Foundational limitations (visual, language, motor, attention, or dysregulation); consider testing appropriateness
Tier 2 deficit	Working memory: discovers then "loses" sorting principle. Facial recognition: Person category difficulty; Sort 33 prompt needed. Affect recognition: Emotion failure with poor Affect Matching (<6/10)	Differentiate by category failure; Affect Matching distinguishes Tier 2 from Tier 3; consider prosopagnosia if Person-specific difficulty
Tier 3 cold deficit	High perseverative errors at category boundaries; low categories completed; elevated nonperseverative or derailment errors; failure to benefit from feedback; Person/Hat completed but Emotion failed despite good Affect Matching (≥8/10)	Executive dysfunction in concept identification, feedback utilization, set-shifting, or inhibition; last pattern indicates integration difficulty with emotional content (ASD, vmPFC dysfunction)
Tier 3 hot deficit	Increasing frustration with errors; impulsive responding; giving up or emotional outbursts; early performance deteriorates with frustration	Emotional dysregulation compromising cognition; relevant for mood disorders, externalizing disorders, vmPFC dysfunction
Tier 4 deficit	Adequate component skills but poor coordination; no strategy adjustment despite poor results; continues ineffective approaches without awareness	Metacognitive monitoring failure; difficulty integrating multiple systems; adequate on isolated measures but struggles with multi-demand tasks

ECOLOGICAL VALIDITY AND FUNCTIONAL IMPLICATIONS

SST's use of social stimuli makes it particularly relevant for predicting real-world functioning in contexts requiring integration of executive control with social–emotional processing.

Academic Functioning

The executive skills assessed by SST—concept identification, feedback utilization, cognitive flexibility, and inhibition—are foundational to academic success. Students with SST deficits may struggle to learn from mistakes on assignments, rigidly adhering to familiar strategies even when feedback indicates they are ineffective. Difficulty discovering implicit rules through trial and error can manifest as trouble understanding unstated teacher expectations or adapting study approaches when initial methods fail. The integration of executive control with social–emotional processing is particularly relevant in classroom settings where students must simultaneously manage academic demands and navigate peer dynamics. Interventions may include explicit instruction in strategy adjustment, structured feedback systems that make implicit expectations concrete, and direct teaching of how to interpret and respond to corrective feedback.

Vocational and Daily Living

Workplace success frequently requires discovering implicit norms through observation and feedback—demands that parallel SST's core requirements. Individuals with SST deficits may have difficulty adjusting to new workplace expectations, understanding unspoken professional conventions, or modifying their approach based on supervisor feedback. Perseverative tendencies may manifest as continuing ineffective work strategies despite clear indications that change is needed. SST's social stimulus content makes it especially relevant for positions requiring customer interaction, team collaboration, or management responsibilities where executive functions must operate on interpersonal information. Beyond the workplace, daily problem-solving often requires adapting behavior based on social feedback by recognizing when an approach isn't working and flexibly shifting to alternatives. Accommodations may include explicit communication of workplace expectations, structured check-ins with supervisors, and mentoring relationships that make implicit norms explicit.

Social Functioning

Individuals who struggle with SST, particularly the Emotion category, may experience significant difficulties in social relationships. They may misinterpret others' emotional expressions, respond inappropriately to social cues, or continue socially ineffective behaviors despite feedback from others. The inability to integrate executive control with emotional processing may manifest as knowing social rules cognitively but failing to apply them flexibly in emotionally laden situations. This pattern—intact cold executive functioning with impaired social–emotional integration—helps explain why some individuals perform adequately on abstract cognitive tasks yet struggle profoundly in interpersonal contexts. Individuals showing the Pattern 3 profile—successful Person and Hat completion but Emotion category failure despite intact affect recognition—may benefit most from social–emotional learning interventions that explicitly teach integration of executive strategies with emotional content, rather than traditional executive function training targeting cognitive flexibility or inhibition in isolation.

PRELIMINARY CLINICAL VALIDATION OF THE D-KEFS ADVANCED SST

During standardization of the D-KEFS Advanced, clinical group studies examined SST's ability to detect executive dysfunction in several populations (Delis & Kaplan, 2025). These preliminary findings warrant replication before drawing firm diagnostic conclusions, but they establish useful reference points for clinical interpretation.

Traumatic Brain Injury

The adult TBI sample ($n = 30$; mean GCS = 8.5) demonstrated statistically lower performance on the majority of SST measures, with eight of 11 scores reaching significance. Effect sizes ranged from moderate to large across these measures. What distinguishes the SST findings from other D-KEFS Advanced results in this population is the absence of time pressure during administration. Whereas the TBI group's deficits on timed measures like the TMT and CWIT reflected slowed processing with preserved accuracy, SST (an untimed task) revealed impairment in the accuracy domain itself. The composite GPI demonstrated stronger differentiation between groups ($d = 0.83$) than did individual process measures examining specific error types. When examining process-level data, difficulties with inhibiting previously reinforced responses emerged as particularly prominent ($d = 0.66$–0.71 for perseverative measures), pointing toward inhibitory control weaknesses as a key contributor to the observed performance pattern.

Specific Learning Disorder-Mathematics

Among the D-KEFS Advanced battery, SST ranked second only to the Tower Test in differentiating the SLD-Math sample ($n = 26$) from matched controls. The composite GPI demonstrated robust separation between groups ($d = 0.87$, $p = 0.01$), while measures of sustained conceptual-level sorting also showed significant differences ($d = 0.69$–0.77). Measures of indexing perseverative tendencies fell in the moderate range. This pattern is noteworthy when juxtaposed with the Verbal Fluency Test results, which showed no meaningful group differences in SLD-Math. The dissociation underscores a critical principle: executive functions are not uniform, and nonverbal reasoning demands—such as those required for abstract sorting and flexible category shifting—appear more closely linked to mathematical competence than rapid verbal retrieval skills. Clinicians evaluating children with mathematics difficulties should consider including measures that tap spatial and nonverbal executive processes rather than relying exclusively on verbally mediated tasks.

Autism Spectrum Disorder

The ASD sample (n = 31) showed significantly elevated error rates compared to matched controls (d = 0.52, p = 0.04), with the GPI falling just at the threshold of statistical significance (d = 0.49, p = 0.05). Perseverative tendencies were elevated at moderate effect sizes (d = 0.39–0.50), though most individual perseverative measures did not achieve significance. A clinically relevant observation emerged from this study: despite the well-established literature documenting facial emotion recognition difficulties in individuals with ASD, participants in this sample successfully engaged with the test's facial affect stimuli and completed sorting requirements. This suggests SST can yield meaningful executive function data in this population without face perception deficits confounding interpretation. The pattern aligns with the broader literature documenting executive challenges in ASD, including difficulties with flexible thinking, maintaining and updating working memory, and strategic problem-solving.

Attention-Deficit/Hyperactivity Disorder

The ADHD sample (n = 55) showed meaningful differentiation from controls across multiple SST measures, with the GPI (d = 0.57, $p < 0.01$) and several error measures reaching significance. This sensitivity is notable because children with ADHD frequently perform within normal limits on structured cognitive testing despite clear real-world executive difficulties. SST's demands—suppressing the tendency to repeat previously successful sorting strategies, shifting flexibly when feedback signals rule changes, and integrating feedback to guide subsequent responses—align closely with the inhibitory control, cognitive flexibility, and self-monitoring weaknesses characteristic of ADHD. However, given the substantial heterogeneity of executive profiles within this diagnostic category, individual pattern analysis remains essential rather than assuming uniform impairment.

> **DON'T FORGET**
>
> Across clinical populations, the GPI consistently demonstrated superior differentiation compared to traditional card-sorting metrics such as perseverative errors or conceptual-level responses examined in isolation. Because this composite integrates multiple performance dimensions, it may serve as an efficient initial indicator of executive dysfunction, with subsequent examination of specific process scores clarifying the nature of observed difficulties.

Mild Cognitive Impairment

The MCI sample (n = 18) did not meet the minimum threshold for reliable statistical analysis; consequently, SST findings for this population are not reported.

STRENGTHS AND WEAKNESSES

SST offers several distinctive strengths for executive function assessment, alongside limitations that clinicians should consider when selecting measures and interpreting results.

Strengths

SST offers several notable advantages for assessing executive functions within a socially relevant context.

Ecological Validity

SST's greatest strength is its use of photographs of actual people with real emotional expressions. This makes the task more similar to real-world social perception than abstract sorting tests, improving the prediction of social functioning difficulties that abstract measures miss. The test assesses how executive functions operate in social contexts, which is how most real-world executive demands occur.

Raised Ceiling

The test successfully addresses ceiling effects common in high-functioning individuals on traditional abstract card sorting tests. The increased difficulty of identifying categories (faces, emotions vs. shapes, colors, numbers) makes SST more sensitive to subtle executive dysfunction that might be missed by measures with lower ceilings.

Accessibility for Color Vision Deficiencies
Unlike the WCST, which relies on color discrimination as one of three primary sorting categories, SST uses Person, Hat, and Emotion categories that do not depend on color perception. This makes the test accessible to individuals with color blindness or color vision deficiencies who would be significantly disadvantaged on traditional card sorting measures.

Digital Administration
The all-digital format dramatically simplifies testing and minimizes examiner-introduced error. Scoring is automatic and standardized. The examiner can focus on observing the examinee's approach and emotional reactions rather than managing materials and tracking complex scoring rules.

Comprehensive Process Scores
The sophisticated process scoring system allows detailed characterization of performance patterns, permitting differentiation between various types of executive dysfunction (concept identification vs. set-shifting vs. inhibition vs. feedback utilization). The GPI provides a psychometrically strong summary score with excellent clinical sensitivity across various populations.

Affect Recognition Differentiation
The optional Affect Matching task enables differentiation between affect recognition deficits (Tier 2) and executive dysfunction affecting the Emotion category (Tier 3). This distinction is critical for accurate diagnosis and intervention planning.

Weaknesses and Limitations

Despite its strengths, SST has several limitations that clinicians should consider when selecting measures and interpreting results.

Floor Limitations
Despite design efforts to lower the floor (Sort 33 prompt), individuals with moderate to severe executive dysfunction may fail to complete even the first category. Meaningful interpretation is difficult when examinees complete zero categories, as it becomes unclear whether the problem is Tier 1/2 limitations or severe Tier 3 executive dysfunction.

Interpretive Complexity
The test's reliance on intact Tier 2 affects recognition and face perception creates interpretive complexity. Determining whether poor performance reflects affect recognition problems, face perception difficulties, executive dysfunction, or some combination requires supplemental testing with measures of facial recognition and affect perception.

Limited Affect Recognition Assessment
SST assesses affect matching rather than true affect recognition or labeling, both in the main sorting task and the optional Affect Matching screening. The primary sorting task can be completed successfully by perceptually matching facial features (mouth configuration, eye shape, eyebrow position) without genuine emotional understanding or the ability to name the emotions being displayed. An examinee could complete all Emotion category sorts through purely visual pattern matching—grouping "faces with upturned mouths" rather than recognizing "happy expressions." Individuals with significant emotion labeling deficits may never be identified if their perceptual matching skills are intact. Individuals with alexithymia, limited emotional vocabulary, difficulty naming emotions or cultural differences in how emotions are interpreted might perform adequately on both the main task and optional Affect Matching. The test therefore may not capture the nuanced affect recognition deficits that compromise real-world social functioning, as everyday social interaction typically requires not just matching similar expressions but identifying and responding appropriately to specific emotional states.

Practice Effects
Despite using different stimuli than traditional abstract card sorting, practice effects remain a concern (Basso et al., 2001; Calamia et al., 2012). Once an examinee understands the general principle that categories change after 10 correct sorts and that Person, Hat, and Emotion are the categories, repeat administration within

typical clinical timeframes (less than one year) may be compromised. This makes SST less suitable for contexts requiring frequent repeat testing, such as annual school evaluations or treatment efficacy studies with multiple assessment points.

Missing Verbal Component

The test provides no measure of sorting generation or verbal explanation of sorting principles, limiting insight into thinking processes compared to tests like the original D-KEFS Sorting Test (Delis et al., 2001). Following administration, asking examinees to describe why they sorted as they did, can provide insight, but general descriptions are not as challenging as the requirement to explain every sort on the D-KEFS Sorting Test.

Front-Loaded Processing Demands

The concept identification demands are front-loaded—discovering Person, Hat, and Emotion categories is most difficult initially. Once identified, these categories are reused in the second cycle. An examinee might struggle with the first three categories but then complete the second cycle efficiently, not because executive dysfunction resolved, but because concept identification became easier. Consider performance patterns across all six categories when interpreting, not just overall summary scores.

ALTERNATIVE MEASURES

When SST's limitations affect interpretability or when specific component abilities require further evaluation, clinicians may consider complementary measures from within the D-KEFS family or from other assessment instruments.

Within the D-KEFS Suite

Several D-KEFS subtests provide complementary or converging evidence for concept formation and cognitive flexibility.

Sorting Test

The original D-KEFS Sorting Test provides complementary information about categorization, cognitive flexibility, and abstract thinking without SST's social–emotional content. The Sorting Test requires examinees to both generate their own sorts and explain the principles they used, revealing thought processes that SST does not assess. Comparing performance clarifies whether categorization difficulties are specific to social stimuli or reflect general conceptual reasoning deficits.

Trail Making Test

The Trail Making Test assesses set-shifting in a more constrained format with clear, visually presented rules. The original D-KEFS version provides Number-Letter Switching, while the D-KEFS Advanced version adds three switching conditions isolating shifting, inhibition, and working memory contributions to multitasking. Comparison helps distinguish between fundamental set-shifting capability (Trail Making) versus problems with set-shifting under ambiguous, feedback-dependent conditions (SST). Intact Trail Making with impaired SST set-shifting suggests the problem is not basic cognitive flexibility but rather difficulty with flexibility under uncertain conditions.

Color-Word Interference Test

This test assesses inhibition in a highly constrained verbal format with clear rules. The original D-KEFS version and D-KEFS Advanced version both provide inhibition and inhibition-switching conditions. Intact Color-Word performance with impaired SST inhibition suggests problems with higher-level conceptual inhibition (suppressing prepotent sorting categories) rather than basic response inhibition (suppressing a prepotent verbal response).

Beyond D-KEFS

Measures outside the D-KEFS family can provide converging evidence or assess related constructs when additional information is needed.

Card Sorting and Set-Shifting Measures

The Wisconsin Card Sorting Test (WCST; Heaton, 1981; Heaton et al., 1993) remains the classic measure of categorization, set-shifting, and perseveration using abstract stimuli (shapes, colors, numbers). SST can serve as an alternate form with reduced practice effects due to different stimulus content, though some practice effects may still occur because both use the same general methodology. Comparing performance clarifies whether difficulties are specific to social stimuli or reflect general card-sorting deficits. The Cambridge Neuropsychological Test Automated Battery Intra-Extra Dimensional Set Shift (CANTAB IED; Cambridge Cognition, 2019) provides more granular analysis of where set-shifting breaks down, systematically increasing difficulty of shifts from simple to complex. It can complement SST by clarifying the specific level at which set-shifting fails.

Face Perception and Recognition Measures

When Person category difficulties suggest possible face perception deficits, standardized assessment of facial recognition abilities helps clarify whether prosopagnosia or related perceptual problems are contributing to SST performance. For children, the NEPSY-II Memory for Faces subtest (Korkman et al., 2007) provides standardized assessment of facial recognition. For adults, the Benton Facial Recognition Test (Benton et al., 1994) assesses ability to match unfamiliar faces across different orientations and lighting conditions. Poor performance on these measures, combined with specific Person category difficulty on SST, suggests face perception deficits rather than executive dysfunction.

Affect Recognition Measures

When Emotion category difficulties persist despite adequate Affect Matching performance, a more comprehensive assessment of emotion perception may be warranted. The NEPSY-II Affect Recognition subtest (Korkman et al., 2007) assesses ability to match facial expressions across different faces, providing a more extensive evaluation than SST's brief screening. For adults, the Mayer-Salovey-Caruso Emotional Intelligence Test (MSCEIT; Mayer et al., 2003) includes face subtests assessing emotion identification. These measures help determine whether subtle affect recognition deficits contribute to SST performance even when the brief Affect Matching screening appears adequate.

Behavior Rating Scales

Executive function rating scales capture real-world executive behaviors that may or may not align with performance-based measures. For children and adolescents, the Behavior Rating Inventory of Executive Function, Second Edition (BRIEF-2; Gioia et al., 2015), Comprehensive Executive Function Inventory (CEFI; Naglieri & Goldstein, 2013), and Delis Rating of Executive Functions (D-REF; Delis, 2012b) provide parent and teacher perspectives on daily executive functioning. For adults, the BRIEF-A (Roth et al., 2005), CEFI Adult (Naglieri & Goldstein, 2017), and D-REF Adult (Delis, 2021) offer self-report and informant-report options. Relevant scales across these measures include Shift (paralleling SST set-shifting demands), Inhibit (suppressing prepotent responses), Emotional Control (managing frustration during challenging tasks), and Plan/Organize (systematic hypothesis testing). Discrepancies between SST performance and rating scale elevations provide diagnostic information: adequate test performance with elevated rating scales may indicate that the structured testing environment does not capture executive challenges that emerge in complex, emotionally meaningful social situations. Conversely, poor SST performance with unremarkable rating scales might suggest test-specific factors such as affect recognition difficulties or unfamiliarity with tablet-based assessment rather than pervasive executive dysfunction.

SUMMARY

The SST represents a significant advancement in executive function assessment by integrating classic card-sorting methodology with ecologically valid social stimuli. By requiring examinees to discover sorting categories of Person, Hat, and Emotion through visual feedback alone, while flexibly shifting between categories as reinforcement contingencies change, SST assesses concept identification, problem-solving, set-shifting, and inhibition in a context more similar to real-world social perception than traditional abstract sorting tasks.

The test's hierarchical structure—with Tier 1 baseline skills, Tier 2 mid-level abilities, Tier 3 executive functions, and Tier 4 metacognition—enables systematic differential diagnosis. This framework helps clinicians determine whether poor performance reflects foundational sensory or perceptual deficits, problems with social perception abilities like affect recognition, or true executive dysfunction. The critical interpretive question is whether difficulties occur specifically when executive control must integrate with social–emotional content, suggesting social executive dysfunction rather than general executive impairment.

The comprehensive scoring system, including the GPI and multiple process scores, allows detailed characterization of performance patterns. SST's primary strengths include ecological validity, raised the ceiling compared to traditional sorting tests, automated digital administration, and comprehensive process scores. Limitations include interpretive complexity when affect recognition or face perception deficits may compromise performance, practice effects limiting utility for repeat testing contexts, and challenges for examinees with severe executive dysfunction.

Interpretation requires integrating quantitative scores with qualitative observations, considering performance across the four-tier framework, examining patterns of scores rather than isolated measures, and contextualizing findings within the broader assessment. SST is particularly valuable for understanding the intersection of executive functioning and social–emotional processing—a critical but often overlooked aspect of adaptive functioning that significantly impacts social relationships, emotion regulation, and real-world problem-solving in complex social contexts.

TEST YOURSELF

1. What is the primary advantage of the Social Sorting Test compared to the traditional Wisconsin Card Sorting Test?

(a) It requires fewer trials to complete.
(b) It uses ecologically valid social stimuli rather than abstract shapes.
(c) It provides verbal feedback instead of visual feedback.
(d) It eliminates the need for set-shifting abilities.

2. In the four-tier hierarchical model for SST, affect recognition is considered a:

(a) Tier 1 baseline skill
(b) Tier 2 mid-level ability
(c) Tier 3 executive function
(d) Confounding variable that should be ignored

3. A 35-year-old client with traumatic brain injury completes the Person and Hat categories efficiently but never completes the Emotion category. Affect Matching performance is 9/10 correct. This pattern most likely indicates:

(a) Prosopagnosia affecting face perception.
(b) Affect recognition deficits compromising emotion sorting.
(c) Executive dysfunction specific to integrating control with emotional content.
(d) Poor test-taking effort.

4. Perseverative errors on SST primarily reflect deficits in:

(a) Visual perception and attention.
(b) Working memory capacity.
(c) Cognitive flexibility and response inhibition.
(d) Concept identification and hypothesis generation.

5. The Sort 33 prompt ("Try matching by the person") is provided to:

(a) All examinees as part of standard administration.
(b) Only examinees who have not completed the Person category by that point.
(c) Any examinee who appears frustrated or confused.
(d) Examinees who make more than 10 perseverative errors.

6. **An examinee completes all six categories but makes numerous derailment errors. This pattern suggests:**
   (a) Severe cognitive inflexibility.
   (b) Problems with concept identification.
   (c) Specific inhibition deficit when facing competing reinforcement.
   (d) Affect recognition impairment.
7. **The Global Performance Index integrates which three components?**
   (a) Perseverative errors, nonperseverative errors, and Other responses
   (b) Categories completed, sorts administered, and percentage correct
   (c) Trials to first category, derailment errors, and conceptual responses
   (d) Person accuracy, Hat accuracy, and Emotion accuracy
8. **High scores on Total Number of Other Responses (sorts that don't match any category) most likely indicate:**
   (a) Excellent cognitive flexibility.
   (b) Strong hypothesis-testing abilities.
   (c) Confusion about task requirements or very poor concept identification.
   (d) Superior executive functioning.
9. **The optional Affect Matching task should NOT be administered to:**
   (a) Examinees who completed Person and Hat but not Emotion.
   (b) Examinees who will need repeat testing in the future.
   (c) Examinees suspected of having affect recognition deficits.
   (d) Examinees over age 60.
10. **A 14-year-old with autism spectrum disorder requires 45 trials to complete the Person category, but then completes Hat and Emotion efficiently with few errors. This pattern suggests:**
   (a) Prosopagnosia affecting only the Person category.
   (b) Initial concept identification difficulty with subsequent learning.
   (c) Progressive cognitive deterioration during testing.
   (d) Inconsistent test-taking effort.

Answer Key: 1-b, 2-b, 3-c, 4-c, 5-b, 6-c, 7-b, 8-c, 9-b, 10-b

REFERENCES

Anderson, S. W., Damasio, H., Tranel, D., & Damasio, A. R. (2006). Long-term sequelae of prefrontal cortex damage acquired in early childhood. *Developmental Neuropsychology, 18*(3), 281–296.

Basso, M. R., Carona, F. D., Lowery, N., & Axelrod, B. N. (2001). Practice effects on the WCST-64 after a one-week interval. *Journal of Clinical and Experimental Neuropsychology, 24*(3), 251–257.

Benton, A. L., Sivan, A. B., Hamsher, K. d., Varney, N. R., & Spreen, O. (1994). *Contributions to Neuropsychological Assessment: A Clinical Manual* (2nd ed.). Oxford University Press.

Calamia, M., Markon, K., & Tranel, D. (2012). Scoring higher the second time around: Meta-analyses of practice effects in neuropsychological assessment. *The Clinical Neuropsychologist, 26*(4), 543–570.

Cambridge Cognition (2019). *CANTAB [Cognitive Assessment Software]*. Cambridge Cognition Ltd.

Delis, D. C. (2012a). Frontal lobe-executive functioning: An overview. In J. Schweitzer & D. Baron (Eds.), *Psychological Foundations of Success for the Medical Professional* (pp. 123–150). Elsevier.

Delis, D. C. (2012b). *Delis Rating of Executive Functions (D-REF)*. Pearson.

Delis, D. C. (2021). *Delis Rating of Executive Functions–Adult (D-REF Adult)*. Pearson.

Delis, D. C., & Kaplan, E. (2025). *Delis-Kaplan Executive Function System–Advanced (D-KEFS Advanced)*. Pearson.

Delis, D. C., Kaplan, E., & Kramer, J. H. (2001). *Delis-Kaplan Executive Function System (D-KEFS)*. Pearson.

Eslinger, P. J., Flaherty-Craig, C. V., & Benton, A. L. (2004). Developmental outcomes after early prefrontal cortex damage. *Brain and Cognition, 55*(1), 84–103.

Gioia, G. A., Isquith, P. K., Guy, S. C., & Kenworthy, L. (2015). *Behavior Rating Inventory of Executive Function, Second Edition (BRIEF-2)*. Psychological Assessment Resources.

Grant, D. A., & Berg, E. A. (1948). A behavioral analysis of degree of reinforcement and ease of shifting to new responses in a Weigl-type card sorting problem. *Journal of Experimental Psychology, 38*, 404–411.

Heaton, R. K. (1981). *Wisconsin Card Sorting Test Manual.* Psychological Assessment Resources.

Heaton, R. K., Chelune, G. J., Talley, J. L., Kay, G. G., & Curtiss, G. (1993). *Wisconsin Card Sorting Test Manual: Revised and Expanded.* Psychological Assessment Resources.

Korkman, M., Kirk, U., & Kemp, S. (2007). *NEPSY–Second Edition (NEPSY-II): Clinical and Interpretive Manual.* Pearson.

Mayer, J. D., Salovey, P., & Caruso, D. R. (2003). *Mayer-Salovey-Caruso Emotional Intelligence Test (MSCEIT)*. Multi-Health Systems.

McKone, E., Crookes, K., & Kanwisher, N. (2009). The cognitive and neural development of face recognition in humans. In M. S. Gazzaniga (Ed.), *The Cognitive Neurosciences* (4th ed., pp. 467–482). MIT Press.

Naglieri, J. A., & Goldstein, S. (2013). *Comprehensive Executive Function Inventory (CEFI)*. Multi-Health Systems.

Naglieri, J. A., & Goldstein, S. (2017). *Comprehensive Executive Function Inventory–Adult (CEFI Adult)*. Multi-Health Systems.

Roth, R. M., Isquith, P. K., & Gioia, G. A. (2005). *Behavior Rating Inventory of Executive Function–Adult Version (BRIEF-A)*. Psychological Assessment Resources.

Slater, A., & Quinn, P. C. (2001). Face recognition in the newborn infant. *Infant and Child Development, 10*(1–2), 21–24.

Stuss, D. T., & Knight, R. T. (eds.) (2013). *Principles of Frontal Lobe Function* (2nd ed.). Oxford University Press.

Suchy, Y. (2023). *Clinical Neuropsychology of Emotion and Motivation*. Routledge.

Nine

SORTING TEST

CLINICAL VIGNETTE

Forty-two-year-old David Chen, an accountant, was referred for neuropsychological evaluation following complaints of difficulty with problem-solving and "mental flexibility" at work. His supervisor noted that David excelled at routine auditing tasks but struggled when projects required novel approaches or creative solutions. David reported feeling "stuck" when encountering unfamiliar problems, often returning to strategies that had worked previously, even when they were clearly inadequate for new situations.

During the D-KEFS Sorting Test, David demonstrated the precise nature of his difficulties. On the Screening Pretest, he read all words accurately and demonstrated intact comprehension. In the Free Sorting condition, David attempted only four sorts across both card sets—well below average for his age group. His descriptions of these sorts were accurate but concrete: "Animals and transportation" and "Big and small." When prompted to find more ways to sort, he repeated these same two categories, unable to generate novel approaches.

The Sort Recognition condition, however, revealed intact concept formation abilities. When the examiner sorted the cards and asked David to identify why they were sorted together, he accurately identified and described almost all of them, including abstract perceptual sorts like "Rounded edges versus straight edges." His performance jumped from the 5th percentile in Free Sorting to the 63rd percentile in Sort Recognition. This dramatic difference between conditions—poor generation paired with strong recognition—indicated a Tier 3 initiation deficit rather than impaired concept formation. David possessed the conceptual reasoning abilities (Tier 3 cold EF) but struggled to spontaneously deploy them without external structure.

The evaluation clarified that David's workplace difficulties stemmed not from poor reasoning but from impaired initiation of problem-solving behavior, a distinction critical for intervention planning. Recommendations focused on environmental modifications rather than cognitive remediation, allowing David to leverage his intact conceptual abilities. Specific strategies included: using project templates that break complex tasks into specific steps, implementing regular check-ins where supervisors prompt David to identify his approach before beginning work, and creating visual prompts (e.g., "What's my strategy?" posted at his workstation) to cue independent problem-solving initiation.

TEST DESCRIPTION

The D-KEFS Sorting Test assesses multiple components of concept formation and problem-solving abilities through a card-sorting paradigm. Appropriate for ages 8–89 years with an administration time of approximately 15–20 minutes, the test uniquely separates the ability to generate sorting concepts from the ability to recognize them—a critical distinction for differential diagnosis and intervention planning. Unlike traditional sorting tasks that provide only a single overall score, the D-KEFS Sorting Test systematically evaluates both the conceptual reasoning underlying sorts and the behavioral execution of sorting responses (Delis et al., 2001).

The test uses two card sets (Standard Form: Sets 1 and 2; Alternate Form: Sets 3 and 4), each containing six cards with both verbal-semantic information (printed words) and visual-perceptual features (colors, sizes, shapes, patterns). Each set can be sorted into multiple target categories—some semantic and some perceptual. The dual modality design allows assessment of both verbal and nonverbal concept formation, revealing whether deficits are modality-specific or generalized.

Condition 1: Free Sorting requires examinees to spontaneously sort cards into two groups of three cards each, according to as many different groups as possible. After each sort, examinees describe the categorization principle they used. This condition assesses spontaneous problem-solving initiation, concept generation, and the ability to shift flexibly between different categorization schemes while inhibiting previously used sorts.

Condition 2: Sort Recognition presents the same card sets sorted by the examiner according to the target sorts. Examinees identify and describe the sorting rule used for each examiner-generated sort. This condition assesses concept recognition and description abilities when the behavioral sorting component is removed.

The contrast between these conditions provides powerful diagnostic information. Strong performance on both conditions suggests intact initiation and concept formation. Poor Free Sorting with strong Sort Recognition indicates initiation deficits despite intact conceptual reasoning. Poor performance on both conditions suggests fundamental concept formation impairment.

CAUTION

The Sorting Test requires sustained engagement across many trials (up to 16+ sorts if the examinee is productive in Free Sorting, plus recognition trials). Examinees with attention difficulties, low frustration tolerance, or motivational issues may show performance declines across the task that reflect fatigue or disengagement rather than true concept formation deficits. Monitor effort and engagement throughout administration.

Rapid Reference 9.1

Sorting Test Overview

Feature	Description
Age range	8–89 years
Administration time	15–20 minutes
Administration format	Paper protocol; two card sets (Standard: Sets 1 & 2; Alternate: Sets 3 & 4)
Stimuli	Six cards per set with verbal-semantic (printed words) and visual-perceptual features (colors, sizes, shapes, patterns)
Conditions	Condition 1: Free sorting (generate sorts); Condition 2: Sort recognition (identify examiner sorts)
Response format	Sort cards into two groups of three; describe sorting principle
Target categories	Eight per set (three verbal-semantic, five visual-perceptual)
Primary constructs	Tier 3 cold EF (concept formation, cognitive flexibility, initiation); generation vs. recognition distinction

HIERARCHICAL TIER ANALYSIS

The Sorting Test can be analyzed through the four-tier framework, with performance reflecting processes ranging from basic perception and language to higher-order metacognitive integration.

Tier 1: Foundational Processes (Nonexecutive)

Several basic cognitive abilities must be intact before the Sorting Test can validly assess executive functions. Unlike tests with minimal foundational demands, the Sorting Test requires coordination of visual, verbal, and motor processes that can each contribute to performance difficulties.

Visual Processing and Perception

Examinees must accurately perceive visual-perceptual features on the cards: colors, sizes, shapes, line thickness, and edge characteristics. Visual discrimination deficits could prevent recognition of subtle perceptual features, particularly the less obvious sorts. The Screening Pretest does not assess these visual abilities, so clinicians should consider visual processing screening if perceptual sorts are disproportionately impaired.

Reading and Vocabulary Knowledge

The Screening Pretest assesses whether examinees can read and comprehend the stimulus words on the cards. Most examinees achieve perfect scores on this screening task. However, limited English vocabulary or reading difficulties could prevent access to verbal-semantic sorts even when concept formation abilities are intact. An examinee unfamiliar with specific category exemplars cannot generate conceptual groupings based on those words.

Expressive Language

Performance on description measures depends heavily on expressive language abilities. An examinee might successfully sort cards by correct concepts but struggle to verbalize the categorization principles, depressing description scores despite intact concept formation. For people with significant expressive language impairments, the manual recommends using the Confirmed/Unconfirmed Target Sorts index as the primary measure, as it assesses sorting accuracy independent of verbal description ability.

Motor Coordination

While less demanding than tests requiring precise motor control, the Sorting Test requires basic ability to manipulate cards and place them into groups. Significant motor impairment could slow performance or make the physical sorting process laborious, potentially increasing frustration or cognitive load. However, the timed test discontinuation criteria are generous (four cumulative minutes excluding time needed to describe the sorts) and minimizes the impact of motor slowing on the results.

Basic Attention and Task Engagement

Examinees must sustain attention across a lengthy task with minimal external reinforcement. The test provides no right/wrong feedback, requiring tolerance for ambiguity and ability to persist without explicit performance indicators. Basic task engagement—understanding and following test instructions, remaining oriented to task goals, and maintaining effort—represents Tier 1 attentional capacity distinct from executive attention control.

> **CAUTION**
>
> The Sorting Test is particularly vulnerable to confounding by vocabulary and expressive language abilities. Low description scores could reflect limited vocabulary, word-finding difficulties, or poor verbal fluency rather than concept formation deficits. Always consider language abilities when interpreting performance, particularly for individuals with language disorders, English Language Learners, or clients with neurological conditions affecting expressive language.

Tier 1 Impairment Pattern

Tier 1 limitations manifest as fundamental difficulties with test prerequisites. An examinee struggling with visual discrimination might confuse colors or miss subtle perceptual features, preventing access to perceptual sorts. Vocabulary limitations could block semantic categorization despite intact abstract reasoning. Expressive language problems might produce low description scores with intact sorting accuracy.

Tier 2: Bridging Processes

Tier 2 processes represent emerging executive control—more complex than foundational abilities but not yet requiring the flexible, strategic deployment characteristic of true executive functions.

Simple Categorical Knowledge

Recognizing that items form semantic categories or that objects can be grouped by perceptual features represents basic semantic knowledge and pattern recognition. This differs from Tier 3 abstract categorical reasoning in an important way: simple categorical knowledge involves retrieving overlearned, conventional groupings rather than generating novel conceptual relationships or flexibly shifting between multiple categorization schemes.

Basic Rule-Following and Set Maintenance
Following the instruction to "sort cards into two groups of three" and maintaining this simple procedural rule across trials represents basic set maintenance. This differs from Tier 3 cognitive flexibility in that it involves maintaining a constant task structure rather than flexibly shifting between different mental sets or categorization principles.

Elementary Inhibition
Avoiding repetition of the exact same sort represents simple response inhibition: remembering what was just done and not doing it again. This differs from the more complex Tier 3 inhibitory demands of suppressing dominant conceptual categories to access less obvious ones.

Procedural Learning
With repeated sorting trials, examinees implicitly learn the task structure and demands. Improvement across trials might reflect procedural learning rather than executive strategy development. Similarly, increased efficiency in the Sort Recognition condition compared to Free Sorting might partly reflect learning from the Free Sorting experience rather than purely reflecting a generation-versus-recognition distinction.

Simple Verbal Working Memory
Holding the examiner's instruction "sort these into two groups" or maintaining awareness of previously used sorts involves basic working memory capacity. This simple maintenance function differs from Tier 3 working memory demands of simultaneously tracking multiple potential categorization schemes while evaluating which to pursue.

Tier 2 Deficit Pattern
Tier 2 Performance shows access to basic categorical knowledge without executive flexibility. These examinees might generate 3–4 conventional sorts but struggle to discover novel or subtle categorization schemes requiring hypothesis generation. They successfully maintain task sets and follow basic rules, but lack the strategic cognitive flexibility for comprehensive category discovery.

Tier 3: Core Executive Functions

The Sorting Test primarily assesses Tier 3 executive functions, particularly in the domains of concept formation, cognitive flexibility, and initiation of problem-solving behavior. Understanding these core demands is essential for accurate interpretation.

Cold Executive Functions
The Sorting Test assesses multiple cold executive functions that operate in the analytical, emotionally neutral domain of categorization and abstract reasoning.

Abstract Categorical Reasoning and Concept Formation (Primary Construct)
The essence of the Sorting Test is identifying abstract conceptual relationships among stimuli, moving beyond surface-level features to recognize underlying commonalities. The test requires hypothesis generation and testing. Examinees must propose potential categorization schemes, evaluate whether card organization fits those schemes, and revise hypotheses when initial approaches fail. This process exemplifies executive control: directing attention strategically, evaluating multiple possibilities, and selecting among competing response options.

The distinction between obvious and subtle sorts highlights the executive demands. Some sorts activate overlearned semantic categories requiring less executive control, while others demand strategic visual analysis and novel conceptual relationship recognition. Some examinees retrieve only conventional categories (Tier 2 categorical knowledge), while others flexibly discover less obvious relationships (Tier 3 concept generation).

The Sort Recognition condition reveals whether poor concept generation reflects true conceptual reasoning deficits versus problems initiating or executing conceptual strategies. Strong recognition despite poor generation indicates intact conceptual reasoning that fails to deploy spontaneously—a dissociation highly informative for intervention planning.

DON'T FORGET

The contrast between Free Sorting and Sort Recognition is the Sorting Test's most diagnostically powerful feature. Strong recognition despite poor generation indicates intact conceptual reasoning that fails to deploy spontaneously—an initiation or executive control problem, not a reasoning deficit. This pattern calls for intervention targeting strategy initiation and self-cueing rather than conceptual skill building.

Cognitive Flexibility and Shifting

After generating one sort, examinees must abandon that conceptual framework and develop an entirely different categorization principle. This requires mental set shifting—releasing attention from one conceptual dimension and redirecting it to another. The test explicitly prohibits repeating previous sorts, requiring active monitoring of which categorization schemes have already been used.

Cognitive flexibility operates at multiple levels on this test. At the most basic level, shifting between verbal sorts requires relatively little flexibility, as they all remain within the semantic domain. Shifting from verbal to perceptual sorts demands greater flexibility: abandoning the verbal-semantic approach entirely and adopting a visual-perceptual strategy. The most demanding flexibility involves discovering multiple perceptual sorts, as these often require noticing increasingly subtle visual features after more obvious patterns are exhausted.

Inhibitory Control and Response Suppression

Successfully completing this test requires inhibiting several types of responses. Examinees must suppress the tendency to repeat previous sorts, inhibit dominant or obvious categorization schemes to discover subtler ones, and resist verbalizing concepts before fully forming them (which could lead to incomplete or inaccurate descriptions). Individuals with disinhibition might impulsively generate sorts without adequate conceptual planning, producing either repeated sorts or nontarget sorts based on hastily conceived principles (Miyake et al., 2000).

The repeated sorts error type specifically reflects inhibitory failure—returning to previously used categorization schemes despite explicit instructions and examiner prompts against repetition. High numbers of repeated sorts, combined with few total attempted sorts, suggest rigid, perseverative thinking where the individual cannot escape from dominant conceptual categories. In some cases, examinees may repeat sorts in response to internal pressure to create more sorts even though they cannot think of new ways to combine the cards.

Executive Working Memory

Beyond simple maintenance (Tier 2), the Sorting Test requires active manipulation of information in working memory. Examinees must simultaneously maintain awareness of previously used sorts, track which conceptual dimensions remain unexplored, evaluate potential new categorization schemes, and monitor whether current groupings satisfy candidate principles. This represents true working memory manipulation: holding multiple pieces of information active while operating on them strategically (Miyake et al., 2000).

The working memory demands intensify as more sorts are generated. Early in Free Sorting, examinees need only avoid repeating one or two previous sorts. Later trials require tracking many already-used categories, increasing the load on executive working memory systems.

Initiation of Problem-Solving Behavior

The Free Sorting condition uniquely assesses spontaneous problem-solving initiation—the ability to independently begin tackling a novel problem without external prompts or structure. Some examinees possess adequate concept formation abilities (demonstrated through Sort Recognition performance) but struggle to spontaneously engage in problem-solving behavior. This initiation deficit might manifest as very few attempted sorts, long latencies before beginning each sort, or passive waiting for examiner direction despite instructions to generate sorts independently (Barkley, 2011).

Low Attempted Sorts scores represent an operational measure of initiation deficits. The contrast between attempted sorts and confirmed correct sorts helps distinguish initiation problems from accuracy issues: few attempts with high accuracy suggests an initiation deficit, while many attempts with low accuracy suggest poor concept formation or hasty, impulsive responding.

Knowledge Transfer to Action

Some examinees can verbalize abstract concepts but struggle to translate that knowledge into behavioral execution. They might accurately describe a potential sorting rule but then group cards incorrectly, or they might demonstrate strong Sort Recognition (identifying examiner-generated sorts) but poor Free Sorting (executing their own sorts). This dissociation between conceptual knowledge and behavioral execution represents an executive dysfunction in translating intention to action.

The Confirmed Correct Sorts measure requires that sorts be "confirmed" by at least partially accurate descriptions, ensuring that correct groupings reflect genuine conceptual understanding rather than chance. The Confirmed/Unconfirmed Target Sorts measure captures accurate sorts regardless of description quality, helping distinguish conceptual accuracy from verbal expression difficulties.

Modality-Specific Concept Formation

The test's dual design—verbal-semantic and visual-perceptual sorts—allows assessment of whether concept formation deficits are broad or modality-specific. Some examinees show disproportionate difficulty with perceptual sorts despite intact verbal sorting, suggesting problems with visual concept formation specifically. Others might demonstrate the opposite pattern, particularly relevant for individuals with language-based learning disabilities who might excel at visual pattern recognition while struggling with verbal categorization. Likewise, English Language Learners may also demonstrate a pattern of stronger visual-perceptual abilities due to their developing language abilities and not because of any innate language-based disorders.

Tier 3 Cold EF Impairment Pattern

Examinees with Tier 3 Cold EF deficits show impaired concept formation, cognitive inflexibility, or initiation difficulties despite intact foundational abilities. Key indicators include a few attempted sorts with dramatic improvement during Sort Recognition (initiation deficit), high repeated sorts despite adequate conceptual accuracy (perseveration), poor performance across both conditions (concept formation deficit), or disproportionate difficulty with verbal versus perceptual sorts (modality-specific impairment). The contrast between Free Sorting and Sort Recognition is particularly diagnostic—strong recognition with weak generation indicates the examinee possesses conceptual reasoning capacity but struggles to deploy it spontaneously.

Hot Executive Functions

While the Sorting Test appears primarily cold and cognitive, hot executive factors significantly affect performance, particularly during extended Free Sorting trials (Casey et al., 2011; Mischel et al., 1989).

Frustration Tolerance and Persistence

The open-ended nature of Free Sorting—with no clear endpoint and no right/wrong feedback—creates frustration for some examinees. After generating several obvious sorts, finding additional categorization schemes requires sustained mental effort and tolerance for increasing difficulty. Some examinees disengage prematurely, giving up when obvious sorts are exhausted rather than persisting through more challenging conceptual discoveries (Mischel et al., 1989).

Frustration might manifest as irritable comments ("I don't see any other ways"), passive waiting ("Are we done yet?"), or premature declarations of completion ("That's all there are"). These hot EF limitations can artificially depress scores that would be higher if emotional regulation were stronger.

Anxiety and Performance Pressure

The ambiguous nature of the task with no clear indication of how many sorts exist or whether performance is adequate can generate anxiety in some examinees. Performance-anxious individuals might experience cognitive interference from worry ("Am I finding enough sorts?"), leading to distraction from the sorting task itself. Alternatively, anxiety might manifest as hasty, impulsive sorting to "get through it quickly," reducing the careful conceptual analysis required for optimal performance.

Tolerance for Ambiguity
The absence of right/wrong feedback requires tolerating uncertainty about performance quality. Some examinees find this ambiguity distressing, repeatedly asking "Is that right?" or seeking reassurance. While examiners must maintain standardization by not providing feedback, the emotional distress generated by ambiguity can interfere with cognitive efficiency for anxiety-prone individuals.

Response to Increasing Difficulty
As obvious sorts are exhausted, task difficulty increases substantially. How examinees respond emotionally to this escalating challenge affects whether they persist or disengage. Some individuals respond to challenge with increased effort (adaptive hot EF), while others respond with frustration-driven withdrawal (maladaptive hot EF), even when cognitive capacity remains adequate for continued performance.

Tier 3 Hot EF Pattern
Examinees with Hot EF difficulties show performance compromised by emotional factors rather than cognitive limitations. They may generate several sorts initially, but deteriorate as frustration builds with the open-ended format and lack of feedback. Observable signs include irritable comments, passive waiting, premature declarations of completion, or rushed sorting without adequate planning. The key diagnostic indicator is that conceptual capacity exists as evidenced by some successful sorts or strong Sort Recognition performance while emotional dysregulation prevents sustained deployment. Behavioral observations during testing distinguish this pattern from Cold EF deficits and indicate that intervention should target frustration tolerance or anxiety management rather than concept formation skills.

CAUTION

Hot executive function difficulties can masquerade as cold EF deficits on the Sorting Test. An examinee with intact concept formation abilities might generate few sorts due to frustration-based disengagement rather than conceptual limitations. Behavioral observations during testing—comments, nonverbal signs of frustration, effort withdrawal—help distinguish between cognitive limitations and emotional regulation difficulties affecting cognitive deployment.

Tier 4: Higher-Order Integration and Metacognition

The Sorting Test makes modest but meaningful demands on Tier 4 metacognitive and integrative processes.

Metacognitive Monitoring and Self-Evaluation
Examinees must monitor their own performance, tracking which sorts they have already generated and evaluating whether candidate sorts represent genuinely novel categorization schemes or unwitting repetitions. This requires stepping back from immediate task engagement to evaluate one's own cognitive processes—a metacognitive function. Some examinees generate repeated sorts not because they cannot avoid repetition but because they fail to monitor whether current ideas match previous ones (Dehn, 2014).

Strategic Approach Selection
More sophisticated examinees develop systematic strategies for discovering sorts: starting with obvious categorical divisions, then examining cards for visual patterns, or methodically checking each potential perceptual dimension. This strategic, organized approach to problem-solving represents Tier 4 integration: coordinating multiple executive processes toward an overarching goal.

In contrast, some examinees approach sorting randomly, grouping cards haphazardly without systematic conceptual analysis. While they might occasionally stumble upon correct sorts, their lack of strategic organization prevents efficient discovery of the full range of categorization possibilities.

Integration of Verbal and Nonverbal Processing
Moving flexibly between verbal-semantic and visual-perceptual sorting modalities requires integrating across different processing systems. Some examinees get "stuck" in one modality, generating all verbal sorts but never shifting to perceptual analysis, or vice versa. Fluid integration across modalities reflects higher-order coordination of different cognitive resources.

DON'T FORGET

A diagnostically powerful pattern on the Sorting Test is the Free Sorting versus Sort Recognition dissociation. Strong recognition despite weak generation indicates problems with initiation, spontaneity, or behavioral execution despite intact conceptual reasoning. This distinction is critical for intervention planning: these individuals do not need concept-building training but rather environmental modifications providing structure and initiation prompts.

Tier 4 Integration Difficulties
Tier 4 Patterns involve metacognitive and strategic deficits. Examinees might possess adequate concept formation abilities (demonstrating this intermittently) but lack systematic, strategic approaches to discovering sorts. They might fail to monitor their own performance, producing repeated sorts without awareness, or generate many overly abstract descriptions without recognizing that single-concept explanations fail to describe both groups. Inconsistent performance with variable quality across trials suggests problems with self-monitoring and strategic organization rather than fundamental cognitive capacity limitations.

Rapid Reference 9.2

Tier Structure at a Glance

Tier	Processes
Tier 1: Foundational processes (nonexecutive)	Visual processing and perception of card features
	Reading and vocabulary knowledge (Screening Pretest)
	Expressive language for descriptions
	Motor coordination for card manipulation
	Basic attention and task engagement
Tier 2: Bridging processes	Simple categorical knowledge (retrieving conventional groupings)
	Basic rule-following and set maintenance
	Elementary inhibition (avoiding exact repetitions)
	Procedural learning across trials
	Simple verbal working memory
Tier 3: Cold executive functions	Abstract categorical reasoning and concept formation
	Cognitive flexibility and set-shifting
	Inhibitory control (suppressing dominant categories)
	Executive working memory (tracking multiple schemes)
	Initiation of problem-solving behavior
	Modality-specific concept formation (verbal vs. perceptual)
Tier 3: Hot executive functions	Frustration tolerance and persistence
	Anxiety management under ambiguity

Tier	Processes
Tier 4: Higher-order integration	Response to increasing difficulty Metacognitive monitoring (tracking previous sorts) Strategic approach selection (systematic vs. random) Integration of verbal and nonverbal processing

ADMINISTRATION

NOTE: Refer to the Examiner's Manual for complete and detailed administration instructions. The Examiner's Manual provides verbatim instructions and clinicians should follow these precisely to ensure standardized administration.

Materials and Setup

For paper-and-pencil administration, the Sorting Test requires the Examiner's Manual, Record Form, Stimulus Booklet, Practice Card Set (shared between Standard and Alternate Forms), Card Sets 1–2 (Standard Form) or 3–4 (Alternate Form), and a timer (Delis et al., 2001). Pearson also offers a partial-digital version, which requires the Q-global Examiner's digital Manual, Stimulus Book, and Stimulus Book Administration Directions, along with the standard Record Form and Card Sets.

Screening Pretest

Before formal testing, administer the Screening Pretest to ensure the examinee can read and comprehend stimulus words. Point to each word on the screening card and ask the examinee to read it aloud. For any word read incorrectly, provide the correct pronunciation. Then define each word, asking the examinee to indicate understanding. For any word the examinee does not know, provide a brief definition. Record the number of reading errors and comprehension errors. Most examinees achieve perfect scores on this screening; significant errors warrant consideration of how vocabulary/reading limitations might affect test performance.

Practice Card Set

Introduce the Practice Card Set (the same set is used for both Standard and Alternate Forms) to familiarize examinees with sorting procedures. Show the cards word-side up in a random, oval arrangement and provide standardized instructions explaining that cards can be sorted into two groups of three cards each in multiple different ways. Demonstrate the first practice sort (circles and squares), grouping cards and describing the categorization principle. Then provide a second Practice trial using historically male names and female names as groups. The Practice Set allows teaching without affecting test scores. Do not discontinue the Practice Set even if the examinee struggles; use it as a teaching opportunity.

Condition 1: Free Sorting

Present Card Set 1 (or Card Set 3 for Alternate Form) cards word-side up in a random, oval arrangement. Instruct the examinee to sort cards into two groups of three cards each, finding as many different ways to sort as possible. After each sort, ask, "How did you group them?" to elicit a description of both groups. Record the physical sort configuration and verbatim description as directed on the Record Form. Refer to the manual for a listing of specific prompts for delayed responding, no description response, new rule violations, overly abstract descriptions, and requests for reminders of previous descriptions.

Start timing when the examinee begins the task. Pause timing when the examinee has completed their sort and begins to describe their sorting strategy. Continue timing after the examinee has provided a description, the cards have been placed and rearranged randomly, and the prompt "Now try to sort them in a different way" has been stated.

Discontinue Rules for Free Sorting

Stop Free Sorting when: (1) the examinee indicates they cannot find any more sorts and declines to continue, (2) cumulative sorting time reaches 240 seconds, OR (3) the examinee has attempted 10 sorts. Do not discontinue early simply because the examinee generates few sorts. Allow them to work until they meet one of these three discontinue criteria. Then present Card Set 2 (or Set 4 for the Alternate Form) and repeat the procedure with the same discontinue rules.

Condition 2: Sort Recognition

For each card set, present the eight target sorts one at a time (same card sets used in Free Sorting) in the order specified in the Examiner's Manual. After displaying each examiner-generated sort, ask, "How did I group them?" Start timing to ensure that the examinee provides a response for each sort within the 45-second time limit. Record verbatim descriptions. Follow the Sort Recognition prompts in the Examiner's Manual for delayed responding and new rule violations. Present all eight sorts for each card set regardless of performance.

BEHAVIORAL OBSERVATIONS

Behavioral observations during Sorting Test administration provide qualitative information for enriching quantitative score interpretation.

Approach to Sorting

Note whether the examinee demonstrates a systematic strategy (e.g., methodically examining each card for features, organizing cards spatially during analysis) versus a haphazard approach (random grouping, little apparent planning). Systematic approaches often correlate with better performance but also reveal preserved executive organization even when scores are depressed by other factors.

Observe whether sorting is impulsive (very rapid grouping with minimal consideration) or deliberate (careful analysis before committing to groups). Impulsive sorting often accompanies disinhibition or low frustration tolerance, while extreme deliberation might reflect anxiety, perfectionism, or perseverative features.

Verbalization Patterns

Some examinees verbalize their thought process extensively during sorting ("Let me see… these could go together… or maybe…"), providing insight into their problem-solving approach. Others work silently, making internal cognitive processes less observable. Rich verbal mediation might compensate for organizational weaknesses, while difficulty verbalizing could reflect expressive language limitations or concrete thinking.

Note the quality of initial description responses. Overly abstract descriptions (single concepts covering both groups) might reflect either conceptual sophistication (recognizing the overarching dimension) or problems with specificity and detail. Concrete, feature-based descriptions suggest difficulty abstracting to categorical level. Circumlocutory descriptions might reflect word-finding difficulties despite intact concepts.

Flexibility and Perseveration

Watch for perseverative tendencies: repeatedly attempting the same sort despite examiner prompts, difficulty shifting from verbal to perceptual sorting (or vice versa), or conceptual rigidity where the examinee insists only a few sorts are possible. Perseveration manifests not just in repeated sorts (scored objectively) but in a resistant, inflexible attitude during testing.

Conversely, note fluid shifting between modalities and creative discovery of novel sorts. Some examinees display remarkable conceptual flexibility, discovering unusual but valid categorization schemes. While nontarget sorts, such creativity suggests strong divergent thinking and conceptual fluency.

Emotional and Motivational Responses

Monitor frustration tolerance as the task progresses. Some examinees remain engaged and persistent even when finding additional sorts becomes difficult, while others show increasing irritability, withdrawal of effort, or passive waiting for the task to end. Comments like "This is stupid," "I can't do this," or "How many more?" signal mounting frustration that might artificially limit performance.

Anxiety about performance often manifests as repeated requests for feedback ("Did I get it right?"), apologetic comments ("I'm probably doing this wrong"), or visible tension. These emotional responses can interfere with cognitive efficiency, consuming working memory resources needed for the sorting task itself.

Note responses to Sort Recognition condition. Some examinees experience relief ("Oh, this is easier!") while others show continued frustration or embarrassment if they failed to discover sorts during Free Sorting that seem obvious when presented by the examiner.

Insight and Metacognitive Awareness

Observe whether examinees demonstrate awareness of task difficulty, monitor their own performance quality, or show insight into their struggles. Comments like "I know I must be missing some, but I just can't see them" indicate metacognitive awareness despite performance limitations. Lack of awareness—confidently declaring completion after generating only 2–3 sorts—might reflect anosognosia or poor self-monitoring.

Similarly, note whether examinees spontaneously self-correct errors, revise descriptions to be more specific, or demonstrate awareness when they have accidentally repeated a previous sort. These metacognitive processes operate at Tier 4 and their presence (or absence) informs tier-based analysis.

SCORING

The Sorting Test provides a complex array of scores reflecting multiple aspects of concept formation and problem-solving. Understanding these measures and their relationships is essential for interpretation (Delis et al., 2001). Refer to and complete the Record Form using scoring criteria. The Examiner's Manual provides examples of responses that correspond to each scoring criterion and figures showing how to complete the Record Form.

Primary Measures

Confirmed Correct Sorts (Condition 1: Free Sorting)

The primary sorting measure counts sorts that meet two criteria: (1) cards are physically grouped according to one of the eight target categorization schemes, and (2) the examinee provides at least a partially accurate description (minimum 1 point per group), confirming the sort was not accidental. This confirmed sorts requirement ensures that correct groupings reflect genuine conceptual understanding rather than chance.

Free Sorting Description Score (Condition 1)

This measures the quality of verbal explanations for each of the two groups for each of the sorts generated during Free Sorting. Each group within a sort receives 0, 1, or 2 description points based on accuracy and specificity. The maximum score is 2 points for each group of a sort and 4 points for the two groups that compose one sort. Novel, correct descriptions to a repeated sort are scored as correct.

- **2 points:** Description reflects the general concept/category accurately and specifically (e.g., using appropriate superordinate or descriptive language).
- **1 point:** Description is partially accurate but too concrete, too general, or overly inclusive.

- **0 points:** Description is inaccurate, irrelevant, overly inclusive, a nonresponse, and most cases of "Not" Statements (describing one group as "not" the other group versus a unique description).

It is important to refer to examples of 2, 1, and 0 point responses in the Examiner's Manual when making scoring decisions.

Sort Recognition Description Score (Condition 2)
Scoring is identical to Free Sorting descriptions, but for examiner-generated sorts.

Combined Conditions 1 + 2 Description Score
This composite combines Free Sorting and Sort Recognition description scaled scores and converts to a new composite scaled score. It represents the most comprehensive measure of description accuracy across both conditions.

Sort Recognition Versus Free Sorting Description Score (Contrast Measure)
This contrast measure compares Sort Recognition description scaled score minus Free Sorting description scaled score, converted to a scaled score (M = 10, SD = 3). Scaled scores ≥13 indicate significantly better recognition than generation, suggesting initiation deficits with intact concept formation. Scaled scores ≤7 indicate better generation than recognition (rare but sometimes seen with perseveration interfering with Sort Recognition).

Optional Measures

Screening Pretest Measures
Word Reading Errors and Word Comprehension Errors. A cumulative percentile rank is provided based on the number of participants in the norming group who demonstrated the same number of errors. The vast majority of examinees (over 90%) achieve perfect scores on this screening. Elevated percentile ranks (indicating more errors than the normative sample) warrant consideration of how vocabulary and reading limitations might affect test performance, particularly on verbal-semantic sorts. When significant errors occur, clinicians should consider supplementary language assessment (e.g., WIAT-4 reading subtests; Wechsler, 2020; Boston Naming Test; Kaplan et al., 2001; WAIS-5 Vocabulary; Wechsler, 2024) to determine whether poor Sorting Test performance reflects language deficits rather than executive dysfunction. The Confirmed/Unconfirmed Target Sorts measure may provide a more valid assessment of concept formation for examinees with notable Screening Pretest difficulties.

Free Sorting—Sorting Measures (Condition 1 Only)
Confirmed Correct Sorts First and Second Card Set. Separates confirmed sort performance on the first card set from performance on the second card set. Comparing performance across card sets may reveal learning-to-learn effects (significantly higher scores on the second set reflecting capacity to acquire more effective problem-solving strategies from experience alone), performance inconsistencies related to non-neurostructural factors (mood, fatigue, effort, medication effects), or provide screening information when time constraints prevent full administration.

Confirmed Correct Verbal Sorts/Confirmed Correct Perceptual Sorts. Separates performance on the three verbal-semantic sorts versus the five visual-perceptual sorts. Allows detection of modality-specific concept formation deficits.

Confirmed/Unconfirmed Target Sorts. Counts target sorts generated regardless of description quality. Useful for examinees with expressive language impairments—measures sorting accuracy independent of verbal ability.

Repeated Sorts. Number of times the examinee produces the same sort more than once (even if prompted against repetition). Reflects perseverative tendencies and cognitive inflexibility. Raw score converts to cumulative percentile rank with higher percentiles indicating more repetition than the normative sample.

Set-Loss Sorts. Based on the number of times that an examinee made a sort but failed to comply with the task demands of forming two groups, with three cards per group. These errors are rare (only 2.2% of the normative sample produces one or more), making even a single set-loss sort potentially significant. Set-loss sorts (e.g., four cards in one group, two in another) may reflect deficits in establishing or maintaining cognitive set.

Nontarget Even Sorts. Each set of six cards can be sorted into two groups, with three cards per group, in 10 possible ways. Eight of those ways are target sorts. The other two sorts are called nontarget even sorts because the examinee divided the cards into two groups evenly but failed to do so according to one of the eight target rules. These errors are relatively common (17.4% of the normative sample makes at least one), and clinical significance depends on the accompanying description: nontarget sorts paired with accurate noncredit descriptions may reflect creative concept formation, while those paired with incorrect descriptions suggest at least some degree of deficient concept formation.

Attempted Sorts. Total number of sorting attempts, including both correct and incorrect sorts. Low attempted sorts (even if those attempted are correct) suggests initiation deficits. Raw score converts to scaled score.

Percent Sorting Accuracy. (Number Confirmed Correct Sorts ÷ Number Attempted Sorts) × 100. This accuracy percentage, when converted to a scaled score, reveals whether low confirmed correct sorts reflects few attempts (initiation deficit) versus many inaccurate attempts (concept formation deficit or impulsivity).

Time-Per-Sort Ratio. Optional normed measure of average time per sort (Total Cumulative Sorting Time ÷ Number of Attempted Sorts). This measure has scaled score norms and can provide clinical information about processing speed, deliberation versus impulsivity, or initiation latencies.

Free Sorting—Description Measures (Condition 1 Only)

Free Sorting Description Score First and Second Card Set. Allows for comparison of description accuracy between Card Set 1 and Card Set 2 in Condition 1. Higher scores on Card Set 2 may reflect learning-to-learn (acquiring more effective problem-solving strategies from experience with Card Set 1), while inconsistent performance across card sets (significantly better on one set in Free Sorting but the opposite pattern in Sort Recognition) may suggest non-neurostructural factors such as mood state, fatigue, effort, or medication effects rather than stable cognitive deficits.

Free Sorting Incorrect Descriptions. Reflects the number of times an examinee reported a specific description of a sorting concept or rule that was incorrect. These include descriptions that do not accurately reflect the target concepts and descriptions that do not match the sort. Any "do not know" responses are not counted for this variable. High numbers suggest concept formation deficits. Qualitative analysis helps: highly concrete/tangential errors signal severe impairment; plausible but inaccurate errors suggest milder deficits.

Free Sorting Repeated Descriptions. The number of times an examinee repeated the same description of a sorting concept or rule within a card set. Repetitions are counted for both correct and incorrect descriptions, but not for "do not know" responses. Reflects perseverative verbal responses distinct from repeated sorts (which reflect perseverative behavioral responses).

Free Sorting Percent Description Accuracy. (Free Sorting Description Raw Score ÷ Number of Attempted Sorts × 4) × 100. Reveals description accuracy relative to productivity which is useful for distinguishing poor descriptions due to limited vocabulary versus poor concept formation.

Sort Recognition (Condition 2 only)

Sort Recognition Description Score First and Second Card Set. Allows for comparison of description accuracy between Card Set 1 and Card Set 2 in Condition 2. Higher scores on Card Set 2 may reflect learning-to-learn (acquiring more effective problem-solving strategies from experience with Card Set 1), while inconsistent performance across card sets (significantly better on one set in Sort Recognition but the opposite pattern in Free Sorting) may suggest non-neurostructural factors such as mood state, fatigue, effort, or medication effects rather than stable cognitive deficits.

Sort Recognition Incorrect Descriptions. Same score criteria as Free Sorting.

Sort Recognition Repeated Descriptions. Same score criteria as Free Sorting.

Combined Description Measures (Conditions 1 and 2).

Combined Description Score Verbal and Perceptual Rules. An examinee's accuracy in describing either the verbal sorting rules or the perceptual sorting rules across Conditions 1 and 2.

Combined No/Do not Know Responses. Number of times examinee did not respond or said "do not know" was summed across Conditions 1 and 2. Elevated counts might reflect initiation deficits, depression/negativity, concept formation problems, or insufficient effort.

Combined Noncredit Descriptions. Responses that are so ubiquitous that they could apply to most card sets and accurately describe how both groups of cards were sorted. These responses are not marked as errors and do not receive description score points.

Combined Overly Abstract Descriptions. Responses that reflect a single, abstract concept that accurately describes both groups and do not explicitly describe how each of the two groups of cards was sorted. An example is "I sorted them by color."

Combined Incorrect Descriptions. The number of times an examinee reported a specific incorrect description of a sorting concept or rule, summed across Conditions 1 and 2.

Combined Repeated Descriptions. Number of repeated descriptions generated by an examinee, summed across Conditions 1 and 2.

Rapid Reference 9.3

Scoring Summary

Score Type	Score Name	What It Measures
Primary measures	Confirmed correct sorts	Sorts with accurate physical grouping AND accurate description
	Free sorting description score	Quality of verbal explanations (0–2 points per group)
	Sort recognition description score	Description quality for examiner-generated sorts
	Combined description score	Composite across both conditions
	Sort recognition vs. free sorting contrast	Recognition minus generation; ≥13 = initiation deficit with intact concepts
Optional sorting measures	Confirmed correct verbal/perceptual sorts	Modality-specific concept formation
	Confirmed/unconfirmed target sorts	Sorting accuracy independent of description quality
	Repeated sorts	Perseverative tendencies; cognitive inflexibility
	Set-loss sorts	Failure to maintain two groups of three; rare but significant
	Attempted sorts	Total attempts; low = initiation deficit
	Percent sorting accuracy	Confirmed ÷ Attempted; distinguishes few attempts from many errors
Optional description measures	Incorrect descriptions	Concept formation deficits
	Repeated descriptions	Verbal perseveration
	No/do not know responses	Initiation, depression, effort, or concept problems
Screening	Word reading/comprehension errors	Tier 1 language limitations

COMMON ADMINISTRATION ERRORS

Several administration mistakes can compromise test validity or scoring accuracy.

Providing Feedback About Correctness

The test specifically prohibits indicating whether sorts are right or wrong. Comments like "Good!" or "Not quite" can alter the examinee's approach and invalidate results. Maintain neutral responses throughout.

Failing to Use the Overly Abstract Clarification Prompt Correctly

When examinees give single-concept descriptions covering both groups, examiners must prompt for a more specific description of each group separately using the exact standardized wording: "Good, but how did you specifically sort each group?" This prompt can only be used ONCE during the entire test administration (not once per sort, but once total). Forgetting this prompt or using it more than once affects scoring validity.

Ignoring Discontinue Criteria

Examiners must apply the three discontinue criteria for Free Sorting: (1) examinee self-discontinues, (2) 240 seconds cumulative sorting time, OR (3) 10 attempted sorts. Continuing beyond these limits or stopping too early affects score validity and normative comparisons.

Forgetting to Stop and Start the Timer

Examiners must repetitively stop the timer when the examinee has completed their sort and begins to describe their sorting strategy, then begin timing again after the examinee has provided a description, the cards have been placed and rearranged randomly, and the prompt "Now try to sort them in a different way" has been stated.

Recording Descriptions Imprecisely

Verbatim recording is essential for accurate scoring. Paraphrasing or summarizing risks losing scoring-relevant details that distinguish between 0, 1, and 2-point responses. For example, recording "animals" when the examinee said "animals that live on farms" loses the specificity that would earn additional points. When in doubt, write exactly what the examinee says and make scoring decisions afterward.

Confusing Card Set Administration Order

For each condition, Card Set 1 (or 3) is always administered first, followed by Set 2 (or 4). Reversing this order affects comparisons between card sets and compromises normative scoring, as the standardization sample completed sets in the prescribed sequence. Additionally, ensure the correct form is used throughout; mixing Standard Form card sets with Alternate Form card sets invalidates results.

Limited Attention to Detail when Scoring

The Sorting Test requires close scrutiny of responses and frequent reference to the numerous examples provided in the Examiner's Manual. Scoring errors are common when examiners attempt to score from memory rather than consulting the manual's detailed response examples. The distinction between 1-point and 2-point descriptions often hinges on subtle differences in specificity and abstraction level that require careful comparison to scoring criteria. Taking time to score accurately—even if it means completing scoring after the session—yields more valid and clinically useful results than rushed scoring during administration.

INTERPRETATION

Sorting Test interpretation requires integrating multiple score types with qualitative observations within a systematic framework that distinguishes foundational limitations from true executive dysfunction.

Using the Hierarchical Framework for Differential Diagnosis

Interpreting Sorting Test performance requires systematic evaluation across tiers to identify where processing breaks down.

Step 1: Rule Out Tier 1 Limitations
Begin by evaluating foundational prerequisites. Did the examinee pass the Screening Pretest with minimal errors? If significant reading or comprehension errors occurred, vocabulary limitations might depress verbal sort performance. Examine whether visual-perceptual difficulties are suspected—would perceptual sort deficits reflect poor visual discrimination rather than concept formation problems? Consider expressive language abilities: Do description scores severely underestimate sorting accuracy (large discrepancy between Confirmed Correct Sorts and Description Scores), suggesting language expression difficulties? If Tier 1 limitations are substantial, higher-tier interpretation becomes tentative, and supplementary language or visual processing assessment is warranted.

Step 2: Evaluate Tier 2 Bridging Processes
Examine whether the examinee demonstrates basic categorical knowledge. Did they successfully generate the most obvious sorts? If performance is limited to simple, conventional categories without discovery of subtler categorization schemes, this suggests Tier 2 functioning: adequate basic knowledge without executive flexibility for novel concept generation. Poor performance on even obvious categories suggests Tier 1–2 limitations in fundamental processing rather than pure executive dysfunction.

Step 3: Analyze Tier 3 Cold Executive Patterns
With Tiers 1–2 intact, evaluate cold executive function capacity. Multiple patterns of Tier 3 dysfunction can emerge on the Sorting Test. Examine whether Free Sorting performance is markedly lower than Sort Recognition. A contrast measure scaled score ≥13 indicates a specific initiation deficit with intact concept formation, where the examinee possesses adequate conceptual reasoning but struggles to deploy it spontaneously without external structure. Poor performance across both conditions suggests fundamental concept formation impairment affecting both generation and recognition. High repeated sorts with moderate attempted sorts indicate cognitive inflexibility and difficulty releasing previous categorization schemes. Finally, compare Confirmed Correct Verbal Sorts versus Confirmed Correct Perceptual Sorts to detect modality-specific deficits—disproportionate impairment in one domain suggests lateralized dysfunction or domain-specific processing limitations rather than generalized concept formation problems.

Step 4: Evaluate Tier 3 Hot Executive Factors
Determine whether emotional regulation factors contributed to performance. Did frustration with the open-ended format or lack of feedback lead to premature disengagement? Some examinees respond to the ambiguity of Free Sorting with visible anxiety, rushing through sorts without adequate conceptual planning or giving up after generating only a few obvious categories. Note whether performance declined across the task in ways suggesting accumulated frustration rather than cognitive fatigue. Behavioral observations during testing—irritable comments, passive waiting, requests to stop—help distinguish hot EF contributions from cold EF limitations, as intervention approaches differ substantially.

Step 5: Assess Tier 4 Integration and Metacognition
For examinees with adequate Tier 3 core functions, evaluate higher-order integration. Is there metacognitive awareness of sorting performance? Examinees who spontaneously recognize they are repeating sorts or who comment on their own difficulty shifting strategies demonstrate intact Tier 4 monitoring. Consider whether the examinee used a systematic strategic approach—methodically exhausting verbal sorts before shifting to perceptual analysis—or approached the task haphazardly without organized planning. Tier 4 deficits manifest as adequate basic concept formation abilities without strategic flexibility or self-monitoring, producing inconsistent performance with repeated sorts that the examinee fails to recognize.

PERFORMANCE PATTERNS AND CLINICAL IMPLICATIONS

Several distinct performance patterns emerge on the Sorting Test, each with different clinical implications for diagnosis and intervention planning.

Performance Patterns

Initiation Deficit with Intact Concept Formation

This pattern shows very few attempted sorts in Free Sorting (often ≤4 across both card sets) with dramatically better Sort Recognition performance. The contrast measure scaled score is typically ≥13, and description scores jump markedly between conditions. These individuals possess adequate conceptual reasoning but struggle to spontaneously engage in problem-solving without external structure. This pattern strongly suggests frontal dysfunction affecting initiation while conceptual reasoning remains intact. Intervention focuses on environmental modifications, providing structure and initiation prompts rather than cognitive remediation targeting concept formation.

Concept Formation Deficit

Poor performance appears across both Free Sorting and Sort Recognition description measures. Examinees generate many incorrect descriptions, achieve few confirmed correct sorts even when many sorts are attempted, and struggle to identify target categories even when the examiner presents them. High noncredit or overly abstract descriptions suggest fundamental difficulties with conceptual reasoning affecting both generation and recognition. This pattern often reflects more diffuse or posterior neurological involvement affecting conceptual processing centers.

Cognitive Inflexibility and Perseveration

Moderate attempted sorts combined with high repeated sorts characterizes this pattern. The examinee generates some sorts but cannot shift away from previously used categorization schemes. Description scores may be adequate for non-repeated sorts, indicating that when novel concepts are accessed, they are correctly identified. The difficulty lies in releasing previous mental sets. Examinees may also show difficulty shifting between verbal and perceptual sorting domains, becoming stuck in one modality throughout testing.

Modality-Specific Deficits

Disproportionate difficulty with either verbal or perceptual sorts suggests domain-specific impairment. Selective impairment in perceptual concept formation (low perceptual sorts with intact verbal sorts) may reflect right hemisphere dysfunction or visual processing deficits. Selective impairment in verbal concept formation may suggest left hemisphere or language-based issues. The Confirmed Correct Verbal Sorts versus Confirmed Correct Perceptual Sorts optional measures help quantify these patterns.

Score Comparisons

Free Sorting Versus Sort Recognition

The contrast between these conditions provides the most diagnostically powerful information. Strong performance on both suggests intact initiation and concept formation. Poor Free Sorting with strong Sort Recognition (contrast scaled score ≥ 13) indicates initiation deficits despite intact conceptual reasoning—a critical distinction because these individuals benefit from environmental structure rather than concept-building interventions. Poor performance on both conditions suggests fundamental concept formation impairment. The rare pattern of better Free Sorting than Sort Recognition may indicate perseveration interfering with recognition trials.

Productivity Versus Accuracy

Compare Attempted Sorts to Confirmed Correct Sorts, or examine the Percent Sorting Accuracy measure. Few attempts with high accuracy suggest initiation deficit where the examinee generates correct sorts when they attempt them, but struggles to spontaneously engage. Many attempts with low accuracy suggest either poor concept formation or hasty, impulsive responding. The Time-Per-Sort Ratio can help distinguish deliberate, effortful processing from impulsive responding.

Verbal Versus Perceptual Sorts

Comparing performance across modalities reveals whether deficits are domain-general or domain-specific. Equivalent impairment across both suggests generalized concept formation difficulties. Selective impairment in one domain guides hypotheses about lateralized dysfunction and informs recommendations. Individuals with perceptual sort deficits may benefit from verbally mediated strategies, while those with verbal sort deficits may benefit from visual organizational supports.

First Versus Second Card Set

Comparing performance across card sets within each condition reveals learning effects or performance inconsistencies. Significantly higher scores on the second set may reflect learning-to-learn—acquiring more effective problem-solving strategies from experience. Inconsistent patterns across card sets (better on one set in Free Sorting but the opposite in Sort Recognition) may suggest non-neurostructural factors such as mood state, fatigue, effort fluctuation, or medication effects rather than stable cognitive deficits.

Rapid Reference 9.4

Distinguishing Tier-Level Deficits

Tier Level	Indicators	Clinical Implications
Tier 1 deficit	Screening pretest errors; modality-specific deficits (all perceptual or all verbal failed); marked description-sorting discrepancy suggesting language vs. conceptual issues	Vocabulary, reading, or expressive language limitations; visual processing deficits; consider language assessment before concluding executive dysfunction
Tier 2 deficit	Only 3–4 conventional sorts; cannot discover subtle categorization schemes; no generation-recognition dissociation; set-loss sorts	Basic categorical knowledge without executive flexibility; difficulty maintaining task rules; intact rule-following but limited hypothesis generation
Tier 3 cold deficit	Initiation: Few attempted sorts but high accuracy, dramatic improvement in sort recognition (contrast ≥13). Inflexibility: Many repeated sorts, cannot shift away from previous schemes. Concept formation: Poor both conditions, many incorrect descriptions. Modality-specific: Disproportionate verbal or perceptual failure	Initiation deficit benefits from external structure; perseveration requires flexibility interventions; concept formation deficit is more diffuse impairment; modality patterns suggest lateralized dysfunction
Tier 3 hot deficit	Behavioral frustration, irritability, or anxiety; premature disengagement; rushed responding; performance decline as task progresses; few sorts due to emotional withdrawal rather than conceptual limitation	Emotional dysregulation compromising cognitive deployment; distinguish from cold deficits via behavioral observation; may need frustration tolerance interventions
Tier 4 deficit	Repeated sorts without awareness; random/haphazard approach without systematic analysis; stuck in one modality; inconsistent performance with variable quality; overly abstract descriptions without recognizing inadequacy	Metacognitive monitoring failure; poor strategic organization; adequate basic abilities but lacks self-monitoring; benefits from explicit strategy training

ECOLOGICAL VALIDITY AND FUNCTIONAL IMPLICATIONS

Sorting Test performance relates to real-world functioning across multiple domains. The core abilities assessed—concept formation, problem-solving initiation, and cognitive flexibility—underlie success in academic, vocational, and social contexts where individuals must spontaneously organize information, generate solutions, and shift approaches when circumstances change.

Academic Functioning

Concept formation abilities directly support academic success across subject areas. Students with Sorting Test deficits may struggle with tasks requiring identification of themes and categories in reading comprehension, organization of written work around conceptual frameworks, classification and comparison activities in science, and understanding mathematical relationships and word problem structures. The Free Sorting–Sort Recognition distinction has particular educational relevance: students who perform adequately when categories are provided (Sort Recognition) but poorly when generating their own organizational schemes (Free Sorting) may appear capable during structured instruction but struggle with independent work requiring self-directed organization. These students benefit from explicit instruction in categorization strategies, graphic organizers that provide conceptual frameworks, and scaffolded approaches that gradually release responsibility for organizational thinking. Modality-specific deficits also inform educational planning. Students with stronger verbal than perceptual concept formation may benefit from verbally mediated learning strategies, while those with the opposite pattern may benefit from visual organizational supports.

Vocational and Daily Living

The executive functions assessed by the Sorting Test support workplace problem-solving and daily adaptive functioning. Concept formation underlies the ability to recognize patterns across situations, categorize information for efficient decision-making, and identify underlying principles that transfer across contexts. Employees with concept formation deficits may struggle to see commonalities across projects, organize tasks by priority or category, or recognize when situations call for similar approaches. The initiation component is particularly relevant vocationally. Individuals with the Free Sorting–Sort Recognition dissociation may perform adequately when given explicit structure and direction, but struggle in roles requiring independent problem identification and self-directed work. These individuals benefit from clearly defined procedures, regular check-ins, checklists that prompt problem-solving steps, and supervisory structures providing external initiation cues. Cognitive flexibility supports adaptation when job demands change, troubleshooting when standard approaches fail, and shifting between different types of tasks throughout the workday. In daily living, concept formation supports organization of household tasks, financial planning requiring categorization of expenses, and medical decision-making involving weighing different factors. Individuals with significant deficits may benefit from environmental supports such as labeled storage systems, categorized shopping lists, and structured routines that reduce demands for spontaneous organization.

Social Functioning

While the Sorting Test uses nonsocial stimuli, the underlying cognitive abilities have social implications. Concept formation supports understanding of social categories and roles, recognition of patterns in others' behavior, and comprehension of social rules that organize interpersonal interactions. Cognitive flexibility enables adaptation to shifting social contexts, recognizing when different situations call for different behavioral approaches and adjusting accordingly. Individuals with cognitive inflexibility may appear rigid in social situations, struggling to shift conversational topics, adapt communication style to different audiences, or recognize when social circumstances have changed. The initiation component affects social engagement—individuals with initiation deficits may have difficulty spontaneously generating conversation topics, initiating social contact, or independently identifying ways to contribute in group settings despite possessing adequate social knowledge. These individuals may benefit from social scripts, conversation starters, and structured social activities that reduce demands for spontaneous social initiation. However, clinicians should interpret social implications cautiously and consider direct assessment of social cognition through measures like the D-KEFS Advanced Social Sorting Test when social functioning is a primary concern.

STRENGTHS AND WEAKNESSES

The Sorting Test offers several distinctive strengths for executive function assessment, alongside limitations that clinicians should consider when selecting measures and interpreting results.

Strengths

The Sorting Test offers several notable advantages for assessing concept formation and cognitive flexibility within a comprehensive executive function evaluation.

Separation of Generation and Recognition

The dual-condition structure uniquely distinguishes spontaneous concept generation from concept recognition—a critical differential diagnosis. This separation helps identify initiation deficits, clarifies whether poor performance reflects reasoning limitations or behavioral execution problems, and guides intervention by identifying whether structure/cueing helps.

Multiple Scoring Dimensions

Unlike single-score sorting tasks, the Sorting Test provides a richly nuanced assessment: sorting accuracy, description quality, productivity (attempted sorts), flexibility (repeated sorts), modality-specific performance (verbal vs. perceptual), and accuracy relative to productivity (percent accuracy measures). This multidimensional scoring allows detection of subtle deficits and specific deficit patterns.

Dual Modality Assessment

Verbal-semantic and visual-perceptual sorts within a single test allow modality comparison, impossible with purely verbal or purely visual tasks. This design reveals whether concept formation deficits are domain-general or modality-specific, informing lateralization hypotheses and treatment planning.

Process-Oriented Scoring

The extensive optional measures capture qualitative aspects of performance: perseveration (repeated sorts/descriptions), disinhibition (many attempted sorts with low accuracy), creative thinking (noncredit descriptions), and conceptual sophistication or vagueness (overly abstract descriptions). These process measures enrich clinical understanding beyond simple accuracy scores.

Alternate Forms

The availability of alternate forms (Card Sets 3–4) allows repeat assessment with minimal practice effects—valuable for monitoring change over time, evaluating intervention effectiveness, or serial assessment in progressive conditions.

Weaknesses and Limitations

Despite its strengths, the Sorting Test has several limitations that clinicians should consider when selecting measures and interpreting results.

Length and Complexity

The test is time-consuming, particularly with highly productive examinees who generate many sorts. The scoring complexity requires careful attention and frequent reference to examples in the Examiner's Manual, which can be time-intensive and potentially limit clinical utility in time-constrained settings.

Vulnerability to Language Confounds

Description scores depend heavily on expressive language abilities. Clients with expressive aphasia, word-finding difficulties, or limited vocabulary may obtain artifactually low description scores despite intact concept formation. While the Confirmed/Unconfirmed Target Sorts measure addresses this for sorting accuracy, description scores remain vulnerable to language confounds.

Open-Ended Nature and Ambiguity

The lack of a clear task endpoint or performance feedback creates ambiguity that some examinees find distressing. Anxiety-prone individuals may underperform due to uncertainty rather than concept formation deficits. The open-ended format also makes the test vulnerable to motivational factors; examinees can easily disengage prematurely.

Cultural and Educational Bias

Familiarity with specific semantic categories varies by cultural background and experience. Educational level affects comfort with abstract categorization tasks. These factors can depress performance for reasons unrelated to executive functioning, particularly affecting verbal sorts where cultural knowledge plays a larger role than in perceptual sorts.

Use of Binary Male and Female Names as a Sort Category

The Practice Set uses male and female names as one of the teaching examples, which may introduce confounds related to naming conventions. Since the test's 2001 publication, cultural associations between names and binary gender categories have become less consistent, with gender-neutral names increasingly common. Beyond these contemporary considerations, examinees from non-Western cultural backgrounds may be less familiar with traditional English gendered name associations. As a result, some examinees may find this sort less intuitive than the perceptual sort (circles and squares), potentially affecting their understanding of task demands before formal testing begins. Examiners should be aware that this teaching example may not provide equivalent practice experience across all examinees.

Hot EF Confounds

While removing negative feedback helps, the test remains vulnerable to hot EF influences: frustration tolerance, persistence, anxiety, and tolerance for ambiguity all affect performance. The test cannot easily separate cold EF concept formation from hot EF factors affecting the deployment of conceptual abilities.

Floor Effects for Severely Impaired

Individuals with severe cognitive impairment may generate zero or very few sorts, producing floor effects that limit discrimination among low-functioning examinees. The test may be too difficult for individuals with intellectual disability, severe dementia, or significant language disorders.

ALTERNATIVE MEASURES

Comprehensive assessment of concept formation and cognitive flexibility often benefits from complementary measures that clarify Sorting Test findings or provide convergent evidence for identified deficits.

Within the D-KEFS Suite

Several D-KEFS subtests provide complementary or converging evidence for concept formation and cognitive flexibility.

Social Sorting Test (D-KEFS Advanced)

This Advanced battery test extends sorting methodology to the social–emotional domain, requiring categorization of faces by emotional expressions and social characteristics. Unlike the original Sorting Test, Social Sorting does not require verbal descriptions. Examinees respond by clicking to indicate their sorting choices, making it useful for individuals with expressive language impairments. Comparing Social Sorting to original Sorting helps distinguish domain-general concept formation abilities from social-specific deficits. Poor Social Sorting with intact D-KEFS Sorting suggests social cognition deficits rather than general concept formation problems—critical for differential diagnosis in autism spectrum disorder, frontotemporal dementia, or right hemisphere dysfunction.

Twenty Questions Test

Both tests assess abstract categorical reasoning, but Twenty Questions uses a constrained hypothesis-testing format requiring yes/no questions to identify a target object, while Sorting uses open-ended generation of categorization schemes. Comparing performance reveals whether deficits extend across different concept formation paradigms. Intact Twenty Questions with poor Sorting may suggest specific difficulty with the open-ended generation demands of Free Sorting. Poor performance on both strengthens evidence for generalized abstract reasoning impairment.

Word Context Test

Assesses verbal deductive reasoning and concept formation through novel word learning from contextual clues. Unlike Sorting's visual-verbal dual modality, Word Context focuses exclusively on verbal-semantic reasoning.

Comparing performance helps clarify whether concept formation deficits are modality-specific (poor Sorting perceptual sorts with intact Word Context suggests visual concept formation deficit) or domain-general (poor performance on both suggests broader abstract reasoning impairment).

Proverbs Test
Measures abstract verbal reasoning through proverb interpretation, requiring examinees to move beyond concrete features to identify abstract principles—similar to the abstraction demands of Sorting. Convergent deficits suggest generalized abstract reasoning problems. Divergent performance helps identify whether difficulties are specific to the categorization demands of Sorting versus the metaphorical interpretation demands of Proverbs.

Trail Making Test (Original and Advanced)
Condition 4 (Number-Letter Switching) and Advanced switching conditions assess cognitive flexibility through sequencing rather than categorization. Convergent deficits across Trail Making switching and Sorting (high repeated sorts, difficulty shifting between verbal and perceptual domains) strengthen evidence for generalized cognitive inflexibility. Divergent performance helps identify whether flexibility deficits are domain-specific or task-specific.

Verbal Fluency Test (Original and Advanced)
Category Fluency conditions require accessing semantic categories efficiently, similar to the semantic categorization demands of Sorting verbal sorts. The Category Switching condition on the original version (Delis et al., 2001) assesses cognitive flexibility through semantic-semantic switching, while the Advanced version (Delis & Kaplan, 2025) increases demands through phonemic-semantic switching and, for ages 14–69, three-rule switching that substantially taxes working memory alongside flexibility. Poor Category Fluency with adequate Sorting verbal sorts might suggest retrieval speed deficits rather than categorical knowledge problems. Poor Sorting with adequate Category Fluency might suggest that the open-ended, generative demands of Sorting are specifically challenging.

Beyond D-KEFS

Measures outside the D-KEFS family can provide converging evidence or be used to assess related constructs when additional information is needed.

Card Sorting Measures
The Wisconsin Card Sorting Test (WCST; Heaton et al., 1993) is the classic measure of concept formation, cognitive flexibility, and perseveration. Unlike D-KEFS Sorting, WCST requires discovering a hidden rule through trial-and-error with feedback and does not require verbal descriptions. Examinees demonstrate their sorting strategy behaviorally, making it useful for examinees with expressive language impairments. WCST emphasizes learning from feedback and rule-discovery, while D-KEFS Sorting emphasizes spontaneous concept generation and verbal explanation of categorization principles. Comparing performance helps distinguish feedback-based learning deficits (poor WCST) from spontaneous generation deficits (poor Free Sorting with better Sort Recognition).

Nonverbal Abstract Reasoning Measures
Several matrix reasoning tests assess nonverbal concept formation and provide useful comparisons to Sorting Test perceptual sorts. Raven's Progressive Matrices (Raven et al., 2018) assesses abstract reasoning through visual pattern completion with clear right/wrong answers and no open-ended generation requirements. Good Ravens with poor Sorting perceptual sorts suggest initiation or open-ended task deficits rather than visual reasoning impairment. The RIAS-2 Odd-Item-Out (Reynolds & Kamphaus, 2015) requires identifying which item does not belong based on visual-perceptual features, tapping visual categorization similar to Sorting's perceptual sorts. WAIS-5/WISC-5 Matrix Reasoning (Wechsler, 2024, 2014) assesses nonverbal reasoning through pattern completion in a structured multiple-choice format. Convergent deficits across these measures and Sorting perceptual sorts strengthen evidence for visual-perceptual concept formation problems; divergent performance helps distinguish structured versus generative reasoning abilities.

Verbal Abstract Reasoning Measures

WAIS-5/WISC-5 Similarities (Wechsler, 2024, 2014) measures verbal abstract reasoning through identifying conceptual relationships between word pairs. Unlike Sorting's open-ended generation, Similarities provides items to be categorized and asks for explicit relationship identification. Comparing performance helps distinguish spontaneous category generation (Sorting) from prompted categorical reasoning (Similarities). Strong Similarities with poor Sorting verbal sorts may suggest the generative demands of Free Sorting are specifically challenging.

Behavior Rating Scales

Executive function rating scales capture real-world behaviors that may or may not align with performance-based measures. For children and adolescents, the Behavior Rating Inventory of Executive Function, Second Edition (BRIEF-2; Gioia et al., 2015), Comprehensive Executive Function Inventory (CEFI; Naglieri & Goldstein, 2013), and Delis Rating of Executive Functions (D-REF; Delis, 2012) provide parent and teacher perspectives on daily executive functioning. For adults, the BRIEF-A (Roth et al., 2005), CEFI Adult (Naglieri & Goldstein, 2017), and D-REF Adult (Delis, 2021) offer self-report and informant-report options. Relevant scales include Shift (cognitive flexibility required for moving between categorization schemes), Initiate (spontaneous generation of sorting approaches), Plan/Organize (systematic strategic approach to discovering sorts), and Working Memory (tracking previous sorts and maintaining categorization principles). Discrepancies between Sorting Test performance and rating scale elevations provide diagnostic information: adequate test performance with elevated rating scales may indicate that the structured one-on-one testing environment with explicit instructions does not capture organizational and flexibility challenges that emerge in unstructured real-world situations requiring spontaneous categorization and problem-solving. Conversely, poor Sorting performance with unremarkable rating scales might suggest test-specific factors such as expressive language demands affecting description scores, performance anxiety in the testing situation, or poor metacognitive awareness of daily organizational difficulties, rather than pervasive executive dysfunction.

SUMMARY

The D-KEFS Sorting Test provides multifaceted assessment of concept formation and problem-solving abilities, uniquely separating spontaneous generation from recognition of categorical relationships. The test's hierarchical demands span from Tier 1 foundational visual-verbal processing through Tier 4 metacognitive integration, with particular emphasis on Tier 3 core executive functions of abstract reasoning, cognitive flexibility, and problem-solving initiation. The dual-condition structure enables powerful differential diagnosis, distinguishing initiation deficits from concept formation problems, generation difficulties from recognition abilities, and modality-specific from generalized deficits (Delis et al., 2001).

Optimal interpretation requires systematic tier-based analysis: ruling out language and visual processing confounds (Tier 1), evaluating basic categorical knowledge (Tier 2), characterizing specific executive deficit patterns (Tier 3), and assessing metacognitive and hot EF factors (Tier 4). A diagnostically valuable pattern—poor Free Sorting with strong Sort Recognition—reveals initiation deficits with intact conceptual reasoning, fundamentally changing intervention approaches from cognitive remediation to environmental modification.

The test's strengths include rich multidimensional scoring, dual modality assessment, separation of generation and recognition, and process-oriented measures capturing perseveration, creativity, and conceptual sophistication. Weaknesses include vulnerability to language confounds, limited visual processing screening, time-intensive administration and scoring, and susceptibility to hot EF factors affecting task engagement.

Integration with complementary measures—Twenty Questions for abstract reasoning convergence, Social Sorting for social–emotional concept formation, Word Context for verbal deductive reasoning, and Wisconsin Card Sorting for feedback-based learning—provides a comprehensive understanding of concept formation abilities across contexts and modalities, enabling nuanced diagnosis and targeted intervention planning.

TEST YOURSELF

1. What is the age range for the D-KEFS Sorting Test?
- (a) 12–89 years
- (b) 8–89 years
- (c) 16–89 years
- (d) 8–79 years

2. Which tier represents the primary executive functions assessed by the Sorting Test?
- (a) Tier 1: Foundational processes
- (b) Tier 2: Bridging processes
- (c) Tier 3: Core executive functions
- (d) Tier 4: Higher-order integration

3. An examinee generates only 3 sorts during Free Sorting but accurately identifies and describes 7 of 8 sorts during Sort Recognition. This pattern most likely indicates:
- (a) Tier 1 visual processing deficits.
- (b) Tier 2 working memory limitations.
- (c) Tier 3 initiation deficit with intact concept formation.
- (d) Tier 4 metacognitive monitoring problems.

4. The Confirmed Correct Sorts measure requires which two criteria to be met?
- (a) Correct physical grouping and completion within the time limit
- (b) Correct physical grouping and at least partially accurate description
- (c) Novel categorization scheme and verbal explanation
- (d) Accurate description and no repeated sorts

5. Which optional measure is most useful for examinees with expressive language impairments?
- (a) Free Sorting Description Score
- (b) Combined Overly Abstract Descriptions
- (c) Confirmed/Unconfirmed Target Sorts
- (d) Free Sorting Percent Description Accuracy

6. High repeated sorts combined with moderate attempted sorts most likely indicate:
- (a) Tier 1 sustained attention deficits.
- (b) Tier 2 procedural learning difficulties.
- (c) Tier 3 cognitive inflexibility and perseveration.
- (d) Tier 4 poor strategic flexibility.

7. An examinee successfully completes all verbal sorts but generates zero correct perceptual sorts. This modality-specific pattern may suggest:
- (a) Expressive language impairment.
- (b) Right hemisphere or visual processing dysfunction.
- (c) Left hemisphere dysfunction.
- (d) Generalized concept formation deficit.

8. The Sort Recognition versus Free Sorting contrast measure scaled score of ≥13 indicates:
- (a) Significantly better generation than recognition abilities.
- (b) Significantly better recognition than generation abilities.
- (c) Equivalent performance across both conditions.
- (d) Invalid test performance requiring readministration.

9. Which behavioral observation would suggest Tier 3 hot executive dysfunction rather than cold executive deficits?

(a) Consistent concrete descriptions across both conditions
(b) Highly repeated sorts without awareness of repetition
(c) Progressive performance decline with visible frustration and irritable comments
(d) Inability to identify examiner-generated sorts during Sort Recognition

10. The overly abstract clarification prompt ("Good, but how did you specifically sort each group?") can be used:

(a) Once per sort when responses are vague.
(b) Once during the entire test administration.
(c) As many times as needed to obtain scorable responses.
(d) Only during Sort Recognition condition.

Answer Key: 1-b, 2-c, 3-c, 4-b, 5-c, 6-c, 7-b, 8-b, 9-c, 10-b

REFERENCES

Barkley, R. A. (2011). *Barkley Deficits in Executive Functioning Scale (BDEFS)*. Guilford Press.

Casey, B. J., Somerville, L. H., Gotlib, I. H., Ayduk, O., Franklin, N. T., Askren, M. K., et al. (2011). Behavioral and neural correlates of delay of gratification 40 years later. *Proceedings of the National Academy of Sciences, 108*(36), 14998–15003.

Dehn, M. J. (2014). *Helping Students Remember: Exercises and Strategies to Strengthen Memory* (2nd ed.). Wiley.

Delis, D. C. (2012). *Delis Rating of Executive Functions (D-REF)*. Pearson.

Delis, D. C. (2021). *Delis Rating of Executive Functions—Adult (D-REF Adult)*. Pearson.

Delis, D. C., & Kaplan, E. (2025). *Delis-Kaplan Executive Function System—Advanced (D-KEFS Advanced)*. Pearson.

Delis, D. C., Kaplan, E., & Kramer, J. H. (2001). *Delis-Kaplan Executive Function System (D-KEFS)*. The Psychological Corporation.

Gioia, G. A., Isquith, P. K., Guy, S. C., & Kenworthy, L. (2015). *Behavior Rating Inventory of Executive Function–Second Edition (BRIEF-2)*. Psychological Assessment Resources.

Heaton, R. K., Chelune, G. J., Talley, J. L., Kay, G. G., & Curtiss, G. (1993). *Wisconsin Card Sorting Test (WCST) Manual: Revised and Expanded*. Psychological Assessment Resources.

Kaplan, E., Goodglass, H., & Weintraub, S. (2001). *Boston Naming Test* (2nd ed.). Pro-Ed.

Mischel, W., Shoda, Y., & Rodriguez, M. L. (1989). Delay of gratification in children. *Science, 244*(4907), 933–938.

Miyake, A., Friedman, N. P., Emerson, M. J., Witzki, A. H., Howerter, A., & Wager, T. D. (2000). The unity and diversity of executive functions and their contributions to complex "frontal lobe" tasks: A latent variable analysis. *Cognitive Psychology, 41*(1), 49–100.

Naglieri, J. A., & Goldstein, S. (2013). *Comprehensive Executive Function Inventory (CEFI)*. Multi-Health Systems.

Naglieri, J. A., & Goldstein, S. (2017). *Comprehensive Executive Function Inventory Adult (CEFI Adult)*. Multi-Health Systems.

Raven, J., Rust, J., Chan, F., & Zhou, X. (2018). *Raven's 2 Progressive Matrices, Clinical Edition*. Pearson.

Reynolds, C. R., & Kamphaus, R. W. (2015). *Reynolds Intellectual Assessment Scales, Second Edition (RIAS-2)*. Psychological Assessment Resources.

Roth, R. M., Isquith, P. K., & Gioia, G. A. (2005). *Behavior Rating Inventory of Executive Function—Adult Version (BRIEF-A)*. Psychological Assessment Resources.

Wechsler, D. (2014). *Wechsler Intelligence Scale for Children* (5th ed.). Pearson.

Wechsler, D. (2020). *Wechsler Individual Achievement Test* (4th ed.). Pearson.

Wechsler, D. (2024). *Wechsler Adult Intelligence Scale* (5th ed.). Pearson.

Ten

TOWER TEST

CLINICAL VIGNETTE

Nine-year-old Lucas Peterson was referred for evaluation following concerns about problem-solving difficulties on math story problems and multistep projects. His teacher reported Lucas understood math concepts when demonstrated, but struggled to determine solution sequences independently. His parents noted he could follow step-by-step LEGO instructions but became frustrated with novel problems requiring his own solution approach.

On the Tower Test, Lucas demonstrated intact Tier 1 abilities (understood rules, manipulated disks easily) and Tier 2 functions (remembered rules, understood goals). However, Tier 3 cold executive functions showed significant impairment. His Total Achievement Score was average (scaled score = 9), but his Mean First-Move Time was extremely brief (1.2 seconds, scaled score = 14), indicating impulsive responding without planning. His Move Accuracy Ratio was impaired (scaled score = 5). For example, he made 18 moves on a 4-move problem, solving through trial-and-error rather than planned sequences.

Most revealing were seven rule violations across testing (placing larger disks on smaller ones), occurring mid-problem when Lucas became focused on intermediate steps (subgoals) like "getting the medium disk out of the way" rather than maintaining awareness of the basic rules. He demonstrated Tier 4 error monitoring, recognizing errors when pointed out, but failed to inhibit rule-violating moves in the moment. Hot EF factors contributed—as problems became harder, he showed increasing frustration, making rapid moves without consideration. When reminded to work carefully to build the tower using the fewest number of moves possible, his performance temporarily improved.

The hierarchical analysis indicated Tier 3 deficits in planning, inhibition of impulsive moves, and maintaining goal hierarchies. Recommendations included explicit planning strategies, external planning tools, and emotion regulation techniques. Six months later, teachers reported significant improvement when he used the planning strategies he was taught.

TEST DESCRIPTION

The Tower Test represents one of neuropsychology's most demanding assessments of spatial planning, working memory, and problem-solving. Based on the classic Tower of Hanoi puzzle, both the original D-KEFS Tower Test (Delis et al., 2001) and the D-KEFS Advanced Tower Test (TWR; Delis & Kaplan, 2025) require examinees to move disks or chips between pegs or tables following specific rules while achieving a target configuration in the minimum number of moves. Unlike some other D-KEFS subtests that assess through Tier 3, the Tower Test engages substantial Tier 4 metacognitive processes—self-monitoring, strategy adjustment, and performance evaluation—making it particularly sensitive to frontal lobe dysfunction.

Original D-KEFS Tower Test

The original version (ages 8–89) consists of nine items administered with physical materials, typically requiring 10–15 minutes to complete. Three wooden pegs hold five disks of graduated sizes. The examiner sets up an initial configuration and shows the examinee a picture of the goal configuration. The examinee must move the disks to match the goal, moving only one disk at a time and never placing a larger disk on top of a smaller one. All nine items end with the same target arrangement: a tower formation with all disks stacked on a single peg. The examiner tracks first-move time, counts moves, identifies rule violations immediately, administers prompts at specified times, and stops the examinee when time limits are reached.

D-KEFS Advanced Tower Test (TWR)

TWR (aged 8–90) modernizes the task through digital administration on a tablet, with administration typically requiring 20–25 minutes. Seventeen items present chips of varying sizes on three tables. The examinee uses a stylus to drag chips between tables. Ten items use solid-colored chips with the rule "never place a larger chip on a smaller one," while seven items use striped chips with the reversed rule "never place a smaller chip on a larger one." This switching component substantially increases cognitive demands. Unlike the original version, where all items end in tower formations, the TWR scatters target configurations across the three tables, preventing examinees from applying a single learned heuristic. The digital interface automatically captures timing data, counts moves, detects rule violations, provides immediate feedback, and calculates all scores.

DON'T FORGET

The Tower Test's diagnostic power lies in distinguishing between different types of planning failures. Poor performance could reflect inadequate preplanning (rushing into action), working memory limitations (forgetting rules mid-problem), inhibitory control deficits (impulsive moves), or metacognitive weaknesses (failing to monitor and adjust strategies). Process scores and behavioral observations differentiate these patterns.

Rapid Reference 10.1

Tower Test Overview

Element	Original D-KEFS Tower	D-KEFS Advanced TWR
Age range	8–89 years	8–90 years
Items	9 items	17 items
Administration time	10–15 minutes	20–25 minutes
Response format	Physical disk manipulation	Stylus-based chip manipulation on tablet
Materials	Examiner's manual, stimulus booklet, record form, wooden base with pegs, disks, timer	Examiner's manual, client device, practitioner device, stylus
Discontinuation	Three consecutive failures	Three consecutive scores of 0 OR move/time limits reached
Primary constructs	Spatial planning, working memory, inhibitory control, problem-solving	Spatial planning, working memory, inhibitory control, cognitive flexibility, problem-solving

CHOOSING BETWEEN ORIGINAL AND ADVANCED VERSIONS

The decision between versions depends on examinee characteristics, referral questions, and clinical context. Each version offers distinct advantages for specific assessment scenarios.

When the Original Version Is Preferred

Ceiling concerns are minimal. If executive deficits are clearly present and moderate to severe, the original version's nine items provide adequate assessment without requiring TWR's extended administration.

Speed of administration is necessary. Generally speaking, the nine items on the original version can be administered faster than the Advanced version of Tower. This varies depending on the response time needed for the nine items.

Cost or equipment constraints exist. TWR requires tablet devices and technical infrastructure that may not be universally available.

Auditory/verbal memory or working memory is limited. Examinees are provided with a listing of basic rules at the bottom of each page on the original version. For the Advanced version, they are required to remember changing verbal directions, which increases the load on auditory memory and working memory.

When the Advanced Version Is Preferred

Higher cognitive ceiling is needed. For intellectually gifted individuals, high-functioning adults, or cases where subtle planning deficits are suspected, the TWR's seventeen items with varied configurations and increased complexity provide better differentiation.

Precise measurement is critical. Automatic timing, move counting, and error detection eliminate measurement error potential in the manual administration. Every move, pause, and error is captured with precision.

Motor limitations exist. While both versions require fine motor control, the stylus-based dragging may accommodate some motor limitations better than manipulating physical disks.

Rule-switching assessment is valuable. The solid-chip/striped-chip switching component with reversed placement rules adds a cognitive flexibility demand absent from the original version.

Contemporary norms are desired. TWR provides updated normative data collected in the 2020s.

When Either Version Works Equally Well

For individuals with average cognitive abilities, no motor impairments, and suspected moderate executive deficits, either version provides a valid planning assessment.

Lucas, at age 9, could have been assessed with either version. TWR's seventeen items with varied configurations and rule switching might have provided a more comprehensive evaluation of his planning abilities, with automatic timing capturing his impulsivity more precisely and immediate error feedback potentially engaging his intact Tier 4 metacognition more effectively. However, the original version provided an adequate assessment of his Tier 3 deficits and was appropriate given the clinical context.

Rapid Reference 10.2

Choosing Between Original and Advanced Versions

Consider Original When	Consider Advanced When
Assessing young children who may struggle with stylus use	Higher cognitive ceiling is needed
Technology limitations exist	Automated scoring precision is important
Motor observation is clinically relevant	Rule-switching assessment is desired
Briefer administration is needed	Process scores (trial-and-error, speed-accuracy) are priorities
Practice effects from prior TWR are a concern	Examiner is managing multiple scoring demands
Examinee has limited technology experience	Contemporary normative data is preferred

HIERARCHICAL TIER ANALYSIS

The Tower Test maps onto a four-tier hierarchical framework that distinguishes foundational abilities from true executive functions and metacognitive processes. Both versions assess through all four tiers of executive functioning; however, it should be noted that this is an expansion of Pearson's model from the D-KEFS Advanced manual, which suggests that TWR only addresses tiers 1 and 2. Given the complexity of the task, it's been expanded to cover all four tiers in this chapter.

Tier 1: Foundational Processes (Nonexecutive)

Tower performance depends on fundamental cognitive processes that must be intact before higher-level executive functions can operate effectively. These foundational requirements remain constant across both versions, though the modality differs between physical and digital administration.

Visuospatial Perception and Processing

Examinees must accurately perceive the relative sizes of disks/chips and their spatial arrangement on pegs/tables. Size discrimination is critical—the entire task depends on distinguishing whether one disk/chip is larger or smaller than another. On the original version, examinees must judge sizes of three-dimensional physical disks in actual space. On TWR, examinees must discriminate sizes of two-dimensional representations on a screen, potentially easier for some individuals and harder for others, depending on their visuospatial processing profiles.

Deficits in visuospatial skills compromise Tower performance independent of planning abilities. An examinee who cannot reliably distinguish chip sizes cannot determine which moves violate rules, rendering planning capacity inaccessible for assessment. Similarly, spatial arrangement comprehension is essential. Examinees must perceive which disk/chip is "on top of" another and visualize how configurations will look after moves. Individuals with posterior cortical dysfunction affecting visual processing may struggle with Tower tasks despite intact frontal planning systems.

Visual Attention and Scanning

The task requires sustained visual attention to monitor multiple disks/chips simultaneously across three pegs/tables. In the original version, examinees must attend to three-dimensional space encompassing physical materials. On TWR, visual attention must scan the tablet screen systematically. Some items present four or five chips requiring tracking of multiple elements and their relationships. Hemispatial neglect following right hemisphere stroke could cause examinees to ignore the leftmost peg/table, fundamentally compromising task performance before planning is even attempted. A visual field cut could require more effort to complete the task and introduce a fatigue factor to the results. Visual attention lapses during the task—briefly "losing track" of which chips are where—can produce errors that mimic planning deficits but actually reflect attentional dysregulation.

Language Comprehension and Auditory Working Memory

The Tower Test's verbal instructions are lengthy and complex, explaining multiple rules, constraints, and goals. Examinees must comprehend multi-clause sentences with embedded conditions: "Move the disks one at a time to make them look like the picture, but you can never put a larger disk on top of a smaller disk, and complete them in as few moves as possible." This places substantial demands on receptive language abilities. Children with developmental language disorders, adults with receptive aphasia, individuals with intellectual disabilities, or English Language Learners may struggle to comprehend instructions independent of planning capacity. Providing verbal feedback during the demonstration item helps, but examinees must still extract and retain the multiple rules from verbal instruction.

Closely related, examinees must hold multiple verbal rules in working memory throughout the task: move only one disk/chip at a time, never place a larger on a smaller (or vice versa for striped chips), complete in as few moves as possible, touch only the top chip in a stack. These rules must remain accessible while spatial planning simultaneously occupies working memory resources. Unlike spatial working memory (an executive function that the test assesses), auditory working memory for verbal rules represents a foundational requirement. Individuals with phonological working memory deficits may know how to plan but lose track of rules mid-problem, producing rule violations that reflect working memory limitations for verbal material rather than planning deficits. Examinees are provided with a listing of basic rules at the bottom of each page on the original version, which provides an advantage over the Advanced version if attempting to reduce confounds from auditory/verbal working memory limitations.

Fine Motor Control and Execution

On the original version, examinees must physically grasp and lift disks of varying sizes. TWR requires stylus control to drag chips accurately. Motor impairments affecting precision grip or hand stability can slow performance, delay completion time if disks are dropped, or cause unintended moves, confounding interpretation of planning abilities. Motor execution speed also matters. Examinees who think quickly but execute moves slowly due to motor limitations may obtain misleading time scores.

Frustration Tolerance and Basic Engagement

Examinees must tolerate initial confusion, persist through challenging items, and maintain effort despite errors. The test can be frustrating, particularly for individuals unaccustomed to puzzle-solving or those with low self-efficacy. Those who disengage when frustrated ("I can't do this," refusing to attempt items) cannot demonstrate their planning capacity regardless of its adequacy. Basic motivational engagement and willingness to tolerate cognitive challenge represent foundational requirements.

Tier 1 Clinical Indicators

Poor performance across all items, including early ones, struggling with the demonstration item despite repeated practice, difficulty understanding what the task requires after repeated explanation, errors suggesting visuospatial confusion (confusing which disk is larger) rather than planning failures, motor difficulties manipulating disks/chips accurately, and disengagement from the task entirely, all suggest Tier 1 limitations. These foundational deficits must be ruled out before attributing poor Tower performance to executive dysfunction.

Tier 2: Bridging Processes

Between foundational abilities and true executive functions lie bridging processes that are somewhat executive in nature but do not represent the high-level planning, problem-solving, and metacognition that constitute the Tower Test's primary targets. These Tier 2 processes are necessary but not sufficient for successful Tower performance.

Rule Following and Constraint Maintenance

The Tower Test involves explicit rules that must be followed consistently: move one at a time, do not violate size-placement rules, and work toward the goal configuration. Successfully applying these rules throughout the task requires basic executive control—maintaining task set, inhibiting rule-violating impulses, and monitoring ongoing behavior against constraints. However, this represents simpler executive control than the strategic planning and problem-solving that the test primarily assesses. Rule following in structured contexts with clear, unchanging constraints (except the solid/striped switching on TWR) is less executively demanding than generating multistep plans or flexibly adjusting strategies.

Individuals can follow rules perfectly yet plan poorly, or alternatively, demonstrate adequate planning concepts but make impulsive rule violations. On TWR, the solid/striped switching adds complexity, because examinees must remember which rule applies to which chip type and switch between opposing rules across items. This engages Tier 2 cognitive flexibility in rule application, distinct from Tier 3 strategic flexibility in planning approaches.

Goal Maintenance and Subgoal Tracking

Examinees must keep the overall goal (matching the target configuration) in mind while working toward it. This goal maintenance functions as a cognitive anchor, guiding move decisions. As examinees work through a problem, they must track progress toward the goal and recognize when they are getting closer versus moving further away.

Many Tower items require establishing subgoals—intermediate configurations that do not match the final goal but are necessary steps toward it. An examinee might need to move the small disk "out of the way" onto an empty peg (temporarily moving away from the goal) to access the medium disk underneath (moving toward the goal). This subgoal tracking requires holding multiple goal states in mind: the ultimate goal, the current subgoal, and monitoring which state is currently being addressed.

Failures at this level manifest as "losing track of where I'm going" or "forgetting what I'm trying to do." Examinees make moves that seem locally reasonable but do not advance toward the goal, suggesting goal maintenance failure rather than planning deficit per se. They may ask, "What am I supposed to do again?" mid-problem, indicating goal-maintenance rather than working-memory-capacity limitation.

Basic Move Sequencing

The easiest Tower items (particularly items 1–3 on the original version, items 1–5 on TWR) require minimal planning. The solution involves straightforward sequential moves without complex branching decision points. Successfully completing these items requires basic sequencing ability: doing first things first, executing moves in logical order, and tracking position in the move sequence. This basic sequencing ability differs from the sophisticated multi-move planning required for difficult items. An examinee who completes early items successfully demonstrates intact Tier 2 sequencing but has not yet demonstrated Tier 3 planning capacity. Conversely, failure on even the simplest items suggests sequencing difficulties that would preclude assessment of higher-level planning.

Tier 2 Clinical Indicators

Adequate performance on early items but deterioration on middle-to-later items suggests intact Tier 2 processes with Tier 3–4 deficits. Consistent rule-following with poor efficiency (excess moves) indicates rule application without strategic planning. Asking "What am I trying to do?" during items suggests goal-maintenance weaknesses. Set-loss errors where examinees briefly forget the rules mid-problem reflect Tier 2 rather than Tier 3–4 failures. Rule violations on early, easy items suggest Tier 2 deficits in basic rule application, while rule violations emerging only on difficult items suggest Tier 3 inhibitory control failures under cognitive load.

Tier 3: Core Executive Functions

The Tower Test's primary assessment targets reside at Tier 3, where both cold and hot executive functions contribute to planning performance in distinct ways.

Cold Executive Functions

The Tower Test's core diagnostic targets reside at Tier 3: the cold executive functions of spatial planning, spatial working memory, inhibitory control, cognitive shifting, and problem-solving. These processes represent the test's core challenges and receive the most extensive assessment across item difficulties.

Spatial Planning and Look-Ahead

The primary cognitive demand of the Tower Test is planning—mentally simulating a sequence of moves before executing them to determine optimal solutions. This forward planning or "look-ahead" requires mentally representing current and future spatial configurations, comparing alternative move sequences, and selecting the sequence achieving the goal in minimum moves.

Planning complexity increases dramatically with item difficulty. On the original Tower Test, item 1 requires one move (trivial planning), item 2 requires two moves (minimal planning), but item 9 requires twenty moves with multiple choice points where the optimal path is not obvious (extensive planning). On TWR, the seventeen items span an even wider difficulty range, with earlier items accessible through simple planning and later items requiring sophisticated multistep planning with look-ahead of several moves.

Spatial Working Memory

Planning requires holding multiple pieces of information simultaneously: (1) the current configuration of disks/chips, (2) the goal configuration, (3) the multiple rules governing moves, (4) potential move sequences being mentally evaluated, (5) the outcomes of moves already executed, and (6) which moves remain to try if the current approach fails.

As Tower items increase in difficulty, adding more disks/chips, creating more complex starting and goal configurations, working memory demands increase. A two-disk problem requires minimal working memory; a five-disk problem requires substantial capacity. Working memory limitations produce characteristic error patterns: forgetting rules mid-problem (particularly on TWR when shifting between solid and striped chips), losing track

DON'T FORGET

Working memory failures and planning failures produce different error patterns and require different interventions. An examinee who articulates good planning strategies verbally but loses track mid-execution has a working memory limitation, not a planning deficit. Intervention should target working memory supports (external tracking, chunking) rather than planning strategy instruction.

of the goal (asking "What am I trying to make again?"), repeating ineffective move sequences (forgetting they already tried that approach), and dramatically worse performance as item complexity increases, even though planning capacity remains constant.

Working memory failures differ from planning failures. An examinee might demonstrate excellent planning concepts verbally ("First I should move this small one, then I can access the medium one...") but then lose track mid-execution and forget what they planned. This represents working memory limitation, not planning deficit per se.

Inhibitory Control and Impulse Regulation

Effective planning requires inhibiting the impulse to immediately execute moves that seem attractive without considering their downstream consequences. Many Tower problems contain "attractive nuisance" moves—moves that appear helpful initially but create more problems later. For example, moving the largest disk onto an empty peg might seem logical because "it gets it out of the way," but if that peg will be needed later as an intermediate staging area, the move creates inefficiency.

Impulsive examinees immediately execute attractive moves without mentally simulating their consequences. They discover the problem only after the move is made, requiring backtracking. This pattern produces high move counts despite adequate planning knowledge. They know what optimal solutions should look like, but cannot inhibit immediate impulses long enough to execute those plans.

Rule violations provide a direct measure of inhibitory control under cognitive load. On easy items with minimal cognitive demands, most examinees maintain perfect rule compliance. On difficult items with high working memory loads and complex planning demands, inhibitory control can fail. Examinees place larger disks on smaller ones despite knowing the rule. These violations typically occur mid-problem when cognitive resources are maximally taxed, not at the beginning when attention to rules is fresh and cognitive demands are less.

TWR's rule-switching component creates additional inhibitory demands. After multiple solid-chip items using "never place larger on smaller," examinees must inhibit that well-practiced rule and apply the opposite rule for striped chips. Perseverative errors (applying solid-chip rules to striped chips) reflect inhibitory failures in suppressing the previously correct response.

Cognitive Flexibility and Strategy Shifting

Examinees who rigidly persist with an ineffective strategy despite accumulating moves demonstrate cognitive inflexibility. They might try the same approach repeatedly—failing, backing up, trying again—without recognizing that their fundamental strategy is flawed. Effective problem-solvers show strategic flexibility: attempting an approach, recognizing it's not working after several moves, and shifting to an alternative strategy. This requires: (1) recognizing the current approach is ineffective (monitoring), (2) generating an alternative approach (planning flexibility), (3) inhibiting continued pursuit of the failing strategy (inhibition), and (4) implementing the new approach (shifting).

TWR's rule-switching assesses a specific type of cognitive flexibility: shifting between opposing rules. After establishing "larger can't go on smaller" across multiple items, examinees must flexibly shift to "smaller can't go on larger" when striped chips appear. Individuals with set-shifting difficulties may show perseveration, continuing to apply the previously correct rule despite clear visual cues (striped pattern) indicating a rule change.

Tier 3 Cold Executive Patterns

Tier 3 deficits produce varied scores and behavioral patterns: Brief first-move times with high move counts but adequate achievement. This is impulsivity without complete planning failure. The examinee can solve problems but does so inefficiently through trial-and-error. Long first-move times but high move counts anyway. In these cases, planning is attempted, but working memory limitations or ineffective planning strategies prevent successful mental simulation. High rule violations, especially mid-problem are situations where inhibitory control fails under cognitive load. The examinee knows rules but cannot maintain inhibition while simultaneously managing planning demands. Achievement and efficiency decline dramatically on later complex items. Here working memory limitations become critical as cognitive load increases. Early items are solved adequately, but later items show collapse. Differential performance on TWR solid versus striped chip items are cases where cognitive flexibility deficits in shifting between opposing rules produce perseverative errors on striped items.

Comparing Original and TWR Tier 3 Demands

The original and Advanced versions differ substantially in Tier 3 demands. TWR's seventeen items versus nine provide more sampling of planning abilities across difficulty levels. The varied target configurations prevent strategy perseveration. Examinees cannot simply apply a "build a tower on the right peg" heuristic across all items. The rule-switching component adds an explicit cognitive flexibility demand. These differences mean high-functioning individuals who perform near ceiling on the original version often show differentiable deficits on TWR, and TWR provides richer data about specific executive process strengths and weaknesses.

Hot Executive Functions

While cold executive functions represent the cognitive machinery of planning and problem-solving, hot executive functions profoundly influence Tower performance through emotional and motivational factors. These hot processes often determine whether intact cold EF capacities are effectively deployed.

Frustration Tolerance and Emotional Regulation

The Tower Test's graduated difficulty structure—problems becoming increasingly complex across items—creates mounting frustration as examinees encounter items beyond their planning capacity. Examinees with strong emotional regulation maintain systematic approaches despite frustration, continuing to plan carefully even when struggling. Those with poor emotional regulation show performance deterioration as frustration escalates: increasingly impulsive moves, more rule violations, abandonment of strategic thinking in favor of random trial-and-error. The relationship between emotional state and performance quality is diagnostically informative—does frustration cause the executive dysfunction, or does executive dysfunction cause frustration?

Motivation and Sustained Effort

Tower requires sustained cognitive effort over 10–20 minutes with increasing challenge. Maintaining effortful planning on later items when early items have already been mastered requires motivation to persist despite difficulty. Some examinees show strong initial performance but deteriorating effort as items become harder, not because planning capacity is exceeded but because motivation wanes. Others maintain consistent effort throughout, demonstrating strong task engagement and achievement motivation.

Impulsivity Under Emotional Load

While Tier 3 cold EF includes basic response inhibition, hot EF encompasses impulsivity specifically triggered by emotional states. An examinee might demonstrate adequate inhibitory control on early, emotionally neutral items but show increasing impulsivity as frustration or anxiety builds on difficult items. This represents hot EF factors overwhelming cold inhibitory capacity rather than a fundamental inhibition deficit.

Performance Anxiety and Self-Doubt

For some examinees, particularly those with histories of academic struggles or prior negative evaluation experiences, the evaluative context of testing triggers anxiety, affecting performance. This differs from cognitive limitations. The planning capacity exists, but anxiety prevents its deployment. Observable indicators include verbal expressions of self-doubt ("I'm bad at these kinds of things"), physiological anxiety signs (trembling hands, rapid breathing), and performance improvement when anxiety is addressed through supportive examiner comments or breaks.

CAUTION

Hot executive factors can look like cold EF deficits. An examinee showing impulsive responding, frequent rule violations, and poor planning efficiency might appear to have a Tier 3 cold EF impairment. However, if these patterns emerge specifically as frustration mounts, improve dramatically after breaks or emotional support, or occur alongside strong metacognitive awareness ("I know I'm being impulsive but I can't help it"), the primary deficit may be hot EF—emotional regulation compromising otherwise intact cold planning capacity. Treatment implications differ: cold EF deficits require cognitive strategy training; hot EF issues require emotional regulation techniques, frustration tolerance building, and anxiety management.

Tier 3 Hot EF Pattern

Hot EF difficulties on the Tower Test produce performance that varies with emotional state rather than remaining consistently impaired. The examinee may demonstrate adequate planning on early items when emotionally regulated but show deteriorating performance as frustration accumulates, such as increasingly impulsive moves, more rule violations, and abandonment of strategic thinking in favor of random trial-and-error. Behavioral observations are essential: visible agitation after failed attempts, negative self-talk, rushing through later items, or requests to stop. The key diagnostic indicator is that planning capacity exists—evidenced by successful early performance or periods of systematic approach—but emotional dysregulation prevents sustained deployment. Performance that improves dramatically after breaks or supportive comments confirms hot EF involvement. This pattern commonly appears in examinees with Attention Deficit Hyperactivity Disorder (ADHD), anxiety disorders, low frustration tolerance, or ventromedial prefrontal dysfunction, and indicates that intervention should prioritize emotional regulation and frustration tolerance before cognitive strategy training.

Tier 4: Higher-Order Integration and Metacognition

The Tower Test's strength among D-KEFS subtests is its substantial Tier 4 assessment. Unlike Color-Word or Trail Making, which proceed rapidly, Tower problems unfold slowly, providing continuous opportunities for examinees to evaluate their progress, detect errors, and adjust strategies.

Self-Monitoring and Error Detection

Effective Tower performance requires continuously monitoring whether the current approach is working. Examinees should detect when they have made errors (rule violations, inefficient moves) and when their strategy is not progressing toward the goal. Some examinees immediately recognize errors—either self-correcting rule violations or verbalizing awareness ("oh no, that wasn't a good move"). Others continue obliviously, piling up ineffective moves without apparent awareness that something is wrong. The Tower Test's immediate auditory error feedback for rule violations makes error detection easier, potentially supporting Tier 4 functioning.

Strategy Evaluation and Adjustment

Metacognition involves evaluating whether the current problem-solving approach is effective and adjusting when it is not. Examinees with strong Tier 4 abilities modify their strategies across items: slowing down and planning more carefully after impulsive failures, breaking complex problems into subgoals, or shifting from trial-and-error to systematic planning. Those with Tier 4 deficits repeat the same ineffective approaches across all items despite accumulating evidence that their strategy is not working.

Performance Awareness and Frustration Tolerance

Metacognition includes awareness of one's own performance quality—recognizing when performance is strong versus problematic. This awareness interacts with hot executive functions: examinees who recognize errors but lack emotional regulation may show increasing frustration and deteriorating performance.

Tier 4 Clinical Indicators

Tier 4 patterns include commenting on errors and self-correcting, slowing down, and planning more carefully after early impulsive failures, asking clarifying questions about rules mid-testing, and adjusting strategy across items. Conversely, Tier 4 deficits appear as repeating identical ineffective strategies across all items and showing no awareness of errors, even when they accumulate.

Rapid Reference 10.3

Tier Structure at a Glance

Tier	Processes
Tier 1: Foundational processes	Visuospatial perception and processing Visual attention and scanning Language comprehension (understanding instructions) Fine motor control (disk/stylus manipulation)
Tier 2: Bridging processes	Rule following and constraint maintenance Goal maintenance and subgoal tracking Basic move sequencing
Tier 3: Cold executive functions	Spatial planning and look-ahead Spatial working memory Inhibitory control and impulse regulation Cognitive flexibility and strategy shifting (especially TWR)
Tier 3: Hot executive functions	Frustration tolerance and emotional regulation Motivation and sustained effort Performance anxiety management
Tier 4: Higher-Order Integration	Self-monitoring and error detection Strategy evaluation and adjustment Performance awareness

ADMINISTRATION

NOTE: Refer to the Examiner's Manual for complete and detailed administration instructions. The Examiner's Manual provides verbatim instructions and clinicians should follow these precisely to ensure standardized administration.

Administration procedures differ substantially between versions but share common principles: establish clear rule understanding, maintain standardized timing and prompting, and observe problem-solving behavior.

Original Version Administration

Materials

For paper-and-pencil administration, the Tower Test requires the Examiner's Manual, Record Form, Stimulus Booklet (easel position), wooden base with three pegs, five wooden disks, and a timer. Pearson also offers a partial-digital version through Q-global digital assets, which requires the Q-global Examiner's Manual, Stimulus Book, and Stimulus Book Administration Directions, along with the base, disks, and timer.

Setup and Instructions

The examiner sets up the apparatus with three wooden pegs and five disks, arranging them according to each item's starting configuration shown in the stimulus book. After showing the examinee the goal picture, the examiner reads standardized instructions emphasizing the rules that are presented on the examinee's side of the easel: move only one disk at a time, never place a larger disk on a smaller one, and solve the puzzle in as few moves as possible.

Test Item Administration

For test items, the examiner must simultaneously: (1) start the timer when the examinee is shown which peg to build on, (2) record time to first move, (3) count and record moves as they occur, including variations that depend on whether they removed their fingers from the disk or not (difficult with rapid responders), (4) watch for and record rule violations and immediately stop the examinee when they occur, (5) point out the error and return the disk to its previous position, (6) track how long the examinee has worked and announce when time has expired, and (7) apply discontinue rules after failing to complete three towers in a row. Less than optimal performance, failure, or rule violations during Item 1 allow for one demonstration of the correct answer and additional explanation of task instructions and rules.

Counting Moves

Careful observation and tracking of the number of moves requires attention to the two criteria for a single move: (1) move initiation requires that the disk be lifted completely off the peg, and (2) move completion requires that the examinee remove their hand from the disk after initiating a move. If the disk is not completely lifted off the peg or the hand is not removed from the disk, it is not counted as a move.

Handling Rule Violations

The first time an examinee violates each rule, stop them, explain the error and return the disk to its last location prior to the rule violation. For all subsequent violations of the same rule, stop them, state that they have made an error and without explaining the specific rule violation, return the disk to its last location. Keep the timer running.

Examiner Demands

This complex administration places substantial demands on the examiner. Missing a rule violation, miscounting moves, or applying incorrect discontinue times introduces measurement error. Experienced examiners develop systems for managing these simultaneous demands—some use tally counters for moves, others develop mental tracking strategies. However, the original Tower remains one of the most challenging D-KEFS subtests to administer reliably, particularly with impulsive examinees who move rapidly or make multiple errors requiring immediate intervention.

The examiner must balance standardized administration with clinical observation. While tracking multiple scoring variables, the examiner should still note planning pauses, verbalizations, frustration indicators, and strategy patterns. This dual demand makes TWR's automated scoring particularly valuable.

Advanced Version Administration

Materials and Setup

TWR requires the Examiner's Manual, Practitioner Device, Client Device, and Stylus. Before beginning, ensure both devices are charged, connected, and the stylus is functional. TWR's digital format eliminates most manual tracking. The Practitioner Device guides the examiner through administration with prompts appearing exactly when needed. The Client Device presents stimuli and registers responses through stylus input.

Demonstration and Practice

The demonstration item is critical because TWR's response demands are unique—lifting, dragging, holding, and releasing chips within a restricted, blue-highlighted area via stylus. Examinees need adequate practice with these mechanics before test items begin. Some examinees, particularly older adults or those with limited technology exposure, may need extended practice. The reset button on the demonstration item allows for reteaching and additional practice until the examinee understands the task. In addition, the first three items provide an additional trial (Trial 2) if Trial 1 is not completed within the time or move limit.

Automated Scoring Features

During test items, the digital interface automatically: (1) captures each move time with tenth-of-a-second precision, (2) counts total moves made, (3) detects rule violations and provides immediate feedback (different sound, red X, shaking chip), (4) prevents further responses until incorrectly placed chips are returned to their last correct position (automatic for size-placement errors), (5) displays notifications on the Practitioner Device when verbal prompts are needed with the specific prompt to read aloud, (6) stops the examinee automatically when move limits or time limits are reached, (7) prompts for discontinuation of the subtest when the discontinue rule of three consecutive item scores of 0 has been met, and (8) scores all measures instantly when testing concludes. The Client Device automatically darkens and becomes inactive for prompts, redirection, or when discontinue criteria have been met. Item discontinue criteria differ from the original D-KEFS in that each trial ends when a certain number of moves have been completed or the time limit runs out.

Behavioral Observation Opportunities

This automation eliminates measurement error from manual administration and frees the examiner to observe behavioral nuances: Does the examinee pause before moves (planning) or move continuously (trial-and-error)? Do they show frustration escalation across items? Do they self-correct in response to error feedback? Do they spontaneously comment on their strategies? These qualitative observations provide critical Tier 4 metacognitive information that quantitative scores alone cannot capture.

Rule Switching

The solid-chip/striped-chip rule switching requires careful attention. Before the first striped-chip item, the software prompts the examiner to explain the rule reversal. The examiner should verify comprehension before proceeding—some examinees initially confuse which rule applies to which chip type. Monitoring for perseverative errors (applying solid-chip rules to striped chips) provides valuable cognitive flexibility data.

Administration Considerations Common to Both Versions

Testing Environment

Examinees should work in quiet, distraction-free environments. The examiner should position materials/tablet to avoid visual obstruction while maintaining the ability to observe the examinee's face and behavior, and for the original version, observe and count the moves made.

Behavioral Observation

Behavioral observation is critical throughout. The examiner should note planning pauses, impulsive moves, verbalizations, frustration indicators, and strategy shifts. These observations often reveal more about executive functioning than scores alone.

Standardization

The examiner should not provide strategy suggestions or hints beyond standardized prompts. Comments like "Think about it first" or "You're going too fast" invalidate standardized administration. The standardized prompts are carefully limited and worded to encourage effort without providing strategy instruction.

Breaks

For examinees showing significant frustration, brief breaks between items are permissible and often clinically informative. If performance improves after breaks, this suggests hot EF factors affecting cold EF capacity or a short attention span that improves with breaks. Document any breaks provided and their effects on subsequent performance.

BEHAVIORAL OBSERVATIONS

Systematic behavioral observation during Tower administration provides essential information for interpreting scores within the hierarchical framework. Both versions offer rich observational opportunities, though the original version's physical manipulation provides additional motor-related observations while TWR's automatic scoring allows more examiner attention to behavioral nuances. For TWR, base rates are provided for a selection of behaviors (see Table 7.9 in the Examiner's Manual), allowing examiners to compare observed behaviors against the frequency at which different age ranges in the normative group exhibited that behavior.

Planning Behaviors and Approach Organization

Watch carefully whether examinees pause before beginning each item. Extended initial pauses suggest active planning while examinees are mentally simulating moves before touching any disks/chips. Immediate action without pauses indicates impulsive trial-and-error approaches. The optimal pattern shows brief pauses on easy items and appropriately longer pauses on difficult items, indicating strategic planning allocation.

Observe whether examinees pause between moves or execute rapid, continuous sequences. Rapid sequences without pauses suggest either excellent preplanning (executing a formulated plan) or thoughtless trial-and-error. Distinguish them by watching for self-corrections. Planners rarely need to undo moves, while trial-and-error responders frequently backtrack. Some examinees show a systematic approach organization, visually scanning all three pegs/tables before each move; others show disorganized scanning without apparent strategic consideration.

Working Memory and Rule-Following Indicators

Rule violations provide critical diagnostic information. Early rule violations (items 1–3 on original, items 1–5 on TWR) likely reflect incomplete rule learning or comprehension difficulties—Tier 1 issues. Rule violations emerging only on difficult items suggest working memory capacity limits or inhibitory control failures under executive demands—Tier 3 issues.

The type of rule violation matters. Moving two disks simultaneously indicates forgetting verbal rules—suggesting auditory working memory limitations (Tier 1–2). Placing larger disks on smaller ones can reflect forgetting the rule, impulsive moves that violate known rules (Tier 2–3), or deliberate rule-breaking when planning has failed. On TWR, applying solid-chip rules to striped-chip items indicates cognitive inflexibility or working memory failures (Tier 3).

Watch for set-loss errors where examinees suddenly "forget what they're doing"—asking "What am I supposed to do again?" or making moves clearly inconsistent with the goal. These suggest goal-maintenance failures (Tier 2) are distinct from planning deficits.

Emotional Regulation and Sustained Effort

Watch for frustration escalation as items become harder: sighing, negative comments, rushing moves, or giving up. Note the relationship between emotional state and performance quality: does frustration produce deterioration (more impulsive moves, more violations) or does performance remain stable despite visible distress?

Brief breaks between items provide diagnostic information. When examinees return with renewed patience and improved performance, this suggests hot EF influences or attention difficulties. When breaks do not help, this suggests cold EF limitations independent of emotional state. Document any breaks and their effects on subsequent performance.

Metacognitive Awareness and Self-Monitoring

Listen for spontaneous verbalizations. Comments like "I think I need to move this one first," "Wait, that won't work," or "This is harder than the last one" indicate explicit metacognitive monitoring (Tier 4). Watch for self-corrections—starting to make a move, then stopping and choosing differently—which demonstrate real-time error monitoring. The absence of self-corrections, even when making rule violations, suggests poor metacognitive awareness.

Watch how examinees respond to error feedback. Immediate incorporation (no further violations of that type) suggests intact learning and adjustment capacity. Continued violations despite feedback suggest poor metacognitive awareness or impaired response regulation. After completing items, some examinees spontaneously evaluate their performance ("I don't think I did that very well"), which indicates awareness of efficiency and solution quality.

Physical and Motor Observations (Original Version)

The original version's physical manipulation reveals motor control quality. Watch how examinees grasp and manipulate disks. Clumsy grasping, dropping disks, difficulty releasing disks precisely, or tremor indicate fine motor limitations that could slow performance independent of planning abilities. Some examinees demonstrate excellent spatial planning but poor motor execution. This dissociation has important implications for real-world functioning. On the original version, watch whether examinees occasionally hover a disk over a peg without placing it; this physical "testing" of a potential move before committing suggests active planning.

SCORING

Both versions provide multiple scores quantifying different aspects of planning and problem-solving, though TWR's automated scoring generates additional process measures unavailable on the original version.

Original D-KEFS Tower Test Scoring

Total Achievement Score

The primary summary score reflects overall planning success. Points are awarded for each item based on the number of moves required to solve the problem within the time limit. For each item, examinees receive points based on move efficiency: solving in minimum moves earns maximum points, while excess moves reduce points according to a conversion table. Maximum score is 30 points (items vary in point value based on difficulty). This score reflects the combined influence of planning, strategy development, rule learning, working memory, inhibition, maintaining cognitive set, and persistence.

Total Achievement represents the test's most comprehensive planning index, integrating preplanning quality, execution efficiency, and ability to avoid excessive trial-and-error. High scores indicate efficient planning, producing near-optimal solutions. Low scores indicate planning deficits resulting in excessive moves, though they do not specify which planning components are compromised.

Mean First-Move Time

Calculated as Total First-Move Times ÷ Number of Items Administered, this score represents the average time from "go" to first move across all completed items. This score indexes planning behavior: extremely brief first-move times indicate impulsivity, moderate times suggest adequate planning, and excessive times may indicate anxiety or working memory overload. Optimal first-move times show appropriate variation—brief on easy items, longer on difficult items. This pattern indicates strategic planning allocation.

Time-Per-Move Ratio

Calculated as Total of Completion Times Across All Items Administered ÷ Total Number of Moves Across All Items Administered, this score compares actual time spent working on the towers, not just the time spent to make their first move. This helps distinguish between examinees who are slow because they are making many moves (poor planning) versus those who are slow because each move takes considerable time (processing speed or motor limitations).

Move Accuracy Ratio

Calculated as Total Number of Moves Across All Items Administered ÷ Total Number of Minimum Moves Required Across All Items Administered, this score compares total moves with the minimum possible moves across items attempted. This ratio is then converted to a scaled score for interpretation. Higher scaled scores reflect efficient problem solving, while lower scaled scores are markers of inefficiency.

Total Rule Violation Score

Number of rule-violating moves across all items (placing a larger disk on a smaller disk; moving more than one disk at a time). This score specifically assesses inhibitory control and rule maintenance under cognitive load. High rule violations despite adequate baseline rule comprehension indicate Tier 3 inhibitory failure rather than Tier 2 rule learning deficits. To account for examinees that may not complete all items, an additional Rule-Violations-Per-Item Ratio is provided (Total Number of Rule Violations Made ÷ Number of Items Administered) and provides a normative cumulative percentile rank.

Rule violations provide critical differential diagnostic information. Frequent violations with adequate achievement scores suggest impulsive execution despite adequate planning concepts—Tier 3 inhibitory control deficits. Frequent violations with poor achievement scores indicate more global executive dysfunction. Violations concentrated on difficult items versus distributed across all items suggest different underlying mechanisms.

D-KEFS Advanced Tower Test (TWR) Scoring

TWR provides several metrics that build upon and extend the original Tower Test scoring system. The digital platform enables automatic calculation of all scores and additional process measures that were difficult or impossible to capture with the manual version.

Core Score

The Global Performance Score is the primary summary score reflecting overall planning success and efficiency. The examinee receives 1 point for successfully completing each item within the move and time limits, plus bonus points for solving items using fewer moves. Correct completion of Trial 2 on the first three items also receives 1 point. The bonus point system rewards spatial planning over rapid, trial-and-error responding. This score integrates planning, working memory, inhibitory control, and problem-solving efficiency.

Process Scores

TWR provides multiple process scores that help differentiate specific aspects of executive functioning.

Global Performance Score for Solid Items and Striped Items

Achievement scores calculated separately for the ten solid-chip items (where the rule is "never place a larger chip on a smaller one") and the seven striped-chip items (where the rule is reversed). Comparing performance on solid versus striped items helps assess cognitive flexibility—the ability to shift between opposing rules. This measure is normed using base rates, with higher base rates reflecting better performance. Disproportionate difficulty on striped items may indicate perseverative application of the first-learned rule or difficulty with rule-switching.

Mean Rule Violations Per Item

Calculated as Total Rule Violations ÷ Number of Items Administered, this score captures the average number of moves that violated instructional rules: size-placement errors (placing wrong-sized chips together) and two-chip errors (attempting to move multiple chips or selecting chips underneath others). This measure is normed using base rates, with higher base rates reflecting fewer violations. Rule violations are clinically significant as they correlate with frontal lobe dysfunction and may indicate working memory deficits (forgetting rules), inhibitory control problems, or impulsivity.

Trial-and-Error Scores

These include 0-Back, 1-Back, and 2-Back Moves, which capture impulsive, trial-and-error responses that do not violate rules but are unproductive because they decrease the chance that the examinee will complete the item in as few moves as possible and obtain bonus points if they eventually solve the item. A 0-back move occurs when the examinee lifts a chip off a table and places it back on the same table. A 1-back move occurs when the examinee lifts a chip off a table, places it on a different table, and then lifts and places it back on the original table. A 2-back move occurs when the examinee lifts a chip off a table, places it on one table, then lifts and places it on a different table, and then lifts and places it back on the original table. This measure is normed using base rates, with higher base rates reflecting fewer trial-and-error moves. Frequent back-moves (particularly 1-back and 2-back) demonstrate poor spatial planning and impulsive responding.

Adjusted Mean Pure Response Time

This score assesses the mean time to make all individual chip moves (both correct moves and rule violations). It yields an age-referenced scaled score reflecting execution speed during active problem-solving—how quickly examinees make individual moves once engaged with the problem. Scaled scores are provided that are based on a cumulative percentage range for adjusted raw score conversion. Extended response times might indicate motor slowness, processing speed limitations, or working memory difficulties requiring extended processing to determine each move.

Adjusted Mean Unproductive Responses

This score quantifies unproductive moves—responses that do not advance toward the solution. TWR distinguishes correct/productive responses (moves that follow rules AND reduce remaining moves needed), correct/unproductive responses (moves that follow rules but do not reduce remaining moves), and incorrect/unproductive responses (rule violations resulting in the chip automatically returned to its last location). Higher scaled scores reflect fewer unproductive moves; lower scores reflect more unproductive moves. This measure captures both rule violations AND technically correct-but-inefficient moves, revealing trial-and-error problem-solving versus planned, efficient strategies.

Contrast Scores

TWR provides regression-based contrast scores that account for expected relationships between measures.

Global Performance Score Solid Versus Striped Items Contrast Base Rate

This score evaluates whether the examinee's performance on striped-chip items is at, above, or below the predicted level given their performance on solid-chip items. It corrects for the methodological problem that simply comparing solid versus striped base rates can be misleading, since the normative sample shows striped items are generally harder and examinees at different performance levels show different typical discrepancies between item types. Low base rates indicate that performance on striped-chip items is lower than predicted, given performance on solid-chip items. Mid-range base rates indicate expected striped-chip performance. High base rates indicate higher than predicted striped-chip performance.

Speed-Accuracy Tradeoff Contrast Score

This score compares the Adjusted Mean Unproductive Responses scaled score to the Adjusted Mean Pure Response Time scaled score. The contrast score provides information regarding whether the examinee has an expected level of accuracy given their pure response speed. In addition, a Speed-Accuracy Tradeoff Graph is provided that indicates whether accuracy was sacrificed for speed, speed was sacrificed for accuracy, both were weaknesses, or both were strengths.

Additional Raw Scores

Total Two-Chip Errors, Total Size-Placement Errors, and Optimal First Move are provided as raw scores, which describe the overall frequency of rule violations or use of the most optimal first move choice.

Behavior Observations

For a selection of behaviors (see Table 7.9 in the Examiner's Manual), base rates are provided that compare the rate at which different age ranges in the normative group also exhibited that behavior.

Rapid Reference 10.4

Scoring Summary

Score Type	Original D-KEFS	Advanced (TWR)
Primary score	Total Achievement Score (points for solving in minimum moves; max 30)	Global Performance Score (completion + bonus points for efficiency)
Planning behavior	Mean First-Move Time (average time before first move; brief = impulsive, excessive = anxiety/overload)	(captured in process scores)
Planning efficiency	Move Accuracy Ratio (total moves ÷ minimum moves; ratio near 1.0 = optimal)	Trial-and-Error Scores (0-Back, 1-Back, 2-Back moves; unproductive but rule-following moves)
Processing speed	Time-Per-Move Ratio (completion time ÷ total moves; slow moves vs. many moves)	Adjusted Mean Pure Response Time (execution speed during moves)
Inhibitory control	Total Rule Violation Score; Rule-Violations-Per-Item Ratio	Mean Rule Violations Per Item (size-placement + two-chip errors)
Cognitive flexibility	(not directly measured)	Global Performance Solid vs. Striped Items; Solid vs. Striped Contrast
Efficiency measure	(not directly measured)	Adjusted Mean Unproductive Responses (rule violations + inefficient moves)
Contrast scores	(not available)	Speed-Accuracy Tradeoff Contrast (accuracy given response speed)

COMMON ADMINISTRATION ERRORS

Given the Tower Test's administration complexity, several errors occur frequently enough to warrant attention.

Failure to Enforce Rule Violations Immediately

The manual specifies that rule violations must be corrected immediately. The examiner must stop the examinee and require them to restore the configuration to the state before the rule-violating move. TWR corrects for rule violations automatically, so this issue is reserved for the original Tower Test. Some examiners may let violations stand, either not noticing them or avoiding confrontation. This invalidates rule violation scores and allows examinees to solve problems through rule-breaking.

Inconsistent Timing and Prompting

First-move timing must begin precisely when the examiner says "go," not when the examinee appears to be thinking. Some examiners delay starting the timer until the examinee reaches for a disk, artificially reducing first-move times.

Incorrect Documentation of Moves

The examiner must carefully observe that the examinee initiated the move (lifted it completely off the peg) and removed their hand from the disk after initiating a move for it to be considered a single move. This requires vigilance as many examinees make moves quickly.

Inadvertent Cueing

Examiner facial expressions, body language, or verbalizations can provide unintended cues. Gasping when the examinee makes a rule violation or showing approval when good moves are made influences performance. The examiner should maintain a neutral, supportive demeanor without signaling error or success.

Over-Assisting on Demonstration Items

While the manual allows demonstrating the solution if needed on Item 1 of the original Tower Test or the TWR demonstration item, some examiners provide excessive help beyond assessment instructions, essentially providing a problem-solving strategy for the examinee. This prevents assessment of the examinee's actual capacity to understand and execute solutions independently.

Poor Behavioral Observation

Because the original version requires tracking multiple variables simultaneously, examiners sometimes focus entirely on scoring mechanics and miss critical behavioral observations. This is why TWR's automated scoring represents a significant advantage—freeing the examiner for observation.

Incomplete Rule Explanation

The instructions are lengthy and complex. Rushing through them or assuming comprehension without verification can result in poor performance reflecting confusion rather than planning deficits.

INTERPRETATION

Interpreting Tower Test performance requires integrating quantitative scores, behavioral observations, and performance patterns within the hierarchical framework. The goal is to determine which tier(s) contain the primary deficits and how these deficits manifest in real-world functioning.

Using the Hierarchical Framework for Differential Diagnosis

Begin interpretation at Tier 1, working upward through the hierarchy. This bottom-up approach prevents misattributing foundational deficits as executive dysfunction.

Step 1: Rule Out Tier 1 Limitations
Did the examinee understand instructions despite repeated explanations? Were early items (items 1–3 on original, items 1–5 on TWR) completed successfully? Were there motor control difficulties affecting physical manipulation (original) or stylus use (TWR)? Did visuospatial perception appear adequate for distinguishing disk/chip sizes? If Tier 1 concerns emerge, seek corroborating evidence from other assessment data. Visuospatial subtests, language comprehension measures, and processing speed indices help determine whether poor Tower performance reflects foundational limitations. When Tier 1 deficits are present, state explicitly that planning capacity could not be adequately assessed due to foundational limitations and recommend targeted assessment of suspected Tier 1 processes.

CAUTION

Tower performance can be compromised by multiple nonexecutive factors, including visuospatial deficits, motor impairments, or language comprehension difficulties. Always consider whether foundational Tier 1 abilities are intact before attributing poor performance to executive dysfunction. Process scores and behavioral observations help determine the appropriate tier of dysfunction.

Step 2: Evaluate Tier 2 Bridging Processes
Were rules followed consistently on easy items? Did rule violations occur primarily on difficult items under cognitive load (suggesting Tier 3 issues) versus distributed across all items (suggesting Tier 2 rule-maintenance problems)? Were subgoals maintained throughout items, or did the examinee lose track of goals mid-problem? Tier 2 difficulties manifest as inconsistent rule application despite apparent understanding, goal-maintenance failures (asking repeatedly "What am I trying to do?"), and adequate completion of simple items with deterioration as complexity increases only modestly. These patterns suggest the bridge between foundational abilities and executive functions is compromised.

Step 3: Analyze Tier 3 Cold Executive Patterns
This represents the Tower Test's primary assessment target. Examine the pattern across planning, working memory, inhibition, cognitive flexibility, and problem-solving. Total Achievement Score and Move Accuracy Ratio quantify planning quality but consider Mean First-Move Time relative to achievement. Brief latencies with poor achievement suggest impulsivity, while extended latencies with poor achievement suggest ineffective planning despite effort. Fragmented performance with frequent pauses between moves suggests working memory limitations, as does deterioration on complex items despite adequate earlier performance. High rule violation counts indicate inhibitory deficits; note whether violations are consistent (cold EF) or concentrated during emotional activation (hot EF). Perseveration on ineffective strategies suggests cognitive rigidity, while consistently high move counts regardless of difficulty indicates trial-and-error rather than planful approaches.

Step 4: Evaluate Tier 3 Hot Executive Factors
Determine whether emotional or motivational factors contributed to performance. Cold executive deficits manifest as consistent planning difficulty independent of emotional state; hot executive dysfunction appears as performance variability related to frustration, anxiety, or engagement. Did performance deteriorate as frustration accumulated? Did rule violations increase when emotionally activated? Did breaks restore performance quality? The critical diagnostic question: Does the examinee demonstrate planning capacity even if inconsistently? Variable performance suggests a hot EF impact on cold EF deployment rather than absent capacity.

Step 5: Assess Tier 4 Integration and Metacognition
Did the examinee demonstrate awareness of their performance quality? Were strategies spontaneously evaluated and adjusted? Strong Tier 4 functioning manifests as spontaneous strategy commentary, appropriate self-corrections, and performance improvement with minimal prompting. Weak Tier 4 functioning shows absent metacognitive awareness, perseveration without adjustment, and failure to benefit from prompts. The presence or

absence of metacognitive awareness shapes intervention planning—examinees with intact self-monitoring can leverage this strength, while combined deficits require interventions addressing both levels.

PERFORMANCE PATTERNS AND CLINICAL IMPLICATIONS

Several characteristic performance patterns emerge on the Tower Test, each with distinct clinical implications for understanding the nature and tier-level of executive dysfunction.

Planning Efficiency Patterns

The relationship between first-move latency and achievement reveals distinct clinical profiles. Brief latencies combined with poor achievement suggest impulsive responding without adequate preplanning. The examinee begins moving before formulating a strategy. These individuals may benefit from explicit instruction to pause and plan, external prompts to think before acting, and structured problem-solving frameworks. Extended latencies combined with poor achievement indicate planning was attempted but proved ineffective, possibly due to working memory limits preventing effective mental simulation or poor strategic knowledge. These individuals may benefit from strategy instruction and worked examples rather than simply more planning time. Moderate latencies with poor achievement suggest adequate planning attempts but poor strategic quality. The examinee takes appropriate time but generates inefficient solutions, indicating a need for explicit strategy training.

Working Memory Patterns

Working memory limitations produce characteristic performance signatures. Fragmented performance with frequent pauses between individual moves suggests examinees cannot hold multistep plans in mind and must replan after each move—a cognitively inefficient approach that increases error risk and time to completion. Rule violations emerging only on difficult items may reflect working memory capacity exceeded under cognitive load rather than inhibitory control deficits. Performance dramatically deteriorates on later complex items, despite adequate performance on earlier items, which strongly suggests working memory capacity limits. These individuals may benefit from external memory supports, chunking strategies, or task simplification in real-world applications.

Inhibitory Control Patterns

The pattern of rule violations provides diagnostic specificity. Violations increasing as frustration mounts suggest hot EF influences on inhibition. The examinee can inhibit when calm, but loses this capacity under emotional activation. Violations consistent across emotional states suggest cold inhibitory control deficits requiring direct inhibition training. Violations specifically at rule-switch points (TWR solid/striped transitions) suggest cognitive inflexibility rather than general inhibition deficit. The examinee can follow rules but struggles to shift between competing rule sets.

Cognitive Flexibility Patterns

On TWR, applying solid-chip rules to striped-chip items or vice versa indicates difficulty shifting between opposing rules—a pattern with implications for any situation requiring alternation between different procedures or mindsets. On both versions, perseveration on ineffective strategies despite poor outcomes suggests cognitive rigidity that may manifest as difficulty adapting approaches when circumstances change. Failure to improve efficiency across items suggests an inability to learn and flexibly apply heuristics developed through experience with earlier problems.

Problem-Solving Style Patterns

Adequate efficiency on middle-difficulty items but poor performance on the most difficult items suggests planning capacity limits with problems exceeding available planning resources. These individuals may function well with moderately complex demands but require support or task modification for highly complex planning. Poor efficiency across all difficulty levels suggests more fundamental problem-solving deficits affecting even simple spatial reasoning. Consistently high move counts despite varying item difficulty indicate trial-and-error approaches rather than planful problem-solving—a pattern often reflecting poor strategy knowledge or failure to engage planning processes.

Hot Executive Function Patterns

Cold executive deficits manifest as consistent planning difficulty independent of emotional state. Performance remains stable even when frustration is minimal. Hot executive dysfunction appears as performance variability related to frustration, anxiety, or engagement. Observable anxiety (trembling hands, self-deprecating comments) corresponding with performance decline suggests emotional interference with otherwise intact planning abilities. Variable performance—strong on some items, poor on others, without clear difficulty progression—suggests hot EF impact on cold EF deployment. These individuals may demonstrate planning capacity under supportive conditions but require emotional regulation support to deploy these abilities consistently.

Metacognitive Patterns

Examinees who recognize their errors but cannot correct them show intact monitoring with impaired control. They know when performance is poor but cannot adjust effectively. Those unaware of poor performance show compromised monitoring requiring external feedback systems for real-world functioning. Spontaneous strategy adjustment during testing indicates strong metacognitive control; perseveration despite recognizing ineffectiveness indicates the monitoring-control dissociation common in frontal dysfunction.

Original Versus Advanced Version Comparisons

When both versions are administered or when compared to clinical research findings, distinctive patterns emerge. Speed-accuracy dissociations—where examinees sacrifice speed to maintain accuracy—may indicate preserved planning capacity with increased cognitive resource demands per step, as observed in TBI samples during clinical validation. TWR's additional rule-switching demands (solid vs. striped chips) may reveal flexibility deficits not apparent on the original version's consistent rule structure. Examinees performing adequately on the original but struggling with TWR rule transitions demonstrate specific flexibility vulnerabilities that would be missed without the Advanced version's opposing-rules format.

Rapid Reference 10.5

Distinguishing Tier-Level Deficits

Pattern	Likely Tier	Clinical Indicators
Early item failures, rule confusion, motor difficulties	Tier 1	Instruction comprehension problems; clumsy manipulation; visuospatial errors
Inconsistent rule application; loses track of goals	Tier 2	Rule violations on easy items; asks "What am I doing?" mid-problem
Poor planning despite intact foundations	Tier 3 Cold	Low Total Achievement; high Move Accuracy Ratio; brief first-move times with poor efficiency
Variable performance tied to emotional state	Tier 3 Hot	Performance deteriorates with frustration; improves after breaks; rule violations increase when stuck
Adequate execution without strategic awareness	Tier 4	No self-correction; perseveration on failed strategies; absent metacognitive commentary

ECOLOGICAL VALIDITY AND FUNCTIONAL IMPLICATIONS

Tower Test performance predicts functioning across multiple domains requiring spatial planning, sequential problem-solving, and goal-directed behavior under constraints.

Academic Functioning

Tower planning relates to multistep problem-solving in mathematics, science experiments, and long-term project completion. Poor Tower performance predicts difficulty with math word problems requiring multistep solutions, science projects demanding planning from conception through execution, and research papers requiring organization of multiple components. Students with Tower deficits may understand individual concepts but struggle to sequence them into coherent solutions. Hot EF influences during Tower testing (frustration leading to rule-breaking when stuck) may predict academic situations where students abandon problem-solving constraints when frustrated, such as giving up on showing work in math problems and guessing answers, or skipping required research steps in lab reports when the methodology becomes confusing.

Vocational and Daily Living

Tower planning correlates with job tasks requiring project management, sequential task execution, and strategic goal pursuit. Professions demanding significant planning—project management, engineering, architecture, computer programming—will be particularly challenging for individuals with Tower deficits. Hot EF difficulties (breaking rules when unable to solve problems) may manifest in workplace shortcuts that violate procedures when tasks become overwhelming, such as skipping quality control or safety steps when behind schedule or circumventing approval processes when standard channels seem too slow. Daily living skills similarly require Tower-like planning: cooking multi-dish meals (coordinating timing of multiple components), financial planning (multistep budgeting), and home organization (systematic cleaning schedules). Hot EF vulnerabilities when stuck may predict real-world behaviors like abandoning recipes mid-preparation when steps do not make sense, making impulsive financial decisions when budgeting feels too complicated, or giving up on organizational systems when maintaining them becomes frustrating.

Social Functioning

Social interactions often require planning and sequencing analogous to Tower demands. Navigating complex social situations—planning how to approach a difficult conversation, sequencing steps to resolve an interpersonal conflict, or organizing a social event—requires the same spatial-sequential reasoning assessed by Tower tasks. Individuals with Tower deficits may struggle with multistep social problem-solving, such as planning how to apologize and repair a damaged relationship or sequencing the steps needed to join a new social group. Hot EF vulnerabilities observed during Tower testing may predict social difficulties when interpersonal problems feel unsolvable, abandoning relationship repair efforts when initial attempts do not work, breaking social "rules" (interrupting, dominating conversations) when frustrated with conversational constraints, or impulsively ending relationships rather than working through sequential conflict resolution steps.

PRELIMINARY CLINICAL VALIDATION OF THE D-KEFS ADVANCED TWR

Clinical group studies conducted during D-KEFS Advanced standardization provide initial evidence of TWR's sensitivity to executive dysfunction across several populations (Delis & Kaplan, 2025). Because the TWR is administered across the full age range (8–90 years), both child and adult clinical groups were tested. These preliminary findings require replication and should not be used as sole diagnostic criteria, but they establish useful reference points for clinical interpretation.

Autism Spectrum Disorder

Children with autism spectrum disorder (ASD; $n = 31$) performed significantly below matched controls on all three TWR measures, with the Global Performance Score yielding a large effect size ($d = 0.89, p < 0.01$). Moderate effect sizes emerged for both Adjusted Mean Pure Response Time ($d = 0.62$, $p = 0.01$) and Adjusted Mean Unproductive Responses ($d = 0.72$, $p < 0.01$). These findings align with documented difficulties in spatial working memory, planning, and problem-solving commonly observed in individuals with ASD. The consistent impairment across both speed and accuracy measures suggests genuine planning deficits rather than a speed-accuracy tradeoff pattern.

Specific Learning Disorder–Mathematics

TWR produced the largest effect sizes among all D-KEFS Advanced tests for the SLD-Math group ($n = 26$), with two measures yielding significant differences and large effect sizes. This sensitivity likely reflects the substantial overlap between spatial planning demands on TWR and the visuospatial reasoning required for mathematical problem-solving. Children who struggle with multistep mathematical operations may share underlying deficits in the spatial working memory and sequential planning processes that TWR assesses. These findings highlight the importance of evaluating executive functioning across modalities—verbal and spatial—when assessing learning difficulties.

Traumatic Brain Injury

Adults with moderate-to-severe traumatic brain injury (TBI; $n = 30$; mean Glasgow Coma Scale = 8.5) demonstrated a distinctive pattern on TWR: large effect sizes for speed-related measures but not for accuracy measures. Specifically, Adjusted Mean Pure Response Time showed significant impairment, while Adjusted Mean Unproductive Responses did not differ significantly from controls. This speed-accuracy dissociation—where individuals with TBI sacrifice speed to maintain accuracy—parallels findings across other D-KEFS Advanced tests in this sample. Clinically, this pattern suggests that planning capacity may be relatively preserved in some individuals with TBI, but the cognitive resources required for each planning step are increased, resulting in slower execution.

Attention-Deficit/Hyperactivity Disorder

Notably, the ADHD group ($n = 55$) did not differ significantly from matched controls on any TWR measure, with negligible effect sizes across Global Performance Score ($d = 0.12$), Adjusted Mean Pure Response Time ($d = -0.03$), and Adjusted Mean Unproductive Responses ($d = 0.11$). This finding contrasts sharply with the same group's significant impairments on other D-KEFS Advanced tests, particularly the Color-Word Interference Test and Trail Making Test. TWR's game-like, interactive format may enhance engagement for individuals with ADHD, and unlike tests requiring sustained rapid responding to repetitive stimuli, TWR presents varied problem-solving challenges that may help maintain attention. Clinicians should recognize that average TWR performance in individuals with ADHD does not rule out executive dysfunction—it may instead reflect a relative strength in spatial planning or the benefits of an engaging task format.

Mild Cognitive Impairment

The mild cognitive impairment (MCI) sample ($n = 18$) was too small for reliable statistical analysis and findings were not reported. Future research with larger samples is needed to establish TWR's sensitivity to early cognitive decline in older adults.

Clinical Implications

These preliminary findings suggest TWR is particularly sensitive to executive dysfunction in ASD and SLD-Math populations, with large effect sizes supporting its utility in these groups. The speed-accuracy dissociation observed in TBI provides clinically meaningful information about preserved versus compromised processes. The lack of sensitivity to ADHD at the group level does not diminish TWR's clinical value but rather highlights its specificity to spatial planning processes that may remain intact in ADHD despite other executive vulnerabilities. As with all clinical group research, substantial individual variability exists within diagnostic categories, and clinicians should interpret TWR performance within the context of comprehensive assessment rather than using it as a standalone diagnostic indicator.

STRENGTHS AND WEAKNESSES

The Tower Test offers distinct advantages for assessing spatial planning and executive functions while also presenting limitations that clinicians should consider when selecting measures and interpreting results.

Strengths

The Tower Test has several notable advantages for assessing spatial planning and executive functions within a comprehensive neuropsychological evaluation.

Unique Assessment of Spatial Planning

The Tower Test assesses complex spatial planning and problem-solving that many other neuropsychological tests do not. While Trail Making assesses sequencing and set-shifting, and Verbal Fluency assesses generativity, Tower uniquely requires mental simulation of potential action sequences and their outcomes.

Multidimensional Process Scores

The process scores differentiate planning quality (Move Accuracy Ratio), planning behavior (Mean First-Move Time), inhibitory control (Rule Violations), and working memory capacity (performance decline on complex items). This multidimensional assessment clarifies which specific executive processes are impaired.

Wide Ability Range

The graduated difficulty structure allows assessment across a wide ability range. Early items are solvable by individuals with significant cognitive limitations, while later items challenge high-functioning adults. TWR's seventeen items further extend this range.

Neuroanatomical Sensitivity

Research demonstrates sensitivity to frontal lobe dysfunction with specificity for lateral prefrontal regions (Yochim et al., 2007). Few neuropsychological tests show such clear anatomical localization.

Rich Behavioral Observation Opportunities

The Tower Test's slow, deliberate pace provides rich opportunities for behavioral observation. Unlike speeded tests, where behavioral observations are limited, Tower performance unfolds over minutes with multiple decision points and opportunities for strategy adjustment. Examining the qualitative process reveals as much as quantitative scores.

Contemporary Normative Data (TWR)

TWR benefits from a recently collected normative sample that reflects current population demographics, enhancing the accuracy of score interpretation across diverse examinees.

Ecological Parallels

The Tower Test's cognitive requirements parallel some aspects of real-world planning demands. Real-world tasks like organizing a trip, troubleshooting a problem, or managing a complex project share certain cognitive elements with Tower tasks: mentally simulating outcomes, selecting among alternative approaches, maintaining goals while managing subgoals, and adjusting strategies when initial approaches fail. However, the ecological validity of Tower performance is limited by its emotionally neutral, structured testing context (see Weaknesses), and performance should be interpreted alongside behavioral rating scales and functional assessment to bridge the assessment–reality gap.

Weaknesses and Limitations

Despite its strengths, the Tower Test has several limitations that clinicians should consider when selecting measures and interpreting results.

Administration Complexity (Original Version)
Administration complexity in the original version creates potential for measurement error. Simultaneous tracking of first-move time, move counting, rule violation detection, and standardized prompting while maintaining behavioral observation is demanding. TWR's automation largely eliminates this weakness but introduces technology dependency.

Limited Ecological Validity for Hot EF Contexts
The Tower Test measures planning and problem-solving in emotionally neutral, structured contexts with clear rules and immediate feedback. Real-world planning often occurs under emotional stress, with ambiguous goals, incomplete information, and delayed feedback. Performance may not predict planning capacity in emotionally charged situations where hot EF factors dominate.

Cultural and Experiential Factors
Cultural and experiential factors may influence performance. Examinees familiar with puzzle games or spatial problem-solving may have an advantaged experience. The task requires tolerance for cognitive challenge and willingness to persist despite difficulty—cultural values around persistence and achievement motivation vary.

Ceiling Effects
The original version's nine items can show ceiling effects in high-functioning individuals, limiting differentiation at the upper range. TWR partially addresses this, but ceiling effects may persist for some examinees.

Substantial Practice Effects
Practice effects are substantial. Repeated administrations show significant improvement, limiting utility for monitoring intervention effects or tracking progressive conditions over short intervals. TWR's different items from the original may allow one-time switching between versions, but repeated TWR administrations show practice effects.

Limited Aging Norms (Original Version)
The original D-KEFS normative sample, collected over two decades ago, may not fully represent current older adult populations, and the upper age range (89 years) may provide less precise estimates for the oldest examinees.

CAUTION

Tower of Hanoi puzzles are widely available as online games and mobile apps. Some examinees may have practiced similar tasks digitally, sometimes extensively. Combined with the substantial practice effects documented for Tower tests, prior exposure can significantly inflate performance. Ask about familiarity with tower puzzles ("Have you ever played puzzle games like this before, either online or in apps?") and interpret results cautiously when examinees report prior exposure. TWR's varied target configurations and rule-switching between solid and striped chips may somewhat mitigate advantages from standard Tower of Hanoi practice, though practice effects remain a significant concern.

ALTERNATIVE MEASURES

Tower tasks represent one approach to assessing spatial planning and problem-solving. Comprehensive executive function assessment benefits from multiple planning measures complementing Tower's strengths and compensating for its limitations. Consider alternatives when Tower is unavailable, when repeated assessment is needed, when Tower results require corroboration or extension, or when cross-test integration illuminates specific executive function patterns.

Within the D-KEFS Suite

Several D-KEFS subtests provide complementary or converging evidence for planning, cognitive flexibility, and related executive functions.

Trail Making Test (Both Versions)

Both Tower and Trail Making assess cognitive flexibility, but through different mechanisms. Trail Making requires following explicit alternation rules (number-letter-number-letter) in a structured, externally guided format, while Tower requires self-directed strategy generation and planning without explicit switching cues. An examinee performing adequately on Trail Making but poorly on Tower demonstrates structured flexibility with impaired self-directed flexibility—planning deficits emerge when external structure is minimal. Conversely, an adequate Tower with impaired Trail Making suggests difficulty with rapid set-shifting even when rules are explicit.

Verbal Fluency Test (Both Versions)

Both Tower and Verbal Fluency require strategic search and retrieval, but Verbal Fluency operates in the verbal domain while Tower operates in the spatial domain. Comparing performance across these tests illuminates domain-specific planning strengths or weaknesses. An examinee with strong Verbal Fluency but weak Tower performance demonstrates intact verbal strategic generation but impaired spatial planning capacity. Consistent deficits across both suggest domain-general strategic thinking and planning weaknesses.

Color-Word Interference Test (Both Versions)

Both Tower and Color-Word assess inhibitory control, but Color-Word requires inhibiting prepotent verbal responses (reading words) while Tower requires inhibiting impulsive motor responses and trial-and-error impulses during planning. Consistent inhibitory control deficits across both tests suggest general inhibition weakness affecting multiple response modalities. Discrepancies suggest modality-specific patterns.

Twenty Questions Test (Original D-KEFS)

Assesses hypothesis-testing strategy, verbal reasoning, and problem-solving through efficient question-asking to identify target items. Like Tower, Twenty Questions requires a strategic approach to generation and evaluation, but in the verbal rather than spatial domain. Comparing Tower and Twenty Questions differentiates spatial versus verbal strategic thinking capacities.

Word Context Test (Original D-KEFS)

Measures verbal reasoning and hypothesis generation through discovering word meanings from context. The strategic search and rule-learning processes parallel Tower's problem-solving demands in the verbal domain. Both require developing and testing hypotheses about solutions.

Sorting Test (Original D-KEFS)

Requires generating sorting rules for cards and flexibly shifting between categorization approaches, assessing verbal and conceptual flexibility with minimal spatial demands. Comparing Tower and Sorting helps determine whether executive weaknesses are specific to spatial planning or extend to verbal conceptual reasoning.

Social Sorting Test (D-KEFS Advanced)

Assesses similar cognitive flexibility and concept formation processes as the original Sorting Test, but incorporates social–emotional stimuli (faces). Comparing Tower and SST performance can illuminate whether planning and flexibility deficits are consistent across domains or whether social–emotional content differentially affects executive performance.

Beyond D-KEFS

Measures outside the D-KEFS family can provide converging evidence or assess related constructs when additional information is needed.

Tower and Maze Tasks

Multiple commercially available tower task variants exist, including the Tower of London–Drexel University (TOL DX; Culbertson & Zillmer, 2005) and the CANTAB Stockings of Cambridge (Cambridge Cognition, 2024). These maintain core tower-task demands while varying specific features such as item difficulties, normative samples, and scoring systems. Tower variants provide alternatives when D-KEFS Tower is unavailable or for repeated assessment requiring different items to minimize practice effects, though substantial practice effects persist across tower task variants. The Porteus Maze Test (Porteus, 1965) requires planning efficient paths through increasingly complex mazes without errors or dead ends, assessing spatial planning in a continuous path-planning context rather than discrete sequential moves.

Working Memory Measures

Tower requires spatial working memory for holding and manipulating spatial configurations during planning. The Digit Span and Letter-Number Sequencing subtests from the Wechsler scales (Wechsler, 2014, 2024) assess verbal working memory. Comparing these measures illuminates whether working memory deficits are domain-general or domain-specific. An examinee with strong verbal working memory but weak Tower performance suggests spatial working memory limitations specifically compromise planning.

Visuospatial Organization Measures

The Rey-Osterrieth Complex Figure Test (Meyers & Meyers, 1995), while primarily assessing visuospatial construction and memory, reflects planning and strategic approach generation during the copy condition. Developmental scoring systems quantify organizational strategy, complementing Tower's explicit planning assessment with evaluation of visuospatial organizational planning in a drawing context.

Card Sorting and Feedback-Based Measures

The Wisconsin Card Sorting Test (Heaton et al., 1993) assesses rule learning, cognitive flexibility, and feedback-based strategy adjustment—executive functions overlapping with but distinct from Tower-assessed planning. WCST requires discovering sorting rules through trial-and-error feedback and shifting rules when they change, assessing conceptual reasoning and set-shifting without the spatial planning component central to Tower tasks. The WCST's feedback-based learning complements Tower's prospective planning demands.

Ecologically Oriented Executive Measures

The Behavioral Assessment of the Dysexecutive Syndrome (BADS; Wilson et al., 1996) includes multiple real-world analogue tasks assessing planning and problem-solving in functionally relevant contexts, including the Zoo Map (route planning with rules) and Six Part Test (organizing multiple tasks within time limits). BADS tasks offer more ecologically valid planning assessment than Tower, helping clarify whether Tower deficits predict real-world planning difficulties or whether compensatory strategies enable adequate functioning despite poor Tower performance.

Behavior Rating Scales

Performance-based measures like Tower assess planning capacity under standardized conditions, but rating scales evaluate how consistently these abilities are deployed in daily life. For children and adolescents, the Behavior Rating Inventory of Executive Function, Second Edition (BRIEF-2; Gioia et al., 2015), Comprehensive Executive Function Inventory (CEFI; Naglieri & Goldstein, 2013), and Delis Rating of Executive Functions (D-REF; Delis, 2012) provide parent and teacher perspectives on daily executive functioning. For adults, the BRIEF-A (Roth et al., 2005), CEFI Adult (Naglieri & Goldstein, 2017), and D-REF Adult (Delis, 2021) offer self-report and informant-report options. Scales particularly relevant to Tower interpretation include Plan/Organize and Working Memory (BRIEF-2/BRIEF-A), Planning and Inhibitory Control (CEFI/CEFI Adult), and Planning, Problem Solving, and Impulse Control (D-REF/D-REF Adult). Discrepancies between Tower performance and rating scale data are clinically meaningful: examinees may demonstrate planning capacity on Tower (structured, clear rules, immediate feedback) but fail to deploy it consistently in daily life (ambiguous demands, delayed feedback, emotional stressors). Conversely, some examinees perform poorly on Tower while functioning adequately through compensatory strategies or environmental supports. Integration of Tower scores with rating scale data helps predict functional planning capacity more accurately than either measure alone.

SUMMARY

The Tower Test provides a comprehensive assessment of spatial planning, working memory, inhibitory control, and metacognition—executive functions critical for complex problem-solving. The hierarchical tier framework guides interpretation, distinguishing foundational visuospatial and comprehension abilities (Tier 1) from basic sequencing and rule application (Tier 2) from executive planning and working memory (Tier 3) from metacognitive self-monitoring and strategy adjustment (Tier 4).

The original version's physical materials and nine-item structure provide a valid assessment for ages 8–89, particularly appropriate for children, cases with clear moderate deficits, and contexts requiring traditional administration. The Advanced version's digital administration, seventeen items, rule-switching component, and automated scoring provide higher ceiling, increased complexity, precise measurement, and contemporary norms for ages 8–90.

Process scores differentiate planning quality, planning behavior, inhibitory control, and working memory capacity, clarifying which specific executive processes contribute to performance patterns. Behavioral observations reveal problem-solving style, metacognitive awareness, emotional regulation, and strategy flexibility—qualitative data essential for complete interpretation.

Integration with other assessment data is critical. Tower performance predominantly reflects cold executive functions in structured, emotionally neutral contexts. Performance may not predict planning capacity when hot EF demands dominate in stressful, ambiguous real-world situations. Behavioral rating scales, functional assessment, and clinical interview data complement Tower results, bridging the assessment-reality gap.

Ultimately, Tower data become clinically meaningful when translated into functional predictions and intervention recommendations. Specific patterns of strengths and weaknesses across tiers, scores, and behavioral observations directly inform individualized interventions targeting the appropriate level—whether foundational skill development, basic cognitive training, executive strategy instruction, metacognitive awareness building, or emotional regulation support.

TEST YOURSELF

1. What is a primary difference in task structure between the original D-KEFS Tower Test and the D-KEFS Advanced Tower Test (TWR)?

(a) The original uses three pegs; the TWR uses four pegs.

(b) The original has all items ending in tower formations; the TWR has varied target configurations.

(c) The original requires verbal responses; the TWR requires motor responses.

(d) The original assesses verbal planning; the TWR assesses spatial planning.

2. According to the tier framework, which tier is primarily assessed by the Tower Test's later, more difficult items?

(a) Tier 1: Foundational abilities

(b) Tier 2: Basic sequencing and rule application

(c) Tier 3: Cold executive functions—planning and problem-solving

(d) Tier 4: Metacognition

3. An examinee obtains a low Total Achievement Score with frequent rule violations and a Mean First-Move Time of 1.5 seconds (very brief). This pattern most likely indicates:

(a) Tier 1 visuospatial processing deficits.

(b) Tier 2 goal-maintenance problems.

(c) Tier 3 impulsive responding with poor inhibitory control.

(d) Tier 4 metacognitive awareness deficits.

4. The TWR's solid-chip and striped-chip items with reversed placement rules specifically assess which Tier 3 executive function?

(a) Spatial working memory capacity

(b) Cognitive shifting and rule flexibility

(c) Preplanning and look-ahead

(d) Problem-solving efficiency

5. An examinee completes early Tower items successfully but makes numerous rule violations only on the most difficult items. This pattern suggests:

(a) Tier 1 foundational deficits affecting all performance.
(b) Tier 2 incomplete rule learning.
(c) Tier 3 inhibitory control failing under cognitive load.
(d) Tier 4 lack of metacognitive awareness.

6. High self-corrections during Tower administration with spontaneous comments like "Wait, that won't work" indicate:

(a) Severe planning deficits.
(b) Poor working memory capacity.
(c) Intact Tier 4 metacognitive awareness and error monitoring.
(d) Tier 1 language comprehension problems.

7. The Tower Test's lack of baseline conditions isolating component skills means that:

(a) The Tower Test is invalid for clinical use.
(b) Poor performance is diagnostically ambiguous without additional assessment data.
(c) All Tower deficits necessarily reflect executive dysfunction.
(d) The test cannot assess planning abilities.

8. When an examinee's Tower performance deteriorates specifically as frustration mounts, with increasing rule violations and impulsive moves, this pattern primarily suggests:

(a) Cold EF deficits independent of emotional state.
(b) Tier 1 foundational processing limitations.
(c) Hot EF factors (emotional regulation) compromising cold EF capacity.
(d) Malingering or poor effort.

9. The Move Accuracy Ratio on the original Tower Test quantifies:

(a) How quickly the examinee responds.
(b) Planning efficiency through excess moves beyond the minimum.
(c) Rule-following accuracy.
(d) Metacognitive awareness.

10. The primary advantage of the TWR's digital administration over the original Tower's physical materials is:

(a) Digital is always easier for examinees.
(b) Automatic timing, scoring, and error detection eliminating measurement error.
(c) Digital requires less examiner training.
(d) All examinees prefer technology-based assessment.

Answer Key: 1-b, 2-c, 3-c, 4-b, 5-c, 6-c, 7-b, 8-c, 9-b, 10-b

REFERENCES

Cambridge Cognition (2024). *CANTAB [Cognitive assessment software]*. Cambridge Cognition Ltd.
Culbertson, W. C., & Zillmer, E. A. (2005). *Tower of London–Drexel University* (2nd ed.). Multi-Health Systems.
Delis, D. C. (2012). *Delis Rating of Executive Functions*. Pearson.
Delis, D. C. (2021). *Delis Rating of Executive Functions—Adult (D-REF Adult)*. Pearson.
Delis, D. C., & Kaplan, E. (2025). *Delis-Kaplan Executive Function System Advanced*. Pearson.

Delis, D. C., Kaplan, E., & Kramer, J. H. (2001). *Delis-Kaplan Executive Function System (D-KEFS).* San Antonio, TX: The Psychological Corporation.

Gioia, G. A., Isquith, P. K., Guy, S. C., & Kenworthy, L. (2015). *Behavior Rating Inventory of Executive Function* (2nd ed.). Psychological Assessment Resources.

Heaton, R. K., Chelune, G. J., Talley, J. L., Kay, G. G., & Curtiss, G. (1993). *Wisconsin Card Sorting Test Manual: Revised and Expanded.* Psychological Assessment Resources.

Meyers, J. E., & Meyers, K. R. (1995). *Rey Complex Figure Test and Recognition Trial: Professional Manual.* Psychological Assessment Resources.

Naglieri, J. A., & Goldstein, S. (2013). *Comprehensive Executive Function Inventory.* Multi-Health Systems.

Naglieri, J. A., & Goldstein, S. (2017). *Comprehensive Executive Function Inventory–Adult.* Multi-Health Systems.

Porteus, S. D. (1965). *Porteus Maze Test: Fifty Years' Application.* Pacific Books.

Roth, R. M., Isquith, P. K., & Gioia, G. A. (2005). *Behavior Rating Inventory of Executive Function–Adult Version.* Psychological Assessment Resources.

Wechsler, D. (2014). *Wechsler Intelligence Scale for Children* (5th ed.). Pearson.

Wechsler, D. (2024). *Wechsler Adult Intelligence Scale* (5th ed.). Pearson.

Wilson, B. A., Alderman, N., Burgess, P. W., Emslie, H., & Evans, J. J. (1996). *Behavioural Assessment of the Dysexecutive Syndrome.* Thames Valley Test Company.

Yochim, B., Baldo, J., Nelson, A., & Delis, D. C. (2007). D-KEFS Trail Making Test performance in patients with lateral prefrontal cortex lesions. Journal of the International Neuropsychological Society, 13(4), 704–709.

Eleven

TRAIL MAKING TEST

CLINICAL VIGNETTE

Fifty-eight-year-old Margaret Foster was referred for neuropsychological evaluation eighteen months poststroke affecting her left frontal lobe. Recently retired from hospital administration, she was considering consulting work but struggled with tasks requiring "keeping multiple things in mind at once." She also reported occasional word-finding difficulties during spontaneous conversation and mild anxiety about her cognitive changes.

On the Trail Making Test, Margaret demonstrated intact Tier 1 abilities on Visual Scanning (scaled score = 9) and adequate Tier 2 sequencing on Number Sequencing (scaled score = 9) and Letter Sequencing (scaled score = 9). However, Number-Letter Switching revealed dramatic Tier 3 impairment (scaled score = 4), including two set-loss errors where she continued connecting numbers instead of switching to letters. Motor Speed was age-appropriate (scaled score = 10), confirming her difficulties reflected mental rather than physical slowing.

Throughout testing, Margaret maintained excellent effort and demonstrated intact self-awareness, frequently commenting, "I know I need to switch but it takes me a moment to shift gears." The hierarchical analysis indicated specific Tier 3 cold executive deficits in cognitive flexibility and set-shifting. Recommendations included breaking complex tasks into single-focus segments, explicit transition cues, and referral for speech-language evaluation to assess verbal fluency given her word-finding concerns.

TEST DESCRIPTION

The Trail Making Test exists in two versions within the D-KEFS family: the original D-KEFS Trail Making Test (Delis et al., 2001) and the D-KEFS Advanced Trail Making Test (TMT; Delis & Kaplan, 2025). Both assess visual-motor sequencing abilities and cognitive flexibility, but they differ in their approach, administration format, and the cognitive demands they place on examinees.

Original D-KEFS Trail Making Test

The original version (ages 8–89) consists of five conditions administered with paper-and-pencil response booklets, typically requiring 5–10 minutes to complete. Administration instructions are available through a paper Examiner's Manual, a digital replication version via Q-global, or a tablet version via Q-interactive. Visual Scanning requires identifying and marking target stimuli across a large visual array; examinees are asked to find and cross out all the 3s. Number Sequencing and Letter Sequencing assess basic sequencing abilities within a visual-motor format; examinees draw lines to connect numbers or letters in order. Number-Letter Switching evaluates cognitive flexibility by requiring alternation between number and letter sequences; examinees are instructed to draw lines in 1-A, 2-B, etc., order. Motor Speed provides a baseline measure of graphomotor speed without cognitive demands; examinees draw over a dotted line quickly.

D-KEFS Advanced Trail Making Test (TMT)

The Advanced version (ages 8–90) is a digitally administered assessment consisting of five conditions, typically requiring 10–20 minutes to complete. Number Sequencing and Letter Sequencing establish baseline sequencing abilities. Number-Letter Switching serves as the classic multitasking condition. Two additional conditions—Switching-Distraction and Switching-Working Memory—provide more cognitively demanding assessments of multitasking under challenging conditions. Switching-Distraction adds visual and auditory distractors to the classic Number-Letter Switching task. Switching-Working Memory removes previously drawn connections from the task, increasing the amount of information needed to be held in working memory.

Both versions share the core construct of assessing cognitive flexibility through number-letter switching, but the Advanced version raises the ceiling through digital presentation, eliminates the separate visual scanning and motor speed conditions, and adds sophisticated multitasking conditions that tax inhibition and working memory more heavily than the original switching task.

DON'T FORGET

The Trail Making Test's diagnostic power lies in its component analysis. Poor switching performance could reflect visual scanning deficits, sequencing difficulties, motor slowness, or true cognitive inflexibility. Use the various assessment conditions to determine which processes are compromised.

Rapid Reference 11.1

Trail Making Test Overview

Element	Original D-KEFS	D-KEFS Advanced
Age range	8–89 years	8–90 years
Conditions	Condition 1: Visual scanning	Condition 1: Number Sequencing
	Condition 2: Number sequencing	Condition 2: Letter Sequencing
	Condition 3: Letter sequencing	Condition 3: Number-Letter Switching
	Condition 4: Number-letter switching	Condition 4: Switching-Distraction
	Condition 5: Motor speed	Condition 5: Switching-Working Memory
Time limits	Conditions 1–3, 5: 150 seconds	Conditions 1–2: 60 seconds
	Condition 4: 240 seconds	Conditions 3–5: 150 seconds
Response format	Paper-and-pencil (examinee draws lines connecting circles)	Touch-screen (examinee touches circles with stylus; lines auto-generated)
Materials	Examiner's manual, stimulus booklet, response booklets, pen, timer	Examiner's manual, client device, practitioner device, stylus
Primary score metric	Completion time in seconds	Mean correct (with errors) connection time
Discontinuation	Time limits; four corrections on practice items	Auto-discontinues at time or error limits
Primary constructs	Cognitive flexibility, visual scanning, processing speed, motor speed	Cognitive flexibility, inhibitory control, working memory

CHOOSING BETWEEN ORIGINAL AND ADVANCED VERSIONS

The decision to use original versus Advanced Trail Making depends on several clinical and practical considerations. Neither version is universally superior; each offers distinct advantages for specific assessment goals and populations.

When the Original Version Is Preferred

Visual-motor assessment is a priority. The paper-and-pencil format provides rich qualitative information about graphomotor control, visual scanning strategies, and approach organization. Clinicians can observe the examinee's physical trail across the page, revealing systematic versus haphazard search patterns.

Motor speed needs direct assessment. The Motor Speed condition quantifies baseline graphomotor speed, essential for determining whether switching difficulties reflect motor slowing rather than cognitive inflexibility. This is particularly valuable for neurological populations where motor deficits may confound executive assessment.

Visual scanning abilities are questionable. The Visual Scanning condition provides normative data on basic visual search and cancellation abilities. For examinees with suspected hemispatial neglect, visual field deficits, or attentional problems, this condition offers valuable diagnostic information.

Traditional format is preferred. Some examinees perform better with familiar paper-and-pencil tasks. Older adults unfamiliar with digital technology or those with previous neuropsychological testing using traditional trail making may benefit from the original format.

When the Advanced Version Is Preferred

Ceiling effects are a concern. High-functioning individuals often complete traditional switching tasks too quickly to reveal subtle deficits. The Advanced version's Switching-Distraction and Switching-Working Memory conditions provide significantly higher cognitive demands, revealing impairments that classic switching tasks miss.

Precise timing is critical. Digital administration captures response times to the tenth of a second, providing more sensitive measurement than manual timing. This precision is valuable for detecting subtle slowing or monitoring treatment effects in high-functioning populations.

Working memory and inhibition need separate assessment. The two additional switching conditions allow differential diagnosis of multitasking impairments. An examinee may perform adequately on basic switching but fail dramatically when distraction or working memory demands increase, revealing specific cognitive vulnerabilities.

Administration efficiency matters. The Advanced version eliminates Visual Scanning and Motor Speed conditions, which most examinees complete easily. This streamlines assessment while maintaining diagnostic sensitivity for cognitive flexibility. Clinicians can still infer visual scanning efficiency from sequencing condition performance, as locating targets in the array requires systematic visual search.

Error analysis is important. Digital administration automatically captures all errors with precise timing, eliminating the need for real-time error tracking while maintaining attention on behavioral observation. This reduces examiner burden and measurement error.

Contemporary norms are preferred. The Advanced version provides updated normative data collected in the 2020s, though Pearson maintains that the original's 2001 norms remain appropriate for most clinical purposes.

When Either Version Works Equally Well

For individuals with average cognitive abilities and no motor or visual impairments, either version provides a valid assessment of cognitive flexibility. The choice may depend on available equipment, examiner preference, or which other D-KEFS subtests are being administered. If using other Advanced subtests, the TMT fits naturally into that assessment. If administering other original subtests, maintaining a consistent format has advantages.

Returning to Margaret

Her stroke affected frontal systems while leaving basic motor and visual functions intact. The original version's component analysis elegantly demonstrated this dissociation—normal Visual Scanning and Motor Speed confirmed intact Tier 1 functions, while impaired Number-Letter Switching localized her deficit to cognitive flexibility. The Advanced version would have eliminated the Visual Scanning and Motor Speed baselines that were diagnostically valuable in her case. However, had Margaret performed adequately on basic switching despite subjective complaints, the Advanced version's more demanding conditions might have revealed her difficulties more clearly.

Rapid Reference 11.2

Choosing Between Original and Advanced Versions

Consider Original When	Consider Advanced When
Direct assessment of visual scanning and motor speed is needed	Higher cognitive ceiling is needed for high-functioning individuals
Graphomotor observation is clinically relevant	Reduced motor demands are important (motor impairment present)
Traditional paper-and-pencil administration is required (forensic, research)	Precise timing and automated error detection are valued
	Contemporary normative comparison from the 2020s is desired
	Differential diagnosis of distraction vs. working memory contributions is needed
	Examiner burden reduction through automated administration is valued

HIERARCHICAL TIER ANALYSIS

Both the original and Advanced Trail Making Tests assess cognitive processes through a hierarchical tier framework. While the Advanced version was explicitly designed with this tiered structure, the original version's tiers emerge from analyzing which conditions tap foundational processes versus true executive demands. Neither test *formally measures* Tier 4 processes—the scored indices are assessed through Tier 3 and lack the metacognitive and higher-order integration demands built into some D-KEFS subtests. However, Tier 4 functioning can be *qualitatively observed* during administration through behaviors such as spontaneous strategy adaptation, self-correction, and metacognitive insight about task demands.

Tier 1: Foundational Processes (Nonexecutive)

Trail Making's Tier 1 demands are substantial and can profoundly affect performance under all conditions. The two versions differ in how these foundational abilities are assessed.

Visual Processing and Scanning

Examinees must efficiently search large visual arrays to locate target stimuli among distractors. Numbers and letters appear in random positions rather than organized rows, requiring systematic visual search. In the original version, the Visual Scanning condition quantifies this directly by having examinees mark all instances of the target stimulus (the number 3) scattered across the page while ignoring other numbers. Poor performance reveals whether visual search deficits underlie subsequent sequencing difficulties.

The Advanced version eliminates the separate Visual Scanning condition, integrating these demands into sequencing tasks. The digital format presents densely packed stimuli with higher visual complexity than the original version. Lines cross each other, unlike the original version, which also creates more complexity when searching. Without a dedicated condition, clinicians must infer visual scanning abilities from sequencing performance.

Graphomotor Speed and Control

In the original version, all paper-and-pencil conditions require drawing lines between circles while maintaining a reasonable speed. The Motor Speed condition isolates this demand—examinees trace over a dotted line as quickly as possible without cognitive requirements. Performance establishes baseline graphomotor speed, essential for interpreting whether slowing on other conditions reflects motor versus cognitive factors. Motor speed varies considerably in neurological populations. Parkinsonism produces bradykinesia affecting all conditions equally; essential tremor may slow drawing without affecting cognitive processes. By quantifying motor speed separately, the test distinguishes physical from cognitive slowing.

The Advanced version's digital format reduces motor demands. Touching circles with a stylus requires basic motor control, but eliminates the continuous drawing requirement. Without a separate Motor Speed condition, clinicians must infer motor abilities from overall performance patterns.

Processing Speed

Individuals with generalized processing speed deficits show proportional slowing across all conditions rather than specific switching impairment. Processing speed reduction is a primary cognitive deficit in multiple sclerosis (Denney et al., 2011; Genova et al., 2009) and subcortical/vascular diseases (Erkinjuntti, 2002). It is also pervasive across tasks following traumatic brain injury (Lange et al., 2005; Dymowski et al., 2015). Normal aging similarly affects trail making performance primarily through processing speed rather than specific executive dysfunction (Salthouse, 2011). When contrast scores remain average despite slow absolute times, interventions should address processing speed through extended time accommodations rather than executive strategy training.

Tier 1 Impairment Pattern

Examinees with Tier 1 deficits show difficulty across all conditions involving that foundational process. Poor Visual Scanning (original version) predicts proportional difficulty on all subsequent conditions as visual search demands increase. Slow Motor Speed suggests proportional slowing across all drawing conditions without specific switching impairment.

The hallmark of Tier 1 deficits is *proportional impact*—all conditions requiring the impaired foundation show difficulty, but relative relationships among conditions remain normal. An examinee with slow processing speed might perform at the 10th percentile on all conditions but show normal contrast scores, indicating switching difficulty is proportional to baseline abilities rather than representing specific executive dysfunction.

CAUTION

Visual Scanning (original version) measures more than simple visual perception. It combines visual processing with sustained attention, inhibitory control (marking only 3s, not other numbers), and basic task persistence. "Normal" Visual Scanning performance doesn't guarantee intact vision; it confirms adequate integration of visual and attentional processes for this task format.

Tier 2: Bridging Processes

Tier 2 represents the bridge between foundational abilities and true executive demands. These processes are more complex than straightforward misperception or motor execution, but don't yet constitute cognitive inflexibility or higher-order executive dysfunction.

Overlearned Sequence Knowledge

Number Sequencing and Letter Sequencing rely heavily on automated sequences acquired early in development. The original version uses sequences 1–16 for numbers and A–P for letters; the Advanced version uses shorter sequences (1–12, A–L), eliminating letters from the middle of the alphabet where individuals with alphabet sequencing difficulties struggle most. These are highly practiced skills that remain robust even in many neurological conditions. However, examinees must track where they are in the sequence while visually scanning for the next item. This creates a dual-task demand: maintaining "I just connected 7, so I need 8" while searching the visual field. For most adults, this places minimal working memory demand because the sequences are so automatic—a single active variable tracking sequence position. Individuals with severe working memory impairment may lose track of sequence position, requiring conscious recitation from the start to determine the next item.

Single-Rule Following

Both sequencing conditions require sustained application of one straightforward rule: connect numbers (or letters) in order. This demands basic rule comprehension, maintenance, and application, but not complex rule manipulation. Set-loss errors are rare in sequencing conditions because only one rule applies. Some examinees with frontal dysfunction demonstrate subtle rule-application problems even on these straightforward conditions.

Basic Selective Attention

Number Sequencing requires attending to numbers while ignoring letters; Letter Sequencing requires the reverse. This demands elementary selective attention, focusing on task-relevant stimuli while filtering distractors. However, the selection is static (always attend to numbers, never to letters) rather than flexible, keeping this demand at Tier 2 rather than Tier 3. The stimulus arrays contain equal numbers of letters and numbers, creating substantial visual distraction that taxes attentional selectivity. The Advanced version intensifies this demand through higher stimulus density. More competing stimuli appear in the visual field (the Client Device screen is smaller than the original version's Response Booklet for each trial, which is two pages wide), though the fundamental selective attention requirement remains the same.

Tier 2 Impairment Pattern

Examinees with Tier 2 deficits struggle with basic sequencing beyond what Tier 1 processes predict. Number Sequencing or Letter Sequencing performance falls below expectations, given normal Visual Scanning and Motor Speed (original) or adequate overall ability level (Advanced). This pattern suggests difficulty with sequence knowledge, working memory for position, or basic selective attention.

Letter Sequencing often reveals Tier 2 problems when Number Sequencing remains adequate. Examinees may need to consciously recite the alphabet from "A" to determine each next letter, creating substantial slowing and increased working memory demand. This reflects differential automaticity rather than executive dysfunction.

Tier 3: Core Executive Functions

Number-Letter Switching represents the core executive demand of Trail Making and requires Tier 3 processes that distinguish executive from nonexecutive cognition. Both versions share this fundamental switching task, though implementation differs. The Advanced version extends Tier 3 assessment through two additional conditions that add interference or working memory demands to baseline switching.

Cold Executive Functions

Cold executive functions on Trail Making involve the cognitive machinery of set-shifting, working memory for alternating rules, and inhibitory control, operating in relatively affect-neutral contexts where logical analysis drives performance.

Mental Set-Shifting

The fundamental executive demand alternates between two mental sets: number sequencing and letter sequencing. Examinees must disengage from one set (numbers), shift attention to the other (letters), and then shift back. This represents cognitive flexibility in its most classic form—the ability to fluidly transition between task demands. Set-shifting requires more than simply knowing both sequences. After connecting 5, the prepotent response is continuing to 6 (same-set continuation). The task requires inhibiting this automatic tendency to instead shift to "E" (cross-set transition).

The original version contains eight "capture stimulus" pairs—consecutive numbers (e.g., 3–4) or letters (e.g., D–E) placed in close proximity. These create a stronger prepotent pull toward set-loss errors. When an examinee connects "3" and sees "4" nearby, the automatic number sequence strongly pulls for connecting to 4 rather than shifting to "D." Examinees who make set-loss errors primarily at capture stimuli may have milder flexibility deficits than those making errors throughout the task.

The Advanced version's digital format modifies shifting demands in subtle ways. Higher stimulus density increases visual search between transitions, potentially taxing shifting more heavily. However, automatic connection line generation reduces motor planning between shifts, and tapping circles requires less fine motor precision than drawing continuous lines.

Working Memory for Alternating Rules

Unlike Number Sequencing (a single rule), Number-Letter Switching requires maintaining two sequences simultaneously—tracking position in the number sequence and the letter sequence—while alternating between them. Examinees must track dual sequences simultaneously, creating a two-variable verbal working memory demand. After connecting "5-E-6," they must remember "I'm at 6 in numbers and E in letters, so next is F." The working memory demand increases with task progression as examinees track higher numbers and later letters. Early connections (1-A-2-B) place minimal demand; later connections require tracking more advanced positions in both sequences.

Inhibition of Automatic Responses

Set-shifting inherently requires inhibition—suppressing the prepotent response (continuing the active sequence) to execute the task-appropriate response (switching sequences). After connecting several numbers in sequence, alternating with letters, (1-A-2-B-3-C-4), the number sequence gains momentum. Connecting "4" strongly activates "5" through automatic association. Inhibiting this to instead shift to "D" requires active suppressive control. At each transition point, examinees must inhibit the automatic response to continue the active sequence. When searching for "E" after connecting "5," multiple intervening numbers and letters create an inhibitory challenge, particularly in the Advanced version, where stimulus density is higher.

Additional Switching Conditions (Advanced Version Only)

The Advanced TMT's signature contribution is two additional switching conditions that add significant interference or working memory demands to baseline switching. These "disrupted multitasking" conditions may reveal executive vulnerabilities invisible on traditional trail making.

Switching-Distraction maintains the alternation task but adds salient, overlearned distractors. Additional visual stimuli and auditory number/letter presentations create powerful prepotent responses that must be inhibited. An examinee searching for "7" might see a distractor "7" that is not in a circle or hear "G" spoken, creating interference precisely when shifting is required. The inhibitory demand increases substantially over baseline switching. Examinees must not only suppress the automatic tendency to continue the active sequence but also resist responding to magnified competing stimuli. Attentional control becomes critical as auditory distractors occur unpredictably.

Switching-Working Memory removes the visual trail of previous connections. The lines fade shortly after being drawn, though the most recently touched circle remains lit until the next selection. While examinees can see their current position, they cannot see where they have been. This eliminates the visual scaffolding that supports performance on other conditions: without visible lines, examinees cannot verify their path, recover easily if they lose track, or benefit from the progressive elimination of options that makes other conditions easier as they proceed. On Number-Letter Switching and Switching-Distraction, completed connections remain visible, effectively crossing off used items and narrowing the visual search with each move. On Switching-Working Memory, all stimuli remain equally available throughout, maintaining consistent search demands from first connection to last. Additionally, this condition starts with A rather than 1, preventing examinees from relying on pairings internalized during earlier conditions (1-A, 2-B, 3-C). The primary working memory demand is maintaining accurate position in both sequences without external verification; examinees must internally track "I'm on 4 in the number sequence and D in the letter sequence" rather than being able to count visible lines to confirm.

Both advanced conditions require coordinating multiple executive functions simultaneously. Switching-Distraction demands inhibiting external interference while maintaining the task set. Switching-Working Memory requires managing spatial memory while executing cognitive shifts. This integration represents higher-order executive function—coordinating multiple control processes toward a complex goal. The dual-condition approach allows differential diagnosis of multitasking impairments. Examinees who struggle specifically with Switching-Distraction may have inhibitory control deficits with adequate working memory. Those struggling specifically with Switching-Working Memory may have working memory limitations with adequate inhibition.

Tier 3 Cold Executive Impairment Pattern

Classic executive dysfunction appears as disproportionate switching difficulty. Number-Letter Switching performance falls below expectations, given adequate foundational abilities. The contrast scores (original version) or regression-based comparison scores (Advanced version) quantify this dissociation—comparing switching to combined sequencing performance.

Set-loss errors particularly indicate Tier 3 deficits, potentially reflecting cognitive inflexibility, inhibitory control deficits, or working memory limitations affecting rule maintenance. Examinees connect multiple same-set items in sequence (1–2–3-4 instead of 1-A-2-B-3-C-4), demonstrating failure to shift between mental sets. Errors clustering at capture stimuli suggest milder flexibility deficits; errors throughout the task indicate more severe set-shifting impairment.

Transition-point slowing without errors suggests a different Tier 3 pattern. Examinees accurately alternate but require substantial time at each shift. This indicates preserved set-shifting capacity but reduced efficiency. They can shift but require cognitive effort to do so. Margaret demonstrated this pattern: accurate switching but dramatically slowed transitions with intact metacognitive awareness of her difficulty.

Hot Executive Functions

Number-Letter Switching primarily assesses cold executive functions—cognitive flexibility, inhibitory control, and working memory for rules. Performance depends more on cognitive capacity than emotional regulation. However, hot EF factors influence performance in predictable ways.

Frustration tolerance

Frustration with switching difficulty often leads to deteriorating performance across the task. Examinees who make early errors may become flustered, leading to increased errors and slowing. This creates a cascade where hot EF dysregulation (decreased frustration tolerance) compounds cold EF deficits (flexibility impairment).

Impulsivity and anxiety

Impulsivity represents another hot EF influence. Some examinees rush through connections without fully processing the alternation rule, leading to set-loss errors from insufficient response inhibition. Others slow dramatically, suggesting anxiety about errors (hot EF) rather than pure cognitive inflexibility (cold EF). The Advanced version's speeded format may heighten anxiety in some examinees, while the digital interface with immediate feedback may increase anxiety in some and reduce uncertainty-driven hesitation in others.

CAUTION

Hot EF factors can appear to be cold EF deficits on Trail Making. An anxious examinee who slows dramatically on Number-Letter Switching might appear to have cognitive inflexibility when the primary problem is anxiety management. Similarly, impulsive examinees may show numerous set-loss errors reflecting poor response inhibition rather than true set-shifting deficits. Behavioral observation must differentiate these patterns.

Tier 3 Hot EF Pattern

Hot EF difficulties on Trail Making produce performance that varies with emotional state rather than cognitive capacity. The examinee may begin Number-Letter Switching adequately but deteriorate as errors accumulate—rushing impulsively after mistakes, slowing dramatically from anxiety, or showing visible frustration that compounds cognitive demands. Error clustering after initial mistakes suggests frustration disrupting subsequent performance rather than consistent cognitive inflexibility. The key diagnostic indicators are: (1) variable performance tied to emotional reactions rather than task difficulty, (2) improvement when given encouragement or brief pauses, and (3) behavioral signs of distress (sighing, negative self-talk, tension) corresponding with performance decline. This pattern commonly appears in examinees with ADHD, anxiety disorders, or low frustration tolerance, and indicates that intervention should address emotional regulation alongside cognitive flexibility strategies.

Tier 4: Higher-Order Integration and Metacognition

Trail Making's scored measures don't formally assess Tier 4 processes—the test provides explicit rules and clear feedback, eliminating the need for self-directed strategy generation or metacognitive problem-solving that characterizes Tier 4 functioning on other D-KEFS subtests. However, qualitative observations during administration can reveal metacognitive abilities that inform clinical interpretation.

Spontaneous Strategy Adaptation

Some examinees begin haphazardly but develop systematic approaches as the task progresses, demonstrating intact metacognitive learning. They recognize what isn't working and adjust accordingly. Others maintain inefficient strategies despite difficulty, suggesting poor self-monitoring and strategy adjustment.

Error Monitoring and Self-Correction

Self-correction before examiner feedback demonstrates error monitoring; the examinee recognizes mistakes and initiates correction. Delayed self-correction after examiner feedback but before being directed to the correct response shows partial awareness. Lack of self-correction despite obvious errors suggests impaired error monitoring or poor task engagement. Note that the Advanced version's digital format limits self-correction opportunities compared to the original version, reducing observational data about this Tier 4 capacity.

Metacognitive Insight

Margaret demonstrated strong Tier 4 functioning through her metacognitive awareness, frequently commenting, "I know I need to switch but it takes me a moment to shift gears." This self-awareness suggested she could benefit from explicit compensatory strategies—a pattern of impaired Tier 3 with preserved Tier 4 that carries favorable prognosis for strategy-based intervention.

These Tier 4 observations provide clinically valuable information even though the test's scored measures capture only Tiers 1–3. Strong performance indicates examinees can shift when explicitly instructed, but this doesn't guarantee they'll recognize when shifting is needed in ambiguous real-world situations. Conversely, poor Trail Making performance may underestimate real-world abilities in individuals who struggle with timed, decontextualized tasks but function adequately when intrinsically motivated.

Rapid Reference 11.3

Tier Structure at a Glance

Tier	Processes
Tier 1: Foundational processes (nonexecutive)	Visual scanning and search
	Graphomotor speed (original)
	Processing speed
Tier 2: Bridging processes	Overlearned sequence knowledge (numbers, letters)
	Single-rule following
	Working memory for sequence position
	Basic selective attention
Tier 3: Cold executive functions	Mental set-shifting (alternating between number and letter sets)
	Inhibition of prepotent responses (resisting sequence continuation)
	Dual-rule working memory
	Interference resistance (Advanced: Switching-Distraction)
	Working memory under load (Advanced: Switching-Working Memory)

Tier	Processes
Tier 3: Hot executive functions	Frustration tolerance and error recovery
	Anxiety management under time pressure
Tier 4: Higher-order integration and metacognition	Self-monitoring and error detection (self-correction before feedback)
	Spontaneous strategy adaptation (shifting from haphazard to systematic scanning)
	Metacognitive insight (awareness of switching difficulty)

ADMINISTRATION

NOTE: Refer to the Examiner's Manual for complete and detailed administration instructions. The Examiner's Manual provides verbatim instructions and clinicians should follow these precisely to ensure standardized administration.

Administration procedures differ between versions primarily in format—paper-and-pencil versus digital tablet—and in the specific conditions administered, but share common principles: ensure task comprehension through practice items, maintain standardized timing and error correction procedures, and observe approach strategies and behavioral responses throughout.

Original D-KEFS Trail Making Test, Paper and Pencil or Q-Global Digital Assets

Materials

For paper-and-pencil administration, the Trail Making Test requires the Examiner's Manual, Record Form, Stimulus Booklet (easel position), five Response Booklets (Visual Scanning, Number Sequencing, Letter Sequencing, Number-Letter Switching, Motor Speed), pen (any color that cannot be erased), and a timer. Pearson's Q-global offers the following digital assets: Examiner's Manual, Stimulus Book, Stimulus Book Administration Directions.

General Administration

All conditions follow a similar format. Present the instructions and allow for training on the practice page of each of the 5 conditions. Administer the timed test trial by opening the Response Booklet and position it horizontally at the examinee's midline. Provide the instructions from the Examiner's Manual and start timing. Keep the timer running while correcting errors and note the completion time when the examinee finishes each task. Most examinees finish well within time limits, but discontinue Visual Scanning, Number Sequencing, Letter Sequencing, and Motor Speed after 150 seconds and Number-Letter Switching after 240 seconds. If the examinee needs the full time allotment, allow the examinee to finish marking an item or drawing a connection before telling them to stop.

Condition 1: Visual Scanning

Instructions are to find and draw a slash through all the 3s on the page. On the practice page, the examiner demonstrates by drawing a slash through one 3 in the upper-left quadrant. Allow the examinee to complete the rest of the sample items and correct any errors they make during the practice set. When administering the timed version of Visual Scanning, do not correct mistakes and allow the examinee to complete the task even if they had difficulty with the practice page.

Conditions 2–3: Number Sequencing and Letter Sequencing

Instructions are to connect numbers in order or letters in order. When providing instructions for the practice page, the examiner traces initial connections with their finger to demonstrate the task. If the examinee cannot complete the practice task after four corrections by the examiner, do not administer the condition and proceed to the next condition. During the timed task, point out mistakes immediately without explaining them by writing an X over the incorrect connection, state that they have made an error, and ask them to proceed from the last correctly connected item.

Condition 4: Number-Letter Switching
Instructions are to alternate between numbers in order and letters in order. Practice and error correction procedures follow the same format as the sequencing conditions. If the examinee cannot complete the practice task after four corrections, do not administer this condition and proceed to Motor Speed.

Condition 5: Motor Speed
Instructions are to draw a line over the dotted line and touch every circle along the path. When providing instructions for the practice page, the examiner traces initial connections with their finger to demonstrate the task. The examinee is told that speed is more important than drawing the line neatly. If the examinee cannot complete the practice task after four corrections by the examiner, do not administer the condition. During the timed task, if the examinee makes an incorrect connection or haphazard line, stop them and redirect them to the dotted line without explaining the error.

Original D-KEFS Trail Making Test, Q-Interactive

Administration and scoring rules for the Q-interactive version of the original D-KEFS are the same as the paper-and-pencil version, but administration via the Practitioner Device reduces examiner demands through providing instructions for each condition, a timer, and automatic scoring after error scores are added manually. The examinee responds to the same five Response Booklets as the pencil-and-paper version. After administration is complete, the examiner can reference the To Do button to manually count and enter error scores for each condition.

D-KEFS Advanced Trail Making Test

Materials and Setup
The Advanced version requires the Practitioner Device (tablet), Client Device (tablet), and Stylus. Place the Client Device flat in landscape orientation and ensure the stylus is charged. Complete the sound check at the beginning of the subtest to ensure audio is at a comfortable level.

Response Format
Examinees respond by touching circles with the stylus. Lines are automatically generated each time a new circle is touched. The last circle touched turns blue if correct and red (with a brief white X) if incorrect. In the Switching-Working Memory condition, the connecting lines and red error warning are briefly displayed and then fade away.

Condition Structure
The five conditions include two baseline sequencing tasks (Number Sequencing, Letter Sequencing) and three switching conditions (Number-Letter Switching, Switching-Distraction, Switching-Working Memory). Each condition includes demonstration, sample, and test items. The software provides automated timing, error detection, and scoring. Switching-Distraction adds visual distractors (numbers and letters not in circles) and auditory distractors. Switching-Working Memory increases working memory load because lines for previously made connections disappear, requiring the examinee to remember previous connections.

Examiner Role
Read instructions verbatim from the Practitioner Device in a natural, conversational manner. When prompts are required after an error, the Client Device darkens, and a notification appears with corrective feedback. Unless notifications appear, do not assist the examinee in locating or selecting responses and do not provide verbal feedback for errors. Encourage effort using neutral prompts like "This is hard for many people" or "Just do your best."

DON'T FORGET

The digital format eliminates common administration errors from paper versions (timing errors, missing set-loss errors, inconsistent error correction) but introduces new considerations. Ensure examinees can physically manipulate the stylus and see the display clearly. Some older adults unfamiliar with digital technology may need additional practice with the stylus before testing begins.

Discontinue Rules

The system automatically discontinues when time or error limits are reached. Number Sequencing and Letter Sequencing: 60-second time limit, 24-error limit. Number-Letter Switching, Switching-Distraction, and Switching-Working Memory: 150-second time limit, 48-error limit. It is recommended to administer all five conditions, but if marked difficulties are noted on early conditions, administering later conditions may not yield useful clinical information and may excessively frustrate the examinee. TMT may be manually discontinued after any condition; Assessment Options notifications appear after Number-Letter Switching and Switching-Distraction to assist with this decision.

BEHAVIORAL OBSERVATIONS

Trail Making provides rich qualitative information beyond quantitative scores. Behavioral observations reveal which tier is compromised and whether hot or cold executive factors predominate.

Approach and Strategy

Visual scanning patterns reveal Tier 1 organization and strategic processing. Systematic scanners develop organized search strategies—working left-to-right, top-to-bottom, or in quadrants. Haphazard scanners jump randomly across the visual field, repeatedly searching the same regions while missing others, suggesting poor spatial organization or inadequate strategy generation. Hand positioning affects visual access in paper-and-pencil administration. Some examinees inadvertently cover circles with their writing hand or arm, then struggle to locate targets that are literally hidden from view. When an examinee repeatedly searches the same visible areas while missing an "obvious" target, clinicians should observe whether hand positioning is blocking visual access before attributing the difficulty to scanning deficits or inattention.

Strategy adaptation reveals Tier 4 functioning through qualitative observation. Some examinees begin haphazardly but develop systematic approaches as the task progresses, demonstrating intact metacognitive learning. They recognize what isn't working and adjust accordingly. Others maintain inefficient strategies despite difficulty, suggesting poor self-monitoring and strategy adjustment. These observations are not captured in scored measures but provide valuable information about higher-order executive integration.

Error Patterns and Self-Correction

Error types reveal specific tier deficits. Sequencing errors (connecting C–E instead of C–D) suggest Tier 1–2 problems: poor sequence knowledge, tracking failures, or perceptual confusion. Set-loss errors (connecting 4–5 instead of 4-D) indicate Tier 3 set-shifting deficits. Capture (distractor) stimulus analysis refines this as set-loss errors only at capture placements suggest milder flexibility impairment than errors throughout the task.

Self-correction reveals Tier 4 metacognitive awareness through observation rather than scored measurement. Immediate self-correction before examiner intervention demonstrates intact error monitoring—the examinee recognizes mistakes and initiates correction. Delayed self-correction after examiner feedback but before being directed to the correct response shows partial awareness. Lack of self-correction despite obvious errors suggests impaired error monitoring or poor task engagement. Note that the Advanced version's digital format limits self-correction opportunities compared to the original version, reducing observational data about this Tier 4 capacity.

Response to error feedback differentiates cold from hot executive factors. Examinees who efficiently incorporate corrections and resume the task demonstrate adequate frustration tolerance. Those who become flustered, lose their place, or require extensive time to resume show hot EF dysregulation. Some show progressive deterioration after errors, such as emotional flooding, compromising cognitive efficiency.

Response Speed and Consistency

Pacing reveals processing efficiency and emotional regulation. Consistent, moderate pacing suggests efficient cognitive processing and good task engagement. Consistently slow pacing may reflect Tier 1 processing speed deficits or a careful/anxious approach. Variable pacing—fast segments alternating with slow periods—suggests inconsistent engagement, strategy shifts, or fatigue effects.

Speed-accuracy trade-offs reveal hot versus cold EF influences. Impulsive examinees rush through connections, making numerous errors they fail to notice until feedback. This reflects poor response inhibition (hot EF) more than cognitive inflexibility (cold EF). Overly cautious examinees slow dramatically to avoid errors, suggesting anxiety (hot EF) rather than pure cognitive limitation.

Emotional and Behavioral Regulation

Frustration tolerance directly impacts performance, particularly on switching conditions. Examinees with good hot EF maintain composure despite difficulty, treating errors as information rather than failure. Those with poor frustration tolerance show visible distress—sighing, negative self-talk, or giving up. Some escalate frustration with each error, creating performance deterioration beyond cognitive limitations.

Anxiety manifestations appear in multiple forms. Performance anxiety produces overcaution, excessive checking, and seeking reassurance. Some examinees repeatedly verify task instructions or their current position in the sequence. Others show physical anxiety signs, including hand tremor, rushed speech, or visible tension.

Impulsivity versus deliberation reveals hot EF's influence on cold EF demands. Impulsive examinees begin connections before fully processing requirements, leading to errors that further compound impulsivity. The key distinction: impulsive examinees make more errors; anxious examinees show more pausing and checking despite adequate accuracy.

SCORING

Both versions provide multiple score types that support hierarchical interpretation, from primary completion measures through contrast scores that isolate executive contributions.

Original D-KEFS Trail Making Test

Completion-Time Scores

Each condition's primary score is the total completion time in seconds, converted to scaled scores. Visual Scanning, Number Sequencing, Letter Sequencing, Number-Letter Switching, and Motor Speed each yield completion time scaled scores. The scaled scores for Number Sequencing and Letter Sequencing sum to create a composite scaled score (Combined Number Sequencing + Letter Sequencing). This composite represents baseline sequencing ability, providing a more stable comparison point for switching performance.

Contrast Measures

These scores reveal whether Number-Letter Switching impairment exceeds what baseline abilities predict. Each contrast measure subtracts a component condition's scaled score from the Number-Letter Switching scaled score, then converts this difference to a new scaled score ($M = 10$, SD = 3). Five contrast measures compare Number-Letter Switching to: Visual Scanning, Number Sequencing, Letter Sequencing, Combined Number Sequencing + Letter Sequencing, and Motor Speed. The Combined Sequencing contrast provides a clinically useful comparison. It determines whether switching difficulty exceeds expectations given basic number and letter sequencing abilities.

Optional Error Scores

Multiple error types provide process-level information. Visual Scanning yields omission errors (missed target 3s) and commission errors (marked nontargets) as age-corrected cumulative percentile ranks. Number Sequencing and Letter Sequencing provide sequencing errors (incorrect number or letter order) and set-loss errors (drawing a line to a letter on Number Sequencing or drawing a line to a number on Letter Sequencing). Number-Letter

Switching provides sequencing errors (incorrect number or letter order) and set-loss errors (connecting letter to letter or number to number instead of switching sets). For conditions 2–5, time-discontinue errors (items not completed due to time limit) are provided as cumulative percentile ranks. A total number of error scores is also provided for Number-Letter Switching, which combines sequencing, set-loss, and time-discontinue errors converted to an age-corrected scaled score.

Set-loss errors particularly indicate executive dysfunction, potentially reflecting cognitive inflexibility, inhibitory control deficits, or working memory limitations affecting rule maintenance. These occur when examinees fail to alternate sets (e.g., connecting 4–5 instead of 4-D on Number-Letter Switching). Base rates are low in the normative sample, making even a few set-loss errors clinically significant.

D-KEFS Advanced Trail Making Test

Core Scaled Scores (Mean Correct (With Errors) Connection Time)

Unlike the original version's total completion time, the Advanced version's primary score is the mean time for each individual correct connection (including time spent making errors prior to making a correct connection), measured to the tenth of a second. This provides more precise measurement and better floor/ceiling characteristics than total time. This method also reduces the impact of difficulty in finding only one target, which could significantly increase overall completion time on the original version. Low scaled scores indicate slow processing; however, interpretation requires examining whether slowness is uniform across conditions (suggesting Tier 1 processing speed deficits) or disproportionate on switching conditions (suggesting Tier 3 executive dysfunction).

Error Scores

Four types of errors are scored across the five TMT conditions: (1) Sequencing errors—incorrect sequence within a set, suggesting difficulty maintaining place in overlearned sequences or momentary attention lapses; (2) Set-loss errors—examinee fails to correctly apply the line-connecting rules for that condition, indicating failure to maintain the active task set, often reflecting working memory or inhibitory control deficits; (3) Discontinue errors—correct responses not completed due to time/error limits for each condition, reflecting overall task failure that may stem from cumulative effects of speed and accuracy problems; and (4) Distraction errors—number of times an examinee touches letters or numbers not in circles on the Switching-Distraction condition, directly measuring susceptibility to interference from salient but irrelevant stimuli. Base rates for each error type are provided for all conditions; errors with low base rates in the general population warrant careful interpretation as they may indicate significant impairment.

Core Combined Index and Error Scores

Provide the sum of various types of performance across different combinations of conditions.

Combined Sequencing Mean Correct (With Errors) Connection Time Index

Sum of this Core Scaled Score for the two baseline conditions, Number and Letter Sequencing, converted to a standard score. This index establishes baseline visual-motor speed and simple sequencing ability. Impairment here constrains interpretation of switching conditions. Poor sequencing baseline means switching difficulties may reflect foundational deficits rather than specific executive dysfunction.

Combined Switching Mean Correct (With Errors) Connection Time Index

Sum of this Core Scaled Score for the three switching conditions (Number-Letter Switching, Switching-Distraction, and Switching-Working Memory) is converted to a standard score. This composite reflects overall cognitive flexibility under varying demands. Compare this score to the Combined Sequencing Index to determine whether switching performance is proportional to baseline abilities or disproportionately impaired.

Combined Switching Total Active Errors (Set-Loss + Sequencing)

Scaled score derived by summing the total set-loss and sequencing errors made across the three switching conditions. High error rates with average speed suggest impulsive responding or poor self-monitoring; high error rates with slow speed suggest pervasive difficulty maintaining task demands despite effortful processing.

Combined Switching Mean Pure Response Speed (Correct or Error Connections)
Mean time to make any connection, whether correct or incorrect, converted to a standard score. This measure captures raw motor-cognitive speed independent of accuracy. Examinees who are slow on this measure but accurate show a cautious, controlled approach; those who are fast but error-prone demonstrate impulsive responding.

Multitasking Index
The sum of the three Mean Correct (With Errors) Connection Time scaled scores for the switching conditions and the Combined Switching Total Active Errors (Set-Loss + Sequencing). This comprehensive index captures both speed and accuracy across all switching demands, providing a global measure of complex multitasking efficiency. Particularly useful for predicting real-world difficulties with divided attention and competing task demands.

Contrast Scores
TMT uses sophisticated regression-based contrasts that statistically adjust for variance and ability-level effects. These provide more accurate comparisons than the original version's scaled-score subtraction method. The regression approach accounts for the fact that higher-difficulty conditions naturally show more variance and that score differences are more common at extreme ability levels. Contrast scaled scores of 7 or below indicate disproportionate difficulty on the more complex condition; scores of 13 or above indicate unexpectedly strong performance on the more complex condition relative to baseline, which may reflect variable effort, specific baseline weaknesses, or genuine cognitive strengths in switching relative to simple sequencing.

Combined Sequencing Versus Number-Letter Switching Mean Correct (With Errors) Connection Time
Compares performance on Number-Letter Switching relative to the two baseline sequencing conditions. This is the primary contrast for identifying specific cognitive flexibility deficits. Low scores (≤7) indicate disproportionate switching difficulty beyond what baseline abilities would predict. The hallmark of Tier 3 executive dysfunction. Average scores (8–12) suggest switching difficulty is proportional to baseline abilities, pointing toward Tier 1 processing speed as the primary limitation.

Number-Letter Switching Versus Switching-Distraction Mean Correct (With Errors) Connection Time
Compares performance on Switching-Distraction relative to performance on the basic switching task (Number-Letter Switching). Low scores indicate specific vulnerability to interference. The examinee can switch adequately in quiet conditions, but breaks down when distraction increases. This pattern commonly appears in ADHD and suggests interventions targeting distraction management and environmental modification.

Number-Letter Switching Versus Switching-Working Memory Mean Correct (With Errors) Connection Time
Compares performance on Switching-Working Memory relative to performance on the basic switching task (Number-Letter Switching). Low scores indicate that adding working memory load disproportionately impairs performance, suggesting limited cognitive capacity for maintaining and manipulating information while switching. This pattern has implications for tasks requiring simultaneous tracking of multiple information streams.

Speed-Accuracy Tradeoff Contrast Score (Combined Switching Mean Pure Response Speed Versus Combined Switching Total Active Errors)
Provides information regarding whether the examinee exhibits an expected level of accuracy given their speed. Allows for parsing whether poor performance reflects slow-but-accurate responding (cautious, effortful processing with intact self-monitoring), fast-but-impulsive errors (poor inhibitory control, inadequate checking), or combined speed and accuracy deficits (pervasive impairment). This directly informs intervention—teaching response slowing and self-checking to impulsive examinees versus addressing processing speed and efficiency in slow-but-accurate ones.

Process Scores

TMT provides extensive process measures revealing performance nuances beyond summary scores.

Mean Pure Response Speed (Correct or Error Connections)
Average speed to make any connection during the three switching conditions. This "raw" speed measure strips away accuracy considerations, revealing basic response tempo. Compare this score to the accuracy measures to understand the examinee's speed-accuracy tradeoff strategy.

Combined Sequencing Total Active Errors (Set-Loss + Sequencing)
Sum of set-loss and sequencing errors across Number and Letter Sequencing, providing overall baseline accuracy. Errors on these relatively simple conditions suggest fundamental difficulties with sustained attention, sequence tracking, or rule following that will compound on more complex switching tasks.

Set-Loss Errors
For each condition, the total number of set-loss errors made (i.e., letter response when it should have been a number and vice versa, or touching a number or letter outside a circle on Switching-Distraction). Set-loss errors on switching conditions reflect failure to maintain the alternating task set where the cognitive system "forgets" which category is currently active. Frequent set-loss errors, especially early in a sequence before fatigue sets in, suggest fundamental set-maintenance deficits rather than simple fatigue or carelessness.

Sequencing Errors
For each condition, the number of sequencing errors made (e.g., connecting to 5 instead of 4). These errors indicate a momentary loss of place in the sequence. Isolated sequencing errors may reflect attention lapses; frequent sequencing errors suggest difficulty with the working memory demand of tracking sequence position while managing other task requirements.

Discontinue Errors
For each condition, the number of correct responses not touched within the time or error limit. High discontinue errors indicate the examinee could not complete the task within limits, which may reflect profound slowing, excessive error-making that consumed time, or both. Examine the pattern—discontinuation due to time limit versus error limit has different implications.

Switching-Distraction Errors
Number of times the examinee touched a number or letter outside a circle during Switching-Distraction. This is a direct measure of interference susceptibility. These errors occur when the examinee responds to stimuli that are visually salient (larger, more prominent) but task-irrelevant. High rates suggest difficulty suppressing prepotent responses to attention-capturing stimuli.

Percent Error Ratio (For Switching Conditions)
Percentage of total connections made (i.e., correct + incorrect) that were incorrect (i.e., errors). High ratios with low base rates in the normative sample often indicate global impairment, inadequate effort, or failure to understand task demands. When error ratios exceed normative expectations substantially, consider validity concerns before interpreting the profile as reflecting genuine cognitive deficits.

Additional Raw Scores

Standard Deviation of Mean Correct (With Errors) Connection Time
Raw standard deviation in the time to make individual connections for each condition. Elevated standard deviations suggest inconsistent attention, fluctuating internal states, fatigue effects across the task, or the disruptive effects of errors on task flow. Some variability is normal; markedly elevated variability (compared to base rates) suggests the examinee's performance was unstable in ways that summary scores may not capture. This can indicate attention regulation difficulties even when mean performance is adequate.

Total Responses
Raw number of responses made for each of the five conditions. Combined with Total Correct Responses, this reveals overall response volume and allows calculation of accuracy rates.

Total Correct Responses

Raw number of correct responses made for each of the five conditions. Lower numbers indicate either slow responding (fewer attempts within time limits) or error-prone responding (attempts made but incorrect). Compare to Total Responses to distinguish these patterns.

Behavior Observations

For a selection of behaviors (see Table 4.5 in the Examiner's Manual), base rates are provided that compare the rate at which different age ranges in the normative group also exhibited that behavior. Behaviors that fall outside normative expectations provide qualitative context for understanding test performance and may reveal cognitive or emotional factors not captured by quantitative scores.

DON'T FORGET

The original and Advanced versions use fundamentally different primary scores (total time vs. mean correct (with errors) connection time). These cannot be directly compared numerically. However, both reveal whether switching is disproportionately impaired relative to baseline abilities—the key clinical question remains the same across versions.

Rapid Reference 11.4

Scoring Summary

Score Type	Original D-KEFS	D-KEFS Advanced
Primary scores	Completion time (seconds) for each condition; converts to scaled scores (*M* = 10, SD = 3)	Mean correct (with errors) connection time for each condition; converts to scaled scores (*M* = 10, SD = 3)
Baseline measures	Visual Scanning, Motor Speed, Number Sequencing, Letter Sequencing, Scaled Scores; Combined Number + Letter Sequencing Composite	Combined Sequencing Mean Correct (With Errors) Connection Time Index (*M* = 100, SD = 15)
Switching measures	Number-Letter Switching Scaled Score	Number-Letter Switching, Switching-Distraction, Switching-Working Memory Scaled Scores; Combined Switching Index
Primary contrast	Number-Letter Switching vs. Combined Number + Letter Sequencing; Subtraction-based	Combined Sequencing vs. Number-Letter Switching; Regression-based
Additional contrasts	Switching vs. Visual Scanning, Number Sequencing, Letter Sequencing, Motor Speed	Number-Letter Switching vs. Switching-Distraction; Number-Letter Switching vs. Switching-Working Memory; Speed-Accuracy Tradeoff
Error scores	Omission/commission (Visual Scanning); sequencing, set-loss, time-discontinue errors; cumulative percentile ranks	Set-loss, sequencing, discontinue, distraction errors; base rates; Combined Switching Total Active Errors
Interpretation	Contrast ≤7 = disproportionate impairment; 8–12 = expected range; ≥13 = relative strength	Same interpretation; regression-based method more accurate at performance extremes

COMMON ADMINISTRATION ERRORS

Several administration errors commonly affect Trail Making validity. Some errors are specific to the paper-and-pencil format, others to the digital administration, and some apply to both versions.

Failing to Maintain Timing During Error Correction (Original)

Examinees' mistakes require immediate correction, but timing continues throughout. Some examiners pause the time while redirecting examinees, invalidating time scores. The correct procedure: mark the error with "X," redirect to the last correct connection, and keep timing.

Over-Explaining Errors Instead of Simple Redirection (Original)

During the timed tasks, when examinees make mistakes, examiners should state "You made an error" and point to where they should resume—nothing more. Explaining why the connection was wrong provides strategy coaching that obscures flexibility deficits.

Incorrect Discontinuation Decisions (Original)

Number Sequencing, Letter Sequencing, Number-Letter Switching, and Motor Speed practice pages have a specific four-error limit before discontinuation. The rule: discontinue if four corrections are needed; proceed if completed with fewer than four errors.

Inadequate Sound Check (Advanced)

Switching-Distraction requires auditory presentation of distractors. Failing to verify adequate volume or testing examinees with hearing impairment without accommodation invalidates this condition.

Providing Verbal Feedback During Test Items (Advanced)

Unlike sample items (where error feedback is provided), test items should receive no verbal examiner feedback beyond neutral encouragement. The digital interface provides visual error feedback; adding verbal feedback alters the task demand.

Prematurely Discontinuing when Examinees Struggle (Both Versions)

Some examiners are tempted to discontinue testing if the examinee makes multiple errors and appears distressed. However, performance under difficulty provides critical diagnostic information. Unless examinees explicitly refuse or show extreme distress requiring clinical intervention, continue until official discontinue criteria are met. Review the manual for specific instructions about when to discontinue administration.

INTERPRETATION

Trail Making interpretation requires systematically working through the tiers to determine where performance breaks down and whether deficits reflect foundational limitations, true executive dysfunction, or hot executive factors influencing cold executive capacity.

Using the Hierarchical Framework for Differential Diagnosis

Trail Making interpretation requires systematically working through the tiers to determine where performance breaks down. This hierarchical approach prevents misattributing foundational deficits as executive dysfunction and ensures interventions target the appropriate level.

Step 1: Rule Out Tier 1 Limitations
Begin by confirming adequate visual-motor processing. On the original version, examine Visual Scanning and Motor Speed performance. Scaled scores of 8 or above indicate adequate foundations for higher-level tasks. On the Advanced version, evaluate Number and Letter Sequencing for signs of visual scanning difficulty (high variability, spatial errors) or motor problems (though motor demands are reduced). The Combined Sequencing Index of 85 or above suggests adequate baseline abilities.

If Tier 1 deficits emerge, determine whether these fully account for switching difficulties or whether additional executive problems exist. Consider general processing speed deficits, neurological conditions affecting motor function, age-related slowing, medications with cognitive side effects, or visual impairments. Critically, processing speed and motor deficits are not executive dysfunction—they represent foundational efficiency limitations. Interventions should target processing speed through extended time accommodations and reduced time pressure rather than executive strategy training.

Step 2: Evaluate Tier 2 Bridging Processes
Assess Number Sequencing and Letter Sequencing performance relative to Tier 1 abilities. Scores below expectations given adequate Visual Scanning and Motor Speed (original) or inconsistent with overall ability level (Advanced) suggest Tier 2 problems. Letter Sequencing often reveals Tier 2 deficits when Number Sequencing remains adequate with difficulty reflecting differential sequence automaticity rather than executive dysfunction.

Examine error patterns on sequencing conditions. Sequencing errors (connecting out of order within a set) suggest working memory limitations for tracking position or gaps in overlearned sequence knowledge. Set-loss errors on baseline conditions (rare but significant) indicate fundamental rule-maintenance problems. If Tier 2 deficits are present, interventions focus on strengthening sequence automaticity, external tracking supports, and reducing concurrent cognitive demands.

Step 3: Analyze Tier 3 Cold Executive Patterns
Examine Number-Letter Switching performance using contrast scores. On the original version, Combined Sequencing contrast scores of 7 or below indicate disproportionate switching difficulty beyond what baseline abilities predict—the hallmark of Tier 3 executive dysfunction. On the Advanced version, the Combined Sequencing vs. Number-Letter Switching contrast serves the same function; additionally, compare performance across the three switching conditions.

Analyze error patterns: set-loss errors particularly indicate true set-shifting impairment. Errors concentrated at capture stimuli suggest milder flexibility deficits than errors distributed throughout the task. Specific difficulty with Switching-Distraction suggests inhibitory control problems under interference; specific difficulty with Switching-Working Memory indicates working memory limitations when visual scaffolding is removed. Interventions for Tier 3 cold EF deficits include explicit transition warnings, task segmentation to reduce switching demands, environmental modifications to minimize multitasking requirements, and cognitive flexibility training.

Step 4: Evaluate Tier 3 Hot Executive Factors
Behavioral observations clarify whether cold EF capacity limitations or hot EF dysregulation primarily drive poor performance. Cold EF deficit pattern: consistent difficulty from task beginning, visible cognitive effort, neutral emotional tone, errors despite adequate effort, and maintained persistence throughout. Hot EF deficit pattern: adequate performance initially that deteriorates as frustration mounts, emotional reactivity to errors, impulsive responding that increases error rates, giving up or rushing through remaining items, and improved performance after encouragement or breaks.

Slow but accurate switching with visible effort and intact metacognitive awareness (Margaret's pattern) indicates cold EF inefficiency without hot EF compromise. Impulsive errors with poor frustration tolerance suggest hot EF dysregulation masquerading as cold EF deficits. Combined patterns show difficulty from the start that worsens with frustration. Interventions for hot EF factors focus on emotional regulation strategies, reducing time pressure, providing encouragement, and teaching self-monitoring for impulsive responding.

Step 5: Assess Tier 4 Integration and Metacognition

Trail Making's scored measures capture Tiers 1–3, but qualitative observations during administration reveal Tier 4 metacognitive abilities. Observe spontaneous strategy adaptation: examinees who begin haphazardly but develop systematic approaches demonstrate intact metacognitive learning. Error monitoring appears in self-correction before examiner feedback. The examinee recognizes mistakes and initiates correction independently. Metacognitive insight manifests as verbal awareness of difficulty, as when Margaret commented, "I know I need to switch but it takes me a moment to shift gears."

Strong Tier 4 functioning with impaired Tier 3 (Margaret's pattern) suggests favorable prognosis for strategy-based intervention—the examinee can recognize and compensate for limitations. Impaired Tier 4 with impaired Tier 3 suggests more pervasive executive dysfunction requiring external supports rather than self-directed strategies. Note that the Advanced version's digital format limits self-correction opportunities, reducing observational data about this capacity.

PERFORMANCE PATTERNS AND CLINICAL IMPLICATIONS

Trail Making performance yields several recognizable patterns, each with distinct clinical implications and intervention considerations. Identifying these patterns helps clinicians move beyond global scores to understand the specific nature of an examinee's flexibility difficulties.

Proportional Slowing Across All Conditions

When Visual Scanning, Motor Speed, both sequencing conditions, and switching on the original version all show similar impairment levels, suspect Tier 1 processing speed or motor deficits. This pattern commonly appears in traumatic brain injury, multiple sclerosis, Parkinson's disease, and normal aging (Genova et al., 2009; Lange et al., 2005; Salthouse, 2011). Relative preservation of contrast scores suggests executive functions remain intact relative to foundational abilities. Interventions should address processing speed through extended time accommodations rather than executive strategy training.

Disproportionate Switching Impairment with Preserved Baselines

Normal Visual Scanning (original only), Motor Speed (original only), and both sequencing conditions with dramatically impaired Number-Letter Switching represent the classic executive dysfunction pattern. Margaret demonstrated this profile—low contrast scores confirmed her switching difficulty exceeded baseline abilities. Error analysis refines interpretation: predominantly set-loss errors indicate set-shifting deficits; mixed error types with high variability suggest working memory or attentional factors compound flexibility problems. Real-world implications include difficulty with multitasking, transitioning between activities, and managing competing task demands. Interventions should include explicit transition warnings, task segmentation, and reducing multitasking requirements.

Differential Impairment Across Advanced Switching Conditions

The Advanced version's three switching conditions enable fine-grained differential diagnosis. Adequate Number-Letter Switching but impaired Switching-Distraction suggests specific vulnerability to interference; intact cognitive flexibility when conditions are quiet, but breakdown when distraction increases. In the D-KEFS Advanced clinical validation studies, a subgroup of children with ADHD (approximately 18%) and over half of adults with moderate-to-severe TBI showed this pattern (Delis & Kaplan, 2025). Adequate Number-Letter Switching but impaired Switching-Working Memory indicates working memory limitations rather than core flexibility deficits. Pilot studies found that a subgroup of children with ADHD had particular difficulty on this condition (Delis & Kaplan, 2025). Impairment across all switching conditions suggests more global executive dysfunction, though relative severity across conditions still provides diagnostic information.

Inconsistent Performance with High Variability

Elevated standard deviations on Advanced version conditions or wildly variable connection times on the original version suggest fluctuating engagement, inconsistent attention, or emotional factors disrupting cognitive efficiency. When combined with low error rates, this pattern can reflect variable sustained attention commonly seen in ADHD (Conners, 2014) or the influence of fluctuating internal states such as mood, pain, or fatigue. When combined with high error rates, the variability may largely reflect the disruptive effect of errors on task flow; however, high error ratios with low base rates can also indicate more global neurocognitive impairment or inadequate effort (Delis & Kaplan, 2025).

Speed-Accuracy Tradeoffs on Advanced Version

Process scores reveal whether examinees sacrifice speed for accuracy, accuracy for speed, or both. Fast mean connection times with high error rates and elevated percent error ratios indicate impulsive responding—prioritizing speed over accuracy. This reflects hot EF factors (impulsivity, poor response inhibition) more than cold EF capacity limitations. Slow mean connection times with low error rates suggest overcaution, possibly anxiety-driven. Very slow times with high error rates may indicate combined cold EF deficits and potentially poor effort, confusion over task demands, or severe global impairment.

Rapid Reference 11.5

Distinguishing Tier-Level Deficits

Tier Level	Indicators	Clinical Implications
Tier 1 deficit	Slow performance across all conditions proportionally; poor Visual Scanning and/or Motor Speed (original) or slow Combined Sequencing Index (Advanced); contrast scores within expected range despite slow absolute performance	Processing speed or foundational visual-motor abilities limit performance; executive functions may be intact relative to foundational capacity; interventions target processing speed accommodations, not flexibility training
Tier 2 deficit	Normal Tier 1 measures but impaired Number and/or Letter Sequencing; Letter Sequencing worse than Number Sequencing; sequencing errors on baseline conditions	Difficulty with overlearned sequences or basic rule application; may reflect differential sequence automaticity (letters less practiced than numbers); interventions target sequence strengthening and basic attention
Tier 3 cold deficit	Normal baselines but disproportionately impaired switching conditions; low contrast scores (≤7); set-loss errors especially at capture stimuli; specific vulnerability on Switching-Distraction (inhibitory control) or Switching-Working Memory (working memory load)	Specific cognitive flexibility deficit; difficulty shifting mental sets despite adequate foundations; interventions target flexibility training, explicit transition cues, reduced multitasking demands, environmental modification
Tier 3 hot deficit	Performance deteriorates after errors or as frustration mounts; adequate initial performance with declining trajectory; visible emotional dysregulation; impulsive errors with poor self-monitoring; improvement with breaks or encouragement	Emotional regulation difficulties compromising cognitive control; hot EF factors overwhelm cold EF capacity; interventions target frustration tolerance, anxiety management, pacing strategies

Tier Level	Indicators	Clinical Implications
Tier 4 deficit	Absence of self-correction before examiner feedback; failure to adapt strategy despite repeated difficulty (persistent haphazard scanning); lack of awareness of switching difficulty; no spontaneous recognition that obstacles can become cues (Switching-Distraction); inability to articulate task demands or own performance quality	Metacognitive limitations affecting self-monitoring and strategy generation; may perform adequately when explicitly instructed but fail to recognize when shifting is needed in ambiguous situations; interventions require external monitoring, explicit strategy instruction, and structured environmental supports rather than self-directed approaches
Combined cold and hot deficit	Poor performance throughout with worsening emotional state; struggles from start with escalating frustration; both cognitive inflexibility and emotional dysregulation evident	Both cognitive limitations and emotional dysregulation present; a comprehensive intervention addressing both cognitive strategies and emotional regulation needed

ECOLOGICAL VALIDITY AND FUNCTIONAL IMPLICATIONS

Trail Making performance connects to multiple real-world domains, though the decontextualized testing format may underestimate or overestimate ecological difficulties depending on the individual.

Academic Functioning

Switching deficits may predict difficulty with multistep math problems requiring alternation between operations, reading comprehension requiring integration of multiple text elements, and note-taking requiring alternation between listening and writing. Visual scanning difficulties affect reading fluency and locating information on busy pages. Processing speed limitations affect timed tests and completing work within typical time frames. Interventions include extended time, reducing multitasking demands in instructions, explicit transition cues between activity components, and teaching systematic visual scanning strategies.

Vocational and Daily Living

Number-Letter Switching directly parallels workplace multitasking, such as alternating between phone calls and email, switching between different software programs, or managing competing task demands. Margaret's consulting difficulties reflected exactly this: managing multiple simultaneous demands in hospital administration required the cognitive flexibility her stroke compromised. Visual scanning deficits can affect driving safety, cooking (monitoring multiple burners), and household organization. Accommodations include task segmentation (completing one task fully before beginning another), minimizing environmental distractions, providing written checklists for multistep tasks, and explicit transition warnings before shifting activities.

Social Functioning

Cognitive inflexibility affects conversational turn-taking, perspective-taking (switching between one's own and others' viewpoints), and adapting behavior to changing social contexts. Visual scanning difficulties may impair social perception—missing facial expressions or social cues in group settings. These deficits often go unrecognized because social demands are implicit. Interventions include explicit social rules, preparation for context transitions, and reducing social multitasking demands (one-on-one interactions rather than groups).

Trail Making's timed, decontextualized format may misrepresent real-world function in both directions. Some individuals perform poorly but function adequately in daily life because real-world tasks provide meaningful context, intrinsic motivation, and unlimited time. Others perform well but struggle ecologically because real-world multitasking involves self-directed goal management and ambiguous transition points absent from structured testing. Rating scales, functional history, and real-world observation remain essential for determining whether Trail Making deficits translate to functional impairment.

PRELIMINARY CLINICAL VALIDATION OF THE D-KEFS ADVANCED TRAIL MAKING TEST

The D-KEFS Advanced standardization included clinical group studies examining the TMT's ability to detect cognitive difficulties across multiple populations (Delis & Kaplan, 2025). Results indicated strong sensitivity, with large effect sizes emerging for adults with traumatic brain injury and children with autism spectrum disorder. Children with ADHD and specific learning disorder–mathematics showed moderate effect sizes—a noteworthy finding for populations that often show variable results on performance-based cognitive measures. These findings are preliminary and require replication; they should inform but not determine diagnostic conclusions.

Traumatic Brain Injury

Adults with moderate-to-severe TBI (n = 30; mean Glasgow Coma Scale = 8.5) demonstrated substantial impairment across all TMT conditions, with effect sizes ranging from d = 1.12 to 1.33 (p<.01). Both the Combined Sequencing Index (d = 1.37) and Combined Switching Index (d = 1.28) effectively distinguished clinical and control groups. Interestingly, the groups did not differ on error rates (d = 0.09 for Combined Switching Total Active Errors), revealing a trade-off wherein individuals with TBI preserved accuracy at the cost of processing speed. This is a pattern that emerged consistently across D-KEFS Advanced tests in this sample.

Examination of individual profiles revealed meaningful diversity within the TBI group. Roughly one-quarter demonstrated comparable slowing across baseline and switching conditions (contrast scores 8–12), pointing toward generalized processing inefficiency rather than specific executive dysfunction. In contrast, approximately one-third showed disproportionate difficulty on switching conditions (contrast scores ≤7), suggesting executive impairment beyond what foundational slowing would predict. Nearly half exhibited a particular breakdown when working memory demands increased in the Switching-Working Memory condition.

Autism Spectrum Disorder

Children with ASD (n = 31) scored significantly lower than matched controls on every TMT condition, with large effect sizes across the board (d = 0.78–1.17, p < 0.01). The strongest group separation occurred on Switching-Working Memory (d = 1.17), though baseline sequencing was also markedly affected (Combined Sequencing Index d = 1.10). Similar to individuals with TBI, children with ASD showed slower performance without corresponding increases in errors, suggesting they prioritized response accuracy. These results correspond with research documenting processing speed, working memory, and cognitive flexibility challenges in ASD. The pervasive impairment spanning both baseline and switching conditions indicates that foundational processing constraints meaningfully affect executive task performance—reinforcing why hierarchical interpretation matters for this population.

Attention-Deficit/Hyperactivity Disorder

Children and adolescents with ADHD (n = 55) showed moderate effect sizes across TMT conditions—a notably strong result for a diagnostic group that frequently fails to show reliable deficits on cognitive testing. The Multitasking Index captured meaningful group differences, likely reflecting TMT's combined demands on sustained attention and set-shifting.

Profile analysis uncovered considerable variability that aggregate scores mask. Approximately one-third of participants performed comparably to controls on both baseline and switching conditions. However, about 22%

showed intact baseline sequencing alongside disproportionately weak switching performance (contrast scores ≤7), revealing specific cognitive flexibility limitations. Another subset (roughly 18%) struggled particularly on Switching-Distraction, suggesting difficulty suppressing responses to visually prominent but task-irrelevant stimuli. Additionally, approximately 16% showed amplified difficulty when working memory load increased on Switching-Working Memory, pointing to working memory as a primary contributor to their multitasking challenges. These diverse profiles—accessible only through contrast scores and condition-level comparisons—illustrate that ADHD manifests through varied executive function patterns rather than a single cognitive fingerprint.

Specific Learning Disorder—Mathematics

Children with SLD-Math (n = 26) produced moderate effect sizes on TMT, with the Multitasking Index showing the clearest group separation ($d = 0.80$, $p < 0.01$). Distinctively, this group showed elevated error rates (Combined Switching Total Active Errors $d = 0.64$, $p = 0.02$), unlike the TBI and ASD samples where speed declined but accuracy held steady. This accuracy vulnerability may stem from shared cognitive demands between Trail Making's sequencing and alternation requirements and the sequential reasoning and mental flexibility needed for mathematical problem-solving. The findings support comprehensive executive function assessment when evaluating learning difficulties, given the process overlap between TMT demands and mathematical reasoning.

Mild Cognitive Impairment

The MCI sample (n = 18 older adults) showed a revealing pattern of selective impairment. The Combined Sequencing Index fell significantly below matched controls with a large effect size, reflecting reduced baseline processing efficiency. However, all three switching conditions—Number-Letter Switching, Switching-Distraction, and Switching-Working Memory—showed no significant group differences. This dissociation indicates that fundamental processing speed bears the impact, while higher-order executive capacities remain relatively spared.

This pattern offers evidence supporting TMT's ability to distinguish between different levels of cognitive dysfunction. Rather than broadly labeling this memory-impaired group as having executive deficits, TMT appropriately localized their difficulties to foundational processing. Clinicians can draw some confidence that the test differentiates where along the cognitive hierarchy problems arise.

Clinical Implications

TMT showed meaningful sensitivity to cognitive difficulties across all clinical groups examined, though the specific patterns differed systematically by diagnosis. The test proved especially effective at identifying impairment in TBI and ASD, where large effect sizes support confident clinical application. The moderate effect sizes in ADHD carry particular significance given how often this population performs within normal limits on standardized cognitive measures.

The subgroup findings carry an important message: belonging to a diagnostic category does not predict a uniform cognitive profile. Each clinical group contained individuals with varying patterns of strengths and weaknesses, and these patterns became visible only through contrast score analysis and condition-level comparison. Relying on single summary scores would obscure clinically meaningful distinctions. These results reinforce the value of systematic, hierarchical interpretation that examines performance across the full range of TMT conditions and contrast measures.

STRENGTHS AND WEAKNESSES

Trail Making offers several advantages for assessing cognitive flexibility while also presenting limitations clinicians should consider when selecting assessment tools and interpreting results.

Strengths

The Trail Making Test offers notable advantages for assessing cognitive flexibility within a comprehensive neuropsychological evaluation.

Hierarchical Component Analysis Isolates Executive from Nonexecutive Deficits
Both versions provide a systematic assessment of component abilities underlying switching performance. The original version directly measures visual scanning and motor speed; both versions assess basic sequencing. Contrast/comparison scores empirically determine whether switching difficulty exceeds baseline expectations, preventing the common error of attributing any poor trail making performance to "executive dysfunction" when foundational deficits may fully explain results.

High Ecological Validity for Multitasking Demands
Number-Letter Switching directly models real-world cognitive flexibility—alternating between mental sets while maintaining both sets active. The task's transparency makes results readily interpretable for referral sources, educators, and families.

Error and Process Scores Reveal Performance Nuances Beyond Completion Time
Error analyses differentiate types of failures: set-loss errors indicate flexibility deficits; sequencing errors suggest working memory or knowledge problems. The Advanced version's extensive process measures (response variability, speed-accuracy tradeoffs, error ratios) provide fine-grained performance parsing supporting differential diagnosis.

Well-Established Psychometric Properties and Extensive Normative Data
Trail making tasks have decades of validation research supporting their use. The original D-KEFS version provides norms across 16 age groups from 8–89 years; the Advanced version covers 8–90 years with updated contemporary norms. Both versions demonstrate strong reliability and validity for assessing cognitive flexibility.

Sensitivity to Subtle Deficits in High-Functioning Individuals (Advanced Version)
Traditional trail making often shows ceiling effects in bright individuals who complete switching tasks too quickly to reveal mild impairment. The Advanced version's Switching-Distraction and Switching-Working Memory conditions provide substantially higher cognitive demands, detecting deficits invisible on standard measures.

Reduced Administration and Scoring Burden (Advanced Version)
Digital administration eliminates manual timing errors, automatically captures precise response latencies, and provides immediate automated scoring. Examiners can focus on behavioral observation rather than vigilantly tracking errors. Score reports generate instantly with all core and process measures calculated.

Contemporary Normative Data (Advanced Version)
The Advanced version provides norms collected in the 2020s, offering more current comparison standards that reflect contemporary demographics and performance expectations.

Weaknesses and Limitations

Despite its strengths, the Trail Making Test has several limitations that clinicians should consider when selecting measures and interpreting results.

Limited Assessment of Self-Directed Cognitive Flexibility
Both versions assess shifting ability when explicitly instructed and provided clear rules—alternating numbers and letters following a demonstrated format. This structured format may overestimate flexibility in individuals who can follow explicit rules but struggle recognizing when shifting is needed or generating appropriate shifts independently. Real-world flexibility often requires identifying that the current approach isn't working and generating alternative strategies without instruction.

Confounding of Multiple Cognitive Processes

Despite component analysis, Number-Letter Switching and the Advanced switching conditions still conflate multiple processes. Poor performance could reflect set-shifting deficits, working memory limitations, inhibitory control problems, processing speed constraints, visual scanning inefficiency, or combinations thereof. While contrast scores help parse contributions, they cannot definitively isolate pure cognitive flexibility from supporting processes.

Switching-Distraction Cues

The number or letter that appears outside a circle is meant to tempt the examinee not to switch sets but continue with the same number or letter sequence. The number or letter remains on the screen after the examinee has resisted the temptation and correctly switched sets. Some examinees have noted that the prior number or letter that remains on the screen then becomes a cue for what they should touch next. For example, if an examinee has just touched "3," a "4" appears on the screen to distract them from switching to "C." The "4" remains on the screen after the examinee correctly touches "C," and for savvy learners, the "4" can be referenced as a cue that it is the next correct answer after again switching sets. This strategic insight, recognizing that an obstacle can be repurposed as a tool, reflects Tier 4 metacognitive learning rather than Tier 3 flexibility per se. Examinees who discover this independently demonstrate spontaneous strategy generation not captured by scored measures. The cues are integrated into norms but may differentially influence performance for those who recognize this pattern versus those who do not, potentially attenuating the distraction effect for metacognitively sophisticated examinees.

Cultural and Linguistic Considerations Limit Applicability

Both versions assume literacy in the English alphabet and familiarity with Western Arabic numerals. Letter sequencing particularly disadvantages individuals educated in nonalphabetic writing systems or multilingual individuals whose primary literacy is not in English. Performance comparisons to monolingual English-speaking norms may misrepresent abilities for linguistically diverse examinees.

Motor and Visual Requirements May Mask or Confound Executive Deficits

The original version's graphomotor demands disadvantage individuals with motor impairments—arthritis, essential tremor, hemiparesis—who may have intact cognitive flexibility but slowed execution. The Advanced version reduces motor demands but introduces challenges, as stylus manipulation may prove difficult for some, and the digital interface creates visual complexity through overlapping connection lines. Visual field deficits, hemispatial neglect, or reduced acuity affect performance on both versions despite normal executive function.

Timed Format May Disproportionately Penalize Some Populations

The emphasis on speed creates performance anxiety in some examinees, particularly those with anxiety disorders, perfectionistic traits, or cultural backgrounds emphasizing accuracy over speed. Time pressure may trigger emotional dysregulation that impairs cognitive efficiency beyond underlying ability limitations. Some neurological populations show generalized psychomotor slowing affecting all timed tasks without specific executive deficits.

Limited Assessment of Hot Executive Functions

Both versions primarily assess cold executive functions—cognitive flexibility, inhibitory control, working memory—with minimal systematic hot EF evaluation. While behavioral observations may reveal frustration tolerance, impulsivity, or anxiety, these observations lack normative data and standardization. The test doesn't systematically measure decision-making under emotional conditions, motivation-driven flexibility, or reward-based shifting.

Advanced Version Eliminates Valuable Baseline Measures

While streamlining improves efficiency, removing Visual Scanning and Motor Speed conditions means these abilities cannot be directly assessed. If Advanced sequencing conditions show impairment, determining whether visual scanning or motor factors contribute requires supplementary testing. For neurological populations where these foundational abilities are commonly affected, losing direct measurement represents a significant limitation.

Dated Normative Data (Original Version)
The original version's norms were collected in the late 1990s and published in 2001. While Pearson maintains these remain clinically appropriate, some clinicians prefer more contemporary normative standards, particularly for populations where secular trends may affect performance expectations.

> **CAUTION**
>
> Neither Trail Making version comprehensively assesses cognitive flexibility. Both measure shifting ability when explicitly cued with clear rules. They provide no information about flexibility in ambiguous situations, self-directed strategy shifting, or adaptation based on feedback. Strong performance indicates ability to shift when instructed; it doesn't guarantee appropriate shifting in complex real-world contexts requiring judgment about when and how to shift.

ALTERNATIVE MEASURES

Trail Making should be interpreted within a comprehensive assessment including complementary measures that assess related but distinct aspects of cognitive flexibility and processing speed.

Within the D-KEFS Suite

Several D-KEFS subtests provide complementary or converging evidence for cognitive flexibility and processing speed.

Design Fluency (Original)
When trail making results are ambiguous or additional cognitive flexibility data are needed, Design Fluency provides a complementary assessment. The figural format eliminates linguistic and literacy demands affecting Letter Sequencing. Switching between filled and empty dots parallels Number-Letter Switching's mental set alternation, but in the visuospatial rather than verbal-sequential domain.

Color-Word Interference Test (Both Versions)
This provides additional inhibitory control assessment, complementing trail making's set-shifting focus. The inhibition task requires suppressing automatic word reading to name ink colors—a different inhibitory demand than suppressing prepotent sequence continuation. The original version includes a switching condition (Inhibition/Switching) directly comparable to Number-Letter Switching.

Tower Test (Both Versions)
Trail making assesses flexibility following explicit alternation rules. Tower Test evaluates planning and problem-solving requiring self-directed strategy generation. Comparing results reveals whether executive deficits involve only rule-following flexibility or extend to strategic planning.

Verbal Fluency Test (Both Versions)
The Category Switching condition assesses generative flexibility—producing responses while alternating between categories—complementing trail making's reactive flexibility assessment, where examinees respond to externally presented stimuli.

Social Sorting Test (D-KEFS Advanced)
Assesses cognitive flexibility within social-cognitive contexts, measuring whether flexibility deficits observed on trail making extend to social categorization and reasoning.

Beyond D-KEFS

Measures outside the D-KEFS family can provide converging evidence or assess related constructs when additional information is needed.

Set-Shifting Measures
The Wisconsin Card Sorting Test (WCST; Heaton et al., 1993) requires discovering sorting rules through trial-and-error, then shifting when rules change without warning. Unlike trail making's explicit alternation instructions, WCST demands recognizing when shifts are needed based solely on feedback—assessing self-directed rule inference and feedback-based shifting that complements trail making's explicit rule switching.

Trail Making Variants

The Comprehensive Trail Making Test (CTMT; Reynolds, 2002) adds complexity through numbered symbols requiring visual search and discrimination, potentially detecting subtle deficits in visual processing speed and complex scanning that D-KEFS trail making misses. The Trails-X (Hartman & Reynolds, 2019) removes numeracy and literacy requirements while increasing adaptive planning demands through its unstructured format with no designated start or end point.

Processing Speed Measures

When trail making shows global slowing across conditions with preserved contrast scores, dedicated processing speed measures help determine whether generalized speed deficits account for performance. WISC-V/WAIS-5 Coding and Symbol Search (Wechsler, 2014, 2024) provides a processing speed assessment independent of the executive demands embedded in trail making tasks.

Motor Function Measures

For individuals with suspected motor impairments, dedicated motor assessments clarify whether trail making difficulties reflect motor limitations rather than cognitive deficits. The Grooved Pegboard Test (Lafayette Instrument, 2015) and Finger Tapping Test (Reitan & Wolfson, 1993) assess fine motor speed and dexterity, helping parse motor contributions to trail making performance—particularly relevant for the original version's graphomotor demands.

Behavioral Rating Scales

Executive function rating scales capture real-world executive behaviors that may or may not align with performance-based measures. For children and adolescents, the Behavior Rating Inventory of Executive Function, Second Edition (BRIEF-2; Gioia et al., 2015), Comprehensive Executive Function Inventory (CEFI; Naglieri & Goldstein, 2013), and Delis Rating of Executive Functions (D-REF; Delis, 2012) provide parent and teacher perspectives on daily executive functioning. For adults, the BRIEF-A (Roth et al., 2005), CEFI Adult (Naglieri & Goldstein, 2017), and D-REF Adult (Delis, 2021) offer self-report and informant-report options. Relevant scales include Shift (paralleling trail making's cognitive flexibility demands) and Working Memory. When trail making performance seems inconsistent with real-world functioning—for example, individuals performing well on trail making but showing elevated Shift scale scores—rating scales clarify whether adequate cognitive flexibility capacity fails to deploy consistently in daily life.

SUMMARY

The Trail Making Test represents one of neuropsychology's most widely used measures, existing in two sophisticated versions within the D-KEFS family. The original D-KEFS Trail Making Test provides comprehensive component analysis through five conditions assessing visual scanning, number sequencing, letter sequencing, number-letter switching, and motor speed. The D-KEFS Advanced Trail Making Test offers a streamlined digital alternative with five conditions—two baseline sequencing tasks and three progressively demanding switching conditions that extend assessment beyond traditional trail making's ceiling.

Both versions excel at hierarchical analysis of performance. The component structure allows clinicians to determine whether impaired switching reflects true cognitive flexibility deficits (Tier 3) or results from foundational problems in visual scanning, motor speed, or processing efficiency (Tier 1) or basic sequencing and rule-following difficulties (Tier 2). Contrast scores quantify whether switching impairment exceeds what baseline abilities predict, distinguishing executive from nonexecutive contributions to performance.

The original version's strengths include direct assessment of visual scanning and motor speed, a paper-and-pencil format familiar to many examinees, and a broad age range (8–89 years) supporting developmental and longitudinal assessment. The Advanced version offers reduced motor demands through digital administration, more precise measurement (response times to 0.1 second), extensive process scores revealing speed-accuracy tradeoffs and response consistency, and critically, higher-level switching conditions (Switching-Distraction and Switching-Working Memory) that detect subtle executive deficits invisible on traditional measures.

Critical limitations apply to both versions. Neither assesses self-directed cognitive flexibility—the ability to recognize when shifting is needed or generate appropriate shifts without explicit instruction. Both measure shifting capacity when rules are clear and transitions are cued; they provide no information about flexibility in ambiguous real-world situations requiring judgment about whether, when, and how to shift. The structured format may overestimate abilities in individuals who can follow explicit rules but struggle with spontaneous, self-directed flexibility. Additionally, both versions primarily assess cold executive functions (cognitive control, inhibition, working memory) with minimal systematic evaluation of hot executive functions (emotional regulation, motivation-driven flexibility, decision-making under affective conditions).

Ecological interpretation requires caution. Trail making's decontextualized, timed format may misrepresent real-world function in both directions. Integration with rating scales, functional history, and naturalistic observation remains essential for determining whether trail making deficits translate to functional impairment.

The hierarchical tier framework guides interpretation and intervention. Tier 1 deficits (visual scanning, motor speed, processing efficiency) require accommodations addressing foundational limitations—extended time, reduced visual complexity, or motor modifications. Tier 2 difficulties (basic sequencing, simple rule-following) benefit from cognitive training, structured practice, or compensatory strategies building automaticity. Tier 3 executive impairments (cognitive flexibility, set-shifting, inhibitory control) warrant metacognitive strategy instruction, explicit transition cues, and environmental modifications reducing multitasking demands.

Margaret's case exemplified ideal trail making interpretation. Her preserved Visual Scanning and Motor Speed confirmed intact Tier 1 functions. Adequate Number and Letter Sequencing demonstrated Tier 2 abilities. Dramatically impaired Number-Letter Switching with significant contrast scores revealed specific Tier 3 cognitive flexibility deficits. Qualitative observations revealed intact Tier 4 functioning; her metacognitive awareness and ability to articulate her difficulties suggested she could benefit from explicit compensatory strategies. This pattern (impaired Tier 3 with preserved Tier 4) carries a favorable prognosis for strategy-based intervention.

When trail making results are ambiguous, alternative measures within and beyond the D-KEFS family provide clarification. These complementary measures, combined with rating scales and functional assessment, create a comprehensive understanding of cognitive flexibility in its multiple forms—structured versus self-directed, verbal versus figural, cold versus hot—ensuring trail making results are interpreted within the broader context of executive functioning and real-world adaptive behavior.

TEST YOURSELF

1. A 45-year-old patient shows impaired performance on Visual Scanning and Motor Speed (original version), with proportionally impaired Number-Letter Switching. Contrast scores are in the average range. This pattern most likely indicates:

(a) Tier 3 cognitive flexibility deficit.
(b) Tier 1 foundational processing deficits affecting all conditions.
(c) Tier 2 sequencing impairment.
(d) Intact executive function with poor effort.

2. On the Advanced version, an examinee performs adequately on Number Sequencing, Letter Sequencing, and Number-Letter Switching, but shows marked impairment on Switching-Distraction with numerous distraction errors. This pattern suggests:

(a) Global executive dysfunction.
(b) Working memory limitations.
(c) Inhibitory control deficits under interference.
(d) Processing speed impairment.

3. Set-loss errors that occur primarily at capture stimulus placements (consecutive numbers or letters in proximity) on Number-Letter Switching most likely indicate:

(a) Severe cognitive inflexibility requiring intensive intervention.
(b) Milder flexibility deficits with vulnerability to spatial interference.
(c) Visual scanning problems.
(d) Working memory impairment.

4. An examinee shows average Number Sequencing but significantly slower Letter Sequencing, with adequate Number-Letter Switching contrast scores. This pattern most likely indicates:

(a) Tier 3 cognitive flexibility deficit.

(b) Tier 1 visual scanning impairment.

(c) Tier 2 differential sequence automaticity.

(d) Hot EF anxiety affecting letter-based tasks.

5. A patient shows adequate Number-Letter Switching completion time but makes numerous set-loss errors. Behavioral observation reveals visible frustration after each error with progressive performance deterioration. This pattern most likely reflects:

(a) Pure cold EF cognitive flexibility deficit.

(b) Hot EF dysregulation compounding mild cold EF limitations.

(c) Tier 1 processing speed deficit.

(d) Inadequate effort.

6. On the original version, the primary difference between the Number Sequencing condition and traditional Trail Making Part A is:

(a) Number Sequencing includes letters in the stimulus array.

(b) Number Sequencing uses different number ranges.

(c) Number Sequencing is untimed.

(d) Number Sequencing appears on one page instead of two.

7. The Advanced TMT's use of mean correct (with errors) connection time instead of total completion time as the primary score provides all of the following advantages EXCEPT:

(a) More precise measurement (to 0.1 second).

(b) Better floor and ceiling than total time.

(c) Allows shorter discontinue times.

(d) Direct comparability to original version completion times.

8. An examinee performs significantly better on original Number-Letter Switching than Advanced Number-Letter Switching despite both being administered within the same evaluation. This discrepancy most likely suggests:

(a) Declining cognitive function between administrations.

(b) Greater difficulty with Advanced version's higher stimulus density or digital format.

(c) Original version was administered incorrectly.

(d) Practice effects benefited original version.

9. A high percent error ratio on Advanced Number-Letter Switching combined with a very slow mean correct (with errors) connection time most likely indicates:

(a) Speed-accuracy tradeoff favoring accuracy.

(b) Impulsive responding favoring speed.

(c) Combined speed and accuracy deficits suggesting global impairment or poor effort.

(d) Adequate cognitive capacity with anxiety.

10. The most clinically useful original version contrast score for determining whether Number-Letter Switching difficulty reflects true cognitive flexibility deficit is:

(a) Switching vs. Visual Scanning.

(b) Switching vs. Motor Speed.

(c) Switching vs. Number Sequencing.

(d) Switching vs. Combined Number Sequencing + Letter Sequencing.

Answer Key: 1-b, 2-c, 3-b, 4-c, 5-b, 6-a, 7-d, 8-b, 9-c, 10-d

REFERENCES

Conners, C. K. (2014). *Conners Continuous Performance Test* (3rd ed.). Multi-Health Systems.

Delis, D. C. (2012). *Delis Rating of Executive Functions.* Pearson.

Delis, D. C. (2021). *Delis Rating of Executive Functions–Adult.* Pearson.

Delis, D. C., & Kaplan, E. (2025). *Delis-Kaplan Executive Function System Advanced.* Pearson.

Delis, D. C., Kaplan, E., & Kramer, J. H. (2001). *Delis-Kaplan Executive Function System (D-KEFS).* Pearson.

Denney, D. R., Gallagher, K. S., & Lynch, S. G. (2011). Deficits in processing speed in patients with multiple sclerosis: Evidence from explicit and covert measures. Archives of Clinical Neuropsychology, 26(2), 110–119.

Dymowski, A. R., Owens, J. A., Ponsford, J. L., & Willmott, C. (2015). Speed of processing and strategic control of attention after traumatic brain injury. Journal of Clinical and Experimental Neuropsychology, 37(10), 1024–1035.

Erkinjuntti, T. (2002). Subcortical vascular dementia. *Cerebrovascular Diseases, 13*(Suppl. 2), 58–60.

Genova, H. M., Hillary, F. G., DeLuca, J., & Wylie, G. (2009). The relationship between executive functioning, processing speed, and white matter integrity in multiple sclerosis. Cognitive Processing, 10(Suppl 2), S218–S220.

Gioia, G. A., Isquith, P. K., Guy, S. C., & Kenworthy, L. (2015). *Behavior Rating Inventory of Executive Function* (2nd ed.) PAR.

Hartman, D. E., & Reynolds, C. R. (2019). *Trails-X. PAR.*

Heaton, R. K., Chelune, G. J., Talley, J. L., Kay, G. G., & Curtiss, G. (1993). *Wisconsin Card Sorting Test manual: Revised and Expanded.* Psychological Assessment Resources.

Lafayette Instrument (2015). *Grooved Pegboard Test User Instructions.* Lafayette Instrument.

Lange, R. T., Iverson, G. L., & Franzen, M. D. (2005). Management of confounding variables in TBI: The role of processing speed in executive function. Applied Neuropsychology, 12(2), 64–71.

Naglieri, J. A., & Goldstein, S. (2013). *Comprehensive Executive Function Inventory.* Multi-Health Systems.

Naglieri, J. A., & Goldstein, S. (2017). *Comprehensive Executive Function Inventory–Adult.* Multi-Health Systems.

Reitan, R. M., & Wolfson, D. (1993). *The Halstead-Reitan Neuropsychological Test Battery: Theory and Clinical Interpretation* ((2nd ed.). ed.). Neuropsychology Press.

Reynolds, C. R. (2002). *Comprehensive Trail-Making Test.* PRO-ED.

Roth, R. M., Isquith, P. K., & Gioia, G. A. (2005). *Behavior Rating Inventory of Executive Function–Adult Version.* PAR.

Salthouse, T. A. (2011). What cognitive abilities are involved in trail-making performance? *Intelligence, 39*(4), 222–232.

Wechsler, D. (2014). *Wechsler Intelligence Scale for Children* (5th ed.). Pearson.

Wechsler, D. (2024). *Wechsler Adult Intelligence Scale* (5th ed.). Pearson.

Twelve

TWENTY QUESTIONS TEST

CLINICAL VIGNETTE

Keisha Williams, a 10-year-old fourth grader, was referred for evaluation due to increasing academic struggles despite average intelligence and strong reading decoding skills. Her parents reported she could memorize facts easily but struggled with comprehension questions asking "why" or "how." Teachers noted she excelled at spelling and math computation but had trouble with word problems and reading inference questions. Previous testing showed average verbal and nonverbal abilities, adequate attention, and no learning disabilities.

During the Twenty Questions Test, Keisha's approach revealed executive-level difficulties. Her first question was "Is it yellow?" (eliminating only 3 objects regardless of answer). After receiving "yes," she asked, "Is it the corn?" When told no, she asked "Is it the banana?" and identified the target. Her Initial Abstraction score of 3 reflected concrete, feature-bound thinking. On subsequent items, she similarly focused on perceptual features (e.g., "Is it red?" "Does it have wings?") rather than superordinate categories like "living things" or "animals." Aside from the first trial, she required 12–15 questions per trial and sometimes asked duplicative questions; for example, asking "Is it a plant?" after already eliminating all plants.

Keisha's performance showed intact Tier 1 functions: accurate object perception and naming, sustained attention, and understanding of the yes/no format. Tier 2 processes were adequate; she maintained the task goal and basic working memory. However, Tier 3 Cold EF approaches revealed significant impairment in abstract categorical reasoning and strategic hypothesis testing. Rather than forming hierarchical categories to systematically eliminate objects, she remained focused on concrete features. Her Repeated Questions indicated difficulty incorporating feedback and adjusting strategy.

The tier-based analysis clarified that Keisha's academic struggles stemmed not from basic skills but from executive-level categorical reasoning deficits—the very abilities needed for reading comprehension requiring inference, organizing essay content thematically, and understanding "why" questions demanding conceptual relationships.

TEST DESCRIPTION

The D-KEFS Twenty Questions Test measures verbal abstract reasoning, hypothesis-testing ability, and the capacity to use categorical thinking to solve problems efficiently. Designed for ages 8 through 89, this test presents examinees with a stimulus page depicting 30 common objects (15 living things, 15 nonliving things). The examinee's task is to identify an unknown target object by asking the fewest yes/no questions possible. The test includes four separate trials.

Twenty Questions also has one alternate form with four alternate trials. The 30 objects can be clustered into conceptual categories and subcategories that differ in the number of objects each contains. At the highest level, examinees can distinguish between living (15 objects) and nonliving (15 objects) things. Mid-level categories include animals (8 objects), plants (7 objects), kitchen items (8 objects), and modes of transportation (7 objects). Lower-level categories such as fruits (3 objects), birds (3 objects), or dishes (3 objects) contain fewer items.

The most efficient problem-solving strategy involves asking questions that eliminate the maximum number of objects regardless of whether the examiner answers "yes" or "no." The question "Is it a living thing?" eliminates exactly 15 objects no matter the response, representing optimal abstract reasoning. In contrast, concrete questions like "Is it yellow?" eliminate only 3 objects with a "no" response (though 27 with a "yes"), reflecting stimulus-bound, inefficient thinking.

Executive functions assessed include the ability to perceive hierarchical category relationships among the 30 objects, formulate abstract yes/no questions that maximize information gain, and incorporate feedback to refine subsequent questions. The test provides three primary scaled scores and three optional process measures, allowing for nuanced analysis of both achievement and the cognitive strategies employed.

DON'T FORGET

The Twenty Questions Test uniquely quantifies the ***level*** of abstraction (via the Initial Abstraction score), separate from efficiency (Total Questions Asked) and weighted achievement. An examinee might identify the target quickly through lucky guessing with concrete questions, but the Initial Abstraction score reveals whether systematic categorical reasoning guided their approach.

Rapid Reference 12.1

Twenty Questions Test Overview

Feature	**Description**
Age range	8–89 years
Administration format	Paper stimulus page with 30 pictured objects
Stimuli	30 common objects: 15 living (animals, plants) and 15 nonliving (kitchen items, transportation); organized into hierarchical categories
Task	Identify unknown target object by asking yes/no questions; use as few questions as possible
Trials	Four trials (alternate form available)
Primary constructs	Tier 3 Cold EF (abstract categorical reasoning, hypothesis generation/testing, feedback utilization, strategic planning)

HIERARCHICAL TIER ANALYSIS

The Twenty Questions Test can be analyzed through the four-tier framework, with performance reflecting processes ranging from basic perception and language to higher-order metacognitive integration.

Tier 1: Foundational Processes (Nonexecutive)

The Twenty Questions Test requires several basic cognitive abilities that must be intact for a valid assessment of executive functions.

Visual Perception and Object Recognition
Visual perception and object recognition form the foundation—examinees must accurately perceive and identify 30 distinct pictured objects on the stimulus page. Poor performance in individuals with visual processing deficits, visual agnosia, or significant visual impairment may reflect perceptual rather than executive dysfunction. Basic color perception is relevant as some objects are presented in distinctive colors (three yellow items, for example), though color blindness does not necessarily prevent successful categorical reasoning.

Object Naming and Semantic Knowledge
Object naming and semantic knowledge represent critical Tier 1 language functions. Examinees must know the names of common objects (e.g., banana, owl, helicopter) and possess basic semantic knowledge about their properties. Individuals with anomia may point to objects effectively (using spatial strategies) without being able to name them, while those with profound semantic deficits may not recognize categorical relationships even when perceptual abilities are intact. The verbal nature of the task means that expressive and receptive language abilities are fundamental requirements. Examinees must comprehend the yes/no question format, understand the examiner's responses, and formulate grammatically coherent questions.

Sustained Attention and Basic Working Memory
Sustained attention throughout the task is essential, as each item may require up to 20 questions and the test focuses on four target items over the respective trials. Individuals with severe attentional dysfunction may lose track of their goal or target item or fail to register the examiner's feedback. Basic working memory allows examinees to hold the target object in mind once identified through their questions and monitor which objects have been eliminated. However, severe anterograde amnesia may cause examinees to ask the same questions repeatedly, not because of perseveration or poor feedback utilization, but because they genuinely cannot remember having asked those questions moments earlier.

Processing Speed
Processing speed affects task efficiency, but is not the primary demand; there is no time limit for question generation. Still, individuals with significantly slowed processing may take longer to scan the stimulus array, retrieve object names, and formulate questions. When slowed processing co-occurs with weakened working memory, the combined effect can compromise monitoring of previous responses, as the examinee may not process feedback quickly enough to consolidate it before moving to the next question.

Tier 1 Impairment Pattern
Examinees with Tier 1 deficits show fundamental problems with object recognition, naming, or sustained attention that pervade the task. They consistently misidentify objects, struggle to maintain focus on the goal, or demonstrate basic language comprehension difficulties. Spatial strategy predominance—repeatedly asking "Is it in this row?" while pointing—may indicate anomia rather than executive dysfunction. Performance shows global difficulty throughout, with no strategic sophistication.

Repeated questions often reflect genuine memory deficits (forgetting previous questions) rather than executive perseveration. The frequency of repetition is diagnostically informative: occasional repetitions after extended questioning may represent normal lapses or mild working memory limitations, whereas frequent repetitions—particularly verbatim repetitions occurring after only a few intervening questions—suggest more significant memory impairment or profound inattention.

Tier 2: Bridging Processes

Tier 2 encompasses abilities that support but do not constitute executive function.

Basic Verbal Reasoning and Mental Flexibility
Basic verbal reasoning allows examinees to understand that a "no" response to "Is it an animal?" eliminates all eight animals from consideration. This straightforward logical inference differs from the higher-order strategic reasoning required at Tier 3. Basic mental flexibility enables examinees to shift from one category to another after

receiving feedback (e.g., moving from "living things" to exploring subcategories within that domain), though this differs from the complex set-shifting and cognitive flexibility demanded at higher tiers.

Goal Maintenance and Procedural Learning

Goal maintenance represents a Tier 2 demand. Examinees must remember they are trying to identify an unknown target object by asking yes/no questions. This differs from Tier 3 planning and strategy in that it involves simply maintaining the basic task parameters rather than formulating sophisticated approaches. Procedural learning occurs as examinees become familiar with the task format, potentially improving across the four items as they grasp the general approach. However, improvement across items may also reflect Tier 3 strategic learning—distinguishing these requires careful observation.

Working Memory

Working memory at this tier involves holding the current category under consideration and remembering which general domains have been eliminated. An examinee might remember "I know it's not an animal" without necessarily maintaining a detailed mental representation of exactly which objects remain possible—that more complex working memory demand belongs to Tier 3.

Pattern Recognition

Pattern recognition abilities allow examinees to notice that objects cluster by various features, though recognizing that these clusters can form hierarchical categories represents higher-order Tier 3 reasoning. An examinee might notice several objects are yellow, or that multiple objects are birds, without necessarily conceptualizing these as strategic categories for systematic elimination.

Tier 2 Deficit Pattern

Individuals with Tier 2 difficulties show adequate perception and language but struggle with bridging functions. They understand the task superficially but lack procedural fluency. They may need frequent goal reminders, struggle with simple working memory for what's been generally eliminated, or show difficulty with basic logical inference that eliminating "animals" also eliminates subordinate categories. Procedural learning across items is minimal.

Tier 3: Core Executive Functions

The Twenty Questions Test primarily assesses Tier 3 executive functions, with cold executive processes driving strategic questioning and hot executive factors influencing performance under evaluative conditions.

Cold Executive Functions

These functions carry the test's central problem-solving demands: abstract categorical reasoning, hypothesis generation and testing, feedback-based flexibility, and the working memory needed to track an evolving strategy.

Abstract Categorical Reasoning (Primary)

The core executive demand of the Twenty Questions Test is abstract categorical reasoning—the ability to perceive hierarchical relationships among objects and form superordinate concepts that subsume multiple items. Examinees must move beyond concrete, stimulus-bound thinking focused on individual objects or salient features to recognize that objects can be organized into nested categories at multiple levels of abstraction.

The hierarchical structure includes: highest level (i.e., living/nonliving dividing 30 objects equally), mid-level categories (e.g., animals, plants, kitchen items, transportation containing 7–8 objects each), and lower-level categories (e.g., fruits, birds, dishes with 2–3 items). The examinee must understand that asking about broader categories provides more information, eliminating more possibilities with each question.

The Initial Abstraction score quantifies this ability by measuring how many objects the examinee's *first* question on each item could eliminate with the *least* favorable answer. "Is it a living thing?" eliminates exactly 15 objects regardless of response (Initial Abstraction = 15). "Is it yellow?" eliminates only 3 objects if "no" (Initial Abstraction = 3), despite eliminating 27 if "yes." Efficient strategy guarantees elimination of half the remaining objects regardless of answer.

DON'T FORGET

The Initial Abstraction score captures the test's key insight: effective categorical reasoning guarantees elimination of objects regardless of the answer. "Is it living?" eliminates exactly 15 objects, whether the answer is yes or no. "Is it yellow?" eliminates only 3 if the answer is no. This distinction between guaranteed versus conditional elimination separates abstract strategic reasoning from concrete guessing.

Individuals with executive dysfunction show characteristic patterns. Many remain stimulus-bound, pulled to salient perceptual features like distinctive colors, size, or paired objects. Others begin with low-level categories or single-object guesses rather than forming superordinate groupings. The stimulus array was deliberately designed with salient visual features (e.g., distinctive colors, paired objects) to elicit concrete thinking in individuals with stimulus-bound tendencies.

Hypothesis and Conceptual Idea Generation

Twenty Questions uniquely requires examinees to spontaneously generate conceptual hypotheses about how objects might be meaningfully organized. Unlike tasks where categories are externally provided (e.g., Sorting Test's Sort Recognition) or response options constrain thinking (e.g., multiple-choice formats), examinees must independently conceive of possible ways to divide the stimulus array.

The hypothesis generation process involves actively searching memory for potential organizing principles—semantic features (e.g., living vs. nonliving), functional properties (e.g., things you eat), perceptual characteristics (e.g., animals vs. birds), or spatial arrangements. Examinees must generate multiple competing hypotheses and evaluate which would most efficiently narrow possibilities. After "Is it living?" receives "yes," the examinee must generate new hypotheses specific to living things: plant versus animal, edible versus inedible.

This iterative hypothesis generation continues throughout each item as the field narrows, requiring increasingly specific conceptual distinctions. Impairment manifests as conceptual poverty, asking the same types of questions repeatedly (e.g., focusing only on color across all items) or struggling to generate new categorical ideas even when current approaches prove inefficient. This pattern differs from amnesia-related repetition: examinees with memory deficits repeat specific questions verbatim after short delays and typically show no awareness of having asked before, whereas those with conceptual poverty demonstrate thematic perseveration across question types (e.g., repeatedly returning to perceptual features like color or size) and may recognize they are "stuck" but cannot generate alternative organizing principles. Some examinees demonstrate adequate categorical knowledge when categories are suggested, but cannot spontaneously generate categorical hypotheses during open-ended problem-solving. This dissociation between recognition and generation of concepts has important real-world implications, as daily tasks often require independently conceiving of multiple approaches rather than selecting from predetermined options.

Hypothesis Testing and Strategic Reasoning

Beyond recognizing categories, examinees must engage in systematic hypothesis testing—formulating questions that maximize information gain. Strategic reasoning requires planning several steps ahead. After "Is it living?" receives "yes," an effective approach asks "Is it a plant?" to distinguish plants from animals. This sequential strategy, where each question is informed by previous responses and designed to systematically narrow possibilities, reflects sophisticated executive planning.

Some examinees lack a strategic approach despite adequate categorical knowledge. They may ask unrelated questions at similar abstraction levels without following a logical decision tree. Others pursue an inefficient elimination strategy, identifying and ruling out categories one at a time rather than using broader divisions.

The Total Weighted Achievement score captures this strategic dimension, awarding most points for identifying targets in 4–5 questions (optimal range), fewer points for either too many (inefficient) or too few (lucky concrete guessing). This inverted U-shaped curve rewards genuine strategic efficiency over fortuitous success.

Cognitive Flexibility and Feedback Utilization

Effective performance requires incorporating examiner feedback to adjust subsequent questions. After "no" to "Is it an animal?" examinees must flexibly shift to exploring other domains rather than perseverating within the animal category. Repeated Questions error scores capture failures in feedback utilization. Asking "Is it a fish?" then later "Does it have fins?" reveals difficulty recognizing these questions identify the same object.

Several neurocognitive mechanisms can underlie poor feedback utilization: perseverative tendencies causing stuck patterns, stimulus-bound individuals pulled to salient features already eliminated, or severe attentional dysfunction preventing adequate feedback processing. At the executive level, poor feedback utilization reflects an inability to flexibly incorporate new information into an evolving problem-solving strategy—maintaining a mental model of remaining possibilities and adjusting systematically.

Set-Loss Questions (e.g., either/or questions, compound questions, non-yes/no questions) represent executive inflexibility, suggesting difficulty maintaining task set or inhibiting inappropriate response formats.

Working Memory for Strategic Information

Tier 3 working memory encompasses maintaining complex, detailed information about the strategic situation. Examinees must track which categories have been ruled out while maintaining mental representation of remaining possibilities, their hierarchical relationships, and which strategic questions would most efficiently narrow the field. This executive working memory component increases as questions progress. After several questions, examinees must simultaneously hold multiple pieces of strategic information while formulating the next optimal query.

The most diagnostically relevant pattern shows intact Tier 1–2 abilities but inability to engage in executive-level categorical reasoning and strategic planning. Initial Abstraction scores are markedly low (0–3), with first questions on concrete features, low-level categories, or single objects. Repeated Questions are common (poor feedback utilization), Set-Loss Questions reveal inability to maintain task set, Total Questions Asked is elevated (often 15–20), and Total Weighted Achievement is low. This pattern shows dissociation from other executive tasks.

Tier 3 Cold EF Impairment Pattern

Examinees with Tier 3 Cold EF deficits demonstrate consistently low Initial Abstraction scores across items, reflecting fundamental difficulty with abstract categorical reasoning rather than situational or emotional factors. Their questions remain concrete and stimulus-bound throughout testing—focusing on perceptual features like color or size, or making single-object guesses—without evidence of hierarchical categorical thinking, even when given ample time. Repeated Questions errors reflect perseverative tendencies or genuine inability to incorporate feedback into strategic adjustment, not memory lapses. Performance does not improve across items despite experience with the task format, and qualitative observation reveals no evidence that emotional factors are disrupting otherwise intact reasoning capacity. These individuals lack the cognitive architecture for spontaneous categorical organization and hypothesis testing.

Hot Executive Functions

Frustration Tolerance and Emotional Regulation

The test naturally taxes frustration tolerance. Examinees using concrete strategies quickly realize they're asking many questions without efficiently narrowing possibilities—provoking frustration. Approaching the 20-question limit without identifying the target creates mounting pressure. Frustration often disrupts executive function. Examinees who begin with categorical reasoning may collapse into impulsive guessing as frustration builds, abandoning systematic reasoning for random guesses driven by emotional dysregulation.

Performance pressure can induce a shift from reflective, strategic reasoning to impulsive responding. The task requires inhibiting multiple inappropriate responses while engaging in complex reasoning—suppressing salient but inefficient questions based on visual features, inhibiting impulse to guess specific objects when categorical strategy feels effortful, restraining learned patterns from previous items when not optimal.

Initial questions may show moderate categorical reasoning, demonstrating capacity for abstract thought. However, performance deteriorates as frustration builds. Later questions become increasingly concrete and impulsive, showing a qualitative shift from systematic to random strategy. Emotional reactivity is observable, response time becomes erratic, and performance varies across items based on emotional state. Success on structured, low-pressure abstract reasoning tasks combined with poor Twenty Questions strongly suggests Hot EF compromise.

> **CAUTION**
>
> Poor performance is often attributed entirely to deficits in abstract reasoning or planning (Cold EF). However, emotional dysregulation, frustration intolerance, and performance anxiety (Hot EF) can substantially compromise categorical reasoning abilities even when capacity for abstract thought remains intact. An examinee demonstrating adequate categorical reasoning on low-pressure tasks but collapsing into concrete thinking on Twenty Questions may have Hot EF rather than Cold EF impairment.

Tier 3 Hot EF Impairment Pattern

Examinees with Hot EF difficulties show performance that varies with emotional state rather than consistent cognitive limitation. Initial questions on some items may demonstrate moderate-to-high abstraction, revealing capacity for categorical reasoning, but performance deteriorates as frustration builds or anxiety mounts. Later questions become increasingly concrete and impulsive, showing a qualitative shift from systematic to random strategy. Observable signs include visible frustration, erratic response timing, self-critical comments, or rushing through questions without strategic consideration. The key diagnostic indicator is variability; these examinees demonstrate that they can reason categorically when emotionally regulated, but lose access to this capacity under emotional load. Success on structured, low-pressure abstract reasoning tasks (e.g., Sorting Test) combined with poor Twenty Questions performance strongly suggests Hot EF compromise rather than Cold EF deficit.

Tier 4: Higher-Order Integration and Metacognition

Tier 4 processes involve the highest level of executive integration—monitoring one's own strategic effectiveness, recognizing when approaches are failing, and flexibly adjusting questioning strategy based on self-evaluation.

Metacognitive Monitoring and Self-Evaluation

At the highest tier, examinees must monitor the effectiveness of their strategy and recognize when their approach is inefficient. This metacognitive awareness manifests in self-corrective comments like "I should be asking bigger categories" or "That question wasn't very good." Spontaneous self-evaluation reflects the ability to step back from the task and assess one's own problem-solving process from a higher-order perspective.

Some examinees demonstrate metacognitive knowledge without implementation. They might say "I know I should start with bigger groups" yet continue asking concrete questions, revealing a dissociation between metacognitive awareness and executive control. Others show the opposite pattern: effective strategy without explicit awareness, successfully employing hierarchical categorization without being able to articulate why their approach is efficient.

Metacognitive monitoring also includes recognizing when questions are redundant before asking them or catching oneself mid-question and reformulating. An examinee might begin "Is it a f—actually, is it an animal?" showing real-time self-monitoring and strategic adjustment.

Strategic Flexibility and Learning Across Items

Performance across the four items provides a window into higher-order learning and strategic adjustment. Some examinees show marked improvement from trial 1 to trial 4 as they recognize more efficient approaches, reflecting strong metacognitive learning abilities. Some may recognize that the target pictures are from different higher-level categories, so they automatically focus on a category that has not been chosen yet. For example, if a picture from the category "mode of transportation" has not been used yet, they will tailor questions toward that category. Others demonstrate the opposite—performance degradation across items as frustration builds or attention wanes, or as they become over-confident and abandon systematic strategy.

The most sophisticated examinees demonstrate flexible strategy adjustment based on the specific strategic situation. They might begin with a mid-level category like "Is it a vehicle?" on one item, but after receiving "no" and facing 23 remaining objects, they recognize on subsequent items the need to start with higher-level distinctions like living versus nonliving.

Integration of Multiple Executive Systems

Twenty Questions requires coordinating several executive processes simultaneously. Examinees must maintain working memory representations while engaging in strategic reasoning, flexibly incorporate feedback while maintaining task set, and pursue systematic categorization while inhibiting concrete impulses. This simultaneous coordination of multiple executive systems represents a Tier 4 demand.

Some individuals perform adequately when executive demands are relatively isolated but struggle when multiple systems must operate in concert. They might demonstrate good categorical reasoning on the Sorting Test (where the categories are externally provided and there is no strategic sequencing) but poor performance on Twenty Questions despite similar categorical knowledge, revealing a Tier 4 integration deficit rather than Tier 3 categorical impairment.

Tier 4 Integration Difficulties

Individual executive components appear adequate—moderate Initial Abstraction, some effective categorical questions, evidence of feedback incorporation—but performance is inefficient overall due to poor integration. Working memory and strategic reasoning are not effectively coordinated. Strategic learning across items is absent despite metacognitive awareness. Performance is worse than individual components would predict.

Rapid Reference 12.2

Tier Structure at a Glance

Tier	Processes
Tier 1: Foundational processes (nonexecutive)	Visual perception and object recognition Object naming and semantic knowledge Receptive/expressive language (yes/no format) Sustained attention across trials Basic working memory (holding target in mind) Processing speed (scanning array, formulating questions)
Tier 2: Bridging processes	Simple verbal reasoning (understanding elimination logic) Basic mental flexibility (shifting categories after feedback) Goal maintenance (remembering task parameters) Procedural learning across trials Working memory for general eliminations Pattern recognition (noticing object clusters)
Tier 3: Cold executive functions	Abstract categorical reasoning (hierarchical relationships) Hypothesis and conceptual idea generation Hypothesis testing and strategic reasoning Cognitive flexibility and feedback utilization Working memory for strategic information
Tier 3: Hot executive functions	Frustration tolerance as questions accumulate Emotional regulation under performance pressure Inhibiting impulsive guessing
Tier 4: Higher-order integration	Metacognitive monitoring and self-evaluation Strategic flexibility and learning across items Integration of multiple executive systems simultaneously

ADMINISTRATION

NOTE: Refer to the Examiner's Manual for complete and detailed administration instructions. The Examiner's Manual provides verbatim instructions and clinicians should follow these precisely to ensure standardized administration.

Materials and Setup

The Twenty Questions Test is administered to examinees ages 8 through 89. Materials needed include the Examiner's Manual, stimulus page from the Stimulus Booklet positioned flat on the table, and the Record Form. The test has two alternate forms, each with four trials. Pearson's Q-global platform offers the following digital assets: Examiner's Manual, Stimulus Book, Stimulus Book Administration Directions.

Standard Instructions

Present the stimulus page and provide standardized instructions explaining that the page shows 30 objects, the examiner is thinking of one, and the examinee's job is to identify it by asking yes/no questions, using as few questions as possible. For each question, provide a clear "yes" or "no" response. Refer to the Examiner's Manual for a list of Prompts used following unusual examinee questions (e.g., refers to one object, compound questions, vague questions). If examinees violate the yes/no format (e.g., either/or, compound questions), prompt them to reformulate.

Recording and Discontinuation

Record all questions verbatim in the order asked, circling Y or N for each response based on the examiner's answer. Continue until the examinee correctly identifies the target or asks 20 questions. If an examinee fails to identify the target object after 20 questions but wants to know which one it is, say, "I can't tell you, but try to guess the next one." There is no discontinue rule; all four trials should be administered.

Accommodations

If an examinee asks clarification questions due to visual problems (e.g., "Is that a fork?"), answer, but do not count it as one of the 20 questions or score it as an error. Examinees may request reminders of previous questions or answers as often as needed—working memory support is permitted.

BEHAVIORAL OBSERVATIONS

Behavioral observations during administration provide critical qualitative data that complement quantitative scores and inform tier-based interpretation.

Approach, Strategy, and Question Patterns

Observe whether examinees pause before first questions to formulate strategy or immediately ask impulsive questions. This observation parallels First-Move Time on the Tower Test, both capture the tendency to plan before acting versus responding impulsively, and consistent patterns across these measures strengthen inferences about planning and inhibitory control. Note whether initial questions reflect high-level categorical thinking (e.g., "Is it living?"), concrete features (e.g., "Is it yellow?"), or single-object guesses. The content and abstraction level of initial questions are particularly diagnostic. Consistency across items versus variability reveals whether the approach represents a stable trait or fluctuating attention, fatigue, or learning.

As items progress, note whether examinees follow logical decision trees based on feedback or ask unconnected questions at similar abstraction levels. Effective patterns show progressive narrowing (e.g., "Is it living?" to "Is it a plant?" then "Is it a flower?"). Response latency patterns provide information. Consistently long pauses may indicate processing speed limitations or careful strategic planning, while increasingly rapid questions might suggest impulsive responding or mounting frustration.

Feedback Utilization and Flexibility

Observe how examinees incorporate feedback. Strong performers demonstrate immediate strategic adjustment, building directly on each answer. Weaker performers may pause uncertainly or ask questions unrelated to the feedback just received. Repeated Questions are particularly informative. Verbatim repetitions occurring shortly after the original question suggest severe memory deficits or profound inattention, while subtle semantic redundancy (e.g., asking about "fish" then later about "things with fins") may reveal poor understanding of hierarchical relationships or inability to maintain mental models of eliminated possibilities. Note also the frequency: occasional repetitions late in an item differ clinically from frequent repetitions throughout.

Set-loss errors often increase as examinees become frustrated or confused. Some catch themselves mid-question and self-correct, demonstrating metacognitive monitoring even if initial formulation was flawed. The relationship between emotional state and cognitive performance is crucial—does frustration lead to strategic collapse or does the examinee maintain a systematic approach despite emotional discomfort?

Emotional Responses

Observe emotional reactions throughout the task. Note visible frustration when questions fail to narrow possibilities efficiently, anxiety as the question count rises, or discouragement after failing to identify a target within 20 questions. Some examinees show mounting pressure through increased response speed, decreased strategic thinking, or self-critical comments ("I'm terrible at this"). Others maintain composure despite difficulty, demonstrating frustration tolerance. The relationship between emotional state and cognitive performance is diagnostically critical. Does frustration lead to abandonment of categorical strategy in favor of impulsive guessing? Does anxiety cause the examinee to second-guess reasonable categorical questions? Does early success breed overconfidence and carelessness on later items? Note whether emotional responses correspond with shifts in abstraction level—examinees whose Initial Abstraction scores decline across items while showing increasing frustration likely have Hot EF factors compromising otherwise adequate Cold EF capacity.

SCORING

The Twenty Questions Test yields three primary scaled scores and three optional process measures, each providing distinct information about categorical reasoning and strategic efficiency.

Primary Measures

Initial Abstraction Score

The Initial Abstraction score quantifies the level of abstract thinking represented by the first question asked on each item. This score measures the minimum number of objects that could be eliminated by the examinee's first question, regardless of whether the examiner's answer is yes or no.

Scoring involves examining the first question and calculating how many objects would be eliminated with a "yes" response and how many with a "no" response. The lower of these two numbers becomes the Initial Abstraction score for that item. For example:

- "Is it a living thing?" eliminates 15 objects if "no" and 15 if "yes"—score = 15
- "Is it an animal?" eliminates 8 objects if "no" and 22 if "yes"—score = 8
- "Is it in the bottom two rows?" eliminates 12 objects if "no" and 18 if "yes"—score = 12
- "Is it yellow?" eliminates 27 objects if "no" and 3 if "yes"—score = 3
- "Is it the banana?" eliminates 29 objects if "no" and 1 if "yes"—score = 1
- "Is it on this page?" eliminates 0 objects (answer is always yes)—score = 0

The raw score can range from 0 to 15 for each item and from 0 to 60 for the total test (summed across all four trials). If an example is not listed in the Examiner's Manual, manually determine the score by looking at the stimulus page and counting all "no" and "yes" options. Sum the scores for all 4 trials. This total raw score is converted to a scaled score corrected for the examinee's age group using the normative tables in the manual.

Total Questions Asked

This achievement measure reflects the total number of yes/no questions asked until the target object is identified for each trial, summed across all four trials. Fewer questions indicate better performance. If an examinee fails to identify the target after 20 questions, their score for that item is 21.

It may be difficult to determine if a yes/no question is valid or counts. If the examinee asks a vague yes/no question but then provides a specific question after being prompted, count it as only one yes/no question. If the examinee asks a yes/no question that the examiner could not answer and was prompted to ask a different question, that unanswerable yes/no question is not counted. If the examinee asks a rule-violation question but then provides a yes/no question after prompting, count it as only one yes/no question (and as an Incorrect Response – see herewith).

For each item, circle the number in the left column to indicate the total number of questions asked, enter that number in its box at the bottom of the column, and then sum for all 4 trials. The raw score is converted to a scaled score corrected for age. Lower raw scores (i.e., fewer questions needed) convert to higher scaled scores, reflecting better performance.

Total Weighted Achievement Score

This scoring system addresses a potential confound in the Total Questions Asked score: examinees who ask highly concrete initial questions might accidentally guess correctly on their first or second question, yielding an artificially inflated score despite poor strategic reasoning.

The weighted achievement system awards points based on an inverted U-shaped curve that rewards optimal performance while penalizing both excessive questions (inefficient strategy) and very few questions (likely lucky guessing unless accompanied by high abstraction):

- 1–2 questions = 1 point (lucky guessing)
- 3 questions = 2 points
- 4–5 questions = 5 points (optimal strategic performance)
- 6–7 questions = 4 points
- 8–10 questions = 3 points
- 11–14 questions = 2 points
- 15–20 questions = 1 point (very inefficient)
- Object not identified = 0 points

CAUTION

When Total Questions Asked is low, but Initial Abstraction is also low, the examinee likely succeeded through lucky guessing rather than strategic reasoning. A low question count can mask concrete thinking if the examinee happened to guess correctly early. Always examine Initial Abstraction alongside Total Questions Asked. The Weighted Achievement Score helps detect this pattern by penalizing quick identification without strategic questioning.

The Record Form accounts for this metric. For each item, circle the number corresponding to the last question asked in the far-right column marked Weighted Achievement Score. Sum this score for all 4 items. The maximum weighted achievement score is 5 points per item, with a total possible raw score of 20 across all four items. This raw score converts to a scaled score corrected for age.

For most examinees, all three primary scores yield similar scaled scores. However, when scores diverge, they provide important diagnostic information. An examinee with low Initial Abstraction (3) but low Total Questions Asked (4) likely got lucky with concrete guessing—their Weighted Achievement score will be low (2 points for 3 questions), reflecting their actually poor strategic reasoning.

Optional Process Measures

Spatial Questions

This measure counts questions attempting to eliminate objects based on location on the stimulus page rather than semantic properties. Examples include "Is it in the bottom row?" or pointing to an object and asking "Is it this one?" without attempting to name it. If an examinee points while also providing semantic information (e.g., "Is it the blue one?" while pointing), score it as verbal rather than spatial.

Spatial Questions occurred infrequently in the normative sample (i.e., only 2.7% of examinees asked any), with no significant age effects. The total raw score summed across all four items is converted to a cumulative percentile rank corrected for the entire normative group (not age-corrected). Percentile ranks below 2% are clinically significant.

While rare in the general population, certain clinical groups may use spatial strategies more frequently. Children with developmental language disorders or adults with aphasia may adopt spatial approaches to compensate for naming difficulties. In these cases, Spatial Questions reflect a Tier 1 language limitation rather than executive dysfunction, and the Initial Abstraction score based on Spatial Questions (which can eliminate 15 objects as effectively as semantic questions) may better reflect strategic reasoning than verbal categorical ability.

Repeated Questions

This error measure counts questions that identify the same object(s) as a previous question within the same item, regardless of whether the questions are verbatim. Examples include:

- Verbatim repetition: asking "Is it a bird?" twice
- Semantic repetition: "Is it a fish?" followed by "Does it have fins?"

Repeated Questions are counted only within items, not across them. If an examinee asks "Is it green?" on trial 1 and again on trial 2, it is not a repeated question error. Repeated Set-Loss Questions (see herewith) are scored as both a repeated question and a Set-Loss Question.

The total raw score (sum across all four trials) converts to a cumulative percentile rank corrected for age. Higher scores (more repetitions) indicate poorer performance. This measure specifically assesses feedback utilization—the ability to incorporate information received and avoid asking questions about already-eliminated possibilities.

Set-Loss Questions

Set-Loss Questions represent rule violations—questions that do not follow the yes/no format. Count the total number across all four trials. Types include:

- Either/or questions: "Is it yellow or green?"
- Compound questions: "Is it a vehicle or an animal?"
- Specification questions: "What kind of car is this?"
- Personalized questions that don't eliminate objects: "Do you like oranges?"
- Tangential questions: "What's that dog's name?"

If an examinee asks a rule-violation question and is prompted to reformulate it as yes/no, count it as one yes/no question (the reformulated version) but also count it as one set-loss error.

Sum the number of Set-Loss Questions across all 4 trials. The total raw score converts to a cumulative percentile rank for the entire normative group (not age-corrected). Percentile ranks below 2% are clinically significant. Set-Loss Questions suggest difficulty maintaining task set, inability to inhibit inappropriate response formats, or severe working memory deficits causing loss of task parameters.

Rapid Reference 12.3

Scoring Summary

Score Type	Score Name	What It Measures
Primary scaled scores	Initial Abstraction Score	Level of abstract thinking on the first question; minimum objects eliminated regardless of yes/no answer (0–15 per item)
	Total Questions Asked	Number of questions to identify target; fewer = better; 21 if not identified after 20
	Total Weighted Achievement	Strategic efficiency with inverted U-curve: 4–5 questions = 5 points (optimal); 1–2 = 1 point (lucky guessing); 15–20 = 1 point (inefficient)
Process measures	Spatial Questions	Location-based questions (e.g., "Is it in the bottom row?"); may indicate anomia or language compensation
	Repeated Questions	Questions identifying same objects as previous; reflects feedback utilization failure or memory deficit
	Set-Loss Questions	Rule violations (either/or, compound, non-yes/no); reflects difficulty maintaining task set

COMMON ADMINISTRATION ERRORS

Several administration errors can compromise test validity. Awareness of these common pitfalls enables quality control and accurate interpretation.

Providing Unclear or Inconsistent Feedback

Examiners sometimes provide ambiguous responses, saying "kind of" or "sort of" rather than a clear "yes" or "no." The task requires binary feedback. If a question is genuinely unanswerable as yes/no (extremely rare), prompt the examinee to reformulate rather than providing qualified responses. Inconsistent feedback across similar questions confuses examinees and invalidates the test.

Inadequate Prompting for Vague or Unanswerable Questions

Refer to the Examiner's Manual for recommended responses to a variety of questions. For example, when examinees ask vague questions (e.g., "Is it big?" "Is it nice?"), examiners must prompt for specificity. Failure to do so and instead arbitrarily answering the vague question results in nonstandard administration. Always prompt: "Could you make your question more specific?" If you do not know the answer to the examiner's question, the Examiner's Manual suggests saying, "That's an excellent question. I'm not sure I know the answer. Try another question.

Revealing Strategy or Providing Hints

Examiners sometimes unconsciously give feedback beyond "yes" or "no," inadvertently teaching a strategy. Comments like "That's a good question" or "You might want to think about bigger groups" compromise standardization and provide executive function scaffolding that masks deficits. Similarly, facial expressions or tone of voice that suggest disappointment when examinees ask concrete questions provide unintended coaching.

Miscounting Questions

Because the test requires recording questions verbatim, counting errors can occur, particularly when prompts for reformulation or vague questions are involved. Remember: a vague question + clarification = 1 question; a rule-violation question + reformulated yes/no version = 1 question (but also 1 Set-Loss Question); unanswerable questions that get reformulated = only the reformulated version counts.

Neglecting to Record Questions Verbatim

Some examiners paraphrase or summarize questions rather than recording them word-for-word. Verbatim recording is essential for accurate scoring of Initial Abstraction (the exact wording determines how many objects are eliminated), Repeated Questions (must determine if questions are truly redundant), and overall quality of categorical reasoning. Without verbatim records, nuanced scoring becomes impossible.

Revealing the Target Object

If an examinee asks 20 questions without identifying the target, do not reveal the target object before proceeding to the next item. If an examinee fails to identify the target object after 20 questions but wants to know which one it is, say, "I can't tell you, but try to guess the next one. Stating that it is against the rules may reduce the examinee's frustration.

INTERPRETATION

Twenty Questions interpretation requires integrating quantitative scores with qualitative analysis of questioning patterns within a systematic framework that distinguishes foundational limitations from true executive dysfunction.

Using the Hierarchical Framework for Differential Diagnosis

The tier-based approach to interpreting Twenty Questions performance follows a systematic decision tree that rules out lower-tier limitations before attributing poor performance to executive dysfunction. This process is crucial because the test's demands span all four tiers, and deficits at any level can result in low scores for different reasons with different intervention implications.

Step 1: Rule Out Tier 1 Limitations

Begin by examining whether basic cognitive abilities compromise performance. Review naming and semantic knowledge—does the examinee recognize and name objects accurately? Children from homes with limited exposure to certain objects or individuals from different cultural backgrounds may not recognize or know names for some items, affecting categorical reasoning, not due to executive deficit, but limited semantic knowledge.

Visual perception deficits appear as difficulty identifying objects, confusion about which object is being discussed, or predominant use of spatial strategies. Sustained attention limitations manifest as forgetting the task goal, asking what they are supposed to be doing, or appearing confused about basic procedures. Severe memory deficits produce Repeated Questions after short delays without apparent awareness of repetition.

If Tier 1 limitations are present, scores will be globally depressed without evidence of any strategic sophistication across any items. Intervention should target the foundational skill rather than executive function training.

Step 2: Evaluate Tier 2 Bridging Processes

If Tier 1 appears intact, consider whether bridging processes support or limit executive performance. Can the examinee maintain the basic goal across questions and items? Do they understand simple logical relationships (that "not an animal" eliminates all animal subcategories)? Is basic working memory sufficient to remember general category information from one question to the next?

Tier 2 difficulties produce a pattern of understanding the task superficially but lacking the cognitive infrastructure for genuine strategic reasoning. Distinguishing Tier 2 from Tier 3 can be subtle. Examining performance on other tasks helps—do they demonstrate understanding of hierarchical relationships on the Sorting Test or verbal subtests? If so, the issue is more likely Tier 3 flexibility than Tier 2 logical reasoning.

Step 3: Analyze Tier 3 Cold Executive Patterns

Once foundational and bridging abilities are established as adequate, examine whether executive dysfunction reflects cold (cognitive) factors. Cold EF impairment manifests in consistently low Initial Abstraction scores across items, predominance of concrete or low-level categorical questions throughout, and difficulty with strategic sequencing regardless of emotional state. The critical diagnostic question: Does the examinee demonstrate capacity for categorical reasoning even if inconsistently? Pure cold EF deficits show consistently poor categorical reasoning regardless of emotional state or task context. The examinee lacks the cognitive architecture for abstract categorical thinking rather than possessing a capacity that becomes inaccessible under emotional load.

Step 4: Evaluate Tier 3 Hot Executive Factors

Behavioral observations reveal emotional regulation affecting executive performance. If initial questions on some items show moderate-to-high abstraction (scores of 7–15) but others show concrete thinking (scores of 0–3), consider whether emotional factors compromise cognitive capacity. Does abstraction deteriorate across items as frustration builds, or improve as the examinee becomes more comfortable? Variable abstraction suggests a hot EF impact. Hot EF compromise appears in the relationship between emotional state and cognitive performance. Observable frustration or anxiety corresponds with qualitative shifts toward more concrete, impulsive questioning. Performance that improves with encouragement or in lower-stakes moments indicates that executive capacity exists but becomes inaccessible under emotional dysregulation.

Step 5: Assess Tier 4 Integration and Metacognition

If the examinee demonstrates individual executive components (i.e., some categorical reasoning, some feedback incorporation, some flexibility) but overall performance remains inefficient, suspect Tier 4 integration deficits. A characteristic score pattern shows moderate Initial Abstraction scores (7–10) combined with elevated Total Questions Asked (15–18), suggesting the capacity for abstract thinking exists but cannot be sustained into an efficient strategy. Variability in Initial Abstraction across items without a clear improvement or deterioration pattern also suggests inconsistent deployment of available executive resources. These individuals can perform executive components in isolation but struggle to coordinate multiple processes simultaneously or sustain sophisticated strategies across extended problem-solving.

Tier 4 difficulties manifest in dissociations between metacognitive knowledge and control. An examinee might articulate understanding of an efficient strategy (e.g., "I should use big categories") while continuing to ask concrete questions. The integration deficit becomes evident when working memory and strategic reasoning demands are both high.

PERFORMANCE PATTERNS AND CLINICAL IMPLICATIONS

Several recognizable performance patterns emerge on the Twenty Questions Test, each with distinct clinical implications and tier-level associations.

Concrete, Stimulus-Bound Pattern

Examinees demonstrating this pattern consistently ask questions about salient perceptual features (e.g., colors, size) or single objects. Initial Abstraction scores are very low (0–5 across all items), with first questions like "Is it yellow?," "Is it big?," or "Is it the banana?" Total Questions Asked is high (often 15–20 per item), and Total Weighted Achievement is low. This pattern suggests significant executive dysfunction in abstract categorical reasoning.

Clinically, these individuals struggle with tasks requiring spontaneous organization of information into conceptual categories. In academic settings, they may have difficulty with reading comprehension questions requiring inference or synthesis, writing essays that organize information thematically, or understanding abstract concepts in math and science. They may perform adequately on rote learning tasks but fail when required to impose organizational structure on information. Vocationally, they may perform well on repetitive tasks but fail at adapting to changing requirements or outcomes. Medically, they may struggle with adapting to new medication strategies or treatment approaches.

This concrete pattern is common following frontal lobe injury, where damage to prefrontal regions disrupts the ability to organize information into abstract categories and employ strategic problem-solving approaches (Stuss & Levine, 2002). In developmental disorders affecting executive function, concrete thinking on Twenty Questions frequently appears in attention-deficit/hyperactive disorder (ADHD), where deficits in behavioral inhibition and executive control compromise abstract reasoning abilities (Willcutt et al., 2005), and in autism spectrum disorder without intellectual disability, where executive dysfunction manifests as difficulty with flexible categorical thinking despite intact basic cognitive abilities (Hill, 2004). In adulthood, this pattern is associated with damage caused by traumatic injuries, medical events with anoxia or ischemia, or underlying neurological diseases. Concrete, stimulus-bound patterns also characterize psychiatric conditions like schizophrenia, where prefrontal dysfunction disrupts higher-order categorical reasoning and strategic hypothesis generation (Goldberg & Weinberger, 1988).

Strategic Inconsistency Pattern

Some examinees show marked variability in abstraction level and efficiency across items. This inconsistency, combined with observable emotional fluctuation, suggests hot EF factors more than stable cognitive limitations. The capacity for strategic reasoning exists but is inconsistently accessed depending on emotional state, confidence, or motivation.

Real-world implications involve unpredictable performance in school and work settings. Teachers and employers may perceive the individual as capable but unmotivated, since they demonstrate competence inconsistently. This pattern may appear in anxiety disorders, ADHD with significant emotional dysregulation, mood disorders affecting executive function, and trauma-related conditions where emotional hyperarousal compromises cognitive control. Intervention focuses on emotional regulation strategies or anxiety management, and may require creating low-pressure environments while they learn new self-regulation skills.

Feedback Utilization Deficits

High rates of Repeated Questions with relatively preserved Initial Abstraction suggest specific difficulty in incorporating feedback and flexibly adjusting strategy. Real-world manifestations may include difficulty learning from mistakes, repeating ineffective approaches despite feedback, and trouble adjusting plans when circumstances change.

This pattern is characteristic of perseverative tendencies in frontal-subcortical dysfunction (Bonelli & Cummings, 2007), cognitive inflexibility in autism spectrum disorder (Leung & Zakzanis, 2014), or working memory limitations severe enough that previous questions are genuinely forgotten (D'Esposito & Postle, 2015). Distinguishing these mechanisms requires examining whether repetitions are verbatim and occur after short delays (memory deficit) versus semantic variations showing perseveration on themes (inflexibility).

Rule Violation Pattern

Frequent Set-Loss Questions (e.g., either/or, compound, or non-yes/no questions) despite reminders suggest difficulty maintaining task set or inhibiting inappropriate response formats. Clinically, this suggests problems with cognitive control and set maintenance that extend beyond this task. These individuals may have difficulty following multistep directions, adhering to specified formats in academic work, complying with procedural rules in work settings, or adapting their typical approach in response to feedback or changing circumstances.

Set-loss questions are common in severe ADHD, where impulsivity overrides format requirements (Mapou, 2009), in frontal lobe dysfunction characterized by set-loss tendencies (Delis et al., 2001), and in cases of working memory deficits so severe that task parameters are quickly forgotten (D'Esposito & Postle, 2015).

COMPARISON BETWEEN MEASURES

Initial Abstraction Versus Total Questions Asked

Comparing these measures reveals the relationship between strategic sophistication (abstraction) and efficiency (questions needed). When both are low (low abstraction, many questions), the interpretation is straightforward: poor categorical reasoning produces inefficient performance.

When abstraction is low but questions asked are also low (lucky guessing), the examinee identified the target quickly through concrete guessing rather than systematic reasoning. The Total Weighted Achievement score correctly identifies this as poor performance despite superficially efficient questioning.

When abstraction is moderate-to-high but many questions are still needed, consider working memory or flexibility deficits. The examinee can generate abstract questions but cannot effectively maintain information about eliminated categories or flexibly adjust based on feedback.

Initial Abstraction Across Items

Examining performance patterns across the four trials reveals consistency of strategic approach or learning. Progressive improvement in Initial Abstraction (trial 1 = 5, trial 2 = 8, trial 3 = 12, trial 4 = 15) accompanied by decreasing Total Questions Asked (trial 1 = 18, trial 2 = 14, trial 3 = 9, trial 4 = 5) suggests good metacognitive learning and strategic adjustment—the examinee recognizes more efficient approaches and successfully applies them.

Progressive deterioration in Initial Abstraction (trial 1 = 12, trial 2 = 10, trial 3 = 5, trial 4 = 3) with increasing Total Questions Asked suggests fatigue, frustration, or attention problems increasingly compromising strategic reasoning. High variability in both Initial Abstraction (8, 3, 15, 5) and Total Questions Asked, without a clear directional pattern, suggests inconsistent deployment of strategic resources. This variability may reflect Hot EF factors (emotional state fluctuations affecting cognitive access) or Tier 3 Cold EF difficulties (unreliable access to categorical reasoning strategies). Distinguishing these requires examining whether variability corresponds with observable emotional changes or occurs independently of affective state.

Optional Measures as Additional Diagnostic Information

Repeated Questions in the context of otherwise good performance (high abstraction, relatively few total questions) suggest specific feedback utilization difficulty rather than global executive dysfunction. In contrast, Repeated Questions combined with poor abstraction and many questions reflect pervasive executive impairment.

Set-Loss Questions occurring predominantly later in items suggest cognitive control deteriorating under working memory load and fatigue. Set-Loss Questions from the beginning suggest a more fundamental difficulty in understanding or maintaining task requirements.

Rapid Reference 12.4

Distinguishing Tier-Level Deficits

Tier Level	Indicators	Clinical Implications
Tier 1 deficit	Consistent object misidentification; attention lapses; language comprehension issues; spatial strategy predominance (pointing without naming); global difficulty throughout	Language remediation, vision correction, attention support; Spatial Questions may indicate anomia rather than executive dysfunction
Tier 2 deficit	Understands task but lacks fluency; needs frequent goal reminders; difficulty with logical inference (eliminating subordinates); poor working memory for general eliminations; minimal learning across items	Bridging skill development; procedural learning support; may benefit from explicit instruction on elimination logic
Tier 3 cold deficit	Low Initial Abstraction (0–3); concrete first questions; poor feedback utilization; high Repeated Questions; Set-Loss Questions; elevated Total Questions Asked (15–20); low Weighted Achievement	Categorical reasoning training; strategic thinking intervention; may show dissociation from recognition-based tasks
Tier 3 hot deficit	Moderate initial abstraction that deteriorates; performance collapse with frustration; variable across items based on affect; observable emotional reactivity; erratic response times	Emotional regulation intervention; anxiety management; low-pressure practice; adequate categorical capacity when calm
Tier 4 deficit	Adequate individual components but inefficient integration; knows strategy but can't sustain it; poor working memory-strategy coordination; absent strategic learning despite metacognitive awareness	Metacognitive training; strategy consolidation; integration practice; performance worse than components predict

ECOLOGICAL VALIDITY AND FUNCTIONAL IMPLICATIONS

Twenty Questions performance relates directly to real-world demands for categorical reasoning, strategic information-gathering, and hypothesis testing across academic, vocational, and social contexts.

Academic Functioning

Categorical reasoning parallels academic demands across subjects. In reading comprehension, students must identify main ideas (superordinate categories) versus supporting details, organize textual information into themes, and make inferences by recognizing relationships among ideas. Examinees with low Initial Abstraction scores may struggle with "main idea" questions, inference, and analysis requiring synthesis.

Essay writing demands hierarchical organization similar to categorical reasoning. The thesis represents the highest abstraction level, topic sentences represent mid-level categories, and supporting details represent lower-level specifics. Students with concrete thinking write lists of details without organizing them thematically. Math and science learning increasingly require abstract conceptual understanding—recognizing that specific problems exemplify broader principles, understanding hierarchical classification systems, and recognizing patterns across phenomena.

Strategic hypothesis testing parallels scientific reasoning and problem-solving. Students must generate hypotheses, test systematically, incorporate feedback, and adjust approaches based on results. Those with poor feedback utilization struggle with trial-and-error learning.

Vocational and Daily Living

Problem-solving in work contexts requires strategic information-seeking and revision. When troubleshooting, individuals must ask strategic questions to narrow possibilities systematically. Concrete thinkers might randomly check components without systematic reasoning. Planning and organization rely on hierarchical thinking, breaking complex projects into phases, tasks, and action steps. Information management requires organizing data into meaningful categories for efficient order and retrieval.

Conversational discourse requires staying on topic at appropriate abstraction levels. Effective communicators adjust abstraction to conversational goals—providing overviews, narrowing to specifics, and returning to broader themes. Examinees with concrete thinking often get lost in irrelevant details, unable to articulate main points. Social problem-solving parallels hypothesis-testing demands, gathering information about others' perspectives, generating and testing solutions, adjusting approaches based on feedback.

Decision-making requires weighing options at various abstraction levels. Choosing a restaurant involves considering broad categories (e.g., cuisine type, price range, distance) before narrowing to specific options. Financial management requires hierarchical planning, such as distinguishing needs from wants, organizing spending into budget categories, tracking specific expenses, and revising the plan when indicated. Medical self-management involves organizing symptoms and behaviors into meaningful patterns for provider communication, tracking the outcomes over time, and adapting to changes when they occur.

Social Functioning

Social interactions require many of the same cognitive processes assessed by Twenty Questions. Effective conversation involves strategic information-gathering—asking questions to understand others' perspectives, experiences, and needs. Individuals with concrete thinking may ask overly specific or tangential questions that fail to build understanding, while those with strong categorical reasoning ask questions that efficiently clarify others' viewpoints. Dating, networking, and building professional relationships all require hypothesis testing about others' interests, intentions, and compatibility.

Feedback utilization is essential for social success. Effective communicators adjust their approach based on others' verbal and nonverbal responses. They recognize when a topic is unwelcome, when more explanation is needed, or when the conversation should shift direction. Individuals who struggle with feedback utilization on Twenty Questions may similarly fail to incorporate social feedback, persisting with conversation topics or approaches despite signals that adjustment is needed.

Abstract categorical reasoning supports understanding of social hierarchies, group dynamics, and relational categories. Navigating workplace politics, family systems, or community organizations requires recognizing how individuals cluster into groups with shared interests, allegiances, or perspectives. Concrete thinkers may miss these larger patterns, focusing on individual interactions without recognizing broader social structures.

Social problem-solving parallels the hypothesis-testing demands of Twenty Questions, gathering information about interpersonal conflicts, generating possible solutions, testing approaches, and adjusting based on outcomes. Individuals with poor strategic reasoning may attempt random solutions without systematic analysis, while those with feedback utilization deficits may repeat ineffective approaches despite evidence that they are not working.

STRENGTHS AND WEAKNESSES

The Twenty Questions Test offers several distinctive strengths for executive function assessment, alongside limitations that clinicians should consider when selecting measures and interpreting results.

Strengths

The Twenty Questions Test has several notable advantages for assessing categorical reasoning and strategic thinking within a comprehensive executive function evaluation.

Explicit Quantification of Abstraction Level

The Initial Abstraction score represents a unique contribution to executive function assessment. Unlike most problem-solving measures that only assess global success or efficiency, Twenty Questions separately quantifies the level of abstract thinking employed. This allows clinicians to distinguish lucky guessing from genuine strategic reasoning, concrete thinking from abstract reasoning, and to track changes in abstraction level across the course of intervention or recovery.

Rich Qualitative Data on Strategic Reasoning

The verbatim recording of questions provides extensive qualitative data about the examinee's problem-solving approach, thought processes, and strategic evolution across items. Clinicians can identify specific patterns: Does the examinee begin abstractly but become concrete as frustration builds? Do they improve across items, suggesting learning? Are Repeated Questions verbatim (memory deficit) or semantic variations (inflexibility)? This information guides differential diagnosis and intervention planning.

Assessment of Feedback Utilization

Few executive function tests explicitly assess the ability to incorporate feedback and adjust strategy accordingly. The repeated questions error measure directly quantifies feedback utilization within items—examinees with low error rates successfully incorporate the examiner's yes/no responses to avoid asking redundant questions. Improvement in Initial Abstraction and reduction in Total Questions Asked across the four items may also reflect strategic learning from experience. Combined with qualitative observation of whether examinees flexibly adjust questions based on answers received, the test provides valuable information about a cognitive process essential for learning, adaptive behavior, and success.

Hierarchically Structured Stimulus Array

The carefully designed categorical hierarchy of the 30 objects allows for a nuanced assessment of abstraction at multiple levels. An examinee might recognize mid-level categories (e.g., animals, plants, vehicles) while missing the higher-level living/nonliving distinction, revealing partial executive capacity. The multiple category levels create a sensitive range of measurement from highly concrete to highly abstract thinking.

Separate Forms for Retesting

The availability of Standard and Alternate Forms with different target objects allows for meaningful retesting to assess change over time or intervention effects. This is valuable in rehabilitation settings, treatment monitoring, and situations where repeated evaluation is necessary.

Game-Like Structure

The structure of Twenty Questions is similar to childhood games like I Spy which can increase motivation. In addition, most assessments ask the examinee questions. Flipping that norm and allowing the examinee to ask the questions can bring a welcome change of pace and increase engagement. The game-like structure of Twenty Questions can also allow anxious or low motivation examinees to become comfortable with the testing process.

Weaknesses and Limitations

Despite its strengths, the Twenty Questions Test has several limitations that clinicians should consider when selecting measures and interpreting results.

Significant Verbal and Language Demands

The test's heavy reliance on verbal abilities limits its utility for examinees with language disorders, bilingual or multilingual examinees whose primary language is not English, or individuals from culturally diverse backgrounds. Poor performance may reflect limited vocabulary, unfamiliarity with object names, or difficulty formulating grammatically complex yes/no questions rather than genuine executive dysfunction. Unlike nonverbal executive measures (e.g., Tower, Design Fluency), Twenty Questions cannot separate language from executive processes.

The assumed categorical structure reflects English semantic organization and Western cultural categories. The grouping of vehicles under "transportation" or distinguishing "kitchen items" as a meaningful category may not be equally salient or automatic across linguistic and cultural backgrounds. This cultural loading limits the test's validity as a pure measure of executive function in diverse populations.

Potential for Lucky Guessing
Despite the weighted achievement scoring system designed to address this issue, examinees can still fortuitously identify targets with concrete initial questions, particularly on the first item. While the Initial Abstraction score captures this distinction, the Total Questions Asked score can be misleadingly favorable.

Statistically, with four trials and 30 objects, random guessing could identify at least one target with a few questions purely by chance. The weighted achievement system partially mitigates this, but the potential for chance success still limits the measure's precision, particularly in brief administrations.

Limited Assessment of Planning Depth
Unlike the Tower Test, which explicitly assesses multistep planning ahead, Twenty Questions does not reveal how many steps ahead the examinee is thinking. The measure captures strategic reasoning retrospectively through the pattern of questions asked, but does not assess metacognitive planning processes explicitly.

Susceptibility to Emotional Factors
While this might be viewed as ecological validity (real-world executive function operates under emotional demands), it also represents a psychometric limitation. Performance variability due to anxiety, frustration, or mood states can obscure the examinee's actual categorical reasoning capacity. Unlike measures with less emotionally evocative demands or shorter duration, Twenty Questions' extended nature and mounting pressure as questions accumulate create hot EF demands that confound cold EF measurement.

An examinee may have intact categorical reasoning abilities that are inaccessible during formal testing due to performance anxiety, but would be evident in low-stakes contexts. The test does not include any conditions that separate cold versus hot demands, making interpretation complicated when emotional factors are prominent.

Working Memory Confound
As items progress and more categories are eliminated, working memory demands increase substantially. Poor performance might reflect working memory limitations rather than strategic reasoning deficits. An examinee with excellent categorical reasoning but limited working memory might formulate good early questions but struggle to maintain the complex mental model needed for later, efficient questioning. The test does not separate these components, and the manual provides limited guidance for disentangling working memory from executive reasoning.

Age Range Limitations
While normed from age 8, many 8–10-year-old children have not yet developed robust categorical reasoning as a stable cognitive capacity. Concrete thinking is developmentally normal in this age range. The test may have limited sensitivity for discriminating executive dysfunction from developmental immaturity in younger school-age children. Floor effects may occur in younger children or individuals with intellectual disabilities.

Conversely, ceiling effects may occur in highly verbal, cognitively sophisticated examinees who quickly employ an optimal strategy across all items. The test's four-trial structure provides a limited measurement range at the upper end, potentially missing subtle executive dysfunction in very high-functioning individuals.

ALTERNATIVE MEASURES

Comprehensive assessment of categorical reasoning and hypothesis testing often benefits from complementary measures that clarify Twenty Questions findings.

Within the D-KEFS Suite

Several D-KEFS subtests provide complementary or converging evidence for categorical reasoning and hypothesis testing.

Sorting Test
Sorting provides an alternative assessment of categorical reasoning with important methodological differences. Free Sorting requires physical card sorting with explicit categorization; Sort Recognition provides categories for identification. Twenty Questions requires spontaneous generation and application in a hypothesis-testing frame-

work. Comparing performance clarifies whether categorical reasoning deficits are absolute (poor on both) or context-dependent—some perform adequately with manipulable materials but poorly on abstract, sequential Twenty Questions.

Word Context Test

This subtest requires deducing word meanings from context clues, involving hypothesis generation and testing, similar to Twenty Questions but with more structured support. Comparing performance distinguishes verbal reasoning capacity from strategic hypothesis testing.

Proverb Test

Proverbs assess verbal abstraction through proverb interpretation, requiring movement from concrete literal to abstract metaphorical thinking, similar to Twenty Questions' demand for abstract categorical reasoning.

Verbal Fluency Test (Original and Advanced)

Category Fluency assesses categorical organization of semantic knowledge. Comparing performance across tests clarifies the nature of categorical reasoning difficulties: examinees demonstrating semantic category knowledge on Verbal Fluency but unable to apply categorical reasoning strategically on Twenty Questions have knowledge not functionally deployed in problem-solving contexts. Conversely, better performance on Twenty Questions (with visual array) than Verbal Fluency (purely verbal) may suggest reliance on external visual cues rather than internal semantic organization. Category Switching assesses cognitive flexibility in shifting between categories, parallel to Twenty Questions flexibility demands.

Trail Making Test (Original and Advanced)

While primarily assessing cognitive flexibility through number-letter switching, Trail Making also requires maintaining task set. The Advanced version adds distraction and working memory conditions. Comparing with Twenty Questions distinguishes visual-motor executive demands from verbal-conceptual demands.

Tower Test (Original and Advanced)

Planning measures requiring multistep sequential planning involve hypothesis generation about move sequences and strategic reasoning. However, planning emphasizes forward planning (anticipating consequences) while Twenty Questions emphasizes categorical organization and feedback-based adjustment. Comparing performance clarifies whether strategic reasoning difficulties are specific to particular executive components.

Beyond D-KEFS

Measures outside the D-KEFS family can provide converging evidence or assess related constructs when additional information is needed.

Nonverbal Abstract Reasoning Measures

Tests such as Raven's Progressive Matrices (Raven et al., 2018) assess nonverbal abstract pattern recognition without verbal demands. Adequate performance on nonverbal abstract reasoning measures, combined with poor Twenty Questions performance, demonstrates that abstract reasoning capacity exists but is compromised when language demands are high.

Set-Shifting and Feedback Utilization Measures

The Wisconsin Card Sorting Test (WCST; Heaton et al., 1993) assesses abstract reasoning, set-shifting, and feedback utilization through nonverbal card sorting. WCST perseverative errors parallel Twenty Questions Repeated Questions—both reflect difficulty incorporating feedback. Comparing performance determines whether feedback utilization deficits are pervasive or modality-specific. Similarly, the Category Test from the Halstead-Reitan battery (Reitan & Halstead 1993) requires abstracting organizing principles from feedback, paralleling Twenty Questions hypothesis-testing demands, but uses visual–spatial rather than verbal–semantic categories. Comparing performance across these measures clarifies whether categorical reasoning difficulties are modality-specific or general.

Verbal Learning Measures with Semantic Organization

Process scores for semantic clustering on tests such as the California Verbal Learning Tests (CVLT-3, Delis et al., 2017) assess whether examinees recognize and utilize categorical relationships in word lists. Examinees demonstrating semantic clustering on verbal learning measures but poor categorical reasoning on Twenty Questions have implicit categorical knowledge that they cannot explicitly and strategically deploy in problem-solving. Conversely, better performance on Twenty Questions than on verbal learning clustering measures may suggest reliance on external visual cues to support categorical organization.

Behavior Rating Scales

Executive function rating scales capture real-world executive behaviors that may or may not align with performance-based measures. For children and adolescents, the Behavior Rating Inventory of Executive Function, Second Edition (BRIEF-2; Gioia et al., 2015), Comprehensive Executive Function Inventory (CEFI; Naglieri & Goldstein, 2013), and Delis Rating of Executive Functions (D-REF; Delis, 2012) provide parent and teacher perspectives on daily executive functioning. For adults, the BRIEF-A (Roth et al., 2005), CEFI Adult (Naglieri & Goldstein, 2017), and D-REF Adult (Delis, 2021) offer self-report and informant-report options. Relevant scales across these measures include Plan/Organize (paralleling strategic reasoning demands), Working Memory (tracking eliminated categories), Shift (cognitive flexibility in adjusting strategy), and Initiate (spontaneous hypothesis generation). Discrepancies between Twenty Questions performance and rating scale elevations provide diagnostic information: adequate test performance with elevated rating scales may indicate that the structured, low-stakes testing environment does not capture executive challenges that emerge in complex, emotionally meaningful daily situations. Conversely, poor Twenty Questions performance with unremarkable rating scales might suggest test-specific factors such as verbal demands or performance anxiety rather than pervasive executive dysfunction.

SUMMARY

The D-KEFS Twenty Questions Test provides a sophisticated assessment of verbal abstract reasoning, hypothesis testing, and strategic problem-solving through identifying an unknown object by asking yes/no questions. The test's unique contribution lies in explicitly quantifying the abstraction level separate from efficiency, allowing clinicians to distinguish genuine strategic reasoning from fortunate guessing.

The hierarchical tier framework reveals that successful performance requires intact foundational abilities (Tier 1: object recognition, naming, attention), bridging processes (Tier 2: simple logical reasoning, goal maintenance), core executive functions (Tier 3: abstract categorical reasoning, hypothesis and conceptual idea generation, strategic hypothesis testing, cognitive flexibility, feedback utilization), and higher-order integration (Tier 4: metacognitive monitoring, strategic learning). Poor performance may reflect deficits at any level, making systematic tier-based differential diagnosis essential.

Primary measures—Initial Abstraction score, Total Questions Asked, and Total Weighted Achievement score—provide complementary perspectives on categorical reasoning and strategic efficiency. Optional process measures quantify approach (spatial versus verbal strategies) and errors (Repeated Questions, Set-Loss Questions) that inform understanding of underlying mechanisms.

Major strengths include explicit abstraction quantification, rich qualitative data about strategic reasoning, assessment of feedback utilization, game-like format, and a carefully designed hierarchical stimulus array. However, significant weaknesses include heavy verbal-language demands, potential for lucky guessing despite weighted scoring, limited planning depth assessment, and susceptibility to emotional factors that may obscure cognitive capacity.

Clinical interpretation requires systematic differential diagnosis, ruling out foundational limitations before attributing poor performance to executive dysfunction, distinguishing cold EF from hot EF contributions, and recognizing that the test's verbal-abstract demands represent only one aspect of executive functioning. Ecological validity is substantial for academic contexts requiring hierarchical organization, essay writing, hypothesis-testing, vocational troubleshooting, planning, and social communication, requiring appropriate abstraction levels.

TEST YOURSELF

1. A 9-year-old begins Twenty Questions by asking, "Is it yellow?" What does this reveal about their approach?

(a) Optimal strategic reasoning.

(b) Concrete, stimulus-bound thinking.

(c) Advanced metacognitive awareness.

(d) Strong feedback utilization skills.

2. An examinee asks, "Is it an animal?" (receives "no"); then later asks, "Does it have four legs?" This error pattern most likely indicates:

(a) Tier 1 visual perception deficit.

(b) Tier 2 logical reasoning limitation.

(c) Tier 3 poor feedback utilization and cognitive inflexibility.

(d) Tier 4 metacognitive monitoring strength.

3. The Initial Abstraction score specifically measures:

(a) Total efficiency in identifying the target.

(b) The minimum number of objects eliminated by the first question, regardless of answer.

(c) How many questions were repeated across items.

(d) Whether the examinee used spatial versus verbal strategies.

4. True or False: An examinee who identifies the target in 2 questions using concrete guessing would receive a higher Total Weighted Achievement score than one who identifies it in 5 questions using a systematic categorical strategy.

5. A high school student demonstrates adequate categorical reasoning on the Sorting Test but very poor performance on Twenty Questions with mounting frustration and increasingly concrete questions. This pattern suggests:

(a) Tier 1 language comprehension deficit.

(b) Tier 2 procedural learning impairment.

(c) Tier 3 Hot EF compromise rather than Cold EF deficit.

(d) Tier 4 superior integration abilities.

6. Set-Loss Questions on Twenty Questions most directly assess:

(a) Abstract categorical reasoning ability.

(b) Hypothesis testing and strategic planning.

(c) Ability to maintain task set and inhibit inappropriate response formats.

(d) Working memory for eliminated categories.

7. An examinee asks, "Is it living?" (eliminates 15 objects regardless of answer) as their first question. Their Initial Abstraction score for this item would be:

(a) 0

(b) 3

(c) 8

(d) 15

8. Which of the following represents the primary Cold EF construct measured by Twenty Questions?

(a) Processing speed.

(b) Abstract categorical reasoning.

(c) Visual-spatial perception.

(d) Expressive language.

9. Spatial Questions on Twenty Questions (e.g., "Is it in the bottom row?") occurred in approximately what percentage of the normative sample?

(a) 2.7%

(b) 5.8%

(c) 9.3%

(d) 15.4%

10. When comparing the three primary scores (Initial Abstraction, Total Questions Asked, Total Weighted Achievement), divergence between them is MOST clinically useful for:

(a) Calculating IQ scores.

(b) Distinguishing lucky guessing from genuine strategic reasoning.

(c) Measuring processing speed.

(d) Assessing visual perception.

Answer Key: 1-b, 2-c, 3-b, 4-false, 5-c, 6-c, 7-d, 8-b, 9-a, 10-b

REFERENCES

Bonelli, R. M., & Cummings, J. L. (2007). Frontal-subcortical circuitry and behavior. *Dialogues in Clinical Neuroscience, 9*(2), 141–151.

Delis, D. C. (2012). *Delis Rating of Executive Function (D-REF).* Pearson.

Delis, D. C. (2021). *Delis Rating of Executive Functions, Adult (D-REF Adult).* Pearson.

Delis, D. C., Kaplan, E., & Kramer, J. H. (2001). *Delis-Kaplan Executive Function System (D-KEFS).* The Psychological Corporation.

Delis, D. C., Kramer, J. H., Kaplan, E., & Ober, B. A. (2017). *California Verbal Learning Test–Third Edition (CVLT-3).* Pearson.

D'Esposito, M., & Postle, B. R. (2015). The cognitive neuroscience of working memory. *Annual Review of Psychology, 66,* 115–142.

Gioia, G. A., Isquith, P. K., Guy, S. C., & Kenworthy, L. (2015). *Behavior Rating Inventory of Executive Function* (second ed.). Psychological Assessment Resources.

Goldberg, T. E., & Weinberger, D. R. (1988). Probing prefrontal function in schizophrenia with neuropsychological paradigms. *Schizophrenia Bulletin, 14*(2), 179–183.

Heaton, R. K., Chelune, G. J., Talley, J. L., Kay, G. G., & Curtiss, G. (1993). *Wisconsin Card Sorting Test Manual: Revised and Expanded.* Psychological Assessment Resources.

Hill, E. L. (2004). Executive dysfunction in autism. *Trends in Cognitive Sciences, 8*(1), 26–32.

Leung, R. C., & Zakzanis, K. K. (2014). Brief report: Cognitive flexibility in autism spectrum disorders: A quantitative review. *Journal of Autism and Developmental Disorders, 44*(10), 2628–2645.

Mapou, R. L. (2009). *Adult Learning Disabilities and ADHD: Research-Informed Assessment.* Oxford University Press.

Naglieri, J. A., & Goldstein, S. (2013). *Comprehensive Executive Function Inventory (CEFI).* Multi-Health Systems.

Naglieri, J. A., & Goldstein, S. (2017). *Comprehensive Executive Function Inventory Adult (CEFI Adult).* Multi-Health Systems.

Raven, J., Rust, J., Chan, F., & Zhou, X. (2018). *Raven's 2 Progressive Matrices.* Pearson: *Clinical Edition.*

Reitan, R. M., & Wolfson, D. (1993). *The Halstead-Reitan Neuropsychological Test Battery: Theory and Clinical Interpretation* (second ed.). Neuropsychology Press.

Roth, R. M., Isquith, P. K., & Gioia, G. A. (2005). *BRIEF-A: Behavior Rating Inventory of Executive Function—Adult Version.* Psychological Assessment Resources.

Stuss, D. T., & Levine, B. (2002). Adult clinical neuropsychology: Lessons from studies of the frontal lobes. *Annual Review of Psychology, 53,* 401–433.

Willcutt, E. G., Doyle, A. E., Nigg, J. T., Faraone, S. V., & Pennington, B. F. (2005). Validity of the executive function theory of attention-deficit/hyperactivity disorder: A meta-analytic review. *Biological Psychiatry, 57*(11), 1336–1346.

Thirteen

VERBAL FLUENCY TEST

CLINICAL VIGNETTE

Fifty-five-year-old Patricia Anderson was referred for neuropsychological evaluation following concerns about word-finding difficulties during impromptu speaking at work. A former college professor now in academic administration, Patricia reported difficulty when called on unexpectedly in meetings or when speaking without preparation, stating, "I know what I want to say, but finding the right words takes longer than it used to." She noted particular difficulty with spontaneous verbal responses when "put on the spot," though her prepared presentations and written communication remained strong. She denied difficulties with reading, language comprehension, or planned speaking engagements.

On the original Verbal Fluency Test, Patricia's Letter Fluency (F, A, S) was impaired (scaled score = 6). She showed delayed initiation, taking 4–6 seconds to produce her first word on each trial, then generated words slowly and inconsistently with long pauses between words. She generated no discernible phonemic clusters and showed no systematic search strategy. She made no rule violations or repetitions (Tier 2 intact). Category Fluency (Animals, Boys' Names) showed relative preservation (scaled score = 9) despite also showing delayed initiation (3–5 seconds before first word). Once initiated, she demonstrated steady production throughout trials with clear semantic clustering evident (farm animals, then pets, then wild animals), suggesting that organized, topic-based retrieval remained relatively intact despite slower overall word access. Category Switching (Furniture/Fruits) was mildly impaired (scaled score = 7), consistent with her overall executive profile but not as severely impaired as Letter Fluency.

On other measures, Patricia's WAIS-5 Vocabulary (Wechsler, 2024) was high average (scaled score = 13), and Boston Naming Test-2 (BNT-2; Kaplan et al., 2001) performance was intact (T-score = 58), confirming strong semantic knowledge appropriate for her educational background. Processing speed measures were average. Her metacognitive awareness was excellent—she accurately recognized that words were "not coming as quickly" across all the fluency tasks and expressed frustration about the delays, particularly noting that even on the animal naming task, she felt slower than she "used to be," despite ultimately generating a reasonable number of words.

The hierarchical analysis indicated Tier 3 cold executive deficits affecting rapid word access and initiation under time pressure, with particular impairment in strategic phonemic retrieval. While both Letter and Category Fluency showed delayed initiation, the disproportionate Letter Fluency impairment (SS = 6) compared to Category Fluency (SS = 9), combined with strong vocabulary/naming performance, distinguished her difficulties from semantic variant primary progressive aphasia (svPPA), where both vocabulary and Category Fluency would be impaired due to semantic knowledge loss. This distinction carries treatment implications: unlike other PPA variants that may respond to cholinesterase inhibitors, svPPA does not. Patricia's pattern explained her functional difficulties: impromptu speaking without preparation was most challenging (requiring rapid, unstructured verbal retrieval), while prepared presentations allowed her to organize thoughts in advance (leveraging her relatively stronger semantic organizational abilities). Follow-up at six months showed stable performance with improved comfort in meetings using strategic preparation techniques (such as preparing key talking points organized by topic in advance, requesting brief moments to gather thoughts before responding, and avoiding situations requiring completely spontaneous verbal generation).

TEST DESCRIPTION

The Verbal Fluency Test assesses the capacity to generate words rapidly under specified constraints, measuring executive control over language production. The test is available in both original D-KEFS format (ages 8–89) and D-KEFS Advanced (VFT) format (ages 8–90), with both versions containing three primary conditions that progressively increase executive demands.

Original Version Structure

The original D-KEFS Verbal Fluency Test includes Letter Fluency (generating words beginning with F, A, and S, each for 60 seconds), Category Fluency (generating Animals and Boys' Names, each for 60 seconds), and Category Switching (alternating between Furniture and Fruits for 60 seconds). Standard and Alternate Forms provide equivalent versions for retesting situations. The Alternate Form substitutes B, H, R for Letter Fluency; Clothing and Girls' Names for Category Fluency; and Vegetables and Musical Instruments for Category Switching.

Advanced Version Structure

The D-KEFS Advanced VFT maintains the Letter Fluency and Category Fluency conditions with modifications: Letter Fluency uses F, A, and S; Category Fluency combines Fruits and Vegetables into a single category (eliminating scoring ambiguity) and also uses Animals. The Switching Fluency condition represents a substantial advancement over the original. Rather than switching between two semantic categories, examinees aged 8–13 and 70–90 switch between phonemic and semantic rules—alternating between Items of Musical Instruments and words beginning with R for one trial and the category Items of Clothing and words beginning with the letter L for the second trial. This phonemic-semantic switching increases cognitive demands significantly compared to semantic-semantic switching. Examinees ages 14–69 complete the same first trial (Musical Instruments and R words) and a three-rule, second trial alternating between L words, Items of Clothing, and B words, substantially increasing working memory and cognitive flexibility demands.

Administration time ranges from 5–10 minutes for the original version to 8–12 minutes for the Advanced version. Both versions use a verbal response format. The original is available in paper-and-pencil and on Q-interactive, which offers digital recording and automated scoring. The Advanced version is available on Q-interactive. Verbal Fluency includes a variety of scaled scores that consider the fluency and accuracy of words produced, competency when switching, and error profiles.

Verbal Fluency demonstrates robust ecological validity. Word generation under constraints mirrors real-world demands, including brainstorming sessions, impromptu speaking, naming items from categories during shopping or planning, and conversational fluency when vocabulary retrieval is challenged. Research demonstrates that Verbal Fluency performance predicts functional communication abilities, vocational success in language-dependent occupations, and academic performance requiring rapid information retrieval (Delis et al., 2001).

> **CAUTION**
>
> Verbal fluency performance varies significantly with education, occupational language exposure, bilingualism, and cultural background. These factors affect both baseline word knowledge (Tier 1) and executive retrieval strategies (Tier 3). An examinee with limited educational opportunities may produce fewer words, not due to executive dysfunction, but due to reduced vocabulary breadth. Similarly, bilingual individuals may access words from multiple languages, requiring careful scoring decisions. Cultural factors influence category knowledge; not all cultures organize semantic categories identically. Always interpret Verbal Fluency scores within the context of the examinee's educational, linguistic, and cultural background.

Rapid Reference 13.1

Verbal Fluency Test Overview

Feature	Original D-KEFS	Advanced (VFT)
Age range	8–89 years	8–90 years
Administration format	Paper-pencil	Digital (Q-interactive)
Letter fluency	F, A, S (60 seconds each)	F, A, S (60 seconds each)
Category fluency	Animals, boys' names (60 seconds each)	Animals; fruits and vegetables combined (60 seconds each)
Switching condition	Category switching: furniture/fruits alternation	Switching fluency: phonemic-semantic alternation (e.g., musical instruments/ R words); ages 14–69 add three-rule trial (L words–clothing–B words)
Primary constructs	Tier 3 cold EF (strategic retrieval, cognitive flexibility, inhibition); Tier 2 (processing speed, working memory)	

CHOOSING BETWEEN ORIGINAL AND ADVANCED VERSIONS

Version selection depends on examinee characteristics, assessment goals, and clinical context. Each version offers distinct advantages for specific situations.

When the Original Version Is Preferred

Comparative Analysis with Existing Data
When an examinee has previous testing using the original version, maintaining consistency enables direct comparison of performance trajectory. Research continuity also favors the original version, given its extensive validation literature spanning over two decades.

Minimizing Cognitive Load
For examinees with known moderate-to-severe executive deficits, the original version's semantic-semantic switching is less demanding than the Advanced version's phonemic-semantic switching, potentially preventing floor effects while still assessing switching capacity.

Access to Alternate Forms is Desired
The original D-KEFS Verbal Fluency Test includes alternate forms (Standard Form: F-A-S, Animals, Boys' Names, Fruits/Furniture; Alternate Form: B-H-R, Clothing, Girls' Names, Vegetables/Musical Instruments), providing options for repeat testing when practice effects are a concern. However, the need for alternate forms in verbal fluency may be less critical than for other cognitive measures. Test–retest studies of the D-KEFS Advanced found no practice effects for Category Fluency and only minimal practice effects (approximately 1/6 SD) for Letter Fluency and Switching Fluency (Delis & Kaplan, 2025), indicating that the test yields highly similar group means when used in repeat examinations. Nevertheless, when retesting is required—particularly for individual cases where even minimal practice effects could influence clinical decision-making—the availability of alternate forms in the original version provides additional flexibility not currently available in the Advanced version.

When the Advanced Version Is Preferred

Maximizing Executive Sensitivity

For high-functioning individuals, subtle executive deficits, or cases where ceiling effects are suspected, the Advanced version's more demanding switching conditions provide superior differentiation. The phonemic-semantic switch and three-rule switching trial increase executive load substantially.

Contemporary Norms

The Advanced version's 2020s normative data better represent current populations.

Clear and Contemporary Categories

The Advanced version addresses scoring ambiguities present in the original version by refining semantic categories. The original D-KEFS used separate Fruits and Vegetables categories on different trials, creating scoring challenges when items could plausibly belong to either category (e.g., avocados and tomatoes are botanically fruits but commonly categorized as vegetables). The Advanced version combines Fruits and Vegetables into a single category on one trial, eliminating these classification dilemmas (Delis & Kaplan, 2025). Additionally, the Advanced version replaces Boys' Names and Girls' Names with more straightforward semantic categories. Studies found that first names elicited variable retrieval approaches. Some individuals generated names of known persons (semantic), others worked through the alphabet systematically (phonemic), while others combined both methods (Koren et al., 2005, as cited in Delis & Kaplan, 2025). These inconsistent strategies complicated interpretation of what cognitive processes were being assessed. Furthermore, evolving naming conventions make gender-based name categorization increasingly unreliable for scoring purposes. The Advanced version's semantic categories (Animals, Fruits and Vegetables, Musical Instruments, Items of Clothing) offer clearer scoring guidelines and minimize examiner judgment during administration and scoring.

Research with Multilevel Switching

When assessment specifically targets cognitive flexibility across different rule types or working memory capacity under switching demands, the Advanced version's three-rule switching trial provides unique data unavailable in the original version.

When Either Version Works Equally Well

Choosing the Q-interactive platform for either version captures exact timing, error types, and patterns with greater accuracy than manual recording, eliminating transcription errors and enabling fine-grained analysis of temporal patterns.

For neurotypical adults ages 14–69 without suspected executive deficits, either version provides a valid fluency assessment. For follow-up evaluations where cross-version comparison is acceptable (recognizing scores aren't directly comparable numerically), either version works, provided interpretation accounts for version differences.

Patricia Anderson's case illustrates version selection considerations. At age 55 with executive concerns affecting rapid word access and high premorbid functioning, the Advanced version would have offered several advantages: its phonemic-semantic switching paradigm (rather than the original's semantic-semantic switching) would have provided more sensitive assessment of her executive flexibility deficits; the three-rule switching condition could have further differentiated working memory contributions from cognitive inflexibility; and the digital error tracking would have captured her temporal patterns (delayed initiation followed by variable production) more precisely. However, the original version successfully identified her executive retrieval pattern through the Letter-Category discrepancy and documented her initiation difficulties across conditions, demonstrating that skilled interpretation and careful behavioral observation can compensate for instrumentation differences when clinical questions are well-formulated.

Rapid Reference 13.2

Choosing Between Original and Advanced Versions

Consider Original When	Consider Advanced When
Examinee is aged 8–13 (either version appropriate)	Subtle executive deficits are suspected in high-functioning individuals
Moderate-to-severe executive deficits are already evident	Higher executive ceiling is needed
Comparing with previous original D-KEFS data	Precise digital error tracking is important
Traditional paper-and-pencil administration is required	Contemporary norms from 2020s are preferred
Digital infrastructure is unavailable	Multilevel working memory assessment is valuable (three-rule switching)
Minimizing executive load on switching is desired	Phonemic-semantic flexibility is assessment target

HIERARCHICAL TIER ANALYSIS

The Verbal Fluency Test assesses executive functions, but successful performance requires intact foundational abilities and emerges from a hierarchy of processes. Both versions map onto the four-tier framework, though the Advanced version's increased complexity amplifies demands at each tier.

Tier 1: Foundational Processes (Nonexecutive)

Verbal Fluency performance depends on fundamental cognitive and linguistic processes that must be intact before executive functions can be validly assessed. These baseline skills are overlearned, automatic abilities required for higher-level executive functions. Consistent with the bottom-up hierarchical effect, Tier 1 deficits typically compromise performance across all three conditions, making it difficult to assess executive capacity.

Motor Articulatory Abilities

Rapid, clear speech production is essential. Dysarthria or motor speech problems impair word generation at the motor level, compromising all conditions independent of executive capacity. Distinguish motor from executive contributions by comparing articulation rate during Verbal Fluency to articulation during conversational speech or when naming objects. If the rate of speech is consistently slow across all speaking contexts, motor factors—not executive dysfunction—explain reduced output. Examinees with motor speech problems produce words slowly and effortfully, even when they know the words, whereas examinees with executive retrieval deficits may articulate quickly once a word comes to mind but struggle to generate words in the first place.

Language Comprehension

Verbal Fluency instructions specify multiple constraints (target letters/categories, no proper names, no numbers, no repetitions, no grammatical variants). Basic comprehension impairments seen in intellectual disability, aphasias, or advanced dementias can affect understanding of task requirements. The Advanced version's Switching Fluency instructions are particularly complex, requiring understanding of alternation rules and, for ages 14–69, three-rule sequencing.

Verbal Semantic Knowledge

Category Fluency explicitly requires semantic knowledge; examinees cannot generate animal names without knowing animals. Reduced vocabulary breadth directly limits word generation ceiling. An examinee with limited education who knows fewer animals will produce fewer words due to semantic store limitations rather than fluency of word retrieval or executive dysfunction. While Letter Fluency emphasizes strategic retrieval more than vocabulary, extremely limited vocabulary constrains performance.

Orthographic Knowledge

Particularly critical for Letter Fluency, examinees must know which letters words begin with—a reading/spelling skill. Individuals with reading disorders may generate set-loss errors, saying words starting with the correct sound but wrong letter (saying "phone" for F words), or may say a reduced number of words per trial. Research shows adolescents with reading disorders demonstrate impaired phonemic fluency but preserved category fluency (Kavé & Sapir-Yogev, 2023).

Sustained Attention

Each 60-second trial requires sustained mental effort. Examinees must maintain attentional focus continuously throughout trials. Attention lapses, even briefly losing focus, cost precious seconds when every word counts. More severe attention deficits (e.g., confusion, delirium, fluctuating consciousness) fundamentally compromise task engagement across all conditions.

Tier 1 Impairment Pattern

Examinees with Tier 1 deficits show reduced word generation across all fluency conditions due to foundational limitations rather than executive dysfunction. Motor speech impairment produces slow, effortful articulation regardless of word accessibility. Language comprehension deficits result in rule violations from misunderstanding rather than forgetting. Limited semantic knowledge constrains Category Fluency output independent of retrieval strategy. Orthographic weaknesses produce Letter Fluency errors (phonetically correct but orthographically wrong responses) or reduced output. Sustained attention deficits create variable performance with mid-trial lapses affecting all conditions. The hallmark is proportional impact: all conditions show difficulty, but contrast scores remain average because the limitation affects baseline fluency rather than executive switching demands specifically.

Tier 2: Bridging Processes

Tier 2 represents the bridge between foundational abilities and executive functions—processes introducing fluid, dynamic demands while remaining relatively structured. When impaired, these skills affect all fluency conditions in ways distinguishable from both Tier 1 foundational deficits and Tier 3 executive dysfunction.

Dual-Level Verbal Working Memory

Examinees must hold task rules in mind while generating responses (first level) and track previously generated words within each trial to avoid repetitions (second level). As more words are generated during a 60-second trial, the working memory load for tracking previous responses increases. Working memory failures manifest as rule violations (saying proper names despite instruction, repeating words, generating grammatical variants) suggesting difficulty maintaining task constraints under cognitive load rather than strategic retrieval failure.

Verbal Processing Speed

The rate at which individuals process verbal information affects how quickly they can generate and articulate words under time pressure. Processing speed represents efficiency independent of knowledge. Individuals can possess extensive vocabularies but demonstrate generally slowed verbal output across all timed language tasks. When processing speed is consistently slow across multiple measures and VFT is proportionally affected across all three conditions, Tier 2 processing efficiency contributes to reduced output rather than executive strategy failure.

Rule Application Consistency

Successfully following Verbal Fluency rules throughout trials requires basic inhibitory control—suppressing rule-violating responses. This is simpler than strategic planning and flexible shifting (Tier 3) but more complex than comprehending instructions (Tier 1). Examinees who understand rules initially but violate them under cognitive load demonstrate Tier 2 rule application difficulties. On Switching, maintaining alternation consistently (not generating multiple words from the same category consecutively) represents the ability to follow Tier 2 rules.

Tier 2 Deficit Pattern

Examinees with Tier 2 deficits demonstrate difficulties with the dynamic, fluid demands of sustained verbal generation beyond simple foundational limitations. Working memory failures manifest as increasing rule violations and repetition errors as trials progress; early performance may be adequate, but cognitive load accumulates. Processing speed limitations produce proportionally slow output across all conditions with normal contrast scores. The examinee generates words at a steady but reduced rate. Rule application difficulties appear as scattered errors throughout trials despite adequate initial comprehension. The examinee knows the rules but cannot consistently maintain them under time pressure. These patterns affect all fluency conditions but remain distinguishable from Tier 3 executive dysfunction, which produces disproportionate impairment on switching conditions relative to baseline Letter and Category Fluency.

Tier 3: Core Executive Functions

Tier 3 represents the Verbal Fluency Test's primary assessment target, where both cold and hot executive functions contribute to word generation performance in distinct ways.

Cold Executive Functions

Tier 3 represents the Verbal Fluency's primary assessment target—executive control over word generation, strategic retrieval, and cognitive flexibility. The conditions differ in executive complexity, with Switching placing substantially greater demands on cognitive flexibility, working memory, and inhibition.

Strategic Word Retrieval

Letter Fluency requires the most executive control, generating words by initial letter demands strategic search through phonological representations. Most individuals adopt systematic strategies: retrieving words by sound clusters (F: fish, flip, flag, then fast, fact, fan) or by semantic categories accessed through initial letters (F: foods, then animals). This strategic search distinguishes executive retrieval from simple vocabulary knowledge. Category Fluency relies more on automatic semantic knowledge access but still requires a systematic search through semantic subcategories (farm animals, then pets, then wild animals). Individuals with executive deficits demonstrate poor strategy use: random retrieval without clustering, early strategy abandonment, and inability to shift to new clusters when current clusters are exhausted. Temporal patterns reveal strategic capacity: adequate retrieval shows steady production throughout trials with discernible clustering; poor retrieval shows an initial burst (automatic high-frequency words) followed by dramatic slowing with no clustering.

Single-Level and Multilevel Cognitive Shifting

On Letter and Category Fluency, shifting occurs within a single strategic level—between phonemic clusters or semantic subcategories. Research by Troyer and colleagues (1998) demonstrated that individuals with focal frontal lesions showed impairment not in responses within clusters but in the ability to switch to new subcategories. Switching requires multilevel shifting: at the strategic search level (phonemic versus semantic retrieval rules) and within cluster subtypes. Category Switching on the original version's semantic-semantic switching (Furniture/Fruits) demands disengaging from one semantic domain, inhibiting continued search, and engaging the alternative domain. Switching Fluency on the Advanced version's phonemic-semantic switching (Musical Instruments/R words) dramatically increases demands by requiring cross-domain strategy shifting. For ages 14–69, the three-rule trial (L words–Clothing–B words) places extreme demands on both cognitive flexibility and working memory simultaneously.

Working Memory for Rules and Sequences

Switching working memory demands exceed baseline conditions substantially. Examinees must simultaneously: (1) maintain awareness of which category/letter is currently active, (2) track the alternation sequence, (3) maintain rules for each category/letter, (4) remember previously generated words across categories to prevent repetitions, and (5) monitor switching accuracy. On the three-rule trial, examinees must track position within a three-item sequence, maintain three distinct rule sets, and prevent nonactive rules from intruding. Working memory failures manifest as losing track of which rule is active, generating words from wrong categories, or confusion about the alternation pattern.

Inhibitory Control

Switching requires robust inhibition. After generating a word from one semantic category, examinees must inhibit the prepotent tendency to continue generating from that category and instead retrieve words from a different semantic category or completely switch to a phonemic strategy. This inhibitory demand is continuous—every switch requires inhibiting the just-active category remaining primed in memory. Set-loss errors (words from wrong categories) indicate inhibitory failure. The Advanced manual notes that phonemic-semantic switching increases inhibitory demands because semantic retrieval is more automatic and requires stronger inhibition to disengage.

Problem-Solving and Initiation

Letter Fluency particularly requires problem-solving: recognizing when current search strategies are exhausted, generating alternative approaches, and adjusting based on success. High-performing examinees flexibly shift strategies mid-trial when productivity slows. Some individuals with executive dysfunction, particularly those with frontal lobe pathology, demonstrate intact knowledge but marked difficulty initiating output, sitting silently before producing words or generating a few words, then stopping despite prompting. This initiation deficit manifests as extremely low word counts with long silent periods, distinct from slowed processing (steady but slow production) or vocabulary limitations (consistent output of few words).

Tier 3 Cold Executive Impairment Pattern

Classic executive dysfunction on Verbal Fluency appears as disproportionate difficulty with strategic retrieval and cognitive flexibility. The hallmark pattern is that Letter Fluency is significantly weaker than Category Fluency despite intact vocabulary and naming—phonemic retrieval requires more executive strategic search than semantically-supported category retrieval. On Switching conditions, examinees show disproportionate impairment relative to baseline fluency (contrast scores ≤7), with set-loss errors indicating failure to maintain alternation rules, reduced switching accuracy despite adequate total word production, or dramatic performance decline when phonemic-semantic switching is required (Advanced version). Temporal patterns reveal strategy failure: strong initial output (automatic high-frequency words) followed by dramatic slowing without evidence of strategic search or clustering. Initiation deficits produce extended latencies before first words and long silent periods despite adequate vocabulary. These patterns localize dysfunction to executive control over retrieval rather than to semantic knowledge or processing efficiency.

> **DON'T FORGET**
>
> Letter Fluency places greater executive demands than Category Fluency. Letter Fluency requires strategic search through phonological representations with minimal semantic support, while Category Fluency can rely more heavily on automatic semantic network activation. Disproportionate Letter Fluency weakness with adequate Category Fluency and intact vocabulary strongly suggests executive strategic retrieval deficits rather than language or vocabulary limitations.

Hot Executive Functions

While Verbal Fluency primarily assesses cold executive functions in emotionally neutral, structured contexts, hot executive factors significantly influence performance. These emotional regulation processes operate at Tier 3, affecting the cold executive capacities described above.

Frustration Tolerance During Cognitive Challenge

Verbal Fluency can be frustrating, particularly for individuals with word-finding difficulties. Examinees who become frustrated when words don't come easily often show progressive performance deterioration across trials. Frustration interferes with continued retrieval effort, strategic thinking, and persistence. Some examinees maintain composure despite difficulty, persistently searching for words. Others visibly become frustrated, make negative self-statements, or give up prematurely. This emotional dysregulation during cognitive challenge compromises otherwise adequate cold executive abilities.

Anxiety and Performance Pressure

Timed tasks induce anxiety in some examinees. The 60-second time limit that is explicitly stated in test instructions creates performance pressure. Anxiety manifests as visible tension, hurried responding without a strategic approach, or performance inhibition, where anxiety blocks word retrieval despite adequate vocabulary. The anxiety about generating too few words paradoxically interferes with word generation, creating a self-fulfilling prophecy. Some examinees who perform adequately on untimed vocabulary tasks may show marked impairment on Verbal Fluency due to anxiety under time pressure rather than true executive or semantic deficits.

CAUTION

Hot executive dysregulation can masquerade as cold executive deficits. An examinee whose performance deteriorates progressively across trials with mounting frustration may appear to have cognitive flexibility or working memory deficits when the primary problem is emotional regulation. Behavioral observations—noting frustration emergence, performance improvement with encouragement, or anxiety interfering with initiation—clarify whether cold capacity limitations or hot dysregulation drives poor performance. This distinction fundamentally changes intervention approaches.

Tier 3 Hot EF Pattern

Hot EF difficulties on Verbal Fluency produce performance that varies with emotional state rather than reflecting stable cognitive limitations. The examinee may begin trials adequately but deteriorate as frustration mounts, showing progressive decline across trials accompanied by visible distress, negative self-statements, or premature cessation. Anxiety manifests as blocked retrieval despite adequate vocabulary, excessive hesitation, or paradoxically rushing without a strategic approach. The key diagnostic indicators are: (1) performance variability tied to emotional state rather than task demands, (2) improvement with encouragement or after brief pauses, (3) behavioral signs of frustration or anxiety corresponding with output decline, and (4) adequate performance on untimed vocabulary measures contrasting with impaired timed fluency. This pattern indicates that intervention should prioritize anxiety management and frustration tolerance strategies before or alongside cognitive retrieval training.

Tier 4: Higher-Order Integration and Metacognition

Tier 4 processes represent the highest level of cognitive control, applying executive functions to monitor and regulate other executive functions. These integrative and metacognitive processes are subtle and often revealed through qualitative observations rather than quantitative scores.

Metacognitive Monitoring

Effective Verbal Fluency performance involves continuously monitoring output quality and productivity: "Am I generating words at a reasonable pace? Is my strategy working? Should I shift approaches?" This metacognitive awareness enables mid-trial strategy adjustments. Patricia Anderson demonstrated intact Tier 4 functioning—she recognized her limited output, expressed frustration about word-finding difficulties, and accurately perceived her performance. Impaired metacognitive monitoring manifests as unawareness of poor performance, continuing ineffective strategies without adjustment, or surprise when informed of low scores.

Strategic Flexibility and Real-Time Adjustment

Tier 4 involves dynamically adjusting the strategy based on ongoing evaluation. An examinee generating F words notices productivity slowing after exhausting "fl-" words, recognizes the pattern, and consciously shifts to a new approach. This represents higher-order executive control. Some examinees demonstrate adequate Tier 3 capacity (capable of strategic retrieval when prompted) but poor Tier 4 regulation (unable to recognize independently when strategy changes are needed).

Effort Regulation and Hot–Cold Integration

Sixty-second trials require sustaining effort throughout. Some examinees give up prematurely despite time remaining; others maintain consistent effort. This effort regulation represents Tier 4 cognitive control—managing motivation and persistence. Additionally, Tier 4 encompasses integration of hot and cold executive systems. Examinees whose performance deteriorates progressively with mounting frustration demonstrate hot–cold integration difficulties; emotional responses interfere with cognitive capacity, and they lack the metacognitive awareness or regulatory capacity to manage this interference. Skilled performers notice frustration emerging and consciously regulate emotions to maintain cognitive performance.

Rapid Reference 13.3

Tier Structure at a Glance

Tier	Processes
Tier 1: Foundational processes (Nonexecutive)	Motor articulatory abilities
	Language comprehension of instructions
	Verbal semantic knowledge (vocabulary breadth)
	Orthographic knowledge (letter-sound correspondence)
	Sustained attention across 60-second trials
Tier 2: Bridging processes	Dual-level verbal working memory (rules + tracking responses)
	Verbal processing speed
	Rule application consistency
Tier 3: Cold executive functions	Strategic word retrieval (phonemic clustering, systematic search)
	Single-level cognitive shifting (within clusters/subcategories)
	Multilevel cognitive shifting (phonemic-semantic switching)
	Working memory for rules and sequences
	Inhibitory control (disengaging from active category)
	Problem-solving and initiation
Tier 3: Hot executive functions	Frustration tolerance during cognitive challenge
	Anxiety management under time pressure
Tier 4: Higher-order integration	Metacognitive monitoring (awareness of productivity/strategy)
	Strategic flexibility and real-time adjustment
	Effort regulation and hot–cold integration

ADMINISTRATION

NOTE: Refer to the Examiner's Manual for complete and detailed administration instructions. The Examiner's Manual provides verbatim instructions and clinicians should follow these precisely to ensure standardized administration.

Original Version Administration

The paper-and-pencil version of the original Verbal Fluency Test requires the Examiner's Manual, Record Form, Stimulus Booklet, and Timer. A digital version of the Examiner's Manual is also available through Q-global. For telepractice administration, Q-global digital assets provide digital stimulus presentation; see Pearson's telepractice guidelines for detailed procedures. If administering using the tablet-based Q-interactive platform, refer to administration instructions herewith for the Advanced version as they approximate the original version when given on Q-interactive. The caveat is that the Switching task directions differ. All examinees aged 8–89 complete all three conditions:

Condition 1: Letter Fluency

Each of three letters (F, A, S on Standard Form; B, H, R on Alternate Form) receives a separate 60-second trial. Instructions specify that examinees should say words beginning with the target letter, excluding proper names (people or places), numbers, and grammatical variants of previously said words. If 15 seconds elapse without a response, the examiner prompts "keep going" (once per trial). If three consecutive words are generated that do not start with the designated letter, the examiner provides one reminder of the letter being used, once per trial. The examiner records responses verbatim in 15-second intervals to enable temporal analysis.

Condition 2: Category Fluency
Examinees generate words from two semantic categories (Animals' and Boys' Names on Standard Form; Items of Clothing and Girls' Names on Alternate Form), each for 60 seconds. Instructions include a reminder that it does not matter what letter the words start with. Similarly, once-per-trial prompting rules apply: "keep going" if 15 seconds elapse without response; one reminder if three consecutive words violate category membership. The examiner records responses verbatim in 15-second intervals.

Condition 3: Category Switching
Examinees alternate between two semantic categories (Furniture and Fruits on Standard Form; Vegetables and Musical Instruments on Alternate Form) for 60 seconds. Instructions specify that examinees should switch back and forth between categories, saying one word from the first category, then one from the second, continuing to alternate. Examinees may start with either category. The "keep going" prompt applies if 15 seconds elapse without response. The first time an examinee generates three consecutive words that are not members of one of the two designated categories, they are reminded to switch and the names of the categories are again provided. The examiner records responses verbatim in 15-second intervals and can use slash marks between words to denote category switches.

Advanced Version Administration

The Advanced version (VFT) uses Q-interactive digital administration on the Practitioner Device with stylus-based response recording. Administration requires only the Practitioner Device—no Client Device is needed. All examinees complete Letter Fluency and Category Fluency conditions identically. Switching Fluency differs by age: examinees aged 8–13 and 70–90 complete two Category-Letter switching trials (two-rule switching), while examinees aged 14–69 complete one two-rule trial and one three-rule trial.

For each Condition, examiners transcribe responses verbatim into the digital response capture area (rectangular, writing spaces that appear on the Practitioner Device) in real time. The system timestamps each response automatically, enabling precise temporal analysis beyond the original version's 15-second intervals. Responses can be altered (add, move, edit, delete, classify, categorize) in review mode following administration. Responses can also be transferred from paper to the Practitioner Device or entered into the capture area using the recording after administration is complete.

All Conditions are discontinued after a 60-second trial. Administer all trials to the examiner's age. Begin timing for each trial after saying the last word of the instructions. Stop timing when 60 seconds have elapsed.

VFT is the only Advanced test in which the examiner must remember when to give prompts because notifications are not automatically triggered. If the examinee provides three incorrect responses in a row, read aloud the specific prompt for that trial. Prompts for each trial are provided on the 3 Errors and the Speech Bubble button. Provide the prompt only once per trial, continuing timing.

Condition 1: Letter Fluency
Three letters (F, A, and S) each receive 60-second trials. Instructions specify the same constraints as the original version: no proper names, numbers, or grammatical variants.

Condition 2: Category Fluency
Two categories are administered: combined Fruits and Vegetables, and Animals. Instructions specify generating names of real animals and combined fruits or vegetables, and note that it doesn't matter which letter they start with.

Condition 3: Switching Fluency
Ages 8–13 and 70–90 Years
Two Category-Letter switching trials are administered: Musical Instruments and R words, then Items of Clothing and L words. Examinees alternate between saying a word from the semantic category and a word beginning with the target letter. They may start with either a category or a letter.

Ages 14–69 Years
The first trial matches the two-rule format mentioned earlier (Musical Instruments and R words). The second trial uses three-rule switching: examinees alternate among L words, Items of Clothing, and B words in sequence. They may begin with any of the three but must maintain the same sequence throughout. This substantially increases working memory and cognitive flexibility demands.

Administration Considerations Common to Both Versions

Timing Precision
Begin timing immediately when the final word of instructions is spoken, not when the examinee begins responding. Stop timing precisely at 60 seconds. If an examinee is mid-word at the time limit, allow completion of that word (credited within the time limit). Timing consistency is critical—variations of even a few seconds can affect word counts, given the time pressure.

Recording Accuracy
Accurate verbatim transcription is essential for scoring. Examiners must write/type quickly during original version administration or digital recording. When examinees speak extremely rapidly, examiners may struggle to keep pace. On the Advanced version, the ability to replay Q-interactive recordings enables verification of unclear responses, a significant advantage over the original version, where ambiguous or missed responses cannot be recovered.

Prompting Consistency
The "keep going" prompt should be given neutrally, with consistent tone and timing. Some examiners inadvertently convey urgency or impatience, while others sound encouraging, potentially influencing performance. Maintain neutral affect throughout. Similarly, rule-reminder prompts should be matter-of-fact, specifying which rule was violated without expressing disapproval or frustration.

Practice Effects
The Advanced version shows minimal practice effects with adequate retest intervals. The Advanced manual reports no practice effects for Category Fluency and only minimal practice effects (approximately 1/6 SD) for Letter Fluency and Switching (Delis & Kaplan, 2025). When retesting is necessary with the original version, using Alternate Forms reduces practice effects further.

BEHAVIORAL OBSERVATIONS

Behavioral observations during Verbal Fluency administration provide critical qualitative information complementing quantitative scores. Careful observation reveals strategy use, emotional responses, effort, and other factors affecting performance.

Response Patterns and Temporal Productivity

Initial response latency, the time from "begin" to first word, indicates initiation capacity. Brief latencies (1–3 seconds) suggest adequate initiation; moderate latencies (4–8 seconds) may reflect careful strategy formulation or mild initiation difficulty; extended latencies (>10 seconds) suggest significant initiation problems, comprehension difficulty, or reduced motivation. Extended latency only on the first trial suggests unfamiliarity or anxiety, while consistent delays across trials suggest initiation deficit.

Temporal productivity patterns reveal executive strategy. High-performing examinees generate words relatively evenly across the 60-second trial. Common dysfunction patterns include strong initial output followed by dramatic slowing (automatic retrieval exhausted without strategic search), very slow starts with improved later production (slow strategy formulation), or sporadic bursts separated by long pauses (fragmented, inefficient search). Listen for clustering—generating multiple words from the same subcategory before switching. Effective clustering indicates strategic search; random generation without clustering suggests strategy absence.

Error Patterns

Set-loss errors (proper names, wrong categories, numbers, grammatical variants) indicate difficulty maintaining task constraints. Early errors suggest initial misunderstanding; late errors suggest rule forgetting under cognitive fatigue; consistent errors suggest working memory or inhibitory control weakness. Repetition errors, saying the same word multiple times within a trial, indicate difficulty tracking previous responses. Early repetitions suggest significant working memory limitation; late repetitions (repeating words from 40–50 seconds earlier) suggest capacity limits under accumulating load.

Strategy Use and Adaptation

Some examinees verbalize strategy overtly ("OK, F… furniture… fan, footstool… foods…"), revealing their approach explicitly. Others employ a strategy covertly, inferred from clustering patterns. The absence of discernible strategy—random word generation, no clustering, frequent long pauses—strongly suggests executive deficit. Watch for strategy abandonment: examinees who begin systematically but stop when initial clusters are exhausted demonstrate strategy capacity but difficulty with flexibility or perseverance. Environmental dependency, exhibited by generating words primarily from visible objects in the room, suggests difficulty with self-generated, internally driven retrieval.

Emotional Regulation and Effort

Observe whether examinees maintain composure or show mounting frustration when words don't come easily. Deteriorating performance across trials accompanied by visible distress, negative self-statements, or premature cessation suggests hot executive dysregulation affecting cold executive capacity. Some examinees maintain vigorous effort throughout; others give up with 20–30 seconds remaining despite time available. Timed tasks induce anxiety in some examinees—visible tension, rushed responding, or statements about pressure. When anxiety appears to impair performance substantially, consider whether scores reflect cognitive capacity or anxiety interference.

SCORING

Verbal Fluency scoring involves classifying responses, calculating primary and process scores, and examining temporal patterns that illuminate the cognitive processes underlying performance.

Classifying Responses

All Q-interactive administration responses must be classified before scoring is possible. After a response is entered, it must be classified as a correct response (meets Condition criteria), a repeated correct response, a set-loss error (does not meet Condition criteria), or a repeated set-loss error. For VRT Switching Fluency trials, examiners must also select which initial letter or semantic category the response belongs to. This categorization is essential for determining whether switches occurred correctly. DK (e.g., states "I don't know how to do this") and NR (provides no response) buttons are also options. If they are selected but responses are entered and classified, scores will be generated.

For the original paper-and-pencil version, notations of any of these can be made on the Record Form to assist with scoring accuracy. For example, an "R" can be written after a repeated response, a word can be circled if it is a set-loss response, and slashes between switching categories can be added if the switch is valid. The Examiner's Manual provides some helpful guidance on responses that do and do not count for each category.

Scores: Original Version—Primary Measures

Letter Fluency Total Correct

Sum all correct responses across the three letter trials (F + A + S or B + H + R). Correct responses begin with the target letter, are not proper names (people or places), are not numbers, are not grammatical variants of previously generated words on that trial and are not repetitions within that trial. Convert the raw total to a scaled score using age-based norms.

Category Fluency Total Correct

Sum all correct responses across the two category trials. Do not count repetitions or grammatical variants.

Category Switching Total Correct Responses

Count all correct responses from both categories combined, independent of switching accuracy. Correct responses include words belonging to the category Furniture or Fruits (or Vegetables or Musical Instruments on Alternate Form) and are not a repetition.

Category Switching Total Switching Accuracy

Count each successful switch between categories. A switch is accurate when a word from Category A is followed by a word from Category B. Switches from Category A to another word from Category A are not switches; switches from Category A to an error word are not switches.

Original Version—Primary Contrast Measures

A scaled score difference score is calculated among two sets of Primary Measures to demonstrate disproportionate impairment. The scaled-score differences are converted to a new scaled score corrected for the total sample.

Letter Fluency Versus Category Fluency

Condition 1 scaled score minus Condition 2 scaled score. This contrast compares phonemic retrieval (generating words by initial letter) to semantic retrieval (generating words from categories). Because Letter Fluency places greater demands on strategic search while Category Fluency relies more heavily on automatic semantic network activation, this contrast isolates the executive retrieval component of verbal fluency.

Category Switching Versus Category Fluency

Condition 3 scaled score minus Condition 2 scaled score. This contrast compares performance requiring alternation between categories to baseline category retrieval without switching demands. The comparison isolates the cognitive flexibility and working memory components added by the switching requirement.

Original Version—Optional Measures

First, Second, Third, Fourth Interval Total Correct

Total number of correct responses generated during each of the 15-second intervals. These scaled scores add a quantitative score to complement observed variations in response speed across the 60-second trial.

Set-Loss Errors and Percent Set-Loss Errors

Sum rule violations across all conditions: proper names, numbers, wrong categories, and grammatical variants are converted to a scaled score. High set-loss error rates may indicate working memory difficulty in maintaining task rules or inhibitory control weakness, allowing rule-violating responses. The Percent score divides the sum by the Number of Total Responses (×100) and provides a method to more evenly assess Set-Loss Errors for those with a high or low number of responses.

Repetition Errors and Percent Repetition Errors

Sum within-trial word repetitions across all conditions, converted to a scaled score. High repetition rates may indicate working memory difficulty, tracking previous responses or reduced monitoring. The Percent score divides the sum by the Number of Total Responses (×100) and provides a method to more evenly assess Repetition Errors for those with a high or low number of responses.

Percent Switching Accuracy

The Total Switching Accuracy score divided by the Number of Total Responses (×100) also provides a method of analyzing accuracy frequency, especially for those with a high or low number of responses.

Scores: Advanced Version—Core Scaled Scores

The Advanced version provides similar scores with modifications reflecting revised conditions.

Letter Fluency Total Correct

Sum correct responses across F, A, and S trials using the same scoring rules as the original version. Digital recording enables precise verification when responses are ambiguous.

Category Fluency Total Correct

Sum correct responses across Animals trial and combined Fruits and Vegetables trial.

Switching Fluency Total Correct

Sum correct words generated across both switching trials, regardless of whether they were said at correct switch points. Count words meeting the category or letter criterion, excluding repetitions and grammatical variants.

Switching Fluency Total Accurate Switches

This score requires careful analysis. On two-rule trials (ages 8–13 and 70–90: both trials; ages 14–69: first trial), count each successful switch between semantic category and letter. On the three-rule trial (ages 14–69 only), switching accuracy is more complex: a switch between two rules (e.g., L word to Clothing) receives 1 point, while a switch including all three rules in sequence (e.g., L word to Clothing to B word) receives 2 points per complete cycle. The Q-interactive system calculates this automatically when responses are properly categorized.

Advanced Version—Index Scores

The Advanced version provides three composite index scores offering a global fluency assessment.

Combined Letter and Category Fluency Total Correct Index

Add scaled scores from Letter Fluency and Category Fluency conditions. This index represents baseline phonemic and semantic fluency capacity, independent of switching demands.

Switching Fluency Total Correct/Switching Accuracy Index

Add scaled scores from Switching Fluency Total Correct and Switching Fluency Total Accurate Switches. This composite recognizes that switching performance reflects both overall word generation and switching precision.

Combined Letter, Category, and Switching Fluency Total Correct Index

Add scaled scores from all three conditions (Letter, Category, Switching Total Correct). This global fluency index represents overall verbal generativity capacity.

Advanced Version—Contrast Scores

Regression-based contrast scaled scores enable direct comparison of baseline fluency versus switching fluency, addressing the question: "Given this examinee's baseline fluency capacity, is their switching performance at the expected level, better than expected, or worse than expected?" The regression-based formula improved upon the original's simple subtraction contrast score method because it accounts for the correlation between the measures. The regression-based scores account for differences in higher and lower ability individuals and the wide variety of relationships among scores. Contrast scores indicate that given the performance on the baseline (less demanding) task, the performance on the more difficult task is above, at, or below the expected level. Scores of 8–12 indicate expected switching performance given the baseline. Scores ≤7 indicate switching performance is lower than predicted—disproportionate switching difficulty suggesting cognitive flexibility or working memory deficits beyond general fluency limitations. Scores ≥13 indicate switching performance exceeds predictions—unexpectedly strong cognitive flexibility given baseline fluency levels. The three contrast scores provided are:

Category Fluency Versus Letter Fluency Total Correct. This contrast compares semantic retrieval (generating words from categories) to phonemic retrieval (generating words by initial letter). Because Category Fluency can rely on automatic semantic network activation while Letter Fluency requires more effortful strategic search through phonological representations, this contrast isolates differential demands between retrieval types.

Combined Letter and Category Fluency Versus Switching Fluency Total Correct. This contrast compares baseline fluency capacity (combined phonemic and semantic retrieval without switching demands) to total word production during switching trials. The comparison determines whether overall word generation under switching conditions matches, exceeds, or falls below expectations given baseline fluency abilities.

Combined Letter and Category Fluency vs. Switching Fluency Total Correct/Switching Accuracy Index. This contrast compares baseline fluency capacity to a composite reflecting both word production and switching precision during alternation trials. By incorporating switching accuracy alongside total output, this comparison captures examinees who generate adequate words but fail to alternate correctly, as well as those who switch accurately but produce fewer total words.

Advanced Version—Process Scores

Total Set-Loss Errors

Sum rule violations across all conditions: proper names, numbers, wrong categories, and grammatical variants, converted to a scaled score. High set-loss error rates may indicate working memory difficulty in maintaining task rules or inhibitory control weakness, allowing rule-violating responses.

Total Repetitions

Sum within-trial word repetitions across all conditions, converted to a scaled score. High repetition rates may indicate working memory difficulty tracking previous responses or reduced monitoring.

Advanced Version—Additional Raw Scores

Nonconverted raw scores are provided as a method to compare performance across each trial. Provided raw scores for each trial are: Total Correct Responses, Total Set-Loss Errors, Total Repetitions, Total Accurate Switches, and Total Responses (correct or incorrect).

Advanced Version—Behavioral Observations

Several base rate scores are provided for a select number of behaviors that examinees may exhibit during assessment. These quantitative scores compliment behavioral observations and provide context for interpreting how behaviors or emotional reactions may have affected an examinee's performance. See Table 5.5 in the Examiner's Manual for a listing.

Rapid Reference 13.4

Scoring Summary

Score Type	Original D-KEFS	Advanced (VFT)
Primary/core scores	Letter Fluency Total Correct	Letter Fluency Total Correct
	Category Fluency Total Correct	Category Fluency Total Correct
	Category Switching Total Correct	Switching Fluency Total Correct
	Category Switching Total Switching Accuracy	Switching Fluency Total Accurate Switches
Contrast scores	Letter vs. Category Fluency (simple subtraction)	Category vs. Letter Fluency (regression-based)
	Category Switching vs. Category Fluency	Combined Letter/Category vs. Switching Total Correct
		Combined Letter/Category vs. Switching Accuracy Index
Index scores	(not available)	Combined Letter and Category Fluency Index
		Switching Total Correct/Accuracy Index
		Combined Letter, Category, and Switching Index
Process scores	Set-Loss Errors; Percent Set-Loss	Total Set-Loss Errors
	Repetition Errors; Percent Repetition	Total Repetitions
	First/Second/Third/Fourth Interval Totals	Trial-by-trial raw scores
	Percent Switching Accuracy	Behavioral observation base rates

COMMON ADMINISTRATION ERRORS

Several administration errors can compromise Verbal Fluency validity. Awareness of these errors enables quality control.

Timing Inaccuracy

Starting timing after the examinee begins responding (rather than when instructions end) artificially reduces time pressure. Stopping timing early or late affects word counts. Use a reliable timer or make sure the tablet start button is initiated; practice timing procedures; and maintain timing discipline throughout administration.

Inconsistent Prompting

The "keep going" prompt should be given after 15 seconds of silence, not sooner or later. Prompting too late reduces the effectiveness of the reminder. Similarly, providing the rule-reminder prompt too readily (after two rather than three violations) or not at all affects standardization. Follow prompting guidelines precisely.

Recording Errors

Missing words due to rapid speech, mishearing words, or writing ambiguously affects scoring accuracy. Develop efficient recording systems, use abbreviations that are clear when reviewing later, and if using Q-interactive, use the recording feature to assure accuracy. On the original version, recording in 15-second intervals enables temporal analysis only if precise timing is maintained while recording.

Overinterpreting or Underinterpreting Borderline Responses

Examiners sometimes make scoring decisions during administration that compromise standardization. Record responses verbatim during administration; make scoring decisions later using scoring guidelines. Avoid real-time interpretation like "That's not really a furniture item" that influences the examinee mid-trial.

Failure to Observe and Document Behavioral Data

Focusing on recording responses verbatim can cause examiners to miss important behavioral observations. After each trial, pause briefly to note observations before beginning the next trial. These qualitative data are as important as scores.

Classification Errors (Q-interactive)

Examiners must classify each response as correct or incorrect and for Switching, classify the category or letter to which the response belongs. Misclassifying responses (marking a clothing item as an L word) corrupts score accuracy. Classify carefully during administration, immediately after administration, or use the recording feature if time has passed.

INTERPRETATION

Interpreting Verbal Fluency performance requires integrating quantitative scores, error patterns, and behavioral observations within the hierarchical framework to determine which tier(s) contain deficits and how these manifest functionally.

Using the Hierarchical Framework for Differential Diagnosis

Step 1: Rule Out Tier 1 Limitations

Before attributing poor Verbal Fluency performance to executive dysfunction, confirm that foundational abilities are adequate. Were instructions understood? Is the rate of speech adequate for rapid verbal output? Are semantic knowledge and vocabulary broadly intact based on other measures? Was attention and engagement adequate across the assessment? Are set-loss errors on Letter Fluency due to orthographic confusion (saying "phone" for F) rather than executive failure? If Tier 1 concerns emerge, state explicitly that executive capacity cannot be adequately assessed due to foundational limitations and recommend a targeted Tier 1 assessment (vocabulary, naming, reading/spelling, articulation evaluation).

Step 2: Evaluate Tier 2 Bridging Processes

Examine error patterns for working memory indicators. High repetition errors and rule violations despite apparent understanding suggest working memory difficulty in maintaining task constraints. Temporal patterns help: adequate early-trial performance followed by deterioration and increased errors suggests working memory capacity limits under accumulating load. Compare Verbal Fluency performance to processing speed measures (WAIS-5/WISC-V Processing Speed Index; Wechsler, 2014, 2024; Color-Word Interference Conditions 1–2). If processing speed is consistently slow and Verbal Fluency is proportionally affected across all three conditions, Tier 2 processing efficiency contributes to reduced output rather than executive strategy failure.

Step 3: Analyze Tier 3 Cold Executive Patterns

This is Verbal Fluency's primary interpretive level. Use the pattern across conditions to identify specific executive deficits. Disproportionate Letter Fluency weakness (Letter Fluency worse than Category Fluency) with adequate vocabulary suggests executive strategic retrieval deficits. The examinee has words available but lacks effective strategies for phonemic search. Temporal pattern showing initial burst followed by dramatic slowing, absence of clustering, and no systematic search strategy confirms executive retrieval failure. Disproportionate Category Fluency weakness (Category Fluency worse than Letter Fluency) with low vocabulary/naming scores suggests semantic memory degradation; with adequate vocabulary, it suggests executive retrieval difficulty accessing intact semantic stores. Disproportionate Switching difficulty relative to baseline fluency indicates cognitive flexibility deficits or multilevel working memory limitations. Examine switching accuracy: adequate total words but poor switching accuracy suggests flexibility/working memory deficits; low total words with adequate accuracy suggests overall fluency limitations without a specific switching deficit.

Step 4: Evaluate Tier 3 Hot Executive Factors

Behavioral observations reveal emotional regulation affecting executive performance. Does frustration emerge and mount across trials, interfering with continued retrieval? Does anxiety about time pressure or word-finding difficulty create visible tension affecting initiation or retrieval? Does performance deteriorate progressively with mounting emotional distress? Do examinees spontaneously recognize and self-correct errors ("no wait, I said that already") or continue generating responses without error awareness? Hot executive dysregulation often masquerades as cold executive deficits: an examinee whose performance deteriorates progressively with frustration may appear to have cognitive flexibility or working memory deficits when the primary problem is emotional regulation. Performance improvement with encouragement, visible frustration interfering with retrieval, or hurried responding without strategy suggest hot EF contributions.

> **DON'T FORGET**
>
> The D-KEFS Advanced VFT demonstrated large effect sizes ($d > 0.80$) in identifying deficits in children with ASD, adults with moderate-to-severe TBI, and older adults with MCI in preliminary clinical validation studies (Delis & Kaplan, 2025). The test did not differentiate children with ADHD or SLD-Math from controls at the group level, though meaningful subgroup heterogeneity emerged on individual analysis—reinforcing the importance of examining individual profiles rather than expecting uniform impairment patterns within diagnostic categories.

Step 5: Assess Tier 4 Integration and Metacognition

Behavioral observations reveal Tier 4 functioning. Does the examinee recognize when performance is weak (metacognitive accuracy)? Patricia Anderson demonstrated intact Tier 4—she recognized her limited output and accurately perceived her difficulty. Does the examinee spontaneously adjust strategies when productivity slows (strategic flexibility) or continue ineffective approaches despite visible failure? Do they maintain effort throughout trials or give up prematurely (effort regulation)? Do they notice frustration emerging and consciously regulate emotions to maintain performance (hot–cold integration), or does emotional dysregulation cascade unchecked? These qualitative indicators distinguish examinees with adequate executive capacity but poor self-regulation from those with fundamental executive deficits.

PERFORMANCE PATTERNS AND CLINICAL IMPLICATIONS

Several characteristic performance patterns emerge on the Verbal Fluency Test, each with distinct clinical implications for understanding the nature and tier-level of executive dysfunction.

Letter Fluency Patterns

Low Letter Fluency with adequate Category Fluency and intact vocabulary suggests executive strategic retrieval deficits. The examinee has words available but lacks effective strategies for phonemic search. Temporal patterns confirm this interpretation: an initial burst of common words followed by dramatic slowing indicates exhaustion of automatic retrieval without strategic search to access additional items. Absence of clustering (phonemic or semantic) and no systematic search strategy further supports executive retrieval failure. These individuals may struggle with any task requiring self-generated structure, benefiting from explicit strategy instruction and external organizational frameworks.

Category Fluency Patterns

Low Category Fluency with low vocabulary and naming scores suggests semantic memory degradation—the knowledge base itself is compromised. This pattern carries particular diagnostic significance in older adults, where semantic retrieval impairment with preserved phonemic retrieval mirrors patterns seen in early Alzheimer's disease progression. Low Category Fluency with adequate vocabulary suggests executive difficulty accessing intact semantic stores; the words exist but retrieval strategies are inefficient. Temporal analysis helps differentiate: semantic degradation shows consistent poverty across the trial, while executive retrieval deficits may show adequate initial output that fails to be sustained.

Switching Condition Patterns

Disproportionate Switching difficulty relative to baseline fluency indicates cognitive flexibility deficits or multilevel working memory limitations. The switching accuracy ratio provides diagnostic specificity: adequate total words but poor switching accuracy suggests flexibility deficits. The examinee generates words but fails to alternate between categories consistently. Low total words with adequate accuracy suggest overall fluency limitations without a specific switching deficit—when words are produced, alternation rules are followed. Low total words with poor accuracy indicate combined productivity and flexibility deficits requiring comprehensive intervention.

Error Patterns

High repetition errors suggest working memory or self-monitoring deficits. The examinee cannot maintain awareness of previously generated responses. Repetitions increasing across the trial indicate working memory capacity limits under accumulating load. High set-loss errors (words not beginning with the target letter or not belonging to the target category) suggest rule maintenance or inhibition deficits. Set-loss errors specifically during switching trials may reflect difficulty maintaining two rule sets simultaneously. Intrusion errors (words from previous trials or unrelated categories) suggest proactive interference or inhibition failure.

Temporal Patterns

Consistent output across time intervals indicates good strategic retrieval and sustained effort—words continue emerging throughout the trial. Initial burst followed by dramatic slowing suggests either poor strategy (exhausting obvious responses without systematic search) or hot EF factors (fatigue, frustration, declining motivation). Slow start followed by improvement suggests warm-up effects or initial anxiety that resolves. Performance deteriorating specifically on later trials (regardless of condition) suggests cumulative fatigue or mounting frustration affecting retrieval efficiency.

Hot Executive Function Patterns

Performance deteriorating progressively with visible frustration or anxiety suggests hot EF interference with otherwise intact retrieval capacity. Hurried responding without an apparent strategy, such as rapid production of obvious words followed by giving up, may indicate anxiety-driven performance or poor frustration tolerance rather than retrieval deficits. Performance improving with encouragement suggests hot EF factors are primary. Self-correction of errors ("no wait, I said that already") indicates intact monitoring despite production difficulties—a positive prognostic indicator suggesting Tier 4 strengths that can support intervention.

Cross-Condition Comparisons

Letter versus Category Fluency dissociations reveal retrieval system differences. Letter worse than Category with intact vocabulary indicates executive-strategic deficits; Category worse than Letter suggests semantic access problems. The contrast score comparing Switching to baseline fluency isolates flexibility demands—disproportionate switching weakness despite adequate baseline indicates specific flexibility vulnerability. When both versions are available, examinees performing adequately on original D-KEFS conditions but struggling with Advanced VFT demands may reveal subtle deficits in sustained strategic retrieval or accumulated cognitive load management.

Rapid Reference 13.5

Distinguishing Tier-Level Deficits

Tier Level	Indicators	Clinical Implications
Tier 1 deficit	Articulation difficulties affecting speech clarity; comprehension questions about instructions; extremely low vocabulary/naming; set-loss errors from orthographic confusion (phone for F); severe inattention across tests	Executive capacity cannot be adequately assessed; recommend Tier 1 assessment (vocabulary, naming, reading/spelling, articulation); interventions focus on foundational skill development
Tier 2 deficit	Rule violations despite understanding instructions; repetition errors increasing as trials progress; slow verbal processing speed across measures; lack of semantic clustering on Category Fluency; inconsistent rule-following under cognitive load	Bridge processes compromised; interventions may target working memory support (external aids, reduced load), processing speed accommodations (extended time), or structured external organization
Tier 3 cold deficit	Poor Letter Fluency with preserved Category Fluency (or reverse); no discernible clustering or strategy use; disproportionate Switching difficulty; adequate knowledge but retrieval failure; few subcategory switches; dramatic slowing after initial burst	Primary executive dysfunction affecting strategic retrieval, cognitive flexibility, or working memory; interventions focus on executive strategy training (clustering strategies, systematic search), compensatory approaches
Tier 3 hot deficit	Progressive performance deterioration with mounting frustration; visible anxiety interfering with initiation or retrieval; hurried responding without strategy; premature cessation due to emotional distress; performance improves with encouragement	Emotional regulation affecting executive performance; interventions focus on frustration tolerance training, anxiety management, self-regulation strategies, performance pressure desensitization
Tier 4 deficit	Poor metacognitive accuracy (unaware of limited output); inability to adjust strategies spontaneously despite demonstrating knowledge when prompted; premature effort withdrawal with time remaining; intact capacity but poor self-regulation	Executive capacity exists but self-monitoring compromised; interventions focus on metacognitive training, self-monitoring strategies, dynamic strategy adjustment practice

ECOLOGICAL VALIDITY AND FUNCTIONAL IMPLICATIONS

Verbal Fluency performance relates directly to real-world situations requiring rapid word retrieval, verbal expression under constraints, and cognitive flexibility in language production.

Academic Functioning

Students regularly face verbal fluency demands. Written expression requires generating content rapidly, particularly during timed essays or creative writing. Brainstorming sessions require generating ideas fluently. Class participation requires formulating responses quickly when called upon. Oral presentations require maintaining verbal fluency while managing anxiety. Students with verbal fluency deficits often struggle with these demands, with teachers reporting "doesn't participate in class discussions," "has ideas but struggles to express them," or "writing is slow and labored despite adequate knowledge." Interventions include advanced planning time before speaking/writing, graphic organizers to structure idea generation, extended time for written work, and strategy instruction in systematic retrieval (using categories to organize thinking).

Vocational and Daily Living

Many occupations require verbal fluency. Sales and customer service positions require fluent verbal expression, generating product information rapidly, and maintaining conversations smoothly. Teaching requires verbal fluency throughout lessons, generating examples spontaneously, and explaining concepts fluidly. Meeting participation across professions requires contributing ideas fluently, responding to questions spontaneously, and brainstorming collaboratively. Management positions require fluent communication during presentations, staff meetings, and problem-solving discussions. Individuals with verbal fluency deficits may struggle with these occupational demands, appearing less knowledgeable than they are due to retrieval difficulties. Workplace accommodations may include allowing written rather than verbal responses when possible, providing questions in advance for meetings, and structuring presentations to minimize extemporaneous speaking.

Beyond the workplace, daily problem-solving often requires generating possible solutions rapidly: troubleshooting technical problems, handling unexpected situations, or brainstorming approaches to challenges. Verbal fluency deficits can slow this process, making individuals appear less capable than they are. Interventions include structured problem-solving approaches, using written lists, and involving others in brainstorming to compensate for reduced self-generated ideas.

Social Functioning

Conversations require verbal fluency—responding to others' comments, contributing to group discussions, and maintaining conversational flow. Individuals with verbal fluency deficits may appear reticent or disinterested when they actually struggle to formulate responses quickly enough for a natural conversational pace. This can affect relationship formation and social integration, which are risk factors for cognitive decline in older individuals. Social situations requiring storytelling, joke-telling, or describing experiences are particularly challenging. Interventions may include educating others about the difficulty, taking time to formulate responses rather than rushing, preparing for relevant topics beforehand, and leveraging strengths in written communication for detailed expression.

Creative expression also demands verbal fluency. Writing fiction, poetry, screenplays, or other creative content requires generating ideas, synonyms, descriptive language, and narrative flow. Individuals with verbal fluency deficits may have creative ideas but struggle with expression. Revision and editing become more important, and extended time for creative projects is often necessary.

PRELIMINARY CLINICAL VALIDATION OF THE D-KEFS ADVANCED VFT

Clinical group studies conducted during D-KEFS Advanced standardization provide initial evidence of VFT's sensitivity to executive dysfunction across several populations (Delis & Kaplan, 2025). These findings require replication and should not be used as sole diagnostic criteria, but they offer useful benchmarks for clinical interpretation.

Autism Spectrum Disorder

Children with ASD ($n = 31$) performed significantly below matched controls across all VFT conditions. Effect sizes were largest for measures tapping semantic retrieval (Category Fluency $d = 1.04$; Switching Fluency $d = 0.93$–1.01) compared to phonemic retrieval (Letter Fluency $d = 0.60$). This semantic-greater-than-phonemic pattern aligns with broader research documenting language and communication differences in ASD populations. Error rates were not elevated, indicating preserved accuracy despite reduced output.

Traumatic Brain Injury

Adults with moderate-to-severe TBI (n = 30; mean Glasgow Coma Scale = 8.5) showed large effect sizes across all VFT conditions (d = 0.96–1.23). Notably, reduced word production occurred without corresponding increases in set-loss errors or repetitions—a pattern suggesting that generalized cognitive slowing, rather than rule-maintenance failure, drove performance decrements. Subgroup analysis revealed that approximately 28% showed both reduced baseline fluency and disproportionately impaired switching (contrast scaled scores $\leq$7), indicating executive dysfunction beyond generalized slowing in this subset.

Mild Cognitive Impairment

The MCI findings (n = 18 older adults) carry particular diagnostic significance. Category Fluency was substantially lower than matched controls (d = 0.85, p = 0.03), while Letter Fluency performance was virtually equivalent between groups. This dissociation, semantic retrieval impaired with phonemic retrieval spared, mirrors the pattern extensively documented in individuals progressing toward Alzheimer's disease, where temporal lobe pathology affecting semantic networks typically precedes frontal involvement (Salmon & Bondi, 2009). Elevated repetition errors also trended toward significance (p = 0.08), consistent with the memory encoding difficulties characteristic of this population. These findings support the clinical utility of the Category versus Letter Fluency contrast score for detecting early cognitive decline.

ADHD and SLD-Math

VFT did not differentiate children with ADHD (n = 55) or SLD-Math (n = 26) from matched controls at the group level, suggesting that rapid rule-based verbal retrieval may represent a relative strength for these populations. However, the ADHD sample showed marked within-group variability: while most participants performed within normal limits, approximately 16% demonstrated average baseline fluency alongside disproportionately weak switching performance (contrast $\leq$7). This subgroup pattern—detectable only through contrast score analysis—indicates specific cognitive flexibility limitations that aggregate statistics obscure. The finding reinforces that diagnostic category membership does not predict uniform executive function profiles.

STRENGTHS AND WEAKNESSES

The Verbal Fluency Test offers several distinctive strengths for executive function assessment, alongside limitations that clinicians should consider when selecting measures and interpreting results.

Strengths

The Verbal Fluency Test offers several notable advantages for assessing executive-controlled word retrieval within a comprehensive neuropsychological evaluation.

Hierarchical Diagnostic Capability

Verbal Fluency's multiple conditions with varying executive demands enable differential diagnosis. The pattern across Letter, Category, and Switching conditions clarifies whether deficits are executive strategic, semantic knowledge-based, or represent specific cognitive flexibility weaknesses. This hierarchical structure aligns naturally with the four-tier framework, enabling systematic analysis from foundational through higher-order processes.

Process Score Richness

Error analysis (set-loss and repetition errors) and temporal interval patterns (original version) provide qualitative richness beyond total score interpretation. These process scores reveal the mechanisms underlying poor performance—working memory limits, inhibitory control weakness, or monitoring deficits—enabling targeted intervention.

Strong Ecological Validity

Verbal fluency directly relates to real-world language use: conversations, meetings, presentations, writing. Performance deficits predict functional communication difficulties, making Verbal Fluency results meaningful for intervention planning.

Brevity and Efficiency

Ten to twelve minutes of administration yield a comprehensive fluency assessment across multiple executive domains. This efficiency enables inclusion in most neuropsychological batteries without excessive time burden.

Clinical Sensitivity

Verbal Fluency demonstrates sensitivity to diverse clinical conditions: traumatic brain injury (Henry & Crawford, 2004a), Parkinson's disease (Henry & Crawford, 2004b), Alzheimer's disease (Henry et al., 2004), mild cognitive impairment (Nutter-Upham et al., 2008), and frontal lobe lesions (Baldo & Shimamura, 1998). This broad clinical utility makes Verbal Fluency valuable across neuropsychological contexts.

Alternate Forms Availability (Original Version)

Standard and Alternate Forms enable retesting while minimizing practice effects, valuable for treatment monitoring, recovery tracking, or repeated assessments in research contexts.

Digital Administration

Q-interactive provides automated timing, response recording, and error detection, improving measurement precision and freeing examiners for behavioral observation.

Advanced Version Enhancements

The phonemic-semantic switching and three-rule switching substantially increase executive demands, improving sensitivity to subtle deficits in high-functioning individuals.

Weaknesses and Limitations

Despite its strengths, the Verbal Fluency Test has several limitations that clinicians should consider when selecting measures and interpreting results.

Cultural and Linguistic Sensitivity

Verbal Fluency is heavily influenced by cultural background, language exposure, and education. Category knowledge varies across cultures. Not all cultures organize semantic categories identically. Letter fluency in English may not translate well to examinees whose primary language uses different orthographic or phonological systems. Bilingual examinees face unique challenges. These cultural-linguistic factors limit cross-cultural validity and require careful interpretation considering examinee background.

Education Confound

Years of education correlate substantially with Verbal Fluency performance, particularly Letter Fluency (Erden Aki et al., 2022). Distinguishing between reduced education and true executive dysfunction remains a significant challenge for clinicians, as the lack of formal schooling often mimics the profile of organic impairment, requiring extreme caution at the lower ends of the educational spectrum.

Dated Normative Data (Original Version)

The original D-KEFS normative data were collected in 2001, now over two decades old. Population changes in education levels, demographic composition, and cognitive stimulation may affect the representativeness of these norms for contemporary examinees, potentially inflating scores relative to current population performance.

Semantic Knowledge Confound

Category Fluency performance depends partly on semantic knowledge breadth. An individual who genuinely knows fewer animals due to cultural background, rural versus urban upbringing, or limited exposure to animal knowledge will produce fewer animal names, not due to executive dysfunction. Disentangling semantic knowledge from executive retrieval requires administering separate vocabulary and semantic knowledge measures.

Ceiling Effects in High-Functioning Individuals (Original Version)
The original version's Letter and Category Fluency sometimes shows ceiling effects in very high-functioning adults, limiting differentiation at superior levels. The Advanced version addresses this partially through increased switching complexity, but even three-rule switching may ceiling in some exceptional individuals.

Floor Effects in Severely Impaired Populations
Individuals with severe executive dysfunction, advanced dementia, or severe intellectual disability may produce only 1–2 words per trial, yielding floor effects that limit meaningful assessment. In such cases, Verbal Fluency provides limited information beyond "severely impaired."

Switching Condition Differences Across Versions
Original and Advanced versions use different switching paradigms (semantic-semantic versus phonemic-semantic), preventing direct numerical comparison. Examiners cannot simply compare an original version Category Switching score to an Advanced version Switching Fluency score without considering that they assess different cognitive demands.

Digital Administration Limitations
While digital administration offers advantages, it requires technological infrastructure (tablet, Internet connectivity, Q-interactive subscription). Settings lacking this infrastructure cannot administer the Advanced version.

Interval Scores Not Available on the Advanced Version
While behavioral observation of fluctuations in performance can still be observed, there are no separate scores for each of the 15-second intervals on the Advanced version.

Use of Binary Male and Female Names as a Category—Original Version
The original D-KEFS Verbal Fluency included Boys' Names and Girls' Names as Category Fluency conditions, which may introduce confounds related to naming conventions. Since the test's 2001 publication, cultural associations between names and binary gender categories have become less consistent, with gender-neutral names increasingly common. Beyond these contemporary considerations, examinees from non-Western cultural backgrounds may have smaller retrieval pools for traditional English gendered names compared to more universal categories such as animals or fruits. As a result, performance on these conditions may reflect cultural and linguistic familiarity rather than pure category fluency ability. Examiners interpreting archival data or using older test forms should consider whether name fluency scores provide equivalent measurement across all examinees.

ALTERNATIVE MEASURES

A comprehensive verbal executive assessment often requires measures beyond the Verbal Fluency Test. This section identifies complementary D-KEFS/D-KEFS Advanced subtests and external measures that clarify Verbal Fluency findings.

Within the D-KEFS Suite

Several D-KEFS subtests provide complementary or converging evidence for fluency, cognitive flexibility, and related executive functions.

Trail Making Test
Trail Making assesses cognitive flexibility through number-letter switching, providing an alternative switching paradigm that is visuomotor rather than verbal. Trail Making complements Verbal Fluency by assessing switching in a different modality, clarifying whether switching deficits are verbal-specific or reflect general cognitive flexibility limitations. Disproportionate Verbal Fluency switching difficulty with adequate Trail Making Number-Letter Switching suggests verbal-domain switching deficits; proportional impairment across both suggests general cognitive inflexibility.

Color-Word Interference Test
Color-Word assesses response inhibition and cognitive flexibility through color-word interference and inhibition-switching conditions. Like Verbal Fluency, Color-Word uses verbal stimuli but focuses on inhibition rather than generativity. Color-Word clarifies whether verbal executive deficits are specific to generative retrieval (Verbal Fluency impaired, Color-Word adequate) or reflect broader verbal inhibitory control problems (both impaired). The original D-KEFS Color-Word Conditions 1–2 provide direct verbal processing speed assessment, recommended by the Advanced manual for interpreting Verbal Fluency performance.

Tower Test
Tower assesses planning, working memory, and inhibition using visuospatial stimuli. It provides a nonverbal executive measure, clarifying whether executive deficits are modality-specific. Poor Verbal Fluency with adequate Tower suggests verbal executive deficits; proportional impairment suggests general executive dysfunction.

Design Fluency Test
Design Fluency assesses visual–spatial generativity and cognitive flexibility, providing the visual–spatial analog to Verbal Fluency. Comparing Verbal Fluency to Design Fluency clarifies modality specificity of fluency deficits. Disproportionate Verbal Fluency impairment with adequate Design Fluency suggests verbal-specific retrieval deficits; proportional impairment suggests general generativity problems.

Sorting Test
Sorting assesses concept formation and cognitive flexibility using both verbal and visual–spatial reasoning. It complements Verbal Fluency by requiring examinees to generate sorting rules rather than generate words within rules, providing a different executive generativity paradigm.

Beyond D-KEFS

Measures outside the D-KEFS family can provide converging evidence or assess related constructs when additional information is needed.

Alternative Phonemic/Semantic Fluency Tasks
When D-KEFS/D-KEFS Advanced is unavailable, other fluency measures can assess verbal generativity, though none provides the comprehensive three-condition design. The Controlled Oral Word Association Test (COWAT; F-A-S letters) from the Multilingual Aphasia Examination (Benton et al., 1994) assesses phonemic fluency but lacks category fluency and switching conditions, limiting differential diagnosis capability.

Semantic Knowledge and Word-Retrieval Measures
Distinguishing whether poor Category Fluency reflects limited semantic stores versus executive retrieval deficits requires measures of vocabulary and naming independent of time pressure. The Boston Naming Test–Second Edition (BNT-2; Kaplan et al., 2001) assesses confrontation naming—poor BNT with poor Category Fluency suggests semantic limitations, while adequate BNT with poor Category Fluency points to executive retrieval deficits. The Peabody Picture Vocabulary Test–Fifth Edition (PPVT-5; Dunn, 2019) assesses receptive vocabulary breadth, and WAIS-5/WISC-V Vocabulary (Wechsler, 2014, 2024) assesses expressive verbal knowledge.

Working Memory Measures
High set-loss errors or repetitions may reflect working memory limitations rather than executive dysfunction per se. WAIS-5/WISC-V Digit Span (particularly Backward and Sequencing) and Letter-Number Sequencing (Wechsler, 2014, 2024) clarify whether rule maintenance difficulties stem from working memory capacity limitations.

Response Inhibition Measures
Verbal fluency requires inhibiting previously generated responses and off-task associations. The Stroop Color and Word Test (Golden & Freshwater, 2002) provides a brief assessment of verbal interference control that complements Verbal Fluency's generative demands.

Cognitive Flexibility Measures

Switching Fluency deficits warrant comparison with other set-shifting paradigms. The Wisconsin Card Sorting Test (WCST; Heaton et al., 1993) assesses flexibility through implicit rule discovery, contrasting with Verbal Fluency's explicit alternation rules; both assess cognitive flexibility but through different mechanisms.

Connected Speech/Discourse Tasks

Formal fluency measures assess word generation under constrained conditions; connected speech tasks reveal fluency in naturalistic communication contexts. The Cookie Theft picture description task from the Boston Diagnostic Aphasia Examination–Third Edition (BDAE-3; Goodglass et al., 2001) provides informal assessment of conversational fluency, word-finding in discourse, and spontaneous language organization—useful when formal fluency scores seem discrepant from observed communication ability.

Behavior Rating Scales

Executive function rating scales capture real-world executive behaviors that may or may not align with performance-based measures. For children and adolescents, the Behavior Rating Inventory of Executive Function, Second Edition (BRIEF-2; Gioia et al., 2015), Comprehensive Executive Function Inventory (CEFI; Naglieri & Goldstein, 2013), and Delis Rating of Executive Functions (D-REF; Delis, 2012) provide parent and teacher perspectives on daily executive functioning. For adults, the BRIEF-A (Roth et al., 2005), CEFI Adult (Naglieri & Goldstein, 2017), and D-REF Adult (Delis, 2021) offer self-report and informant-report options. Relevant scales across these measures include Initiate (paralleling word generation initiation demands), Working Memory (tracking previously generated words and maintaining task rules), Shift (cognitive flexibility required for switching conditions), and Plan/Organize (strategic retrieval and clustering approaches). Discrepancies between Verbal Fluency performance and rating scale elevations provide diagnostic information: adequate test performance with elevated rating scales may indicate that the structured, quiet testing environment does not capture word retrieval challenges that emerge in fast-paced conversations, workplace meetings, or emotionally charged discussions. Conversely, poor Verbal Fluency performance with unremarkable rating scales might suggest test-specific factors such as performance anxiety under timed conditions, unfamiliarity with testing demands, or poor metacognitive awareness of daily word-finding difficulties rather than pervasive executive dysfunction.

SUMMARY

The Verbal Fluency Test provides a comprehensive assessment of executive-controlled language production, measuring strategic retrieval, cognitive flexibility, working memory, and monitoring across three conditions with progressively increasing executive demands. The hierarchical tier framework guides interpretation, distinguishing foundational language and semantic knowledge (Tier 1: motor articulation, comprehension, vocabulary, orthographic knowledge, word-retrieval skills) from bridging processes (Tier 2: dual-level working memory, verbal processing speed, basic rule-following) from core executive functions (Tier 3: strategic retrieval, cognitive flexibility, inhibition, working memory for rules, with both cold executive processes in structured contexts and hot executive factors like frustration tolerance and anxiety management) from higher-order integration (Tier 4: metacognitive monitoring, strategic flexibility, effort regulation, and hot–cold system integration).

The original version's three-condition structure (Letter Fluency, Category Fluency, Category Switching) provides a valid assessment for ages 8–89, with particular value for its extensive validation literature, availability of alternate forms, and phonemic fluency assessment using F-A-S (the most commonly used and researched letter combination). The Advanced version's enhanced switching conditions, particularly phonemic-semantic switching and three-rule switching for ages 14–69, provide higher executive ceiling, increased sensitivity to subtle deficits, and contemporary norms with precise digital measurement for ages 8–90.

Process scores differentiate strategic retrieval capacity, cognitive flexibility, working memory, and monitoring quality, clarifying which specific executive processes contribute to performance patterns. Error analysis (set-loss versus repetition errors) reveals the mechanisms of difficulty—rule maintenance failures versus response tracking failures versus inhibitory control weaknesses. Temporal patterns on the original version (initial burst with slowing versus steady production) reveal strategy use and fatigue effects. Behavioral observations reveal metacognitive awareness, emotional regulation, effort allocation, and strategy sophistication, which provide qualitative data essential for complete interpretation and distinguishing cold executive capacity from hot executive dysregulation.

Integration with other assessment data is critical. Verbal Fluency reflects primarily cold executive functions in emotionally neutral, structured contexts with explicit constraints. Performance may not predict verbal executive functioning when hot executive demands dominate in emotionally charged, ambiguous real-world situations. Semantic knowledge measures (vocabulary, naming) clarify whether category fluency deficits reflect semantic store limitations or executive retrieval failures. Processing speed measures clarify whether reduced fluency reflects general efficiency constraints or specific executive strategy limitations. Other executive measures (Trail Making, Color-Word Interference, Tower) clarify whether executive deficits are verbal-specific or reflect broader dysfunction. Behavioral rating scales and functional assessment complement Verbal Fluency results, bridging the assessment-reality gap.

Ultimately, Verbal Fluency data become clinically meaningful when translated into functional predictions and intervention recommendations. Specific patterns of strengths and weaknesses across conditions, error types, and behavioral observations directly inform individualized interventions targeting the appropriate level: foundational skill development (Tier 1: vocabulary enrichment, reading/spelling instruction, articulation therapy), processing support (Tier 2: working memory aids, extended time, reduced cognitive load), executive strategy instruction (Tier 3: clustering strategies, systematic search training, cognitive flexibility exercises, emotional regulation support), or metacognitive development (Tier 4: self-monitoring training, strategic adjustment practice, hot–cold integration). The examinee's real-world verbal fluency challenges—in meetings, academic writing, brainstorming sessions, social conversations, or creative expression—are understood through the lens of hierarchical analysis, enabling interventions that address root causes rather than surface symptoms.

TEST YOURSELF

1. According to Pearson's hierarchical tier framework for Verbal Fluency, which of the following represents a Tier 1 foundational process rather than an executive function?

(a) Strategic phonemic word retrieval.
(b) Cognitive flexibility during category switching.
(c) Verbal semantic knowledge and vocabulary breadth.
(d) Working memory for maintaining task rules.

2. A 45-year-old examinee produces 8, 7, and 9 words on Letter Fluency (F, A, S), but generates 22 and 20 words on Category Fluency (Animals, Fruits/Vegetables). Vocabulary and naming scores are average. This pattern most likely indicates:

(a) Semantic memory degradation.
(b) Executive strategic retrieval deficit.
(c) Generalized processing speed limitation.
(d) Poor test-taking effort.

3. The D-KEFS Advanced VFT's phonemic-semantic switching (e.g., alternating between Clothing items and L words) differs from the original version's semantic-semantic switching (e.g., Furniture-Fruits) primarily in:

(a) Time allowed per trial.
(b) Number of words required.
(c) Executive demand level—cross-domain strategy shifting is more demanding than within-domain switching.
(d) Scoring procedures for errors.

4. **High repetition errors combined with high late-trial set-loss errors (rule violations emerging only after 40+ seconds) most directly suggest:**
   (a) Reduced test-taking effort or malingering.
   (b) Working memory capacity limits under accumulating cognitive load.
   (c) Semantic memory degradation.
   (d) Poor initial instruction comprehension.
5. **On the Advanced VFT, the three-rule switching trial (L words–Clothing–B words) for ages 14–69 primarily assesses which combination of Tier 3 executive functions?**
   (a) Initiation and response inhibition.
   (b) Multilevel verbal working memory and multilevel cognitive shifting.
   (c) Semantic knowledge and strategic retrieval.
   (d) Processing speed and sustained attention.
6. **An examinee generates 15 words in the first 30 seconds of a Letter Fluency trial (F words), then only 2 words in the final 30 seconds despite prompting, with no rule violations or repetitions. This temporal pattern most likely indicates:**
   (a) Tier 1 articulation difficulty affecting speech production.
   (b) Tier 2 processing speed limitation.
   (c) Tier 3 executive strategy failure—initial automatic retrieval exhausted without effective strategic search.
   (d) Tier 4 premature effort withdrawal.
7. **When an examinee's Category Fluency performance is significantly weaker than Letter Fluency performance AND vocabulary/naming measures are also low, the most likely interpretation is:**
   (a) Executive strategic retrieval deficit specific to semantic search.
   (b) Semantic memory degradation affecting semantic stores (Tier 1).
   (c) Cognitive flexibility deficit.
   (d) Working memory limitation affecting rule maintenance.
8. **The Advanced VFT's Combined Letter and Category Fluency vs. Switching Fluency Total Correct/ Switching Accuracy Index contrast scaled score of 6 indicates:**
   (a) Switching performance is within the expected range, given baseline fluency.
   (b) Switching performance exceeds expectations, given baseline fluency.
   (c) Switching performance is worse than predicted, suggesting disproportionate cognitive flexibility/working memory difficulty.
   (d) Invalid test results requiring readministration.
9. **Which of the following behavioral observations would most strongly suggest intact Tier 4 metacognitive functioning despite Tier 3 executive deficits?**
   (a) High error rate without apparent awareness or concern.
   (b) Generating words at a steady pace without clustering or strategy.
   (c) Spontaneously recognizing difficulty, expressing frustration about limited output, and accurately perceiving performance quality.
   (d) Continuing ineffective strategy without adjustment throughout trials.
10. **A clinician should prefer the D-KEFS Advanced VFT over the original version when:**
   (a) The examinee is 10 years old.
   (b) Forensic evaluation requires comparison with extensive prior testing using the original version.
   (c) Assessment targets subtle executive deficits in a high-functioning adult where increased switching demands and precise error measurement are valuable.
   (d) Traditional paper-pencil administration is required due to lack of digital infrastructure.

Answer Key: 1-c, 2-b, 3-c, 4-b, 5-b, 6-c, 7-b, 8-c, 9-c, 10-c

REFERENCES

Baldo, J. V., & Shimamura, A. P. (1998). Letter and category fluency in patients with frontal lobe lesions. *Neuropsychology, 12*(2), 259–267.

Benton, A. L., Hamsher, K. d S., & Sivan, A. B. (1994). *Multilingual Aphasia Examination* (3rd ed.). Psychological Assessment Resources.

Delis, D. C. (2012). *Delis Rating of Executive Functions (D-REF)*, Pearson.

Delis, D. C. (2021). *Delis Rating of Executive Functions—Adult (D-REF Adult)*. Pearson.

Delis, D. C., & Kaplan, E. (2025). *Delis-Kaplan Executive Function System—Advanced (D-KEFS Advanced)*. Pearson.

Delis, D. C., Kaplan, E., & Kramer, J. H. (2001). *Delis-Kaplan Executive Function System (D-KEFS)*. Pearson.

Dunn, D. M. (2019). *Peabody Picture Vocabulary Test* (5th ed.). NCS Pearson.

Erden Aki, Ö., Alkan, B., Demirsöz, T., Velibaşoğlu, B., Taşdemir, T., Piri Erbaş, S., Selvi, K., Ergenç, İ., Barişkin, E., Özdemir, P., & Demir, B. (2022). Effects of age, gender and education on phonemic and semantic verbal fluency. *Türk Psikiyatri Dergisi, 33*(1), 53–64.

Gioia, G. A., Isquith, P. K., Guy, S. C., & Kenworthy, L. (2015). *Behavior Rating Inventory of Executive Function* (2nd ed.). PAR.

Golden, C. J., & Freshwater, S. M. (2002). *Stroop Color and Word Test: A Manual for Clinical and Experimental Uses*. Stoelting.

Goodglass, H., Kaplan, E., & Barresi, B. (2001). *Boston Diagnostic Aphasia Examination* (3rd ed.). Pro-Ed.

Heaton, R. K., Chelune, G. J., Talley, J. L., Kay, G. G., & Curtiss, G. (1993). *Wisconsin Card Sorting Test Manual: Revised and Expanded*. Psychological Assessment Resources.

Henry, J. D., & Crawford, J. R. (2004a). A meta-analytic review of verbal fluency performance in patients with traumatic brain injury. *Neuropsychology, 18*(4), 621–628.

Henry, J. D., & Crawford, J. R. (2004b). Verbal fluency deficits in Parkinson's disease: A meta-analysis. *Journal of the International Neuropsychological Society, 10*(4), 608–622.

Henry, J. D., Crawford, J. R., & Phillips, L. H. (2004). Verbal fluency performance in dementia of the Alzheimer's type: A meta-analysis. *Neuropsychologia, 42*(9), 1212–1222.

Kaplan, E., Goodglass, H., & Weintraub, S. (2001). *Boston Naming Test* (2nd ed.). Pro-Ed.

Kavé, G., & Sapir-Yogev, S. (2023). Differences between semantic and phonemic verbal fluency in adolescents with reading disorders. *Archives of Clinical Neuropsychology, 38*(1), 126–130.

Koren, R., Kofman, O., & Berger, A. (2005). Analysis of word clustering in verbal fluency of school-aged children. *Archives of Clinical Neuropsychology, 20*(8), 1087–1104.

Naglieri, J. A., & Goldstein, S. (2013). *Comprehensive Executive Function Inventory (CEFI)*. Multi-Health Systems.

Naglieri, J. A., & Goldstein, S. (2017). *Comprehensive Executive Function Inventory Adult (CEFI Adult)*. Multi-Health Systems.

Nutter-Upham, K. E., Saykin, A. J., Rabin, L. A., Roth, R. M., Wishart, H. A., Pare, N., & Flashman, L. A. (2008). Verbal fluency performance in amnestic MCI and older adults with cognitive complaints. *Archives of Clinical Neuropsychology, 23*(3), 229–241.

Roth, R. M., Isquith, P. K., & Gioia, G. A. (2005). *Behavior Rating Inventory of Executive Function—Adult Version (BRIEF-A)*. PAR.

Salmon, D. P., & Bondi, M. W. (2009). Neuropsychological assessment of dementia. *Annual Review of Psychology, 60*, 257–282.

Troyer, A. K., Moscovitch, M., Winocur, G., Alexander, M. P., & Stuss, D. (1998). Clustering and switching on verbal fluency: The effects of focal frontal- and temporal-lobe lesions. *Neuropsychologia, 36*(6), 499–504.

Wechsler, D. (2014). *Wechsler Intelligence Scale for Children* (5th ed.). NCS Pearson.

Wechsler, D. (2024). *Wechsler Adult Intelligence Scale* (5th ed.). NCS Pearson.

Fourteen

WORD CONTEXT TEST

CLINICAL VIGNETTE

Thirteen-year-old Darren Thompson was referred for an evaluation due to declining academic performance despite average intelligence test scores. His seventh-grade teachers reported that Darren seemed to understand material when presented in class but struggled with assignments requiring him to "put it all together." Reading comprehension was particularly challenging when passages required inference across multiple paragraphs, and he often missed the main ideas despite understanding individual sentences.

On the Word Context Test, Darren's performance revealed an intriguing pattern across the hierarchical tiers. He demonstrated intact Tier 1 foundational abilities, understanding each clue sentence individually and generating responses that showed adequate vocabulary and language comprehension for his age. His Tier 2 bridging processes also appeared intact, as he could maintain attention across all five sentences and follow the basic task requirements. However, his Tier 3 executive functioning revealed significant deficits. On one item, after hearing "You blorf several times a day," Darren responded, "Eat." When presented with the second clue, "People blorf when they're thirsty," he shifted to "swallow," then to "pour" for the third clue, "You blorf liquids." Each response was plausible for the individual sentence, but ignored information from previous clues, earning him only 1 point on this item when he finally arrived at the correct response on the fifth sentence.

This pattern of applicable but shifting responses occurred across multiple items, yielding a Total Consecutively Correct scaled score of 6 and a Consistently Correct Ratio scaled score of 5. His performance demonstrated adequate deductive reasoning at the single-sentence level but prominent deficits in information integration and cognitive flexibility—core Tier 3 executive functions. Notably, Darren showed increasing frustration as testing progressed, commenting, "I hate these kinds of puzzles" and rushing through later items, making quick decisions. Hot executive factors appeared to exacerbate his cold executive difficulties. This profile suggested that Darren's academic struggles stemmed not from fundamental language or reasoning deficits but from impaired ability to integrate multiple streams of information—the skill required for synthesizing textbook content, lecture notes, and class discussions into cohesive understanding. Recommendations focused on explicit instruction in integration strategies, graphic organizers that visually represented relationships between pieces of information, and emotion regulation techniques for managing frustration during complex synthesis tasks.

TEST DESCRIPTION

The D-KEFS Word Context Test (Delis et al., 2001), appropriate for ages 8 through 89, assesses verbal executive functions through a deductive reasoning paradigm. Originally developed by Edith Kaplan at Brooklyn College in collaboration with developmental psychologist Heinz Werner, the task was designed to study how children acquire word meanings (Werner & Kaplan, 1952). The test's evolution into a neuropsychological instrument reflects its capacity to assess multiple executive functions in the verbal domain.

The examinee's task is to discover the meaning of 10 made-up "mystery words" based on progressively informative clue sentences. Each mystery word appears in five sentences presented sequentially, with all previously shown sentences remaining visible. The first sentence provides only vague, overly inclusive clues

DON'T FORGET

The Word Context Test provides a unique assessment of deductive reasoning, moving from general categorical information to specific conclusions. This contrasts with inductive reasoning tasks like the Wechsler Similarities subtest (Wechsler, 2014, 2024), which require identifying superordinate categories from specific exemplars. Understanding this distinction helps clarify which aspect of verbal reasoning is impaired when performance diverges across these measures.

CAUTION

The Word Context Test places substantial demands on language comprehension and verbal expression. Individuals with developmental language disorders, acquired aphasia, or those who are English language learners may obtain low scores due to fundamental linguistic deficits rather than executive dysfunction. Always assess basic language abilities through complementary measures before attributing poor Word Context performance to executive deficits.

(e.g., "Most people need to limur in the morning."), while each subsequent sentence offers increasingly specific information. The examinee generates one hypothesis after each sentence, attempting to identify the word's meaning. Critically, once the correct response is identified, the examinee must maintain that response across remaining sentences—a requirement that distinguishes this test from simple word-learning tasks.

The test yields five core normed measures: Total Consecutively Correct (the primary achievement measure), Consistently Correct Ratio, Repeated Incorrect Responses, No/Don't Know Responses, and Correct-to-Incorrect Errors. This scoring system captures not just whether the examinee eventually identifies the correct meaning but how efficiently they reach that conclusion and whether they maintain set once established. The test typically requires 15–20 minutes to administer and provides rich qualitative data about an examinee's reasoning process, flexibility, and integration abilities.

The test's ecological validity derives from its similarity to real-world situations requiring integration of multiple information sources to reach conclusions (Burgess et al., 1998; Chaytor & Schmitter-Edgecombe, 2003). Students must synthesize information from textbooks, lectures, and discussions to understand concepts. Professionals integrate data from reports, conversations, and observations to make decisions. When determining the meaning of unknown words when reading, listening to conversations, or learning a foreign language, we often use the meaning of words surrounding an unknown word to help us determine the unknown word's meaning. The Word Context Test's requirement to progressively narrow hypotheses based on accumulating evidence mirrors these everyday cognitive demands, making it particularly valuable for understanding functional difficulties in academic and professional contexts.

Rapid Reference 14.1

Word Context Test Overview

Element	Description
Age range	8–89 years
Administration time	15–20 minutes
Structure	10 items, each with 5 progressive clue sentences containing a made-up "mystery word"
Response format	Verbal hypothesis generation; one response per sentence
Materials	Examiner's Manual, Stimulus Booklet (easel format), Record Form; digital versions available through Q-global Digital Assets
Discontinuation	None—administer all 10 items; all 5 sentences per item, regardless of when correct response emerges
Primary constructs	Deductive reasoning, information integration, cognitive flexibility
Key feature	Novel stimuli prevent reliance on crystallized knowledge; assesses top-down (general to specific) reasoning

HIERARCHICAL TIER ANALYSIS

The Word Context Test can be analyzed through the tiered framework, with performance primarily reflecting processes from Tier 1 foundational abilities through Tier 3 executive functions. Unlike some D-KEFS subtests, Word Context does not substantively assess Tier 4 higher-order integration; metacognitive processes on this task are better conceptualized as extensions of Tier 3 functioning.

Tier 1: Foundational Processes (Nonexecutive)

Before executive functions can be assessed, several foundational processes must be intact.

Auditory Processing and Language Comprehension
Understanding each clue sentence as presented requires adequate auditory processing and receptive language abilities. The test requires comprehension of moderately complex sentence structures and the ability to extract meaning from sentences containing unfamiliar words in context. Individuals with auditory processing disorders, receptive language deficits, or hearing impairments may struggle to understand the clue sentences themselves, independent of any executive dysfunction.

Lexical-Semantic Knowledge
Understanding the known words within each clue sentence depends on vocabulary breadth and depth. The examinee must possess adequate vocabulary to comprehend words like "vocal cords," "convex," or "implement." Limited vocabulary restricts the examinee's ability to fully process the clues, leading to low scores that reflect knowledge deficits rather than reasoning impairments. This is particularly relevant when assessing individuals with limited educational backgrounds or English language learners. The test's scoring guidelines recognize this challenge by crediting responses that capture the general concept even when precise terminology is lacking.

Expressive Language Abilities
Communicating hypotheses verbally requires sufficient expressive language capacity. While the scoring guidelines emphasize reasoning over linguistic precision, a minimum level of expressive capacity is required to convey understanding. Individuals with expressive aphasia, significant word-finding difficulties, or severe articulation disorders may understand the correct meaning but struggle to communicate their hypothesis. A comprehensive aphasia assessment (Goodglass & Kaplan, 1987) may be warranted when language limitations are suspected. Basic word retrieval, the ability to access and produce specific lexical items, is a foundational language skill distinct from the semantic flexibility required to search strategically within conceptual domains, which represents Tier 3 executive processing described herewith.

> **CAUTION**
>
> Before concluding that poor Word Context performance reflects executive deficits, assess vocabulary through standardized receptive and expressive vocabulary measures. Significant discrepancies between vocabulary and Word Context scores warrant careful analysis of which clues the examinee appeared to understand versus which may have been incomprehensible due to limited word knowledge.

Basic Sustained Attention
Maintaining engagement across the five sentences of each item and across all 10 items requires adequate attentional capacity. The test does not make extraordinary attentional demands—sentences are brief, and there are natural breaks between items—but examinees must maintain sufficient attention to process each sentence and remember previous clues. Processing speed at Tier 1 is less critical than on many D-KEFS subtests, as the task is untimed and the examiner controls pacing.

Tier 1 Impairment Pattern
Tier 1 deficits manifest differently depending on which foundational process is compromised. Auditory processing or language comprehension deficits appear as consistent difficulty across all items, with responses suggesting limited comprehension of clue sentences themselves; supporting evidence includes difficulty following complex verbal instructions and frequent requests for repetition. Lexical-semantic deficits produce errors concentrated on items containing unfamiliar vocabulary. The examinee may reason well on items with common words but fail items requiring knowledge of terms like "convex" or "implement"; corroborating evidence includes low vocabulary scores on standardized measures. Expressive language deficits create a different pattern: the examinee may demonstrate understanding through partial responses, gestures, or circumlocution but struggle to produce the target word

despite apparent comprehension; word-finding pauses, self-corrections, and frustration with articulation suggest expressive rather than reasoning limitations. Basic attention deficits manifest as inconsistent performance across items unrelated to difficulty level, with declining engagement, missed clue information, or requests to repeat sentences that were adequately heard.

Tier 2: Bridging Processes

Basic Rule-Following and Task Orientation

Understanding and adhering to task demands requires foundational procedural awareness. Examinees must generate one hypothesis per sentence, take their best guess, and continue providing responses even after identifying the correct meaning. These requirements represent procedural knowledge about the task rather than executive control. Most examinees grasp these rules readily during the practice item.

Categorical Thinking

Generating responses that fit within the broad category implied by a single clue sentence requires elementary semantic categorization abilities. This represents basic semantic activation (sometimes termed abductive inference)—accessing knowledge networks related to the clue content—rather than the complex deductive reasoning required to narrow possibilities across multiple clues.

Response Inhibition

Refraining from blurting out multiple responses per sentence or continuing to respond after all five sentences have been presented requires foundational impulse control. This differs from the more complex inhibition required at Tier 3 to suppress a previous hypothesis when new evidence conflicts with it.

Recognition of Novelty

Understanding that these are made-up words requiring hypothesis generation rather than retrieval of known definitions requires basic metacognitive awareness. This metacognitive awareness, recognizing that standard vocabulary knowledge won't apply, represents a bridging process between basic comprehension and executive reasoning.

Tier 2 Deficit Pattern

Tier 2 Bridging Deficits appear as difficulty maintaining task orientation or following basic task rules. These are uncommon in Word Context, given its straightforward structure, but individuals with significant cognitive impairment may struggle with the basic concept of generating hypotheses for made-up words or following the one-response-per-sentence rule.

Tier 3: Core Executive Functions

Tier 3 represents the core executive functions that the Word Context Test is designed to assess. These processes can be divided into cold executive functions—the cognitive mechanisms underlying deductive reasoning, information integration, and hypothesis testing—and hot executive functions involving frustration tolerance, anxiety management, and sustained motivation. Accurate interpretation requires distinguishing between these domains, as intervention approaches differ substantially.

Cold Executive Functions

Cold executive functions represent the purely cognitive aspects of executive control, operating on logical and analytical processes independent of emotional valence. On the Word Context Test, several interrelated cold executive processes contribute to successful performance, with deductive reasoning and information integration representing the primary demands.

Deductive Reasoning

Executive functions encompass the cognitive processes that enable goal-directed behavior through flexible adaptation to changing demands (Diamond, 2013). On the Word Context Test, deductive reasoning represents the primary cold executive function assessed. Deduction involves moving from general principles to specific conclusions—the opposite of induction's movement from specific instances to general rules. Each clue sentence provides categorical information, and the examinee must deduce which specific entity satisfies all the provided categories. This top-down reasoning process requires analyzing overly inclusive information and progressively narrowing possibilities as additional constraints are added.

The quality of deductive reasoning becomes apparent in the nature of incorrect responses. When an examinee responds "fire" to "A blorf can be hot or cold," they demonstrate impaired deduction, focusing on the "hot" feature while ignoring that the entity must also be capable of being cold. This pattern of responses that fit partial but not complete clue information characterizes deductive reasoning deficits.

Information Integration and Synthesis

Integration and synthesis distinguish Word Context Test performance from simpler reasoning tasks. The examinee must not treat each sentence in isolation but must actively integrate new clues with previous information to progressively narrow hypotheses. This requires maintaining the accumulated constraint set in working memory while evaluating whether a new clue confirms, narrows, or contradicts the current hypothesis. Strong performers demonstrate this integration by offering increasingly specific responses that respect all previous clues.

Many examinees with executive dysfunction generate responses that fit individual sentences but ignore previous clues—the pattern Darren exhibited in the clinical vignette. This failure to integrate across information sources appears frequently in individuals with frontal lobe dysfunction (Lezak et al., 2012; Waltz et al., 1999) and significantly impacts the Total Consecutively Correct score.

> **DON'T FORGET**
>
> The Word Context Test's most diagnostically revealing pattern is responses that fit individual sentences but ignore previous clues. This failure to integrate across information sources, generating "fire" because something "can be hot" while ignoring the clue that it must also be cold, appears frequently in frontal lobe dysfunction and distinguishes integration deficits from vocabulary or language limitations.

Hypothesis Generation and Testing

Hypothesis generation involves formulating potential meanings based on available evidence and implicitly testing whether those hypotheses fit new information. Strong performers engage in active hypothesis testing, generating possibilities after early clues and then evaluating whether each new sentence supports or refutes their hypothesis. Weak performers often engage in associative responding, generating the first word that comes to mind in response to each new sentence rather than systematically evaluating hypotheses.

The difference between hypothesis-testing and associative responding becomes particularly apparent on items where strong semantic associates might mislead. When hearing "A carpenter uses a flim every day," the examinee using hypothesis-testing thinks: "I said 'tool' for the last sentence about fixing things; does 'tool' work here? Yes, carpenters use tools." The examinee engaging in associative responding thinks: "Carpenter... wood!" and shifts to a new response despite previously identifying the correct meaning.

Cognitive Flexibility and Set-Shifting

Shifting and cognitive flexibility enables the examinee to abandon incorrect hypotheses when new evidence conflicts with them. After responding "music" to the first sentence of an item, the flexible thinker recognizes that the second sentence ("People do this multiple times per day") contradicts this hypothesis, because not everyone listens to music multiple times daily. This recognition prompts set-shifting to a new hypothesis consistent with both sentences.

The Repeated Incorrect Responses score directly quantifies flexibility deficits. Examinees who rigidly maintain incorrect responses across multiple sentences despite contradictory clues demonstrate impaired cognitive flexibility. Examinees who rigidly maintain incorrect responses across multiple sentences despite contradictory clues demonstrate impaired cognitive flexibility—a pattern consistent with frontal systems dysfunction. Similar flexibility deficits may manifest on other D-KEFS measures, including perseverative errors on Color-Word Interference Condition 4, reduced switching productivity on Verbal Fluency Category Switching, and inefficient strategy adjustment on Twenty Questions. This convergent pattern strengthens diagnostic confidence when present.

Executive Working Memory

Working memory involves actively manipulating and integrating multiple pieces of information simultaneously—the constraint set from previous sentences (all visible but requiring active consideration), the new information from the current sentence, and potential hypotheses being evaluated. The examinee must track their own previous responses, maintain awareness of accumulating constraints, and evaluate new clues against this integrated knowledge base. This active manipulation and integration distinguishes executive working memory from passive storage.

Semantic Flexibility

Accessing multiple related concepts within semantic domains supports effective hypothesis generation and refinement. While basic word retrieval is a Tier 1 foundational ability, the capacity to flexibly search within semantic domains, accessing various related terms to find one that precisely fits accumulating constraints, represents Tier 3 executive processing.

Tier 3 Cold EF Impairment Pattern

Tier 3 Cold Executive Deficits produce the most common impairment pattern. Deductive reasoning deficits appear as responses addressing only partial clue information, integration deficits manifest as responses ignoring previous clues, and flexibility deficits show in perseveration on incorrect hypotheses despite contradictory evidence. These patterns occur despite adequate language comprehension and working memory capacity.

Hot Executive Functions

Hot executive functions involve the motivational and emotional aspects of executive control that influence how effectively cold executive processes are deployed. Despite its ostensibly cognitive demands, the Word Context Test creates conditions that engage hot executive processes through uncertainty, ambiguity, and the absence of performance feedback.

Frustration Tolerance and Emotional Regulation

These issues significantly impact Word Context Test performance despite its ostensibly "cold" cognitive demands (Zelazo & Carlson, 2012). The test structure creates multiple opportunities for frustration: early clues provide insufficient information for confident responses, requiring the examinee to guess with high uncertainty. This emotional discomfort can lead some examinees to refuse to respond (No/Don't Know responses) or to become increasingly disengaged as the test progresses.

Individuals with poor frustration tolerance may become derailed after several difficult items. Their reasoning abilities remain intact, but emotional dysregulation interferes with cognitive performance. They may answer rapidly without fully considering their response to "get it over with," abandon systematic reasoning in favor of random guessing, or become oppositional.

Performance Anxiety and Self-Consciousness

Willingness to generate hypotheses—particularly after early clues when the correct answer isn't obvious—can be affected by concerns about appearing incompetent. The instruction to "take a guess even if you're not sure" runs counter to many individuals' preferred performance style. Those who pride themselves on accuracy and worry about appearing incompetent may resist guessing, producing elevated No/Don't Know responses despite possessing adequate reasoning abilities.

CAUTION

Hot executive dysfunction can appear as cold executive deficits on the Word Context Test. An examinee who becomes anxious and disengaged might produce a low Total Consecutively Correct score that superficially resembles impaired deductive reasoning. However, the pattern of No/Don't Know responses, behavioral observations of anxiety or frustration, and performance history can distinguish these presentations. Always consider whether emotional factors, rather than cognitive limitations, explain poor performance, as the intervention approaches differ dramatically.

Persistence and Sustained Motivation

Continued engagement across 10 items when early items are challenging, and success isn't immediate, requires adequate effort regulation. The capacity to delay gratification and sustain effort toward future goals represents a core hot executive function with well-documented real-world consequences (Mischel et al., 1989). The test provides minimal external reinforcement. The examiner cannot confirm correct responses during administration, leaving the examinee uncertain about performance quality. Individuals with motivational deficits or low frustration tolerance may disengage after several items, producing effort-related low scores distinct from reasoning deficits.

Tier 3 Hot EF Pattern

Tier 3 Hot Executive Dysfunction appears as performance deteriorating with increasing frustration or disengagement despite preserved reasoning ability. Early items demonstrate good reasoning, but later items show rapid, unconsidered responses or increased No/Don't Know responses. Behavioral observations reveal frustration, anxiety, or declining motivation rather than confusion.

Note on Tier 4

The Word Context Test does not substantively assess Tier 4 higher-order integration processes. While metacognitive awareness and strategy adjustment may influence performance, these functions are better conceptualized as extensions of Tier 3 self-monitoring and cognitive flexibility rather than distinct higher-order integration demands.

Rapid Reference 14.2

Tier Structure at a Glance

Tier	Processes
Tier 1: Foundational processes (nonexecutive)	Auditory processing and language comprehension
	Lexical-semantic knowledge (vocabulary for clue words)
	Expressive language for communicating hypotheses
	Basic sustained attention across items
Tier 2: Bridging processes	Basic rule-following and task orientation
	Elementary categorical thinking (single-sentence level)
	Basic response inhibition (one response per sentence)
	Recognition that mystery words require reasoning, not retrieval
Tier 3: Cold executive functions	Deductive reasoning—general to specific (PRIMARY)
	Information integration and synthesis across clues
	Hypothesis generation and testing
	Cognitive flexibility and set-shifting
	Executive working memory (active manipulation)
	Semantic flexibility
Tier 3: Hot executive functions	Frustration tolerance with uncertainty
	Performance anxiety and self-consciousness
	Persistence and sustained motivation

Note: Word Context does not substantively assess Tier 4 higher-order integration. Metacognitive processes on this task are better conceptualized as Tier 3 functions.

ADMINISTRATION

NOTE: Refer to the Examiner's Manual for complete and detailed administration instructions. The Examiner's Manual provides verbatim instructions and clinicians should follow these precisely to ensure standardized administration.

Materials

The Word Context Test requires minimal materials: the Examiner's Manual, Record Form and Stimulus Booklet positioned in its easel format facing the examinee. Digital versions of the Examiner's Manual, Stimulus Booklet, and Stimulus Book Administration Directions are available through Pearson's Q-global Digital Assets.

General Administration

Administration begins with clear instructions establishing the task structure: the examinee should imagine being in a foreign country with a different language, and sentences will provide progressive clues about the mystery word meanings. The instructions emphasize guessing after each sentence, even when clues seem insufficient, taking one guess per sentence, and maintaining a response if it continues to fit subsequent sentences or changing it if a better answer emerges.

The practice item serves multiple purposes beyond familiarizing the examinee with the task format. It allows assessment of basic comprehension of instructions, provides an opportunity to observe reasoning approach, and permits the examiner to ensure the examinee understands that responses need not be verbatim from the sentences. For each sentence, feedback responses are provided in the Examiner's Manual and on the examiner's side of the Stimulus Booklet.

For each test item, the examiner presents the mystery word pronunciation, reads the first sentence aloud while the examinee views it, and prompts for a response. After the examinee responds, the examiner proceeds to the next sentence without providing feedback about correctness. This neutral stance—neither confirming correct responses nor correcting errors—represents a critical administrative requirement.

If the examinee does not respond within 15 seconds or says "I don't know," the examiner should prompt: "Take a guess even if you are not sure." If the examinee continues not responding after the prompt, the examiner records "no response" or "don't know" and proceeds to the next sentence.

Recording Responses

Recording responses requires verbatim transcription of the examinee's exact words. This proves essential for accurate scoring and for qualitative analysis of reasoning quality. The quality of verbatim recording directly impacts scoring accuracy and qualitative interpretation. Also record a Q if the prompt required a Query, or an NR or DK if there is no response. For each sentence, circle Y if the response is correct, or N if it is not.

Within each item, for the first sentence with a correct response, circle the corresponding raw score under the First Sentence Correct column or a 0 if there were no correct responses. After all five responses have been provided, circle the raw score for the first sentence that is correct and continues to be correct until the end of the item under the First Sentence Consecutively Correct column. For example, if the examinee is correct for responses 1 and 2, incorrect for response 3, and correct for responses 4 and 5, a 2 would be circled because it corresponds to response 4. Response 4 is the first of the consecutive correct responses until the end of the item.

Within each item, record the number of Repeated Incorrect Responses, No/Don't Know Responses, and Correct-to-Incorrect Errors that the examinee made for each item. Correct-to-incorrect responses occur when an examinee provides a correct response but then switches to an incorrect response before the end of the item.

Discontinue Rules

Word Context contains no discontinue rule—all 10 items must be administered regardless of performance. Even when an examinee provides the correct response before all five sentences within an item are presented, all five sentences must be read and responses obtained for each.

BEHAVIORAL OBSERVATIONS

Behavioral observations during Word Context administration provide qualitative information for enriching quantitative score interpretation.

Response Quality and Reasoning Approach

The sophistication of responses reveals reasoning quality independent of correctness. Responses integrating information from multiple sentences demonstrate more sophisticated reasoning than single-feature responses. The progression of responses within an item illuminates reasoning processes: Are responses becoming increasingly specific as clues accumulate, or does each response seem unrelated to previous ones?

Observing whether incorrect responses fit provided clues distinguishes deductive reasoning ability from flexibility. An examinee generating responses that fit individual clues but ignore previous information demonstrates intact deduction but impaired integration. Response specificity and precision vary meaningfully, some identify precise terms while others provide accurate but circumlocutory descriptions.

Behavioral and Emotional Indicators

Frustration tolerance becomes observable as testing progresses. Some examinees maintain consistent engagement while others show increasing frustration through sighing, negative self-statements, or rushing through items. The point at which frustration emerges matters: immediate frustration suggests low tolerance (hot executive deficit) while gradual emergence suggests normal response to accumulated challenge.

Response latency patterns provide clues about processing demands. Latencies increasing within items suggest working memory load or integration difficulties. Unusually brief latencies paired with low-quality responses may signal disengagement. The response to uncertainty reveals emotional regulation effectiveness. Some examinees tolerate ambiguity with equanimity, while others become anxious or oppositional.

SCORING

The Word Context Test yields one primary achievement measure and four optional process measures, each capturing different aspects of verbal deductive reasoning performance. Together, these scores enable clinicians to distinguish efficient reasoning from eventual success, identify specific patterns of cognitive inflexibility or disengagement, and differentiate cold executive deficits from hot executive interference.

Primary Measure: Total Consecutively Correct

The Total Consecutively Correct score represents the primary achievement measure and captures the examinee's efficiency in correctly identifying and maintaining mystery word meanings as more clues present. For each item, scoring begins when the examinee first provides the correct response and continues through all remaining sentences in which the correct response is maintained. An examinee who identifies the correct response on sentence 2 and maintains that response through sentences 3–5 earns 4 points for that item. An examinee who identifies the correct response on sentence 5 earns only 1 point. Failure to identify the correct meaning across all five sentences yields 0 points for that item. The total score is calculated by adding the Consecutively Correct scores for all items.

This scoring approach rewards both early identification and consistency of correct responding. The consecutively correct requirement distinguishes the Word Context Test from tasks where a single correct response earns full credit.

Scoring requires careful attention to response meaning rather than precise wording. A response is scored correct if it reflects the general concept of the mystery word, not if it uses the exact target word. The scoring guidelines emphasize giving the benefit of the doubt when responses are reasonably close, prioritizing reasoning assessment over expressive precision.

Optional Process Measures

Consistently Correct Ratio

The Consistently Correct Ratio (Total Consecutively Correct Raw Score ÷ First Sentence Correct Raw Score) quantifies the examinee's efficiency by comparing total consecutively correct scores to total sum first-sentence correct scores. High ratios indicate efficient early identification and consistent maintenance of correct responses. Low ratios suggest that correct meanings were identified, but not identified early, or were identified but not maintained across subsequent sentences.

Repeated Incorrect Responses

The Repeated Incorrect Responses score quantifies cognitive flexibility by counting how many times an incorrect response is repeated within the same item. Summed across all items, this measure provides a scaled score indicating flexibility of thinking. High raw scores result in low scaled scores and suggest perseverative thinking and difficulty abandoning unsuccessful hypotheses. Higher scaled scores indicate better performance, meaning fewer raw repetitions.

No/Don't Know Responses

This score counts instances where the examinee provides no response or states "I don't know" even after the standard prompt to guess. Approximately 39.8% of the normative sample produced at least one such response, indicating that some no/don't know responding represents normal performance variation. Raw scores are converted to cumulative percentile ranks, with high raw scores representing lower percentile ranks. Low percentiles for no/don't know responses arise from multiple causes requiring differential diagnosis: conservative response style in anxious individuals, depression or poor motivation, or severe reasoning deficits.

Correct-to-Incorrect Errors

This is a measure of set-loss errors that correct response is given and then abandoned in favor of an incorrect response on the immediately following sentence. Raw scores are converted to cumulative percentile ranks, with high raw scores representing lower percentile ranks. Low percentiles suggest poor metacognitive monitoring, inadequate integration, or susceptibility to distraction by salient features in new sentences. Approximately 34% of the normative sample made at least one correct-to-incorrect error.

Qualitative Scoring Considerations

Beyond standardized scores, qualitative analysis of response patterns enriches interpretation substantially. Recording whether incorrect responses fit clue information distinguishes reasoning quality from reasoning correctness. Systematic tracking of when correct responses emerge reveals efficiency patterns. Error analysis proves particularly informative: categorizing incorrect responses as applicable versus nonapplicable reveals deductive reasoning quality.

Rapid Reference 14.3

Scoring Summary

Score Type	Score Name	What It Measures
Primary scaled score	Total consecutively correct	Efficiency of identifying correct meanings early and maintaining them; points awarded from first correct response through maintained correct responses
Process measures	Consistently correct ratio	Efficiency ratio (Total Consecutively Correct ÷ First Sentence Correct); low ratio = eventual success but inefficient
	Repeated incorrect responses	Cognitive flexibility; counts repeated incorrect responses within items; elevated = perseverative thinking, difficulty abandoning unsuccessful hypotheses
	No/don't know responses	Response withholding pattern; elevated may indicate anxiety, perfectionism, depression, disengagement, or severe reasoning deficits
	Correct-to-incorrect errors	Set maintenance; correct response given then abandoned; elevated = poor metacognitive monitoring or distraction by salient features

COMMON ADMINISTRATION ERRORS

Although administration requirements are streamlined, several administration errors can compromise Word Context Test validity.

Providing Feedback

Providing feedback about response correctness represents the most serious administration error. Comments like "good" or "not quite" provide external executive support by confirming or disconfirming hypotheses, invalidating the assessment of independent reasoning.

Failing to Complete All Sentences

Failing to present all five sentences of an item when the correct response is identified early violates standardized procedures and prevents calculation of key process measures. Always complete all five sentences regardless of when correct responses emerge.

Insufficient or Excessive Prompting

Insufficient prompting when the examinee states "I don't know" can artificially elevate No/Don't Know Responses scores. The standardized procedure requires one prompt when the examinee doesn't respond. Conversely, excessive prompting or coaching invalidates results.

Paraphrasing Clue Sentences

Paraphrasing clue sentences rather than reading them verbatim changes the information available to the examinee. Always read sentences exactly as written.

Recording and Scoring Errors

Recording and scoring First Sentence Consecutively Correct, Repeated Incorrect Responses, and Correct-to-Incorrect Errors requires vigilance, and mistakes compromise both standardized scoring and qualitative analysis. Strong administration requires legible, complete verbatim transcription and attention to recording and scoring rules.

INTERPRETATION

Word Context Test interpretation requires integrating quantitative scores with qualitative analysis of response patterns within a systematic framework that distinguishes foundational limitations from true executive dysfunction.

Using the Hierarchical Framework for Differential Diagnosis

Word Context Test interpretation begins by systematically evaluating performance across tiers to identify where breakdown occurs. Always evaluate tiers hierarchically from bottom to top.

Step 1: Rule Out Tier 1 Limitations
Before concluding executive dysfunction, ensure foundational language processes are intact. Review vocabulary and language performance from other measures in the battery. Was language comprehension adequate for understanding clue sentences? Were there signs of word-finding difficulty that might have prevented articulation of correct responses? Did the examinee appear to understand the vocabulary used in the clues (e.g., "vocal cords," "convex")? Was basic sustained attention adequate across the 10 items? Significant discrepancies between Word Context and vocabulary measures (Word Context substantially lower) suggest executive deficits may be primary. Similarly low scores across

Word Context and vocabulary measures suggest fundamental language limitations require attention before executive conclusions can be drawn. Consider English language proficiency and educational background when relevant.

Step 2: Evaluate Tier 2 Bridging Processes
If Tier 1 appears intact, assess basic task orientation and rule-following. Did the examinee understand that these are made-up words requiring hypothesis generation rather than vocabulary retrieval? Could they adhere to basic task structure—one response per sentence, continuing to respond even after identifying the correct meaning? Did they grasp the concept of maintaining a correct response across subsequent sentences? Difficulty with these straightforward task requirements suggests impaired task orientation, though this is uncommon given the Word Context Test's simple procedural structure. Tier 2 deficits may manifest as confusion about the basic task concept or inability to follow the one-response-per-sentence format.

Step 3: Analyze Tier 3 Cold Executive Patterns
With Tiers 1–2 intact, examine the pattern of Tier 3 cold executive functioning. Was the Total Consecutively Correct score low despite adequate vocabulary? Did responses fit individual sentences but ignore previous clues (integration deficit)? Was the Repeated Incorrect Responses score elevated, suggesting perseverative thinking and flexibility deficits? Did the examinee demonstrate hypothesis-testing behavior or associative responding? Did responses progressively narrow with accumulating clues, or did each response seem unrelated to previous ones? Low Total Consecutively Correct with average Repeated Incorrect suggests integration problems without marked perseveration. Low Total Consecutively Correct with elevated Repeated Incorrect adds flexibility deficits, suggesting more extensive executive dysfunction.

Step 4: Evaluate Tier 3 Hot Executive Factors
Determine whether emotional or motivational factors contributed to performance. Cold executive deficits manifest as consistent reasoning difficulty independent of emotional state. Hot executive dysfunction appears as performance variability related to frustration, anxiety, or engagement. Did performance deteriorate across items as frustration accumulated? Were No/Don't Know Responses elevated, potentially reflecting anxiety about guessing or discomfort with uncertainty? Did the examinee show visible frustration, rushing, or disengagement? The Correct-to-Incorrect Errors pattern sometimes signals hot executive interference. Anxiety leads examinees to abandon correct responses despite intact reasoning. Compare early-item versus late-item performance to identify fatigue or motivational decline.

Note on Tier 4
Unlike many D-KEFS subtests, Word Context does not require a separate Tier 4 analysis. As discussed in the Hierarchical Tier Analysis section, this test does not substantively assess higher-order integration processes; metacognitive elements are better conceptualized as Tier 3 functioning for this task.

PERFORMANCE PATTERNS AND CLINICAL IMPLICATIONS

Several characteristic performance patterns emerge on the Word Context Test, each with distinct clinical implications and intervention considerations.

Isolated Low Total Consecutively Correct

Isolated Low Total Consecutively Correct suggests global difficulty with deductive reasoning, integration, and flexibility. Real-world implications include difficulty synthesizing information from multiple sources, trouble reaching conclusions when evidence is complex, and challenges with problem-solving requiring progressive hypothesis refinement.

Academic implications prove particularly significant. Students struggle to combine information presented across different contexts and formats. Reading comprehension suffers when texts require drawing connections across sections. Research papers and essays demanding integration of multiple sources present a particular difficulty. Professionally, these deficits affect roles requiring decision-making from incomplete or distributed information—project coordinators weighing input from multiple stakeholders, diagnosticians integrating test results with clinical history, or researchers synthesizing findings across studies.

Low Total Consecutively Correct with High Repeated Incorrect Responses

Low Total Consecutively Correct with High Repeated Incorrect Responses indicates flexibility deficits as primary limitation. Real-world implications include difficulty adapting when initial approaches fail and challenges in environments requiring frequent strategy adjustment. This pattern is associated with frontal lobe dysfunction and requires flexibility training and metacognitive strategies for recognizing when approaches should change.

Low Total Consecutively Correct with High No/Don't Know Responses

Low Total Consecutively Correct with High No/Don't Know Responses requires differential diagnosis. When combined with behavioral observations of anxiety or perfectionism, this suggests hot executive dysfunction—discomfort with uncertainty despite adequate reasoning. When combined with low motivation indicators, this may reflect insufficient engagement. Intact performance on other verbal reasoning tasks despite high Word Context no/don't know responses suggests hot executive factors.

High Correct-to-Incorrect Errors

High Correct-to-Incorrect Errors suggests that poor tolerance for ambiguity leads to abandoning correct responses when subsequent sentences create momentary confusion, or susceptibility to salient features in new sentences. This pattern has particular relevance for test-taking difficulties. Students who "overthink" questions, second-guess correct answers, and change responses from correct to incorrect show similar processes.

Total Consecutively Correct Versus Repeated Incorrect Responses

Total Consecutively Correct versus Repeated Incorrect Responses distinguishes integration from flexibility deficits. Low Total with average Repeated Incorrect suggests integration problems without marked perseveration. Low Total with elevated Repeated Incorrect adds flexibility deficits, suggesting more extensive frontal dysfunction.

No/Don't Know Responses Across Items

No/Don't Know Responses across items reveal patterns over time. Clustering in later items suggests fatigue or declining motivation. Random distribution suggests discomfort with uncertainty. Very low no/don't know responses indicate good uncertainty tolerance—positive hot executive functioning.

Rapid Reference 14.4

Distinguishing Tier-Level Deficits

Tier Level	Indicators	Clinical Implications
Tier 1 deficit	Low Word Context WITH low Vocabulary; difficulty comprehending clue sentences; limited expressive language for hypotheses; attention lapses across items	Language limitations confound executive interpretation; address foundational language skills before targeting executive functions
Tier 2 deficit	Difficulty following one-response-per-sentence rule; treats mystery words as real words to retrieve rather than concepts to deduce; inconsistent task orientation	Bridging processes compromised; may benefit from explicit instruction about task demands and structured support

Tier Level	Indicators	Clinical Implications
Tier 3 cold deficit	Low Total Consecutively Correct WITH average Vocabulary; elevated Repeated Incorrect Responses (perseveration); responses fit individual clues but fail to integrate across sentences; no discernible hypothesis-testing strategy	True executive integration deficits; target deductive reasoning strategies, information synthesis, and flexibility training
Tier 3 hot deficit	Good early items with deteriorating later items; elevated No/Don't Know Responses with visible anxiety; rushing or disengagement under frustration	Emotional regulation affecting executive performance; address frustration tolerance, anxiety management, and motivation

Note: Word Context does not substantively assess Tier 4 higher-order integration.

ECOLOGICAL VALIDITY AND FUNCTIONAL IMPLICATIONS

Word Context Test performance predicts functioning across multiple domains requiring information synthesis and deductive reasoning.

Academic Functioning

Reading comprehension beyond literal understanding requires holding concepts in working memory and integrating information across text to identify themes and understand complex concepts. Students with Word Context deficits struggle with advanced reading despite adequate decoding. Writing requiring complex arguments from multiple sources poses challenges. Science education requires integrating observations, results, and frameworks. Students may understand individual facts but struggle applying principles to novel situations.

Vocational and Daily Living

Many professional roles require synthesizing information to reach conclusions—managers integrating reports for decisions, healthcare providers synthesizing client data for diagnoses, and legal professionals integrating case law and facts. Problem-solving in complex contexts requires hypothesis generation, testing, and refinement. Teachers must integrate content knowledge, pedagogy, and student needs; technical writers integrate specifications and user needs. Healthcare management for chronic conditions requires integrating symptoms, schedules, recommendations, and activities for effective self-care decisions. Financial planning requires integrating income, expenses, goals, and conditions. Poor integration leads to fragmented approaches where advice is followed in isolation.

Social Functioning

Social problem-solving requires integrating multiple information pieces—what someone said, their emotional state, the context, and history—to understand situations and respond appropriately. Perspective-taking requires deducing others' mental states from behavioral cues. Conflict resolution requires synthesizing multiple perspectives to generate solutions addressing all needs.

STRENGTHS AND WEAKNESSES

The Word Context Test offers distinct advantages for assessing verbal executive functions while also presenting limitations that clinicians should consider when selecting measures and interpreting results.

Strengths

The Word Context Test offers several notable advantages for assessing verbal deductive reasoning within a comprehensive executive function evaluation.

Novel Stimuli. The Word Context Test provides a relatively pure assessment of verbal deductive reasoning by using novel stimuli that prevent reliance on crystallized knowledge.

Progressive Structure. The test's progressive structure with accumulating clues creates a sophisticated measure of information integration.

Rich Process Measures. Rich process measures distinguish the Word Context Test from many reasoning tasks, providing only total scores, enabling clinicians to distinguish integration deficits from flexibility problems, anxiety from reasoning impairment, and inefficiency from inability.

Set Maintenance Assessment. The test's requirement to maintain correct responses across multiple sentences assesses set maintenance—an important executive function often overlooked by tasks crediting single correct responses.

Qualitative Analysis. Qualitative analysis possibilities enrich interpretation beyond standardized scores.

Efficient Administration. The test's moderate administration time (15–20 minutes) provides substantial executive function information efficiently.

Weaknesses and Limitations

The Word Context Test offers several notable advantages for assessing verbal deductive reasoning within a comprehensive executive function evaluation.

CAUTION

The vocabulary confound requires particular attention with culturally and linguistically diverse examinees (Ardila, 2005; Manly, 2008; Nell, 2000). Clues reference concepts more familiar in mainstream American culture, and vocabulary choices reflect English language structure and idiom. An individual from another cultural background with excellent reasoning ability might perform poorly due to cultural/linguistic factors rather than executive dysfunction.

Vocabulary Confound

Heavy reliance on vocabulary knowledge creates the test's primary weakness. Examinees who don't know that "vocal cords" produce sound or "convex" means outwardly curved cannot use those clues effectively, regardless of reasoning ability. This proves particularly problematic when assessing individuals with limited education, English language learners, or those with vocabulary deficits due to language-based learning disabilities.

Working Memory Demands

Limited working memory capacity represents another significant confound. Examinees must hold prior answers in mind while processing new sentences—a working memory demand that increases as more sentences accumulate.

Ceiling Effects

The test's limited range at the upper end creates ceiling effects for individuals with superior verbal executive functions.

Score Reliability

Single-item unreliability affects score stability more than on tests with more items. With only 10 items contributing to the Total Consecutively Correct score, random factors affecting performance on one or two items can substantially impact the total score.

Construct Overlap

The test cannot distinguish deductive reasoning deficits from integration deficits with complete precision. Hot executive factors can confound cold executive assessment in ways that prove difficult to fully disentangle.

Aging Norms

The original D-KEFS normative data, collected over two decades ago, may not fully represent contemporary populations.

ALTERNATIVE MEASURES

When Word Context Test results require clarification or when foundational abilities need separate evaluation, several alternative measures can provide convergent evidence or help isolate specific cognitive processes.

Within the D-KEFS Suite

Several D-KEFS subtests provide complementary or converging evidence for verbal abstract reasoning and hypothesis testing.

D-KEFS Proverbs Test

Proverbs assess verbal abstract reasoning but through inductive rather than deductive processes. Where Word Context requires deducing specific meanings from general categorical information (top-down), Proverbs requires inducing abstract principles from concrete sayings (bottom-up). Comparing performance across these measures helps distinguish reasoning direction deficits.

D-KEFS Sorting Test

Sorting requires verbal description of categorization principles, providing another measure of verbal reasoning and concept formation. Comparing Word Context and Sorting performance helps distinguish reasoning direction (deductive versus categorical abstraction) and the perception-to-verbal-description pathway.

D-KEFS Twenty Questions Test

This subtest assesses verbal hypothesis testing through yes/no questioning to identify target objects, sharing the Word Context Test's hypothesis-testing and information integration requirements. Both tests require progressively narrowing possibilities based on accumulating information and shifting strategies when hypotheses prove unproductive.

Beyond D-KEFS

Measures outside the D-KEFS family can provide converging evidence or assess related constructs when additional information is needed.

Verbal Abstraction Measures

Inductive reasoning tasks such as the Wechsler Similarities subtest (Wechsler, 2014, 2024) measure bottom-up verbal abstraction, while Word Context measures top-down (deductive) reasoning. Comparing performance across these complementary approaches clarifies whether abstraction difficulties are global or specific to one reasoning direction.

Nonverbal Reasoning Measures

Nonverbal reasoning tests such as Raven's 2 Progressive Matrices (Raven et al., 2018) provide a comparison of reasoning ability independent of language. Discrepancies between nonverbal reasoning (strong) and Word Context (weak) suggest language or verbal integration deficits rather than global reasoning impairment.

Verbal Memory Measures

List learning tests such as the California Verbal Learning Test, Third Edition (CVLT-3; Delis et al., 2017) assess verbal memory functions that can confound Word Context performance. Comparing Word Context with verbal memory measures helps clarify whether integration deficits reflect executive dysfunction or stem from memory limitations.

Language Measures

Naming tests such as the Boston Naming Test (Kaplan et al., 1983) or comprehensive language batteries, assess foundational language abilities critical for interpreting Word Context performance. Administering language measures helps clarify whether poor Word Context performance reflects executive deficits versus fundamental language limitations.

Behavior Rating Scales

Executive function rating scales capture real-world executive behaviors that may or may not align with performance-based measures. For children and adolescents, the Behavior Rating Inventory of Executive Function, Second Edition

(BRIEF-2; Gioia et al., 2015), Comprehensive Executive Function Inventory (CEFI; Naglieri & Goldstein, 2013), and Delis Rating of Executive Functions (D-REF; Delis, 2012) provide parent and teacher perspectives on daily executive functioning. For adults, the BRIEF-A (Roth et al., 2005), CEFI Adult (Naglieri & Goldstein, 2017), and D-REF Adult (Delis, 2021) offer self-report and informant-report options. Relevant scales across these measures include Working Memory (tracking accumulated clues), Shift (cognitive flexibility in adjusting hypotheses), and Plan/Organize (strategic approach to integrating information). Discrepancies between Word Context performance and rating scale elevations provide diagnostic information: adequate test performance with elevated rating scales may indicate that the structured testing environment with visible clues does not capture integration challenges that emerge in fast-paced, verbally demanding daily situations without external supports. Conversely, poor Word Context performance with unremarkable rating scales might suggest test-specific factors such as vocabulary limitations or performance anxiety rather than pervasive executive dysfunction.

SUMMARY

The D-KEFS Word Context Test provides a sophisticated assessment of verbal executive functions through deductive reasoning using made-up words and progressively informative clues. The test's primary strength lies in assessing information integration and deductive reasoning using novel stimuli that prevent reliance on crystallized knowledge. Rich process measures enable distinction among integration deficits, flexibility problems, and hot executive factors—distinctions crucial for targeted intervention.

Effective interpretation requires systematic hierarchical analysis beginning with Tier 1 language foundations. Vocabulary knowledge and language comprehension must be adequate before executive function conclusions can be drawn. Tier 2 task orientation must be intact, though this rarely poses difficulty given the test's straightforward structure. Only after ruling out foundational limitations can poor performance be confidently attributed to Tier 3 executive deficits in deductive reasoning, information integration, or cognitive flexibility.

The test's most significant weakness involves vocabulary confounds disproportionately affecting individuals with limited education, language-based learning disabilities, or diverse linguistic backgrounds. These confounds necessitate careful integration with other measures, particularly vocabulary and language assessments, before attributing poor performance to executive dysfunction.

Clinical utility centers on differential diagnosis of verbal reasoning deficits and understanding integration failures affecting academic and occupational functioning. The test proves particularly valuable for evaluating individuals who struggle with synthesis despite adequate basic abilities and distinguishing reasoning capacity from reasoning efficiency. The hierarchical framework fundamentally shapes interpretation—clinicians systematically evaluate Tier 1 language foundations, Tier 2 task orientation, and Tier 3 cold and hot executive functions. This approach prevents misdiagnosis, guides targeted intervention, and ensures language support isn't mislabeled as executive function training.

TEST YOURSELF

1. What type of reasoning does the Word Context Test primarily assess?

(a) Inductive reasoning (specific to general).
(b) Deductive reasoning (general to specific).
(c) Analogical reasoning.
(d) Spatial reasoning.

2. An examinee generates responses that fit each individual clue sentence but ignores information from previous clues. This pattern most likely reflects a deficit in:

(a) Basic vocabulary knowledge.
(b) Information integration.
(c) Auditory processing.
(d) Task orientation.

3. **What is the most important step before attributing poor Word Context performance to executive dysfunction?**
   (a) Administering additional executive function measures.
   (b) Assessing vocabulary and language abilities.
   (c) Obtaining a detailed developmental history.
   (d) Ruling out visual processing deficits.
4. **An examinee repeats the same incorrect response across multiple sentences despite contradictory clues. Which process score best captures this pattern?**
   (a) Consistently Correct Ratio.
   (b) No/Don't Know Responses.
   (c) Correct-to-Incorrect Errors.
   (d) Repeated Incorrect Responses.
5. **An examinee performs well on early items but shows declining performance with rushed responses and visible frustration on later items. This pattern suggests:**
   (a) Progressive cognitive fatigue from Tier 1 deficits.
   (b) Worsening deductive reasoning across the test.
   (c) Hot executive factors interfering with performance.
   (d) Inadequate task orientation.
6. **How does the Word Context Test differ from the Wechsler Similarities subtest?**
   (a) Word Context is nonverbal; Similarities is verbal.
   (b) Word Context uses top-down reasoning; Similarities uses bottom-up reasoning.
   (c) Word Context measures vocabulary; Similarities measures executive function.
   (d) Word Context is timed; Similarities is untimed.
7. **Why does vocabulary knowledge create a significant confound on the Word Context Test?**
   (a) The test directly measures crystallized vocabulary.
   (b) Unknown words in clues cannot be used for reasoning regardless of executive ability.
   (c) Vocabulary and executive functions are the same construct.
   (d) The scoring system penalizes imprecise word choices.
8. **An examinee correctly identifies a mystery word on sentence 2 but then abandons it for an incorrect response on sentence 3. This Correct-to-Incorrect error pattern suggests difficulty with:**
   (a) Initial hypothesis generation.
   (b) Basic language comprehension.
   (c) Set maintenance and metacognitive monitoring.
   (d) Processing speed.
9. **Why does the Word Context Test not include Tier 4 in its hierarchical analysis?**
   (a) Tier 4 processes are not relevant to verbal tasks.
   (b) The test was not designed to measure higher-order functions.
   (c) Metacognitive processes are better conceptualized as Tier 3 for this task.
   (d) Only nonverbal tests assess Tier 4.

10. When assessing an English language learner who requests clarification on vocabulary words within the clues, the clinician should:

(a) Discontinue testing immediately.

(b) Provide definitions to ensure valid results.

(c) Consider linguistic factors when interpreting results and seek converging evidence.

(d) Assume executive dysfunction is present.

Answer Key: 1-b, 2-b, 3-b, 4-d, 5-c, 6-b, 7-b, 8-c, 9-c, 10-c

REFERENCES

Ardila, A. (2005). Cultural values underlying psychometric cognitive testing. *Neuropsychology Review, 15*(4), 185–195.

Burgess, P. W., Alderman, N., Evans, J., Emslie, H., & Wilson, B. A. (1998). The ecological validity of tests of executive function. *Journal of the International Neuropsychological Society, 4*(6), 547–558.

Chaytor, N., & Schmitter-Edgecombe, M. (2003). The ecological validity of neuropsychological tests: A review of the literature on everyday cognitive skills. *Neuropsychology Review, 13*(4), 181–197.

Delis, D. C. (2012). *Delis Rating of Executive Functions (D-REF)*. Pearson.

Delis, D. C. (2021). *Delis Rating of Executive Functions—Adult (D-REF Adult)*. Pearson.

Delis, D. C., Kaplan, E., & Kramer, J. H. (2001). *Delis-Kaplan Executive Function System (D-KEFS)*. The Psychological Corporation.

Delis, D. C., Kramer, J. H., Kaplan, E., & Ober, B. A. (2017). *California Verbal Learning Test–Third Edition (CVLT-3)*. Pearson.

Diamond, A. (2013). Executive functions. *Annual Review of Psychology, 64*, 135–168.

Gioia, G. A., Isquith, P. K., Guy, S. C., & Kenworthy, L. (2015). *Behavior Rating Inventory of Executive Function–Second Edition (BRIEF-2)*. Psychological Assessment Resources.

Goodglass, H., & Kaplan, E. (1987). *Boston Diagnostic Aphasia Examination*. Lea & Febiger.

Kaplan, E., Goodglass, H., & Weintraub, S. (1983). *Boston Naming Test*. Lea & Febiger.

Lezak, M. D., Howieson, D. B., Bigler, E. D., & Tranel, D. (2012). *Neuropsychological Assessment* (5th ed.). Oxford University Press.

Manly, J. J. (2008). Critical issues in cultural neuropsychology: Profit from diversity. *Neuropsychology Review, 18*(3), 179–183.

Mischel, W., Shoda, Y., & Rodriguez, M. L. (1989). Delay of gratification in children. *Science, 244*(4907), 933–938.

Naglieri, J. A., & Goldstein, S. (2013). *Comprehensive Executive Function Inventory (CEFI)*. Multi-Health Systems.

Naglieri, J. A., & Goldstein, S. (2017). *Comprehensive Executive Function Inventory Adult (CEFI Adult)*. Multi-Health Systems.

Nell, V. (2000). *Cross-Cultural Neuropsychological Assessment: Theory and Practice*. Lawrence Erlbaum Associates.

Raven, J., Rust, J., Chan, F., & Zhou, X. (2018). *Raven's 2 Progressive Matrices, Clinical Edition (Raven's 2)*. Pearson.

Roth, R. M., Isquith, P. K., & Gioia, G. A. (2005). *Behavior Rating Inventory of Executive Function—Adult Version (BRIEF-A)*. PAR.

Waltz, J. A., Knowlton, B. J., Holyoak, K. J., Boone, K. B., Mishkin, F. S., de Menezes Santos, M., Thomas, C. R., & Miller, B. L. (1999). A system for relational reasoning in human prefrontal cortex. *Psychological Science, 10*(2), 119–125.

Wechsler, D. (2014). *Wechsler Intelligence Scale for Children* (5th ed.). NCS Pearson.

Wechsler, D. (2024). *Wechsler Adult Intelligence Scale* (5th ed.). NCS Pearson.

Werner, H., & Kaplan, E. (1952). The acquisition of word meanings: A developmental study. *Monographs of the Society for Research in Child Development, 15*(1), Serial No. 51.

Zelazo, P. D., & Carlson, S. M. (2012). Hot and cool executive function in childhood and adolescence: Development and plasticity. *Child Development Perspectives, 6*(4), 354–360.

Part III

INTEGRATION

Fifteen

CROSS-SUBTEST INTEGRATION AND SYNTHESIS

CLINICAL VIGNETTE

Robert Jackson, a 45-year-old attorney, was referred for a neuropsychological evaluation six months following a moderate traumatic brain injury sustained in a car accident. He reported persistent difficulties with mental flexibility and multitasking that were affecting his work performance, particularly when managing multiple cases simultaneously.

Cognitive testing revealed above-average intellectual functioning (FSIQ = 115) with strong verbal reasoning (VCI = 118) and a relative weakness in processing speed (PSI = 94). D-KEFS administration produced an initially puzzling pattern across flexibility measures. Verbal Fluency Category Switching Total Correct was impaired (SS = 5), suggesting cognitive flexibility weakness. However, Trails Number-Letter Switching was solidly average (SS = 10), and Sorting Confirmed Correct Sorts was above average (SS = 12). Three tests ostensibly measuring flexibility had produced varied results. RISK performance was average across all indices, with appropriate risk calibration and no evidence of impulsive decision-making, ruling out hot executive dysfunction as a contributing factor.

Tier-based analysis clarified the pattern. Robert's Letter Fluency (SS = 7) and Category Fluency (SS = 8) were both below expectations for his verbal intelligence, indicating reduced verbal generativity across all fluency conditions—not just switching. The Category Switching weakness reflected this broader generativity limitation compounded by switching demands, not isolated flexibility impairment. Trails and Sorting, which assess flexibility without requiring rapid verbal generation, revealed intact set-shifting ability when generativity demands were removed. The intact RISK performance confirmed that Robert's difficulties were specific to speeded verbal tasks rather than reflecting broader executive or decision-making impairment.

The integrated interpretation identified a Tier 2 processing efficiency weakness affecting speeded verbal production rather than a Tier 3 cognitive flexibility deficit. Recommendations emphasized accommodations for time pressure and verbal retrieval demands rather than cognitive flexibility intervention. At six-month follow-up, Robert reported improved work functioning after receiving rehabilitation services and implementing strategies to reduce time pressure during complex verbal tasks.

This vignette illustrates why cross-subtest integration matters. The individual subtest chapters in Part II provide the tools for interpreting each measure; this chapter addresses how to synthesize findings when those measures tell different stories.

THE CHALLENGE OF INTEGRATION

Executive function assessment rarely involves a single test. Clinicians administer multiple D-KEFS subtests, embed them within broader neuropsychological batteries, and supplement with rating scales and observations. This multimethod approach is critical because no single measure captures the complexity of executive functioning. But it creates an interpretive challenge: what do you do when test results seemingly disagree?

The temptation might be to average or summarize across measures, describing overall executive functioning as impaired, borderline, or intact. This approach obscures more than it reveals. A person with severely impaired inhibition but intact planning has a fundamentally different clinical profile than someone with the reverse pattern, even if their abilities overall tend to cluster in the average range. Collapsing across domains loses the very specificity that makes assessment valuable.

Equally problematic is over-interpreting isolated findings. A single low score invites elaborate explanation—perhaps this represents a circumscribed deficit, a task-specific weakness, or a meaningful dissociation. But isolated scores can also reflect measurement error, momentary lapses in attention, fatigue effects, or transient emotional interference. The question is not whether a finding *can* be explained but whether it *should* be.

The hierarchical tier framework introduced in Chapter 3 provides a systematic alternative to both averaging and over-interpretation. By organizing findings according to the level at which processing breaks down, clinicians can identify patterns that transcend individual tests and distinguish meaningful discrepancies from noise. This chapter presents strategies for building tier-based profiles across the D-KEFS battery and integrating those profiles with broader assessment data.

BUILDING A TIER-BASED PROFILE ACROSS THE BATTERY

The interpretive sequence introduced in Chapter 3—rule out Tier 1, evaluate Tier 2, distinguish Tier 3 cold and hot, assess Tier 4—applies not just to individual subtests but to the battery as a whole. Each subtest chapter in Part II applies this sequence to a single measure; here we apply it across measures simultaneously. The goal remains the same: identify the lowest tier at which consistent weakness appears, recognizing that deficits at lower tiers contaminate performance at higher tiers.

Tier 1: Foundational Processes (Nonexecutive)

Tier 1 encompasses the foundational abilities—motor speed, visual acuity, basic attention, basic language comprehension, and fundamental perceptual processing—that are prerequisites for higher-order performance but are not themselves independent executive functions. As discussed in Chapter 3, these foundations must be evaluated first because weakness here will ripple through all subsequent tiers. Different D-KEFS subtests place different demands on these foundations, creating opportunities to identify Tier 1 limitations through cross-subtest patterns.

Motor demands are highest on the original Trails (continuous drawing), Design Fluency (rapid drawing), and the original Tower (physical manipulation of discs). A client with motor weakness may show impaired performance across these subtests even with intact executive functioning. The D-KEFS provides baseline conditions to isolate these demands: Trails Visual Scanning and Motor Speed conditions, Design Fluency Condition 1 (filled dots only), and observation of motor execution during Tower. When baseline conditions are weak across multiple motor-demanding subtests, the pattern points clearly to Tier 1 limitations. Motor speed should be distinguished from processing speed (a Tier 2 process). Motor speed reflects the physical execution of movement with minimal cognitive involvement, while processing speed involves cognitively mediated operations—perceiving stimuli, making decisions, and coordinating responses. An examinee with motor slowing will be slow to draw but may identify targets at normal speed; a person with processing speed weakness will be slow across all cognitively demanding tasks regardless of motor demands.

Language demands are highest on Verbal Fluency, Word Context, Proverb Test, and Twenty Questions. Clients with word-finding difficulties or English Language Learners may struggle on these subtests regardless of executive capacity. The pattern again provides a clue: if weakness appears selectively on verbally mediated subtests while nonverbal measures (Trails, Design Fluency, Tower) remain intact, suspect Tier 1 language limitations rather than executive dysfunction. Chapter 2's discussion of language development reminds us that these foundational abilities have their own developmental trajectories, which is particularly relevant when assessing children whose language skills may still be consolidating.

Visual and perceptual demands are prominent on Trails (following paths, distinguishing targets from distractors), Design Fluency (perceiving dot arrays, recognizing design configurations), Tower (perceiving spatial relationships among discs and pegs), Sorting (discriminating card features), and SST (processing facial features and clothing details). People with visual acuity limitations, visual field deficits, or basic perceptual processing weaknesses may struggle on these subtests independent of executive capacity. The pattern of selective weakness on visually demanding subtests with preserved performance on verbally mediated measures (Verbal Fluency, Proverb Test, Word Context) suggests Tier 1 visual-perceptual limitations. Visual-perceptual foundations should be distinguished from higher-order visuospatial reasoning. Basic perception involves accurately seeing and discriminating stimuli, while visuospatial reasoning involves mentally manipulating spatial information, which engages Tier 3 processes. An examinee who cannot accurately perceive the disc configuration on Tower has a different problem than one who perceives accurately but cannot mentally simulate move sequences.

Basic attentional demands, maintaining focus on straightforward, repetitive tasks without significant cognitive load, also represent Tier 1 foundations. Baseline conditions like Color Naming, Word Reading, Visual Scanning, and the sequencing conditions on Trails assess this foundational attention. Examinees who show attention lapses, lose their place, or drift off-task during these low-demand conditions likely have Tier 1 attentional limitations that will affect all subsequent performance. This differs from Tier 2 sustained attention, which involves maintaining focus under cognitive load or interference—a distinction examined in the following section.

The critical principle: When Tier 1 weakness is identified on one subtest, check for converging evidence across other subtests with similar foundational demands. If the pattern holds, Tier 1 limitations likely explain the broader profile. If Tier 1 weakness is isolated to a single subtest, consider task-specific factors before concluding that foundational components are impaired.

> **DON'T FORGET**
>
> Always rule out foundational deficits before attributing poor performance to executive dysfunction—across every subtest, every time. A comprehensive Tier 1 evaluation at the battery level prevents the common error of interpreting motor slowing as planning impairment, language limitations as verbal reasoning deficits, or visual processing weakness as cognitive inflexibility.

Tier 2: Bridging Processes

Tier 2 processes bridge foundational abilities and true executive functions. These bridging skills support executive functioning without being full-fledged executive functions themselves, and they are engaged by virtually every D-KEFS subtest, making Tier 2 the most common source of cross-subtest convergence and the most frequent alternative explanation when apparent executive deficits appear. Key Tier 2 processes include processing speed, basic working memory maintenance, sustained attention under cognitive load, basic rule-following and set maintenance, goal maintenance, elementary inhibition of rule violations, and procedural learning. Importantly, some cognitive processes—particularly working memory, attention, and inhibition—can function at multiple tiers depending on task complexity. Simple maintenance of information represents Tier 2 working memory, while active manipulation engages Tier 3 executive working memory. Basic attention to repetitive tasks is a Tier 1 foundation, while sustaining attention under interference represents Tier 2. Following explicit task rules requires Tier 2 basic inhibition, while suppressing prepotent responses under interference demands Tier 3 inhibitory control. Recognizing these gradations is essential for accurate cross-subtest integration.

Processing speed demands vary considerably across the battery. Trails, Color-Word Interference, Verbal Fluency, and Design Fluency are heavily speeded; performance depends substantially on how quickly the examinee can execute responses. Sorting, Tower, Twenty Questions, and Word Context are less speed-focused or untimed, reducing processing speed influence. When impairment appears selectively on speeded subtests with relatively preserved performance on less speeded measures, Tier 2 processing speed weakness is the likely explanation. This pattern is particularly common in older adults, as discussed in Chapter 2's section on aging-related changes, and in clients recovering from traumatic brain injury.

Working memory demands vary across the battery, but the critical integration question is whether a task requires basic maintenance (Tier 2) or active manipulation (Tier 3). Tier 2 working memory involves holding task rules in mind, tracking one's position in a sequence, or maintaining basic procedural information, which are demands present across virtually all D-KEFS subtests. Every subtest requires examinees to remember instructions and maintain a task set, representing baseline Tier 2 working memory. Tier 3 executive working memory, by contrast, requires simultaneously tracking multiple pieces of information while actively manipulating or integrating them. Twenty Questions places heavy Tier 3 working memory demands as examinees must track eliminated items, maintain mental representations of remaining possibilities and their hierarchical relationships, and evaluate which questions would most efficiently narrow the field. Tower engages Tier 3 working memory when examinees must hold the goal state and multiple subgoals in mind while mentally simulating move sequences. Word Context escalates from Tier 2 to Tier 3 as clues accumulate. Early clues require straightforward maintenance, but integrating information across all five clues to deduce meaning requires active manipulation. When weakness appears selectively on high-manipulation subtests (e.g., Tower, Twenty Questions, and later Word Context items) with preserved performance on tasks requiring only maintenance, the pattern suggests Tier 3 executive working memory limitations. The D-KEFS Advanced Trails Switching-Working Memory condition specifically stresses working memory by removing visual aids—connecting lines disappear after being made. Selective difficulty on this condition, with intact standard Number-Letter Switching, implicates working memory as a contributor to multitasking difficulties, though clinicians must determine whether the limitation reflects Tier 2 maintenance capacity or Tier 3 manipulation under load.

Attention demands exist across tiers and must be parsed carefully during integration. As noted in the preceding section, basic sustained attention to low-demand tasks represents a Tier 1 foundation. Examinees who show attention lapses on these low-demand conditions likely have Tier 1 attentional limitations affecting all subsequent performance. Tier 2 sustained attention involves maintaining focus under cognitive load or interference—the demand present during Stroop Inhibition, Number-Letter Switching, or any condition requiring effortful processing over time. When performance deteriorates over the course of a subtest (early items stronger than later items) or when errors cluster in subtests administered later in the session, Tier 2 attention or fatigue factors warrant consideration. Verbal Fluency's 60-second trials require continuous effortful output; Tower items can extend several minutes for complex problems; the full Sorting administration involves eight card sets requiring persistent engagement. This interpretive challenge becomes particularly relevant for D-KEFS Advanced Trails, where the Switching-Distraction and Switching-Working Memory conditions follow standard Number-Letter Switching. Poor performance on these latter conditions could reflect their specific added demands or fatigue effects. Differential patterns help disentangle this: if one advanced condition is impaired while the other remains intact, the specific cognitive demand is more likely responsible than global fatigue. Cross-battery context also informs interpretation. If other tests administered late in the session show preserved performance, attentional fatigue becomes a less compelling explanation.

Rule-following and set maintenance—the ability to consistently apply explicit task rules throughout administration—underlies valid assessment of higher-tier functions. Tower requires following "move one disk at a time" and size-placement rules; Verbal Fluency prohibits proper names and repetitions; Design Fluency demands exactly four connected lines per design; Sorting requires "two groups of three." Frequent rule violations despite apparent comprehension suggest Tier 2 difficulties rather than Tier 3 executive dysfunction.

Goal maintenance involves keeping the task objective in mind while working toward it. Tower requires holding the target configuration in mind across extended problem-solving; Twenty Questions requires remembering that the goal is identifying an unknown object. Examinees who ask "What am I supposed to do again?" mid-task or make responses disconnected from task goals demonstrate Tier 2 goal maintenance weakness rather than Tier 3 planning deficits.

Basic inhibition, suppressing rule-violating behaviors when rules are explicit and unchanging, differs from Tier 3 inhibitory control, which requires suppressing prepotent responses under interference or flexibly applying inhibition based on changing demands. An examinee who cannot consistently use four lines on Design Fluency has a different problem than one who cannot suppress the reading response on Color-Word Interference.

Procedural learning—becoming more efficient through task familiarity—can mimic executive improvement. When performance improves across Sorting trials or Twenty Questions items, clinicians must distinguish Tier 2 procedural learning from Tier 4 strategic adaptation. Procedural learning reflects implicit familiarization; strategic adaptation reflects conscious modification of approach based on self-monitoring.

The integration question at Tier 2 is whether mid-level weakness is the bottleneck limiting performance across the battery. If so, subtests that minimize Tier 2 demands (e.g., Sorting's untimed format) should reveal relatively stronger performance than those that maximize them (e.g., Trails' speeded format). Contrast scores, emphasized throughout the subtest chapters in Part II, provide critical information: if contrast scores are normal despite weak absolute scores, Tier 2 factors are likely the primary constraint rather than executive dysfunction.

Tier 3: Core Executive Functions

Tier 3 encompasses the cognitive processes most clinicians have in mind when they refer to "executive functions"—the deliberate, effortful mental operations that organize and regulate goal-directed behavior. At the battery level, Tier 3 assessment asks whether patterns of weakness reflect genuine executive dysfunction now that foundational and bridging processes have been ruled out. The D-KEFS assesses both cold executive functions (cognitive processes operating in emotionally neutral contexts) and hot executive functions (regulatory processes engaged when emotion, motivation, or reward are involved). Both domains merit systematic cross-subtest integration.

Cold Executive Functions

With Tiers 1 and 2 evaluated across the battery, the clinician can now examine Tier 3 cold executive functions with greater confidence that weakness represents genuine executive dysfunction rather than contamination from below. Some Tier 3 constructs exist only at this level: cognitive flexibility, generativity and fluency, planning and problem-solving, abstract reasoning and concept formation, hypothesis testing, and feedback utilization. Others represent the complex end of processes that also appear at lower tiers: executive working memory (active manipulation rather than basic maintenance), complex inhibitory control (suppressing prepotent responses under interference rather than following explicit rules), and strategic attentional allocation (flexibly directing attention based on task demands rather than basic focus on a single task). The D-KEFS battery allows clinicians to evaluate these constructs across multiple measures, creating opportunities for convergent validation but also for apparent discrepancies that require reconciliation.

Cognitive flexibility is assessed by Trails Number-Letter Switching, Verbal Fluency Switching conditions, Color-Word Interference Inhibition/Switching, Sorting, and Design Fluency Condition 3. As the individual subtest chapters detail, these tests share the requirement to shift between mental sets but differ in their additional demands: motor speed for the original Trails, verbal retrieval for Verbal Fluency, and inhibition for Color-Word Interference. A true cognitive flexibility deficit should manifest across multiple measures; an isolated weakness suggests task-specific factors rather than core inflexibility.

Generativity and fluency are assessed by Verbal Fluency (all conditions), Design Fluency (all conditions), and, to some extent, Twenty Questions and Word Context. The key distinction is between verbal and nonverbal generativity: selective weakness in one domain with preservation in the other suggests modality-specific rather than domain-general fluency impairment. The opening vignette illustrates this point—Robert's apparent flexibility deficit was actually a verbal generativity weakness that affected fluency conditions differentially.

Planning and problem-solving are assessed by Tower (planning and execution), Sorting (concept identification and hypothesis testing), Twenty Questions (strategic question generation), and Word Context (deductive integration). Convergent weakness across these measures suggests broad planning or problem-solving deficits; isolated weakness raises questions about task-specific demands.

Tier 3 inhibitory control—suppressing prepotent responses under interference—is assessed most directly by Color-Word Interference Inhibition condition and, in the D-KEFS Advanced, by Trails Switching-Distraction, which adds visual and auditory distractors that must be inhibited while maintaining the switching task. This complex inhibition differs from Tier 2 basic inhibition, which involves following explicit rules without the added challenge of interference or competing response tendencies. Additional inhibition data come from error analysis across the battery (intrusions on Verbal Fluency, rule violations on Tower, repetitions across subtests) though clinicians must determine whether errors reflect Tier 2 rule-following failures or Tier 3 inhibitory control breakdowns. Rule violations on early, straightforward Tower items suggest Tier 2 difficulties with basic rule application; violations emerging only on complex items under cognitive load suggest Tier 3 inhibitory control failures. As the Color-Word Interference chapter discusses, the distinction between inhibition failure and impulsivity is also clinically important: inhibition deficits produce errors even with adequate effort and motivation, while impulsivity reflects inadequate response modulation that may respond to cueing or strategy instruction.

Abstract reasoning and concept formation—the ability to identify underlying principles, form categories, and think beyond concrete features—is assessed most directly by Sorting (identifying conceptual groupings), Proverb Test (extracting metaphorical meaning), and Twenty Questions (recognizing hierarchical category structures). Convergent weakness across these measures suggests broad abstract reasoning deficits; isolated weakness on one measure may reflect task-specific factors such as verbal demands on Proverb Test or perceptual demands on Sorting.

Hypothesis testing involves generating and systematically evaluating potential solutions. Twenty Questions requires forming categorical hypotheses and refining them based on feedback; Word Context demands generating hypotheses about word meaning and revising them as clues accumulate; Sorting involves hypothesizing potential grouping principles and testing them against the card features. Weakness in hypothesis testing often manifests as random or unsystematic responding rather than strategic elimination of possibilities.

Feedback utilization—the ability to modify strategy based on performance information—cuts across Sorting (adjusting categorization approach after sorts are confirmed or rejected), Twenty Questions (refining questions based on yes/no responses), SST (using correct/incorrect feedback to identify sorting dimensions), and RISK (calibrating risk tolerance based on outcomes). Examinees who persist with ineffective strategies despite clear feedback demonstrate feedback utilization deficits distinct from the strategies themselves. This pattern is particularly important because it may respond to intervention: examinees who can use feedback when explicitly directed to attend to it have better prognoses than those who cannot incorporate feedback, even with support.

Hot Executive Functions

The D-KEFS Advanced includes the Risk–Reward Decision Test (RISK) as a dedicated measure of hot executive functions—risk tolerance, delay of gratification, and decision-making under uncertainty. For adults administered this test, RISK provides the primary hot EF data. But as the RISK chapter emphasizes, hot executive functioning also manifests in behavioral observations across the battery, extending hot EF assessment to all ages and populations.

Frustration tolerance reveals itself when examinees encounter difficulty. How does the examinee respond to failure on Tower? Does performance deteriorate after a difficult item, suggesting emotional interference with subsequent cognitive processing? Does the client show visible signs of agitation during challenging portions of Color-Word Interference or give up prematurely on Twenty Questions? These patterns, observed qualitatively across subtests, provide converging evidence about hot EF functioning even without formal hot EF measures.

Emotional inhibition is observed through behavioral responses to challenge throughout testing. Examinees with hot EF weakness may verbalize frustration, show physical signs of agitation, or abandon effortful processing in favor of impulsive responses. Chapter 3's discussion of the hot–cold distinction reminds us that these regulatory processes are dissociable from cold cognitive abilities. A client may demonstrate sophisticated planning on Tower while simultaneously showing poor frustration tolerance when that planning fails.

Anxiety, particularly performance anxiety, affects examinees differently than frustration. Anxious examinees may show excessive caution, extended response latencies, self-deprecating comments, or physiological signs of distress even on tasks within their ability level. On timed measures like Trails or Color-Word Interference, anxiety often produces a speed-accuracy tradeoff favoring accuracy at the expense of speed; on Tower, it may manifest as reluctance to commit to moves or excessive checking.

Effort regulation involves sustaining motivated engagement across demanding tasks. Examinees with effort regulation difficulties may start strong but fade as cognitive demands accumulate, show variable engagement across subtests based on perceived interest or difficulty, or demonstrate adequate ability on brief tasks but deteriorate on extended ones like Sorting or Verbal Fluency's 60-second trials. This pattern differs from Tier 2 attentional fatigue in that it reflects motivational rather than capacity limitations—the examinee could sustain effort but doesn't.

Impulsivity—responding before adequately processing task demands—cuts across measures as rushed responses, premature commitment to strategies, and errors of commission. On Tower, impulsive examinees show brief first-move times with high move counts; on Twenty Questions, they ask specific-object questions rather than categorical ones; on RISK, they select rapidly without apparent deliberation. Impulsivity represents hot EF dysregulation distinct from cold EF inhibitory control deficits, though both produce errors; the distinction lies in whether adequate processing occurred before the response.

The hot–cold integration question is whether deficits appear in one domain, the other, or both. When RISK or behavioral indicators suggest hot EF weakness but cold EF measures are intact, real-world functioning may be more impaired than the test scores suggest. Hot EF problems often emerge only in emotionally charged situations, not replicated by standard cognitive tests or in structured testing environments. When cold EF measures are impaired but hot EF indicators are intact, the client may function better in real life than predicted by cognitive scores, as adequate emotional regulation allows compensation for cognitive limitations.

Tier 4: Higher-Order Integration and Metacognition

Tier 4 encompasses metacognition, strategic coordination, and the integration of multiple executive processes in service of complex goals. As Chapter 3 notes, these higher-order functions are difficult to assess directly but reveal themselves through patterns across the battery and qualitative observations within subtests. At the battery level, Tier 4 assessment involves stepping back from individual scores to observe how the examinee manages the overall testing experience.

Strategic adaptation across the battery provides Tier 4 information, though this is typically observed qualitatively rather than measured through formal learning curves that are integrated into some memory batteries. Does the client's approach to later Tower items reflect lessons learned from earlier failures? Does the examinee's initial abstraction level on Twenty Questions improve across trials, shifting from specific guesses early on to more efficient categorical questions as they learn what works? Observed improvement in strategic approach suggests intact Tier 4 capacity; persistent use of ineffective strategies despite repeated failure, when component skills are adequate, suggests Tier 4 weakness.

Error awareness and self-correction are related but distinct Tier 4 indicators. Examinees who recognize their errors demonstrate metacognitive monitoring; those who can also correct them demonstrate intact executive control over their own cognitive processes. The distinction matters clinically: an examinee who notices errors but cannot fix them has a different profile than one who remains unaware of errors entirely. On Color-Word Interference, self-corrected errors indicate intact monitoring despite response execution difficulty; uncorrected errors suggest either failed monitoring or inability to override the initial response. On Tower, examinees who recognize ineffective move sequences but persist anyway differ from those who show no awareness that their approach isn't working. Those who persist without awareness of difficulty, particularly when errors are obvious to the examiner, show compromised self-evaluation. This can be assessed across subtests by noting whether the client shows any recognition that responses are incorrect or strategies ineffective, and whether that recognition translates into behavioral adjustment. As several subtest chapters note, qualitative observations of error awareness and self-correction often provide more Tier 4 information than any single scored measure.

The integration question at Tier 4 is whether the examinee can coordinate multiple processes when tasks demand it. Some people show intact performance on subtests assessing isolated executive functions but struggle when multiple demands converge. The most complex D-KEFS conditions—Trails Advanced Switching-Distraction, Color-Word Interference Inhibition/Switching, Sorting with multiple valid sorts—provide windows into Tier 4 integration.

Rapid Reference 15.1

Tier-Based Constructs Across the D-KEFS Battery

Construct	Primary Subtests	Additional/Supporting Subtests
Tier 1: Foundational processes		
Motor speed	Trails (original), Design Fluency, Tower (original)	—
Language comprehension	Verbal Fluency, Word Context, Proverb Test, Twenty Questions	—
Visual-perceptual processing	Trails, Design Fluency, Tower, Sorting, SST	—
Basic attention	Baseline conditions: Color Naming, Word Reading, Visual Scanning, Trails sequencing	—
Tier 2: Bridging processes		
Processing speed	Trails, Color-Word Interference, Verbal Fluency, Design Fluency (heavily speeded)	Sorting, Tower, Twenty Questions, Word Context (minimal)

Construct	Primary Subtests	Additional/Supporting Subtests
Basic working memory (maintenance)	All subtests	—
Sustained attention	Verbal Fluency, Tower, Sorting	Stroop Inhibition, Number-Letter Switching
Rule-following/set maintenance	Tower, Verbal Fluency, Design Fluency, Sorting	—
Goal maintenance	Tower, Twenty Questions	—
Basic inhibition (rule compliance)	Design Fluency	Tower, Verbal Fluency
Procedural learning	Sorting, Twenty Questions	—
Tier 3: Cold executive functions		
Cognitive flexibility	Trails Number-Letter Switching, Verbal Fluency Switching, CWI Inhibition/Switching, Sorting, Design Fluency Condition 3	—
Generativity/fluency (verbal)	Verbal Fluency (all conditions)	Twenty Questions, Word Context
Generativity/fluency (nonverbal)	Design Fluency (all conditions)	—
Planning/problem-solving	Tower, Sorting, Twenty Questions, Word Context	—
Inhibitory control (complex)	CWI Inhibition, Advanced Trails Switching-Distraction	Error analysis across battery
Abstract reasoning/concept formation	Sorting, Proverb Test, Twenty Questions	—
Hypothesis testing	Twenty Questions, Word Context, Sorting	—
Feedback utilization	Sorting, Twenty Questions, SST, RISK	—
Executive working memory (manipulation)	Twenty Questions, Tower, Word Context (later items), Advanced Trails Switching-Working Memory	—
Tier 3: Hot executive functions		
Risk tolerance/delay of gratification	RISK	—
Frustration tolerance	Behavioral observation across battery	Tower, CWIT, Twenty Questions
Emotional inhibition	Behavioral observation across battery	—
Effort regulation	Behavioral observation across battery	Verbal Fluency, Sorting
Impulsivity	RISK, behavioral observation	Tower (first-move time), Twenty Questions
Tier 4: Higher-order integration		
Strategic adaptation	Qualitative observation	Tower, Twenty Questions
Error awareness/self-correction	Qualitative observation	CWIT, Tower
Multiprocess coordination	Advanced Trails Switching-Distraction, CWIT Inhibition/Switching, Sorting (multiple valid sorts)	—

Note: CWIT = Color-Word Interference Test; SST = Social Sorting Test.

CONVERGENT AND DIVERGENT PATTERNS

With tier-based profiles constructed across the battery, clinicians face the interpretive challenge of reconciling findings that converge, diverge, or fall somewhere in between. This section addresses how to handle each scenario.

When Findings Converge

Convergent patterns, weakness appearing across multiple measures of the same construct, strengthen diagnostic confidence. When Trails switching, Verbal Fluency switching, and Sorting all reveal flexibility deficits in the absence of Tier 1 or 2 explanations, the case for cognitive inflexibility is robust. The clinician can describe the pattern with confidence, link it to functional implications, and recommend targeted interventions.

Convergence also helps build clinical narratives that translate findings into meaningful communication. A person showing converging evidence of planning weakness (Tower deficits, inefficient Twenty Questions strategy, real-world organization complaints) presents a coherent story that can be communicated to referral sources and translated into actionable recommendations. The narrative is stronger than any individual finding and more useful than a list of disconnected test scores.

However, convergent weakness requires careful consideration of shared method variance. Multiple speeded tests showing impairment may reflect processing speed weakness (Tier 2) rather than converging evidence of executive dysfunction (Tier 3). Multiple verbal measures showing weakness may reflect language limitations (Tier 1) rather than specific executive deficits. The tier framework helps disentangle these patterns by requiring evaluation of lower-tier explanations before attributing convergent weakness to higher-tier deficits.

> **CAUTION**
>
> The Seduction of Consistency. Convergent findings feel satisfying but can reflect shared method variance rather than shared construct. A weakness appearing across all timed tests may reflect processing speed, not the executive functions each test nominally measures. Always ask: what do these tests have in common *besides* the construct I'm trying to measure?

When Findings Diverge

Divergent patterns, discrepancies between tests ostensibly measuring the same construct, are more common than clean convergence and often more informative. But the first question when facing divergence is not what it means but whether it is meaningful at all.

Single-test anomalies arise from countless sources: momentary attention lapses, environmental disruption, hot EF flare-ups in response to perceived failure, examiner error, random measurement variability, or test-taking factors unrelated to the construct of interest. A low score on one flexibility measure with intact scores on others could represent a genuine dissociation, or it could represent noise. The isolated finding itself cannot distinguish these possibilities.

The critical question is whether the discrepancy replicates. If divergent patterns transcend multiple tests, appearing consistently across measures with different task demands and different methods, they likely reflect something meaningful about the client's cognitive profile. If divergence is isolated to a single test with no corroborating evidence, interpret cautiously. A single weak measure is not yet a finding nor a pattern—it is a hypothesis to be tested.

The implication is that divergence often signals the need for more data, whether by testing, interview, background history, or observation in real-world settings, not immediate interpretation. When initial assessment produces discrepancies, the professional approach is to acknowledge uncertainty and, where possible, gather more data to clarify the pattern. A conclusion based on inadequate data is worse than no conclusion at all. The adult case example later in this chapter illustrates this principle in action.

> **CAUTION**
>
> Don't Over-Interpret Isolated Findings. A single unexpected score is not a pattern. Before constructing elaborate explanations for why Trails switching was impaired but Verbal Fluency switching was intact, consider simpler possibilities: the examinee was fatigued, distracted, or experiencing a momentary hot EF breakdown. Gather more data before treating the discrepancy as diagnostically meaningful.

Hot–Cold Dissociations as a Special Case

Divergence between hot and cold executive functions represents a particularly important pattern because it predicts different real-world outcomes. This dissociation is not a measurement artifact to be explained away but a clinically meaningful finding that shapes recommendations.

Examinees with intact cold EF but impaired hot EF often appear competent in structured assessment settings but struggle with emotionally charged real-world decisions. They know what they should do, but cannot execute when it matters. As Chapter 2's developmental discussion notes, this pattern is common in adolescents whose cognitive abilities have matured ahead of their emotional regulation systems (Steinberg, 2017). It also appears in clients with orbitofrontal damage, who may retain cognitive flexibility on testing while showing impaired real-world decision-making (Bechara et al., 1994; Messina et al., 2021), and in various psychiatric conditions affecting emotional control.

The reverse pattern—impaired cold EF with intact hot EF—is also clinically meaningful. These individuals struggle with cognitive demands but maintain adequate emotional regulation, allowing compensation through persistence, help-seeking, and environmental support. Their real-world functioning may exceed test predictions because they navigate their limitations more effectively.

Identifying Strengths and Compensatory Resources

The tier framework applies equally to strengths and weaknesses. Just as convergent weakness across multiple measures strengthens confidence in a deficit, convergent strength across measures identifies reliable cognitive resources. A client showing intact processing speed across Trails, Color-Word Interference, and Verbal Fluency has a confirmed Tier 2 strength. An examinee demonstrating strong cognitive flexibility across multiple switching conditions has a verified Tier 3 resource. These strengths matter clinically—not just as "areas of intact functioning" to note in passing, but as active assets that inform intervention planning. The same systematic cross-subtest analysis used to identify weaknesses should be applied to identify what an individual does well.

Strengths at one tier can compensate for weaknesses at another, but clinicians can only understand this if they identify both aspects. Strong verbal reasoning (Tier 3) can support a client with processing speed weakness (Tier 2) through verbal mediation strategies. Intact metacognitive monitoring (Tier 4) can help an examinee with inhibition deficits (Tier 3) catch and correct errors. Solid emotional regulation (Tier 3 hot) can sustain effort despite cognitive flexibility limitations (Tier 3 cold). Conversely, understanding which potential compensatory resources are *not* available is equally important. A person with both planning deficits and metacognitive weakness has fewer internal resources to draw upon and may need more external support. Chapter 16 addresses how to translate identified strengths into intervention recommendations that leverage what works to address what doesn't.

WEIGHTING FINDINGS

The process of integration inevitably requires weighting some findings more heavily than others. Not all scores are equal: some subtests provide better information than others for specific referral questions; some scores are more interpretively robust than others; some patterns carry more diagnostic weight than others.

D-KEFS test selection should be driven by referral questions. Planning concerns warrant Tower and Twenty Questions; flexibility concerns warrant Trails, Verbal Fluency switching, and Sorting; inhibition concerns warrant Color-Word Interference and Advanced Trails. When referral questions are specific, primary weight should go to subtests most relevant to those questions, with other measures providing context and convergent validation.

Contrast scores often carry more weight than absolute scores for tier-based interpretation. As emphasized throughout the subtest chapters in Part II, a client with slow absolute performance but normal contrast scores demonstrates that executive processes are intact despite processing speed limitations. An examinee with average absolute performance but impaired contrast scores shows executive weakness masked by strong foundational abilities. The contrast score isolates the executive contribution, making it more interpretively useful than the absolute score alone.

Process scores and error analyses carry more weight when they converge with primary scores. Elevated repetition errors on Verbal Fluency are more concerning if they accompany weak total production and appear across Letter and Category conditions. Isolated error elevation with otherwise normal performance may represent a response style (liberal responding) rather than a cognitive deficit.

Base rates provide essential context for interpreting patterns. A score pattern that appears in 40% of the normative sample is less clinically significant than one appearing in 5%. The D-KEFS manuals provide base rate information for many patterns; consulting this information prevents over-interpretation of common variability. When a pattern is rare in the normative sample but fits the clinical picture, diagnostic confidence increases; when a pattern is common even in healthy individuals, caution is warranted.

Rapid Reference 15.2

Common Cross-Subtest Patterns and Their Interpretations

Pattern	Likely Interpretation	Clinical Action
Tier 1 patterns		
Weak motor-demanding subtests (original Trails, Design Fluency, original Tower) with intact verbal measures	Tier 1 motor limitations; executive scores contaminated	Evaluate motor function independently; consider Advanced versions with reduced motor demands
Weak verbal subtests (VF, Word Context, Proverb Test, Twenty Questions) with intact nonverbal measures (Trails, Design Fluency, Tower)	Tier 1 language limitations rather than executive dysfunction	Evaluate language abilities independently; weight nonverbal executive measures more heavily
Weak visually demanding subtests (Trails, Design Fluency, Tower, Sorting, SST) with intact verbal measures	Tier 1 visual-perceptual limitations	Evaluate visual processing independently; weight verbal executive measures more heavily
Weak baseline conditions across multiple subtests (Trails Motor Speed, CWIT Color Naming/Word Reading)	Tier 1 foundational weakness; all executive scores should be interpreted cautiously	Identify specific foundational limitation before interpreting executive conditions
Tier 2 patterns		
Weak speeded subtests (Trails, CWIT, VF, DF) with intact untimed measures (Sorting, Tower, Twenty Questions, Word Context)	Tier 2 processing speed weakness rather than executive dysfunction	Examine contrast scores to confirm; recommend accommodations for speed rather than EF intervention
Weak absolute scores across battery with normal contrast scores	Tier 2 factors (speed, attention) are the bottleneck; executive efficiency intact relative to baseline	Focus on lower-tier factors in recommendations
Declining performance over course of testing; errors clustering late in subtests or session	Tier 2 sustained attention or fatigue factors	Scores from later testing may underestimate true ability; consider retesting critical measures when fresh
Rule violations on early, straightforward items despite apparent comprehension	Tier 2 rule-following/set maintenance difficulty	Distinct from Tier 3 inhibitory control; may respond to external cueing and structure

Pattern	Likely Interpretation	Clinical Action
Tier 3 cold patterns		
Impaired switching across Trails, VF, CWIT, and Sorting with intact baseline conditions	Convergent evidence of Tier 3 cognitive flexibility deficit	High diagnostic confidence; target flexibility in intervention
Isolated switching weakness on one subtest with intact switching on others	Likely task-specific factors, measurement error, or momentary fluctuation	Consider additional testing before diagnosing flexibility deficit
Weak Verbal Fluency (all conditions) with intact Design Fluency	Modality-specific verbal generativity weakness, not domain-general fluency impairment	Distinguish from language limitations (Tier 1) by examining non-fluency verbal measures
Weak Design Fluency with intact Verbal Fluency	Modality-specific nonverbal generativity weakness	Consider visuospatial and motor contributions
Weak high-manipulation tasks (Tower, Twenty Questions, later Word Context items) with preserved performance on maintenance-only tasks	Tier 3 executive working memory limitation	Distinct from Tier 2 working memory capacity
Rule violations emerging only on complex items under cognitive load (not on early/simple items)	Tier 3 inhibitory control failure under demand	Distinct from Tier 2 basic rule-following difficulty
Tier 3 hot patterns		
Cold EF measures intact; RISK impaired and/or frustration/impulsivity observed across subtests	Hot–cold dissociation; real-world functioning likely worse than cold EF scores predict	Compare with rating scale data; prioritize emotional regulation in recommendations
Cold EF measures impaired; RISK intact and behavioral regulation adequate throughout testing	Reverse hot–cold dissociation; patient may function better than cold scores predict	Adequate emotional regulation may compensate for cognitive limitations in real-world settings
Tier 4 patterns		
Persistent use of ineffective strategies despite repeated failure, when component executive skills are adequate	Tier 4 metacognitive weakness; impaired strategic adaptation	May require explicit metacognitive coaching rather than skill-based intervention
Self-corrected errors across subtests	Intact metacognitive monitoring despite response execution difficulty	Better prognosis; can leverage self-monitoring in intervention
Uncorrected errors with no apparent awareness of difficulty	Compromised metacognitive monitoring	May require external feedback systems; limited insight-oriented intervention potential

INTEGRATIVE CASE EXAMPLES

The following examples illustrate cross-subtest integration principles. Each case demonstrates a specific interpretive challenge and its resolution through tier-based analysis. Note that these cases, like the vignettes throughout Part II, embed D-KEFS findings within larger batteries—executive function assessment should not occur in isolation. Similar score profiles in different individuals may warrant alternative interpretations depending on history, referral question, behavioral observations, and collateral data; these examples demonstrate the reasoning process rather than fixed interpretive rules.

Example 1: Child (Age 9)—Rule Out Lower Tiers First

Jason Grant was referred for ADHD evaluation following teacher concerns about inattention and disorganization. WISC-V results showed average Verbal Comprehension (VCI = 102), Visual Spatial (VSI = 98), Fluid Reasoning (FRI = 101) indices, but low Processing Speed (PSI = 78). Working Memory was low average (WMI = 88). WIAT-4 revealed adequate writing abilities but slow production of written material.

D-KEFS Trails showed weak absolute scores: Visual Scanning SS = 7, Number Sequencing SS = 6, Letter Sequencing SS = 6, Number-Letter Switching SS = 5, and Motor Speed SS = 7. At first glance, the Number-Letter Switching score appeared to confirm executive dysfunction—a finding that might support an ADHD diagnosis. However, comparison of contrast scores told a different story. The Number-Letter Switching versus Combined Number and Letter Sequencing contrast scaled score was 10—exactly average. The weak switching score reflected slow processing across all conditions, not specific switching difficulty.

Verbal Fluency showed a parallel pattern: Letter Fluency SS = 7, Category Fluency SS = 8, Category Switching Total Correct SS = 6, but Switching Accuracy SS = 10. Jason was slow to generate words across all conditions, but the accuracy of his switching, correct alternations relative to words produced, was normal.

Integration: The convergent pattern across WISC-V PSI, Trails, and Verbal Fluency pointed to Tier 2 processing speed as the bottleneck. What appeared to be executive dysfunction on initial inspection was actually speed limitation affecting all speeded tasks equivalently. As Chapter 2's discussion of developmental considerations reminds us, processing speed continues developing through childhood and shows considerable individual variation. Jason's profile suggested immature processing speed rather than executive dysfunction. Recommendations emphasized accommodations for processing speed (extended time, reduced written output demands, chunked assignments) and building automaticity in foundational academic skills to reduce processing load, rather than executive function intervention targeting flexibility or inhibition that was not actually impaired.

Example 2: Adolescent (Age 16)—Hot–Cold Dissociation

Anna Klein was referred following impulsive decision-making and risk-taking behavior despite strong academic performance. Her parents described her as "knowing the right thing but doing the wrong thing," particularly with peers. WAIS-5 scores were uniformly strong: FSIQ = 118, VCI = 122, VSI = 117, FRI = 115, WMI = 112, PSI = 108.

D-KEFS cold executive measures showed no deficits. Trails Advanced Number-Letter Switching SS = 12 with an average Switching-Distraction score (SS = 11), indicating she handled the added complexity without difficulty. Verbal Fluency Category Switching SS = 11; Color-Word Interference Inhibition SS = 13, Inhibition/Switching SS = 12; Sorting Confirmed Sorts SS = 11. Anna demonstrated intact cognitive flexibility, fluency, inhibition, and concept formation across the battery. Cold EF was clearly not the problem.

However, behavioral observations told a different story. During Tower administration, Anna showed visible frustration during challenging items, sighing loudly and making self-critical comments. On one item, she abandoned a reasonable strategy after an early mistake and made impulsive moves that violated rules—moves she immediately recognized as errors. Likewise, her verbal mediation during Sorting included frustrated comments when she couldn't immediately identify sorts.

BRIEF-2 ratings from both parents showed clinically elevated Emotional Control (T = 72) and Inhibit (T = 68) scales, with normative Behavioral Regulation Index scores. Parent narrative described Anna as "emotionally reactive to frustration" and "prone to impulsive decisions when upset."

Integration: The dissociation between intact cold EF test scores and elevated hot EF indicators (behavioral observations, rating scales) explained Anna's clinical presentation. Her cognitive abilities were mature; her emotional regulation was not. This is the developmental pattern Chapter 2 describes as typical of adolescence, when prefrontal cognitive systems mature ahead of ventromedial emotional regulation systems. Recommendations focused on emotional regulation strategies, decision-making supports for high-stakes situations, and psychoeducation about the hot–cold distinction for both Anna and her parents. Traditional cognitive strategy training would have missed the point entirely.

Example 3: Adult (Age 34)—When Divergence Requires More Data

Levi Finch presented six months post-concussion with persistent cognitive complaints, primarily difficulty with multitasking and mental flexibility at work. WAIS-5 showed intact reasoning (VCI = 108, VSI = 109, FRI = 112) with mildly low Working Memory (WMI = 92).

Initial D-KEFS testing produced a discrepancy that didn't immediately cohere. Verbal Fluency Category Switching Total Correct was impaired (SS = 5) with low Switching Accuracy (SS = 6), suggesting genuine flexibility difficulty. However, Trails Number-Letter Switching was average (SS = 10) with an average contrast score (SS = 10). He appeared to have impaired verbal switching but intact visual-motor switching.

Several explanations were possible. Perhaps the deficit was modality-specific, affecting verbal but not visual-motor flexibility. Perhaps fatigue or attention fluctuation affected one test but not the other. Perhaps one score was simply measurement error. The isolated discrepancy didn't support a confident interpretation in any direction.

Rather than forcing an interpretation, the clinician administered additional measures at a follow-up session. Sorting Confirmed Correct Sorts was average (SS = 10), Color-Word Interference Inhibition/Switching was average (SS = 9), and RISK performance showed appropriate risk calibration with no impulsivity indicators. With three of four flexibility measures in the average range, only Verbal Fluency Category Switching was impaired, and intact hot EF on RISK, the pattern became clearer: the Verbal Fluency weakness likely reflected task-specific factors—perhaps the combination of generativity and switching demands—rather than core flexibility impairment. The follow-up testing transformed an uninterpretable discrepancy into a coherent profile. Recommendations focused on monitoring rather than intervention, with the report framing the isolated weakness as task-specific rather than indicative of flexibility dysfunction warranting treatment. If flexibility concerns emerged functionally, the Wisconsin Card Sorting Test could provide additional clarifying data.

Example 4: Older Adult (Age 71)—Distinguishing Speed from Executive Decline

Eleanor Parker was referred by her primary care physician for cognitive evaluation following her own concerns about declining mental sharpness. The referral question was whether changes represented normal aging or early dementia. WAIS-5 showed a characteristic aging pattern: preserved Verbal Comprehension (VCI = 112) and relative weakness on Processing Speed (PSI = 88). WMS-5 memory scores were low average (Immediate Memory Index = 92, Delayed Memory Index = 94), within expectations for age.

D-KEFS Color-Word Interference produced concerning-looking absolute scores: Color Naming SS = 7, Word Reading SS = 8, Inhibition SS = 6, Inhibition/Switching SS = 5. A surface-level reading might suggest progressive executive decline, particularly given the low Inhibition/Switching score.

However, contrast scores revealed a different picture. The Inhibition versus Color Naming contrast scaled score was 9—average. The Inhibition/Switching versus Combined Inhibition plus Color Naming contrast scaled score was 8—also within normal limits. Eleanor was slower across all conditions, consistent with her WAIS-5 PSI, but her inhibitory control and switching efficiency relative to her own baseline were preserved.

Trails Advanced showed the same pattern: weak absolute scores across all conditions, but average contrast scores when switching was compared to other conditions. RISK was administered to assess decision-making capacity, an area of concern in early dementia; her performance was age-appropriate with no evidence of impaired risk calibration or reward sensitivity that might suggest ventromedial dysfunction. Verbal Fluency total words were in the low average range across conditions, but her clustering and switching strategies were observed and effective.

Integration: The convergent pattern of weak absolute scores with preserved contrast scores across multiple subtests indicated Tier 1/2 slowing rather than Tier 3 executive decline. Eleanor's executive functions were intact relative to her processing speed baseline—she was slower, not less capable. This pattern aligns with the developmental trajectories reviewed in Chapter 2: Tier 1–2 processing

> **DON'T FORGET**
>
> Contrast scores are your friend. Absolute scores confound executive functions with foundational abilities. Contrast scores isolate the executive contribution by comparing executive conditions to baseline conditions. When absolute scores are weak but contrast scores are normal, the weakness lies at Tier 1 or 2, not Tier 3 or 4. When contrast scores are weak regardless of absolute performance, executive functions are impaired independent of foundational abilities.

speed shows the most consistent age-related decline, while Tier 3 executive functions may remain relatively preserved when processing demands are accounted for through contrast scores. The normal RISK performance provided additional reassurance that higher-order decision-making remained intact. Feedback emphasized that her cognitive changes were consistent with normal aging rather than pathological decline, reducing her anxiety significantly. Recommendations focused on accommodating speed limitations (allowing more time, reducing time pressure) rather than cognitive rehabilitation for executive dysfunction.

SUMMARY

Cross-subtest integration transforms a collection of individual findings into a coherent clinical picture. The hierarchical tier framework provides the organizing principle: identify the lowest tier showing consistent weakness, use convergent patterns across subtests to strengthen diagnostic confidence, and treat divergent patterns as signals that may require additional data rather than immediate interpretation.

Effective integration requires weighting findings appropriately, prioritizing contrast scores over absolute scores, primary measures over isolated process scores, and convergent patterns over isolated findings. It also requires humility: single-test anomalies may reflect noise rather than signal and forcing interpretations on inadequate data serves no one.

The hot–cold distinction adds a critical dimension to integration. Divergence between cold EF test scores and hot EF indicators (behavioral observations, rating scales, RISK performance) predicts real-world functioning better than either source alone. People with intact cold EF but impaired hot EF may appear competent in testing but struggle in emotionally charged real-world situations; those with impaired cold EF but intact hot EF may exceed test-based predictions through emotional resilience and adaptive compensation.

The goal of integration is not a summary score or global characterization but a differentiated profile that guides intervention. Accurate integration is necessary but not sufficient—a coherent tier-based profile that sits in a report drawer helps no one. The next chapter addresses the translation challenge: how to communicate tier-based findings to non-clinicians and how to generate recommendations that address the actual level of dysfunction rather than generic intervention lists.

TEST YOURSELF

1. When multiple speeded D-KEFS subtests show weakness but untimed measures are relatively preserved, the most likely explanation involves deficits at which tier?

(a) Tier 1
(b) Tier 2
(c) Tier 3 Cold EF
(d) Tier 3 Hot EF

2. A client shows impaired Trails Number-Letter Switching but intact Verbal Fluency Category Switching and average Sorting performance. What is the most appropriate next step?

(a) Diagnose a specific visual-motor switching deficit.
(b) Consider the isolated finding as likely noise and interpret with caution or administer additional measures.
(c) Average the scores to determine overall flexibility.
(d) Diagnose generalized cognitive inflexibility.

3. Contrast scores are particularly valuable because they:

(a) Are more reliable than absolute scores.
(b) Isolate executive contributions from foundational abilities.
(c) Eliminate the need for baseline conditions.
(d) Provide normative comparisons across age groups.

4. An examinee with intact cold EF scores but impaired RISK performance and elevated BRIEF-2 Emotional Control is most likely to:

(a) Function better in real life than cold EF scores predict.

(b) Function worse in real life than cold EF scores predict.

(c) Show consistent functioning across structured and unstructured settings.

(d) Require cognitive flexibility intervention.

5. When interpreting convergent weaknesses across multiple subtests, clinicians should be cautious about:

(a) Shared method variance creating artificial convergence.

(b) The possibility that findings reflect true deficits.

(c) Referral source bias.

(d) Client motivation.

6. A 72-year-old individual shows weak absolute scores on Color-Word Interference Inhibition (SS = 6) but an average contrast score comparing Inhibition to Color Naming (SS = 10). This pattern most likely reflects:

(a) Age-related inhibitory decline.

(b) Processing speed weakness with intact inhibition.

(c) Dementia-related executive dysfunction.

(d) Test anxiety affecting performance.

7. Which of the following patterns would MOST strongly support Tier 3 cognitive flexibility impairment?

(a) Impaired Trails Number-Letter Switching with intact contrast score.

(b) Impaired switching on Trails only, with average Verbal Fluency and Sorting.

(c) Impaired switching across Trails, Verbal Fluency, and Color-Word Interference with intact baseline conditions.

(d) Impaired switching on all subtests with equally impaired baseline conditions.

8. Behavioral observations of frustration tolerance during testing provide information primarily about:

(a) Tier 2 sustained attention.

(b) Tier 3 cold executive functions.

(c) Tier 3 hot executive functions.

(d) Tier 4 metacognition.

9. When initial D-KEFS testing produces a discrepancy that doesn't clearly fit known patterns, the most appropriate response is to:

(a) Select the interpretation that best fits the referral question.

(b) Average discrepant scores to find the true level of functioning.

(c) Acknowledge uncertainty and consider additional testing to clarify the pattern.

(d) Weight the lower score more heavily as it reflects true impairment.

10. Base rate information from the D-KEFS manual is useful for integration because it helps clinicians:

(a) Convert raw scores to scaled scores.

(b) Determine whether a pattern is common or rare in the normative sample.

(c) Calculate confidence intervals around scores.

(d) Identify which subtests to administer.

Answer Key: 1-b, 2-b, 3-b, 4-b, 5-a, 6-b, 7-c, 8-c, 9-c, 10-b

REFERENCES

Bechara, A., Damasio, A. R., Damasio, H., & Anderson, S. W. (1994). Insensitivity to future consequences following damage to human prefrontal cortex. *Cognition, 50*(1–3), 7–15.

Messina, I., Sambin, M., Palmieri, A., & Viviani, R. (2021). The role of the orbitofrontal cortex in the experience and regulation of emotions: A systematic review. *Frontiers in Psychology, 12*, 718931.

Steinberg, L. (2017). *Adolescents* (11th ed.). McGraw-Hill Education.

Sixteen

FROM ASSESSMENT TO ACTION

CLINICAL VIGNETTE

Ella McMathers, a 12-year-old seventh grader, was referred for reevaluation after two years of intervention following an attention-deficit/hyperactivity disorder (ADHD) diagnosis. Despite consistent 504 plan implementation, medication management, and parent training, her teachers and parents reported minimal improvement in the difficulties that prompted the original evaluation.

Review of the previous neuropsychological report revealed a thorough assessment with a clear diagnosis. The recommendations section listed common ADHD interventions: preferential seating, extended time, breaks during testing, organizational support, homework accommodations, behavioral intervention, parent training, social skills group, and several others. All had been implemented. None had produced meaningful change.

Reevaluation using tier-based analysis clarified why. WISC-V showed average processing speed (PSI = 102) and working memory (WMI = 98). The accommodations for these domains, while reasonable for ADHD generally, weren't addressing Ella's actual weaknesses. D-KEFS cold executive measures were intact: Trails Number-Letter Switching SS = 10, Color-Word Interference Inhibition SS = 11, Sorting Confirmed Correct Sorts SS = 10. However, BRIEF-2 parent and teacher ratings showed marked elevations on Emotional Control ($T = 71$ and $T = 74$) and Shift ($T = 68$ and $T = 70$) scales. Behavioral observations during testing revealed significant frustration when problems became difficult—irritability, reactivity, and abandonment of effective strategies in favor of impulsive responses.

The tier analysis identified Tier 3 hot executive dysfunction as the core issue. Ella possessed the cognitive capacity to plan, shift, and inhibit but couldn't deploy these abilities when emotionally activated. This pattern is consistent with Chapter 2's discussion of hot–cold developmental trajectories: hot executive functions mature more slowly than cold cognitive abilities, and some children show pronounced asymmetry between what they can do under optimal conditions and what they actually do when emotions run high. The original recommendations were replaced with new ones: emotional regulation skill-building with her therapist, a classroom plan for de-escalation when frustration mounted, and modified expectations during high-stress periods like testing weeks. Within six months, Ella's functioning had improved more than in the previous two years of well-intentioned but poorly targeted intervention.

THE TRANSLATION PROBLEM

Neuropsychological assessment generates data: scores, patterns, contrasts, observations. The challenge is translating that data into something meaningful. A scaled score of 5 on Verbal Fluency Category Switching means nothing to a parent, teacher, or treatment provider. Even diagnostic labels—"executive dysfunction," "cognitive flexibility deficit"—describe problems without providing solutions.

The tier framework provides a translation structure. Rather than listing which tests were impaired, the clinician identifies *where* in the processing hierarchy the breakdown occurs. This reframes the clinical question from "What's wrong?" to "What's getting in the way?" This is a question that points naturally toward intervention.

Consider two clients, both with impaired Tower Test performance. Individual A shows Tier 2 weakness: slow processing speed and limited working memory constrain planning capacity. Individual B shows Tier 3 weakness: adequate speed and working memory, but genuine difficulty generating and evaluating strategic options. The same low score has entirely different intervention implications. Individual A needs accommodations that reduce processing demands: more time, external working memory supports, simplified problem presentation. Individual B needs strategy training: explicit instruction in planning approaches, practice with systematic evaluation of options. Treating both clients identically because they share difficulties related to "planning impairment" doesn't make sense.

> **DON'T FORGET**
>
> Same score, different intervention. A low score on any executive measure can arise from multiple sources. The tier framework asks not just "what is impaired?" but "why is it impaired?" Two clients with identical Tower Test scores may need completely different interventions—one needs accommodations for processing demands, the other needs strategy training for planning. The score alone doesn't tell you which.

The tier framework also prevents a common error: recommending executive function intervention for problems that aren't executive in nature. When Tier 1 or Tier 2 weaknesses explain poor performance, executive strategy training is unlikely to help. You cannot train someone to use strategies they lack the foundational capacity to implement. Accommodations for lower-tier limitations must precede or accompany interventions targeting higher-tier functions.

EXPLAINING THE TIER FRAMEWORK TO NON-CLINICIANS

The tier framework is a clinical tool, but its value extends beyond the clinician's interpretation. When examinees, families, educators, and treatment providers understand the framework, they can better understand the assessment findings and participate more meaningfully in intervention planning. The challenge is communicating these concepts without jargon.

Language for Parents and Families

Parents want to understand their child's difficulties in terms that make intuitive sense. The tier framework can be explained through a building metaphor: "Think of cognitive abilities like a building. The foundation—things like how quickly the brain processes information, how much it can hold in mind at once—supports everything above it. The upper floors are the executive functions: planning, flexibility, and self-control. When we test, we're trying to figure out which floor has the problem. Is the foundation shaky, or is the structure above it where the issue lies? This matters because the repair strategy is completely different. You don't fix a cracked foundation by redecorating the top floor."

For a child with Tier 2 processing speed weakness affecting apparent executive performance, the explanation might be: "Your son's executive functions—his ability to plan, switch between tasks, stay organized—are actually intact. The issue is processing speed, which is like the clock speed of a computer. Everything takes him longer, which makes complex tasks pile up before he can manage them. The good news is that when we give him more time, he can do what other kids do. The intervention isn't teaching him new strategies, it's giving him the time his brain needs to use the strategies he already has."

For a child with genuine Tier 3 executive dysfunction, the framing shifts: "Your daughter's foundational abilities are solid. She processes information quickly and can hold plenty in mind at once. The issue is at the executive level, specifically cognitive flexibility. She has trouble shifting gears when circumstances change. This isn't about effort or motivation; it's how her brain is wired right now. The intervention is teaching her explicit strategies for recognizing when shifts are needed and how to make them, because this doesn't come naturally to her the way it does for some kids."

Hot–cold dissociations require particular care in explanation because they can sound like the child is being willful: "The testing showed something interesting: your son can do all these tasks when he's calm and focused. His 'thinking' executive functions are fine. But the executive functions that manage emotions—staying regulated when frustrated, not acting impulsively when upset—those are weaker. This explains why he seems capable in some situations but falls apart in others. It's not that he doesn't know what to do; it's that strong emotions override his ability to do it. The intervention focuses on emotion regulation, not cognitive strategies."

Language for Schools and Educators

Educators need practical translation. They want to know what to do differently in the classroom, and they need to understand why those accommodations or interventions are warranted. Abstract discussions of executive function theory are less useful than concrete guidance tied to specific classroom situations.

For IEP teams and classroom teachers, tier-based explanations help justify specific accommodations: "The testing shows that Aiden's difficulties stem from processing speed, not executive function per se. He understands concepts as quickly as his peers, but producing output—writing, completing worksheets, showing his work—takes significantly longer. The accommodation of extended time isn't giving him an unfair advantage; it's leveling the playing field by removing a bottleneck that isn't related to what you're actually trying to assess or teach."

When the issue is hot executive functioning, educators benefit from understanding why a student may perform inconsistently: "Sofia's profile shows intact cognitive abilities but significant weakness in what we call 'hot' executive functioning, which includes managing emotions in the moment. In the structured testing environment, she performed well. But the classroom has distractions, social dynamics, and unpredictable events that overwhelm her regulatory capacity. The strategies that help are environmental: predictable routines, advance warning of transitions, a designated cool-down space, and coaching on recognizing when she's escalating."

Sometimes the most important communication is explaining why generic interventions haven't worked: "The previous evaluation recommended organizational supports, which makes sense for executive dysfunction generally. But Carlos's organizational difficulties stem from working memory limitations, not planning deficits. He can create organizational systems just fine, but he can't hold enough information in mind to use them consistently. External memory supports—checklists, visual schedules, written instructions he can refer back to—will help more than teaching him to plan better."

Language for Treatment Providers

Therapists, physicians, and other treatment providers need to understand how the assessment findings relate to their own interventions. For a therapist providing intervention, the tier analysis shapes treatment targets: "The tier analysis suggests that Mia, a 28-year-old accountant, has apparent planning difficulties that are secondary to slow processing speed. She can plan, but she runs out of time before she can execute. Therapy focused on planning strategies may be less helpful than therapy focused on accepting and accommodating her slower pace. This includes managing frustration about needing more time, advocating for workplace accommodations, and developing realistic expectations for task completion."

For occupational therapists or rehabilitation specialists designing skill-building programs, tier identification prevents misdirected effort: "The evaluation shows that Owen, a 48-year-old returning to work after a stroke, has difficulties with organization that stem from working memory limitations, not planning deficits. Previous interventions tried to teach him organizational strategies, like prioritization systems, breaking projects into steps, and time management techniques. But learning and applying those strategies requires holding multiple pieces of information in mind simultaneously, which is exactly what he struggles to do. The goal isn't teaching more sophisticated organizational thinking, it's providing external supports simple enough that they don't tax working memory: a single visual checklist rather than a multistep system, phone alerts rather than mental reminders, one task visible at a time rather than a complex planner."

When hot executive dysfunction is the primary finding, treatment providers benefit from understanding why traditional cognitive approaches may fall short: "Testing showed intact cognitive flexibility, planning, and inhibition but behavioral observations and rating scales revealed significant emotional dysregulation. Traditional executive function coaching that focuses on strategies and skills is unlikely to help because the cognitive skills are already present. Treatment should focus on emotion regulation: recognizing escalation, de-escalation techniques, and building frustration tolerance. The goal is helping this 36-year-old professional access the executive abilities she already has when workplace stress or interpersonal conflict triggers emotional reactivity."

Language for Adult Clients

Adults seeking evaluation often arrive with years of confusion about why they struggle with tasks others find easy. Tier-based explanation can provide clarity and reduce self-blame.

For an adult with Tier 2 processing speed limitations: "Your thinking is fine—your processing speed is slow. You understand things as quickly as anyone else, but executing tasks takes you longer. This isn't about intelligence or effort. It's like having a computer with a great processor but a slow hard drive. The work gets done accurately, but it just takes more time. The implication is that you need to build more time into your schedule, advocate for deadline flexibility when possible, and stop comparing your pace to people whose brains simply run faster."

For an adult with Tier 3 cold executive dysfunction: "Your foundational abilities are solid, but the executive control system, the part that organizes, prioritizes, and sequences, isn't keeping up. This explains why you can understand complex information but struggle to break projects into steps, or why you know what you need to do but can't figure out where to start. The good news is that executive strategies can be learned. It takes more explicit effort for you than for others, but with the right tools and practice, you can build systems that work."

For an adult with hot executive dysfunction: "Your cognitive abilities are intact. You can plan, organize, and problem-solve as well as anyone when you're calm. The difficulty is maintaining access to those abilities when emotions run high. Under stress or frustration, the executive functions that would normally guide your behavior become harder to access. This is why you might make decisions in the heat of the moment that you wouldn't make when calm, or why you know exactly what you should do but can't seem to do it when it matters. The intervention focuses on emotion regulation—learning to recognize when you're escalating, developing strategies to bring arousal down, and creating space between the emotional trigger and your response so your thinking has a chance to engage."

Rapid Reference 16.1

Explaining Tier-Based Findings to Different Audiences

Audience	Key Framing	Example Language
Parents/families	Building metaphor: foundation vs. upper floors; different floors require different repairs	"The foundation—things like how quickly the brain processes information—supports everything above it. You don't fix a cracked foundation by redecorating the top floor."
	Tier 2 (e.g., processing speed)	"Your son's executive functions are actually intact. The issue is processing speed—like the clock speed of a computer. The intervention isn't teaching new strategies—it's giving him the time his brain needs."
	Tier 3 Cold	"Her foundational abilities are solid. The issue is at the executive level. This isn't about effort—it's how her brain is wired right now. The intervention is teaching explicit strategies."
	Tier 3 Hot	"Your son can do all these tasks when he's calm. But the executive functions that manage emotions are weaker. It's not that he doesn't know what to do; strong emotions override his ability to do it."
Schools/educators	Practical translation tied to classroom situations; justify specific accommodations	"The testing shows that Aiden's difficulties stem from processing speed, not executive function. Extended time isn't giving him an unfair advantage; it's leveling the playing field."

Audience	Key Framing	Example Language
	Explaining inconsistency	"Sofia's profile shows intact cognitive abilities but weakness in 'hot' executive functioning. The classroom has distractions and unpredictable events that overwhelm her regulatory capacity."
	Explaining failed interventions	"Carlos's organizational difficulties stem from working memory limitations, not planning deficits. He can create systems—he can't hold enough in mind to use them. External supports will help more than teaching him to plan better."
Treatment providers	Shape treatment targets based on tier analysis	"Mia's planning difficulties are secondary to slow processing speed. Therapy focused on planning strategies may be less helpful than therapy focused on accommodating her slower pace."
	Prevent misdirected effort	"Jason's difficulties with organization stem from working memory limitations. The goal isn't teaching more sophisticated organizational thinking—it's providing external supports simple enough that they don't tax working memory."
	Hot EF primary finding	"Traditional executive function coaching focusing on strategies is unlikely to help because the cognitive skills are already present. Treatment should focus on emotion regulation."
Adult clients	Reduce self-blame; provide clarity	Tier 2: "Your thinking is fine—your processing speed is slow. This isn't about intelligence or effort. It's like having a computer with a great processor but a slow hard drive."
		Tier 3 Cold: "Your foundational abilities are solid, but the executive control system isn't keeping up. The good news is that executive strategies can be learned."
		Tier 3 Hot: "Your cognitive abilities are intact when you're calm. The difficulty is maintaining access to those abilities when emotions run high. The intervention focuses on emotion regulation."

WHEN TESTS AND REAL LIFE DIVERGE

A well-conducted assessment creates optimal conditions for performance: a quiet room, one-on-one attention, structured tasks, clear instructions, and managed time pressure. This is by design—we want to measure capacity under favorable conditions. But real life rarely offers these conditions. The classroom is noisy, social situations are unpredictable, work deadlines are externally imposed, and emotional stressors don't pause for cognitive tasks.

This means that test performance represents a ceiling of what someone *can* do when conditions are right. It may or may not reflect what they actually *do* when conditions are typical. The discrepancy between capacity and daily performance is not measurement error. It is clinically meaningful data.

Rating Scales as Ecological Indicators

Rating scales like the BRIEF-2 and BRIEF-A, D-REF and D-REF-A, and CEFI and CEFI Adult capture executive functioning as it manifests in daily life. Parents, teachers, and self-reporters describe behavior in naturalistic settings: home, school, work, and social situations. These environments include the distractions, emotional provocations, and unpredictable demands that testing environments deliberately minimize.

When test scores and rating scales converge—both showing executive weakness, or both showing intact functioning—interpretation is straightforward and diagnostic confidence is high. Divergence between these sources is also clinically meaningful, though it requires more interpretation.

Intact test scores with elevated rating scales suggest that capacity exists but isn't deployed in daily life. This is the hallmark of hot executive dysfunction. The person can perform when calm, focused, and supported, but emotional dysregulation, distraction, or insufficient motivation derails performance in real-world contexts. Ella's profile in the opening vignette illustrates this pattern: intact D-KEFS performance, elevated BRIEF-2 ratings. The testing environment controlled the very variables that cause her difficulty in daily life. Intervention for this pattern focuses on bridging the gap between capacity and deployment, including emotion regulation skills, environmental modifications, motivational supports.

Impaired test scores with normal rating scale results are less common but do occur. This pattern requires careful interpretation. It may indicate that the testing environment itself was problematic—anxiety, poor effort, fatigue, or other factors suppressing performance. Alternatively, the person may have Tier 1 or Tier 2 limitations that they naturally accommodate in daily life (taking more time, avoiding time-pressured situations, relying on external supports) but cannot work around during standardized testing. It may also reflect compensatory strategies that work in daily life but cannot be applied during testing, or that rating scale respondents have inaccurate perceptions through accommodation to the person's difficulties or limited observation opportunities. Interpretation requires careful consideration of test-taking behavior and behavioral observations to determine which explanation is most plausible.

The RISK Test provides a direct measure of hot executive functioning, but it too occurs in a structured setting. Behavioral observations during testing, frustration tolerance, response to failure, persistence under difficulty, supplement RISK scores by capturing hot EF manifestations in real time. As discussed in Chapter 15, these observations often align more closely with rating scale elevations than cold EF test scores do.

Communicating About Ecological Validity

When explaining divergence between tests and rating scales to families, the capacity-deployment distinction provides a useful frame: "The testing shows what your daughter can do when conditions are ideal—quiet room, one-on-one support, no distractions. Her abilities are there. But the rating scales show that she's not able to use those abilities consistently at school or home. The issue isn't capability; it's deployment. Something in real-world environments is getting in the way. Our job is to figure out what that something is and address it directly."

The reverse pattern, impaired test scores with normal rating scales, requires a different explanation: "The testing showed slower processing speed than we'd expect, but teachers and parents report he keeps up fine at school and home. This actually makes sense: in daily life, he's had years to develop workarounds. He avoids time-pressured situations, takes longer on homework than his peers but gets it done, and has learned to give himself extra time without even thinking about it. The testing strips away those compensations and measures raw processing speed. Both pictures are true: he has a real limitation, and he's learned to manage it effectively. Our job is to make sure his accommodations are formalized so he doesn't have to work so hard to compensate."

In written reports, the intact-tests/elevated-ratings divergence should be explicitly noted and interpreted: "Performance-based testing revealed intact inhibitory control (Color-Word Interference Inhibition SS = 11), while parent and teacher ratings on the BRIEF-2 Inhibit scale were clinically elevated (T = 70 and T = 68, respectively). This divergence suggests that the client possesses the cognitive capacity for inhibition but is unable to employ it consistently in naturalistic settings, likely due to emotional or motivational factors that were controlled in the testing environment. Intervention should focus on supports for real-world deployment rather than cognitive skill-building."

The reverse pattern warrants its own report language: "Performance-based testing revealed slow processing speed (PSI = 82), while parent and teacher ratings on the BRIEF-2 were within normal limits across all scales. This divergence suggests that the person has developed effective compensatory strategies that support adequate

DON'T FORGET

Tests show capacity, rating scales show deployment. Performance-based tests measure what someone ***can*** do under optimal conditions. Rating scales measure what they actually ***do*** in daily life. When these diverge, the divergence itself is the finding. Intact test scores with elevated ratings indicate hot executive dysfunction—capacity exists but isn't deployed when conditions aren't optimal.

daily functioning despite underlying processing limitations. However, they are also working twice as hard to get the same results. Formal accommodations, particularly extended time, should be implemented to reduce the compensatory burden and ensure that his processing speed does not become a barrier as academic demands increase."

FROM UNDERSTANDING TO ACTION

The purpose of assessment is intervention. A beautifully interpreted profile that generates no actionable recommendations has failed its purpose. The tier framework naturally generates intervention directions because it identifies the level at which functioning breaks down. Of course, effective intervention planning extends beyond tier identification. The individual's developmental history, cultural context, family and school resources, co-occurring conditions, prior intervention response, and personal goals all shape which recommendations are appropriate and feasible. The tier framework provides the cognitive roadmap; these broader factors determine how that roadmap is navigated.

Tier-Based Intervention Principles

The sections that follow outline intervention approaches matched to each tier. These are intervention categories, not comprehensive intervention lists. Whole books address executive function interventions, including Dawson and Guare's (2018) *Executive Skills in Children and Adolescents* and Meltzer's (2010) *Promoting Executive Function in the Classroom* for school-age populations, Kennedy's (2017) *Coaching College Students with Executive Function Problems*, Dawson and Guare's (2016) *The Smart but Scattered Guide to Success* for adults, and Solanto's (2011) *Cognitive-Behavioral Therapy for Adult ADHD: Targeting Executive Dysfunction* for clinicians treating adults with executive dysfunction. The goal here is to match the tier to the intervention type. Once you know an individual needs Tier 2 working memory supports rather than Tier 3 strategy training, you can consult those resources for specific techniques. Without that tier-level understanding, even the best intervention repository won't help you choose wisely.

Tier 1

When foundational abilities are impaired—motor speed, basic language, perceptual processing, basic attention—the first question is whether the limitation can be directly addressed. Some Tier 1 impairments respond to prosthetic correction: glasses or contacts for visual acuity, hearing aids for hearing loss, and appropriate lighting for low vision. When prosthetic correction is possible, it should be implemented before any cognitive assessment is interpreted; otherwise, we risk attributing to executive dysfunction what is actually uncorrected sensory impairment. Color blindness, which affects performance on Color-Word Interference and other color-dependent tasks, cannot be corrected but must be identified and accommodated.

When Tier 1 limitations cannot be directly corrected, accommodation becomes the primary strategy. Foundational capacities cannot be trained in the same way as strategic skills can. A client with motor slowing will not become faster through practice. A person with language limitations will not suddenly acquire vocabulary through cognitive rehabilitation. The goal of accommodation is to reduce or remove demands on the impaired foundation, allowing higher-level abilities to express themselves despite foundational constraints. For motor limitations, this means reducing graphomotor demands, allowing typed responses, and not penalizing slow production. For language limitations, it means simplifying verbal instructions, allowing nonverbal response modes, and assessing knowledge through demonstration rather than explanation. For perceptual limitations, it means reducing visual complexity, allowing enlarged materials, and minimizing visual search demands. Basic attentional limitations—difficulty maintaining focus even on straightforward, low-demand tasks—call for environmental modifications that reduce competing stimuli: quiet workspaces, minimized visual clutter, and removal of distracting objects. Unlike Tier 2 sustained attention difficulties, which emerge under cognitive load, Tier 1 attentional limitations affect even basic tasks and require consistent environmental control rather than task-specific accommodations.

Tier 2

Limitations in processing speed, sustained attention, and related bridging processes create bottlenecks that constrain higher-level functioning. Intervention combines accommodation with targeted support. Processing speed weakness calls for extended time on all speeded tasks, reduced time pressure in daily activities where possible, and helping the person develop realistic expectations for how long tasks will take. Self-advocacy around time needs becomes an important skill. Sustained attention difficulties call for breaking long tasks into shorter segments, building in scheduled breaks, environmental modifications to reduce distraction, and identifying and working with natural attention rhythms rather than against them.

Rule-following and set maintenance difficulties—inconsistent application of explicit rules despite apparent comprehension—benefit from external cueing systems that prompt rule adherence at key moments. Visual reminders posted in the work environment, verbal prompts from teachers or supervisors, and checklists that require explicit confirmation of rule compliance all support consistent rule application. The intervention puts the reminder "in the world" rather than relying on internal maintenance.

Goal maintenance limitations respond to similar external supports. Visual representations of the goal state, frequent check-ins that redirect attention to the objective, and breaking long tasks into shorter segments with explicit goal reminders at each transition help keep the target in mind. When someone asks, "What am I supposed to be doing?" mid-task, the environment should provide the answer.

Basic inhibition difficulties at Tier 2, failing to suppress rule-violating behaviors when rules are explicit and unchanging, differ from Tier 3 inhibitory control deficits and require different interventions. Tier 2 basic inhibition responds to environmental restructuring that removes opportunities for rule violation, explicit reminders at choice points, and consistent external consequences. The person isn't struggling to suppress a prepotent response under interference; they're struggling to maintain rule compliance over time. Structure and cueing, not inhibition training, address this limitation.

Procedural learning (becoming more efficient through task repetition) can be leveraged therapeutically when intact and accommodated when impaired. Individuals with strong procedural learning benefit from consistent routines that allow automaticity to develop; those with weak procedural learning need continued external support even for familiar tasks, as the expected efficiency gains may not materialize.

Working memory intervention differs by tier. Tier 2 working memory limitations involve basic maintenance capacity—holding information in mind while using it. External supports that reduce maintenance demands are the primary intervention: written instructions, reference materials, checklists, visual schedules, and reference materials during complex tasks. The intervention isn't strengthening working memory; it's circumventing the limitation. Tier 3 executive working memory limitations involve manipulation under load—actively reorganizing or integrating information while maintaining it. These higher-level demands can respond to strategy training: chunking information, verbal rehearsal strategies, and systematic approaches to complex integration tasks. The distinction matters: someone with Tier 2 maintenance limitations needs information externalized; someone with Tier 3 manipulation limitations may benefit from learning strategies to manage complex information more efficiently.

> **CAUTION**
>
> You cannot train what you cannot build. Recommending executive strategy training for Tier 1 or Tier 2 limitations sets everyone up for failure. A client with a slow processing speed will not become faster through planning instruction. A person with working memory limitations cannot learn their way to a larger capacity. Accommodations must precede or accompany strategy training, and for some limitations, accommodation is the intervention.

Tier 3 Cold

Cold executive function limitations call for strategy training. When foundational and bridging abilities are intact, but executive functions are impaired, the person has the raw cognitive capacity but lacks the executive control to deploy it effectively. Unlike Tier 1 and 2 limitations, Tier 3 cold deficits can respond to explicit instruction. Cognitive flexibility deficits benefit from explicit instruction in recognizing when shifts are needed, practice with structured shift cues before expecting spontaneous shifts, and verbal mediation strategies that prompt consideration of alternatives. Generativity deficits respond to structured brainstorming techniques, cueing strategies to prompt retrieval, and practice generating alternatives in low-stakes situations. Planning deficits call for explicit instruction in planning frameworks, think-aloud modeling of planning processes, and external planning tools like graphic organizers and step-by-step templates.

Abstract reasoning and concept formation deficits—difficulty identifying underlying principles or forming categories—benefit from explicit instruction in looking for patterns, structured frameworks for categorization, and practice with graded materials that make abstract relationships increasingly explicit. Teaching the person to ask "what do these have in common?" or "what's the underlying rule?" can scaffold reasoning that doesn't occur spontaneously.

Hypothesis testing deficits respond to structured problem-solving frameworks that make the hypothesis-test-revise cycle explicit. Teaching systematic elimination strategies, encouraging verbal mediation of the testing process ("if this is true, then I should see…"), and practicing with problems that have clear feedback support development of systematic approaches. The goal is to make implicit reasoning processes explicit and sequential.

Feedback utilization deficits, difficulty modifying strategy based on performance information, require intervention that makes feedback salient and connects it explicitly to strategy adjustment. Some individuals can use feedback when explicitly directed to attend to it; for these individuals, cueing systems that highlight feedback and prompt strategy review may be sufficient. Others struggle to incorporate feedback even with support; these individuals need more structured external guidance in the feedback-adjustment loop, with a coach or supervisor explicitly identifying what the feedback indicates and what adjustment is warranted.

Inhibitory control deficits at Tier 3 involve suppressing prepotent responses under interference. The challenge isn't remembering the rule but overriding a strong competing response. Strategy training can help: verbal self-instruction to pause before responding, identification of high-risk situations where prepotent responses are strongest, environmental modification to reduce temptation, and practice with response delay in graduated contexts. Unlike Tier 2 basic inhibition, which responds primarily to environmental structure, Tier 3 inhibitory control can improve with explicit strategy development.

Tier 3 Hot

Hot executive dysfunction requires intervention targeting emotional regulation rather than cognitive strategy. The person may already know what to do; the problem is doing it when emotions run high. Intervention focuses on recognizing physiological and emotional signs of dysregulation, developing de-escalation strategies such as deep breathing, taking space, or cognitive reframing, and building tolerance for frustration through graduated exposure. Environmental modifications to reduce emotional triggers are often essential. For children and adolescents, parent coaching is frequently necessary; adults in the environment need to recognize escalation, provide co-regulation, and avoid inadvertently intensifying emotional responses. For adults, intervention may involve individual therapy focused on self-regulation skills, workplace coaching to identify environmental triggers, or couples/family work when dysregulation affects close relationships. Repairing after dysregulated episodes without shame helps prevent secondary emotional problems from compounding the primary executive weakness.

Tier 4

Deficits at this level involve impaired self-monitoring, strategic coordination, and metacognitive awareness. Intervention focuses on making implicit processes explicit. Self-monitoring supports include external feedback systems such as checklists, observer cues, and recorded review of performance. Explicit instruction in self-evaluation, frequent pauses for "how am I doing?" checks, and calibration exercises comparing self-assessment to objective measures all build metacognitive capacity. Strategic coordination benefits from explicit prioritization frameworks, practice coordinating multiple demands in structured settings, and coaching on when to shift strategies versus persist. Metacognitive development comes through think-aloud practice during problem-solving, reflection after task completion, identification of personal patterns across situations, and goal-setting that incorporates self-knowledge. For adults in professional contexts, Tier 4 intervention often includes workplace coaching focused on self-monitoring during meetings and collaborative tasks, structured reflection on project outcomes, and developing self-advocacy skills for communicating cognitive needs to supervisors and colleagues. Adults living independently benefit from building personal systems for self-evaluation—regular review of how strategies are working, adjustment based on outcomes, and realistic calibration of what they can manage without external support.

Rapid Reference 16.2

Tier-Based Intervention Examples

Tier	Core Principle	Intervention Category	Specific Examples
Tier 1	Accommodate; foundations cannot be trained	Prosthetic correction (when possible)	Glasses, hearing aids, appropriate lighting
		Reduce demands on impaired foundation	Reduce graphomotor demands; allow typed responses; simplify verbal instructions; allow nonverbal response modes; reduce visual complexity; quiet workspace
Tier 2	Accommodate + targeted support; circumvent limitations	Processing speed	Extended time; reduced time pressure; realistic task-duration expectations; self-advocacy for time needs
		Sustained attention	Break tasks into segments; scheduled breaks; environmental modifications; work with natural attention rhythms
		Rule-following/set maintenance	External cueing systems; visual reminders; verbal prompts; checklists requiring explicit confirmation
		Goal maintenance	Visual goal representations; frequent check-ins; explicit goal reminders at transitions
		Basic inhibition	Environmental restructuring; explicit reminders at choice points; consistent external consequences
		Working memory (maintenance)	Written instructions; reference materials; checklists; visual schedules; information externalized
		Procedural learning	Leverage through consistent routines (if intact); continued external support (if impaired)
Tier 3 cold	Strategy training; explicit instruction in executive skills	Cognitive flexibility	Explicit instruction in recognizing when shifts are needed; structured shift cues; verbal mediation strategies
		Generativity	Structured brainstorming techniques; cueing strategies; practice in low-stakes situations
		Planning	Explicit instruction in planning frameworks; think-aloud modeling; graphic organizers; step-by-step templates
		Abstract reasoning/ concept formation	Explicit pattern instruction; categorization frameworks; graded materials; "what do these have in common?" scaffolding
		Hypothesis testing	Structured problem-solving frameworks; systematic elimination strategies; verbal mediation of testing process

Tier	Core Principle	Intervention Category	Specific Examples
		Feedback utilization	Make feedback salient; explicit connection to strategy adjustment; cueing systems; structured external guidance
		Inhibitory control	Verbal self-instruction to pause; identify high-risk situations; environmental modification; response delay practice
		Working memory (manipulation)	Chunking; verbal rehearsal strategies; systematic approaches to complex integration
Tier 3 hot	Emotion regulation; the person knows what to do but cannot do it when emotions are high	Recognition and de-escalation	Recognize physiological/emotional signs of dysregulation; deep breathing; taking space; cognitive reframing
		Environmental modification	Reduce emotional triggers; predictable routines; advance warning of transitions; designated cool-down space
		For children/ adolescents	Parent coaching; co-regulation; avoid intensifying emotional responses; repair without shame
		Build tolerance	Graduated exposure to frustration
Tier 4	Metacognitive coaching; make implicit processes explicit	Self-monitoring	External feedback systems (checklists, observer cues, recorded review); explicit self-evaluation instruction; "how am I doing?" checks; calibration exercises
		Strategic coordination	Explicit prioritization frameworks; practice coordinating multiple demands; coaching on when to shift vs. persist
		Metacognitive development	Think-aloud practice; reflection after task completion; identify personal patterns; goal-setting incorporating self-knowledge

Leveraging Strengths in Recommendations

Effective recommendations address weaknesses, but the best recommendations also leverage strengths. Chapter 15 emphasized identifying convergent strengths across the battery; here, those strengths become intervention tools. When an examinee has strong verbal reasoning but weak visual–spatial planning, recommendations should explicitly incorporate verbal mediation—talking through spatial problems, using verbal labels for visual information, and converting diagrams to written steps. When processing speed is slow, but reasoning is strong, recommendations should create time for that reasoning to operate rather than forcing quick responses that bypass the examinee's best thinking. When hot executive functions are intact but cold executive functions are weak, recommendations can harness emotional investment and motivation to sustain effort through cognitively demanding tasks.

The principle is straightforward: work with the individual's cognitive profile, not against it. A recommendation that requires a client to rely on an impaired process will fail. A recommendation that routes around weakness by leveraging strength has a chance. This means explicitly noting in recommendations not just what the examinee struggles with, but what resources support the intervention: "Because verbal reasoning is a strength, use verbal self-instruction strategies to support planning" is more actionable and more likely to succeed than "Use planning strategies" alone. When strengths are limited and multiple tiers show weakness, recommendations must rely more heavily on external supports and environmental modifications, and expectations for independent compensation should be calibrated accordingly.

PRINCIPLES FOR WRITING RECOMMENDATIONS

Recommendations should flow naturally from the tier analysis. Each recommendation should connect explicitly to an identified weakness and explain why that particular intervention addresses that particular problem. This connection between finding and recommendation is what transforms a generic list into a targeted intervention plan.

Specificity is essential. "Executive function support" tells no one what to do. "Provide written instructions for multistep tasks because working memory limitations make it difficult to hold verbal instructions in mind while executing them" tells everyone exactly what to do and why. The recommendation names the intervention, identifies the underlying deficit, and explains the mechanism by which the intervention addresses the deficit. This level of specificity allows implementers to adapt the recommendation to their context while maintaining fidelity to its purpose.

Prioritization matters more than volume. Twelve recommendations overwhelm families and educators, leading to inconsistent implementation or abandonment. Three to five targeted recommendations, clearly prioritized, are more likely to be enacted effectively (Elias et al., 2021; Postal & Armstrong, 2013). Focus on interventions that address the most impairing difficulties or that create cascading benefits, addressing a foundational bottleneck, for example, may improve functioning across multiple domains without requiring domain-specific interventions for each.

Matching intervention to the tier prevents wasted effort. Recommending strategy training for foundational limitations sets everyone up for failure. Recommending accommodations when the person has the capacity to develop skills with proper instruction sells them short. Recommending cognitive strategies for hot executive dysfunction misses the mark. The tier analysis should directly inform whether accommodation, support, strategy training, emotion regulation, or metacognitive coaching is the appropriate intervention category.

Recommendations must be implementable by the people who will implement them. School recommendations must fit within what schools can actually do legally, logistically, and practically. Parent recommendations must fit within family capacity, accounting for time, resources, and competing demands. Workplace accommodation recommendations must be reasonable given job demands and employer resources. Treatment recommendations must match available services in the community. A brilliant recommendation that can't or won't be implemented helps no one.

Finally, recommendations should build in evaluation—some way to determine whether the intervention is actually helping. Without this, ineffective interventions persist too long while effective ones may be abandoned prematurely.

> **CAUTION**
>
> Avoid generic recommendation lists. Recommendations copied from templates or applied uniformly across diagnoses rarely produce meaningful change. The value of tier-based assessment lies in generating recommendations that address ***this*** person's specific profile. If the recommendations could have been written without the assessment, the assessment hasn't done its job.

SUMMARY

Assessment without translation is incomplete. The tier framework provides a structure for moving from test scores to meaningful understanding to targeted intervention. By identifying the level at which processing breaks down, clinicians can explain findings in terms that non-clinicians understand, generate recommendations that address actual sources of dysfunction, and predict which interventions are likely to help.

The translation process requires attention to ecological validity. Performance-based tests capture capacity under optimal conditions; rating scales capture deployment in daily life. Divergence between these sources is not an error; it is information about the gap between what someone can do and what they actually do. Hot executive dysfunction often manifests as exactly this divergence: intact cold EF on testing, impaired functioning in real-world settings where emotional regulation matters.

Recommendations should flow naturally from tier analysis. Tier 1 and Tier 2 limitations call for accommodation and support—you cannot train what you cannot build. Tier 3 cold limitations call for strategy training—explicit instruction in executive skills that don't develop naturally. Tier 3 hot limitations call for emotion regulation work—the person knows what to do, but cannot do it when emotions are high. Tier 4 limitations call for metacognitive coaching—building self-awareness and strategic self-regulation.

The preceding chapters have focused on interpreting D-KEFS findings and translating them into action. But clinicians rarely use only one battery, and the interpretive challenges addressed throughout this book—the impurity problem, the hot–cold distinction, the need to identify the level at which processing breaks down—arise in every evaluation. The final chapter considers how tier-based thinking travels beyond the D-KEFS, becoming a clinical lens that shapes interpretation regardless of which instruments are in the clinician's hands.

TEST YOURSELF

1. A client shows intact performance on all cold EF measures but has clinically elevated BRIEF-2 scores across multiple scales. What does this divergence most likely indicate?

(a) The testing was invalid due to poor effort.
(b) Hot executive dysfunction affected real-world deployment.
(c) The rating scale respondents were unreliable.
(d) Tier 1 limitations affected daily functioning.

2. For an examinee with Tier 2 working memory limitations, the most appropriate primary intervention is:

(a) Strategy training for planning skills.
(b) Emotion regulation coaching.
(c) External memory supports such as checklists and written instructions.
(d) Metacognitive self-monitoring practice.

3. When explaining the tier framework to parents, using a building metaphor helps because:

(a) It makes the clinician sound more professional.
(b) It illustrates that foundation problems require different repairs than upper-floor problems.
(c) It emphasizes that executive functions are more important than foundational abilities.
(d) It simplifies the explanation by eliminating technical details.

4. A school requests recommendations for a student with Tier 3 cognitive flexibility deficits. Which recommendation is most appropriate?

(a) Extended time on all assignments.
(b) Preferential seating near the teacher.
(c) Explicit instruction in recognizing when mental shifts are needed.
(d) Reduced homework load.

5. The primary reason why generic executive function recommendations may fail is that they:

(a) Are too difficult for schools to implement.
(b) Don't account for the specific tier at which dysfunction occurs.
(c) Require too much parent involvement.
(d) Are based on outdated research.

6. **Rating scales like the BRIEF-2 are valuable in executive function assessment primarily because they:**
   (a) Are more reliable than performance-based tests.
   (b) Capture functioning in naturalistic settings that differ from testing conditions.
   (c) Provide diagnosis-specific information.
   (d) Are faster to administer than standardized tests.
7. **For a person with Tier 3 hot executive dysfunction, the most appropriate intervention focus is:**
   (a) Planning strategy instruction.
   (b) Extended time accommodations.
   (c) Emotion regulation skill-building.
   (d) External memory supports.
8. **When test scores show impairment but rating scales are normal, the clinician should first consider:**
   (a) Dismissing the test results as invalid.
   (b) Whether state factors affected testing or compensatory strategies support daily functioning.
   (c) Diagnosing a learning disability.
   (d) Recommending immediate intervention based on test results.
9. **Recommendations should be prioritized rather than exhaustive because:**
   (a) Insurance companies limit the number of recommendations allowed.
   (b) Fewer, targeted recommendations are more likely to be implemented effectively.
   (c) Clinicians should not tell schools or families what to do.
   (d) Most clients only have one or two deficits.
10. **The statement "You cannot train what you cannot build" refers to the principle that:**
    (a) Some clients are untreatable.
    (b) Strategy training is ineffective for all executive deficits.
    (c) Tier 1 and 2 limitations require accommodation rather than skill training.
    (d) Executive functions cannot be improved through intervention.

Answer Key: 1-b, 2-c, 3-b, 4-c, 5-b, 6-b, 7-c, 8-b, 9-b, 10-c

REFERENCES

Dawson, P., & Guare, R. (2016). *The Smart But Scattered Guide to Success: How to Use Your Brain's Executive Skills to Keep Up, Stay Calm, and Get Organized at Work and at Home*. Guilford Press.

Dawson, P., & Guare, R. (2018). *Executive Skills in Children and Adolescents: A Practical Guide to Assessment and Intervention* (3rd ed.). Guilford Press.

Elias, J., Zimak, E., Sherwood, A., MacDonald, B., Lozano, N., Long, J., & Larsen, A. D. (2021). Do parents implement pediatric neuropsychological report recommendations? *The Clinical Neuropsychologist, 35*(6), 1117–1133.

Kennedy, M. R. T. (2017). *Coaching College Students with Executive Function Problems*. Guilford Press.

Meltzer, L. (2010). *Promoting Executive Function in the Classroom*. Guilford Press.

Postal, K., & Armstrong, K. (2013). *Feedback that Sticks: The Art of Effectively Communicating Neuropsychological Assessment Results*. Oxford University Press.

Seventeen

THE TIER FRAMEWORK AS A CLINICAL LENS

BEYOND THE D-KEFS

The hierarchical tier framework highlighted throughout this book emerged from the interpretive challenges inherent in executive function assessment. The D-KEFS Advanced manual, developed by Pearson in collaboration with Dean Delis and colleagues, explicitly organized interpretation around tiered analysis, distinguishing foundational processes from bridging abilities from executive functions proper. This book extends and operationalizes that approach. But the framework's utility extends far beyond a single test battery. The impurity problem—the reality that every test measures multiple processes simultaneously—is universal. Every cognitive measure confounds the construct it intends to assess with foundational abilities, processing efficiency, and regulatory factors. The tier framework provides a systematic approach to disentangling these contributions regardless of which instruments are in the clinician's hands.

This final chapter considers how tier-based thinking applies to assessment more broadly. The goal is not comprehensive coverage of every assessment instrument but rather illustration of how the framework generalizes. Clinicians who internalize this approach will find themselves asking the same questions—What tier is the bottleneck? What's the simplest explanation for this pattern? What would I need to see to rule out lower-tier contributions?—whether they are interpreting a D-KEFS profile, a Wechsler battery, a memory assessment, or an academic achievement evaluation.

THE IMPURITY PROBLEM IS UNIVERSAL

The impurity problem, introduced in Chapter 3, refers to the inescapable reality that complex cognitive tasks recruit multiple processes. A test designed to measure executive planning also requires motor execution, visual perception, working memory, and processing speed. Poor performance could reflect weakness at any of these levels. The D-KEFS addresses this through baseline conditions and contrast scores; other instruments handle it differently or not at all. But the interpretive challenge remains constant across all assessment.

Consider the Wechsler intelligence scales: Block Design is classified as a measure of visual–spatial processing, and it is. But performance also depends on motor speed and coordination (manipulating blocks), processing speed (working within time limits), planning (approaching the design systematically), and executive monitoring (checking work against the model). A child with motor difficulties will struggle on Block Design regardless of visual–spatial ability. A child with slow processing speed will lose bonus points even with accurate constructions. A child with poor planning will approach designs haphazardly despite adequate perception. The "visual–spatial" score is contaminated by all these factors.

The same analysis applies to any complex cognitive measure. Coding and Symbol Search assess processing speed but require visual discrimination, motor coordination, sustained attention, and following novel rules. Digit Span assesses working memory but requires auditory processing, attention, and adequate initial encoding before manipulation can occur. Vocabulary assesses crystallized knowledge but requires word retrieval, verbal expression, and adequate hearing. No cognitive test is pure.

APPLYING TIER-BASED THINKING BEYOND D-KEFS

The Wechsler scales don't provide the baseline-to-complex condition structure that makes D-KEFS interpretation so systematic. But tier-based thinking still applies through cross-subtest pattern analysis. The examples that follow use Wechsler subtests for illustration, but the same logic applies to the Woodcock-Johnson, WRAML, NEPSY-II, or any other assessment battery. The goal is not comprehensive instruction in interpreting any particular instrument but rather demonstration of how tier-based questions generalize.

When a child shows weakness across multiple timed subtests (Coding, Symbol Search, Block Design with time bonuses, Cancellation) with relative strength on untimed measures (Vocabulary, Similarities, Matrix Reasoning without time pressure), the pattern suggests Tier 2 processing speed as the bottleneck. The weakness isn't in any single domain—it's in the efficiency with which all domains can be executed. Intervention implications follow: extended time accommodations, reduced emphasis on speed, and recognition that the child's abilities exceed what timed measures suggest.

When weakness appears selectively on working memory measures (Digit Span, Picture Span, Letter-Number Sequencing) with preserved performance elsewhere, Tier 2 working memory limitations become the hypothesis. This pattern suggests difficulty will emerge on any task requiring simultaneous holding and manipulation of information, regardless of domain. An adult with this profile may struggle with multistep instructions at work, managing complex projects, and following lengthy conversations, not because of deficits in those specific domains but because working memory capacity constrains performance across them all.

When an individual shows intact processing speed and working memory but struggles specifically with novel problem-solving tasks (Matrix Reasoning, Figure Weights, Arithmetic reasoning) despite adequate foundational abilities, Tier 3 cold executive contributions become relevant. The person can execute quickly, can hold information in mind, but struggles with the flexible reasoning and strategic thinking these tasks demand.

The interpretive logic parallels D-KEFS interpretation: rule out Tier 1, evaluate Tier 2, then consider Tier 3 cold and hot, and assess Tier 4 through qualitative observation. The difference is that Wechsler scales require the clinician to construct this analysis from cross-subtest patterns and behavioral data rather than reading it from built-in contrast scores.

APPLYING TIER-BASED THINKING TO MEMORY ASSESSMENT

Memory assessment illustrates the tier framework particularly well because memory tests generate multiple scores that can be systematically compared to identify the level of breakdown.

On the CVLT-3 or similar list-learning tests, consider the client who shows poor initial acquisition (Trials 1–5) but normal retention (minimal loss from Trial 5 to Long Delay) and normal recognition (accurate discrimination of targets from foils). This pattern indicates Tier 2 encoding inefficiency—difficulty getting information in—rather than Tier 3 memory consolidation or storage problems. The information that gets encoded is retained and accessible; the bottleneck is in the initial learning process. Intervention focuses on encoding strategies and additional learning opportunities rather than memory rehabilitation per se.

Contrast this with the examinees who show adequate acquisition but poor retention (significant loss from immediate to delayed recall) and impaired recognition. This pattern suggests genuine Tier 3 memory consolidation or storage deficits. The information was encoded, but did not stick. This is a fundamentally different problem requiring a different clinical conceptualization and intervention.

The WMS-5 and similar batteries provide additional tier-relevant information through comparison of immediate versus delayed recall, free recall versus cued recall versus recognition, and verbal versus visual memory. Each comparison illuminates where the memory system breakdown occurs. Is the problem getting information in (encoding), keeping it there (consolidation), or getting it back out (retrieval)? These questions map onto tier-based analysis: foundational sensory processing, working memory encoding, executive strategic retrieval, and memory storage itself.

APPLYING TIER-BASED THINKING TO ACHIEVEMENT ASSESSMENT

Achievement testing might seem distant from executive function assessment, but tier-based thinking applies here too. Academic skills depend on foundational abilities, processing efficiency, and executive control. Weaknesses at any level affect achievement outcomes.

Reading difficulties illustrate this clearly. A child may struggle with reading fluency because of phonological processing deficits (Tier 1 language foundations), slow processing speed (Tier 2 efficiency), poor sustained attention (Tier 2 attention), difficulty with decoding strategy application (Tier 3 cold executive), or anxiety that disrupts performance (Tier 3 hot executive). The intervention for each is entirely different. Phonological training addresses Tier 1. Extended time addresses Tier 2 speed. Attention supports address Tier 2 attention. Strategy instruction addresses Tier 3 cold. Anxiety intervention addresses Tier 3 hot. A reading score alone cannot distinguish these possibilities; pattern analysis across measures can.

Mathematics difficulties similarly decompose across tiers. Foundational number sense and fact retrieval (Tier 1), processing speed for calculation fluency (Tier 2), working memory for multistep problems (Tier 2), planning and strategy selection for word problems (Tier 3 cold), and frustration tolerance for challenging material (Tier 3 hot) all contribute to math performance. A comprehensive evaluation examines each level to identify where intervention should target.

Written expression may be the most tier-complex academic domain. Motor execution for handwriting (Tier 1), processing speed for written production (Tier 2), working memory for holding ideas while transcribing (Tier 2), planning and organization for composition (Tier 3 cold), generativity for idea production (Tier 3 cold), self-monitoring for editing (Tier 4), and frustration tolerance for the inherently effortful task (Tier 3 hot) all contribute. A student's writing difficulties could originate at any of these levels, and effective intervention depends on accurate identification of the bottleneck. Though framed here in terms of school-age learners, the same tier-based analysis applies to adults in vocational rehabilitation, those returning to school later in life, or individuals recovering from acquired brain injuries who must relearn academic skills.

THE HOT–COLD DISTINCTION BEYOND D-KEFS

The distinction between hot and cold executive functions, central to D-KEFS Advanced interpretation through the RISK Test, applies across all assessment contexts. Rating scales like the BRIEF-2 and BRIEF-A, D-REF and D-REF-A, and CEFI and CEFI Adult capture hot executive functioning—emotional regulation, behavioral inhibition under real-world conditions, frustration tolerance—in ways that performance-based tests typically cannot.

When a comprehensive evaluation reveals intact cold executive functioning on performance-based measures but elevated concerns on rating scales, the hot–cold dissociation explains the pattern regardless of which specific tests were administered. The individual can perform when calm and focused, but cannot deploy those abilities when emotionally activated. This finding emerges from the pattern across data sources, not from any single instrument.

Behavioral observations during testing provide hot executive data regardless of the battery administered. How does the person respond to difficulty? Does frustration derail performance on later items? Does anxiety about timed tests suppress processing speed scores below true capacity? Does the client give up prematurely or persist despite challenge? These observations, combined with rating scale data, illuminate hot executive functioning in ways that cold cognitive tests cannot.

The practical implication is that clinicians already possess the data needed to evaluate hot executive functioning in most comprehensive evaluations. Rating scales are standard practice; behavioral observations occur whether or not they're systematically recorded. The interpretive move is integration, comparing what performance-based tests reveal about capacity with what rating scales and observations reveal about deployment. The capacity-versus-deployment distinction discussed in Chapter 16 is, at its core, a hot–cold distinction. When capacity exceeds deployment, hot executive factors are typically responsible.

The developmental trajectories outlined in Chapter 2 also inform hot–cold interpretation regardless of which instruments are used. An adolescent showing intact cognitive flexibility on any measure but poor real-world adaptability fits the maturational pattern in which cold systems mature ahead of hot regulatory systems. An older adult whose test performance has declined but whose emotional regulation remains strong may compensate effectively despite cognitive losses. These developmental expectations travel with the framework, not with any particular test.

ERRORS AS WINDOWS

Dean Delis, reflecting on the process approach philosophy that underlies the D-KEFS, recalled Edith Kaplan's observation: "Errors are the best window into brain function, and it really is true."

This principle extends to all assessment. Errors often reveal more than correct responses because they illuminate *how* processing breaks down, not just *that* it breaks down. The type of error—intrusion versus omission, perseverative versus random, self-corrected versus unrecognized—provides tier-relevant information.

Intrusion errors on memory tests (stating words that weren't on the list) suggest different problems than omission errors (failing to recall words that were). Perseverative errors on any task (repeating previous responses inappropriately) suggest different problems than random errors. Self-corrected errors suggest intact monitoring with impaired initial execution; uncorrected errors suggest impaired monitoring itself. This distinction provides Tier 4 information—self-correction indicates intact metacognitive monitoring, while failure to recognize errors suggests impaired self-awareness.

Across any battery, attending to error patterns enriches interpretation beyond what summary scores provide. The person who makes many errors but catches them demonstrates different functioning than the individual who makes few errors, who differs from the client who makes many errors without awareness. Same score, different profiles, different tier implications, different interventions.

A WAY OF THINKING

The tier framework is ultimately not about the D-KEFS specifically. It is a way of thinking about assessment that applies whenever clinicians face the interpretive challenge of disentangling what a test score actually means.

The questions are always the same:

- What foundational abilities does this task require, and are they intact?
- What processing efficiency demands does this task place, and are they met?
- What executive control does this task require, and is it present?
- Is the problem cold (cognitive) or hot (emotional-regulatory)?
- Where is the lowest level at which I see consistent weakness?

These questions apply to the WISC as much as the D-KEFS, to the CVLT as much as the Tower Test, to the WIAT as much as Verbal Fluency. The specific tests provide data; the framework provides meaning.

DON'T FORGET

The framework transcends the instrument. Tier-based thinking applies to all cognitive assessment, not just D-KEFS interpretation. Every cognitive test confounds multiple processes. The clinical task is always to identify the lowest level at which breakdown occurs, using pattern analysis across measures rather than relying on any single score.

Rapid Reference 17.1

Tier-Based Questions Across Any Assessment

Tier	Key Questions
Tier 1	Are sensory, motor, and language foundations intact? Could perceptual or motor limitations explain this score?
Tier 2	Is processing speed, working memory, or sustained attention constraining performance? Would untimed conditions, reduced memory load, or shorter task segments change the picture?
Tier 3 cold	With lower tiers accounted for, is there evidence of executive dysfunction in flexibility, planning, inhibition, or generativity?
Tier 3 hot	Do rating scales or behavioral observations suggest emotional regulation difficulties not captured by cognitive testing?
Tier 4	Does the individual show awareness of errors? Do they adapt strategy based on feedback?
Integration	Where is the lowest level at which consistent weakness appears? What is the simplest explanation for this pattern?

WHAT THIS FRAMEWORK OFFERS

The tier framework is not the only way to interpret assessment data, but it offers specific advantages over common alternatives.

Compared to relying on summary scores and index composites, tier-based thinking identifies mechanism rather than merely documenting impairment. A low Processing Speed Index tells you something is slow; tier analysis tells you whether that slowness is the primary problem or a downstream consequence of something else. A weak Working Memory Index confirms difficulty holding information in mind; tier analysis distinguishes whether this reflects storage limitations, attentional lapses during encoding, or executive control failures during manipulation. The same summary score can have different meanings depending on what's happening at other tiers—clinically signficant findings that summary scores alone cannot reveal.

Compared to diagnosis-first interpretation, approaching data with an expected profile in mind and fitting findings to it, tier-based thinking reduces confirmatory bias. The framework asks the same questions regardless of referral concern: What do the foundations look like? Where is the bottleneck? The diagnosis emerges from the pattern rather than shaping how the pattern is perceived. This discipline is particularly valuable when referral questions are leading ("rule out ADHD") or when preliminary information creates strong expectations.

Compared to treating all low scores as equivalent evidence of dysfunction, the framework distinguishes constraint from deficit. A client with slow processing speed will produce many low scores on timed measures, but those scores reflect the same underlying limitation, not multiple independent problems. Without tier-based analysis, the clinician might describe impairments in "processing speed, cognitive flexibility, and inhibition" when the accurate description is "processing speed limitations affecting performance across executive measures." The first interpretation implies three targets for intervention; the second implies one. Getting it right matters for the people who will live with the recommendations. The framework also clarifies what can be trained versus what must be accommodated. You cannot train what you cannot build. Tier 1 and Tier 2 limitations require accommodation; Tier 3 deficits may respond to strategy instruction.

The framework also systematically identifies strengths—not just where breakdown occurs, but where processing remains intact. Convergent strength across measures is as interpretively meaningful as convergent weakness. These strengths become intervention tools, enabling recommendations that route around weakness by leveraging capacity rather than fighting against the cognitive profile.

CAUTION

The framework structures thinking; it doesn't replace it. Tier-based analysis provides scaffolding for interpretation, but ambiguous cases will remain ambiguous. Conflicting data will still conflict. The framework tells you what questions to ask—it cannot guarantee clear answers. Clinical judgment remains essential.

CLOSING REFLECTIONS

The tier framework structures interpretation, but it does not replace clinical judgment. Ambiguous cases will remain ambiguous. Conflicting data will still conflict. Some examinees will present with profiles that resist clean categorization despite systematic analysis. The framework tells you what questions to ask; it cannot guarantee clear answers.

What distinguishes skilled interpretation from score reporting is not access to a better framework but willingness to sit with uncertainty while continuing to reason carefully. The framework provides scaffolding for that reasoning. It ensures that obvious explanations are considered before exotic ones, that lower-tier contributions are ruled out before higher-tier deficits are invoked, that convergent patterns carry more weight than isolated findings. But the clinician must still weigh the evidence, tolerate ambiguity when evidence is thin, and make reasoned judgments that go beyond what any algorithm could generate.

Experienced clinicians often apply something like tier-based reasoning without naming it. They sense when a low score doesn't fit and probe for alternative explanations. They notice when a client's struggles in daily life exceed what cold cognitive testing would predict and think about hot executive factors. They resist attributing planning deficits to examinees whose slow processing speed would explain the same Tower Test performance. The framework makes this intuitive process explicit. It can be an aid to trainees who haven't yet developed clinical intuition, as well as experienced clinicians when intuition fails or cases fall outside familiar patterns.

We return, finally, to purpose. Assessment exists to help people. The referral question is never really "What are the scores?" but rather "What is getting in this person's way, and what would help?" A report that catalogues impairments without identifying mechanism has documented a problem without understanding it. A profile that identifies the bottleneck—the specific level at which processing breaks down—points toward intervention. The tier framework keeps this purpose in view by refusing to stop at "what" and insisting on "where" and "why."

The D-KEFS and D-KEFS Advanced, with their baseline conditions and contrast scores and process measures, were designed for exactly this kind of analysis. But the interpretive philosophy extends beyond any single battery. The impurity problem is universal; the need to distinguish foundational limitations from executive dysfunction is constant; the question of whether emotional regulation is compromising cognitive capacity arises in every clinic and classroom. Clinicians who learn to think in tiers will find themselves thinking that way about every evaluation they conduct—not because the D-KEFS taught them a scoring system, but because it taught them a way of understanding what test scores mean and what they fail to capture.

That is the contribution we hope this book has made.

TEST YOURSELF

1. The impurity problem in cognitive assessment refers to:

(a) Contamination of test materials affecting validity.

(b) The reality that cognitive tests measure multiple processes simultaneously.

(c) Errors in test scoring and administration.

(d) The influence of cultural factors on test performance.

2. When applying tier-based thinking to Wechsler batteries, weakness across all timed subtests with preserved untimed performance most likely suggests:

(a) Tier 1 motor impairment.

(b) Tier 2 processing speed limitations.

(c) Tier 3 executive dysfunction.

(d) Tier 4 metacognitive deficits.

3. On a list-learning memory test, poor acquisition with normal retention and recognition indicates:

(a) Storage deficits.

(b) Retrieval deficits.

(c) Encoding inefficiency.

(d) Consolidation failure.

4. The hot–cold executive function distinction can be assessed in any evaluation through:

(a) Performance-based tests only.

(b) Rating scales and behavioral observations combined with test scores.

(c) Neuroimaging.

(d) Interview alone.

5. According to Edith Kaplan, what provides the "best window into brain function"?

(a) Processing speed

(b) Global scores

(c) Errors

(d) Contrast measures

6. Tier-based thinking applies to achievement assessment because:
   (a) Achievement tests are executive function measures.
   (b) Academic skills depend on foundational, efficiency, and executive processes.
   (c) Achievement tests include baseline conditions.
   (d) Reading and math are Tier 3 functions.

7. The primary advantage of the tier framework compared to traditional score interpretation is that it:
   (a) Eliminates the need for standardized testing.
   (b) Identifies the level at which processing breaks down.
   (c) Provides diagnostic labels.
   (d) Reduces assessment time.

8. When an individual shows intact cold EF on testing but elevated BRIEF-2 scores, this pattern:
   (a) Indicates invalid test results.
   (b) Suggests hot–cold dissociation regardless of which performance tests were used.
   (c) Means the rating scales are unreliable.
   (d) Is uninterpretable.

9. Self-corrected errors versus uncorrected errors provide information about:
   (a) Test difficulty.
   (b) Metacognitive monitoring (Tier 4).
   (c) Processing speed.
   (d) Motor control.

10. The tier framework is best understood as:
   (a) A D-KEFS-specific scoring system.
   (b) A way of thinking about cognitive assessment that applies across instruments.
   (c) A replacement for standardized testing.
   (d) A diagnostic classification system.

Answer Key: 1-b, 2-b, 3-c, 4-b, 5-c, 6-b, 7-b, 8-b, 9-b, 10-b

INDEX